OXFORD WORLD'S CLASSICS

RICHARD BRINSLEY SHERIDAN

The Rivals
The Duenna
A Trip to Scarborough
The School for Scandal
The Critic

Edited with an Introduction and Notes by
MICHAEL CORDNER

OXFORD
UNIVERSITY PRESS

OXFORD
UNIVERSITY PRESS

Great Clarendon Street, Oxford OX2 6DP

Oxford University Press is a department of the University of Oxford.
It furthers the University's objective of excellence in research, scholarship,
and education by publishing worldwide in

Oxford New York

Auckland Bangkok Buenos Aires Cape Town Chennai
Dar es Salaam Delhi Hong Kong Istanbul Karachi Kolkata
Kuala Lumpur Madrid Melbourne Mexico City Mumbai Nairobi
São Paulo Shanghai Taipei Tokyo Toronto

Oxford is a registered trade mark of Oxford University Press
in the UK and in certain other countries

Published in the United States
by Oxford University Press Inc., New York

British Library Cataloguing in Publication Data

Data available

Library of Congress Cataloging in Publication Data

Sheridan, Richard Brinsley, 1751–1816.
The rivals; The duenna; A trip to Scarborough; The school for
scandal; The critic / edited by Michael Cordner.
(Oxford world's classics)
Includes bibliographical references (p.   ).
I. Cordner, Michael.   II. Title.   III. Title: Duenna.
IV. Title: Trip to Scarborough.   V. Title: School for scandal.
VI. Title: Critic.   VII. Series: Oxford world's classics
(Oxford University Press)
PR3681.C67   1998   822'.6—dc21   97–50491

ISBN 0–19–282567–4

6

Typeset by Best-set Typesetter Ltd., Hong Kong
Printed in Great Britain by
Clays Ltd., St Ives plc

OXFORD ENGLISH DRAMA

General Editor: MICHAEL CORDNER
Associate General Editors: PETER HOLLAND · MARTIN WIGGINS

THE SCHOOL FOR SCANDAL
AND OTHER PLAYS

RICHARD BRINSLEY SHERIDAN (1751–1816) was the son of Thomas Sheridan, actor, theatre-manager, and educationalist, and Frances Sheridan, dramatist and novelist. He was born in Dublin but mainly educated in England. His elopement with the distinguished singer Elizabeth Linley caused a sensation and embroiled him in two duels. He abandoned legal training after the success of the rewritten version of *The Rivals* in January 1775 and consolidated his theatrical reputation with the triumphant première of the opera *The Duenna* in November that year. On David Garrick's retirement in 1776 he became manager of the Theatre Royal in Drury Lane, for which he wrote *A Trip to Scarborough*, *The School for Scandal*, and *The Critic* over the next three years. Although he continued to manage Drury Lane for two more decades, his election as Member of Parliament in 1780 initiated a new stage of his career, in which he gave priority to his political ambitions over his theatrical involvements, and he was to write only one more full-length play, *Pizarro* (premièred in 1799). But major political office always eluded him, and he died in poverty. In contrast, his three finest comedies, *The Rivals*, *The School for Scandal*, and *The Critic*, have an unbroken history of successful stage performance from their premières to today.

MICHAEL CORDNER is Reader in the Department of English and Related Literature at the University of York. His editions include George Farquhar's *The Beaux' Stratagem*, the *Complete Plays* of Sir George Etherege, *Four Comedies* of Sir John Vanbrugh, and *Four Restoration Marriage Comedies*. He is completing a book on *The Comedy of Marriage 1660–1737*.

PETER HOLLAND is Professor of Shakespeare Studics and Director of the Shakespeare Institute, University of Birmingham.

MARTIN WIGGINS is a Fellow of the Shakespeare Institute and Lecturer in English at the University of Birmingham.

OXFORD ENGLISH DRAMA

J. M. Barrie
Peter Pan and Other Plays

Aphra Behn
The Rover and Other Plays

George Farquhar
The Recruiting Officer and Other Plays

John Ford
'Tis Pity She's a Whore and Other Plays

Ben Jonson
The Alchemist and Other Plays

Ben Jonson
The Devil is an Ass and Other Plays

D. H. Lawrence
The Widowing of Mrs Holroyd and Other Plays

Christopher Marlowe
Doctor Faustus and Other Plays

John Marston
The Malcontent and Other Plays

Thomas Middleton
Women Beware Women and Other Plays

A Mad World, My Masters and Other Plays

Richard Brinsley Sheridan
The School for Scandal and Other Plays

J. M. Synge
The Playboy of the Western World and Other Plays

John Webster
The Duchess of Malfi and Other Plays

Oscar Wilde
The Importance of Being Earnest and Other Plays

William Wycherley
The Country Wife and Other Plays

Court Masques
ed. David Lindley

Eighteenth-Century Women Dramatists
ed. Melinda Finberg

Five Romantic Plays
ed. Paul Baines and Edward Burns

Four Jacobean Sex Tragedies
ed. Martin Wiggins

Four Restoration Marriage Plays
ed. Michael Cordner

Four Revenge Tragedies
ed. Katharine Maus

London Assurance and Other Victorian Comedies
ed. Klaus Stierstorfer

The New Woman and Other Emancipated Woman Plays
ed. Jean Chothia

The Roaring Girl and Other City Comedies
ed. James Knowles and Eugenen Giddens

CONTENTS

Acknowledgements   vi

Introduction   vii

Note on the Text   xlvi

Sheridan's Playhouses   xlviii

Select Bibliography   lii

A Chronology of Richard Brinsley Sheridan   lv

THE RIVALS   1

THE DUENNA   87

A TRIP TO SCARBOROUGH   145

THE SCHOOL FOR SCANDAL   203

THE CRITIC   289

Explanatory Notes   339

Glossary   429

ACKNOWLEDGEMENTS

I AM grateful for the generous help I have received in the preparation of this edition, especially from Richard and Marie Axton, John Barrell, Anne Barton, Jacques Berthoud, Jordi Coral, John Roe, and Geoffrey Wall. Nick Havely has been an indispensable guide in coping with the difficulties of Sheridan's curious Italian. The greatest debt, as always, is to Niccy.

MICHAEL CORDNER

INTRODUCTION

The Rivals

FOUR days before the première of Sheridan's first play at the Theatre Royal in Covent Garden, David Garrick reported in a letter to a friend that *The Rivals* had 'rais'd great Expectation in the Public'.[1] *The Morning Chronicle* later recorded that before the first performance it was similarly 'deemed the *ne plus ultra* of Comedy' by the Covent Garden actors;[2] and the theatre's management was equally confident, telling Sheridan 'in the most flattering terms that there is not a doubt of its success' and that 'the least shilling I shall get (if it succeeds) will be six hundred pounds' (*Letters*, i. 39).[3]

In the event, however, the première was a disaster. 'A Friend to Comedy', reviewing it in *The Morning Chronicle*, underlined the scale of the disappointment:

Our expectations have been some time raised with the hope that they were at last to produce us a truly good comedy; the hour of proof arrives, and we are presented with a piece got up with such flagrant inattention, that half the per- formers appear to know nothing of their parts, and the play itself is a *full hour* longer in the representation than any piece on the stage.—This last circum- stance is an error of such a nature as shows either great obstinacy in the author, or excessive ignorance in the managers . . . (Price, i. 46)

The reviewers constantly harped on the actors' ill-preparedness; but Sheridan also came in for a substantial share of the blame. The full indictment ranged from the charge that the role of Sir Lucius O'Trig- ger was fundamentally misconceived—'a blunder of the first brogue'—to pained regret at the fledgeling dramatist's indulgence 'in many low quibbles and barbarous puns that disgrace the very name of comedy' (Price, i. 45–6). Some reviews contained encouraging words about Sheridan's future prospects as a dramatist. According to *The London Packet*, there was 'room for expectation, that when the author's

---

[1] David Garrick, *Letters*, ed. David M. Little and George M. Kahrl (Cambridge, Mass., 1963), iii. 985.

[2] Richard Brinsley Sheridan, *Dramatic Works*, ed. Cecil Price (Oxford, 1973), i. 39. Future quotations in the Introduction from this edition will be identified in the text by editor's name and volume and page number.

[3] Volume and page references in the text for Sheridan letters are to Sheridan, *Letters*, ed. Cecil Price (Oxford, 1966).

judgment is matured, the town may see a good play of his writing' (Price, i. 41). But the verdict was almost unanimous that the performance on 17 January 1775 had in no way fulfilled the hopes so industriously built up for it.

The eighteenth-century theatre was a place of peremptory judgements, in which many new plays failed to reach a second performance after comparably bathetic premières. But Sheridan, presumably encouraged by his ally Thomas Harris, the Covent Garden manager, refused to accept defeat. The strategy he employed to secure his comedy's resurrection was, as he recorded in the preface he later wrote for it, of a kind 'which the author is informed has not before attended a theatrical trial' (ll. 16–17). It involved a sophisticated use of those very newspapers which had documented his initial failure.

The 1770s were the decade in which theatrical criticism came of age in English journalism. By the end of it 'hardly one of the larger newspapers failed to carry paragraphs on the [London] performances, and even in more or less responsible manner to criticize them', and a 'new play was sure to be reported in about a dozen newspapers'.[4] Journalistic hostility could help seal a play's fate, but an enterprising author could also seek to use the newspapers to his own advantage. Within a day or two of the disastrous première, according to the *St James's Chronicle*, Sheridan had 'by an Advertisement promised some necessary Alterations' to his play and thus implicitly begged the public to 'suspend their Judgement till a farther Hearing'. The *Chronicle* concluded that 'it would be illiberal on this Submission and Address to the Public, to make any severe Remarks on the Fable or conduct of 'Sheridan's comedy (Price, i. 42). His surprise move had given him a crucial breathing-space and perhaps toned down some, at least, of the hostile criticism of *The Rivals* which might otherwise have been published. It had also proclaimed his unqualified acceptance of the supreme authority of his audience's verdicts.

Within the brief space of ten days he radically rewrote his play, and on 28 January its second performance earned a warmer response from both spectators and reviewers. *The Morning Chronicle*, testifying to the deftness of Sheridan's tactics, expressed the wish that 'it was the general custom for authors to withdraw their pieces after a first performance, in order to remove the objectionable passages, heighten the favourite characters, and generally amend the play' and registered its verdict that Sheridan 'therefore, from motives of candour and

[4] Charles Harold Gray, *Theatrical Criticism in London to 1795* (New York, 1931), 191.

encouragement, is entitled to the patronage and favour of a generous public' (Price, i. 50). His quick-witted manipulation of public opinion foreshadows his later skills as manager of the press for the Rockingham Whigs.[5] It also alerts us to the subsequent unlikelihood of his ever again straying far from what his audience would tolerate.

The survival of the manuscript copy of *The Rivals* submitted for licensing to the Lord Chamberlain before the first performance allows us to map in detail the kinds of change Sheridan introduced in the course of his rewriting. He adjusted and streamlined the plot. Stung by the charge that Sir Lucius was a 'villainous . . . portrait of an Irish gentleman' (Price, i. 47), he also comprehensively reshaped that role, allowing the character to display more dignity and common sense. But in some ways the most interesting of Sheridan's alterations are the frequent local adjustments of phrasing and wordplay. One reviewer complained that Sheridan 'has here and there mistaken ribaldry for humour, at which the audience seemed displeased' (Price, i. 45). Bowing to that displeasure, Sheridan bowdlerized his own text.

The tyro playwright had a taste for risqué puns and sexual innuendo. A prime offender had been Sir Anthony Absolute, who originally rebuked his son, in the following suggestive terms, for his apparent reluctance to woo Lydia: 'So lifeless a Clod as you should not dare to approach the Arms of such glowing Beauty—to lie like a Cucumber, on a hot bed'. The annoyed father also responded to the discovery that the 'trinket' Jack claims to be taking to Lydia is a sword with the command: 'get along, you Fool, and let her know you have better Trinkets than that'. Both these remarks, and numerous others like them, were now excised. Mrs Malaprop too needed taming. In the revised play she no longer follows her description of Sir Lucius as 'thou barbarous Van Dyke' (5.3.201) with the lewder insult of 'thou inhuman goat', nor arrives on the duelling field, crying, 'O mercy, I am glad to see you all Horizontal on your Legs'. Similarly, her worry that Sir Lucius might 'Perforate my Mistery' was tempered into a concern that he might 'dissolve my mystery' (5.3.193).[6] His play's initial failure had given Sheridan a bracing lesson in the decorums the Georgian playhouse required its playwrights to observe.

In the first version of the comedy, Sir Lucius, Bob Acres, and Fag

---

[5] Lucyle Werkmeister, *The London Daily Press 1772–1792* (Lincoln, Nebr. 1963), 10–11 and 13–14.

[6] Sheridan, *The Rivals, A Comedy. As it was first Acted at the Theatre-Royal in Covent-Garden. Edited from the Larpent Ms.*, ed. Richard Little Purdy (Oxford, 1935), 47, 104, 115, 113, and 115.

are all allowed to commit verbal blunders. In revising it, Sheridan sensibly confined this trait to Mrs Malaprop alone. Mistaking and misapplying words in this fashion is, of course, a familiar comic prop. In some productions I have seen, nothing more has been invited from the audience by the player of the part than a smug sense of superiority at Mrs Malaprop's hapless mangling of her 'oracular tongue' (3.3.69). Whatever degree of verbal sophistication individual spectators may themselves possess, such reductive playing licenses them to feel complacently superior to the linguistic bathos Sheridan's character constantly generates. In 1830 Leigh Hunt worked from different assumptions, when he observed that 'One of the pleasant things in being present at this comedy is to see how *Mrs. Malaprop's* blunders are hailed by the persons around you. It furnishes a curious insight into the respective amounts of their reading and education.'[7] This assumes that being fully alert to all her mistakings requires a level of linguistic sophistication not likely to be possessed in equal measure by all those watching the play. Leigh Hunt is confident that he is one of the (possibly very few) truly qualified spectators in this respect, and he finds his pleasure sharpened by his neighbours' failure to keep abreast of the subtleties of Sheridan's wordplay.

It is not only audience members who have been misled. Mrs Malaprop's verbal excursions have frequently confused the play's editors. In her denunciation of Lydia as 'a little intricate hussy' (1.2.192), for instance, 'intricate' has been glossed as a mistake for 'ingrate', meaning 'ungrateful', or for 'obstinate'.[8] But is this really necessary? She could perfectly logically be using it to mean 'perplexingly complex', and therefore, by extension, 'deceitful', which would neatly fit her feelings about her niece. Editors are too easily assuming that she will invariably go wrong in attempting any ambitious or adventurous use of language. But this time the last laugh may be hers. Similarly, in her next speech, when she dubs Sir Anthony 'an absolute misanthropy' (lines 197–8), the noun is clearly a misjudgement, but what about the adjective? It carries at least three meanings here: (1) complete, (2) authoritarian, and (3) displaying the characteristics of the males of the Absolute family. There is no reason to deny Mrs Malaprop the credit for this piece of dexterity. But she will then emerge as a character who

---

[7] Leigh Hunt, *Dramatic Criticism 1808–1831*, ed. Lawrence Huston Houtchens and Carolyn Houtchens (New York, 1949), 250.

[8] Sheridan, *The Rivals*, ed. Elizabeth Duthie (London, 1979), 25; Sheridan, *Major Dramas*, ed. George Henry Nettleton (Boston, 1906), 322.

can switch in consecutive words between deft punning and verbal catastrophe, and also therefore as a much more interesting proposition for an intelligent actress.[9]

In other passages where Mrs Malaprop blunders, Sheridan still ensures that what she says contains revelations of its own. When she pronounces that she would wish any daughter of hers to be a 'mistress of orthodoxy' (1.2.224), the context tells us that the last word is a slip for 'orthography'; but the slip also testifies to a truth, since she would certainly want her daughter to be a 'mistress of orthodoxy' as well—that is, she should comply with perfect ease and fluency with all pre-vailing social decorums. Mrs Malaprop contrives to speak nonsense and a kind of sense simultaneously.[10] A well-judged performance of the line needs to register both those perceptions, not just one of them. That challenge is evaded every time an actress bedecks her perfor-mance of Mrs Malaprop with 'exorbitant make-up', 'Rabelaisian padding', and 'pantomime costume'.[11] Such excesses too often disfig-ure modern productions of these plays.

Sheridan also uses her mistakings to generate proleptic irony. Mrs Malaprop's use of 'interceded' when she intended 'intercepted' (3.3.38) in her first encounter with Captain Absolute acquires retro-spectively an extra significance, since an eighteenth-century meaning of this verb is 'to act as a go-between', which is the service she is unknow-ingly about to perform for Lydia and 'Beverley'. Her unintended word-play spotlights how completely she is being outmanœuvred. Similarly, when she hopes that Sir Anthony will report Lydia to Jack as 'not wholly illegible' (1.2.252), she may have meant 'ineligible'; but 'illegi-ble', in the sense of 'indecipherable, incomprehensible', is also brought enrichingly into play, since this is indeed how Lydia often appears to her aunt. To Jack, however, Lydia is totally comprehensible, her every response foreseen throughout the comedy. Once again we are being reminded how totally outgunned Mrs Malaprop already is.

This kind of irony is particularly apt to Sheridan's tactics in *The Rivals*. The play belongs to a lengthy tradition of European comedy in which elderly relatives prescribe for their heirs marital fates the

---

[9] For other examples of passages where editors have mistakenly assumed blunders by Mrs Malaprop, see the notes to 1.2.216 and 263, 3.3.30, and 4.2.10–11 and 16.

[10] For other instances of verbal mishaps which are yet revelatory, see the notes to 1.2.161, 173, and 184, and to 3.3.12.

[11] Ronald Hayman, *The First Thrust: The Chichester Festival Theatre* (London, 1975), 161. The description is of Margaret Leighton as Mrs Malaprop in the 1971 Chichester production.

latter seek to resist. Sheridan's key variation on this model is to reduce the resulting combat to a form of shadow-play by one simple adjust-ment to the standard plot. Because Beverley and Jack are the same person, Sir Anthony and Mrs Malaprop are placed in the paradoxical situation of exerting what authority they can muster to enforce unions Lydia and the Captain only appear to oppose and which the spectators can be confident they will eventually embrace with alacrity. The fits of anger and other symptoms of outrage provoked in the elders along the way are therefore passionately indulged at the moment, but also always fated to be rendered transitory by subsequent revelations. Sheridan's writing for his principals constantly prepares the way for that final domestic harmony. A 1966 reviewer praised Sir Ralph Richardson's 'exhilarating performance' of Sir Anthony for his ability in the quarrel scenes to convey the character's insistence *both* that 'his son should obey him implicitly' *and* 'that he should have the spirit to show defi-ance'.[12] Patriarchal outrage fuelled the scenes' climaxes; fond pride prepared for eventual reconciliation. Sheridan frequently requires such Janus-faced dexterity from his actors.

His admiration for the plays of William Congreve means that the father/son rows in *The Rivals* sometimes recall the collisions between Sir Sampson and Valentine in Congreve's *Love for Love* (1695). Thus, Sir Anthony's furious crescendo, 'I'll disown you, I'll disinherit you, I'll unget you!'(2.1.428–9), echoes his predecessor's 'Are not you my slave? Did not I beget you? And might not I have chosen whether I would have begot you or not?'[13] But in Congreve's play the quarrel between father and son is deeply rooted, intensifies harshly in their mutual rivalry for Angelica's favours, and ends in total alienation. In contrast, Sir Anthony savours Lydia's charms luxuriously, but always recognizes that '*Youth's the season made for joy*' (4.2.151–2), and that the best he can now hope for is to be an excited and approving observer of his son's conquest of her. Consequently, where Restoration comedy characteristically finds its subject in radical confrontation and the eventual subjugation of one character by another, *The Rivals* designs its characters so that all their quarrels will be evanescent and ensures that its audience will throughout be snugly confident of this.

As a result, the comic energy of individual scenes in *The Rivals* derives scarcely at all from narrative tension, but depends almost entirely upon the deft juxtaposition of characters and a delight in the

[12] D. A. N. Jones, 'When the Bad Bleed', *New Statesman*, 14 Oct. 1966, 563.

[13] William Congreve, *Comedies*, ed. Eric S. Rump (Harmondsworth, 1985), 243.

incongruous and eccentric behaviour these carefully contrived encounters elicit from their principal participants. Stuart Tave has mapped the process by which in the third quarter of the eighteenth century 'pride and contempt were eliminated from the generally accepted theory' of the comic and 'a more joyful and kindly theory of laughter, based on incongruity, was established as the convention'. Among other illustrations of this, he cites Alexander Gerard's 1759 definition of 'incongruity' as 'a surprising and uncommon mixture of *relation* and *contrariety* in things'.[14] That is a category into which it is easy to fit both Mrs Malaprop's idiosyncratic oscillations between linguistic deftness and incompetence and Sir Anthony's simultaneous experiencing of both fury and delight at his son's behaviour. It also applies to the set-piece displays of most of the play's other main characters—to Bob Acres's ability, for instance, to combine heroic ambition and enervating terror as he confronts the prospect of fighting a duel and Faulkland's amorous obsession with, and constant self-generated distrust of, his fiancée Julia.

The theories Tave describes are part of an attempt to vindicate at least certain kinds of laughter by grounding them in benevolent feelings. In 1762 Lord Kames, in an influential passage, sought to distinguish between the 'risible' and the 'ridiculous', the former raising 'an emotion of laughter that is altogether pleasant', the latter an emotion that 'is qualified with that of contempt'. He argued that 'I avenge myself of the pain a ridiculous object gives me by a laugh of derision'; whereas a 'risible object . . . gives me no pain: it is altogether pleasant by a certain sort of titillation, which is expressed externally by mirthful laughter'.[15] In these terms, the laughter in which Sheridan specializes in *The Rivals* belongs predominantly to the category of the 'risible'. Even Mrs Malaprop, in an inventive, nuanced performance, will provoke a response in which embryonic contempt soon gives way to a form of delighted celebration. Here, for example, is a graphic description of the finest performance of the role—by Geraldine McEwan at the National Theatre in 1983—I have witnessed:

Geraldine McEwan's Malaprop is neither bumbling lady brontosaurus nor dyslexic Lady Bracknell, but a woman whose pride is her intellect and whose weakness is to set it challenges it has never been trained to meet. She is like Sisyphus with his stone, for ever flexing her mental muscles, seizing on

[14] Stuart M. Tave, *The Amiable Humorist: A Study in the Comic Theory and Criticism of the Eighteenth and Early Nineteenth Centuries* (Chicago and London, 1960), 74–5.
[15] Ibid. 76–7.

intransigent words, and trying to shove them into impossible places. It is a task that, understandably enough, brings her moments of self-doubt, even panic; and, when she thinks she's accomplished it, the relief on that solemn, superior face of hers is marvellous to see. But it is also an obsession, a compulsive need to prove and reassure herself: so much so that Miss McEwan can get away with increasing the number of malapropisms provided by her author. Her last sentence, 'Men are all barbarians', quite plausibly becomes 'Men are all Bavarians'; and off she stalks, nostrils quivering, to find new words to conquer.[16]

Another celebration of McEwan's achievements, this time by Katharine Worth, pinpoints how much of the role's potential she had succeeded in realizing:

McEwan conveyed an impression of someone with more energy than she could find outlet for; someone who longed to inhabit—and partly did—a more interesting world of the mind than that conventionally assigned to a middle-aged woman of her class and time. Curiously, she brought to mind another scatter-brained misquoter, from a very different realm, Beckett's Winnie [in *Happy Days*]. Like her, McEwan's Malaprop fished about in her memory for expressive words, sayings, proverbs, lines from Shakespeare. Her failures . . . were comical, as they have to be, but, again like Winnie's, indicated something aspiring in the character which the audience could not afford to despise. How many of them, after all, could fill in correctly for her at every point? . . . Gaps in the audience's laughter usually show where the erudite joke has gone beyond them and they are obliged to share in her all-too-human tendency to error.[17]

Such bravura playing stimulates and feeds an appetite in its audience for yet further and more extreme displays of the behaviour and invention which have already so delighted it. William Hazlitt, paying tribute to another first-rate performance in *The Rivals*, that of James Dodd as Acres, thought such histrionic athleticism the fundamental demand Sheridan had imposed upon his players. Because of the 'extravagance of the poet's conception', imaginative investment on an unusual scale by the leading actors was a *sine qua non* for a successful staging:

In proportion, therefore, as the author has overdone the part, it calls for a greater effort of animal spirits, and a peculiar aptitude of genius in the actor to go through with it, to humour the extravagance, and to seem to take a real and cordial delight in caricaturing himself. Dodd was the only actor we remember who realised this ideal combination of volatility and phlegm, of

---

[16] Benedict Nightingale, 'Absolutely', *New Statesman*, 22 Apr. 1983, 31–2.
[17] Katharine Worth, *Sheridan and Goldsmith* (London, 1992), 129.

slowness of understanding with levity of purpose, of vacancy of thought and vivacity of gesture. Acres's affected phrases and apish manners used to sit upon this inimitable actor with the same sort of bumpkin grace and conscious self-complacency as the new cut of his clothes. In general, this character is made little of on the stage; and when left to shift for itself, seems as vapid as it is forced.[18]

Sheridan writes brilliantly for his performers and has accordingly won plaudits from generation after generation of England's finest actors.[19] But, as Hazlitt's remarks remind us, Sheridan's exemplary craftsmanship demands an answering brilliance in his players. Characters constructed upon such ostentatiously conventional and narrow principles—the angry father, the intellectually overambitious lady, etc.—can easily dwindle into stale repetitiveness unless the local precision of the writing is matched by a comparable variety and ingenuity in the playing; and that requires the highest powers in the actors. George Bernard Shaw's comment on Sheridan's comedies contains an important truth, as long as the phrase I have printed in italics is given equal weight with the rest of his statement:

Sheridan wrote for the actor as Handel wrote for the singer, setting him a combination of strokes, which, *however difficult some of them may be to execute finely*, are familiar to all practised actors as the strokes which experience has shewn to be proper to the nature and capacity of the stage-player as a dramatic instrument.[20]

That neatly captures Sheridan's characteristic combination of intense conservatism, innate theatricality, and technical precision. He is especially exacting vocally, as James Boaden makes clear in narrating the problems Mrs Jordan faced in tackling roles Sheridan had created for the preceding generation of leading actresses:

The fact is, that Sheridan's ear was made up to this artificial cadence in the drama. His own declamation was of the old school; and when you read either his *School for Scandal* or his *Critic*, you discover the *tune* to which, like a composer, he had set every line in them. Accordingly, a natural actress, like Mrs.

---

[18] William Hazlitt, 'Introduction' to W. Oxberry (ed.), *The New English Drama* (1818), repr. in Peter Davison (ed.), *Sheridan, Comedies: A Casebook* (London, 1986), 86–7.
[19] For tributes by David Garrick, Sir Henry Irving, and Sir John Gielgud respectively, for instance, see Arthur Murphy, *The Life of David Garrick, Esq.* (London, 1801), ii. 145; W. Fraser Rae, *Sheridan: A Biography* (London, 1896), ii. 322; John Gielgud, *Stage Directions* (London, 1963), 76.
[20] George Bernard Shaw, *Our Theatres in the Nineties* (London, 1932), ii. 170.

Jordan, was all abroad in this *antithetic* and *pointed* speech; it did not suit her manner, and was against her judgment or her feeling, whichever you call it; and in Sheridan's opinion, which I know was a sincere one, she could not 'speak a line' of Cora [in *Pizarro*]. But she felt the situation keenly, and played with as much zeal as could be wished.[21]

As an actor framed by nature and training to meet Sheridan's demands, Boaden offers Thomas King, the original Sir Peter Teazle and Puff:

The language of common parlance was not for his mouth. He converted every thing into epigram; and although no man's utterance was more rapid, yet the *ictus* fell so smartly upon the point, his tune was so perfect, and the members of his sentences were so well antagonized, that he spoke all such composition with more effect than any man of his time. Those who remember his delivery of Touchstone's degrees of the lie, and Puff's recapitulation of his own mendicant and literary arts, will have no difficulty in assenting to my remark.[22]

Such gifts are rare in any generation. McEwan's triumph, however, demonstrates that they are not totally the monopoly of Sheridan's original actors.

The Duenna

With *The Rivals* securely ensconced in the repertoire, Sheridan might have been expected to rest on his laurels for a time. Instead, by the end of 1775 Sheridan produced two more plays. The first was a brief farce, *St Patrick's Day; or, The Scheming Lieutenant*, composed partly in gratitude to Lawrence Clinch, whose performance as Sir Lucius in the revised version of *The Rivals* had contributed crucially to its success. This was then followed by the first performance on 21 November of *The Duenna*, 'one of the most successful operas ever staged'. It achieved the astonishing total of seventy-five performances in its first season and 'was constantly given all over Britain until the 1840s, when Covent Garden staged it for the last time'.[23] The first newspaper notices produced a rich crop of superlatives, calling it, for instance, 'the best comic opera since the time of Gay' and acclaiming it for 'the richness of the plot, the strong and natural connection and succession of incident, the drollery and contrast of situation, and the humour of

---

[21] James Boaden, *The Life of Mrs. Jordan* (London, 1831), i. 23–4.

[22] James Boaden, *Memoirs of the Life of John Philip Kemble, Esq.* (London, 1825), i. 60.

[23] Roger Fiske, *English Theatre Music in the Eighteenth Century* (London, 1973), 414.

the dialogue' (Price, i. 206 and 211). It also in time earned the applause of more renowned admirers, including Samuel Johnson, William Hazlitt, and Lord Byron.[24]

Sheridan's planning of *The Duenna* demonstrates his outstanding flair for the optimal use of available resources. In turning to opera he was responding to a powerful theatrical current. Between the summer of 1776 and the century's end, 'of the twelve most performed main pieces six were operas, four were plays by Shakespeare, and two were modern plays'.[25] It also enabled him to put to work the formidable musical talents of the family into which he had recently married. Both his father-in-law and brother-in-law were accomplished musicians and composers, and Elizabeth Linley, his wife, was one of the outstanding singers of her generation.[26] The original manuscript of the libretto is in Elizabeth's handwriting, and it seems likely that Sheridan, lacking musical training, leaned greatly on her advice. He was, however, a swift learner, and his letters to his father-in-law, Thomas Linley the Elder, explaining how he wished his words to be set, are characteristically precise. Thus, he wanted Carlos's air at the end of Act 1 to match exactly the strengths of Michael Leoni, the Italian tenor who was to play the role:

I want him to show himself advantageously in the six lines, beginning 'Gentle maid'. I should tell you, that he sings nothing well but in a plaintive or pastoral style; and his voice is such as appears to me always to be hurt by much accompaniment. I have observed, too, that he never gets so much applause as when he makes a cadence. Therefore my idea is, that he should make a flourish at 'Shall I grieve thee?' and return to 'Gentle maid', and so sing that part of the tune again. After that, the two last lines, sung by the three, with the persons only varied, may get them off with as much spirit as possible. The second act ends with a *slow* glee, therefore I should think the two last lines in question had better be brisk, especially as Quick and Mrs. Mattocks are concerned in it. (*Letters*, i. 89)

He has no inhibitions about issuing firm directions to his father-in-law, and that confidence grows from his capacity to observe a performer's strengths and capitalize upon them.

---

[24] James Boswell, *The Life of Johnson*, ed. G. B. Hill, rev. L. F. Powell (Oxford, 1934), iii. 115–16; William Hazlitt, 'On the Comic Writers of the Last Century', in *Collected Works*, ed. A. R. Waller and Arnold Glover (London, 1903), viii. 164; Lord Byron, *Letters and Journals*, ed. Leslie A. Marchand, iii. (London, 1974), 239.

[25] Fiske, *English Theatre Music*, 412.

[26] For the Linley family, the authoritative work is Clementina Black, *The Linleys of Bath*, 3rd edn. (London, 1971).

Sheridan's choice of plot and setting in *The Duenna* is rooted in a lengthy stage tradition of 'Spanish honour' dramas.[27] David Garrick, for example, had often appeared in his own adaptation of the Duke of Buckingham's 1660s rewriting of one of the earliest examples of the mode, John Fletcher's *The Chances* (*c.*1617). *The Duenna* includes many of the characteristic features of the genre—daughters escaping, or being evicted, from their fathers' houses, confusions of identity on nocturnal streets, congenitally jealous gallants only too eager to draw their swords on the slightest provocation, and so on. *The Chances*, for instance, contains two characters named Constantia, one an honourable woman fleeing from family tyranny, the other a whore. The former, mistaken for the latter, faces a sequence of tense, potentially compromising encounters. In another version of the Spanish plot the mistakes of the night test the leading male character's honour as multiplying confusions confront him with difficult choices between competing obligations. A popular example of this variant can be found in the first great comic success of the Restoration stage, Sir Samuel Tuke's *The Adventures of Five Hours* (1663).

Sheridan has no wish to put his characters through comparable ordeals. A characteristic moment in *The Duenna* occurs when Don Jerome evicts Louisa onto a dark street where 'yonder is some fellow skulking' (1.4.3). The anticipated threat never materializes. Louisa, left alone in the darkness, wishes that her best friend might be with her and has her wish immediately granted. In similar circumstances in *The Chances*, the chaste Constantia was allowed no comforting female companionship to alleviate her situation. Her forlorn plight as the object of pursuit and contumely explored how vulnerable a gentlewoman might be to the loss of her reputation once exiled from the family which might oppress but would also protect her. In this kind of play the night's confusions open the possibility that the distinction between chaste woman and whore can easily become irreparably blurred. In *The Duenna*, Louisa's desire that Clara might be with her is qualified by the thought that Clara's 'prudery would condemn' her flight from her father (1.5.11); but, simultaneously, the absconding Clara is rejecting the thought of contacting Louisa because 'her notions of filial duty are so severe, she would certainly betray me' (ll. 14–15). They then recognize each other and happily embrace. The

---

[27] The full history of this genre remains to be written; but the exploration of it has been begun in John Loftis, *The Spanish Plays of Neo-Classical England* (New Haven and London, 1973).

thought that their nocturnal antics might open them to censure is invoked in order to be discounted. Sheridan consistently purges all the situations he derives from the 'Spanish honour' drama, denuding them of threat, and making the night a safe place for ladies of impeccable virtue.

The early contrast between Ferdinand's tense distrustfulness and Antonio's cynical 'levity' (1.2.117) recalls many comparable male pairings in earlier 'Spanish honour' plays, including *The Adventures of Five Hours*. The two men's respective humours are played off neatly against each other in 1.2, climaxing with the nicely contrasted airs with which that scene concludes. But no significant dramatic consequences flow from this opposition. Antonio's insouciant boast that he would always betray a friend rather than a mistress (1.2.105–16) remains merely a boast. And within a few scenes his 'levity', which so riled Ferdinand, has been abandoned, so that, when Isaac asserts that 'you are no honest fellow, if love can't make a rogue of you' (2.4.63–4), Antonio takes the sober line against him, asking, 'And could you reconcile it to your conscience, to supplant your friend?' (ll. 60–1). The character who is by then displaying 'levity' is Isaac, constantly convulsed with laughter in (misguided) admiration of his own Machiavellian cunning, and inviting Louisa and Antonio to share the laugh with him.

G. Wilson Knight has argued that 'Perhaps Sheridan's most typifying trick is his way of showing people being amused at a situation wherein the audience knows that it is they themselves who are being fooled' and observed, with only slight exaggeration, that *The Duenna* 'is made almost entirely from this type of dramatic irony'.[28] Early responses to the play also remarked on this. Charles Dibdin, no friend of Sheridan's, still celebrated 'the *aside* speeches of *Isaac*'; 'shewing beforehand how clearly he shall himself be taken in by his different attempts to deceive others, is the most artful species of anticipation that ever was practised, and shews a judgment of theatrical effect powerful, new, and extraordinary' (Price, i. 213). The premise from which Isaac's role is developed is laid out for us before his first entry: he possesses a 'passion for deceit, and tricks of cunning', but 'the fool predominates so much over the knave, that . . . he is generally the dupe of his own art' (1.3.59–61). Almost every self-regarding move he makes helps to bring the lovers' aims closer to fruition; and his crowing enjoyment of his own brilliance invites and legitimizes the laughter

---

[28] G. Wilson Knight, *The Golden Labyrinth: A Study of British Drama* (London, 1962), 185.

bestowed on him by the other characters and the spectators. If Antonio's early 'levity' in preferring '*A breach of social faith*' to a friend to disloyalty to a mistress (1.2.115–16) had been translated into action, the comedy might have moved into morally problematic territory, as numerous earlier 'Spanish honour' plays had been designed to do; but Sheridan refuses to follow his own cue and once again prefers an ingeniously anodyne reinvention of his dramatic inheritance.

As a result, the progress of Antonio, Louisa, and Clara through the night begins to resemble a tourist trip. At one moment, indeed, in tones appropriate to the philosophical travellers in Samuel Johnson's *Rasselas* (1759), Antonio proposes to Louisa that, since 'You have already been diverted by the manners of a nunnery', it might be a pleasurable next step to 'see whether there is less hypocrisy among the holy fathers' (3.3.80–2). All narrative urgency has disappeared. Because of their anti-Catholic satire, the early Italian translations of *The Duenna* omit the friars scenes. It is remarkably easy to do this. They can be removed without any effect on the opera's smooth progress towards its ending. A model for these scenes has plausibly been discovered in John Dryden's *The Spanish Friar* (1680), whose exuberantly fleshly Father Dominick can certainly claim a family resemblance to Sheridan's friars; but Father Dominick is intrinsic to the earlier play's design in a way that cannot be claimed for his descendants in *The Duenna*. Dryden's masterpiece is an intricate meditation on piety and treachery in times of civil turmoil, and through both its plots variations are woven on those preoccupations. A friar who jubilantly exploits his calling for profit and who considers no chicanery beneath him qualifies naturally as a key figure in Dryden's design. Sheridan's friars are, in contrast, merely another item on the varied menu he is setting before his audience and, as such, were applauded in the early reviews (Price, i. 208).

The songs were, of course, fundamental to the success of *The Duenna*. Linda V. Troost has recently argued that Sheridan devotes his 'dialogue to the elaborate plotting' and 'economically leaves the development of character to the music'.[29] This looks questionable to me. Many of the lyrics seem to me rather to indulge passing moods without any lasting consequence for our perception of the character who sings them. We have already noted how little relationship Antonio's '*Friendship is the bond of reason*' air (1.2.105 ff.) has to his subsequent

[29] Linda V. Troost, 'The Characterizing Power of Song in Sheridan's *The Duenna*', *Eighteenth-Century Studies*, 20 (1986–7), 155.

behaviour. Similarly, Don Jerome waxes briefly rakish in '*When the maid whom we love*' (2.1.87 ff.), and Louisa, waiting for her lover, considers sententiously '*What bard*' it was who first bestowed wings on Cupid (2.4.5 ff.). In each case, the pleasure of the moment appears to be the predominant motive behind the movement into song, not careful calculation of how a particular song can contribute to a larger design. *The Duenna* is a triumph of the anecdotal.

In this respect, it is an extreme instance of a tendency characteristic of all Sheridan's writing for the stage. Martin Meisel has explored the development of a new dramaturgy in the late eighteenth century. He contrasts it with an older style of play creation, in which 'the building block of the play was transitive'—that is, each 'piece of the dramatic whole typically came from somewhere, or led somewhere, or both'. In this dramaturgy, 'however peripatetic the course of the play, however divided its plots or contrived for the accommodation of turns, the standard remains an unfolding continuum'. In contrast, in the new dramaturgy, of which he judges Sheridan to be a principal practitioner,

the [scenic] unit is intransitive; it is in fact an achieved moment of stasis, a picture. The play creates a series of such pictures, some of them offering a culminating symbolic summary of represented events, while others substitute an arrested situation for action and reaction. Each picture, dissolving, leads not into consequent activity, but to a new infusion and distribution of elements from which a new picture will be assembled or resolved. The form is serial discontinuity, like that of the magic lantern, or the so-called 'Dissolving Views.'[30]

In 1840, Edward Mayhew explored the 'modern theory . . . that *dramatic success is dependent on situations*'. He explained that

To theatrical minds the word 'situation' suggests some strong point in a play likely to command applause; where the action is wrought to a climax, where the actors strike attitudes, and form what they call 'a picture,' during the exhibition of which a pause takes place; after which the action is renewed, not continued, and advantage of which is frequently taken to turn the natural current of the interest.[31]

Mayhew exemplifies this with an analysis of the screen scene in *The School for Scandal*; but numerous moments from *The Duenna* would have served his purpose just as well. In Meisel's terms, it is the product

---

[30] Martin Meisel, *Realizations: Narrative, Pictorial, and Theatrical Arts in Nineteenth-Century England* (Princeton, 1983), 38.

[31] Edward Mayhew, *Stage Effect: Or, The Principles Which Command Dramatic Success in the Theatre* (London, 1840), 44.

of a 'pictorial dramaturgy . . . organizing a play as a series of achieved situations, or effects'.[32]

Sheridan's is a pastiche opera—that is, its musical score is an eclectic combination of traditional ballads, other composers' established successes, and new tunes (provided in this case by the Linleys, father and, more frequently, son). Between 1775 and 1835 five editions of the vocal score were published, but no edition of the orchestral score or parts was ever printed. 'Hence one of the greatest operatic successes London has ever known is now totally neglected.'[33] Roger Fiske, the author of those words, has gone a long way towards remedying that situation by his researches; but we still await the major stage revival which his work has rendered possible. Sheridan's libretto has, however, spurred other composers to action. Prokofiev used it for his opera *The Betrothal in the Monastery*. He saw two possibilities in it for the composer: 'to underline in the music the comic side of the work' or 'to rely on the romantic aspect'.[34] He favoured the second, though he did not entirely neglect the comic possibilities, especially in a 'bravura chorus of the carousing monks ("The bottle's the sun of our life") . . . followed by a decorous, ascetic chant, which is interrupted by the drunken exclamations' of one of the friars.[35] The première of Prokofiev's opera was forestalled by the German invasion of the Soviet Union in 1941, and its first performance was consequently delayed until 1946. A year earlier, the exiled Catalan composer Roberto Gerhard had come upon a copy of Sheridan's play on a market-stall in Cambridge and, without commission or hope of performance, immediately began to plan a setting of it. *The Duenna*, his first and only opera, was completed in 1947 and premièred in a BBC radio broadcast in 1949. It had to wait until 1992 for its first stage production. Gerhard's music, though often exuberant and celebratory, also has a sadder, darker undertow. Don Jerome's suavely matter-of-fact speech about his dead wife becomes, most remarkably, an expression of genuine loss, with a solo violin etching out the old man's grief. Similarly, the final festivities are undercut by an offstage chorus of beggars and recurrent musical references to a penitential chant first heard at the opera's beginning. It is one of the paradoxes of this extraordinary

[32] Meisel, *Realizations*, 41.

[33] Roger Fiske, 'A Score for *The Duenna*', *Music and Letters*, 42 (1961), 132.

[34] Claude Samuel, *Prokofiev*, trans. Miriam John (London, 1971), 140.

[35] Israel V. Nestyev, *Prokofiev*, trans. Florence Jonas (Stanford, Calif., 1961), 391.

labour of love that Gerhard systematically reintroduces those graver preoccupations Sheridan had so carefully excluded from his original text.[36]

A Trip to Scarborough

With Garrick's retirement in 1776 Sheridan became one of the owners of Drury Lane and its manager. His first season there produced a frenetic burst of administrative activity; but audiences were naturally impatient for the first play of his written for his new company. Disappointment was therefore natural when his initial offering, *A Trip to Scarborough*, proved to be, not a new comedy, but an adaptation of John Vanbrugh's *The Relapse; or, Virtue in Danger* (1696). *The Relapse* was a favourite repertory piece for seventy years after its première, though gradually subjected to accelerating bowdlerization. By the late 1760s, however, changing taste meant that the tide was turning against it, and it 'was acted in the London theatres only on one occasion in the ten years after 7 May 1766' (Price, i. 554). John Lee, the disastrous Sir Lucius in the first performance of *The Rivals*, had carved out one of its plots—Fashion's attempt to snatch the heiress Hoyden from his brother, Lord Foppington—to produce a short farce, *The Man of Quality*, performed at Covent Garden on 27 April 1773. It achieved some further performances, but enjoyed no real success. Although it is a piece of nondescript hackwork, Lee's experiment may have alerted Sheridan to the possibility of undertaking his own adaptation. He was perhaps especially encouraged to do so by the performances of James William Dodd as Foppington and Frances Abington as Hoyden, roles they would also adorn in *A Trip to Scarborough*.[37]

The Relapse had been one of the prime targets of Jeremy Collier's wrath in his notorious attack on the contemporary drama in 1698. Collier impugned both Vanbrugh's technical competence—he dubbed the play 'a Heap of Irregularities'—and his moral probity. He asserted that his '*Play* perverts the End of *Comedy*: Which . . . ought to regard Reformation, and publick Improvement. But the *Relapser* had a more fashionable Fancy in his Head.' Accordingly, the play's 'Moral is

---

[36] A recording of Gerhard's opera, by Opera North and conducted by Antoni Ros Marbá, is now available on CD (Chan 9520(2)).

[37] Amy Elizabeth Smith, 'Casting and the Manager's Role in Sheridan's *A Trip to Scarborough*', *Theatre Notebook*, 47 (1993), 170–2.

vitious: It points the wrong way, and puts the *Prize* into the wrong Hand'.[38]

Sheridan acts on both of Collier's objections. He tidies the play remorselessly, linking its two stories in ways Vanbrugh had not bothered to attempt. The quartet of potential adulterers in the comedy's other plot, for example, now become co-conspirators in the hoodwinking of Foppington; whereas in *The Relapse* characters from the two plots share the stage on two social occasions, but otherwise lead separate existences. In addition, Sheridan signposts his characters' moods and motives with a zeal nowhere paralleled in Vanbrugh's text. In *A Trip*, the marriage-broker on her first entry must immediately proclaim her resentful distrust of Foppington. In *The Relapse*, the same information emerges fluently later in the scene. At moments like this, Sheridan seems to trust his audience's intelligence less than Vanbrugh did his.

The other aspect of the changes he introduces is exemplified by the transformation of Vanbrugh's homosexual marriage-broker, with his extrovert attraction to Fashion's inviting flesh, into the drably business-like Mrs Coupler, whose only concern is with her profit margins. Decorums of the 1770s made some alteration of this kind unavoidable; but the loss in adrenalin is palpable. Vanbrugh's scene is alive with delight at its own outrageousness; Sheridan's manages to do little more than carry the narrative forward.

In the Fashion/Foppington plot Sheridan's taming of Vanbrugh proceeds along straightforward, but rigorous, lines. Thus, Lory can be allowed to say, in a line borrowed with some insignificant variations from *The Relapse*, 'I'm glad to find I was not so well acquainted with the strength of your conscience as with the weakness of your purse' (1.1.49–50); but Fashion cannot be permitted to retort, as in *The Relapse*, 'Methinks, sir, a person of your experience should have known that the strength of the conscience proceeds from the weakness of the purse' (1.2.61–3).[39] That even such a modest cynicism is beyond the pale indicates how tight the constraints were within which Sheridan believed himself to be working.

The physical and sexual explicitness of much of Vanbrugh's writing must similarly be neutered. Hoyden's delight at the thought of being

[38] Jeremy Collier, *A Short View of the Immorality, and Profaneness of the English Stage* (London, 1698), 231, 211, and 210.

[39] Act, scene, and line references for quotations from *The Relapse* in the introduction are from the text of the play in Sir John Vanbrugh, *Four Comedies*, ed. Michael Cordner (Harmondsworth, 1989).

married twice to Fashion (*A Trip*, 4.1.137–9) can no longer be capped, and glossed, by her aside about the pleasure of the 'two wedding-nights' this will entail (*Relapse*, 4.1.128). Nor can she be allowed to assert defiantly that she will put on her 'laced smock, though I am whipped till the blood run down my heels for't' (3.4.31–2). In *The Relapse*, the body is often graphically envisaged, while, in *A Trip to Scarborough*, its nakedness and indignity are masked from view.

Sheridan's alterations to the Fashion/Foppington plot consist mainly of this kind of systematic chastening of the dialogue. The principal events, though telescoped into a smaller compass, remain essentially as in *The Relapse*. With the other plot his interventions are more radical. In Vanbrugh's play Berinthia and Worthy (renamed Townly by Sheridan), themselves ex-lovers, conspire together to lure Amanda and Loveless into adultery. The first part of the plan works smoothly, with Loveless triumphantly bearing Berinthia offstage in his arms by the middle of Act 4. Amanda proves more difficult to conquer; and, as the play ends, her spirited resistance seems to have converted Worthy into a chastely platonic devotee, though he himself is unsure 'How long this influence may last' (5.4.160).

The direction Sheridan's recasting of Vanbrugh's story will take is indicated when Fashion, hearing of Townley's interest in Amanda, confidently asserts that the latter's friendship with her husband 'will prevent your pursuing' it 'too far' (1.1.124–5). In *The Duenna*, Antonio was at least allowed to proclaim in a song a willingness to sacrifice friendship to eros. In *A Trip*, such behaviour is declared ungentlemanly from the start. Vanbrugh's Worthy and Berinthia acknowledged no such impediment to the satisfaction of their desires. Sheridan must therefore eliminate their duplicitous conspiracy and reinvent their relationship. In place of their past love-affair, Sheridan inserts a courtship, with view to marriage, which has been stalled by mutual misunderstandings. Piqued by the other's behaviour, each entertains briefly the thought of turning for solace to an adulterous affair. But their entertaining of this idea is tentative and frequently checked by doubts and scruples. Vanbrugh's Berinthia ends one scene with a pleasurable anticipation of the adulterous fate awaiting Amanda: 'she seems to me to be in as fair a way—as a boy is to be a rogue, when he's put clerk to an attorney' (4.2.131–2). Sheridan retains the comparison, but his Berinthia applies it to herself: 'I seem to be in as fair a way to lose my gallant colonel, as a boy is to be a rogue, when he's put clerk to an attorney' (3.2.136–7). In *A Trip*, Berinthia preserves little of her predecessor's witty relish for engineering the sexual education of the ingenuous; her thoughts turn more naturally to the perplexities of her own situation and the risks she runs of losing Townly as her future husband.

Vanbrugh's Loveless, like Sheridan's, reports a recent visit to the playhouse. He saw there a comedy with a story rather like his own— of a husband who had committed adultery, repented, and been forgiven by his virtuous wife—but the playwright had added the husband's relapse into further infidelity and catalogued the 'train of mischiefs' (2.1.61) which as a consequence befell him. Loveless claimed to have been affected by this moral fable and consequently checked his eyes from admiring a beautiful woman seated near him. That beauty is, of course, Berinthia, and in *The Relapse* Loveless's progress into adultery with her brings with it no 'train of mischiefs' to punish him for his backsliding. Vanbrugh is encouraging his spectators to be very self-aware about their own responses. If the play Loveless witnessed had a moral effect upon him, however temporary, what will the effect be upon spectators of enjoying a comedy in which adulterers escape unpunished? The seduction scene between Berinthia and Loveless climaxes with a famous moment when, settled comfortably in her lover's arms, she *whispers*, 'Help, help, I'm ravished, ruined, undone. O Lord, I shall never be able to bear it' (4.3.78–9). An audience which laughs with her has been taught to recognize the implications of its laughter.

The play Vanbrugh's Loveless watches has no relevance to Sheridan's Loveless, since he has no adulterous past to worry about. Sheridan therefore omits that passage. He retains much of the rest of the sequence, but turns the original debate between husband and wife about the immorality of the contemporary—i.e. 1690s—drama into a conversation about whether Restoration comedy should be banished from the 1770s stage, or whether, as Loveless argues, ''twould surely be a pity to exclude the productions of some of our best writers for want of a little wholesome pruning, which might be effected by anyone who possessed modesty enough to believe that we should preserve all we can of our deceased authors, at least till they are outdone by the living ones' (2.1.21–6). Sheridan is, immodestly, identifying himself as possessed of the appropriate 'modesty' to effect that task.

He still allows an Act 4 meeting between Loveless and Berinthia in her dressing-room; but where Vanbrugh's seduction scene begins with a Loveless eager for 'a chase of five hours' (4.3.4), Sheridan's Loveless seems merely to want to talk to Berinthia and is even unsure if he can 'muster up assurance to show' himself 'when she comes' (4.3.5–6).

Vanbrugh's Berinthia enters, excited at having left Amanda and Worthy alone together at cards and thinking fondly of Loveless's attractions; while, in *A Trip*, she enters on edge because she has had to 'sit and hear' Townly 'compliment Amanda to my face' (ll. 13–14). The erotic energy of Vanbrugh's writing is thus cancelled, and the eventual encounter between them is consequently brief, unproductive, and, in any case, soon aborted by Amanda's arrival to speak with Berinthia. From concealment, Loveless hears their conversation and for the first time learns of what might have developed between his wife and Townly. The scene ends, not, as in *The Relapse*, with an exuberant exit to offstage love-making, but with Loveless, the chastened spectator, moralizing on how a wife's 'virtues can atone her husband's sins' (l. 80).

Sheridan weaves variations on the same effect in what one of the first reviewers hailed as the 'entire new scene in the fifth [act], producing the *denouement* in a different and improved manner'; while another reported that 'The moonlight scene is quite new, and, in our judgment, the best in the piece' (Price, i. 556–7). The scene—5.1—was not, in fact, entirely new, but reprocesses material from Vanbrugh's 5.4 encounter between Amanda and Worthy. What *is* totally new is that it begins with brief exchanges between Loveless and Berinthia, which are again interrupted by Amanda's entry. Loveless and Berinthia then watch from hiding, but in view of the audience, Amanda's rejection of her wooer. The experience shames and subdues them:

BERINTHIA Don't you think we steal forth two very contemptible creatures?
LOVELESS Why, tolerably so, I must confess.
BERINTHIA And do you conceive it possible for you ever to give Amanda the least uneasiness again?
LOVELESS No, I think we never should, indeed. (5.1.99–104)

This, I take it, is Sheridan's deft reply to Vanbrugh's refusal to allow Loveless's career as adulterer to confirm the moral lesson of the play he watched. In *A Trip* Loveless and Berinthia's experiences as spectators have the reformative effect 1770s expectations would also demand of the ideal theatre event. *The Relapse*, and the playhouse, had been redeemed for morality despite all Vanbrugh's best efforts; and in the process Sheridan had produced another comedy which, after a mixed initial critical response, would in due course settle comfortably into a secure place in the repertoire.

One result of that was the prolonged banishment of Vanbrugh's masterpiece from the stage. As late as 1950 Harold Hobson felt the need to reassure his readers that a London company was indeed right to stage *The Relapse* instead of Sheridan's adaptation.[40] The pendulum of taste has now once again swung in Vanbrugh's favour; but *A Trip to Scarborough* has been allowed a further lease of life, thanks to Alan Ayckbourn's decision to exercise his own formidable skills on it. His reshaping of Sheridan's play, however, is at least as radical as Gerhard's reworking of *The Duenna*, since it blows 'Sheridan's unification of Vanbrugh's double-plot sky high' and turns 'it into three, not two, disconnected plots set in three distinct historical periods—1800, 1940 and 1980—only associated by the nominal continuity provided by the names of the characters'.[41]

The School for Scandal

Arnold Hare has observed that *A Trip to Scarborough* may have been important to Sheridan mainly 'as a preparation for the writing of his next comedy, *The School for Scandal*, which opened on 8 May of the same year'.[42] The combative union of the Teazles certainly recalls the careers of numerous unhappy spouses in Restoration marriage comedy, a comic mode of which *The Relapse* is itself a prime example. Several generations of post-1660 dramatists—from Etherege's *She Would If She Could* (1668) and Shadwell's *Epsom Wells* (1672) to Southerne's *The Wives' Excuse* (1691) and Farquhar's *The Beaux' Stratagem* (1707)—had anatomized marriages in disarray or terminal catastrophe.[43] Their precedents had in turn fed a lengthy series of eighteenth-century comedies mapping the same territory. *The School for Scandal* is indebted to some of these later works; but, as his work as reviser of *The Relapse* confirms, Sheridan was also well aware of those late seventeenth-century masterpieces which originated the comic mode to which he was now making an original contribution.

If *A Trip to Scarborough* allows us to watch him at work purifying Vanbrugh, the survival in manuscript of two brief and inchoate

---

[40] Harold Hobson, *Theatre 2* (London, 1950), 8.

[41] Hugh Haughton, reviewing its première in the *Times Literary Supplement*, 7 Jan. 1983, repr. in Malcom Page (ed.), *File on Ayckbourn* (London, 1989), 70.

[42] Arnold Hare, *Richard Brinsley Sheridan* (Windsor, 1981), 25.

[43] On this genre, see Robert D. Hume, 'Marital Discord in English Comedy from Dryden to Fielding', *Modern Philology*, 74 (1976–7), 248–72; Michael Cordner, 'Marrage Comedy after the 1688 Revolution: Southerne to Vanbrugh', *Modern Language Review*, 85 (1990), 273–89.

playlets, 'The Slanderers' and 'Sir Peter Teazle', permits us to glimpse
some of the processes which lay behind the creation of one of his masterpieces. Both playlets mingle extended sequences of performable
dialogue with passages where Sheridan hastily jots down ideas about
plot and costume, fragments of dialogue, and promising aphorisms.
The dramatist revealed is one who, eager to waste nothing, records all
his ideas as they occur. Many of these passing thoughts eventually find
a place in the completed script.

Between them, the two playlets introduce many of the principal
characters of the eventual comedy, including Lady Sneerwell, Mrs
Candour, the Teazles, and two brothers of dissimilar temperament and
competing interests, who are not yet, however, named Joseph and
Charles. Among the numerous refinements and recastings which lay
ahead was a wholesale chastening of language and motive. Young
Pliant, for instance, Joseph's predecessor, is given a franker statement
of his cynical manipulation of his brother's declining reputation than
Joseph is allowed to utter (p. 98).[44] Domestic warfare between the
Teazles is similarly conducted in the playlet with a ruthlessness carefully avoided in the equivalent scenes in The School for Scandal. The
earlier Lady Teazle can reply to her husband's question, 'if I were to
die what would you do', with the curt response, 'countermand my new
Brocade' (p. 84), and reward his 'Then you never had a Desire to please
me or add to my Happiness' with the punishing 'Seriously I never
thought about you' (p. 86). After the screen's collapse, this Lady Teazle
frankly states that 'seduced—by that smooth tong'd Gentleman—I
forgot my Duty—and Integrity—and came here to give him an opportunity to make love to me' (p. 128)—a confession for which The School
for Scandal provides no equivalent. Comparable softenings occur
throughout. Thus, where Mrs Candour refers in the completed play
to 'a house of no extraordinary fame' (1.1.217–18), she had originally
bluntly named a 'Bagnio', i.e. a brothel (p. 36).[45]

Sheridan therefore revised his own first thoughts in exactly the
manner he had recently reworked The Relapse. Roughing out ideas for
a new play, he writes with a freedom and directness which needs to be

[44] Page references for quotations from 'The Slanderers' and 'Sir Peter Teazle' are to
the invaluable edition of the manuscripts in Bruce Redford (ed.), The Origins of 'The
School for Scandal' (Princeton, 1986).
[45] Yet further chastening lay ahead. In the 1890s, William Archer reported that an
actress had the makings of 'the best Mrs Candour of our day', but that she was 'reduced
to the merest shadow by the bowdlerisation of the dialogue' (The Theatrical 'World' for
1893 (London, 1894), 275).

disciplined before the finished script can be safely submitted to the judgement of a 1770s audience. This also means that the manuscript scenes are often closer in their notation of matrimonial mayhem to the terse, bruising confrontations characteristic of such Restoration texts as Otway's *Friendship in Fashion* (1677) and Vanbrugh's *The Provoked Wife* (1697) than is the dialogue provided for the Teazles in the script premièred at Drury Lane in May 1777.

Despite Sheridan's debts to his formidable dramatic inheritance, some of his earliest reviewers were struck by the contemporaneity of the play he had produced, praising the zeal with which he had arraigned 'Detraction and Hypocrisy . . . the prevailing vices of the times', and testifying that, though scandal 'indeed is quite coeval with the world, and has proved the bane of society in all ages', it 'never stared mankind in the face as in our modern times'. For its services against this reigning monster, another reviewer declared the play to be 'one of the keenest and best pointed satires in the English language' (Price, i. 312, 314, and 319). In contrast, modern commentators have often regarded this area of the play as problematic. Andrew Schiller, for instance, writes that 'The fact is that scandal has nothing to do with the outcome of the Teazle problem'; while Patricia Meyer Spacks finds it impossible to read the scenes in the scandal school as satiric. She remarks that 'much of the entertainment this comedy provides for readers or audiences derives from its interludes of verbal extravagance', among which she includes 'the fiction-making of the scandal-mongers', a 'fiction-making' the play's spectators are as likely to relish for its carefree exuberance as condemn for its unwholesomeness or perniciousness.[46]

The relationship between wit, laughter, and morality is debated at an early point in the play itself. Maria stakes out the moral high ground for herself by declaring that 'wit loses its respect with me when I see it in company with malice'. Joseph moralizes mellifluously in reply: 'to smile at the jest which plants a thorn in another's breast is to become a principal in the mischief'. But Lady Sneerwell counters powerfully with the claim that 'There's no possibility of being witty without a little ill nature. The malice of a good thing is the barb that makes it stick' (1.1.147–53). In performance the neatness of that last aphorism often earns applause. Sheridan here borrows a technique from Vanbrugh and encourages in his spectators an unusual alertness to the

---

[46] Andrew Schiller, '*The School for Scandal*: The Restoration Unrestored', *PMLA* 71 (1956), 699; Patricia Meyer Spacks, *Gossip* (Chicago and London, 1985), 144.

implications of their own laughter. As a result, he leaves them in no doubt that the laughter this play provokes is not always of a kind Maria would approve.

Nor, however, is its predominant style of wit truly barbed. As Patricia Meyer Spacks points out, what an audience most relishes in the scandalmongers' chatter is their recurrent lift-offs into unmitigated fantasy, a point emphasized in their brilliant last appearance, as they compete with each other to establish the truthfulness of their own, totally fictional, versions of events in the Teazle household after the collapse of the screen. Their self-propelling loquacity becomes a spectacle as relishable as Mrs Malaprop's wrestlings with language had been. Censure plays little part in an audience's response here.

The effect of the scandalmongers upon the principal characters' misperceptions of each other is potentially a graver matter. Sir Peter's misreading of Charles, for instance, has been fed by, though it does not originate in, the scandals circulating about him. The rancorous mischief caused by the theft or loss of reputation is a habitual preoccupation of Restoration comedy, from Alithea's plight in the concluding scenes of Wycherley's *The Country Wife* (1675) to Mrs Friendall's desperate struggle to preserve her social standing in Southerne's *The Wives' Excuse* (1691). In *The School for Scandal*, those laws no longer hold. When the screen's fall reveals Lady Teazle, the least of her concerns is how her reputation in London society generally will suffer. She is totally focused on how her husband will now regard her. In this sense, it is true that the scandal plot is not linked to the fate of the Teazles in the way an earlier style of comedy might have ensured. Far from being a weakness, however, that may be one of the comedy's distinctive strengths.

In 'Sir Peter Teazle', the matrimonial quarrel proceeds along familiar lines. A servant shows the husband the latest of his wife's unpaid bills, and a confrontation ensues about her extravagant style of life. His disapproval is countered by her indifference, and insults are traded in a formulaic fashion. In *The School for Scandal*, lines from the earlier scene, refurbished and sharpened, crop up in the Teazles' two major set-pieces; but the whole nature of their mutual dealings has been tonally transformed. In particular, Sheridan now makes both partners satirically astute, not only about the other's weaknesses, but also about the way in which they themselves are vulnerable to ridicule. Thus, Sir Peter's belittling evocation of the rural boredom from which he rescued his wife, and her role in it, is taken up and energetically elaborated by her (2.1.36–45). The good humour she displays here is, of course, also one of her weapons. At the end of their second duologue, Sir Peter, annoyed that, despite his best efforts, she has successfully maintained her poise, is determined that next time 'she shan't keep her temper' (3.1.268–9). Yet that very poise entrances him. As he has earlier told us, 'I think she never appears to such advantage as when she's doing everything in her power to plague me' (2.1.106–7). If Lady Sneerwell was certain that 'The malice of a good thing is the barb that makes it stick', then the Teazles' quarrels may provide a paradoxical instance of that truth. The playful composure of the wife's wit fashions the barb which guarantees the continuance of her husband's devotion to her, regardless of the annoyance, even fury, she may provoke in him in the process. Similarly, her constant possession of that wit in their quarrels speaks of her certainty that she is secure of his devotion. A style of duologue which in Restoration comedy characteristically explores bitter feelings of estrangement, imprisonment, and betrayal within a union which cannot legally be ended breeds here a quite different mode of encounter, in which satiric wit itself provides some of the cement which will ensure the marriage's continuance. As Sir Peter confesses, 'with what a charming air she contradicts everything I say, and how pleasingly she shows her contempt of my authority' (2.1.103–4). The play's ending will demand of Lady Teazle a new, if perhaps temporary, submissiveness; but her husband's feelings for her are intimately entwined with his relish for the aplomb with which she has defied and spoofed him. She will in the end leave the scandal club, just as he will banish its members from his house; but the bond which unites them is partly fashioned from the talent for satiric mockery which drew her to the club in the first place.

Devising the apt performance style to match the delicate balance of Sheridan's writing here can sometimes elude even the greatest of actors. That, at least, was T. C. Worsley's judgement on Laurence Olivier's performance of Sir Peter in his own production of the play. What concerned him was Olivier's enthusiasm for 'the possibilities of pathos' in the role:

This pathos comes out into the open in the second quarrel scene with Lady Teazle. At the beginning of this scene, it will be remembered, husband and wife have at last agreed to agree, until Sir Peter proceeds to spoil it all with '. . . in all our little quarrels, my dear, if you recollect my love, you always began first.' So up it flares again between them, a full-scale row, which is suddenly brought to a dead stop by Lady Teazle's exclaiming of a baronet she refused that he would have been a much better match—'for his estate was just as good as yours, and he has broke his neck since we were married.' They are on opposite sides of the stage as she says this, and that thrust brings the quarrel and our laughter to a sudden hush. The pause is lengthened and dragged; Sir Peter's jaw visibly falls: he suddenly looks quite broken. She, with her back to him, feels that she has gone too far, and would like to make amends, but cannot find the way to, and finally, out of embarrassment as it seems, picks up her raillery again and exits on the wave of it, leaving him still shattered. . . . It is a most affecting moment, affectingly played, though at once the difficulty of this interpretation of the part reveals itself. It leaves badly in the air Sir Peter's curtain line, about her keeping her temper: 'I'll not bear her presuming to keep her temper. No! She may break my heart but she shall not keep her temper.' This is, after all, in the spirit of pure artificial comedy, which we cannot suddenly switch back to out of the extreme of pathos.[47]

Far grosser sentimentalities had been inflicted on the play in earlier productions. Arthur C. Sprague records a Victorian performance in which, at the end of the screen scene, Lady Teazle 'touched and tried to kiss her husband's hand . . . ; then went tottering towards the door of "the hated room", with enough strength left, however, to repulse Joseph who attempted to help her; and at last abandoned herself to hysterical grief'. Charles Surface, too, has succumbed to comparable excesses, as in an 1874 staging in which, while Sir Oliver stands 'anxious to become the purchaser of his own picture, the young man kneels on the settee before it and is lost in a reverie of old days and old kindnesses'.[48] Historical distance renders such excesses ridiculous to us. It may be more difficult for us to gauge the aptness to Sheridan's design of the climax of the screen scene in the 1972 National Theatre production, with 'a marriage lying momentarily in ruins as Lady Teazle cowers in a corner like a frightened rabbit caught in a car's headlights and a stricken Sir Peter pulls his wig over his brows'.[49]

Debate about how exactly the play might best be served began early. A letter of 12 May 1777 recorded Garrick's view that 'the Characters upon the Stage at the falling of the Screen Stand too long before they speak' and that 'tho they should be astonish'd & a little petrify'd, yet it may be carry'd to too great a length'.[50] This, however, was a matter

---

[47] T. C. Worsley, *The Fugitive Art: Dramatic Commentaries 1947–1951* (London, 1952), 55–6.

[48] Arthur C. Sprague, 'In Defence of a Masterpiece: *The School for Scandal* Re-examined', in G. E. Duthie (ed.), *English Studies Today*, Third Series (Edinburgh, 1964), 131–2.

[49] Michael Billington, *One Night Stands: A Critic's View of Modern British Theatre* (London, 1993), 16.

[50] David Garrick, *Letters*, iii. 1163.

of local finessing. Forty-seven years later, larger issues had come into play. Charles Lamb could boast that 'Amidst the mortifying circumstances attendant upon growing old, it is something to have seen' *The School for Scandal* 'in its glory'. But he sadly concluded that his time would never again see it 'in its glory'. He recollected fondly Palmer's playing of Joseph—'the gay boldness, the graceful solemn plausibility, the measured step, the insinuating voice—to express it in a word—the downright *acted* villany [*sic*] of the part, so different from the pressure of conscious actual wickedness,—the hypocritical assumption of hypocrisy,—which made Jack so deservedly a favourite in that character'. Lamb believed that 'the present generation of playgoers'—'more virtuous than myself, or more dense'—would no longer relish such playing:

John Palmer was twice an actor in this exquisite part. He was playing to you all the while that he was playing upon Sir Peter and his lady. You had the first intimation of a sentiment before it was on his lips. His altered voice was meant to you, and you were to suppose that his fictitious co-flutterers on the stage perceived nothing at all of it. What was it to you if that half-reality, the husband, was over-reached by the puppetry—or the thin thing (Lady Teazle's reputation) was persuaded it was dying of a plethory? The fortunes of Othello and Desdemona were not concerned in it. Poor Jack has past from the stage in good time, that he did not live to this our age of seriousness. The pleasant old Teazle *King*, too, is gone in good time. His manner would scarce have past current in our day. We must love or hate—acquit or condemn—censure or pity—exert our detestable coxcombry of moral judgment upon every thing. Joseph Surface, to go down now, must be a downright revolting villain—no compromise—his first appearance must shock and give horror—his specious plausibilities, which the pleasurable faculties of our fathers welcomed with such hearty greetings, knowing that no harm (dramatic harm even) could come, or was meant to come of them, must inspire a cold and killing aversion.[51]

Palmer's other roles included Iago; but if Lamb's fervent account can be trusted, his playing of Joseph did not attempt to call on the depth of malignity and threat that the Shakespearean role demands. Instead, the effect achieved was a kind of acting in italics—in Lamb's dizzying phrase, 'the hypocritical assumption of hypocrisy'—and requiring a knowingness of response from the spectator almost equal to that with which the performance of the role had itself been calculated.

[51] Charles Lamb, 'On the Artificial Comedy of the Last Century', in Roy Park (ed.), *Lamb as Critic* (London and Henley, 1980), 65–7.

Sheridan designed even minor supporting roles in *The School for Scandal* with a careful eye to the proven qualities and specialisms of the actors who would play them. The fact that Palmer's nickname was Plausible Jack and that, in one contemporary account, he was always, on stage and off, '*acting* the man of superior accomplishments' suggests how snugly the part must have fitted him.[52] Major plays, however, if they are to survive in the repertoire, must be performable by actors other than those for whom they were originally written; and, equally, they must prove amenable to reinterpretation in changed cultural circumstances, where new audiences place different demands on them. From one perspective, therefore, Lamb runs the risk of denying the play any further stage history; but, from another, the warning he offers about the stylistic demands the play sets is one which future performers would do well to bear in mind.

Twentieth-century actors have rarely attempted a reading of Joseph as a 'downright revolting villain'. The emphasis instead has tended to be, sometimes almost belittlingly, on the implications of his surname. Harley Granville Barker congratulated John Gielgud on his 1939 performance of the part in these terms: 'the best J.S. I remember or am likely to encounter. . . . I liked your dandyism, and shallowness. Just—for me—the right value'; while a reviewer of Gielgud's later 1962 production reported, less enthusiastically, that 'John Neville's Joseph has no depth at all'.[53] Some more recent productions have been less inclined to read Joseph as so accomplishedly smooth. The tension underpinning the deceitfulness has accordingly been allowed to show, to the extent even, in Jonathan Miller's 1972 National Theatre production, of his 'executing at one point a great leap of relief'.[54] As Ronald Pickup, who played Joseph, reported, this was part of a wholesale rethinking of how to stage Sheridan:

Rather than just playing Surface as the ultimate smoothie in very well-oiled Haymarket style, Jonathan encouraged me to play him as an edgy, neurotic figure, as a man who lives on that kind of hypocritical level would have to be. This fitted in with the style of his production—there was a strong feeling early on of these smelly rooms, of the body odour of the characters and the murky

---

[52] The brilliance with which Sheridan fitted roles to actors is explored in Christian Deelman, 'The Original Cast of *The School for Scandal*', *Review of English Studies*, NS 13 (1962), 257–66.

[53] Eric Salmon (ed.), *Granville Barker and his Correspondents: A Selection of Letters by Him and to Him* (Detroit, 1986), 417; H.G.M., in *Theatre World*, 448 (May 1962), 9.

[54] Kenneth Hurren, 'Low Society', *Spectator*, 20 May 1972, 782.

lighting. There was nothing prettified about it at all, which was very arresting for our audiences. It made the play much fresher, and brought a lot of younger audiences into the theatre.[55]

Derek Mahon, reviewing the production, reported that

Instead of the well-heeled world of high fashion to which, traditionally, we think of the Sneerwell claque and the Teazles as belonging, Miller proposes something with rather less surface glitter—a relatively obscure, down-at-heel social set in which everyone's affairs, not just those of the improvident Charles, are in a pretty tatty condition.

He welcomed the 'further satirical dimension' this added to the play, but he found the production's overall effect interesting, but counterproductive:

the problem is that in reducing Sheridan's characters to this all-too-human scale, Miller forfeits the panache which is vital to the dramatic momentum of the play, so that although his production is never less than interesting it's never more than that either.[56]

Mahon's objection, though expressed very differently, has a great deal in common with Lamb's a century and a half earlier. In each case the charge is that a formulaic earnestness has suppressed the text's true vitality. Yet Pickup's interpretation of Joseph is not without textual justification, since the play makes it clear that his manœuvrings are not always flawlessly executed. In 1.1, Lady Sneerwell has the mischievous pleasure of reminding him that he has misjudged his audience: 'O lud, you are going to be moral and forget that you are among friends' (ll. 108–9). At other moments, there are hints that his disguises control him, not he them, and that this may potentially work to his disadvantage. In his brief solo at the end of 2.2, he wanly attempts, but fails, to decipher quite how it is that he has managed to become Lady Teazle's 'serious lover' (l. 241). A similar sign of incomplete control is perhaps detectable in the moment when, yawning, he '*throws away the book*' (4.3.112), but then proceeds to boast to Sir Peter about his addiction to books, 'the only things I am a coxcomb in' (ll. 115–16).

When Sheridan was writing the play, his father appeared at Drury Lane as Maskwell in Congreve's *The Double Dealer* (1693). Recollections of that character and play leave their imprint on *The School for Scandal*. Like Joseph's, Maskwell's objective is marriage to a wealthy heiress, as a preliminary to which he conducts an affair with the wife

---

[55] Michael Romain, *A Profile of Jonathan Miller* (Cambridge, 1992), 149.
[56] Derek Mahon, 'Sheridan's Nonentities', *Listener*, 18 May 1972, 665.

of an older man who is his friend and also seeks to discredit and dislodge the rival gallant who already enjoys the heiress's favour. Maskwell, however, would easily satisfy precisely those instincts in 1820s audiences which Lamb disparaged. His soliloquy on the ruthlessness he espouses as his goddess identifies him as a determined enemy to all the bonds which unite family and society.[57] As a result, beside Maskwell, Joseph may look puny indeed. His predecessor's carefully wrought and ambitiously various plots lead to explosions of rage, threatened violence, and the only just averted transfer of a substantial estate into his hands and away from the rightful heir. In contrast, Joseph's earnest plotting, devoted to gaining Maria as his wife, is principally defeated by his own failure to see that he must extricate himself from the developing relationship with Lady Teazle. This adept of hypocrisy is also addicted to hypocrisy, unable to avoid exercising his gifts on yet another inviting victim, even if, in the process, he begins to destabilize his own designs. For the steely manipulativeness of a character like Lovemore in Southerne's masterpiece, *The Wives' Excuse*, remorselessly tracking the virtuous wife he aims to seduce and then cast aside, Sheridan substitutes a plotter whose plausibility is not accompanied by the tactical resource and self-control which should attend it. Consequently, in the end, Joseph 'hurts nobody but himself'.[58] In this suave late contribution to the marriage comedy genre, Sheridan totally reinvents both the libertine Machiavel and the dynamic of the quarrels within the play's central marriage to produce a work which, while at every point displaying detailed indebtedness to its predecessors, still remains utterly distinctive.

The Critic

The Critic, first performed on 30 October 1779, was, in part, provoked by the political and military crisis of the preceding summer. The government's desultory conduct of the continuing American war was already arousing controversy, when France's recognition in 1778 of the independence of Britain's American colonies and accompanying declaration of war against Britain faced the country with the prospect of invasion. In June 1779 Spain too declared war on Britain, and in August 'news reached the Admiralty that the French and Spanish

---

[57] Congreve, *Comedies*, 151–2.
[58] James Morwood, *The Life and Works of Richard Brinsley Sheridan* (Edinburgh, 1985), 77.

fleets had slipped past the British squadron and were in the Channel' (Price, ii. 465). Panic ensued, accompanied by bitter criticism of the administration's lack of preparedness and incapacity to respond intelligently and urgently now that the crisis appeared to be so desperate. British incompetence found its mirror image in French and Spanish ineptitude, and as a result the invasion never occurred. But, even when the lifting of the immediate threat became apparent, uneasiness about the future remained. The political mayhem of the summer had raised serious doubts about the country's capacity to defend itself, and the newspapers printed gloomy predictions that the nation 'was a declining power' and laments about 'the critical situation in which the British Empire now stands' (Price, ii. 465). The state of the navy was central to the debate. The lower ranks were praised while those at the top were branded for betraying their subordinates' bravery. In the words of the *Public Advertiser*, 5 October 1779, 'Courage and true Valour abound in our Fleets and Armies, though a stigmatized Coward directs the War; and there are [those] who are wakeful and watchful for their Country's Good, though North [the much vilified Prime Minister] sleeps in the Storm that his senseless misrule has raised' (Price, ii. 465–6).

The dangerous summer of 1779 prompted many to recall another occasion when England had been threatened with a sea invasion. The Spanish Armada of 1588 was recollected in political speeches and memoranda, and its defeat celebrated in *The Prophecy; or, Queen Elizabeth at Tilbury*, a pantomime pastiche performed at Sadler's Wells that summer. Its likely author was the manager of Sadler's Wells, Thomas King, for whom Sheridan wrote the role of Puff in *The Critic*. Puff's own Spanish Armada extravaganza alludes, therefore, both to current national events and to the theatre's response to those events.

Vividly contemporary in its immediate inspiration, *The Critic* also has roots deep in a hundred years of playhouse history. Its prologue's reference to the days 'When Villiers criticized what Dryden writ' (l. 6) provides the apt clue. *The Rehearsal* (1671), by George Villiers, Duke of Buckingham, memorably pilloried John Dryden as Bayes, incompetent playwright and virtuoso of 'the new way of writing' heroic drama (1.1.151–2).[59] Bayes is one of those 'fellows that scorns to imitate Nature; but are given altogether to elevate and surprise' (1.1.38–9). In his plays, 'every line surprises you, and brings in new matter' (1.1.157–8). His ultimate devotion is to the goddess of novelty,

---

[59] Quotations from the play are taken from George Villiers, Duke of Buckingham, *The Rehearsal*, ed. D. E. L. Crane (Durham, 1976).

no matter how crazed and incoherent her inspirations may be. His characteristic answer to a sceptical question about why he made a particular playwriting decision is: 'because it's new; and that's it I aim at' (2.1.61). *The Rehearsal* charts his latest play's uneasy progress towards performance, as the unfortunate actors grapple with a text which constantly baffles them. As one of them depressedly remarks, 'I can't guess for my life what humour I'm to be in: whether angry, melancholy, merry, or in love. I don't know what to make on't' (1.1.146–9). Incomprehension, however, is something Bayes is inured to. As the symptoms of his incompetence multiply before us, his defiance of the actors' distrust and his audience's puzzlement also intensifies: 'As long as I know my things are good, what care I, what they say?' (3.1.87–8). In the end, the long-suffering players abandon the rehearsal, and Bayes abandons them. His play will never achieve performance; but he threatens to take up a new career as satirist, in order to excoriate both actors and spectators.

For a play whose immediate inspiration was so personal and local, *The Rehearsal* enjoyed a surprising longevity as a repertory piece. David Garrick, for instance, played Bayes ninety-one times, performing the part for the last time in 1772. The play's freshness in performance was partly sustained by a frequent updating of its references.[60] Garrick's interest in Bayes also extended to writing his own playlet, *The Meeting of the Company*, first performed at Drury Lane on 12 November 1774, in which Buckingham's character pompously instructed the mutinous players in new styles of acting, according to 'Bayes's Art of Acting; or The Worst Equal to the Best'.[61] *The Meeting of the Company* was only the latest in an extended series of eighteenth-century metatheatrical playscripts which derive part of their inspiration from Buckingham's extraordinary improvisation.[62] *The Critic* belongs in this line of descent, as its overt recollections of lines and situations in the Restoration text proclaim. Its pious imitation of its dramatic ancestor was attended by an unforeseen consequence. So great was *The Critic*'s popularity that it effectively ended *The*

[60] George Winchester Stone, Jr., and George M. Kahrl, *David Garrick: A Critical Biography* (Carbondale and Edwardsville, Ill., 1979), 477–80.
[61] David Garrick, *The Meeting of the Company; or, Bayes's Art of Acting*, in *Plays*, ed. Harry William Pedicord and Fredrick Louis Bergmann (Carbondale and Edwardsville, Ill., 1980), ii. 244.
[62] See e.g. V. C. Clinton-Baddeley, *The Burlesque Tradition in the English Theatre after 1660* (London, 1952); D. F. Smith and M. L. Lawhon, *Plays about the Theatre in England, 1737–1800; Or, The Self-Conscious Stage from Foote to Sheridan* (Lewisburg, Pa., 1979).

Rehearsal's stage-life. Within a few years Buckingham's play had vanished from the active repertory.

Sheridan radically reshapes the model he inherited. In his play, Puff and the actors may on occasion disagree, but the blank incomprehension which divides playwright and performer in *The Rehearsal* is not repeated; and there is never any doubt that their joint activity will finally yield a theatre performance, even if not within the time-scale of *The Critic* itself. Similarly, Puff, although frequently nettled by it, remains compliant with the actors' cutting of his script; he shows no trace of Bayes's haughty insistence on the supremacy of his own inspiration. And, where Bayes worshipped novelty, Puff is happy to announce that 'I don't attempt to strike out anything new; but I take it I improve on the established modes' (2.1.459–60). Puff and his actors are at one in their devotion to 'the established modes'. What they produce 'scorns to imitate Nature' just as much as Bayes's creations had done, but for an exactly opposite reason. Bayes refused adamantly to follow any established pattern; Puff's devotion to theatrical precedent is so total that questions of plausibility and historical realism never enter his head. His answer to any challenge is, in effect, to assert that tried and tested theatrical convention sanctifies what he does.

The early reviewers recognized that Sheridan had particular targets in view. Most notoriously, Sir Fretful Plagiary—a portrait, according to *The Morning Post*, 'strongly etched in *aqua fortis*' (Price, ii. 476)—was immediately identified as a caricature of the playwright Richard Cumberland, whose play, *The Battle of Hastings*, had been 'accepted by Sheridan for production at Drury Lane after it had been rejected at Covent Garden' (Price, ii. 469). The likeness was intensified by the actor's imitating Cumberland's style of dress. The result was denounced by one review as 'directly and grossly personal' (Price, ii. 479); but others observed the spectacle with greater equanimity. *The Public Advertiser*, for instance, celebrating Sheridan's achievement as 'at once original and striking', went on: 'Whether Sir *Fretful Plagiary* is drawn from nature, or is only the coinage of Fancy, we will not determine; but if the former is the Case, the Original certainly bids as fair for an enduring Ridicule as Dryden in *Bayes*' (Price, ii. 477–8).

Ridicule may be the principal ingredient in Sir Fretful's portrait, but self-observation plays its part. As one reviewer pointed out, Sheridan was as capable as Sir Fretful of feeling 'angry and offended' at newspaper comment (Price, ii. 471); and self-reference is also present in Sir Fretful's assertion that his new play is 'remarkably short', lasting only 'three hours and a half' (1.1.291 and 296–7). The first performance of *The Rivals* notoriously lasted more than four hours, and reviews of Sheridan first performances regularly include references to the need for cutting. *The Critic* itself was, as *The Morning Chronicle* reported, 'considerably heightened and improved, in consequence of its having been judiciously altered and curtailed' (Price, ii. 480) between its first and second performances. Equally, Puff's devotion to following theatrical precedent mirrors his creator's own inclination. Puff would have understood the reasons for Sheridan's attempt to persuade Sarah Siddons not to depart from convention in her performance of Lady Macbeth's sleepwalking. Siddons intended to lay down her candle, so as not to impede her frenzied rubbing of her hands. Her predecessors had held the candle throughout the scene, and Sheridan was convinced that this departure would not be tolerated by the audience. Siddons ignored his frantic advice and proved him wrong. Like Puff's, Sheridan's unwillingness to offend his audience could mean that he hemmed himself in with unnecessary constraints.[63]

Mrs Dangle's mockery of her husband's myopic obsession with matters theatrical at a time of national crisis is another instance of Sheridan's mingling of satiric derision and self-implication in *The Critic*. While writing the play, Sheridan was energetically contributing to the opposition's propaganda war against North's conduct of national affairs; and within a year of its first performance his election as a Member of Parliament launched him on the political career which henceforward took priority over his theatrical activities. The justifiability of spending time on playhouse labours at such a juncture is, if anything, more relevant to Sheridan's situation than to Dangle's.

From one perspective, Puff's Spanish Armada spectacular conclusively demonstrates the contemporary theatre's political irrelevance. The events of 1588 had been invoked during the summer and autumn crisis as a rebuke to contemporary pusillanimity and ineptitude and as an exemplification of the heroism to which 1770s Britain should aspire. Puff's *Spanish Armada* does all it can to evade such contemporary application. Perversely consigning Elizabeth I to the green room, it looks for its excitements to stories of thwarted private loves, entirely fashioned out of dramatic stock. Puff's fidelity to the 'received point among poets, that where history gives you a good heroic outline for a play, you may fill up with a little love at your own discretion' (2.1.11–13) is total. He thus incarnates a theatrical culture whose

---

[63] Dennis Bartholomeusz, *Macbeth and the Players* (Cambridge, 1969), 119.

hackneyed and diminished notion of the tragic strips it of all political reverberations.

Unlike Puff's, Sheridan's play is by no means apolitical. Burghley's silent appearance is a moment which brilliantly combines theatrical self-awareness and political satire. The incident is deftly introduced by Puff's hope that 'the Lord High Treasurer is perfect; if he is but perfect!' (3.1.102–3). *The Morning Post* praised Puff's 'discovering so much anxiety for the performer being perfect in a character that had not a syllable to utter'; and, on first hearing, we are indeed likely to assume that 'perfect' bears its common theatrical meaning, i.e., 'in complete control of his lines'. It is only in retrospect that we will realize that Puff instead meant something like 'has perfectly mastered all my instructions for his mime'. Puff's subsequent recitation of all he hopes the actor will have conveyed 'by that shake of the head' (l. 119)—a multi-layered judgement on the parlous state of the nation—may on one level be ridiculous, since the actor's impersonation of Burghley is likely to have conveyed no such information. But, on another level, as *The Morning Post* also recorded, '*Puff's* interpretation of that Prime Minister's *thoughts*' was a well-timed 'stroke of political satire' (Price, ii. 477). The manuscript of *The Critic* was only sent to the Lord Chamberlain for licensing the day before its first performance. Sheridan was frequently dilatory in these matters, and he may only have completed the script at the very last moment. It has been suspected, however, that he was also attempting to slip something past the censor, whose inevitably hasty reading of the text in such circumstances would be unlikely to detect the subversive implications of a performer's mute display.[64] The significance of Burghley's silence was, however, easily decoded by the audience as a reference to the near catatonic inactivity of Lord North throughout the invasion crisis and afterwards. North was in a deeply depressive state, overwhelmed by events and wishing to abandon office, but prevented by George III from doing so. What Puff interprets as an image of fatherly solicitude for the nation is offered by Sheridan as a derisory caricature of the politician on whom opposition contumely was principally focused. Sheridan never showed himself defter than in the devising of this extraordinary combination of metatheatrical gamesmanship— in G. Wilson Knight's words, 'what questions of dramatic art and

---

[64] On the late submission of the manuscript, see John Loftis, 'Political and Social Thought in the Drama', in Robert D. Hume (ed.), *The London Theatre World, 1660–1800* (Carbondale and Edwardsville, Ill., 1980), 276–7.

literature in collaboration or opposition does it not raise?'[65]—and deadly political mockery.[66]

Sheridan devises the concluding spectacle of sea-battle and triumphant processional with comparable cunning. In modern production this scene can degenerate into easy mockery of an earlier generation's naïve notion of stage splendour. In 1779 its impact must have been quite different. The designs were the work of Philippe Jacques de Loutherbourg, imported by David Garrick in 1772 to revolutionize the scenic arts at Drury Lane.[67] The reviewer in the *St James's Chronicle* praised De Loutherbourg for 'the most charming Scenes' with which he decorated *The Critic's* second and third acts (Price, ii. 481). But it is in the climactic naval engagement and display of '*all the English rivers and their tributaries*' that his ingenuity must have been most exercised. The mid- to late 1770s had witnessed a vogue for plays showing ships at sea, including an intricate representation of a naval review in *Alfred* at Drury Lane in 1773, also designed by De Loutherbourg. His sets for the concluding scene of *The Critic* may have included parodic references to some of these earlier spectacles; but their effect cannot have been simply parodic. Sheridan and he had collaborated the preceding winter on *The Camp*, a massive success, which climaxed with a view of Coxheath military camp and, in the words of one reviewer, a representation of 'the Right Wing of The Camp, and the Regiments in Motion, which exceeds every Thing in Scenery we have ever seen' (Price, ii. 712). The performance then concluded with a rousing chorus. Puff's tragedy demands a spectacle not easily distinguishable in kind from the display which audiences had cheered at Drury Lane in the preceding season. An element of self-mockery on Sheridan's part is clearly involved here. But, at the same time, he has placed at Puff's disposal the best state-of-the-art ingenuity a profoundly talented designer could provide. In *The Rehearsal* Bayes's stupidity was manifested in his inability to make intelligent use of the

[65] Knight, *The Golden Labyrinth*, 187.

[66] In modern productions, the play's original political resonance is inevitably lost; and Burghley's appearance, in a great actor's hands, can yield an effect opposite to that which Sheridan planned. In the 1945 Old Vic staging, Ralph Richardson was, according to the *Punch* review, 'speechless yet in spate'. The reviewer asked: 'Has Burleigh's shaking of the head ever been more portentous? It implies all that Puff wants it to suggest—and a great deal more besides' (John Miller, *Ralph Richardson: The Authorized Biography* (London, 1995), 99).

[67] For a more extensive account, see Christopher Baugh, 'Philippe James de Loutherbourg and the Early Pictorial Theatre: Some Aspects of its Cultural Context', *Themes in Drama*, 9 (1987), 99–128.

resources his theatre offered him. Much more ambiguously, Puff ecstatically mobilizes some of the most innovatory resources of the contemporary playhouse and puts them to use in a way which recollects Sheridan's own most recent success.

The spectacle is enhanced by musical accompaniment. Sheridan's choice of music is carefully premeditated. The march from Handel's *Judas Maccabaeus*, for instance, brings associations of victory in war. In the oratorio, it celebrates the triumph of the eponymous Israelite warrior over the Syrians; but it is also relevant that Handel had composed the work in 1746 in celebration of the defeat by William, Duke of Cumberland, George III's younger son, of the army of the Young Pretender at Culloden. So, Sheridan's use of it plays against the débâcle of 1779 memories of an earlier, effective response to an invasion threat by a Catholic force. The musical allusion begins to restore to a play about the Spanish Armada some of the political appositeness to which Puff is otherwise deaf. The use of 'Rule, Britannia' works in a similar way. It had been composed by Thomas Arne for *The Masque of Alfred*, which relates another island victory against foreign invaders, this time the Danes. It was a later, revised version of this masque which, when staged at Drury Lane in 1773, included the large-scale representation of a naval review De Loutherbourg designed. So the tune's use here both places the current spectacle within a longer tradition of such resonant stage displays and once again rebukes a decadent present with recollections of a heroic past.[68] Until the 1770s patriotic rhetoric had been one of the opposition's distinctive cards; but during that decade the king had begun to try to deploy comparable language to his own purposes.[69] The concluding episode of *The Critic* resists that tactic and stigmatizes the present government as unworthy of their inheritance as Britons. Yet all this is happening within the context of a spectacle generated by the much mocked and buffeted Puff. It also perfectly exemplifies his earlier profession of devotion to 'situation and stage-effect, by which the greatest applause may be obtained without the assistance of language, sentiment or character' (3.1.138–40).

The Critic, in its Janus-faced manœuvring, bears the imprint of an

---

[68] The significance of the music in this scene is helpfully explored by Eric S. Rump, 'Sheridan, Politics, the Navy, and the Musical Allusions in the Final Scene of *The Critic*', *Restoration and 18th Century Theatre Research*, 2nd ser., 6 (1991), 30–4.

[69] Hugh Cunningham, 'The Language of Patriotism, 1750–1914', *History Workshop*, 12 (Autumn 1981), 9–12; Linda Colley, 'The Apotheosis of George III: Loyalty, Royalty and the British Nation 1760–1820', *Past and Present*, 102 (Feb. 1984), 94–129.

extraordinarily talented dramatist, whose invention remains fresh and vivid, but whose faith in theatre itself may be diminishing. With *The Critic*, the fertile period of Sheridan's career as playwright ended. Ahead lay many years of playhouse management, in which his attention to his duties was spasmodic and unpredictable, and a few collaborative projects (like the pantomime *Robinson Crusoe* and the spectacular *The Glorious First of June*, both of which extended the partnership with De Loutherbourg). He would produce only one further full-scale work, the tragedy *Pizarro* (premièred at Drury Lane in May 1799). An enormous success in its own day, it seems unlikely to be revived on the modern stage, but it has recently been prompting fresh critical interest.[70] Of the works produced between 1775 and 1779 a very different story can be told. All five have a twentieth-century stage history, and three of them, *The Rivals*, *The School for Scandal*, and *The Critic*, have never been out of the repertoire since their first performance. Biographers and critics have often regretted that Sheridan abandoned his playwriting career so early. But surely the better response is to celebrate how much he contrived to achieve in four short years in the late 1770s.

[70] See e.g. Joseph W. Donohue, Jr., *Dramatic Character in the English Romantic Age* (Princeton, 1970), 125–56; John Loftis, 'Whig Oratory on Stage: Sheridan's *Pizarro*', *Eighteenth-Century Studies*, 8 (1974–5), 454–72; Sara Suleri, *The Rhetoric of British India* (Chicago and London, 1992), 68–74.

NOTE ON THE TEXT

ONE of my earliest decisions as General Editor of the drama series of which this edition is part was to invite Cecil Price to undertake a Sheridan volume for it. My respect and admiration for the enormous achievement represented by his two-volume edition of Sheridan's *Dramatic Works* (Oxford, 1973) made this an inevitable choice. To my delight, he accepted the invitation and was experimenting with a modernization of the screen scene in *The School for Scandal*, when a tragic recurrence of an earlier illness forced him to abandon the project. The present volume is dedicated to the memory of a great Sheridan scholar.

In subsequently undertaking the editing of these Sheridan plays myself, my intention has been to fulfil the original goal of making the riches of Cecil Price's scholarship available in a new form to a wider readership. A few minor slips in the 1973 printing of the plays have been silently corrected, and at three points (*The Rivals*, Prologue on the tenth night, lines 3 and 11–12, and *A Trip to Scarborough*, 1.2.145), for reasons explained in the accompanying explanatory notes, I have had the temerity to differ from the readings on which my predecessor had settled. But, in every other respect, the five plays included here are direct modernizations of the texts in Price's edition.

The complexity of the manuscript and printed materials for Sheridan's plays presents an exacting challenge to his editor; and the punctilious energy and imaginative clarity with which Cecil Price confronted that challenge are exemplary. In his two-volume masterwork he traces in great detail the variety of the sources with which he was dealing and the thinking underpinning his editorial decisions. For *The Rivals*, his copy-text was the 1775 first edition, with occasional new readings from the 1776 third edition (believed to have Sheridan's authority) and a few corrections of errors from the 1784/5 fourth edition. His text of *The Duenna* is based on the first authoritative printing in 1794, but admits readings from manuscript sources 'where they appear to correct errors or even to make better sense' (i. 222), plus some songs omitted from the 1794 edition. His copy-text for *A Trip to Scarborough* is the 1781 first edition, with some variants admitted from the licensing manuscript. *The School for Scandal* is the most intractable problem Sheridan sets his editors. Price based his edition of it 'on the manuscripts . . . that are in Sheridan's handwriting or bear some traces of it', collated with the copy sent to the Lord Chamberlain for licensing (i. 349). The 1781 first edition was his source for *The Critic*, with 'few and minor corrections' (ii. 489). In the explanatory notes in this volume, the various editions are, where necessary, identified by their date in italics—*1781* for the first printing of *The Critic*, and so on.

The texts have here been modernized in spelling and punctuation. Standard forms have been adopted for character names in stage directions and in speech prefixes. It is also series-practice to use character names, not 'he', 'she', or 'they', in stage directions; these changes have also been made without each being separately recorded. The usual modern forms—for example, 'whispers to' for the copy-text's 'whispers'—have also been used in stage directions where the original employs a now archaic form; and, apart from *'exit'* and *'exeunt'*, Latin forms in stage directions—for instance, *'solus'* for *'alone'*—have been silently translated. In addition, the copy-texts sometimes have *'exit'* for a multiple departure or *'exeunt'* for a solitary one; the necessary adjustments have been made without comment. Finally, series practice is for a scene's concluding stage direction to take the form of a simple *'exit'* or *'exeunt'* without the relevant characters' names, unless the direction requires different characters to do different things. This too has been silently standardized. Any other editorial additions to, or alterations of, stage directions are identified by being enclosed in square brackets.

Sheridan's three most famous plays have been often re-edited. Though my overwhelming debt is to Cecil Price's work, I have also learned much from the following editions in particular: *The Major Dramas*, ed. George Henry Nettleton (Boston, 1906); *Plays and Poems*, ed. R. Crompton Rhodes (Oxford, 1933), 3 vols.; *The Rivals*, ed. Elizabeth Duthie (London, 1979); *The School for Scandal*, ed. F. W. Bateson (London, 1979); *The Critic*, ed. David Crane (London, 1989).

SHERIDAN'S PLAYHOUSES

THE Licensing Act of 1737 restricted the production of the drama of the spoken word to the two patent playhouses, the Theatres Royal in Covent Garden and Drury Lane. Sheridan's playwriting career was therefore shaped by the nature of these two renowned auditoria and their clientele. The first two plays in this volume were premièred at Covent Garden, and the remaining three at Drury Lane, of which Sheridan was by then also manager.

Both theatres combined a large forestage, enabling a close, intimate relationship between actors and audience, with a substantial scenic stage behind the proscenium, where a realist illusion could be created by means of wings, borders, shutters, drops, and ground rows. For Sheridan's plays, the overwhelming majority of the action would happen on the forestage, with most entrances and exits being through the forestage doors on either side, and in front, of the proscenium arch. These theatres could accommodate large numbers of spectators—a packed house at Drury Lane could be as many as 2,300 people—but the use of the forestage ensured intimacy of address to the audience, an effect enhanced by the fact that some of the spectators' boxes were right over the stage, adjacent to the proscenium doors. These were auditoria, therefore, where the art of the aside—especially sudden confidences or ironic remarks in the midst of other dialogue—could thrive.

On the scenic stage, the fundamental units of scenery were the shutters, held in place by grooves on the raked floor and supported by battens above. There were five or six of these grooves behind the proscenium. These allowed frequent variation of locale and also per-mitted 'discovery scenes', where the shutters for the preceding scene were drawn apart to reveal the performers for the next scene already in place. David Garrick, Sheridan's predecessor in control of Drury Lane, was responsible for a variety of significant refurbishments and modernizations there. His investment in scenes and machines was especially ambitious. By the time he retired in 1776 he was spending six times as much on scenery and scene painters' salaries as in the first year of his management.[1] The splendour of what had been achieved

---

[1] Kalman A. Burnim, *David Garrick Director* (Pittsburgh, 1961), 74–5.

was praised by foreign visitors, one of whom wrote in 1774 that he found 'the decorations lavish, the effects dazzling, the changes as frequent as demanded'.[2]

In 1771 Garrick crowned his reforms by appointing Philippe Jacques de Loutherbourg as scene designer at Drury Lane. A distinguished painter in a thoroughgoing romantic style, De Loutherbourg proved a radical innovator as a theatre craftsman. He altered Drury Lane's methods of scene-shifting and installed new machinery. He commanded complete control of a production's visual characteristics, producing models from which carpenters, painters, and machinists were required to work. His aim was a unified stage-picture, a project not attempted in England since the work of Inigo Jones on court masques in the first half of the seventeenth century. He also transformed stage lighting, achieving subtler transitions and multiplying the range of effects available. As a result of his innovations, 'England became a pioneer in romantic scenery and for the first time led, and did not follow, the Continent'.[3] He continued at Drury Lane after Garrick's retirement. The most zestful product of his collaborations with Sheridan is the spectacular bravado of the final scene of *The Critic*.

The hardy spectators who patronized Drury Lane and Covent Garden sat on backless benches. They still, however, demanded lengthy programmes. The convention was that each evening performance should consist of two major dramatic pieces, a five-act comedy or tragedy or three-act musical, followed by an afterpiece, a shorter comedy, farce, or pantomime. There would also be pre-performance and entr'acte music. The complete running time could be five hours or more. At its first performance, *The Critic* was an afterpiece to a staging of *Hamlet*.

This was not a docile audience. Approval and disapproval were both vociferously expressed. Despite the increasing subtlety of stage lighting, the great chandeliers over the auditorium were left undimmed during the performance. Sheridan's spectators were therefore visible to each other, and interaction between them, and between them and the players, was continuous. Audiences, however, had a great deal to applaud. Drury Lane, in particular, fielded a distinguished acting company, and Sheridan was adept at tailoring his characters to the

---

[2] Sybil Rosenfeld, *A Short History of Scene Design in Great Britain* (Oxford, 1973), 75.
[3] Ibid. 87.

specific strengths of the available player. Especially warm testimony to the extraordinariness of what was consequently achieved is provided by James Boaden's celebration of *The School for Scandal* in early performance:

I think his comedy was better *spoken*, in all its parts, than any play that I have witnessed upon the stage. And I can safely add that, as to the acting of it, every change, to the present hour, has been a sensible diminution of the original effect. The lingered sentiment of Palmer—the jovial smartness of Smith—the caustic shyness of King—the brilliant loquacity of Abington—however congenial to the play, have long been silent.[4]

More is involved here than an old man's sentimental preference for former days. Boaden elsewhere charts a social transformation which has, for him, rendered archaic and unrecreatable the social codes Sheridan and his players took for granted:

The fine gentleman in comedy was then very different from what it has since become—it was regulated by higher manners, and seemed indeed born in polished life and educated in drawing-rooms. The dress kept the performer up to the character. It was necessary to wear the sword, and to manage it gracefully. As the hair was dressed and powdered, the hat was supported under the arm. The mode of approaching the lady was more respectful, and it required the most delicate address to lead and seat her upon the stage. It will be recollected that ladies wore the hoop, and in all the brilliancy of court dress, appeared very formidable beings. The flippancy of the modern style makes a bow look like a mockery: it does not seem naturally to belong to a man in pantaloons and a plain blue coat, with a white or a black waistcost. . . . Should we therefore venture back to the lace and embroidery, the swords and bags of the last age? I think not: the difference from our present costume would excite a laugh. What is the result unfortunately?—We drop, or impoverish the comedies.[5]

Thus early in their stage history is posed the crucial challenge of finding an effective, *modern* style for staging Sheridan's masterpieces.

The subsequent performance tradition has also generated divided opinions about what kind of stage design will best serve the plays. In the 1870s and 1880s, for instance, the Bancrofts revived *The Rivals* and *The School for Scandal* with a 'painstaking reproduction of scenes of eighteenth-century life', based on devoted and lavish historical

---

[4] James Boaden, *Memoirs of Mrs. Siddons* (London, 1827), i. 111–12.
[5] James Boaden, *Memoirs of the Life of John Philip Kemble, Esq.* (London, 1825), i. 51–2.

1

research.[6] Henry James remarked of this manner of staging *The School for Scandal* that 'The spectacle . . . was brilliant and the furniture very clever, being made up for the most part of genuine antiques of the Teazle period, in which the strongest opera-glass was challenged to detect a flaw'.[7] This tradition of lavish historical pictorialism has survived strongly into the twentieth century.[8] But there is also a powerful counter-tradition, which recognizes the relatively spare furnishings of Sheridan's own stage and, therefore, supplies 'a minimum of furniture' in order to keep the action and narrative uncluttered and fluid.[9]

Further information on Sheridan's theatres and actors can be found in: Mark S. Auburn, 'Theatre in the Age of Garrick and Sheridan', in James Morwood and David Crane (eds.), *Sheridan Studies* (Cambridge, 1995), 7–46; Michael R. Booth, Richard Southern, Frederick and Lise-Lone Marker, and Robertson Davies, *The Revels History of Drama in English, vi. 1759–1880* (London, 1975); Kalman A. Burnim, *David Garrick Director* (Pittsburgh, 1961); Roger Fiske, *English Theatre Music in the Eighteenth Century* (London, 1973); Philip H. Highfill, Jr., Kalman A. Burnim, and Edward A. Langhans (eds.), *A Biographical Dictionary of Actors, Actresses, Musicians, Dancers, Managers and Other Stage Personnel in London, 1660–1800* (Carbondale and Edwardsville, Ill., 1973–93), 16 vols.; Leo Hughes, *The Drama's Patrons: A Study of the Eighteenth Century London Audience* (Austin, Tex., and London, 1971); Robert D. Hume (ed.), *The London Theatre World, 1660–1800* (Carbondale and Edwardsville, Ill., 1980); Richard Leacroft, *The Development of the English Playhouse* (London and New York, 1973); James J. Lynch, *Box, Pit and Gallery: Stage and Society in Johnson's London* (Berkeley and Los Angeles, 1953); Allardyce Nicoll, *The Garrick Stage: Theatres and Audience in the Eighteenth Century* (Manchester, 1980); Harry William Pedicord, *The Theatrical Public in the Time of Garrick* (New York, 1954); Cecil Price, *Theatre in the Age of Garrick* (Oxford, 1973); Sybil Rosenfeld, *A Short History of Scene Design in Great Britain* (Oxford, 1973); George Winchester Stone, Jr. (ed.), *The Stage and the Page: London's 'Whole Show' in the Eighteenth-Century Theatre* (Berkeley and Los Angeles, 1981).

[6] Michael R. Booth, *Victorian Spectacular Theatre 1850–1910* (London, 1981), 23.
[7] Henry James, *The Scenic Art: Notes on Acting and the Drama 1872–1901* (London, 1949), 16.
[8] See e.g. Michael Mullin, *Design by Motley* (Newark, NJ, 1996), 189–90.
[9] Harcourt Williams, *Four Years at the Old Vic 1929–1933* (London, 1935), 213.

SELECT BIBLIOGRAPHY

SHERIDAN'S life has attracted an extended series of biographers. The substantive works, however, are the older ones: Thomas Moore, *Memoirs of the Life of the Right Honourable Richard Brinsley Sheridan* (London, 1825), 2 vols.; W. Fraser Rae, *Sheridan: A Biography* (London, 1896), 2 vols.; Walter Sichel, *Sheridan: From New and Original Material* (London, 1909), 2 vols.; R. Crompton Rhodes, *Harlequin Sheridan: The Man and the Legends* (Oxford, 1933). Some of their successors—for instance, Madeleine Bingham, *Sheridan: The Track of a Comet* (London, 1972)—are fluently written and pleasant to read, but add little either factually or interpretatively. Others have been little more than potboilers. Published in 1997, however, was a biography— Fintan O'Toole, *A Traitor's Kiss: The Life of Richard Brinsley Sheridan* (London, 1997)—which opens up new perspectives by foregrounding Sheridan's Irishness. Documents about Sheridan's life and early responses to him have been gathered in E. H. Mikhail (ed.), *Sheridan: Interviews and Recollections* (London, 1989).

The foundation stones of modern Sheridan scholarship are the devoted editorial labours of Cecil Price—the three-volume *Letters* (Oxford, 1966) and two-volume *Dramatic Works* (1973). All subsequent work on the plays derives its impetus from Price's magisterial achievements.

The manuscript of *The Rivals* submitted for licensing has survived, thus allowing us to read it as it was before the drastic revision provoked by the failure of its first performance. This manuscript has been edited, and informatively introduced, by Richard Little Purdy (Oxford, 1935). The two playlets from which *The School for Scandal* eventually developed have also been edited by Bruce Redford as *The Origins of 'The School for Scandal'* (Princeton, 1986).

Katharine Worth has written a comparative study of *Sheridan and Goldsmith* (London, 1992). Book-length studies devoted to Sheridan's plays which contain interesting commentary include Mark S. Auburn, *Sheridan's Comedies: Their Contexts and Achievements* (Lincoln, Nebr., and London, 1977); Jean Dulck, *Les Comedies de R. B. Sheridan: Étude Littéraire* (Paris, 1962); Jack D. Durant, *Richard Brinsley Sheridan* (Boston, 1975); John Loftis, *Sheridan and the Drama of Georgian England* (Oxford, 1976); and James Morwood, *The Life and Works of*

Richard Brinsley Sheridan (Edinburgh, 1985). Peter Davison (ed.), *Sheridan: Comedies* (London, 1986), provides an attractive sampling of writing on Sheridan from the 1770s to the mid-1980s; and James Morwood and David Crane (eds.), *Sheridan Studies* (Cambridge, 1995) is especially worth consulting for the essays by Christopher Reid, Christopher Clayton, and Marc Baer investigating aspects of his political career in ways which illuminate his dramatic achievements and techniques.

Articles which explore more than one of his plays include: Robert Hogan, 'Plot, Character, and Comic Language in Sheridan', in A. R. Braunmuller and J. C. Bulman (eds.), *Comedy from Shakespeare to Sheridan* (Newark, NJ, 1988), 274–85; Christine S. Wiesenthal, 'Representation and Experimentation in the Major Comedies of Richard Brinsley Sheridan', *Eighteenth-Century Studies*, 25 (1991–2), 309–30; and Elizabeth M. Yearling, 'The Good-Natured Heroes of Cumberland, Goldsmith, and Sheridan', *Modern Language Review*, 67 (1972), 490–500. The few pages on Sheridan in G. Wilson Knight, *The Golden Labyrinth: A Study of British Drama* (London, 1962), are suggestive and incisive.

Aspects of the stage-history of the plays are illuminatingly charted in Mark S. Auburn, 'The Pleasures of Sheridan's *The Rivals*: A Critical Study in the Light of Stage History', *Modern Philology*, 72 (1974–5), 256–70; Mita Choudhury, 'Sheridan, Garrick, and a Colonial Gesture: *The School for Scandal* on the Calcutta Stage', *Theatre Journal*, 46 (1994), 303–21; Christian Deelman, 'The Original Cast of *The School for Scandal*', *Review of English Studies*, NS 13 (1962), 257–66; George H. Nettleton, 'Sheridan's Introduction to the American Stage', *PMLA* 65 (1950), 163–82; and Arthur C. Sprague, 'In Defence of a Masterpiece: *The School for Scandal* Re-examined', in G. E. Duthie (ed.), *English Studies Today*, 3rd ser. (Edinburgh, 1964), 125–35.

Roger Fiske's crucial work on the music for *The Duenna* appears in 'A Score for *The Duenna*', *Music and Letters*, 42 (1961), 132–41, and his *English Theatre Music in the Eighteenth Century* (London, 1972). Linda V. Troost has more recently discussed 'The Characterizing Power of Song in Sheridan's *The Duenna*', *Eighteenth-Century Studies*, 20 (1986–7), 153–72.

Articles worth consulting on *The School for Scandal* include John Dolman, Jr., 'A Laugh Analysis of *The School for Scandal*', *Quarterly Journal of Speech*, 16 (1930), 432–45; J. R. de J. Jackson, 'The Importance of Witty Dialogue in *The School for Scandal*', *Modern Language*

Notes, 76 (1961), 601—7; Leonard L. J. Leff, 'The Disguise Motif in Sheridan's *The School for Scandal*', *Educational Theatre Journal*, 22 (1970), 350–60; and Andrew Schiller, '*The School for Scandal*: The Restoration Unrestored', *PMLA* 71 (1956), 694–704. An editorial approach to the play different from Cecil Price's is mapped by F. W. Bateson, 'The Application of Thought to an Eighteenth-Century Text: *The School for Scandal*', in René Wellek and Alvaro Ribeiro (eds.), *Evidence in Literary Scholarship: Essays in Memory of James Marshall Osborn* (Oxford, 1979), 321–35.

The Critic is set within a larger tradition of burlesque comedy by V. C. Clinton-Baddeley, *The Burlesque Tradition in the English Theatre after 1660* (London, 1952); D. F. Smith, *The Critics in the Audience of the London Theatres from Buckingham to Sheridan* (Albuquerque, N. Mex., 1953); and D. F. Smith and M. L. Lawhon, *Plays about the Theatre in England, 1737–1800; Or, The Self-Conscious Stage from Foote to Sheridan* (Lewisburg, Pa., 1979). Two brief, but helpful, essays on its final scene are V. C. Rudolph, ' "Exit *Thames* Between His Banks": An Emblem of Order in Sheridan's *The Critic*', *Theatre Survey*, 16 (1975), 93–5; and Eric S. Rump. 'Sheridan, Politics, the Navy and the Musical Allusions in the Final Scene of *The Critic*', *Restoration and 18th Century Theatre Research*, 2nd ser. 6 (1991), 30–4. Philip K. Jason, 'A Twentieth-Century Response to *The Critic*', *Theatre Survey*, 15 (1979), 51–8, explores the play's metatheatrical implications, but entirely without reference to its political reverberations.

A wider perspective on the comedy of the mid-to-late eighteenth century is provided by Richard W. Bevis's authoritative and engaging *The Laughing Tradition: Stage Comedy in Garrick's Day* (London, 1980), and two important articles by Robert D. Hume, 'The Multi-farious Forms of Eighteenth-Century Comedy' and 'Goldsmith and Sheridan and the Supposed Revolution of "Laughing" against "Sentimental" Comedy', both in Hume's *The Rakish Stage: Studies in English Drama, 1660–1800* (Carbondale and Edwardsville, Ill., 1983), 214–44 and 312–55. We still await the truly comprehensive account of sentimentalism in the drama we need; but, in the meantime, Arthur Sherbo, *English Sentimental Drama* (East Lansing, Mich., 1957), and Frank H. Ellis, *Sentimental Comedy: Theory and Practice* (Cambridge, 1991), begin to map the territory.

A CHRONOLOGY OF
RICHARD BRINSLEY SHERIDAN

1751   30 October: born at 12 Dorset Street, Dublin, son of Thomas and Frances Sheridan.

1757   Attends Samuel Whyte's grammar school in Dublin.

1760   The Sheridan family moves to London.

1762–8   Richard Brinsley attends Harrow School.

1764   Thomas Sheridan's financial problems trigger his removing the family to France. Richard Brinsley remains at Harrow, but under the (distant) care of his uncle, Richard Chamberlayne, a London surgeon.

1766   22 September: Frances Sheridan dies at Blois in France.

1770   The Sheridan family moves to Bath.

1771   Richard Brinsley publishes *The Love Epistles of Aristanetus*, a translation from Greek.

1772   18 March: elopes to France with Elizabeth Linley. Thomas Matthews, Elizabeth's admirer, publishes an insulting account of Sheridan, branding him a liar and a treacherous scoundrel. Matthews, in effect, had issued Sheridan a challenge.

        4 May: Richard Brinsley fights a first duel with Thomas Matthews.

        1 July: fights his second duel with Matthews.

        27 August: to Waltham Abbey in Essex to study law.

1773   6 April: begins legal training in the Middle Temple. Marries Elizabeth Linley at Marylebone Church in London. They live in a cottage at Burnham Grove.

1774   Moves to a house in Orchard Street, London. Writes in November to his father-in-law that he has been seriously at work on a book.

1775   17 January: première of *The Rivals* at the Theatre Royal in Covent Garden. Unfavourable reception prompts its immediate withdrawal for rewriting.

        28 January: revised version of *The Rivals* is first performed and earns favourable response.

        2 May: première of *St Patrick's Day* at Covent Garden Theatre.

        17 November: birth of first son, Thomas.

        21 November: première of *The Duenna* at Covent Garden.

1776   24 June: on David Garrick's retirement, Sheridan signs an agreement which makes over Garrick's half of Drury Lane Theatre to Sheridan and two partners.

        21 September: new Drury Lane season opens under Sheridan's management.

1777   24 February: première of *A Trip to Scarborough* at Drury Lane.

14 March: elected a member of Samuel Johnson's exclusive Literary Club.

8 May: première of *The School for Scandal* at Drury Lane.

1778   Acquires remaining half-share in ownership of Drury Lane.

15 November: première of *The Camp* at Drury Lane.

1779   30 October: première of *The Critic* at Drury Lane.

1780   12 September: elected Member of Parliament for Stafford.

23 September: makes first parliamentary speech.

2 November: elected to Brooks's Club, the fashionable Whig fraternity.

1781   21 January: first performance of *Robinson Crusoe* at Drury Lane.

1782   March: appointed Under-Secretary of State in Lord Rockingham's cabinet.

1783   2 April: becomes Secretary of Treasury in the coalition government under Lord North and Charles James Fox.

1787   7 February: advances the charge against Warren Hastings in the House of Commons.

1788   13 February: the trial of Warren Hastings begins. Sheridan makes his first speech against Hastings in Westminster Hall. He makes further speeches on 3, 6, 10, and 13 June.

14 August: Thomas Sheridan, his father, dies.

1789   Sir Joshua Reynolds paints Sheridan's portrait. On the outbreak of the French Revolution, Fox and Sheridan favour the anti-monarchist side.

1790   Quarrels with Edmund Burke over the French Revolution.

1791   4 June: the last performance in the Drury Lane Theatre. The building had been condemned.

1792   30 March: birth of Mary Sheridan (the product of Elizabeth Sheridan's affair with Lord Edward Fitzgerald).

28 June: death of Elizabeth Sheridan.

1793   23 October: death of Mary Sheridan.

1794   12 March: the new Drury Lane Theatre opens.

1795   27 April: marries Hester Jane Ogle, daughter of the Dean of Winchester.

1796   14 January: birth of second son, Charles Brinsley Sheridan.

1799   24 May: first performance of *Pizarro* at Drury Lane.

1804   Offered the receivership of the Duchy of Cornwall by the Prince of Wales; but a prior promise of the office to General Lake takes precedence.

1806   Becomes Treasurer of the Navy in Lord Grenville's administration. Charles James Fox dies and is succeeded by Sheridan as Member of Parliament for Westminster.

Surrenders the directorship of his theatre to his eldest son.

Sheridan's elder brother, Charles Francis, dies.

1807   Defeated in election at Westminster. Becomes Member of Parliament for Ilchester.

1809   24 February: the new Drury Lane Theatre burns down.

1811   Becomes chief adviser to the Prince of Wales.

1812   21 July: makes final parliamentary speech (in support of the war with France).

October: defeated in parliamentary election.

Loses the favour of the Prince of Wales.

The rebuilt Drury Lane Theatre opens.

1813   August: imprisoned for debt.

1814   May: arrested for debt. (There may have been other intervening arrests.)

1816   7 July: dies at 17 Savile Row.

13 July: buried in Westminster Abbey.

THE RIVALS

A Comedy

PREFACE

A preface to a play seems generally to be considered as a kind of closet-prologue,° in which, if his piece has been successful, the author solicits° that indulgence from the reader which he had before experienced from the audience. But as the scope and immediate object of a play is to please a mixed assembly in representation,° whose judgement in the theatre at least is decisive, its degree of reputation is usually as determined° as public, before it can be prepared for the cooler tribunal of the study.° Thus, any farther solicitude° on the part of the writer becomes unnecessary at least, if not an intrusion; and if the piece has been condemned in the performance, I fear an address to the closet, like an appeal to posterity, is constantly regarded as the procrastination of a suit from a consciousness of the weakness of the cause.° From these considerations, the following comedy would certainly have been submitted to the reader without any further introduction than what it had in the representation, but that its success has probably been founded on a circumstance which the author is informed has not before attended a theatrical trial, and which consequently ought not to pass unnoticed.

I need scarcely add that the circumstance alluded to was the withdrawing of the piece, to remove those imperfections in the first representation which were too obvious to escape reprehension, and too numerous to admit of a hasty correction.° There are few writers, I believe, who, even in the fullest consciousness of error, do not wish to palliate the faults which they acknowledge, and, however trifling the performance, to second their confession of its deficiencies by whatever plea seems least disgraceful to their ability. In the present instance, it cannot be said to amount either to candour or modesty in me to acknowledge an extreme inexperience and want of judgement on matters in which, without guidance from practice or spur from success, a young man° should scarcely boast of being an adept. If it be said that under such disadvantages no-one should attempt to write a play, I must beg leave to dissent from the position, while the first point of experience that I have gained on the subject is a knowledge of the candour° and judgement with which an impartial public distinguishes between the errors of inexperience and incapacity, and the indulgence which it shows even to a disposition° to remedy the defects of either.

It were unnecessary to enter into any farther extenuation of what was thought exceptionable in this play, but that it has been said that the managers should have prevented some of the defects before its 40
appearance to the public—and, in particular, the uncommon length of the piece as represented the first night.° It were an ill return for the most liberal and gentlemanly conduct on their side, to suffer any censure to rest where none was deserved. Hurry in writing has long been exploded as an excuse for an author. However, in the dramatic 45
line, it may happen that both an author and a manager may wish to fill a chasm in the entertainment of the public° with a hastiness not alto-gether culpable. The season was advanced when I first put the play into Mr Harris's° hands. It was at that time at least double the length of any acting comedy. I profited by his judgement and experience in 50
the curtailing of it, till, I believe, his feeling for the vanity of a young author got the better of his desire for correctness, and he left many excrescences remaining, because he had assisted in pruning so many more. Hence, though I was not uninformed that the acts were still too long, I flattered myself that, after the first trial,° I might with safer 55
judgement proceed to remove what should appear to have been most dissatisfactory. Many other errors there were, which might in part have arisen from my being by no means conversant with plays in general,° either in reading or at the theatre. Yet I own that, in one respect, I did not regret my ignorance; for as my first wish 60
in attempting a play was to avoid every appearance of plagiary, I thought I should stand a better chance of effecting this from being in a walk which I had not frequented, and where consequently the progress of invention was less likely to be interrupted by starts of rec-ollection. For on subjects on which the mind has been much informed, 65
invention is slow of exerting itself. Faded ideas float in the fancy like half-forgotten dreams; and the imagination in its fullest enjoyments becomes suspicious of its offspring and doubts whether it has created or adopted.

With regard to some particular passages which on the first night's 70
representation seemed generally disliked, I confess that if I felt any emotion of surprise at the disapprobation, it was not that they were disapproved of, but that I had not before perceived that they deserved it. As some part of the attack on the piece was begun too early to pass for the sentence of judgement,° which is ever tardy in condemning, it 75
has been suggested to me that much of the disapprobation must have arisen from virulence of malice° rather than severity of criticism. But

as I was more apprehensive° of there being just grounds to excite the latter than conscious of having deserved the former, I continue not to believe that probable, which I am sure must have been unprovoked. However, if it was so, and I could even mark° the quarter from whence it came, it would be ungenerous° to retort; for no passion suffers more than malice from disappointment.° For my own part, I see no reason why the author of a play should not regard a first night's audience as a candid and judicious friend attending in behalf of the public at his last rehearsal. If he can dispense with° flattery, he is sure at least of sincerity, and even though the annotation be rude,° he may rely upon the justness of the comment. Considered in this light, that audience, whose *fiat*° is essential to the poet's claim, whether his object° be fame or profit, has surely a right to expect some deference to its opinion, from principles of politeness at least, if not from gratitude.

As for the little puny critics, who scatter their peevish strictures in private circles and scribble at every author who has the eminence of being unconnected with them, as they are usually spleen-swollen° from a vain idea of increasing their consequence,° there will always be found a petulance and illiberality in their remarks, which should place them as far beneath the notice of a gentleman, as their original° dullness had sunk them from the level of the most unsuccessful author.

It is not without pleasure that I catch at an opportunity of justifying myself from the charge of intending any national reflection in the character of Sir Lucius O'Trigger.° If any gentlemen opposed the piece from that idea, I thank them sincerely for their opposition; and if the condemnation of this comedy, however misconceived the provocation, could have added one spark to the decaying flame of national attachment to the country supposed to be reflected on, I should have been happy in its fate, and might with truth have boasted that it had done more real service in its failure than the successful morality of a thousand stage-novels° will ever effect.

It is usual, I believe, to thank the performers in a new play for the exertion of their several abilities. But where, as in this instance, their merit has been so striking and uncontroverted as to call for the warmest and truest applause from a number of judicious audiences, the poet's after-praise comes like the feeble acclamation of a child to close the shouts of a multitude. The conduct, however, of the principals in a theatre° cannot be so apparent to the public. I think it therefore but justice to declare that from this theatre, the only one I can speak of

80

85

90

95

100

105

110

115

5

from experience, those writers who wish to try the dramatic line will meet with that candour and liberal attention, which are generally allowed to be better calculated to lead genius into excellence than either 120 the precepts of judgement° or the guidance of experience.

THE AUTHOR

6

THE CHARACTERS OF THE PLAY

Sir Anthony Absolute°   *Mr Shuter*
Captain Absolute   *Mr Woodward*
Faulkland°   *Mr Lewis*
Bob Acres°   *Mr Quick*
Sir Lucius O'Trigger°   *Mr Clinch*
Fag°   *Mr Lee Lewis*
David   *Mr Dunstall*
Coachman   *Mr Fearon*
[Errand-boy]
[Servant in Bob Acres's lodgings]
[Servant in Mrs Malaprop's lodgings]
[Servant to Julia]

Mrs Malaprop°   *Mrs Green*
Lydia Languish°   *Miss Barsanti*
Julia   *Mrs Bulkley*
Lucy   *Mrs Lessingham*
[Maid to Julia]

SCENE: BATH

Time of action: within one day

Prologue°

By the author

Spoken by Mr Woodward and Mr Quick

*Enter Sergeant-at-law, and Attorney following and giving a
paper*°

SERGEANT What's here? A vile cramp hand! I cannot see°
Without my spectacles.
ATTORNEY [*aside*]   He means his fee.—
          The Attorney gives the Sergeant-at-law money
Nay, Mr Sergeant, good sir, try again.
SERGEANT The scrawl improves.
          The Attorney gives the   Sergeant-at-law more money
                              O come, 'tis pretty plain.
Hey! How's this? Dibble! Sure it cannot be!°   5
A poet's brief! A poet and a fee!°
ATTORNEY Yea, sir! Though *you* without reward, I know,
Would gladly plead the muses' cause.
SERGEANT   So, so!
ATTORNEY And if the fee offends, your wrath should fall
On me.
SERGEANT   Dear Dibble, no offence at all.   10
ATTORNEY Some sons of Phoebus in the courts we meet—°
SERGEANT And fifty sons of Phoebus in the Fleet!°
ATTORNEY Nor pleads he worse, who with a decent sprig
Of bays adorns his legal waste of wig.°
SERGEANT Full-bottomed heroes thus, on signs, unfurl   15
A leaf of laurel in a grove of curl!°
Yet tell your client that, in adverse days,
This wig is warmer than a bush of bays.°
ATTORNEY Do you then, sir, my client's place supply,
Profuse of robe, and prodigal of tie.°   20
Do you, with all those blushing powers of face
And wonted bashful hesitating grace,
Rise in the court and flourish on the case.°
          Exit Attorney
SERGEANT For practice then suppose—this brief will show it—
Me, Sergeant Woodward, counsel for the poet.   25

9

Used to the ground, I know 'tis hard to deal°
With this dread court, from whence there's no appeal.
No tricking here, to blunt the edge of law,
Or, damned in equity, escape by flaw;
But, judgement given, your sentence must remain.   30
No writ of error lies to Drury Lane!°
Yet when so kind you seem, 'tis past dispute
We gain some favour, if not costs of suit.°
No spleen is here! I see no hoarded fury.
I think I never faced a milder jury!   35
Sad else our plight!—where frowns are transportation,°
A hiss the gallows, and a groan damnation!
But such the public candour, without fear
My client waives all right of challenge here.°
No newsman from *our* session is dismissed,°   40
Nor wit nor critic *we* scratch off the list.
His faults can never hurt another's ease;
His crime, at worst, a bad attempt to please.
Thus, all respecting, he appeals to all,°
And by the general voice will stand or fall.°   45

Prologue

By the author

Spoken on the tenth night by Mrs Bulkley°

Granted our cause, our suit and trial o'er,
The worthy sergeant need appear no more.°
In pleading, I a different client choose.°
He served the poet; I would serve the muse.
Like him, I'll try to merit your applause,   5
A female counsel in a female's cause.
  Look on this form, where humour, quaint and fly,°
Dimples the cheek and points the beaming eye;
Where gay invention seems to boast its wiles
In amorous hint and half-triumphant smiles;   10
While her light mask or covers satire's strokes
Or hides the conscious blush her wit provokes.°
Look on her well. Does she seem formed to teach?
Should you *expect* to hear this lady preach?
Is grey experience suited to her youth?   15
Do solemn sentiments become that mouth?
Bid her be grave, those lips should rebel prove°
To every theme that slanders mirth or love.
  Yet, thus adorned with every graceful art
To charm the fancy and yet reach the heart,   20
Must we displace her? And instead advance
The goddess of the woeful countenance,
The sentimental muse! Her emblems view—°
The Pilgrim's Progress and a sprig of rue!°
View her, too chaste to look like flesh and blood,   25
Primly portrayed on emblematic wood!
There fixed in usurpation should she stand,
She'll snatch the dagger from her sister's hand;°
And, having made her votaries weep a flood,
Good heaven, she'll end her comedies in blood—   30
Bid Harry Woodward break poor Dunstall's crown;
Imprison Quick, and knock Ned Shuter down;
While sad Barsanti, weeping o'er the scene,
Shall stab herself, or poison Mrs Green!°

Such dire encroachments to prevent in time 35
Demands the critic's voice, the poet's rhyme.
Can our light scenes add strength to holy laws!
Such puny patronage but hurts the cause.
Fair virtue scorns our feeble aid to ask,
And moral truth disdains the trickster's mask. 40
For here their favourite stands, whose brow, severe°
And sad, claims youth's respect and pity's tear,
Who, when oppressed by foes her worth creates,
Can point a poniard at the guilt she hates.

1.1

A street in Bath°

Coachman crosses the stage.° Enter Fag, looking after him

FAG What! Thomas!—Sure 'tis he?—What! Thomas! Thomas!

COACHMAN Hey! Od's° life! Mr Fag! Give us your hand, my old° fellow-servant.

FAG Excuse my glove,° Thomas. I'm devilish glad to see you, my lad. Why, my prince of charioteers, you look as hearty! But who the deuce thought of seeing you in Bath!   5

COACHMAN Sure, Master, Madam Julia, Harry, Mrs Kate, and the postilion be all come!

FAG Indeed!

COACHMAN Ay!° Master thought another fit of the gout was coming   10 to make him a visit; so he'd a mind to gi't the slip, and, whip, we were all off at an hour's warning.°

FAG Ay, ay! Hasty in everything, or it would not be Sir Anthony Absolute!

COACHMAN But tell us, Mr Fag, how does young Master! Od, Sir   15 Anthony will stare to see the captain here!

FAG I do not serve Captain Absolute now.

COACHMAN Why sure!

FAG At present I am employed by Ensign Beverley.

COACHMAN I doubt, Mr Fag, you ha'n't changed for the better.   20

FAG I have not changed, Thomas.

COACHMAN No! Why, didn't you say you had left young Master?

FAG No. Well, honest Thomas, I must puzzle you no farther. Briefly then: Captain Absolute and Ensign Beverley are one and the same person.   25

COACHMAN The devil they are!

FAG So it is indeed, Thomas; and the ensign half of my master being on guard at present, the captain has nothing to do with me.

COACHMAN So, so! What, this is some freak, I warrant! Do tell us, Mr Fag, the meaning o't. You know I ha' trusted you.°   30

FAG You'll be secret, Thomas?

COACHMAN As a coach-horse.

FAG Why then, the cause of all this is L-O-V-E°—love, Thomas, who, as you may get read to you, has been a masquerader ever since the days of Jupiter.°   35

COACHMAN Ay, ay; I guessed there was a lady in the case. But pray, why does your master pass only for ensign? Now if he had shammed general indeed—

FAG Ah, Thomas, there lies the mystery o' the matter. Harkee, Thomas. My master is in love with a lady of a very singular taste—   40 a lady who likes him better as a half-pay° ensign than if she knew he was son and heir to Sir Anthony Absolute, a baronet with three thousand a year!

COACHMAN That is an odd taste indeed! But has she got the stuff, Mr Fag? Is she rich, hey?   45

FAG Rich! Why, I believe she owns half the stocks!° Zounds, Thomas, she could pay the national debt as easy as I could my washer-woman! She has a lapdog that eats out of gold.° She feeds her parrot with small pearls, and all her thread-papers are made of bank-notes!   50

COACHMAN Bravo! Faith! Od! I warrant she has a set of thousands° at least. But does she draw kindly with° the captain?

FAG As fond as pigeons.

COACHMAN May one hear her name?

FAG Miss Lydia Languish. But there is an old tough aunt in the way;   55 though, by the bye, she has never seen my master, for he got acquainted with Miss while on a visit in Gloucestershire.

COACHMAN Well, I wish they were once harnessed together in matrimony. But pray, Mr Fag, what kind of a place is this Bath? I ha' heard a deal of it. Here's a mort o' merry-making,   60 hey?

FAG Pretty well, Thomas, pretty well. 'Tis a good lounge. In the morning we go to the Pump Room,° though neither my master nor I drink the waters. After breakfast we saunter on the Parades° or play a game at billiards. At night we dance. But damn the place, I'm   65 tired of it. Their regular hours stupefy me. Not a fiddle nor a card after eleven!° However, Mr Faulkland's gentleman° and I keep it up a little in private parties. I'll introduce you there, Thomas; you'll like him much.

COACHMAN Sure I know Mr Du Peigne.° You know his master is to   70 marry Madam Julia.

FAG I had forgot. But, Thomas, you must polish° a little; indeed you must. Here now, this wig! What the devil do you do with a *wig*, Thomas?° None of the London whips of any degree of ton wear *wigs* now.   75

COACHMAN More's the pity! More's the pity, I say. Od's life, when I heard how the lawyers and doctors had took to their own hair, I thought how 'twould go next. Od rabbit it!° When the fashion had got foot on the Bar, I guessed 'twould mount to the box!° But 'tis all out of character, believe me, Mr Fag. And, lookee, 80 I'll never gi' up mine; the lawyers and doctors may do as they will.

FAG Well, Thomas, we'll not quarrel about that.

COACHMAN Why, bless you, the gentlemen of they professions ben't all of a mind; for in our village now, tho'ff° Jack Gauge the excise- 85 man° has ta'en to his carrots,° there's little Dick the farrier swears he'll never forsake his bob, though all the college° should appear with their own heads!

FAG Indeed! Well said, Dick! But hold—mark!° Mark, Thomas!

COACHMAN Zooks, 'tis the captain! Is that the lady with him? 90

FAG No, no! That is Madam Lucy, my master's mistress's maid. They lodge at that house. But I must after him to tell him the news.

COACHMAN Od, he's giving her money! Well, Mr Fag—

FAG Good-bye, Thomas. I have an appointment in Gyde's Porch° this evening at eight. Meet me there, and we'll make a little party. 95

Exeunt severally

1.2

A dressing-room in Mrs Malaprop's lodgings

Lydia Languish sitting on a sofa with a book in her hand.
Lucy, as just returned from a message

LUCY Indeed, ma'am, I transferred° half the town in search of it. I don't believe there's a circulating library° in Bath I ha'n't been at.

LYDIA And could not you get *The Reward of Constancy?*°

LUCY No, indeed, ma'am. 5

LYDIA Nor *The Fatal Connection?*°

LUCY No, indeed, ma'am.

LYDIA Nor *The Mistakes of the Heart?*°

LUCY Ma'am, as ill luck would have it, Mr Bull° said Miss Sukey Saunter° had just fetched it away. 10

LYDIA Heigh-ho! Did you inquire for *The Delicate Distress?*°

LUCY Or *The Memoirs of Lady Woodford?*° Yes, indeed, ma'am. I asked everywhere for it; and I might have brought it from Mr

Frederick's,° but Lady Slattern Lounger, who had just sent it home, had so soiled and dog's-eared it,° it wa'n't fit for a Christian to read.   15

LYDIA Heigh-ho! Yes, I always know when Lady Slattern has been before me. She has a most observing thumb, and, I believe, cherishes her nails for the convenience of making marginal notes. Well, child, what *have* you brought me?   20

LUCY O, here, ma'am. (*Taking books from under her cloak, and from her pockets*) This is *The Gordian Knot*,° and this *Peregrine Pickle*.° Here are *The Tears of Sensibility*° and *Humphry Clinker*.° This is *The Memoirs of a Lady of Quality, Written by Herself*,° and here the second volume of *The Sentimental Journey*.°   25

LYDIA Heigh-ho! What are those books by the glass?°

LUCY The great one is only *The Whole Duty of Man*,° where I press a few blondes, ma'am.

LYDIA Very well. Give me the sal volatile.

LUCY Is it in a blue cover, ma'am?   30

LYDIA My smelling-bottle, you simpleton!

LUCY O, the drops!—Here, ma'am.

LYDIA Hold! Here's someone coming. Quick, see who it is.
        Exit Lucy
Surely I heard my cousin Julia's voice!
        Enter Lucy

LUCY Lud, ma'am, here is Miss Melville.   35

LYDIA LANGUISH Is it possible!
        Enter Julia
My dearest Julia, how delighted am I!
        Lydia Languish and Julia embrace
How unexpected was this happiness!

JULIA True, Lydia, and our pleasure is the greater. But what has been the matter? You were denied to me at first!°   40

LYDIA Ah, Julia, I have a thousand things to tell you! But first inform me what has conjured you to Bath? Is Sir Anthony here?

JULIA He is. We are arrived within this hour, and I suppose he will be here to wait on° Mrs Malaprop as soon as he is dressed.°

LYDIA Then, before we are interrupted, let me impart to you some of   45
my distress! I know your gentle nature will sympathize with me, though your prudence may condemn me! My letters have informed you of my whole connection° with Beverley; but I have lost him, Julia! My aunt has discovered our intercourse° by a note she intercepted, and has confined me ever since! Yet, would you believe it?   50

She has fallen absolutely in love with a tall Irish baronet she met
one night since we have been here, at Lady Macshuffle's rout.°

JULIA You jest, Lydia!

LYDIA No, upon my word. She really carries on a kind of correspondence with him, under a feigned name though, till she chooses to   55
be known to him; but it is a Delia or a Celia,° I assure you.

JULIA Then, surely, she is now more indulgent to her niece.

LYDIA Quite the contrary. Since she has discovered her own frailty,
she is become more suspicious of mine. Then I must inform you of
another plague! That odious Acres is to be in Bath today; so that I   60
protest I shall be teased° out of all spirits!

JULIA Come, come, Lydia, hope the best. Sir Anthony shall use his
interest° with Mrs Malaprop.

LYDIA But you have not heard the worst. Unfortunately I had quarrelled with my poor Beverley, just before my aunt made the dis-   65
covery, and I have not seen him since, to make it up.

JULIA What was his offence?

LYDIA Nothing at all! But, I don't know how it was, as often as we had
been together, we had never had a quarrel! And somehow I was
afraid he would never give me an opportunity. So, last Thursday, I   70
wrote a letter to myself, to inform myself that Beverley was at that
time paying his addresses to° another woman. I signed it 'your
friend unknown', showed it to Beverley, charged him with his falsehood, put myself in a violent passion, and vowed I'd never see him
more.   75

JULIA And you let him depart so and have not seen him since?

LYDIA 'Twas the next day my aunt found the matter out. I intended
only to have teased him three days and a half, and now I've lost him
forever.

JULIA If he is as deserving and sincere as you have represented him   80
to me, he will never give you up so. Yet consider, Lydia; you tell me
he is but an ensign, and you have thirty thousand pounds!

LYDIA But you know I lose most of my fortune, if I marry without
my aunt's consent, till of age;° and that is what I have determined
to do, ever since I knew the penalty. Nor could I love the man who   85
would wish to wait a day for the alternative.

JULIA Nay, this is caprice!

LYDIA What, does Julia tax me with caprice! I thought her lover Faulkland had inured her to it.

JULIA I do not love even *his* faults.   90

LYDIA But apropos—you have sent to him, I suppose?

JULIA Not yet, upon my word; nor has he the least idea of my being in Bath. Sir Anthony's resolution° was so sudden, I could not inform him of it.

LYDIA Well, Julia, you are your own mistress, though under the pro- 95
tection of Sir Anthony.° Yet have you, for this long year, been a slave to the caprice, the whim, the jealousy of this ungrateful Faulkland, who will ever delay assuming the right of a husband, while you suffer him to be equally imperious as a lover.

JULIA Nay, you are wrong entirely. We were contracted° before my 100
father's death. *That,* and some consequent embarrassments,° have delayed what I know to be my Faulkland's most ardent wish. He is too generous° to trifle on such a point. And for his character, you wrong him there too. No, Lydia, he is too proud, too noble to be jealous. If he is captious, 'tis without dissembling; if fretful, 105
without rudeness. Unused to the fopperies of love, he is negligent of the little duties expected from a lover. But, being unhackneyed° in the passion, his affection is ardent and sincere; and as it engrosses his whole soul, he expects every thought and emotion of his mistress to move in unison with his. Yet, though his pride calls 110
for this full return,° his humility makes him undervalue those qualities in him, which would entitle him to it; and, not feeling why he should be loved to the degree he wishes, he still suspects that he is not loved enough. This temper,° I must own, has cost me many unhappy hours; but I have learned to think myself his debtor 115
for those imperfections which arise from the ardour of his attachment.°

LYDIA Well, I cannot blame you for defending him. But tell me candidly, Julia. Had he never saved your life, do you think you should have been attached to him as you are? Believe me, the rude blast 120
that overset your boat was a prosperous gale of love to him.

JULIA Gratitude may have strengthened my attachment to Mr Faulkland, but I loved him before he had preserved me. Yet surely that alone were an obligation sufficient.

LYDIA Obligation! Why, a water-spaniel would have done as much. 125
Well, I should never think of giving my heart to a man because he could swim!

JULIA Come, Lydia, you are too inconsiderate.

LYDIA Nay, I do but jest.—What's here?
    Enter Lucy in a hurry

LUCY O ma'am, here is Sir Anthony Absolute just come home with 130
your aunt.

LYDIA They'll not come here.—Lucy, do you watch.
    Exit Lucy

JULIA Yet I must go. Sir Anthony does not know I am here, and if we
meet, he'll detain me, to show me the town. I'll take another opportunity of paying my respects to Mrs Malaprop,° when she shall   135
treat me, as long as she chooses, with her select words so ingeniously
misapplied, without being mispronounced.°
    Enter Lucy

LUCY O lud, ma'am, they are both coming upstairs.

LYDIA Well, I'll not detain you, coz.° Adieu, my dear Julia, I'm sure
you are in haste to send to Faulkland. There—through my room   140
you'll find another staircase.

JULIA Adieu.
    Lydia Languish and Julia embrace. Exit Julia

LYDIA Here, my dear Lucy, hide these books. Quick, quick. Fling
Peregrine Pickle under the toilet. Throw *Roderick Random*° into the
closet. Put *The Innocent Adultery*° into *The Whole Duty of Man*.   145
Thrust *Lord Aimworth*° under the sofa. Cram Ovid° behind the
bolster. There—put *The Man of Feeling*° into your pocket. So, so.
Now lay Mrs Chapone° in sight, and leave Fordyce's *Sermons*° open
on the table.

LUCY O burn it, ma'am, the hairdresser has torn away° as far as   150
'Proper Pride'.

LYDIA Never mind; open at 'Sobriety'. Fling me Lord Chesterfield's
Letters.° [*Sitting down*] Now for 'em.
    Enter Mrs Malaprop and Sir Anthony Absolute

MRS MALAPROP There, Sir Anthony, there sits the deliberate° simpleton, who wants to disgrace her family and lavish herself on a   155
fellow not worth a shilling!

LYDIA Madam, I thought you once—

MRS MALAPROP You thought, Miss! I don't know any business
you have to think at all; thought does not become a young woman.
But the point we would request of you is, that you will promise to   160
forget this fellow—to illiterate° him, I say, quite from your memory.

LYDIA Ah, madam, our memories are independent of our wills. It is
not so easy to forget.

MRS MALAPROP But I say it is, Miss. There is nothing on earth so
easy as to forget, if a person chooses to set about it. I'm sure I have   165
as much forgot your poor dear uncle as if he had never existed; and
I thought it my duty to do so. And let me tell you, Lydia, these
violent memories don't become a young woman.

SIR ANTHONY Why, sure she won't pretend° to remember what she's ordered not! Ay, this comes of her reading!   170

LYDIA What crime, madam, have I committed to be treated thus?

MRS MALAPROP Now don't attempt to extirpate° yourself from the matter; you know I have proof controvertible° of it. But tell me, will you promise to do as you're bid? Will you take a husband of your friends'° choosing?   175

LYDIA Madam, I must tell you plainly, that had I no preference for anyone else, the choice you have made would be my aversion.°

MRS MALAPROP What business have you, Miss, with 'preference' and 'aversion'? They don't become a young woman; and you ought to know, that as both always wear off, 'tis safest in matrimony to begin   180
with a little 'aversion'. I am sure I hated your poor dear uncle before marriage as if he'd been a blackamoor; and yet, Miss, you are sensible° what a wife I made! And when it pleased heaven to release me from him, 'tis unknown what tears I shed!° But suppose we were going to give you another choice, will you promise us to give up this   185
Beverley?

LYDIA Could I belie my thoughts so far as to give that promise, my actions would certainly as far belie° my words.

MRS MALAPROP Take yourself to your room. You are fit company for nothing but your own ill humours.   190

LYDIA Willingly, ma'am. I cannot change for the worse.
     Exit Lydia Languish

MRS MALAPROP There's a little intricate° hussy for you!

SIR ANTHONY It is not to be wondered at, ma'am; all this is the natural consequence of teaching girls to read. Had I a thousand daughters, by heaven, I'd as soon have them taught the black art as   195
their alphabet!

MRS MALAPROP Nay, nay, Sir Anthony, you are an absolute misanthropy.°

SIR ANTHONY In my way hither, Mrs Malaprop, I observed your niece's maid coming forth from a circulating library! She had a book   200
in each hand; they were half-bound volumes, with marble covers!° From that moment I guessed how full of duty I should see her mistress!

MRS MALAPROP Those are vile places, indeed!

SIR ANTHONY Madam, a circulating library in a town is as an ever-   205
green tree of diabolical knowledge!° It blossoms through the year! And depend on it, Mrs Malaprop, that they who are so fond of handling the leaves will long for the fruit at last.

MRS MALAPROP Fie, fie, Sir Anthony, you surely speak laconically!°

SIR ANTHONY Why, Mrs Malaprop, in moderation, now, what would   210
you have a woman know?

MRS MALAPROP Observe me,° Sir Anthony. I would by no means
wish a daughter of mine to be a progeny° of learning; I don't think
so much learning becomes a young woman. For instance, I would
never let her meddle with Greek, or Hebrew, or algebra, or simony,°   215
or fluxions,° or paradoxes,° or such inflammatory° branches
of learning. Neither would it be necessary for her to handle any of
your mathematical, astronomical, diabolical instruments. But, Sir
Anthony, I would send her, at nine years old, to a boarding-school,
in order to learn a little ingenuity and artifice.° Then, sir, she should   220
have a supercilious° knowledge in accounts; and as she grew up,
I would have her instructed in geometry,° that she might
know something of the contagious° countries. But above all,
Sir Anthony, she should be mistress of orthodoxy,° that she might
not misspell and mispronounce words so shamefully as girls   225
usually do, and likewise that she might reprehend° the true meaning
of what she is saying. This, Sir Anthony, is what I would have a
woman know; and I don't think there is a superstitious° article in
it.

SIR ANTHONY Well, well, Mrs Malaprop, I will dispute the point no   230
further with you; though I must confess that you are a truly moderate and polite arguer, for almost every third word you say is on
my side of the question. But, Mrs Malaprop, to the more important point in debate. You say you have no objection to my proposal.

MRS MALAPROP None, I assure you. I am under no positive engage-   235
ment with Mr Acres,° and as Lydia is so obstinate against him,
perhaps your son may have better success.

SIR ANTHONY Well, madam, I will write for the boy directly. He
knows not a syllable of this yet, though I have for some time had
the proposal in my head. He is at present with his regiment.   240

MRS MALAPROP We have never seen your son, Sir Anthony; but I
hope no objection on his side.

SIR ANTHONY Objection! Let him object if he dare! No, no, Mrs
Malaprop, Jack knows that the least demur puts me in a frenzy
directly. My process was always very simple. In their younger days,   245
'twas 'Jack, do this'. If he demurred, I knocked him down; and if
he grumbled at that, I always sent him out of the room.

MRS MALAPROP Ay, and the properest way, o' my conscience!
Nothing is so conciliating° to young people as severity. Well, Sir

Anthony, I shall give Mr Acres his discharge, and prepare Lydia to   250
receive your son's invocations;° and I hope you will represent *her*
to the captain as an object not altogether illegible.°

SIR ANTHONY Madam, I will handle the subject prudently. Well, I
must leave you. And let me beg you, Mrs Malaprop, to enforce this
matter roundly to the girl. Take my advice; keep a tight hand. If   255
she rejects this proposal, clap her under lock and key; and if you
were just to let the servants forget to bring her dinner for three or
four days, you can't conceive how she'd come about!

    Exit Sir Anthony Absolute

MRS MALAPROP Well, at any rate I shall be glad to get her from under
my intuition.° She has somehow discovered my partiality for Sir   260
Lucius O'Trigger. Sure, Lucy can't have betrayed me! No, the girl
is such a simpleton, I should have made her confess it. (*Calls*) Lucy!
Lucy!—Had she been one of your artificial° ones, I should never
have trusted her.

    Enter Lucy

LUCY Did you call, ma'am?   265

MRS MALAPROP Yes, girl. Did you see Sir Lucius while you was out?

LUCY No, indeed, ma'am, not a glimpse of him.

MRS MALAPROP You are sure, Lucy, that you never mentioned—

LUCY O gemini, I'd sooner cut my tongue out.

MRS MALAPROP Well, don't let your simplicity be imposed on.   270

LUCY No, ma'am.

MRS MALAPROP So, come to me presently,° and I'll give you another
letter to Sir Lucius. But mind, Lucy. If ever you betray what you
are entrusted with, unless it be other people's secrets to me, you
forfeit my malevolence° forever, and your being a simpleton shall   275
be no excuse for your locality.°

    Exit Mrs Malaprop

LUCY Ha, ha, ha! So, my dear simplicity, let me give you a little respite.
(*Altering her manner*) Let girls in my station be as fond as they please
of appearing expert and knowing in their trusts. Commend me to
a mask of silliness, and a pair of sharp eyes for my own interest   280
under it! Let me see to what account I have turned my simplicity
lately. (*Looks at a paper*) 'For abetting Miss Lydia Languish in a
design of running away with an ensign! In money, sundry times,
twelve pound twelve;° gowns five; hats, ruffles, caps, etc., etc., numberless! From the said ensign, within this last month, six guineas   285
and a half.' About a quarter's pay!° 'Item, from Mrs Malaprop, for
betraying the young people to her'—when I found matters were

likely to be discovered—'two guineas, and a black paduasoy. Item, from Mr Acres, for carrying divers letters'—which I never delivered—'two guineas, and a pair of buckles. Item, from Sir Lucius O'Trigger, three crowns, two gold pocket-pieces,° and a silver snuff-box!' Well done, simplicity! Yet I was forced to make my Hibernian believe that he was corresponding, not with the aunt, but with the niece; for, though not over-rich, I found he had too much pride and delicacy to sacrifice the feelings of a gentleman to the necessities of his fortune.

    Exit

2.1

Captain Absolute's lodgings

Captain Absolute and Fag

FAG Sir, while I was there, Sir Anthony came in. I told him you had sent me to inquire after his health, and to know if he was at leisure to see you.

ABSOLUTE And what did he say on hearing I was at Bath?

FAG Sir, in my life I never saw an elderly gentleman more astonished! He started back two or three paces, rapped out a dozen interjectural oaths, and asked, what the devil had brought you here!

ABSOLUTE Well, sir, and what did you say?

FAG O, I lied, sir. I forget the precise lie; but you may depend on't, he got no truth from me. Yet, with submission, for fear of blunders in future, I should be glad to fix what *has* brought us to Bath, in order that we may lie a little consistently. Sir Anthony's servants were curious, sir, very curious indeed.

ABSOLUTE You have said nothing to them?

FAG O, not a word, sir, not a word. Mr Thomas, indeed, the coachman, whom I take to be the discreetest of whips—

ABSOLUTE 'Sdeath, you rascal! You have not trusted him!

FAG O, *no*, sir—no, no, not a syllable, upon my veracity! He was, indeed, a little inquisitive; but I was sly, sir, devilish sly. 'My master', said I, 'honest Thomas'—you know, sir, one says 'honest' to one's inferiors—'is come to Bath to *recruit*'°—yes, sir, I said 'to *recruit*'—and whether for men, money, or constitution, you know, sir, is nothing to him, nor anyone else.

ABSOLUTE Well, '*recruit*' will do. Let it be so.

FAG O, sir 'recruit' will do surprisingly. Indeed, to give the thing an air,° I told Thomas that your honour had already enlisted five disbanded chairmen,° seven minority waiters,° and thirteen billiard-markers.°

ABSOLUTE You blockhead, never say more than is necessary.

FAG I beg pardon, sir; I beg pardon. But, with submission, a lie is nothing unless one supports it. Sir, whenever I draw on my invention for a good current lie, I always forge endorsements as well as the bill.°

ABSOLUTE Well, take care you don't hurt your credit by offering too much security. Is Mr Faulkland returned?

FAG He is above, sir, changing his dress.

ABSOLUTE Can you tell whether he has been informed of Sir
Anthony's and Miss Melville's arrival?

FAG I fancy not, sir; he has seen no one since he came in, but his gentleman, who was with him at Bristol. I think, sir, I hear Mr Faulk-   40
land coming down.

ABSOLUTE Go, tell him I am here.

FAG (*going*) Yes, sir.—I beg pardon, sir, but should Sir Anthony call,
you will do me the favour to remember that we are '*recruiting*', if
you please.   45

ABSOLUTE Well, well.

FAG And in tenderness to my character,° if your honour could bring
in the chairmen and waiters, I shall esteem it as an obligation; for
though I never scruple a lie to serve my master, yet it hurts one's
conscience to be found out.   50

   Exit Fag

ABSOLUTE Now for my whimsical friend. If he does not know that his
mistress° is here, I'll tease him a little before I tell him.

   Enter Faulkland

Faulkland, you're welcome to Bath again; you are punctual in your
return.

FAULKLAND Yes; I had nothing to detain me, when I had finished the   55
business I went on. Well, what news since I left you? How stand
matters between you and Lydia?

ABSOLUTE Faith, much as they were. I have not seen her since our
quarrel; however, I expect to be recalled every hour.

FAULKLAND Why don't you persuade her to go off with you at once?   60

ABSOLUTE What, and lose two thirds of her fortune? You forget that,
my friend. No, no; I could have brought her to that long ago.

FAULKLAND Nay then, you trifle too long. If you are sure of *her*,
propose to the aunt in your own character,° and write to Sir
Anthony for his consent.   65

ABSOLUTE Softly, softly; for though I am convinced my little
Lydia would elope with me as Ensign Beverley, yet am I by no
means certain that she would take me with the impediment of
our friends' consent, a regular humdrum wedding, and the
reversion of a good fortune on my side.° No, no; I must prepare her   70
gradually for the discovery, and make myself necessary to her,
before I risk it. Well, but, Faulkland, you'll dine with us today at
the hotel?

FAULKLAND Indeed I cannot; I am not in spirits to be of such a party.

ABSOLUTE By heavens, I shall forswear your company. You are the   75
most teasing, captious, incorrigible lover! Do love like a man.

FAULKLAND I own I am unfit for company.

ABSOLUTE Am not *I* a lover? Ay, and a romantic one too? Yet do I carry
everywhere with me such a confounded farrago of doubts, fears,
hopes, wishes, and all the flimsy furniture of a country miss's brain?   80

FAULKLAND Ah, Jack, your heart and soul are not, like mine, fixed
immutably on one only object. You throw for a large stake, but,
losing, you could stake and throw again; but I have set my sum of
happiness on this cast,° and not to succeed were to be stripped of all.

ABSOLUTE But, for heaven's sake, what grounds for apprehension can   85
your whimsical brain conjure up at present?

FAULKLAND What grounds for apprehension did you say? Heavens,
are there not a thousand! I fear for her spirits—her health—her life.
My absence may fret her; her anxiety for my return, her fears for me,
may oppress her gentle temper. And for her health—does not every   90
hour bring me cause to be alarmed? If it rains, some shower may
even then have chilled her delicate frame! If the wind be keen, some
rude blast may have affected her! The heat of noon, the dews of the
evening, may endanger the life of her, for whom only I value mine.
O, Jack, when delicate and feeling souls are separated, there is not a   95
feature in the sky, not a movement of the elements, not an aspira-
tion° of the breeze, but hints some cause for a lover's apprehension!

ABSOLUTE Ay, but we may choose whether we will take the hint or
not. So then, Faulkland, if you were convinced that Julia were well
and in spirits, you would be entirely content.   100

FAULKLAND I should be happy beyond measure. I am anxious only
for that.

ABSOLUTE Then, to cure your anxiety at once, Miss Melville is in
perfect health, and is at this moment in Bath.

FAULKLAND Nay, Jack, don't trifle with me.   105

ABSOLUTE She is arrived here with my father within this hour.

FAULKLAND Can you be serious?

ABSOLUTE I thought you knew Sir Anthony better than to be surprised at a sudden whim of this kind. Seriously then, it is as I tell
you, upon my honour.   110

FAULKLAND My dear friend!—[*Calling offstage*] Hollo, Du Peigne, my
hat!—My dear Jack! Now nothing on earth can give me a moment's
uneasiness.
      Enter Fag

FAG Sir, Mr Acres, just arrived, is below.

ABSOLUTE Stay, Faulkland. This Acres lives within a mile of Sir   115
Anthony, and he shall tell you how your mistress has been ever since
you left her.—Fag, show the gentleman up.
    Exit Fag

FAULKLAND What, is he much acquainted in the family?

ABSOLUTE O, very intimate. I insist on your not going. Besides, his
character will divert you.   120

FAULKLAND Well, I should like to ask him a few questions.

ABSOLUTE He is likewise a rival of mine—that is, of my other
self's—for he does not think his friend Captain Absolute ever
saw the lady in question; and it is ridiculous enough to hear
him complain to me of one Beverley, a concealed skulking rival,   125
who—

FAULKLAND Hush! He's here.
    Enter Bob Acres

ACRES Ha, my dear friend, noble captain, and honest Jack, how dost
thou? Just arrived, faith, as you see. [*To Faulkland*] Sir, your humble
servant. [*To Captain Absolute*] Warm work on the roads, Jack. Od's   130
whips and wheels,° I've travelled like a comet, with a tail of dust all
the way as long as the Mall.°

ABSOLUTE Ah, Bob, you are indeed an eccentric planet, but we know
your attraction hither. Give me leave to introduce Mr Faulkland to
you. Mr Faulkland, Mr Acres.   135

ACRES [*to Faulkland*] Sir, I am most heartily glad to see you. Sir, I
solicit your connections.°—Hey, Jack! What, this is Mr Faulkland,
who—?

ABSOLUTE Ay, Bob, Miss Melville's Mr Faulkland.

ACRES Odso! She and your father can be but just arrived before me. I   140
suppose you have seen them.—Ah, Mr Faulkland, you are indeed
a happy man.

FAULKLAND I have not seen Miss Melville yet, sir. I hope she enjoyed
full health and spirits in Devonshire?

ACRES Never knew her better in my life, sir, never better. Od's blushes   145
and blooms, she has been as healthy as the German Spa.°

FAULKLAND Indeed! I did hear that she had been a little indisposed.

ACRES False, false, sir; only said to vex you. Quite the reverse, I assure
you.

FAULKLAND There, Jack, you see she has the advantage of me; I had   150
almost fretted myself ill.

ABSOLUTE Now are you angry with your mistress for not having been
sick.

FAULKLAND No, no, you misunderstand me. Yet surely a little trifling
indisposition is not an unnatural consequence of absence from   155
those we love. Now confess. Isn't there something unkind in this
violent, robust, unfeeling health?

ABSOLUTE O, it was very unkind of her to be well in your absence, to
be sure!

ACRES Good apartments, Jack.   160

FAULKLAND Well, sir, but you were saying that Miss Melville has been
so *exceedingly* well. What then, she has been merry and gay, I
suppose? Always in spirits, hey?

ACRES Merry? Od's crickets,° she has been the belle and spirit of the
company wherever she has been. So lively and entertaining! So full   165
of wit and humour!

FAULKLAND There, Jack, there. O, by my soul, there is an innate levity
in woman that nothing can overcome. What, happy and I away!

ABSOLUTE Have done. How foolish this is! Just now you were only
apprehensive for your mistress's *spirits*.   170

FAULKLAND Why, Jack, have I been the joy and spirit of the company?

ABSOLUTE No, indeed, you have not.

FAULKLAND Have I been lively and entertaining?

ABSOLUTE O, upon my word, I acquit you.

FAULKLAND Have I been full of wit and humour?   175

ABSOLUTE No, faith; to do you justice, you have been confoundedly
stupid indeed.

ACRES What's the matter with the gentleman?

ABSOLUTE He is only expressing his great satisfaction at hearing that
Julia has been so well and happy.—That's all, hey, Faulkland?   180

FAULKLAND O, I am rejoiced to hear it. Yes, yes, she has a *happy*
disposition!

ACRES That she has indeed. Then she is so accomplished. So sweet a
voice, so expert at her harpsichord, such a mistress of flat and sharp,
squallante, rumblante, and quiverante!° There was this time   185
month°—od's minims and crotchets, how she did chirrup at Mrs
Piano's° concert!

FAULKLAND There again! What say you to this? You see she has been
all mirth and song. Not a thought of me!

ABSOLUTE Foh, man! Is not music the food of love?°   190

FAULKLAND Well, well, it may be so. Pray Mr—what's his damned
name?—do you remember what songs Miss Melville sung?

ACRES Not I, indeed.

ABSOLUTE Stay now. They were some pretty, melancholy, purling
   stream° airs, I warrant. Perhaps you may recollect. Did she sing   195
   'When absent from my soul's delight'?°

ACRES No, that wa'n't it.

ABSOLUTE Or 'Go, gentle gales!'°—(sings) 'Go, gentle gales!'

ACRES O no, nothing like it! Od's, now I recollect one of them. (Sings)
   'My heart's my own, my will is free'.°   200

FAULKLAND Fool! Fool that I am! To fix all my happiness on such a
   trifler! 'Sdeath, to make herself the pipe and balladmonger° of a
   circle! To soothe her light heart with catches and glees! What can
   you say to this, sir?

ABSOLUTE Why, that I should be glad to hear my mistress had been   205
   so merry, sir.

FAULKLAND Nay, nay, nay; I am not sorry that she has been happy.
   No, no; I am glad of that. I would not have had her sad or sick. Yet
   surely a sympathetic heart would have shown itself even in the
   choice of a song. She might have been temperately healthy, and   210
   somehow plaintively gay. But she has been dancing too, I doubt not!

ACRES What does the gentleman say about dancing?

ABSOLUTE He says the lady we speak of dances as well as she sings.

ACRES Ay, truly, does she. There was at our last race-ball°—

FAULKLAND Hell and the devil! There! There! I told you so, I told   215
   you so! O, she thrives in my absence! Dancing! But her whole feelings have been in opposition with mine! I have been anxious, silent,
   pensive, sedentary. My days have been hours of care, my nights of
   watchfulness. She has been all health! spirit! laugh! song! dance! O,
   damned, damned levity!   220

ABSOLUTE For heaven's sake, Faulkland, don't expose yourself so.°
   Suppose she has danced, what then? Does not the ceremony of
   society often oblige—

FAULKLAND Well, well, I'll contain myself. Perhaps, as you say, for
   form sake.—What, Mr Acres, you were praising Miss Melville's   225
   manner of dancing a minuet, hey?

ACRES O I dare insure her for that;° but what I was going to speak of
   was her country-dancing.° Od's swimmings,° she has such an air
   with her!

FAULKLAND Now disappointment on her! Defend this, Absolute!   230
   Why don't you defend this? Country-dances! Jigs and reels! Am I
   to blame now? A minuet I could have forgiven. I should not have
   minded that; I say I should not have regarded a minuet. But country-

dances? Zounds! Had she made one in a *cotillion*,° I believe I could
have forgiven even that. But to be monkey-led° for a night! To run   235
the gauntlet° through a string of amorous palming puppies! To
show paces like a managed° filly! O Jack, there never can be but *one*
man in the world, whom a truly modest and delicate° woman ought
to pair with in a *country-dance*; and even then the rest of the couples
should be her great uncles and aunts!   240

ABSOLUTE Ay, to be sure! Grandfathers and grandmothers!

FAULKLAND If there be but one vicious mind in the set, 'twill spread like
a contagion. The action of their pulse beats to the lascivious movement of the jig. Their quivering, warm-breathed sighs impregnate
the very air. The atmosphere becomes electrical to love, and each   245
amorous spark darts through every link of the chain!° I must leave
you. I own I am somewhat flurried; and that confounded looby has
perceived it. (*Going*)

ABSOLUTE Nay, but stay, Faulkland, and thank Mr Acres for his good
news.   250

FAULKLAND Damn his news!
    Exit Faulkland

ABSOLUTE Ha, ha, ha! Poor Faulkland! Five minutes since 'nothing
on earth could give him a moment's uneasiness!'

ACRES The gentleman wa'n't angry at my praising his mistress, was
he?   255

ABSOLUTE A little jealous, I believe, Bob.

ACRES You don't say so? Ha, ha? Jealous of me! That's a good joke.

ABSOLUTE There's nothing strange in that, Bob. Let me tell you, that
sprightly grace and insinuating manner of yours will do some mischief among the girls here.   260

ACRES Ah, you joke! Ha, ha! Mischief! Ha, ha! But you know I am not
my own property; my dear Lydia has forestalled me.° She could
never abide me in the country, because I used to dress so badly. But,
od's frogs and tambours,° I shan't take matters so here. Now ancient
madam° has no voice in it. I'll make my old clothes know who's   265
master. I shall straightway cashier the hunting-frock and render my
leather breeches incapable.° My hair has been in training some time.

ABSOLUTE Indeed!

ACRES Ay; and tho'ff the side-curls are a little restive, my hind-part
takes to it very kindly.°   270

ABSOLUTE O, you'll polish, I doubt not.

ACRES Absolutely, I propose so. Then if I can find out this Ensign

Beverley, od's triggers and flints,° I'll make him know the difference o't.

ABSOLUTE Spoke like a man. But pray, Bob, I observe you have got 275
an odd kind of a new method of swearing.

ACRES Ha, ha! You've taken notice of it. 'Tis genteel,° isn't it? I
didn't invent it myself, though; but a commander in our militia°—
a great scholar, I assure you—says that there is no meaning in
the common oaths, and that nothing but their antiquity makes 280
them respectable, because, he says, the ancients would never
stick to an oath or two, but would say 'By Jove!' or 'By Bacchus!'
or 'By Mars!' or 'By Venus!' or 'By Pallas' according to the
sentiment.° So that to swear with propriety, says my little major,
the 'oath should be an echo to the sense';° and this we call the oath 285
referential, or sentimental swearing. Ha, ha, ha! 'Tis genteel, isn't
it?

ABSOLUTE Very genteel, and very new indeed; and I dare say will supplant
all other figures of imprecation.

ACRES Ay, ay; the best terms will grow obsolete. Damns have had their 290
day.

Enter Fag

FAG Sir, there is a gentleman below desires to see you. Shall I show
him into the parlour?

ABSOLUTE Ay, you may.

ACRES Well, I must be gone. 295

ABSOLUTE Stay.—Who is it, Fag?

FAG Your father, sir.

ABSOLUTE You puppy, why didn't you show him up directly?

Exit Fag

ACRES You have business with Sir Anthony. I expect a message
from Mrs Malaprop at my lodgings. I have sent also to my dear 300
friend Sir Lucius O'Trigger. Adieu, Jack. We must meet at night,
when you shall give me a dozen bumpers° to little Lydia.

ABSOLUTE That I will with all my heart.

Exit Bob Acres

Now for a parental lecture. I hope he has heard nothing of the business
that has brought me here. I wish the gout had held him fast in 305
Devonshire, with all my soul!

Enter Sir Anthony Absolute

Sir, I am delighted to see you here, and looking so well! Your sudden
arrival at Bath made me apprehensive for your health.

SIR ANTHONY Very apprehensive, I dare say, Jack. What, you are
recruiting here, hey?   315

ABSOLUTE Yes, sir, I am on duty.

SIR ANTHONY Well, Jack, I am glad to see you, though I did not
expect it, for I was going to write to you on a little matter of business. Jack, I have been considering that I grow old and infirm, and
shall probably not trouble you long.   320

ABSOLUTE Pardon me, sir, I never saw you look more strong and
hearty; and I pray frequently that you may continue so.

SIR ANTHONY I hope your prayers may be heard with all my heart.
Well then, Jack, I have been considering that I am so strong
and hearty, I may continue to plague you a long time. Now, Jack,   325
I am sensible that the income of your commission, and what I
have hitherto allowed you, is but a small pittance° for a lad of your
spirit.

ABSOLUTE Sir, you are very good.

SIR ANTHONY And it is my wish, while yet I live, to have my boy   330
make some figure° in the world. I have resolved, therefore, to fix
you at once in a noble independence.

ABSOLUTE Sir, your kindness overpowers me. Such generosity makes
the gratitude of reason more lively than the sensations even of filial
affection.   335

SIR ANTHONY I am glad you are so sensible of my attention°—and
you shall be master of a large estate in a few weeks.

ABSOLUTE Let my future life, sir, speak my gratitude; I cannot express
the sense I have of your munificence. Yet, sir, I presume you would
not wish me to quit the army?   340

SIR ANTHONY O, that shall be as your wife chooses.

ABSOLUTE My wife, sir!

SIR ANTHONY Ay, ay, settle that between you; settle that between you.

ABSOLUTE A *wife*, sir, did you say?

SIR ANTHONY Ay, a wife. Why, did not I mention her before?   345

ABSOLUTE Not a word of her, sir.

SIR ANTHONY Odso, I mustn't forget *her*, though. Yes, Jack, the independence I was talking of is by a marriage. The fortune is saddled
with a wife. But I suppose that makes no difference.

ABSOLUTE Sir! Sir! You amaze me!   350

SIR ANTHONY Why, what the devil's the matter with the fool? Just
now you were all gratitude and duty.

ABSOLUTE I was, sir. You talked to me of independence and a fortune,
but not a word of a wife.

SIR ANTHONY Why, what difference does that make? Od's life, sir, if 355
you have the estate, you must take it with the livestock on it, as it
stands!

ABSOLUTE If my happiness is to be the price, I must beg leave to
decline the purchase. Pray, sir, who is the lady?

SIR ANTHONY What's that to you, sir? Come, give me your promise 360
to love and to marry her directly.

ABSOLUTE Sure, sir, this is not very reasonable—to summon my
affections for a lady I know nothing of!

SIR ANTHONY I am sure, sir, 'tis more unreasonable in you to *object*
to a lady you know nothing of. 365

ABSOLUTE Then, sir, I must tell you plainly that my inclinations° are
fixed on another. My heart is engaged to an angel.

SIR ANTHONY Then pray let it send an excuse. It is very sorry, but
business° prevents its waiting on her.

ABSOLUTE But my vows are pledged to her. 370

SIR ANTHONY Let her foreclose, Jack; let her foreclose. They are not
worth redeeming.° Besides, you have the angel's vows in exchange,
I suppose; so there can be no loss there.

ABSOLUTE You must excuse me, sir, if I tell you, once for all, that in
this point I cannot obey you. 375

SIR ANTHONY Harkee, Jack. I have heard you for some time with
patience. I have been cool, quite cool; but take care. You know I am
compliance itself, when I am not thwarted—no one more easily led,
when I have my own way; but don't put me in a frenzy!

ABSOLUTE Sir, I must repeat it. In this I cannot obey you. 380

SIR ANTHONY Now, damn me, if ever I call you Jack again while I
live!

ABSOLUTE Nay, sir, but hear me.

SIR ANTHONY Sir, I won't hear a word; not a word! Not one word!
So give me your promise by a nod, and I'll tell you what, Jack—I 385
mean, you dog—if you don't, by—

ABSOLUTE What, sir, promise to link myself to some mass of ugliness!
To—

SIR ANTHONY Zounds, sirrah, the lady shall be as ugly as I choose. She
shall have a hump on each shoulder. She shall be as crooked as the 390
Crescent.° Her one eye shall roll like the bull's in Cox's Museum.°
She shall have a skin like a mummy and the beard of a Jew. She shall be
all this, sirrah! Yet I'll make you ogle her all day, and sit up all night to
write sonnets on her beauty.

ABSOLUTE This is reason and moderation indeed! 395

SIR ANTHONY None of your sneering, puppy! No grinning, jackanapes!

ABSOLUTE Indeed, sir, I never was in a worse humour for mirth in my life.

SIR ANTHONY 'Tis false, sir! I know you are laughing in your sleeve.°   400
I know you'll grin when I am gone, sirrah!

ABSOLUTE Sir, I hope I know my duty better.

SIR ANTHONY None of your passion, sir! None of your violence, if you please! It won't do with me, I promise you.

ABSOLUTE Indeed, sir, I never was cooler in my life.   410

SIR ANTHONY 'Tis a confounded lie! I know you are in a passion in your heart; I know you are, you hypocritical young dog! But it won't do.

ABSOLUTE Nay, sir, upon my word.

SIR ANTHONY So you will fly out!° Can't you be cool, like me?   415
What the devil good can *passion* do! *Passion* is of no service, you impudent, insolent, overbearing reprobate! There you sneer again! Don't provoke me! But you rely upon the mildness of my temper. You do, you dog! You play upon the meekness of my disposition! Yet take care. The patience of a saint may be overcome at last!   420
But mark! I give you six hours and a half to consider of this. If you then agree, without any condition, to do everything on earth that I choose, why, confound you, I may in time forgive you. If not, zounds, don't enter the same hemisphere with me! Don't dare to breathe the same air, or use the same light with me;   425
but get an atmosphere and a sun of your own! I'll strip you of your commission; I'll lodge a five-and-threepence° in the hands of trustees, and you shall live on the interest. I'll disown you, I'll disinherit you, I'll unget you! And damn me, if ever I call you Jack again!   430

Exit Sir Anthony Absolute

ABSOLUTE (*alone*) Mild, gentle, considerate father, I kiss your hands. What a tender method of giving his opinion in these matters Sir Anthony has! I dare not trust him with the truth. I wonder what old, wealthy hag it is that he wants to bestow on me! Yet he married himself for love, and was in his youth a bold intriguer° and a gay   435
companion!

Enter Fag

FAG Assuredly, sir, our father is wrath to a degree. He comes down stairs eight or ten steps at a time, muttering, growling, and thumping the banisters all the way. I, and the cook's dog, stand bowing at

the door. Rap! He gives me a stroke on the head with his cane; bids   440
me carry that to my master; then, kicking the poor turnspit° into
the area,° damns us all for a puppy triumvirate! Upon my credit,
sir, were I in your place, and found my father such very bad
company, I should certainly drop his acquaintance.

ABSOLUTE Cease your impertinence, sir, at present. Did you come in   445
for nothing more? Stand out of the way.

Captain Absolute pushes Fag aside, and exits

FAG (*alone*) So! Sir Anthony trims my master. He is afraid to reply to
his father, then vents his spleen° on poor Fag! When one is vexed
by one person, to revenge one's self on another who happens to
come in the way is the vilest injustice! Ah, it shows the worst   450
temper, the basest—

Enter Errand-boy

ERRAND-BOY Mr Fag! Mr Fag! Your master calls you.

FAG Well, you little, dirty puppy, you need not bawl so!—The meanest
disposition! The—

ERRAND-BOY Quick, quick, Mr Fag.   455

FAG '*Quick, quick*', you impudent jackanapes! Am I to be commanded
by you too? You little, impertinent, insolent, kitchen-bred—

Exit Fag, kicking and beating the Errand-boy

2.2

The North Parade

Enter Lucy

LUCY So. I shall have another rival to add to my mistress's list—
Captain Absolute. However, I shall not enter his name till my purse
has received notice in form.° Poor Acres is dismissed! Well, I have
done him a last friendly office, in letting him know that Beverley
was here before him. Sir Lucius is generally more punctual, when   5
he expects to hear from his 'dear Dalia',° as he calls her. I wonder
he's not here! I have a little scruple of conscience from this deceit;
though I should not be paid so well, if my hero knew that Delia was
near fifty, and her own mistress.

Enter Sir Lucius O'Trigger

SIR LUCIUS Ha, my little embassadress! Upon my conscience I have   10
been looking for you; I have been on the South Parade this half-
hour.

35

LUCY (*speaking simply°*) O gemini! And I have been waiting for your worship here on the North.

SIR LUCIUS Faith, maybe that was the reason we did not meet; and it is very comical too, how you could go out and I not see you, for I was only taking a nap at the Parade coffee-house, and I chose the *window* on purpose that I might not miss you.

LUCY My stars! Now I'd wager a sixpence I went by while you were asleep.

SIR LUCIUS Sure enough it must have been so. And I never dreamt it was so late, till I waked. Well, but, my little girl, have you got nothing for me?

LUCY Yes, but I have. I've got a letter for you in my pocket.

SIR LUCIUS O faith! I guessed you weren't come empty-handed. Well, let me see what the dear creature says.

LUCY There, Sir Lucius.

Lucy gives Sir Lucius O'Trigger a letter

SIR LUCIUS (*reads*) 'Sir, there is often a sudden incentive° impulse in love, that has a greater induction° than years of domestic combination. Such was the commotion° I felt at the first superfluous° view of Sir Lucius O'Trigger.' Very pretty, upon my word. 'Female punctuation° forbids me to say more. Yet let me add, that it will give me joy infallible° to find Sir Lucius worthy the last criterion of my affections.°—Delia.' Upon my conscience, Lucy, your lady is a great mistress of language. Faith, she's quite the queen of the dictionary; for the devil a word dare refuse coming at her call, though one would think it was quite out of hearing.

LUCY Ay, sir, a lady of her experience.

SIR LUCIUS Experience! What, at seventeen?

LUCY O true, sir; but then she reads so. My stars, how she will read off-hand!

SIR LUCIUS Faith, she must be very deep read to write this way. Though she is rather an arbitrary writer too, for here are a great many poor words pressed° into the service of this note, that would get their *habeas corpus*° from any court in Christendom.

LUCY Ah, Sir Lucius, if you were to hear how she talks of you!

SIR LUCIUS O, tell her I'll make her the best husband in the world, and Lady O'Trigger into the bargain! But we must get the old gentlewoman's consent and do everything fairly.

LUCY Nay, Sir Lucius, I thought you wa'n't rich enough to be so nice!°

SIR LUCIUS Upon my word, young woman, you have hit it. I am so poor that I can't afford to do a dirty action. If I did not want money

I'd steal your mistress and her fortune with a great deal of pleasure. However, my pretty girl (*gives her money*), here's a little something to buy you a ribbon; and meet me in the evening, and I'll give you an answer to this. So, hussy, take a kiss beforehand, to put you in mind. 55

> *Sir Lucius O'Trigger kisses Lucy*

LUCY O lud, Sir Lucius! I never seed such a gemman!° My lady won't like you if you're so impudent.

SIR LUCIUS Faith, she will, Lucy. That same—foh, what's the name of it?—*modesty!*—is a quality in a lover more praised by the women than liked. So, if your mistress asks you whether Sir Lucius ever gave you a kiss, tell her *fifty*, my dear. 60

LUCY What, would you have me tell her a lie?

SIR LUCIUS Ah, then, you baggage, I'll make it a truth presently. 65

LUCY For shame now! Here is someone coming.

SIR LUCIUS [*trying to kiss her*] O faith, I'll quiet your conscience!

> *Sir Lucius O'Trigger sees Fag. Exit Sir Lucius O'Trigger,*
> *humming a tune. Enter Fag*

FAG So, so, ma'am, I humbly beg pardon.

LUCY O lud! Now, Mr Fag, you flurry one so.

FAG Come, come, Lucy, here's no one by. So a little less simplicity, with a grain or two more sincerity, if you please. You play false with us, madam. I saw you give the baronet a letter. My master shall know this; and if he don't call him out,° I will. 70

LUCY Ha, ha, ha! You gentlemen's gentlemen are so hasty. That letter was from Mrs Malaprop, simpleton. She is taken with Sir Lucius's address. 75

FAG How! What tastes some people have! Why, I suppose I have walked by her window an hundred times. But what says our young lady? Any message to my master?

LUCY Sad news, Mr Fag! A worse rival than Acres! Sir Anthony Absolute has proposed his son. 80

FAG What, Captain Absolute?

LUCY Even so. I overheard it all.

FAG Ha, ha, ha! Very good, faith. Goodbye, Lucy; I must away with this news. 85

LUCY Well, you may laugh, but it is true, I assure you. (*Going*) But, Mr Fag, tell your master not to be cast down by this.

FAG O, he'll be so disconsolate!

LUCY And charge him not to think of quarrelling with young Absolute. 90

FAG Never fear! Never fear!
LUCY Be sure bid him keep up his spirits.
FAG We will, we will.

   Exeunt severally

3.1

The North Parade

Enter Captain Absolute

ABSOLUTE 'Tis just as Fag told me, indeed. Whimsical enough, faith! My father wants to *force* me to marry the very girl I am plotting to run away with! He must not know of my connection with her yet awhile. He has too summary a method of proceeding in these matters. However, I'll read my recantation instantly. My conversion   5
is something sudden, indeed; but I can assure him it is very *sincere*. So, so, here he comes. He looks plaguy gruff.

Captain Absolute steps aside. Enter Sir Anthony Absolute

SIR ANTHONY No, I'll die sooner than forgive him. '*Die*', did I say? I'll live these fifty years to plague him. At our last meeting, his impudence had almost put me out of temper. An obstinate, pas-   10
sionate, self-willed boy! Who can he take after? This is my return for getting him before all his brothers and sisters!—for putting him, at twelve years old,° into a marching regiment, and allowing him fifty pounds a year, beside his pay, ever since? But I have done with him; he's anybody's son for me. I never will see him more. Never—   15
never—never—never.°

ABSOLUTE [*aside*] Now for a penitential face.

SIR ANTHONY Fellow, get out of my way.

ABSOLUTE Sir, you see a penitent before you.

SIR ANTHONY I see an impudent scoundrel before me.   20

ABSOLUTE A sincere penitent. I am come, sir, to acknowledge my error, and to submit entirely to your will.

SIR ANTHONY What's that?

ABSOLUTE I have been revolving, and reflecting, and considering on your past goodness, and kindness, and condescension to me.°   25

SIR ANTHONY Well, sir?

ABSOLUTE I have been likewise weighing and balancing what you were pleased to mention concerning duty, and obedience, and authority.

SIR ANTHONY Well, puppy?

ABSOLUTE Why then, sir, the result of my reflections is a resolution   30
to sacrifice every inclination of my own to your satisfaction.

SIR ANTHONY Why, now you talk sense—absolute° sense. I never heard anything more sensible in my life. Confound you; you shall be Jack again.

ABSOLUTE I am happy in the appellation.   35

SIR ANTHONY Why, then, Jack, my dear Jack, I will now inform you
    who the lady really is. Nothing but your passion and violence, you
    silly fellow, prevented my telling you at first. Prepare, Jack, for
    wonder and rapture; prepare. What think you of Miss Lydia
    Languish?   40

ABSOLUTE Languish! What, the Languishes of Worcestershire?

SIR ANTHONY Worcestershire! No. Did you never meet Mrs Mala-
    prop and her niece, Miss Languish, who came into our country°
    just before you were last ordered to your regiment?

ABSOLUTE Malaprop! Languish! I don't remember ever to have   45
    heard the names before. Yet, stay! I think I do recollect something.
    Languish! Languish! She squints, don't she? A little, red-haired
    girl?

SIR ANTHONY Squints? A red-haired girl! Zounds, no.

ABSOLUTE Then I must have forgot; it can't be the same person.   50

SIR ANTHONY Jack! Jack! What think you of blooming, love-
    breathing seventeen?

ABSOLUTE As to that, sir, I am quite indifferent. If I can please you
    in the matter, 'tis all I desire.

SIR ANTHONY Nay, but, Jack, such eyes! Such eyes! So innocently   55
    wild! So bashfully irresolute! Not a glance but speaks and kindles
    some thought of love! Then, Jack, her cheeks! Her cheeks, Jack!
    So deeply blushing at the insinuations° of her tell-tale eyes!
    Then, Jack, her lips! O, Jack, lips smiling at their own dis-
    cretion; and if not smiling, more sweetly pouting, more lovely in   60
    sullenness!

ABSOLUTE [aside] That's she indeed. Well done, old gentleman!

SIR ANTHONY Then, Jack, her neck. O Jack! Jack!

ABSOLUTE And which is to be mine, sir, the niece or the aunt?

SIR ANTHONY Why, you unfeeling, insensible puppy, I despise you.   65
    When I was of your age, such a description would have made me
    fly like a rocket! The *aunt*, indeed! Od's life, when I ran away with
    your mother, I would not have touched anything old or ugly to gain
    an empire.

ABSOLUTE Not to please your father, sir?   70

SIR ANTHONY To please my father! Zounds, not to please—O my
    father! Odso! Yes, yes! If my father indeed had desired—that's
    quite another matter. Though he wa'n't the indulgent father that I
    am, Jack.

ABSOLUTE I dare say not, sir.   75

SIR ANTHONY But, Jack, you are not sorry to find your mistress is so
 beautiful.

ABSOLUTE Sir, I repeat it: if I please you in this affair, 'tis all I desire.
 Not that I think a woman the worse for being handsome; but, sir,
 if you please to recollect, you before hinted something about a   80
 hump or two, one eye, and a few more graces of that kind. Now,
 without being very nice, I own I should rather choose a wife of mine
 to have the usual number of limbs, and a limited quantity of back;
 and though *one* eye may be very agreeable, yet as the prejudice has
 always run in favour of *two*, I would not wish to affect a singular-   85
 ity° in that article.

SIR ANTHONY What a phlegmatic sot it is! Why, sirrah, you're an
 anchorite!—a vile insensible stock! You a soldier! You're a walking
 block,° fit only to dust the company's regimentals on! Od's life, I've
 a great mind to marry the girl myself!   90

ABSOLUTE I am entirely at your disposal, sir. If you should think of
 addressing Miss Languish yourself, I suppose you would have me
 marry the *aunt*; or if you should change your mind and take the old
 lady, 'tis the same to me. I'll marry the *niece*.

SIR ANTHONY Upon my word, Jack, thou'rt either a very great hypo-   95
 crite, or—but, come, I know your indifference on such a subject
 must be all a lie. I'm sure it must. Come, now. Damn your demure
 face! Come, confess, Jack! You have been lying, ha'n't you? You have
 been playing the hypocrite, hey? I'll never forgive you, if you ha'n't
 been lying and playing the hypocrite.   100

ABSOLUTE I'm sorry, sir, that the respect and duty which I bear to you
 should be so mistaken.

SIR ANTHONY Hang your respect and duty! But come along with me.
 I'll write a note to Mrs Malaprop, and you shall visit the lady
 directly.   105

ABSOLUTE Where does she lodge, sir?

SIR ANTHONY What a dull question? Only on the Grove° here.

ABSOLUTE O, then I can call on her in my way to the coffee-house.

SIR ANTHONY In your way to the coffee-house! You'll set your heart
 down° in your way to the coffee-house, hey? Ah, you leaden-   110
 nerved, wooden-hearted dolt! But come along, you shall see her
 directly; her eyes shall be the Promethean torch° to you. Come
 along! I'll never forgive you, if you don't come back stark mad with
 rapture and impatience. If you don't, egad, I'll marry the girl
 myself!   115

 Exeunt

3.2

Julia's dressing-room
Faulkland, alone

FAULKLAND They told me Julia would return directly; I wonder
she is not yet come! How mean does this captious, unsatisfied
temper of mine appear to my cooler judgement! Yet I know not
that I indulge it in any other point; but on this one subject, and
to this one subject, whom I think I love beyond my life, I am   5
ever ungenerously fretful and madly capricious! I am conscious
of it; yet I cannot correct myself! What tender, honest joy spark-
led in her eyes when we met! How delicate was the warmth of her
expressions! I was ashamed to appear less happy, though I had
come resolved to wear a face of coolness and upbraiding. Sir   10
Anthony's presence prevented my proposed expostulations.
Yet I must be satisfied that she has not been so *very* happy in my
absence. She is coming! Yes! I know the nimbleness of her tread,
when she thinks her impatient Faulkland counts the moments of
her stay.   15

Enter Julia

JULIA I had not hoped to see you again so soon.

FAULKLAND Could I, Julia, be contented with my first welcome,
restrained as we were by the presence of a third person?

JULIA O Faulkland, when your kindness can make me thus happy, let
me not think that I discovered something of coldness in your first 20
salutation.

FAULKLAND 'Twas but your fancy, Julia. I *was* rejoiced to see you—
to see you in such health. Sure I had no cause for coldness?

JULIA Nay then, I see you have taken something ill. You must not
conceal from me what it is.   25

FAULKLAND Well then, shall I own to you that my joy at hearing
of your health and arrival here, by your neighbour Acres, was
somewhat damped by his dwelling much on the high spirits you
had enjoyed in Devonshire—on your mirth, your singing,
dancing, and I know not what! For such is my temper, Julia, that   30
I should regard every mirthful moment in your absence as a
treason to constancy. The mutual tear that steals down the cheek of
parting lovers is a compact that no smile shall live there till they
meet again.

JULIA Must I never cease to tax my Faulkland with this teasing minute   35
caprice? Can the idle reports of a silly boor weigh in your breast
against my tried affection?

FAULKLAND They have no weight with me, Julia. No, no; I am happy
if you have been so. Yet only say that you did not sing with *mirth*;
say that you *thought* of Faulkland in the dance.   40

JULIA I never can be happy in your absence. If I wear a countenance of
content, it is to show that my mind holds no doubt of my Faulkland's
truth. If I seemed sad, it were to make malice triumph, and say that I
had fixed my heart on one who left me to lament his roving° and my
own credulity. Believe me, Faulkland, I mean not to upbraid you,   45
when I say that I have often dressed sorrow in smiles, lest my friends
should guess whose unkindness had caused my tears.

FAULKLAND You were ever all goodness to me. O, I am a brute, when
I but admit a doubt of your true constancy!

JULIA If ever, without such cause from you as I will not suppose pos-   50
sible, you find my affections veering but a point,° may I become a
proverbial scoff for levity and base ingratitude.

FAULKLAND Ah, Julia, that *last* word is grating to me. I would I had
no title° to your *gratitude*! Search your heart, Julia; perhaps what
you have mistaken for love is but the warm effusion of a too thank-   55
ful heart!

JULIA For what quality must I love you?

FAULKLAND For no quality! To regard me for any quality of mind or
understanding were only to *esteem* me. And, for person,° I have
often wished myself deformed, to be convinced that I owed no   60
obligation *there* for any part of your affection.

JULIA Where nature has bestowed a show of nice attention in the features of a man,° he should laugh at it as misplaced. I have seen men
who in *this* vain article° perhaps might rank above you; but my heart
has never asked my eyes if it were so or not.   65

FAULKLAND Now this is not well from *you*, Julia. I despise person in
a man. Yet, if you loved me as I wish, though I were an Ethiop,°
you'd think none so fair.

JULIA I see you are determined to be unkind. The *contract*° which my
poor father bound us in gives you more than a lover's privilege.   70

FAULKLAND Again, Julia, you raise ideas that feed and justify my
doubts. I would not have been more free. No, I am proud of my
restraint.° Yet—yet—perhaps your high respect alone for this
solemn compact has fettered your inclinations, which else had made
a worthier choice. How shall I be sure, had you remained unbound   75

in thought and promise, that I should still have been the object of
your persevering love?

JULIA Then try me now. Let us be free as strangers as to what is past.
My heart will not feel more liberty!

FAULKLAND There now! So hasty, Julia! So anxious to be free! If your   80
love for me were fixed and ardent, you would not loose your hold,
even though I wished it!

JULIA O, you torture me to the heart! I cannot bear it.

FAULKLAND I do not mean to distress you. If I loved you less, I should
never give you an uneasy moment. But hear me. All my fretful   85
doubts arise from this: women are not used to weigh and separate
the motives of their affections. The cold dictates of prudence, gratitude, or filial duty may sometimes be mistaken for the pleadings of
the heart. I would not boast; yet let me say that I have neither age,
person, or character to found dislike on; my fortune such as few   90
ladies could be charged with *indiscretion* in the match. O Julia, when
love receives such countenance° from *prudence*, nice minds will be
suspicious of its *birth*.

JULIA I know not whither your insinuations would tend. But as they
seem pressing to insult me, I will spare you the regret of having   95
done so. I have given you no cause for this!

Exit Julia in tears

FAULKLAND In tears! Stay, Julia. Stay but for a moment. The door is
fastened! Julia! My soul! But for one moment. I hear her sobbing!
'Sdeath, what a brute am I to use her thus! Yet stay. Ay, she is
coming now. How little resolution there is in woman! How a few   100
soft words can turn them! No, faith! she is *not* coming either. Why,
Julia, my love, say but that you forgive me, come but to tell me that.
Now, this is being *too* resentful. Stay! She *is* coming too. I thought
she would. No *steadiness* in anything! Her going away must have
been a mere trick then. She shan't see that I was hurt by it. I'll affect   105
indifference. (*Hums a tune; then listens*) No, zounds, she's *not*
coming! Nor don't intend it, I suppose. This is not *steadiness*, but
obstinacy. Yet I deserve it. What, after so long an absence, to quarrel
with her tenderness! 'Twas barbarous and unmanly! I should be
ashamed to see her now. I'll wait till her just resentment is abated;   110
and when I distress her so again, may I lose her forever, and be
linked instead to some antique virago, whose gnawing passions and
long-hoarded spleen shall make me curse my folly half the day and
all the night!

Exit

3.3

Mrs Malaprop's lodgings

Mrs Malaprop, with a letter in her hand, and Captain Absolute

MRS MALAPROP Your being Sir Anthony's son, Captain, would itself be a sufficient accommodation;° but, from the ingenuity° of your appearance, I am convinced you deserve the character here given of you.

ABSOLUTE Permit me to say, madam, that as I never yet have had the 5 pleasure of seeing Miss Languish, my principal inducement in this affair at present is the honour of being allied to Mrs Malaprop, of whose intellectual accomplishments, elegant manners, and unaffected learning no tongue is silent.

MRS MALAPROP Sir, you do me infinite honour! I beg, Captain, you'll 10 be seated.

Mrs Malaprop and Captain Absolute sit

Ah, few gentlemen, nowadays, know how to value the ineffectual° qualities in a woman! Few think how a little knowledge becomes a gentlewoman! Men have no sense now but for the worthless flower of beauty! 15

ABSOLUTE It is but too true indeed, ma'am. Yet I fear our ladies should share the blame. They think our admiration of *beauty* so great, that *knowledge* in *them* would be superfluous. Thus, like garden-trees, they seldom show fruit, till time has robbed them of the more specious° blossom. Few, like Mrs Malaprop and the 20 orange-tree, are rich in both at once!

MRS MALAPROP Sir, you overpower me with good-breeding. [*Aside*] He is the very pineapple° of politeness!—You are not ignorant, Captain, that this giddy girl has somehow contrived to fix her affections on a beggarly, strolling,° eavesdropping ensign, whom none 25 of us have seen, and nobody knows anything of.

ABSOLUTE O, I have heard the silly° affair before. I'm not at all prejudiced against her on *that* account.

MRS MALAPROP You are very good, and very considerate, Captain. I am sure I have done everything in my power since I exploded° the 30 affair! Long ago I laid my positive conjunctions° on her never to think on the fellow again. I have since laid Sir Anthony's preposition° before her; but I'm sorry to say she seems resolved to decline every particle° that I enjoin her.

ABSOLUTE It must be very distressing indeed, ma'am.   35

MRS MALAPROP O, it gives me the hydrostatics° to such a degree! I
thought she had persisted° from corresponding with him; but
behold, this very day I have interceded° another letter from the
fellow! I believe I have it in my pocket.

ABSOLUTE (*aside*) O the devil! My last note!   40

MRS MALAPROP Ay, here it is.

ABSOLUTE (*aside*) Ay, my note indeed! O the little traitress Lucy.

MRS MALAPROP There, perhaps you may know the writing.

Mrs Malaprop gives Captain Absolute the letter.

ABSOLUTE I think I have seen the hand before. Yes, I *certainly must*
have seen this hand before.   45

MRS MALAPROP Nay, but read it, Captain.

ABSOLUTE (*reads*) 'My soul's idol, my adored Lydia!' Very tender
indeed!

MRS MALAPROP Tender! Ay, and profane too, o' my conscience!

ABSOLUTE 'I am excessively alarmed at the intelligence you send me.   50
The more so as my new rival—'

MRS MALAPROP That's *you*, sir.

ABSOLUTE '—has universally the character of being an accomplished
gentleman and a man of honour.' Well, that's handsome enough.

MRS MALAPROP O, the fellow has some design° in writing so.   55

ABSOLUTE That he had. I'll answer for him, ma'am.

MRS MALAPROP But go on, sir; you'll see presently.

ABSOLUTE 'As for the old weather-beaten she-dragon who guards
you—' Who can he mean by that?

MRS MALAPROP *Me*, sir, *me*; he means *me* there. What do you think   60
now? But go on a little further.

ABSOLUTE Impudent scoundrel! '—it shall go hard but I will elude
her vigilance, as I am told that the same ridiculous vanity, which
makes her dress up her coarse features and deck her dull chat with
hard words which she don't understand—'   65

MRS MALAPROP There, sir! An attack upon my language! What do
you think of that? An aspersion upon my parts of speech! Was ever
such a brute! Sure if I reprehend° anything in this world, it is the
use of my oracular° tongue and a nice derangement of epitaphs!°

ABSOLUTE He deserves to be hanged and quartered! Let me see. '—   70
same ridiculous vanity—'

MRS MALAPROP You need not read it again, sir.

ABSOLUTE I beg pardon, ma'am. '—does also lay her open to
the grossest deceptions from flattery and pretended admiration'—

an impudent coxcomb!—'so that I have a scheme to see you shortly   75
with the old harridan's consent, and even to make her a go-between
in our interviews.' Was ever such assurance!°

MRS MALAPROP Did you ever hear anything like it? He'll elude my
vigilance, will he? Yes, yes! Ha, ha! He's very likely to enter these
doors! We'll try who can plot best!   80

ABSOLUTE So we will, ma'am; so we will. Ha, ha, ha! A conceited
puppy. Ha, ha, ha! Well, but, Mrs Malaprop, as the girl seems so
infatuated by this fellow, suppose you were to wink at her corresponding with him for a little time. Let her even plot an elopement
with him. Then do you connive at her escape, while *I*, just in the   85
nick,° will have the fellow laid by the heels,° and fairly° contrive to
carry her off in his stead.

MRS MALAPROP I am delighted with the scheme. Never was anything
better perpetrated!

ABSOLUTE But, pray, could not I see the lady for a few minutes now?   90
I should like to try her temper° a little.

MRS MALAPROP Why, I don't know; I doubt she is not prepared for
a visit of this kind. There is a decorum in these matters.

ABSOLUTE O lord, she won't mind *me*. Only tell her Beverley—

MRS MALAPROP Sir!   95

ABSOLUTE (*aside*) Gently, good tongue.

MRS MALAPROP What did you say of Beverley?

ABSOLUTE O, I was going to propose that you should tell her, by way
of jest, that it was Beverley who was below.° She'd come down fast
enough then. Ha, ha, ha!   100

MRS MALAPROP 'Twould be a trick she well deserves. Besides, you
know the fellow tells her he'll get my consent to see her. Ha, ha!
Let him if he can, I say again. (*Calling*) Lydia, come down here!—
He'll make me a 'go-between in their interviews'! Ha, ha, ha!—
Come down, I say, Lydia!—I don't wonder at your laughing. Ha,   105
ha, ha! His impudence is truly ridiculous.

ABSOLUTE 'Tis very ridiculous, upon my soul, ma'am. Ha, ha, ha!

MRS MALAPROP The little hussy won't hear. Well, I'll go and tell her
at once who it is. She shall know that Captain Absolute is come to
wait on her. And I'll make her behave as becomes a young woman.   115

ABSOLUTE As you please, ma'am.

MRS MALAPROP For the present, Captain, your servant. Ah, you've not
done laughing yet, I see. 'Elude my vigilance'! Yes, yes. Ha, ha, ha!
        Exit Mrs Malaprop

ABSOLUTE Ha, ha, ha! One would think now that I might throw off

all disguise at once, and seize my prize with security. But such is   120
Lydia's caprice, that to undeceive her were probably to lose her. I'll
see whether she knows me.

> *Captain Absolute walks aside, and seems engaged in looking at*
> *the pictures. Enter Lydia Languish*

LYDIA What a scene am I now to go through! Surely nothing can be
more dreadful than to be obliged to listen to the loathsome
addresses of a stranger to one's heart. I have heard of girls perse-   125
cuted as I am, who have appealed in behalf of their favoured lover
to the generosity of his rival. Suppose I were to try it. There stands
the hated rival! An officer too! But, O, how unlike my Beverley! I
wonder he don't begin. Truly he seems a very negligent wooer!
Quite at his ease, upon my word! I'll speak first.—Mr Absolute.   130

ABSOLUTE Madam.

> *Captain Absolute turns round*

LYDIA O heavens! Beverley!

ABSOLUTE Hush! Hush, my life! Softly! Be not surprised!

LYDIA I am so astonished!—and so terrified!—and so overjoyed! For
heaven's sake, how came you here?   135

ABSOLUTE Briefly:° I have deceived your aunt. I was informed that
my new rival was to visit her this evening, and, contriving to have
him kept away, have passed myself on *her* for Captain Absolute.

LYDIA O, charming! And she really takes you for young Absolute?

ABSOLUTE O, she's convinced of it.   140

LYDIA Ha, ha, ha! I can't forbear laughing to think how her sagacity
is overreached!

ABSOLUTE But we trifle with our precious moments; such another
opportunity may not occur. Then let me now conjure my kind, my
condescending° angel, to fix the time when I may rescue her from   145
undeserved persecution, and with a licensed° warmth plead for my
reward.

LYDIA Will you then, Beverley, consent to forfeit that portion° of my
paltry wealth, that burden on the wings of love?

ABSOLUTE O come to me, rich only thus, in loveliness. Bring no portion   150
to me but thy love. 'Twill be generous in you, Lydia, for well you know
it is the only dower your poor Beverley can repay.

LYDIA [*aside*] How persuasive are his words! How charming will
poverty be with him!

ABSOLUTE Ah, my soul, what a life will we then live? Love shall be   155
our idol and support! We will worship him with a monastic strict-
ness, abjuring all worldly toys, to centre every thought and action

there. Proud of calamity, we will enjoy the wreck of wealth, while
the surrounding gloom of adversity shall make the flame of our
pure love show doubly bright. By heavens, I would fling all goods   160
of fortune from me with a prodigal hand to enjoy the scene where
I might clasp my Lydia to my bosom, and say the world affords no
smile to me but here! (*Embracing her*). (*Aside*) If she holds out now
the devil is in it!

LYDIA [*aside*] Now could I fly with him to the antipodes! But my per-   165
secution is not yet come to a crisis.

    Enter Mrs Malaprop, listening

MRS MALAPROP (*aside*) I'm impatient to know how the little hussy
deports herself.

ABSOLUTE So pensive, Lydia! Is then your warmth abated?

MRS MALAPROP [*aside*] 'Warmth abated'! So! She has been in a   170
passion, I suppose.

LYDIA No; nor ever can while I have life.

MRS MALAPROP [*aside*] An ill-tempered little devil! She'll be in a
passion all her life, will she?

LYDIA Think not the idle threats of my ridiculous aunt can ever have   175
any weight with me.

MRS MALAPROP [*aside*] Very dutiful, upon my word!

LYDIA Let her choice be Captain Absolute, but Beverley is mine.

MRS MALAPROP [*aside*] I am astonished at her assurance! To his face!
This is to his face!   180

ABSOLUTE (*kneeling*) Thus then let me enforce my suit.

MRS MALAPROP Ay, poor young man! Down on his knees entreating
for pity! I can contain° no longer.—[*To Lydia*] Why, thou vixen! I
have overheard you.

ABSOLUTE (*aside*) O confound her vigilance!   185

    [*Captain Absolute rises*]

MRS MALAPROP Captain Absolute, I know not how to apologize for
her shocking rudeness.

ABSOLUTE (*aside*) So, all's safe, I find.—I have hopes, madam, that
time will bring the young lady—

MRS MALAPROP O, there's nothing to be hoped for from her! She's   190
as headstrong as an allegory° on the banks of Nile.

LYDIA Nay, madam, what do you charge me with now?

MRS MALAPROP Why, thou unblushing rebel, didn't you tell this
gentleman to his face that you loved another better? Didn't you say
you never would be his?   195

LYDIA No, madam, I did not.

MRS MALAPROP Good heavens, what assurance! Lydia, Lydia, you
ought to know that lying don't become a young woman! Didn't you
boast that Beverley, that stroller Beverley, possessed your heart?
Tell me that, I say.   200

LYDIA 'Tis true, ma'am, and none but Beverley—

MRS MALAPROP Hold; hold, assurance! You shall not be so rude.

ABSOLUTE Nay, pray, Mrs Malaprop, don't stop the young lady's
speech. She's very welcome to talk thus; it does not hurt *me* in the
least, I assure you.   205

MRS MALAPROP You are *too* good, Captain, *too* amiably patient.—But
come with me, Miss.—Let us see you again soon, Captain. Remember what we have fixed.

ABSOLUTE I shall, ma'am.

MRS MALAPROP Come, take a graceful leave of the gentleman.   210

LYDIA May every blessing wait on my Beverley, my loved Bev—

MRS MALAPROP Hussy! I'll choke the word in your throat! Come
along, come along.

   Exeunt severally, Captain Absolute kissing his hand to Lydia,
   Mrs Malaprop stopping her from speaking

3.4

Bob Acres's lodgings

Bob Acres (as just dressed°) and David

ACRES Indeed, David; do you think I become it so?°

DAVID You are quite another creature, believe me, Master, by the mass!
An we've any luck, we shall see the Devon monkeyrony° in all the
print-shops° in Bath!

ACRES Dress *does* make a difference, David.   5

DAVID 'Tis all in all,° I think. Difference! Why, an you were to go now
to Clod Hall, I am certain the old lady° wouldn't know you. Master
butler wouldn't believe his own eyes, and Mrs Pickle° would cry,
'Lard preserve me!'. Our dairy-maid would come giggling to the
door, and I warrant Dolly Tester,° your honour's favourite, would   10
blush like my waistcoat. Oons, I'll hold a gallon° there a'n't a dog
in the house but would bark, and I question whether Phillis° would
wag a hair of her tail!

ACRES Ay, David, there's nothing like *polishing*.°

DAVID So I says of your honour's boots; but the boy never heeds me!   15

ACRES But, David, has Mr De la Grace° been here? I must rub up my balancing, and chasing, and boring.°

DAVID I'll call again, sir.

ACRES Do; and see if there are any letters for me at the post-office.

DAVID I will. By the mass, I can't help looking at your head! If I hadn't   20
been by at the cooking, I wish I may die if I should have known the dish again myself!

Exit David. Bob Acres comes forward, practising a dancing step

ACRES Sink, slide, coupee.° Confound the first inventors of cotillions, say I! They are as bad as algebra to us country gentlemen. I can walk a minuet easy enough when I'm forced! And I have been   25
accounted a good stick° in a country-dance. Od's jigs and tabors, I never valued° your cross-over to couple, figure in, right and left;° and I'd foot it with e'er a captain in the county! But these outlandish heathen allemandes and cotillions are quite beyond me! I shall never prosper at 'em; that's sure. Mine are true-born English legs; they   30
don't understand their cursed French lingo! Their *pas*° this, and *pas* that, and *pas* t'other! Damn me, my feet don't like to be called paws! No, 'tis certain I have most antigallican° toes!

Enter Servant

SERVANT Here is Sir Lucius O'Trigger to wait on you, sir.

ACRES Show him in.   35

[Exit Servant.] Enter Sir Lucius O'Trigger

SIR LUCIUS Mr Acres, I am delighted to embrace you.

ACRES My dear Sir Lucius, I kiss your hands.

SIR LUCIUS Pray, my friend, what has brought you so suddenly to Bath?

ACRES Faith, I have followed Cupid's jack-o'-lantern° and find myself   40
in a quagmire° at last. In short, I have been very ill-used, Sir Lucius. I don't choose to mention names, but look on me as a very ill-used gentleman.

SIR LUCIUS Pray, what is the case? I ask no names.

ACRES Mark me, Sir Lucius. I fall as deep as need be in love with a   45
young lady. Her friends take my part. I follow her to Bath, send word of my arrival, and receive answer that the lady is to be otherwise disposed of. This, Sir Lucius, I call being ill-used.

SIR LUCIUS Very ill, upon my conscience. Pray, can you divine the cause of it?   50

ACRES Why, there's the matter. She has another lover, *one* Beverley, who, I am told, is now in Bath. Od's slanders and lies, he must be at the bottom of it.

SIR LUCIUS A rival in the case, is there? And you think he has sup-
planted you unfairly?   55

ACRES *'Unfairly'*! To be sure he has. He never could have done it fairly.

SIR LUCIUS Then sure you know what is to be done!

ACRES Not I, upon my soul!

SIR LUCIUS We wear no swords here,° but you understand me.

ACRES What! Fight him!   60

SIR LUCIUS Ay, to be sure.° What can I mean else?

ACRES But he has given me no provocation.

SIR LUCIUS Now, I think he has given you the greatest provocation in
the world. Can a man commit a more heinous offence against
another than to fall in love with the same woman? O, by my soul,   65
it is the most unpardonable breach of friendship!

ACRES 'Breach of *friendship*'! Ay, ay. But I have no acquaintance with
this man. I never saw him in my life.

SIR LUCIUS That's no argument at all. He has the less right then to
take such a liberty.   70

ACRES Gad, that's true. I grow full of anger, Sir Lucius! I fire apace!°
Od's hilts and blades, I find a man may have a deal of valour in him,
and not know it! But couldn't I contrive to have a little right of my
side?°

SIR LUCIUS What the devil signifies *right*, when your *honour* is con-   75
cerned? Do you think Achilles, or my little Alexander the Great,°
ever inquired where the right lay? No, by my soul! They drew their
broadswords, and left the lazy sons of peace to settle the justice of
it.

ACRES Your words are a grenadier's march° to my heart! I believe   80
courage must be catching! I certainly do feel a kind of valour rising
as it were—a kind of courage, as I may say. Od's flints, pans, and
triggers, I'll challenge him directly!

SIR LUCIUS Ah, my little friend, if we had Blunderbuss Hall° here, I
could show you a range of ancestry, in the O'Trigger line, that   85
would furnish the New Room,° every one of whom had killed his
man! For though the mansion-house and dirty acres have slipped
through my fingers, I thank heaven our honour, and the family pictures, are as fresh as ever.

ACRES O, Sir Lucius, I have had ancestors too! Every man of 'em   90
colonel or captain in the militia! Od's balls and barrels,° say no
more! I'm braced for it. The thunder of your words has soured the
milk of human kindness° in my breast! Zounds, as the man in the
play says, 'I could do such deeds!'°

SIR LUCIUS Come, come, there must be no passion at all in the case. 95
These things should always be done civilly.

ACRES I must be in a passion, Sir Lucius; I must be in a rage. Dear
Sir Lucius, let me be in a rage, if you love me. Come, here's pen
and paper. (*Sits down to write*) I would the ink were red! Indite, I
say, indite! How shall I begin? Od's bullets and blades, I'll write a 100
good bold hand, however.

SIR LUCIUS Pray compose yourself.

ACRES Come. Now shall I begin with an oath? Do, Sir Lucius, let me
begin with a damme.°

SIR LUCIUS Foh, foh, do the thing *decently* and like a Christian. Begin 105
now. 'Sir—'

ACRES [*writing*] That's too civil by half.

SIR LUCIUS 'To prevent the confusion that might arise—'

ACRES Well.

SIR LUCIUS '—from our both addressing the same lady—' 110

ACRES Ay, there's the reason. '—same lady—' Well?

SIR LUCIUS '—I shall expect the honour of your company—'

ACRES Zounds, I'm not asking him to dinner.

SIR LUCIUS Pray be easy.

ACRES Well then. '—honour of your company—' 115

SIR LUCIUS '—to settle our pretensions°—'

ACRES Well.

SIR LUCIUS Let me see; ay, Kingsmead Fields° will do. '—in
Kingsmead Fields.'

ACRES So, that's done. Well, I'll fold it up presently; my own crest, a 120
hand and dagger, shall be the seal.°

SIR LUCIUS You see now this little explanation will put a stop at once
to all confusion or misunderstanding that might arise between you.

ACRES Ay, we fight to prevent any misunderstanding.

SIR LUCIUS Now, I'll leave you to fix your own time. Take my advice, 125
and you'll decide it this evening if you can. Then, let the worst
come of it,° 'twill be off your mind tomorrow.

ACRES Very true.

SIR LUCIUS So I shall see nothing more of you, unless it be by letter,
till the evening. I would do myself the honour to carry your 130
message;° but, to tell you a secret, I believe I shall have just such
another affair on my own hands. There is a gay captain here, who
put a jest on me lately, at the expense of my country,° and I only
want to fall in with° the gentleman, to call him out.

ACRES By my valour, I should like to see you fight first! Od's 135

life, I should like to see you kill him, if it was only to get a little
lesson.

SIR LUCIUS I shall be very proud of instructing you. Well, for the
present.° But remember now, when you meet your antagonist, do
everything in a mild and agreeable manner. Let your courage be as   140
keen, but at the same time as polished, as your sword.

Exeunt severally

4.1

Bob Acres's lodgings

Bob Acres and David

DAVID Then, by the mass, sir, I would do no such thing. Ne'er a Sir
Lucius O'Trigger in the kingdom should make me fight, when I
wa'n't so minded. Oons, what will the old lady say, when she hears
o't!

ACRES Ah, David, if you had heard Sir Lucius! Od's sparks and   5
flames, he would have roused your valour.

DAVID Not he, indeed. I hates such bloodthirsty cormorants.° Lookee,
Master, if you'd wanted a bout at boxing, quarter-staff, or short-
staff,° I should never be the man to bid you cry off. But, for your
cursed sharps and snaps,° I never knew any good come of 'em.   10

ACRES But my *honour*, David, my *honour*! I must be very careful of my
honour.

DAVID Ay, by the mass, and I would be very careful of it; and I think
in return my *honour* couldn't do less than to be very careful of *me*.

ACRES Od's blades, David, no gentleman will ever risk the loss of his   15
honour!

DAVID I say then, it would be but civil in *honour* never to risk the
loss of a *gentleman*. Lookee, Master, this *honour* seems to me to be
a marvellous false friend—ay, truly, a very courtier-like° servant.
Put the case I was a gentleman, which, thank God, no one can   20
say of me. Well, my honour makes me quarrel with another
gentleman of my acquaintance. So, we fight. (Pleasant enough°
that.) Boh!° I kill him! (The more's my luck.) Now, pray who gets
the profit of it? Why, my *honour*. But put the case that he kills me!
By the mass, I go to the worms, and my honour whips over to° my   25
enemy!

ACRES No, David; in that case, od's crowns and laurels, your honour
follows you to the grave!

DAVID Now, that's just the place where I could make a shift to do
without it.°   30

ACRES Zounds, David, you're a coward! It doesn't become my valour
to listen to you. What, shall I disgrace my ancestors! Think of that,
David; think what it would be to disgrace my ancestors!

DAVID Under favour,° the surest way of not disgracing them is to keep
as long as you can out of their company. Lookee now, Master, to go   35

to them in such haste, with an ounce of lead° in your brains, I should think might as well be let alone. Our ancestors are very good kind of folks; but they are the last people I should choose to have a visiting acquaintance with.

ACRES But, David, now, you don't think there is such very, very, *very*   40
great danger, hey? Od's life, people often fight without any mischief done!

DAVID By the mass, I think 'tis ten to one against you! Oons, here to meet some lion-headed fellow, I warrant, with his damned double-barrelled swords and cut-and-thrust pistols!° Lord bless us, it   45
makes me tremble to think o't! Those be such desperate bloody-minded weapons! Well, I never could abide 'em! From a child I never could fancy 'em! I suppose there a'n't so merciless a beast in the world as your loaded pistol!

ACRES Zounds, I *won't* be afraid. Od's fire and fury, you shan't make   50
me afraid! Here is the challenge, and I have sent for my dear friend Jack Absolute to carry it for me.

DAVID Ay, i' the name of mischief, let *him* be the messenger. For my part, I wouldn't lend a hand to it for the best horse in your stable. By the mass, it don't look like another letter! It is, as I may say, a   55
designing and malicious-looking letter, and, I warrant, smells of gunpowder like a soldier's pouch! Oons, I wouldn't swear it mayn't go off!

ACRES Out, you poltroon! You ha'n't the valour of a grasshopper.

DAVID Well, I say no more. 'Twill be sad news, to be sure, at Clod Hall!   60
But I ha' done. How Phillis will howl when she hears of it! Ay, poor bitch, she little thinks what shooting her master's going after! And I warrant old Crop,° who has carried your honour, field and road, these ten years, will (*whimpering*) curse the hour he was born.

ACRES It won't do, David. I am determined to fight. So get along, you   65
coward, while I'm in the mind.

Enter Servant

SERVANT Captain Absolute, sir.

ACRES O, show him up.

Exit Servant

DAVID Well, heaven send we be all alive this time tomorrow.

ACRES What's that? Don't provoke me, David!   70

DAVID (*whimpering*) Good-bye, Master.

ACRES Get along, you cowardly, dastardly, croaking raven.°

Exit David. Enter Captain Absolute

ABSOLUTE What's the matter, Bob?

ACRES A vile, sheep-hearted blockhead! If I hadn't the valour of St
George° and the dragon to boot—   75
ABSOLUTE But what did you want with me, Bob?
ACRES O—there.
      Bob Acres gives Captain Absolute the challenge
ABSOLUTE(*aside*) 'To Ensign Beverley.' So, what's going on now?—
Well, what's this?
ACRES A challenge!   80
ABSOLUTE Indeed! Why, you won't fight him, will you, Bob?
ACRES Egad, but I will, Jack. Sir Lucius has wrought me to it.° He
has left me full of rage; and I'll fight this evening, that so much
good passion mayn't be wasted.
ABSOLUTE But what have I to do with this?   85
ACRES Why, as I think you know something of this fellow, I
want you to find him out for me, and give him this mortal defiance.°
ABSOLUTE Well, give it to me, and trust me he gets it.
ACRES Thank you, my dear friend, my dear Jack; but it is giving you
a great deal of trouble.   90
ABSOLUTE Not in the least; I beg you won't mention it. No trouble in
the world, I assure you.
ACRES You are very kind. What it is to have a friend! You couldn't be
my second, could you, Jack?
ABSOLUTE Why, no, Bob, not in *this* affair; it would not be quite so   95
proper.°
ACRES Well then, I must get my friend Sir Lucius. I shall have your
good wishes, however, Jack.
ABSOLUTE Whenever he° meets you, believe me.
      Enter Servant
SERVANT Sir Anthony Absolute is below, inquiring for the captain.   100
ABSOLUTE I'll come instantly.
      [*Exit Servant*]
Well, my little hero, success attend you. (*Going*)
ACRES Stay, stay, Jack. If Beverley should ask you what kind of a man
your friend Acres is, do tell him I am a devil of a fellow, will you,
Jack?   105
ABSOLUTE To be sure I shall. I'll say you are a determined dog, hey,
Bob!
ACRES Ay, do, do; and if that frightens him, egad perhaps he mayn't
come. So tell him I generally kill a man a week, will you, Jack?
ABSOLUTE I will, I will; I'll say you are called in the country fighting 110
Bob!

ACRES Right, right. 'Tis all to prevent mischief; for I don't want to
take his life if I clear my honour.

ABSOLUTE No! That's very kind of you.

ACRES Why, you don't wish me to kill him, do you, Jack?   115

ABSOLUTE No, upon my soul, I do not. (*Going*) But a devil of a fellow,
hey?

ACRES True, true. But stay, stay, Jack. You may add that you never saw
me in such a rage before—a most devouring rage!

ABSOLUTE I will, I will.   120

ACRES Remember, Jack—a determined dog!

ABSOLUTE Ay, ay, fighting Bob!

>   *Exeunt severally*

4.2

>   *Mrs Malaprop's lodgings*

>   *Mrs Malaprop and Lydia Languish*

MRS MALAPROP Why, thou perverse one! Tell me what you can object
to him? Isn't he a handsome man? Tell me that. A genteel man? A
pretty figure of a man?

LYDIA (*aside*) She little thinks whom she is praising!—So is Beverley,
ma'am.   5

MRS MALAPROP No caparisons,° Miss, if you please! Caparisons
don't become a young woman. No! Captain Absolute is indeed a
fine gentleman!

LYDIA (*aside*) Ay, the Captain Absolute *you* have seen.

MRS MALAPROP Then he's *so* well-bred, *so* full of alacrity° and adu-   10
lation!°—and has *so* much to say for himself, in such good language
too! His physiognomy° so grammatical! Then his presence is so
noble! I protest, when I saw him, I thought of what Hamlet says°
in the play: 'Hesperian curls! The front of Job himself! An eye, like
March, to threaten at command! A station, like Harry Mercury,   15
new—' Something about kissing on a hill. However, the similitude°
struck me directly.

LYDIA (*aside*) How enraged she'll be presently when she discovers her
mistake!

>   *Enter Servant*

SERVANT Sir Anthony and Captain Absolute are below, ma'am.   20

MRS MALAPROP Show them up here.

>   *Exit Servant*

Now, Lydia, I insist on your behaving as becomes a young woman. Show your good breeding at least, though you have forgot your duty.

LYDIA Madam, I have told you my resolution. I shall not only   25
give him no encouragement, but I won't even speak to or look at him.

> *Lydia Languish flings herself into a chair, with her face*
> *from the door. Enter Sir Anthony Absolute and Captain*
> *Absolute*

SIR ANTHONY Here we are, Mrs Malaprop, come to mitigate the frowns of unrelenting beauty; and difficulty enough I had to bring this fellow. I don't know what's the matter; but if I hadn't held him   30
by force, he'd have given me the slip.

MRS MALAPROP You have infinite trouble, Sir Anthony, in the affair. I am ashamed for the cause! (*Aside to Lydia*) Lydia, Lydia, rise, I beseech you! Pay your respects!°

SIR ANTHONY I hope, madam, that Miss Languish has reflected on the   35
worth of this gentleman, and the regard due to her aunt's choice and *my* alliance.° (*Aside to Captain Absolute*) Now, Jack, speak to her!

ABSOLUTE (*aside*) What the devil shall I do!—You see, sir, she won't even look at me whilst you are here. I knew she wouldn't! I told you so. Let me entreat you, sir, to leave us together!   40

> *Captain Absolute seems to expostulate° with Sir Anthony*
> *Absolute*

LYDIA (*aside*) I wonder I ha'n't heard my aunt exclaim yet! Sure she can't have looked at him! Perhaps their regimentals are alike, and she is something blind.

SIR ANTHONY I say, sir, I won't stir a foot yet.

MRS MALAPROP I am sorry to say, Sir Anthony, that my affluence°   45
over my niece is very small. (*Aside to Lydia*) Turn round, Lydia. I blush for you!

SIR ANTHONY May I not flatter myself that Miss Languish will assign what cause of dislike she can have to my son! (*Aside to Captain Absolute*) Why don't you begin, Jack? Speak, you puppy, speak!   50

MRS MALAPROP It is impossible, Sir Anthony, she can have any. She will not *say* she has. (*Aside to Lydia*) Answer, hussy! Why don't you answer?

SIR ANTHONY Then, madam, I trust that a childish and hasty predilection will be no bar to Jack's happiness. (*Aside to Captain*   55
Absolute) Zounds, sirrah, why don't you speak?

LYDIA (*aside*) I think my lover seems as little inclined to conversation as myself. How strangely blind my aunt must be!

ABSOLUTE Hem, hem! Madam—hem!

> *Captain Absolute attempts to speak, then returns to Sir*
> *Anthony Absolute*

Faith, sir, I am so confounded!—and so—so—confused! I told you   60
I should be so, sir. I knew it. The—the—tremor of my passion
entirely takes away my presence of mind.

SIR ANTHONY But it don't take away your voice, fool, does it? Go up
and speak to her directly!°

> *Captain Absolute makes signs to Mrs Malaprop to leave them*
> *together*

MRS MALAPROP Sir Anthony, shall we leave them together? (*Aside to*   65
Lydia) Ah, you stubborn little vixen!

SIR ANTHONY Not yet, ma'am, not yet! (*Aside to Captain Absolute*)
What the devil are you at? Unlock your jaws, sirrah,° or—

> *Captain Absolute draws near Lydia Languish*

ABSOLUTE (*aside*) Now heaven send she may be too sullen to look
round! I must disguise my voice. (*Speaks in a low hoarse tone*) Will   70
not Miss Languish lend an ear to the mild accents of true love? Will
not—

SIR ANTHONY What the devil ails the fellow? Why don't you speak
out? Not stand croaking like a frog in a quinsy?

ABSOLUTE The—the—excess of my awe, and my—my—my   75
modesty, quite choke me!

SIR ANTHONY Ah, your *modesty* again! I'll tell you what, Jack. If you
don't speak out directly, and glibly too, I shall be in such a rage!—
Mrs Malaprop, I wish the lady would favour us with something
more than a side-front!   80

> *Mrs Malaprop seems to chide Lydia Languish*

ABSOLUTE [*aside*] So! All will out, I see!

> *Captain Absolute goes up to Lydia Languish, speaks softly*

Be not surprised, my Lydia; suppress all surprise at present.

LYDIA (*aside*) Heavens, 'tis Beverley's voice! Sure he can't have
imposed on Sir Anthony too!

> *Lydia Languish looks round by degrees, then starts up*

Is this possible! My Beverley! How can this be? My Beverley?   85

ABSOLUTE (*aside*) Ah, 'tis all over.

SIR ANTHONY Beverley! The devil. Beverley! What can the girl mean?
This is my son, Jack Absolute!

MRS MALAPROP For shame, hussy, for shame! Your head runs so on
that fellow, that you have him always in your eyes! Beg Captain   90
Absolute's pardon directly.

LYDIA I see no Captain Absolute, but my loved Beverley!

SIR ANTHONY Zounds, the girl's mad! Her brain's turned by reading!

MRS MALAPROP O' my conscience, I believe so!—What do you mean
by Beverley, hussy? You saw Captain Absolute before today; there   95
he is, your husband that shall be.

LYDIA With all my soul, ma'am. When I refuse my Beverley—

SIR ANTHONY O, she's as mad as Bedlam!° Or has this fellow been
playing us a rogue's trick? Come here, sirrah! Who the devil are
you?   100

ABSOLUTE Faith, sir, I am not quite clear myself; but I'll endeavour
to recollect.

SIR ANTHONY Are you my son, or not? Answer for your mother,° you
dog, if you won't for me.

MRS MALAPROP Ay, sir, who are you? O mercy! I begin to suspect!   105

ABSOLUTE (aside) Ye powers of impudence befriend me!—Sir
Anthony, most assuredly I am your wife's son; and that I sincerely
believe myself to be *yours* also, I hope my duty has always shown.—
Mrs Malaprop, I am your most respectful admirer, and shall be
proud to add *affectionate nephew*.—I need not tell my Lydia that she   110
sees her faithful Beverley, who, knowing the singular° generosity of
her temper, assumed that name, and a station which has proved a
test of the most disinterested° love, which he now hopes to enjoy
in a more elevated character.°

LYDIA (sullenly) So! There will be no elopement after all!   115

SIR ANTHONY Upon my soul, Jack, thou art a very impudent fellow!°
To do you justice, I think I never saw a piece of more consummate
assurance!

ABSOLUTE O, you flatter me, sir; you compliment. 'Tis my *modesty*,
you know, sir, my *modesty* that has stood in my way.   120

SIR ANTHONY Well, I am glad you are not the dull, insensible
varlet you pretended to be, however! I'm glad you have made a fool
of your father, you dog; I am. So this was your *penitence*, your *duty*,
and *obedience*! I thought it was damned sudden! You 'never
heard their names before', not you! 'What, Languishes of Worces-   125
tershire', hey? 'If you could please me in the affair, 'twas all you
desired!' Ah, you dissembling villain! (*Pointing to Lydia*) What, she
squints, don't she? A little red-haired girl! Hey? Why, you hypocritical young rascal, I wonder you a'n't ashamed to hold up your
head!   130

ABSOLUTE 'Tis with difficulty, sir. I *am* confused, very much confused, as you must perceive.

MRS MALAPROP O lud! Sir Anthony! A new light breaks in upon me! Hey! How! What! Captain, did *you* write the letters then? What! Am I to thank *you* for the elegant compilation° of 'an old weather-beaten she-dragon', hey? O mercy! Was it *you* that reflected on my parts of speech?   135

ABSOLUTE Dear sir, my modesty is overpowered at last, if you don't assist me. I shall certainly not be able to stand it!

SIR ANTHONY Come, come, Mrs Malaprop. We must forget and forgive. Od's life, matters have taken so clever° a turn all of a sudden, that I could find in my heart to be so good-humoured, and so gallant!° Hey, Mrs Malaprop!   140

MRS MALAPROP Well, Sir Anthony, since *you* desire it, we will not anticipate the past. So mind, young people. Our retrospection will now be all to the future.°   145

SIR ANTHONY Come, we must leave them together; Mrs Malaprop, they long to fly into each other's arms, I warrant!—Jack, isn't the *cheek* as I said, hey? And the eye, you rogue! And the lip, hey?— Come, Mrs Malaprop, we'll not disturb their tenderness; theirs is   150 the time of life for happiness! (*Sings*) '*Youth's the season made for joy.*'° Hey! Od's life, I'm in such spirits. I don't know what I couldn't do! (*Gives his hand to Mrs Malaprop*) Permit me, ma'am. (*Sings*) '*Tol-de-rol!*' Gad, I should like a little fooling myself. [*Sings*] '*Tol-de-rol! de-rol!*'   155

> *Exit Sir Anthony Absolute singing, and handing*° *Mrs Malaprop. Lydia Languish sits sullenly in her chair*

ABSOLUTE (*aside*) So much thought bodes me no good.—So grave, Lydia!

LYDIA Sir!

ABSOLUTE (*aside*) So! Egad! I thought as much! That damned mono-syllable has froze me!—What, Lydia, now that we are as happy in   160 our *friends' consent* as in our *mutual vows*—

LYDIA (*peevishly*) *Friends' consent*, indeed!

ABSOLUTE Come, come; we must lay aside some of our romance.° A little *wealth* and *comfort* may be endured after all. And for your fortune, the lawyers shall make such settlements as—°   165

LYDIA *Lawyers*! I *hate* lawyers!

ABSOLUTE Nay then, we will not wait for the lingering forms,° but instantly procure the licence° and—

LYDIA The *licence*! I *hate* licence!

ABSOLUTE O my love! *Be* not so unkind! (*Kneeling*) Thus let me   170 entreat—

LYDIA Pshaw! What signifies kneeling, when you know I *must* have you?

ABSOLUTE (*rising*) Nay, madam, there shall be no constraint upon your inclinations, I promise you. If I have lost your *heart*, I resign   175
the rest. (*Aside*) Gad, I must try what a little *spirit* will do.

LYDIA (*rising*) Then, sir, let me tell you, the interest you had there was acquired by a mean, unmanly imposition,° and deserves the punishment of fraud. What, you have been treating *me* like a *child*, humouring my romance, and laughing, I suppose, at your   180
success!

ABSOLUTE You wrong me, Lydia, you wrong me. Only hear—

LYDIA (*walking about in heat*) So, while *I* fondly° imagined we were deceiving my relations, and flattered myself that I should outwit and incense them *all*, behold, my hopes are to be crushed   185
at once by my aunt's consent and approbation! And *I* am *myself* the only dupe at last! (*Taking a miniature from her bosom*) But here, sir, here is the picture—Beverley's picture!—which I have worn, night and day, in spite of threats and entreaties! There, sir, (*flings it to him*) and be assured I throw the original from my heart   190
as easily!

ABSOLUTE Nay, nay, ma'am, we will not differ as to that. Here, (*taking out a picture*) *here* is Miss Lydia Languish. What a difference! Ay, *there* is the heavenly assenting smile that first gave soul and spirit to my hopes! Those are the lips which sealed a vow, as yet   195
scarce dry in Cupid's calendar! And *there* the *half*-resentful blush, that *would* have checked the ardour of my thanks. Well, all that's past! All over indeed! There, madam. In *beauty*, that copy is not equal to you, but in my mind its merit over the original, in being still the same, is such—that—I cannot find in my heart to *part*   200
with it.

　　　Captain Absolute puts the miniature up again°

LYDIA (*softening*) 'Tis *your own* doing, sir. I, I, I suppose you are perfectly satisfied.

ABSOLUTE O, most certainly. Sure now this is much better than being in love! Ha, ha, ha! There's some spirit in *this*! What signifies break-   205
ing some scores of solemn promises? All that's of no consequence, you know. To be sure people will say that Miss didn't know her own mind; but never mind that. Or perhaps they may be ill-natured enough to hint that the gentleman grew tired of the lady and forsook her; but don't let that fret you.   210

LYDIA There's no bearing his insolence.

> *Lydia Languish bursts into tears. Enter Mrs Malaprop and Sir*
> *Anthony Absolute*

MRS MALAPROP (*entering*) Come, we must interrupt your billing and
cooing a while.

LYDIA (*sobbing*) *This* is *worse* than your treachery and deceit, you base
ingrate!   215

SIR ANTHONY What the devil's the matter now! Zounds, Mrs
Malaprop, this is the *oddest billing* and *cooing* I ever heard! But what
the deuce is the meaning of it? I'm quite astonished!

ABSOLUTE Ask the lady, sir.

MRS MALAPROP O mercy! I'm quite analysed° for my part! Why,   220
Lydia, what is the reason of this?

LYDIA Ask the *gentleman*, ma'am.

SIR ANTHONY Zounds, I shall be in a frenzy! Why, Jack, you are not
come out to be anyone else, are you?

MRS MALAPROP Ay, sir, there's no more *trick*, is there? You are not   225
like Cerberus,° *three* gentlemen at once, are you?

ABSOLUTE You'll not let me speak. I say the *lady* can account for *this*
much better than I can.

LYDIA Ma'am, you once commanded me never to think of Beverley
again. *There* is the man. I now obey you; for, from this moment, I   230
renounce him forever.

> *Exit Lydia Languish*

MRS MALAPROP O mercy, and miracles! What a turn here is. Why,
sure, Captain, you haven't behaved disrespectfully to my niece?

SIR ANTHONY Ha, ha, ha! Ha, ha, ha! Now I see it. Ha, ha, ha! Now
I see it. You have been too lively, Jack.   235

ABSOLUTE Nay, sir, upon my word—

SIR ANTHONY Come, no lying, Jack. I'm sure 'twas so.

MRS MALAPROP O lud! Sir Anthony!—O fie, Captain!

ABSOLUTE Upon my soul, ma'am—

SIR ANTHONY Come, no excuses, Jack. Why, your father, you rogue,   240
was so before you. The blood of the Absolutes was always impatient. Ha, ha, ha! Poor little Lydia! Why, you've frightened her, you
dog! You have!

ABSOLUTE By all that's good, sir—

SIR ANTHONY Zounds, say no more, I tell you! Mrs Malaprop shall   245
make your peace.—You must make his peace, Mrs Malaprop. You
must tell her 'tis Jack's way. Tell her 'tis all our ways; it runs in the
blood of our family!—Come, get on, Jack. Ha, ha, ha!—Mrs
Malaprop, a young villain!

Sir Anthony Absolute pushes Captain Absolute out

MRS MALAPROP O, Sir Anthony!—O fie, Captain!   250

Exeunt severally

4.3

The North Parade

Enter Sir Lucius O'Trigger

SIR LUCIUS I wonder where this Captain Absolute hides himself.
Upon my conscience, these officers are always in one's way in love-
affairs. I remember I might have married Lady Dorothy Carmine,°
if it had not been for a little rogue of a major, who ran away with
her before she could get a sight of me! And I wonder too what it is   5
the ladies can see in them to be so fond of them, unless it be a touch
of the old serpent in 'em, that makes the little creatures be caught,
like vipers with a bit of red cloth.° Ha, isn't this the captain coming?
Faith, it is! There is a probability of succeeding° about that fellow
that is mighty provoking! Who the devil is he talking to?   10

Sir Lucius O'Trigger steps aside. Enter Captain Absolute

ABSOLUTE To what fine purpose I have been plotting! A noble reward
for all my schemes, upon my soul! A little gipsy! I did not think her
romance could have made her so damned absurd either. 'Sdeath, I
never was in a worse humour in my life. I could cut my own throat,
or any other person's, with the greatest pleasure in the world!   15

SIR LUCIUS [*aside*] O, faith, I'm in the luck of it! I never could have
found him in a sweeter temper for my purpose. To be sure I'm just
come in the nick! Now to enter into conversation with him, and so
quarrel genteelly.

Sir Lucius O'Trigger goes up to Captain Absolute

With regard to that matter, Captain, I must beg leave to differ in   20
opinion with you.

ABSOLUTE Upon my word then, you must be a very subtle disputant,
because, sir, I happened just then to be giving no opinion at all.

SIR LUCIUS That's no reason. For give me leave to tell you, a man may
think an untruth as well as *speak* one.   25

ABSOLUTE Very true, sir. But if the man never utters his thoughts, I
should think they *might* stand a *chance* of escaping controversy.

SIR LUCIUS Then, sir, you differ in opinion with me, which amounts
to the same thing.

ABSOLUTE Harkee, Sir Lucius. If I had not before known you to be a   30
gentleman, upon my soul, I should not have discovered it at this
interview; for what you can drive at, unless you mean to quarrel
with me, I cannot conceive!

SIR LUCIUS (*bowing*) I humbly thank you, sir, for the quickness of your
apprehension; you have named the very thing I would be at.   35

ABSOLUTE Very well, sir. I shall certainly not baulk your inclinations;
but I should be glad you would please to explain your motives.

SIR LUCIUS Pray, sir, be easy. The quarrel is a very pretty quarrel as
it stands; we should only spoil it by trying to explain it. However,
your memory is very short, or you could not have forgot an affront   40
you passed on me within this week. So no more, but name your time
and place.°

ABSOLUTE Well, sir, since you are so bent on it, the sooner the better.
Let it be this evening, here by the Spring Gardens.° We shall
scarcely be° interrupted.   45

SIR LUCIUS Faith, that same interruption in affairs of this nature
shows very great ill-breeding. I don't know what's the reason, but
in England, if a thing of this kind gets wind,° people make such a
pother, that a gentleman can never fight in peace and quietness.
However, if it's the same to you, Captain, I should take it as a par-   50
ticular kindness, if you'd let us meet in Kingsmead Fields, as a little
business will call me there about six o'clock, and I may dispatch
both matters at once.

ABSOLUTE 'Tis the same to me exactly. A little after six, then, we will
discuss this matter more seriously.   55

SIR LUCIUS If you please, sir. There will be very pretty small-sword
light, though it won't do for a long shot. So that matter's settled,
and my mind's at ease.

> *Exit Sir Lucius O'Trigger. Enter Faulkland, meeting Captain
> Absolute*

ABSOLUTE Well met. I was going to look for you. O, Faulkland! All
the demons of spite and disappointment have conspired against me!   60
I'm so vexed, that if I had not the prospect of a resource° in being
knocked o' the head° by and by, I should scarce have spirits to tell
you the cause.

FAULKLAND What can you mean? Has Lydia changed her mind? I
should have thought her duty and inclination would now have   65
pointed to the same object.

ABSOLUTE Ay, just as the eyes do of a person who squints. When her
love eye was fixed on *me*, t'other, her *eye* of *duty*, was finely

obliqued.° But when duty bid her point *that* the same way, off
t'other turned on a swivel and secured its retreat with a frown!   70

FAULKLAND But what's the resource you—

ABSOLUTE O, to wind up the whole, a good-natured Irishman here
has (*mimicking Sir Lucius*) begged leave to have the pleasure of
cutting my throat, and I mean to indulge him. That's all.

FAULKLAND Prithee, be serious.   75

ABSOLUTE 'Tis fact, upon my soul. Sir Lucius O'Trigger—you know
him by sight—for some affront, which I am sure I never intended,
has obliged me to meet him this evening at six o'clock. 'Tis on that
account I wished to see you. You must go with me.°

FAULKLAND Nay, there must be some mistake, sure. Sir Lucius shall   80
explain himself, and I dare say matters may be accommodated.° But
this evening, did you say? I wish it had been any other time.

ABSOLUTE Why? There will be light enough. There will, as Sir Lucius
says, 'be very pretty small-sword light, though it won't do for a long
shot'. Confound his long shots!   85

FAULKLAND But I am myself a good deal ruffled by a difference I have
had with Julia. My vile tormenting temper has made me treat her
so cruelly, that I shall not be myself till we are reconciled.

ABSOLUTE By heavens, Faulkland, you don't deserve her.

    Enter Servant. He gives Faulkland a letter. [Exit Servant]

FAULKLAND O Jack, this is from Julia! I dread to open it. I fear it may   90
be to take a last leave, perhaps to bid me return her letters, and
restore—O, how I suffer for my folly!

ABSOLUTE Here, let me see. (*Takes the letter and opens it*) Ay, a final
sentence indeed! 'Tis all over with you, faith!

FAULKLAND Nay, Jack, don't keep me in suspense.   95

ABSOLUTE Hear then. 'As I am convinced that my dear Faulkland's
own reflections have already upbraided him for his last unkindness
to me, I will not add a word on the subject. I wish to speak with
you as soon as possible. Yours ever and truly, Julia.' There's stub-
bornness and resentment for you!   100

    Captain Absolute gives Faulkland the letter

Why, man, you don't seem one whit the happier at this.

FAULKLAND O, yes, I am; but—but—

ABSOLUTE Confound your *buts*. You never hear anything that would
make another man bless himself, but you immediately damn it with
a *but*.   105

FAULKLAND Now, Jack, as you are my friend, own honestly. Don't you
think there is something forward, something indelicate in this haste

to forgive? Women should never sue for reconciliation; *that* should *always* come from us. *They* should retain their coldness till *wooed* to kindness, and their *pardon*, like their *love*, should 'not unsought be won'.° 110

ABSOLUTE   I have not patience to listen to you; thou'rt incorrigible! So say no more on the subject. I must go to settle a few matters. Let me see you before six, remember, at my lodgings. A poor industrious devil like me, who have toiled and drudged and plotted to gain 115 my ends, and am at last disappointed by other people's folly, may in pity be allowed to swear and grumble a little; but a captious sceptic in love, a slave to fretfulness and whim, who has no difficulties but of *his own* creating, is a subject more fit for ridicule than compassion! 120

Exit Captain Absolute

FAULKLAND   I feel his reproaches! Yet I would not change this too exquisite nicety for the gross content with which *he* tramples on the thorns of love. His engaging me in this duel has started an idea in my head, which I will instantly pursue. I'll use it as the touchstone of Julia's sincerity and disinterestedness. If her love prove true and 125 sterling ore, my name will rest on it with honour! And once I've stamped it there, I lay aside my doubts forever.° But if the dross of selfishness, the allay of pride, predominate, 'twill be best to leave her as a toy for some less cautious fool to sigh for.

Exit

5.1

Julia's dressing-room

Julia, alone

JULIA How this message has alarmed me! What dreadful accident can he mean! Why such charge to be alone? O Faulkland! How many unhappy moments, how many tears have you cost me!

Enter Faulkland,° muffled up° in a riding-coat

What means this? Why this caution, Faulkland?

FAULKLAND Alas, Julia, I am come to take a long farewell.°   5

JULIA Heavens, what do you mean?

FAULKLAND You see before you a wretch, whose life is forfeited.° Nay, start not! The infirmity of my temper has drawn all this misery on me. I left you fretful and passionate. An untoward accident drew me into a quarrel. The event is, that I must fly this kingdom   10 instantly. O Julia, had I been so fortunate as to have called you mine entirely before this mischance had fallen on me, I should not so deeply dread my banishment!

JULIA My soul is oppressed with sorrow at the *nature* of your misfortune. Had these adverse circumstances arisen from a less fatal   15 cause, I should have felt strong comfort in the thought that I could *now* chase from your bosom every doubt of the warm sincerity of my love. My heart has long known no other guardian. I now entrust my person to your honour; we will fly together. When safe from pursuit, my father's will may be fulfilled,° and I receive a legal claim   20 to be the partner of your sorrows and tenderest comforter. Then on the bosom of your wedded Julia you may lull your keen regret to slumbering; while virtuous love, with a cherub's hand, shall smooth the brow of upbraiding thought and pluck the thorn from compunction.   25

FAULKLAND O Julia, I am bankrupt in gratitude! But the time is so pressing, it calls on you for so hasty a resolution. Would you not wish some hours to weigh the advantages you forgo, and what little compensation poor Faulkland can make you beside his solitary love?

JULIA I ask not a moment. No, Faulkland, I have loved you for yourself; and if I now, more than ever, prize the solemn engagement   30 which so long has pledged us to each other, it is because it leaves no room for hard aspersions on my fame and puts the seal of duty to an act of love. But let us not linger. Perhaps this delay—

FAULKLAND 'Twill be better I should not venture out again till dark.   35
Yet am I grieved to think what numberless distresses will press
heavy on your gentle disposition!

JULIA Perhaps your fortune may be forfeited by this unhappy act.° I
know not whether 'tis so; but sure that alone can never make us
unhappy. The little I have will be sufficient to *support* us; and *exile*   40
never should be splendid.

FAULKLAND Ay, but in such an abject state of life my wounded pride
perhaps may increase the natural fretfulness of my temper, till I
become a rude,° morose companion, beyond your patience to
endure. Perhaps the recollection of a deed my conscience cannot   45
justify may haunt me in such gloomy and unsocial fits, that I shall
hate the tenderness that would relieve me, break from your arms,
and quarrel with your fondness!

JULIA If your thoughts should assume so unhappy a bent, you will the
more want some mild and affectionate spirit to watch over and   50
console you—one who, by bearing *your* infirmities with gentleness and resignation, may teach you *so* to bear the evils of your
fortune.

FAULKLAND Julia, I have proved you to the quick,° and with this
useless device° I throw away all my doubts. How shall I plead to be   55
forgiven this last unworthy effect of my restless, unsatisfied disposition?

JULIA Has no such disaster happened as you related?

FAULKLAND I am ashamed to own that it was all pretended. Yet in
pity, Julia, do not kill me with resenting a fault which never can be   60
repeated. But, sealing this once my pardon, let me tomorrow, in the
face of heaven, receive my future guide and monitress, and expiate
my past folly by years of tender adoration.

JULIA Hold, Faulkland! That you are free from a crime which I before
feared to name, heaven knows how sincerely I rejoice! These are   65
tears of thankfulness for that! But that your cruel doubts should
have urged you to an imposition° that has wrung my heart gives me
now a pang more keen than I can express!

FAULKLAND By heavens, Julia—

JULIA Yet hear me. My father loved you, Faulkland, and you pre-   70
served the life that tender parent gave me. In his presence I pledged
my hand—*joyfully* pledged it—where before I had given my heart.
When, soon after, I lost that parent, it seemed to me that provi-
dence° had, in Faulkland, shown me whither to transfer, without a
pause, my grateful duty, as well as my affection. Hence I have been   75

content to bear from you what pride and delicacy would have forbid
me from another. I will not upbraid you by repeating how you have
trifled with my sincerity.

FAULKLAND I confess it all! Yet hear—

JULIA After such a year of trial, I might have flattered myself that I   80
should not have been insulted with a new probation of my sincerity, as cruel as unnecessary! I now see it is not in your nature to be
content, or confident, in love. With this conviction,° I never will be
yours. While I had hopes that my persevering attention and unre-
proaching kindness might in time reform your temper, I should   85
have been happy to have gained a dearer influence over you; but I
will not furnish you with a licensed power° to keep alive an incorrigible fault, at the expense of one who never would contend with
you.

FAULKLAND Nay, but, Julia, by my soul and honour, if after this—   90

JULIA But one word more. As my faith has once been given to you, I
never will barter it with another.° I shall pray for your happiness
with the truest sincerity; and the dearest blessing I can ask of heaven
to send you will be to charm you from that unhappy temper, which
alone has prevented the performance of our solemn engagement.   95
All I request of *you* is, that you will yourself reflect upon this infirmity; and when you number up the many true delights it has
deprived you of, let it not be your *least* regret that it lost you the
love of one, who would have followed you in beggary through the
world!   100

    Exit Julia

FAULKLAND She's gone!—forever! There was an awful° resolution
in her manner, that riveted me to my place. O fool! Dolt! Barbarian! Cursed as I am with more imperfections than my fellow-
wretches, kind fortune sent a heaven-gifted° cherub to my aid, and,
like a ruffian, I have driven her from my side! I must now haste to   105
my appointment. Well, my mind is tuned for such a scene. I shall
wish only to become a principal° in it, and reverse the tale my
cursed folly put me upon forging here.° O love! Tormentor!
Fiend!—whose influence, like the moon's,° acting on men of dull
souls, makes idiots of them, but, meeting subtler° spirits, betrays   110
their course and urges sensibility to madness!

    Exit Faulkland. Enter Maid and Lydia Languish

MAID My mistress, ma'am, I know, was here just now. Perhaps she is
only in the next room.

    Exit Maid

LYDIA Heigh-ho! Though he has used me so, this fellow runs strangely in my head. I believe one lecture from my grave cousin will make me recall him.
    Enter Julia
O Julia, I am come to you with such an appetite for consolation. Lud, child, what's the matter with you? You have been crying! I'll be hanged, if that Faulkland has not been tormenting you!

JULIA You mistake the cause of my uneasiness. Something *has* flurried me a little. Nothing that you can guess at. (*Aside*) I would not accuse Faulkland to a sister!

LYDIA Ah, whatever vexations you may have, I can assure you mine surpass them. You know who Beverley proves to be?

JULIA I will now own to you, Lydia, that Mr Faulkland had before informed me of the whole affair. Had young Absolute been the person you took him for, I should not have accepted your confidence° on the subject without a serious endeavour to counteract your caprice.

LYDIA So, then, I see I have been deceived by everyone! But I don't care; I'll never have him.

JULIA Nay, Lydia—

LYDIA Why, is it not provoking, when I thought we were coming to the prettiest distress imaginable, to find myself made a mere Smithfield bargain° of at last? There had I projected one of the most sentimental° elopements!—so becoming a disguise!—so amiable a ladder of ropes! Conscious° moon, four horses, Scotch parson,° with such surprise to Mrs Malaprop, and such paragraphs in the newspapers! O, I shall die with disappointment.

JULIA I don't wonder at it!

LYDIA Now—sad reverse!—what have I to expect, but, after a deal of flimsy preparation, with a bishop's licence and my aunt's blessing, to go simpering up to the altar, or perhaps be cried three times° in a country church, and have an unmannerly fat clerk ask the consent of every butcher in the parish to join John Absolute and Lydia Languish, *spinster*! O, that I should live to hear myself called spinster!

JULIA Melancholy, indeed!

LYDIA How mortifying to remember the dear delicious shifts I used to be put to, to gain half a minute's conversation with this fellow! How often have I stole forth, in the coldest night in January, and found him in the garden, stuck like a dripping statue! There would

he kneel to me in the snow, and sneeze and cough so pathetically!
He shivering with cold, and I with apprehension! And while the
freezing blast numbed our joints, how warmly would he press me   155
to pity his flame, and glow with mutual ardour! Ah, Julia, that was
something like being in love.

JULIA If I were in spirits, Lydia, I should chide you only by laughing
heartily at you. But it suits more the situation of my mind, at
present, earnestly to entreat you not to let a man, who loves you   160
with sincerity, suffer that unhappiness from your *caprice*, which I
know too well caprice can inflict.

LYDIA O lud, what has brought my aunt here!
    Enter Mrs Malaprop, Fag, and David

MRS MALAPROP So! So! Here's fine work! Here's fine suicide, parricide,° and simulation° going on in the fields, and Sir Anthony not   165
to be found to prevent the antistrophe!°

JULIA For heaven's sake, madam, what's the meaning of this?

MRS MALAPROP That gentleman can tell you; 'twas he enveloped° the
affair to me.

LYDIA (*to Fag*) Do, sir. Will you inform us?   170

FAG Ma'am, I should hold myself very deficient in every requisite that
forms the man of breeding, if I delayed a moment to give all the
information in my power to a lady so deeply interested in° the affair
as you are.

LYDIA But quick! Quick, sir!   175

FAG True, ma'am; as you say, one should be quick in divulging matters of
this nature; for should we be tedious, perhaps while we are flourish-
ing° on the subject, two or three lives may be lost!

LYDIA O patience! [*To Mrs Malaprop*] Do, ma'am, for heaven's sake,
tell us what is the matter!   180

MRS MALAPROP Why, murder's the matter! Slaughter's the matter!
Killing's the matter! But he can tell you the perpendiculars.°

LYDIA Then, prithee, sir, be brief.

FAG Why then, ma'am, as to murder, I cannot take upon me to say;
and as to slaughter, or manslaughter, that will be as the jury finds   185
it.

LYDIA But who, sir—who are engaged in this?

FAG Faith, ma'am, one is a young gentleman whom I should be very
sorry anything was to happen to—a very pretty-behaved gentleman!
We have lived much together, and always on terms.°   190

LYDIA But who is this? Who! Who! Who!

FAG My master, ma'am, my master; I speak of my master.

LYDIA Heavens! What, Captain Absolute!

MRS MALAPROP O, to be sure, you are frightened now!

JULIA But who are with him, sir?   195

FAG As to the rest, ma'am, this gentleman can inform you better than I.

JULIA (to David) Do speak, friend.

DAVID Lookee, my lady; by the mass, there's mischief going on! Folks don't use to meet for amusement with firearms, firelocks,   200 fire-engines, fire-screens, fire-office, and the devil knows what other crackers besides!° This, my lady, I say, has an angry favour.°

JULIA But who is there beside Captain Absolute, friend?

DAVID My poor master—under favour, for mentioning him first. You   205 know me, my lady. I am David, and my master, of course, is, or *was*, Squire Acres. Then comes Squire Faulkland.

JULIA [to Mrs Malaprop] Do, ma'am, let us instantly endeavour to prevent mischief.

MRS MALAPROP O fie, it would be very inelegant in us. We should   210 only participate° things.

DAVID Ah, do, Mrs Aunt, save a few lives. They are desperately given,° believe me. Above all, there is that bloodthirsty Philistine,° Sir Lucius O'Trigger.

MRS MALAPROP Sir Lucius O'Trigger! O mercy! Have they drawn   215 poor little dear Sir Lucius into the scrape? Why, how, how you stand, girl! You have no more feeling than one of the Derbyshire putrefactions!°

LYDIA What are we to do, madam?

MRS MALAPROP Why, fly with the utmost felicity,° to be sure, to   220 prevent mischief.—Here, friend, you can show us the place?

FAG If you please, ma'am, I will conduct you.—David, do you look° for Sir Anthony.

      Exit David

MRS MALAPROP Come, girls! This gentleman will exhort° us.— Come, sir, you're our envoy.° Lead the way, and we'll precede.°   230

FAG Not a step before the ladies for the world!

MRS MALAPROP You're sure you know the spot.

FAG I think I can find it, ma'am; and one good thing is, we shall hear the report of the pistols as we draw near, so we can't well miss them. Never fear, ma'am, never fear.   235

      Exeunt, Fag talking

74

5.2

The South Parade°

Enter Captain Absolute, putting his sword under his greatcoat

ABSOLUTE A sword seen in the streets of Bath would raise as great an
alarm as a mad dog.° How provoking this is in Faulkland! Never
punctual! I shall be obliged to go without him at last. O, the devil!
Here's Sir Anthony! How shall I escape him?

> *Captain Absolute muffles up his face and takes a circle° to go
> off. Enter Sir Anthony Absolute*

SIR ANTHONY How one may be deceived at a little distance! Only that   5
I see he don't know me, I could have sworn that was Jack! Hey!
Gad's life, it is! Why, Jack! What are you afraid of? Hey! Sure I'm
right! Why, Jack! Jack Absolute!

> *Sir Anthony Absolute goes up to Captain Absolute*

ABSOLUTE Really, sir, you have the advantage of me. I don't remember ever to have had the honour. My name is Saunderson, at your   10
service.

SIR ANTHONY Sir, I beg your pardon. I took you—hey! Why, zounds,
it is. Stay.

> *Sir Anthony Absolute looks up to Captain Absolute's face*

So, so. Your humble servant, Mr Saunderson! Why, you scoundrel,
what tricks are you after now?   15

ABSOLUTE O, a joke, sir, a joke! I came here on purpose to look for
you, sir.

SIR ANTHONY You did! Well, I am glad you were so lucky. But what
are you muffled up so for? What's this for? Hey?

ABSOLUTE 'Tis cool, sir, isn't it? Rather chilly somehow. But I shall   20
be late; I have a particular engagement.

SIR ANTHONY Stay. Why, I thought you were looking for me? Pray,
Jack, where is't you are going?

ABSOLUTE Going, sir!

SIR ANTHONY Ay; where are you going?   25

ABSOLUTE Where am I going?

SIR ANTHONY You unmannerly puppy!

ABSOLUTE I was going, sir, to—to—to—to Lydia—sir, to Lydia—to
make matters up° if I could. And I was looking for you, sir, to—
to—   30

SIR ANTHONY To go with you, I suppose. Well, come along.

ABSOLUTE O, zounds, no, sir! Not for the world! I wished to meet with

you, sir, to—to—to—You find it cool, I'm sure, sir; you'd better
not stay out.

SIR ANTHONY Cool! Not at all. Well, Jack, and what will you say to   35
Lydia?

ABSOLUTE O, sir, beg her pardon, humour her, promise and vow. But
I detain you, sir. Consider the cold air on your gout.

SIR ANTHONY O, not at all, not at all! I'm in no hurry. Ah, Jack, you
youngsters, when once you are wounded here. (*Putting his hand to*   40
Captain Absolute's breast) Hey, what the deuce have you got here?

ABSOLUTE Nothing, sir, nothing.

SIR ANTHONY What's this? Here's something damned hard!

ABSOLUTE O, trinkets, sir, trinkets! A bauble for Lydia!

SIR ANTHONY Nay, let me see your taste. (*Pulls Captain Absolute's coat*   45
open. The sword falls) Trinkets! A bauble for Lydia! Zounds, sirrah,
you are not going to cut her throat, are you?

ABSOLUTE Ha, ha, ha! I thought it would divert° you, sir, though I
didn't mean to tell you till afterwards.

SIR ANTHONY You didn't? Yes, this is a very diverting trinket, truly.   50

ABSOLUTE Sir, I'll explain to you. You know, sir, Lydia is romantic,
devilish romantic, and very absurd, of course. Now, sir, I intend, if
she refuses to forgive me, to unsheath this sword, and swear I'll fall
upon its point and expire at her feet!

SIR ANTHONY Fall upon a fiddle-stick's end! Why, I suppose it is the   55
very thing that would please her. Get along, you fool.

ABSOLUTE Well, sir, you shall hear of my success; you shall hear. 'O,
Lydia, forgive me, or this pointed steel—', says I.

SIR ANTHONY 'O, booby, stab away, and welcome', says she. Get
along! And damn your trinkets!   60

Exit Captain Absolute. Enter David, running

DAVID Stop him! Stop him! Murder! Thief! Fire! Stop fire! Stop
fire!—O, Sir Anthony! Call! Call! Bid 'em stop! Murder! Fire!

SIR ANTHONY Fire! Murder! Where?

DAVID Oons, he's out of sight! And I'm out of breath, for my part! O,
Sir Anthony, why didn't you stop him? Why didn't you stop him?   65

SIR ANTHONY Zounds, the fellow's mad! Stop whom? Stop Jack?

DAVID Ay, the captain, sir! There's murder and slaughter—

SIR ANTHONY Murder!

DAVID Ay, please you,° Sir Anthony, there's all kinds of murder, all
sorts of slaughter to be seen in the fields. There's fighting going on,   70
sir, bloody sword-and-gun fighting!

SIR ANTHONY Who are going to fight, dunce?

DAVID Everybody that I know of, Sir Anthony. Everybody is going to fight—my poor master, Sir Lucius O'Trigger, your son the captain— 75

SIR ANTHONY O, the dog! I see his tricks. Do you know the place?

DAVID Kingsmead Fields.

SIR ANTHONY You know the way?

DAVID Not an inch; but I'll call the mayor, aldermen, constables, churchwardens and beadles.° We can't be too many to part them. 80

SIR ANTHONY Come along! Give me your shoulder!° We'll get assistance as we go. The lying villain! Well, I shall be in such a frenzy. So, this was the history of his damned trinkets! I'll bauble him!

Exeunt

5.3

Kingsmead Fields

Sir Lucius and Bob Acres, with pistols

ACRES By my valour, then, Sir Lucius, forty yards° is a good distance. Od's levels and aims, I say it is a good distance!

SIR LUCIUS Is it for muskets or small fieldpieces? Upon my conscience, Mr Acres, you must leave those things to me. Stay now. I'll show you. 5

Sir Lucius O'Trigger measures paces along the stage

There now. That is a very pretty distance, a pretty gentleman's distance.

ACRES Zounds, we might as well fight in a sentry-box! I tell you, Sir Lucius, the farther he is off, the cooler I shall take my aim.

SIR LUCIUS Faith, then I suppose you would aim at him best of all if 10 he was out of sight!

ACRES No, Sir Lucius; but I should think forty or eight-and-thirty yards—

SIR LUCIUS Foh, foh, nonsense! Three or four feet between the mouths of your pistols is as good as a mile. 15

ACRES Od's bullets, no! By my valour, there is no merit in killing him so near. No, my dear Sir Lucius, let me bring him down at a long shot—a long shot, Sir Lucius, if you love me!

SIR LUCIUS Well, the gentleman's friend and I° must settle that. But tell me now, Mr Acres. In case of an accident, is there any little will 20 or commission I could execute for you?

ACRES I am much obliged to you, Sir Lucius; but I don't understand—

SIR LUCIUS Why, you may think there's no being shot at without a little risk; and if an unlucky bullet should carry a quietus with it, I say it will be no time then to be bothering you about family matters. 25

ACRES A quietus!

SIR LUCIUS For instance, now, if that should be the case, would you choose to be pickled° and sent home? Or would it be the same to you to lie here in the Abbey?° I'm told there is very snug lying in the Abbey. 30

ACRES Pickled! Snug lying in the Abbey! Od's tremors, Sir Lucius, don't talk so!

SIR LUCIUS I suppose, Mr Acres, you never were engaged in an affair of this kind before? 35

ACRES No, Sir Lucius, never before.

SIR LUCIUS Ah, that's a pity! There's nothing like being used to a thing. Pray now, how would you receive the gentleman's shot?

ACRES Od's flies,° I've practised that. (*Puts himself into an attitude°*) There, Sir Lucius, there. A side-front, hey? Od, I'll make myself small enough. I'll stand edgeways. 40

SIR LUCIUS Now, you're quite out;° for if you stand so when I take my aim—(*Levelling at him*)

ACRES Zounds, Sir Lucius! Are you sure it is not cocked?

SIR LUCIUS Never fear. 45

ACRES But—but—you don't know; it may go off of its own head!

SIR LUCIUS Foh, be easy! Well, now if I hit you in the body, my bullet has a double chance; for if it misses a vital part on your right side, 'twill be very hard if it don't succeed on the left!

ACRES A vital part! 50

SIR LUCIUS But, there—fix yourself so. (*Placing him*) Let him see the broad side of your full front. There. Now a ball or two may pass clean through your body, and never do any harm at all.

ACRES Clean through me! A ball or two clean through me!

SIR LUCIUS Ay, may they; and it is much the genteelest attitude into the bargain. 55

ACRES Lookee, Sir Lucius. I'd just as lief° be shot in an awkward posture as a genteel one. So, by my valour, I will stand edgeways.

SIR LUCIUS (*looking at his watch*) Sure they don't mean to disappoint us. Ha? No, faith; I think I see them coming. 60

ACRES Hey! What! Coming!

SIR LUCIUS Ay. Who are those yonder getting over the stile?

ACRES There are two of them, indeed! Well, let them come, hey, Sir
  Lucius! We—we—we—we—won't run.

SIR LUCIUS Run!   65

ACRES No, I say, we *won't* run, by my valour!

SIR LUCIUS What the devil's the matter with you?

ACRES Nothing—nothing—my dear friend—my dear Sir Lucius—
  but—I—I—I don't feel quite so bold, somehow—as I did.

SIR LUCIUS O fie! Consider your honour!   70

ACRES Ay—true—my honour. Do, Sir Lucius, edge in a word or two
  every now and then about my honour.

SIR LUCIUS (*looking*) Well, here they're coming.

ACRES Sir Lucius, if I wa'n't with you, I should almost think I was
  afraid. If my valour should leave me! Valour will come and go.   75

SIR LUCIUS Then, pray keep it fast, while you have it.

ACRES Sir Lucius, I doubt it is going. Yes, my valour is certainly going!
  It is sneaking off! I feel it oozing out, as it were, at the palms of my
  hands!

SIR LUCIUS Your honour, your honour! Here they are.   80

ACRES O mercy! Now that° I were safe at Clod Hall! Or could be shot
  before I was aware!

        Enter Faulkland and Captain Absolute

SIR LUCIUS Gentlemen, your most obedient. Ha, what, Captain
  Absolute! So, I suppose, sir, you are come here, just like myself, to
  do a kind office first for your friend, then to proceed to business on 85
  your own account.

ACRES What, Jack! My dear Jack! My dear friend!

ABSOLUTE Harkee, Bob, Beverley's at hand.

SIR LUCIUS Well, Mr Acres, I don't blame your saluting the gentleman civilly. (*To Faulkland*°) So, Mr Beverley, if you'll choose your 90
  weapons, the captain and I will measure the ground.

FAULKLAND *My* weapons, sir?

ACRES Od's life, Sir Lucius, I'm not going to fight Mr Faulkland.
  These are my particular friends.

SIR LUCIUS What, sir, did not you come here to fight Mr Acres?   95

FAULKLAND Not I, upon my word, sir.

SIR LUCIUS Well, now, that's mighty provoking! But I hope, Mr
  Faulkland, as there are three of us come on purpose for the game,
  you won't be so cantankerous as to spoil the party by sitting out.

ABSOLUTE O pray, Faulkland, fight to oblige Sir Lucius.   100

FAULKLAND Nay, if Mr Acres is so bent on the matter.

ACRES No, no, Mr Faulkland; I'll bear my disappointment like a

Christian.—Lookee, Sir Lucius, there's no occasion at all for me to fight; and if it is the same to you, I'd as lief let it alone.

SIR LUCIUS Observe me, Mr Acres; I must not be trifled with. You   105
have certainly challenged somebody, and you came here to fight him. Now, if that gentleman is willing to represent him, I can't see, for my soul, why it isn't just the same thing.

ACRES Why, no, Sir Lucius; I tell you 'tis one Beverley I've challenged—a fellow, you see, that dare not show his face! If *he* were   110
here, I'd make him give up his pretensions directly!

ABSOLUTE Hold, Bob, let me set you right. There is no such man as Beverley in the case. The person who assumed that name is before you; and as his pretensions are the same in both characters, he is ready to support them in whatever way you please.   115

SIR LUCIUS Well, this is lucky. Now you have an opportunity—

ACRES What, quarrel with my dear friend Jack Absolute! Not if he were fifty Beverleys! Zounds, Sir Lucius, you would not have me be so unnatural.

SIR LUCIUS Upon my conscience, Mr Acres, your valour has *oozed*   120
away with a vengeance!

ACRES Not in the least! Od's backs and abettors,° I'll be your second with all my heart; and if you should get a quietus, you may command me entirely. I'll get you a *snug lying* in the *Abbey here*, or *pickle* you and send you over to Blunderbuss Hall, or anything of   125
the kind, with the greatest pleasure.

SIR LUCIUS Foh, foh, you are little better than a coward!

ACRES Mind, gentlemen, he calls me a *coward*. '*Coward*' was the word, by my valour!

SIR LUCIUS Well, sir?   130

ACRES Lookee, Sir Lucius. 'Tisn't that I mind the word '*coward*'; '*coward*' may be said in joke. But if you had called me a *poltroon*, od's daggers and balls—

SIR LUCIUS Well, sir!

ACRES I should have thought you a very ill-bred man.   135

SIR LUCIUS Foh, you are beneath my notice.

ABSOLUTE Nay, Sir Lucius, you can't have a better second than my friend Acres. He is a most *determined* dog, called in the country *fighting Bob*. He generally *kills a man a week*. Don't you, Bob?

ACRES Ay, at home!   140

SIR LUCIUS Well then, Captain, 'tis we must begin. So come out, my little counsellor (*draws his sword*), and ask the gentleman whether he will resign the lady, without forcing you to proceed against him?

ABSOLUTE Come on then, sir. (*Draws*) Since you won't let it be an
amicable suit,° here's *my reply*.   145
    Enter Sir Anthony Absolute, David, Mrs Malaprop, Lydia
    Languish and Julia

DAVID Knock 'em all down, sweet Sir Anthony. Knock down my
master in particular,° and bind his hands over to their good
behaviour!°

SIR ANTHONY Put up,° Jack, put up, or I shall be in a frenzy. How
came you in a duel, sir?   150

ABSOLUTE Faith, sir, that gentleman can tell you better than
I; 'twas he called on me, and you know, sir, I serve his majesty.°

SIR ANTHONY Here's a pretty fellow; I catch him going to cut a
man's throat, and he tells me he serves his majesty! Zounds, sirrah,
then how durst you draw the king's sword against one of his   155
subjects?

ABSOLUTE Sir, I tell you! That gentleman called me out, without
explaining his reasons.

SIR ANTHONY Gad, sir, how came you to call my son out, without
explaining your reasons?   160

SIR LUCIUS Your son, sir, insulted me in a manner which my honour
could not brook.

SIR ANTHONY Zounds, Jack, how durst you insult the gentleman in
a manner which his honour could not brook?

MRS MALAPROP Come, come, let's have no honour before ladies.°——   165
Captain Absolute, come here. How could you intimidate° us so?
Here's Lydia has been terrified to death for you.

ABSOLUTE For fear I should be killed, or escape, ma'am?

MRS MALAPROP Nay, no delusions° to the past. Lydia is convinced.——
Speak, child.   170

SIR LUCIUS With your leave, ma'am, I must put in a word here. I
believe I could interpret the young lady's silence. Now mark.

LYDIA What is it you mean, sir?

SIR LUCIUS Come, come, Delia, we must be serious now; this is no
time for trifling.   175

LYDIA 'Tis true, sir; and your reproof bids me offer this gentleman
my hand, and solicit the return of his affections.

ABSOLUTE O, my little angel, say you so?——Sir Lucius, I perceive
there must be some mistake here. With regard to the affront which
you affirm I have given you, I can only say that it could not have   180
been intentional. And as you must be convinced that I should not
fear to support a real injury,° you shall now see that I am not

ashamed to atone for an inadvertency. I ask your pardon. But for
this lady, while honoured with her approbation, I will support my
claim against any man whatever.   185

SIR ANTHONY Well said, Jack, and I'll stand by you, my boy.

ACRES Mind, I give up all my claim. I make no pretensions to anything in the world; and if I can't get a wife without fighting for her,
by my valour, I'll live a bachelor.

SIR LUCIUS Captain, give me your hand. An affront handsomely   190
acknowledged becomes an obligation.° And as for the lady, if she
chooses to deny her own handwriting here—
         Sir Lucius O'Trigger takes out letters

MRS MALAPROP [*aside*] O, he will dissolve my mystery!°—Sir Lucius,
perhaps there's some mistake. Perhaps I can illuminate—

SIR LUCIUS Pray, old gentlewoman, don't interfere, where you have   195
no business.—Miss Languish, are you my Delia, or not?

LYDIA Indeed, Sir Lucius, I am not.
         Lydia Languish and Captain Absolute walk aside

MRS MALAPROP Sir Lucius O'Trigger, ungrateful as you are, I own
the soft impeachment.° Pardon my blushes; I am Delia.

SIR LUCIUS You Delia! Foh, foh, be easy!°   200

MRS MALAPROP Why, thou barbarous Van Dyke,° those letters are
mine. When you are more sensible of my benignity, perhaps I may
be brought to encourage your addresses.

SIR LUCIUS Mrs Malaprop, I am extremely sensible of your condescension; and whether you or Lucy have put this trick upon me, I   205
am equally beholden to you.—And to show you I'm not ungrateful, Captain Absolute, since you have taken that lady from me, I'll
give you my Delia into the bargain.

ABSOLUTE I am much obliged to you, Sir Lucius; but here's our
friend, fighting Bob, unprovided for.   210

SIR LUCIUS Ha, little valour! Here, will you make your fortune?

ACRES Od's wrinkles, no! But give me your hand, Sir Lucius; forget
and forgive. But if ever I give you a chance of *pickling* me again,
say Bob Acres is a dunce; that's all.

ABSOLUTE Come, Mrs Malaprop, don't be cast down. You are in your   215
bloom yet.

MRS MALAPROP O Sir Anthony! Men are all barbarians.
         All retire but Julia and Faulkland°

JULIA [*aside*] He seems dejected and unhappy, not sullen. There was
some foundation, however, for the tale he told me. O woman, how
true should be your judgement, when your resolution is so weak!   220

FAULKLAND Julia, how can I sue for what I so little deserve? I dare not presume; yet hope is the child of penitence.

JULIA O, Faulkland, you have not been more faulty in your unkind treatment of me, than I am now in wanting inclination to resent it. As my heart honestly bids me place my weakness to the account of   225
love, I should be ungenerous not to admit the same plea for yours.

FAULKLAND Now I shall be blessed indeed!

Sir Anthony Absolute comes forward

SIR ANTHONY What's going on here? So, you have been quarrelling too, I warrant. Come, Julia, I never interfered before; but let me have a hand in the matter at last. All the faults I have ever seen in   230
my friend Faulkland seemed to proceed from what he calls the *delicacy* and *warmth* of his affection for you. There, marry him directly, Julia; you'll find he'll mend surprisingly!

The rest come forward

SIR LUCIUS Come now, I hope there is no dissatisfied person, but what is content; for as I have been disappointed myself, it will be very   235
hard if I have not the satisfaction of seeing other people succeed better.

ACRES You are right, Sir Lucius.—So, Jack, I wish you joy—Mr Faulkland the same.—Ladies, come now. To show you I'm neither vexed nor angry, od's tabors and pipes, I'll order the fiddles in half   240
an hour to the New Rooms, and I insist on your all meeting me there.

SIR ANTHONY Gad, sir, I like your spirit; and at night we single lads will drink a health to the young couples, and a husband to Mrs Malaprop.   245

FAULKLAND Our partners are stolen from us, Jack—I hope, to be congratulated by each other.° Yours for having checked in time the errors of an ill-directed imagination, which might have betrayed an innocent heart; and mine, for having, by her gentleness and candour, reformed the unhappy temper of one, who by it made   250
wretched whom he loved most, and tortured the heart he ought to have adored.

ABSOLUTE Well, Faulkland, we have both tasted the bitters, as well as the sweets, of love—with this difference only, that *you* always prepared the bitter cup for yourself, while *I*—   255

LYDIA Was always obliged to *me* for it, hey, Mr Modesty? But come, no more of that. Our happiness is now as unallayed as general.

JULIA Then let us study to preserve it so; and while hope pictures to us a flattering scene of future bliss, let us deny its pencil those

colours which are too bright to be lasting. When hearts deserving   260
happiness would unite their fortunes, virtue would crown them
with an unfading garland of modest, hurtless flowers; but ill-
judging passion will force the gaudier rose into the wreath, whose
thorn offends them, when its leaves are dropped!

[*Exeunt*]

Epilogue

By the author

Spoken by Mrs Bulkley°

Ladies, for *you*, I heard our poet say,°
He'd try to coax some moral from his play.
'One moral's plain,' cried I, 'without more fuss:
Man's social happiness all rests on us.
Through all the drama, whether damned or not,°   5
Love gilds the scene, and women guide the plot.
From every rank obedience is our due.
D'ye doubt? The world's great stage shall prove it true.'
    The cit, well-skilled to shun domestic strife,
Will sup abroad; but, first, he'll ask his wife.   10
John Trot, his friend, for once will do the same;°
But, then, he'll just step home to tell his dame.
    The surly squire at noon resolves to rule,
And half the day, 'Zounds, madam is a fool!'
Convinced at night, the vanquished victor says,°   15
'Ah, Kate, you women have such coaxing ways!'
    The jolly toper chides each tardy blade,
Till reeling Bacchus calls on love for aid;
Then with each toast he sees fair bumpers swim,
And kisses Chloe on the sparkling brim!°   20
    Nay, I have heard that statesmen, great and wise,
Will sometimes counsel with a lady's eyes.°
The servile suitors watch her various face;
She smiles preferment, or she frowns disgrace,
Curtsies a pension here, there nods a place.   25
    Nor with less awe, in scenes of humbler life,
Is viewed the mistress, or is heard the wife.
The poorest peasant of the poorest soil,
The child of poverty and heir to toil,
Early from radiant love's impartial light   30
Steals one small spark, to cheer his world of night.
Dear spark!—that oft through winter's chilling woes
Is all the warmth his little cottage knows!
    The wand'ring tar, who, not for years, has pressed°

The widowed partner of his day of rest,   35
On the cold deck, far from her arms removed,
Still hums the ditty which his Susan loved;°
And while around the cadence rude is blown,
The boatswain whistles in a softer tone.°
    The soldier, fairly proud of wounds and toil,°   40
Pants for the triumph of his Nancy's smile;
But ere the battle, should he list her cries,°
The lover trembles, and the hero dies!
That heart, by war and honour steeled to fear,
Droops on a sigh, and sickens at a tear!   45
    But ye more cautious, ye nice judging few,
Who give to beauty only beauty's due,
Though friends to love, ye view with deep regret
Our conquests marred and triumphs incomplete,
Till polished wit more lasting charms disclose,   50
And judgement fix the darts which beauty throws!
In female breasts did sense and merit rule,
The lover's mind would ask no other school.
Shamed into sense, the scholars of our eyes,
Our beaux from gallantry would soon be wise—   55
Would gladly light, their homage to improve,
The lamp of knowledge at the torch of love!

THE DUENNA
A Comic Opera

THE CHARACTERS OF THE PLAY

Don Jerome	*Mr Wilson*
Ferdinand	*Mr Mattocks*
Antonio	*Mr Dubellamy*
Carlos	*Mr Leoni*
Isaac Mendoza	*Mr Quick*
Father Paul	*Mr Mahon*
[Father Francis]	
[Father Augustine]	
Lopez	*Mr Wewitzer*
Lewis	*Mr Castevens*
[Two Masks]	
[Servants to Don Jerome]	
[A Porter]	
[Friars]°	
Louisa	*Mrs Mattocks*
Clara	*Miss Brown*
Margaret, the Duenna°	*Mrs Green*
[Maid to Louisa]	
[Maid to Clara]	
[Masqueraders]	

[SCENE: SEVILLE]

88

1.1

A street

Enter Lopez, with a dark-lantern

LOPEZ Past three o'clock! So! A notable hour for one of my regular disposition to be strolling like a bravo through the streets of Seville. Well, of all services, to serve a young lover is the hardest. Not that I am an enemy to love; but my love and my master's differ strangely.° Don Ferdinand is much too gallant to eat, drink or sleep; now, my love gives me an appetite. Then I am fond of dreaming of my mistress, and I love dearly to toast her. This cannot be done without good sleep and good liquor; hence my partiality to a feather-bed and a bottle. What a pity now, that I have not further time for reflections; but thy master expects thee, honest Lopez, to secure his retreat from Donna Clara's window, as I guess.

Music without°

Hey! Sure I heard music! So! So! Who have we here? O, Don Antonio, my master's friend, come from the masquerade to serenade my young mistress, Donna Louisa, I suppose! So! We shall have the old gentleman up presently. Lest he should miss his son, I had best lose no time in getting to my post.

Exit Lopez. Enter Antonio, with masks and music°

ANTONIO [*sings*]

SONG

(Soft Symphony)°

Tell me, my lute, can thy fond strain°
So gently speak thy master's pain,
So softly sing, so humbly sigh,
That though my sleeping love shall know
Who sings, who sighs below,
Her rosy slumbers shall not fly?
Thus may some vision whisper more
Than ever I dare speak before.

FIRST MASK Antonio, your mistress will never wake while you sing so dolefully; love, like a cradled infant, is lulled by a sad melody.

ANTONIO I do not wish to disturb her rest.

FIRST MASK The reason is, because you know she does not regard you
  enough, to appear if you waked her.   30
ANTONIO Nay, then I'll convince you. (*Sings*)

> The breath of morn bids hence the night;°
> Unveil those beauteous eyes, my fair,
> For till the dawn of love is there,
>   I feel no day, I own no light.°   35

LOUISA (*replies from a window*)
> Waking, I heard thy numbers chide;°
> Waking, the dawn did bless my sight.
> ''Tis Phoebus sure that woos', I cried,
> 'Who speaks in song, who moves in light'.°

DON JEROME (*from a window*)
> What vagabonds are these I hear   40
> Fiddling, fluting, rhyming, ranting,
> Piping, scraping, whining, canting?
>   Fly, scurvy minstrels, fly.

TRIO

LOUISA   *Nay, prithee, father, why so rough?*
ANTONIO   *An humble lover I.*   45
JEROME   *How durst you, daughter, lend an ear*
              To such deceitful stuff?
              Quick from the window fly.
LOUISA   *Adieu, Antonio!*
ANTONIO   *Must you go?*
LOUISA and ANTONIO
              We soon perhaps may meet again,   50
              For though hard fortune is our foe,
              The god of love will fight for us.
JEROME   *Reach me the blunderbuss.*
ANTONIO and LOUISA
              The god of love, who knows our pain—
JEROME   *Hence, or these slugs are through your brain.*   55

Exeunt severally

1.2

A piazza

Enter Ferdinand and Lopez

LOPEZ Truly, sir, I think that a little sleep once in a week or so—

FERDINAND Peace, fool; don't mention sleep to me.

LOPEZ No, no, sir, I don't mention your low-bred, vulgar, sound sleep; but I can't help thinking that a genteel slumber, or half an hour's dozing, if it were only for the novelty of the thing—   5

FERDINAND Peace, booby, I say.—O Clara, dear, cruel disturber of my rest.

LOPEZ And of mine too.

FERDINAND 'Sdeath! To trifle with me at such a juncture as this! Now to stand on punctilios! Love me? I don't believe she ever did.   10

LOPEZ Nor I either.

FERDINAND Or is it that her sex never know their desires for an hour together?

LOPEZ Ah, they know them oftener than they'll own them.

FERDINAND Is there in the world so inconsistent a creature as Clara?   15

LOPEZ I could name one.

FERDINAND Yes; the tame fool who submits to her caprice.

LOPEZ [*aside*] I thought he couldn't miss it.

FERDINAND Is she not capricious, teasing, tyrannical, obstinate, perverse, absurd, ay, a wilderness of faults and follies? Her looks   20
are scorn, and her very smiles—'sdeath, I wish I hadn't mentioned her smiles, for she does smile such beaming loveliness and fascinating brightness. O death and madness, I shall die if I lose her.

LOPEZ [*aside*] O, those damned smiles have undone all.

FERDINAND [*sings*]

AIR

Could I her faults remember,°   25
  Forgetting every charm,
Soon would impartial reason
  The tyrant love disarm.
But when, enraged, I number
  Each failing of her mind,   30
Love still suggests her beauty,
  And sees, while reason's blind.

LOPEZ Here comes Don Antonio, sir.

FERDINAND Well, go you home. I shall be there presently.

LOPEZ [*aside*] Ah, those cursed smiles.   35

     Exit Lopez. Enter Antonio

FERDINAND Antonio, Lopez tells me he left you chanting before our
door. Was my father waked?

ANTONIO Yes, yes; he has a singular affection for music, so I left him
roaring at his barred window, like the print of Bajazet in the cage.°
And what brings you out so early?   40

FERDINAND I believe I told you that tomorrow was the day fixed
by Don Pedro and Clara's unnatural stepmother for her to enter
a convent, in order that her brat might possess her fortune.°
Made desperate by this, I procured a key to the door, and bribed
Clara's maid to leave it unbolted. At two this morning I entered,   45
unperceived, and stole to her chamber. I found her waking and
weeping.

ANTONIO Happy Ferdinand!

FERDINAND 'Sdeath, hear the conclusion. I was rated° as the most
confident° ruffian, for daring to approach her room at that hour of   50
night.

ANTONIO Ay, ay, this was at first.

FERDINAND No such thing! She would not hear a word from me, but
threatened to raise her father if I did not instantly leave her.

ANTONIO Well; but at last?   55

FERDINAND At last! Why, I was forced to leave the house as I came
in.

ANTONIO And did you do nothing to offend her?

FERDINAND Nothing, as I hope to be saved. I believe I might snatch
a dozen or two kisses.   60

ANTONIO Was that all? Well, I think I never heard of such assurance.°

FERDINAND Zounds, I tell you I behaved with the utmost respect.

ANTONIO O lord, I don't mean you, but in her. But, harkee, Ferdinand, did you leave your key with them?

FERDINAND Yes; the maid who saw me out took it from the   65
door.

ANTONIO Then, my life for it,° her mistress elopes after you.

FERDINAND Ay, to bless some rival perhaps. I am in a humour to
suspect everybody. You loved her once, and thought her an angel,
as I do now.   70

ANTONIO Yes, I loved her till I found she wouldn't love me, and then
I discovered that she hadn't a good feature in her face. [*Sings*]

AIR

I ne'er could any lustre see°
In eyes that would not look on me.
I ne'er saw nectar on a lip,   75
But where my own did hope to sip.
Has the maid who seeks my heart
Cheeks of rose untouched by art?°
I will own the colour true,
When yielding blushes aid their hue.   80

Is her hand so soft and pure?
I must press it to be sure;
Nor can I be certain then
Till it, grateful, press again.°
Must I with attentive eye   85
Watch her heaving bosom sigh?
I will do so when I see
That heaving bosom sigh for me.

Besides, Ferdinand, you have full security in my love for
your sister.° Help me there, and I can never disturb you with   90
Clara.

FERDINAND As far as I can consistently with the honour of our family,
you know I will; but there must be no eloping.

ANTONIO And yet, now, you would carry off Clara.

FERDINAND Ay, that's a different case. We never mean that others   95
should act to our sisters and wives as we do to theirs. But tomorrow Clara is to be forced into a convent.

ANTONIO Well, and am not I as unfortunately circumstanced? Tomorrow your father forces Louisa to marry Isaac, the Portuguese. But
come with me, and we'll devise something, I warrant.   100

FERDINAND I must go home.

ANTONIO Well, adieu.

FERDINAND But, Antonio, if you did not love my sister, you have too
much honour and friendship to think of supplanting me with Clara.

ANTONIO [*sings*]

AIR

Friendship is the bond of reason;°   105
But if beauty disapprove,
Heaven absolves all other treason
In the heart that's true to love.

> *The faith which to my friend I swore*
> *As a civil oath I view;*   110
> *But to the charms which I adore,*
> *'Tis religion to be true.*

> *Then if to one I false must be,*
> *Can I doubt which to prefer—*
> *A breach of social faith with thee,*   115
> *Or sacrilege to love and her?*

Exit Antonio

FERDINAND There is always a levity in Antonio's manner of replying
to me on this subject that is very alarming. 'Sdeath, if Clara should
love him after all. [*Sings*]

AIR

> *Though cause for suspicion appears,°*   120
> *Yet proofs of her love too are strong;*
> *I'm a wretch if I'm right in my fears,*
> *And unworthy of bliss if I'm wrong.*
> *What heartbreaking torments from jealousy flow,*
> *Ah, none but the jealous, the jealous can know.*   125

> *When blessed with the smiles of my fair,*
> *I know not how much I adore;*
> *Those smiles let another but share,*
> *And I wonder I prized them no more.*
> *Then whence can I hope a relief from my woe,*   130
> *When the falser she seems still the fonder I grow.*

Exit

1.3

A room in Don Jerome's house

Enter Louisa and the Duenna

LOUISA But, my dear Margaret, my charming duenna, do you think
we shall succeed?

DUENNA I tell you again I have no doubt on't; but it must be instantly
put to the trial. Everything is prepared in your room, and for the   5
rest we must trust to fortune.

LOUISA My father's oath was never to see me till I had consented to—

DUENNA 'Twas thus I overheard him say to his friend, Don Guzman: 'I will demand of her tomorrow, once for all, whether she will consent to marry Isaac Mendoza. If she hesitates, I will make a solemn oath never to see or speak to her till she returns to her duty.' These were his very words.

LOUISA And on his known obstinate adherence to what he has once said, you have formed this plan for my escape. But have you secured my maid in our interest?

DUENNA She is a party in the whole.° But remember, if we succeed, you resign all right and title in little Isaac the Jew over to me.

LOUISA That I do with all my soul. Get him if you can, and I shall wish you joy° most heartily. He is twenty times as rich as my poor Antonio. [*Sings*]

AIR

Thou canst not boast of fortune's store,°
My love, while me they wealthy call;
But I was glad to find thee poor,
For with my heart I'd give thee all.
And then the grateful youth shall own
I loved him for himself alone.

But when his worth my hand shall gain,
No word or look of mine shall show
That I the smallest thought retain
Of what my bounty did bestow.
Yet still his grateful heart shall own
I loved him for himself alone.

DUENNA I hear Don Jerome coming. Quick, give me the last letter I brought you from Antonio. You know that is to be the ground of my dismission. I must slip out to seal it up as undelivered.°

Exit the Duenna. Enter Don Jerome and Ferdinand

JEROME What, I suppose you have been serenading too! Eh! Disturbing some peaceable neighbourhood with villainous catgut° and lascivious piping? Out on't! You set your sister here a vile example. But I come to tell you, madam, that I'll suffer no more of these midnight incantations,° these amorous orgies that steal the senses in the hearing, as they say Egyptian embalmers serve mummies, extracting the brain through the ears.° However, there's an end of your frolics. Isaac Mendoza will be here presently, and tomorrow you shall marry him.

LOUISA Never while I have life.   45

FERDINAND Indeed, sir, I wonder how you can think of such a man
for a son-in-law.

JEROME Sir, you are very kind to favour me with your sentiments.°
And pray, what is your objection to him?

FERDINAND He is a Portuguese in the first place.   50

JEROME No such thing, boy: he has forsworn his country.

LOUISA He is a Jew.

JEROME Another mistake: he has been a Christian these six weeks.

FERDINAND Ay, he left his old religion for an estate, and has not had
time to get a new one.   55

LOUISA But stands like a dead wall between church and synagogue,
or like the blank leaves between the Old and New Testament.

JEROME Anything more?

FERDINAND But the most remarkable part of his character is his
passion for deceit and tricks of cunning.   60

LOUISA Though at the same time the fool predominates so much over
the knave, that I am told he is generally the dupe of his own art.°

FERDINAND True. Like an unskilful gunner, he usually misses his aim
and is hurt by the recoil of his own piece.

JEROME Anything more?   65

LOUISA To sum up all, he has the worst fault a husband can have: he's
not my choice.

JEROME But you are his; and choice on one side is sufficient. Two
lovers should never meet in marriage. Be you sour as you please; he
is sweet-tempered, and, for your good fruit, there's nothing like   70
engrafting on a crab.°

LOUISA I detest him as a lover, and shall ten times more as a husband.

JEROME I don't know that; marriage generally makes a great change.
But, to cut the matter short, will you have him or not?

LOUISA There is nothing else I could disobey you in.   75

JEROME Do you value your father's peace?

LOUISA So much, that I will not fasten on him the regret of making
an only daughter wretched.

JEROME Very well, ma'am. Then mark me. Never more will I see or
converse with you till you return to your duty. No reply. This and   80
your chamber shall be your apartments. I never will stir out without
leaving you under lock and key, and when I'm at home no creature
can approach you but through my library. We'll try who can be most
obstinate. Out of my sight. There remain till you know your duty.

Don Jerome pushes Louisa out

FERDINAND Surely, sir, my sister's inclinations should be consulted   85
in a matter of this kind, and some regard paid to Don Antonio,
being my particular friend.

JEROME That, doubtless, is a very great recommendation. I certainly
have not paid sufficient respect to it.

FERDINAND There is not a man living I would sooner choose for a   90
brother-in-law.

JEROME Very possible; and if you happen to have e'er a sister, who is
not at the same time a daughter of mine, I'm sure I shall have no
objection to the relationship. But at present, if you please, we'll
drop the subject.   95

FERDINAND Nay, sir, 'tis only my regard for my sister makes me
speak.

JEROME Then pray, sir, in future, let your regard for your father make
you hold your tongue.

FERDINAND I have done, sir. I shall only add a wish that you would   100
reflect what at our age you would have felt, had you been crossed
in your affection for the mother of her you are so severe to.

JEROME Why, I must confess I had a great affection for your mother's
ducats; but that was all, boy. I married her for her fortune, and she
took me in obedience to her father, and a very happy couple we   105
were. We never expected any love from one another, and so we were
never disappointed. If we grumbled a little now and then, it was
soon over, for we were never fond enough to quarrel; and when the
good woman died, why, why, I had as lief° she had lived, and I wish
every widower in Seville could say the same. I shall now go and get   110
the key of this dressing-room. So, good son, if you have any lecture
in support of disobedience to give your sister, it must be brief; so
make the best of your time, d'ye hear?

    Exit Don Jerome

FERDINAND I fear, indeed, my friend Antonio has little to hope for.
However, Louisa has firmness, and my father's anger will probably   115
only increase her affection. In our intercourse with the world, it is
natural for us to dislike those who are innocently the cause of our
distress; but, in the heart's attachment, a woman never likes a man
with ardour till she has suffered for his sake.

    Noise [*offstage*]

So! What bustle is here? Between my father and the duenna too. I'll   120
e'en out of the way.

    Exit Ferdinand. Enter Don Jerome, with a letter, pulling in the
    Duenna

JEROME I'm astonished! I'm thunder-struck! Here's treachery and
conspiracy with a vengeance!° You Antonio's creature,° and chief
manager of this plot for my daughter's eloping! You that I placed
here as a scarecrow.   125

DUENNA What?

JEROME A scarecrow. To prove a decoy-duck!° What have you to say
for yourself?

DUENNA Well, sir, since you have forced that letter from me and discovered my real sentiments, I scorn to renounce 'em. I am Antonio's   130
friend, and it was my intention that your daughter should
have served you as all such old tyrannical sots should be served. I
delight in the tender passions and would befriend all under their
influence.

JEROME The tender passions! Yes, they would become° those impen-   135
etrable features. Why, thou deceitful hag, I placed thee as a guard
to the rich blossoms of my daughter's beauty. I thought that
dragon's front of thine would cry aloof° to the sons of gallantry;°
steel traps and spring guns° seemed writ in every wrinkle of it. But
you shall quit my house this instant. The tender passions, indeed!   140
Go, thou wanton sibyl,° thou amorous woman of Endor,° go!

DUENNA You base, scurrilous, old—but I won't demean myself by
naming what you are. Yes, savage, I'll leave your den; but I suppose
you don't mean to detain my apparel. I may have my things, I
presume.   145

JEROME I took you, mistress, with your wardrobe on. What have you
pilfered, hey?

DUENNA Sir, I must take leave of my mistress. She has valuables of
mine; besides, my cardinal and veil are in her room.

JEROME Your veil, forsooth! What, do you dread being gazed at? Or   150
are you afraid of your complexion? Well, go take your leave, and get
your veil and cardinal! So, you quit the house within these five
minutes! In, in; quick!

        Exit the Duenna

Here was a precious plot of mischief! These are the comforts
daughters bring us. [*Sings*]   155

AIR

If a daughter you have, she's the plague of your life;°
No peace shall you know, though you've buried your wife.
At twenty she mocks at the duty you taught her;
O, what a plague is an obstinate daughter.

> *Sighing and whining,*   160
> *Dying and pining,*
> *O, what a plague is an obstinate daughter.*
>
> *When scarce in their teens they have wit to perplex us;*
> *With letters and lovers forever they vex us;*
> *While each still rejects the fair suitor you've brought her.*   165
> *O, what a plague is an obstinate daughter.*
> *Wrangling and jangling,*
> *Flouting and pouting,*
> *O, what a plague is an obstinate daughter.*

Enter Louisa, dressed as the Duenna, with cardinal and veil,
seeming to cry

JEROME This way, mistress, this way. What, I warrant, a tender   170
parting! So! Tears of turpentine down those deal cheeks. Ay, you
may well hide your head. Yes, whine till your heart breaks, but I'll
not hear one word of excuse. So, you are right to be dumb. This
way, this way.

Exeunt Don Jerome and Louisa. Enter the Duenna

DUENNA So speed you well,° sagacious Don Jerome! O, rare effects of   175
passion and obstinacy. Now shall I try whether I can't play the fine
lady as well as my mistress; and if I succeed, I may be a fine lady
for the rest of my life. I'll lose no time to equip myself.°

Exit

1.4

The court° before Don Jerome's house

Enter Don Jerome and Louisa

JEROME Come, mistress, there is your way. The world lies before
you; so troop, thou antiquated Eve, thou original sin.° Hold,
yonder is some fellow skulking. Perhaps it is Antonio. Go to him,
d'ye hear, and tell him to make you amends, and as he has got you
turned away,° tell him I say it is but just he should take you himself.   5
Go.

Exit Louisa

So! I am rid of her, thank heaven! And now I shall be able to keep
my oath, and confine my daughter with better security.

Exit

1.5

The piazza

Enter Clara and her Maid

MAID But where, madam, is it you intend to go?

CLARA Anywhere to avoid the selfish violence of my mother-in-law°
and Ferdinand's insolent importunity.

MAID Indeed, ma'am, since we have profited by Don Ferdinand's key
in making our escape, I think we had best find him, if it were only   5
to thank him.

CLARA No—he has offended me exceedingly.

Clara and her Maid retire.° Enter Louisa

LOUISA [*aside*] So, I have succeeded in being turned out of doors; but
how shall I find Antonio? I dare not inquire for him for fear of being
discovered. I would send to my friend Clara, but that I doubt her   10
prudery° would condemn me.

MAID [*to Clara*] Then suppose, ma'am, you were to try if your friend
Donna Louisa would not receive you.

CLARA No, her notions of filial duty are so severe, she would certainly
betray me.   15

LOUISA [*aside*] Clara is of a cold temper, and would think this step of
mine highly forward.

CLARA Louisa's respect for her father is so great, she would not credit
the unkindness of mine.

Louisa turns and sees Clara and her Maid

LOUISA [*aside*] Ha! Who are those? Sure one is Clara. If it be, I'll trust   20
her. (*Advances*) Clara!

CLARA Louisa! And in masquerade° too!

LOUISA You will be more surprised when I tell you that I have run
away from my father.

CLARA Surprised indeed! And I should certainly chide you most   25
horridly, only that I have just° run away from mine.

LOUISA My dear Clara!

Louisa and Clara embrace

CLARA Dear sister truant! And whither are you going?

LOUISA To find the man I love, to be sure. And I presume you would
have no aversion to meet with my brother.   30

CLARA Indeed I should. He has behaved so ill to me, I don't believe I
shall ever forgive him. [*Sings*]

AIR

When sable night, each drooping plant restoring,°
    Wept o'er the flowers her breath did cheer,
As some sad widow, o'er her babe deploring,   35
    Wakes its beauty with a tear;
When all did sleep, whose weary hearts did borrow
    One hour from love and care to rest,
Lo, as I pressed my couch in silent sorrow,
    My lover caught me to his breast.   40
      He vowed he came to save me
      From those who would enslave me!
        Then kneeling,
        Kisses stealing,
Endless faith he swore.   45
      But soon I chid him thence,
      For had his fond pretence
      Obtained one favour then,
      And he had pressed again,
I feared my treacherous heart might grant him more.   50

LOUISA Well, for all this, I would have sent him to plead his pardon,
but that I would not yet awhile have him know of my flight. And
where do you hope to find protection?

CLARA The lady abbess of the convent of St Catherine is a relation
and kind friend of mine. I shall be secure with her, and you had   55
best go thither with me.

LOUISA No; I am determined to find Antonio first. And as I live, here
comes the very man I will employ to seek him for me.

CLARA Who is he? He's a strange figure!

LOUISA Yes, that sweet creature is the man whom my father has fixed   60
on for my husband.

CLARA And will you speak to him? Are you mad?

LOUISA He is the fittest man in the world for my purpose; for, though
I was to have married him tomorrow, he is the only man in Seville
who, I am sure, never saw me in his life.   65

CLARA And how do you know him?

LOUISA He arrived but yesterday, and he was shown me from the
window as he visited my father.

CLARA Well, I'll be gone.

LOUISA Hold, my dear Clara; a thought has struck me. Will you give   70
me leave to borrow your name as I see occasion?

CLARA It will but disgrace you; but use it as you please. I dare
not stay. (*Going*) But, Louisa, if you should see your brother, be
sure you don't inform him that I have taken refuge with the dame
prior of the convent of St Catherine, on the left-hand side of the   75
piazza which leads to the church of St Anthony.

LOUISA Ha, ha, ha! I'll be very particular in my directions where he
may not find you.

Exeunt Clara and her Maid

So! My swain yonder has done admiring himself and draws nearer.

Louisa retires. Enter Isaac, with a pocket glass, and Carlos

ISAAC (*looking in the glass*) I tell you, friend Carlos, I will please myself   80
in the habit° of my chin.

CARLOS But, my dear friend, how can you think to please a lady with
such a face?

ISAAC Why, what's the matter with the face? I think it is a very engaging face; and I am sure a lady must have very little taste, who could   85
dislike my beard.

Isaac sees Louisa

See now! I'll die if here is not a little damsel struck with it already.

LOUISA Signor, are you disposed to oblige a lady who greatly wants
your assistance?

Louisa unveils

ISAAC Egad, a very pretty black-eyed girl; she has certainly taken a   90
fancy to me, Carlos.—First, ma'am, I must beg the favour of your
name.

LOUISA (*aside*) So! It's well I am provided.—My name, sir, is Donna
Clara D'Almanza.

ISAAC [*aside*] What! Don Guzman's daughter! I'faith, I just now heard   95
she was missing.

LOUISA But, sure, sir, you have too much gallantry and honour to
betray me, whose fault is love.

ISAAC [*aside*] So! A passion for me! Poor girl!—Why, ma'am, as for
betraying you, I don't see how I could get anything by it; so you   100
may rely on my honour. But, as for your love, I am sorry your case
is so desperate.

LOUISA Why so, signor?

ISAAC Because I'm positively° engaged to another. A'n't I, Carlos?

LOUISA Nay, but hear me.   105

ISAAC No, no; what should I hear for? It is impossible for me to court you in an honourable way; and, for anything else, if I were to comply now, I suppose you have some ungrateful brother, or cousin, who would want to cut my throat for my civility. So, truly, you had best go home again.   110

LOUISA (*aside*) Odious wretch!—But, good signor, it is Antonio D'Ercilla, on whose account I have eloped.

ISAAC How! What! It is not with me then that you are in love?

LOUISA No, indeed it is not.

ISAAC Then you are a forward, impertinent simpleton! And I shall   115 certainly acquaint your father.

LOUISA Is this your gallantry?

ISAAC Yet hold. Antonio D'Ercilla, did you say? Egad, I may make something of this. Antonio D'Ercilla?

LOUISA Yes, and if ever you hope to prosper in love, you will bring   120 me to him.

ISAAC By St Iago,° and I will too.—[*Aside, to Carlos*] Carlos, this Antonio is one who rivals me, as I have heard, with Louisa. Now, if I could hamper him with this girl, I should have the field to myself, hey, Carlos! A lucky thought, isn't it?   125

CARLOS Yes, very good; very good.

ISAAC Ah, this little brain is never at a loss. Cunning Isaac! Cunning rogue!—Donna Clara, will you trust yourself a while to my friend's direction?

LOUISA May I rely on you, good signor?   130

CARLOS Lady, it is impossible I should deceive you. [*Sings*]

AIR

> Had I a heart for falsehood framed,°
>   I ne'er could injure you;
> For though your tongue no promise claimed,
>   Your charms would make me true.   135
> To you no soul shall bear deceit,
>   No stranger offer wrong;
> But friends in all the aged you'll meet,°
>   And lovers in the young.
>
> But when they learn that you have blessed   140
>   Another with your heart,
> They'll bid aspiring passion rest
>   And act a brother's part.
> Then, lady, dread not here deceit,
>   Nor fear to suffer wrong;   145

> *For friends in all the aged you'll meet,*
> *And brothers in the young.*

ISAAC Conduct the lady to my lodgings, Carlos. I must haste to Don
Jerome.—Perhaps you know Louisa, ma'am. She is divinely handsome, isn't she?   150

LOUISA You must excuse me not joining with you.

ISAAC Why, I have heard it on all hands.°

LOUISA Her father is uncommonly partial to her; but I believe you
will find she has rather a matronly air.

ISAAC Carlos, this is all envy.—You pretty girls never speak well of   155
one another. (*To Don Carlos*) Harkee, find out Antonio, and I'll
saddle him with this scrape,° I warrant! O, 'twas the luckiest
thought.—Donna Clara, your very obedient.—Carlos, to your post.

ISAAC and LOUISA [*sing*]

DUET

ISAAC   *My mistress expects me, and I must go to her,°*
           Or how can I hope for a smile?   160

LOUISA   *Soon may you return a prosperous wooer,*
           But think what I suffer the while:
           Alone and away from the man whom I love,
           In strangers I'm forced to confide.°

ISAAC   *Dear lady, my friend you may trust, and he'll prove*   165
           Your servant, protector, and guide.

CARLOS [*sings*]

AIR

> *Gentle maid, ah, why suspect me?*
> *Let me serve thee—then reject me.*
> *Canst thou trust, and I deceive thee?*
> *Art thou sad, and shall I grieve thee?*   170
> *Gentle maid, ah, why suspect me?*
> *Let me serve thee—then reject me.*

LOUISA, ISAAC, and CARLOS [*sing*]

TRIO

LOUISA   *Never may'st thou happy be,*
                If in aught thou'rt false to me.

ISAAC   *Never may he happy be,*   175
                If in aught he's false to thee.

CARLOS	*Never may I happy be,*
	If in aught I'm false to thee.
LOUISA	*Never may'st thou, etc.*
ISAAC	*Never may he, etc.*
CARLOS	*Never may I, etc.*

180

Exeunt

2.1

A library in Don Jerome's house

Enter Don Jerome and Isaac

JEROME Ha, ha, ha! Run away from her father, has she? Given him the slip! Ha, ha, ha! Poor Don Guzman!

ISAAC Ay; and I am to conduct her to Antonio, by which means you see I shall hamper him so that he can give me no disturbance with your daughter. This is a trap, isn't it? A nice stroke of cunning, hey! 5

JEROME Excellent! Excellent! Yes, yes, carry her to him, hamper him by all means. Ha, ha, ha! Poor Don Guzman! An old fool! Imposed on by a girl!

ISAAC Nay, they have the cunning of serpents. That's the truth on't.

JEROME Pshaw! They are cunning only when they have fools to deal 10
with. Why don't my girl play me such a trick? Let her cunning overreach my caution, I say. Hey, little Isaac!

ISAAC True, true; or let me see any of the sex make a fool of me. No, no, egad, little Solomon, as my aunt used to call me, understands tricking a little too well. 15

JEROME Ay, but such a driveller as Don Guzman.

ISAAC And such a dupe as Antonio.

JEROME True; sure never were seen such a couple of credulous simpletons. But come, 'tis time you should see my daughter. You must carry on the siege by yourself, friend Isaac. 20

ISAAC Sure, you'll introduce me?

JEROME No; I have sworn a solemn oath not to see or speak to her till she renounces her disobedience. Win her to that, and she gains a father and a husband at once.

ISAAC Gad, I shall never be able to deal with her alone. Nothing keeps 25
me in such awe as perfect beauty. Now there is something consoling and encouraging in ugliness. [*Sings*]

SONG

Give Isaac the nymph who no beauty can boast,°
But health and good humour to make her his toast.
If straight, I don't mind whether slender or fat; 30
And six feet or four—we'll ne'er quarrel for that.

Whate'er her complexion, I vow I don't care;
If brown it is lasting, more pleasing if fair.
And though in her cheeks I no dimples should see,
Let her smile, and each dell is a dimple to me.   35

Let her locks be the reddest that ever were seen,
And her eyes may be e'en any colour but green;
For in eyes, though so various in lustre and hue,
I swear I've no choice—only let her have two.

'Tis true I'd dispense with a throne on her back;°   40
And white teeth, I own, are genteeler than black.
A little round chin too's a beauty, I've heard;
But I only desire she mayn't have a beard.

JEROME You will change your note, my friend, when you've seen
Louisa.   45

ISAAC O, Don Jerome, the honour of your alliance—

JEROME Ay, but her beauty will affect you. She is, though I say it,
who am her father, a very prodigy. There you will see features
with an eye like mine. Yes, i'faith, there is a kind of wicked
sparkling, something of a roguish brightness that shows her to be   50
my own.

ISAAC Pretty rogue!

JEROME Then, when she smiles, you'll see a little dimple in one cheek
only. A beauty it is certainly; yet you shall not say which is prettiest—the cheek with the dimple, or the cheek without.   55

ISAAC Pretty rogue!

JEROME Then the roses on those cheeks are shaded with a sort of
velvet down, that gives a delicacy to the glow of health.

ISAAC Pretty rogue!

JEROME Her skin pure dimity, yet more fair, being spangled here and   60
there with a golden freckle.

ISAAC Charming pretty rogue!

JEROME and ISAAC [*sing*]

DUET

JEROME   *Dominion was given°*
                      To beauty from heaven,
                        Pleasing bondage to the mind!   65
                      Will you then alone
                      Its worship disown?°

ISAAC   *Never!—could I favour find;*

> *But when for my pain*
> *I meet with disdain—*   70

JEROME   *Coax her, kiss her, till she's kind.*

JEROME Come, courage, man. You must not be dismayed if you find
Louisa a little haughty at first.

ISAAC Pray how is the tone of her voice?

JEROME Remarkably pleasing. But if you could prevail on her to sing,   75
you would be enchanted. She is a nightingale, a Virginia nightingale.° But come, come; her maid shall conduct you to her
antechamber.

ISAAC Well, egad, I'll pluck up resolution and meet her frowns
intrepidly.   80

JEROME Ay, woo her briskly. Win her and give me a proof of your
address, my little Solomon.

ISAAC But hold. I expect my friend Carlos to call on me here. If he
comes, will you send him to me?

JEROME I will.—Lauretta, come.°—She'll show you to the room.   85
What! Do you droop? Here's a mournful face to make love with.°
[*Sings*]

SONG

> *When the maid whom we love°*
> *No entreaties can move,*
>   *Who'd lead a life of pining?*
> *If her charms will excuse*   90
> *The fond rashness we use*
>   *—Away with idle whining!*
>
> *Never stand like a fool*
> *With looks sheepish and cool—*   95
>   *Such bashful love is teasing;*
> *But with spirit address,*
> *And you're sure of success*
>   *—For honest warmth is pleasing.*
>
> *Nay, though wedlock's your view,*   100
> *Like a rake if you'll woo,*
>   *Girls sooner quit their coldness;*
> *They know beauty inspires*
> *Less respect than desires*
>   *—Hence love is proved by boldness.*   105

Exeunt

2.2

Louisa's dressing-room

Enter Maid and Isaac

MAID Sir, my mistress will wait on you presently.

　　　Maid goes to the door°

ISAAC When she's at leisure. Don't hurry her.

　　　Exit Maid

I wish I had ever practised a love-scene. I doubt I shall make a poor
figure. I couldn't be more afraid if I was going before the Inquisition.° So! The door opens. Yes, she's coming. The very rustling   5
of her silks has a disdainful sound.

　　　Enter the Duenna, dressed as Louisa

Now daren't I look round for the soul of me.° Her beauty will
certainly strike me dumb if I do. I wish she'd speak first.

DUENNA Sir, I attend your pleasure.

ISAAC (*aside*) So! The ice is broke, and a pretty civil beginning too!—   10
Hem! Madam—Miss—I'm all attention.

DUENNA Nay, sir, 'tis I who should listen, and you propose.

ISAAC [*aside*] Egad, this isn't so disdainful neither. I believe I may
venture to look. No, I daren't; one glance of those roguish sparklers
would fix me again.   15

DUENNA You seem thoughtful, sir. Let me persuade you to sit down.

ISAAC (*aside*) So, so; she mollifies apace.° She's struck with my figure;
this attitude° has had its effect.

DUENNA Come, sir, here's a chair.

ISAAC Madam, the greatness of your goodness overpowers me. That   20
a lady so lovely should deign to turn her beauteous eyes on one so.°

　　　The Duenna takes his hand. Isaac turns and sees her

DUENNA You seem surprised at my condescension.°

ISAAC Why, yes, madam, I am a little surprised at—at—(*Aside*)
Zounds, this can never be Louisa! She's as old as my mother.

DUENNA But former prepossessions give way to my father's   25
commands.

ISAAC (*aside*) Her father! Yes, 'tis she then. Lord, lord, how blind some
parents are!

DUENNA Signor Isaac.

ISAAC [*aside*] Truly, the little damsel was right; she has rather a   30
matronly air indeed! Ah, 'tis well my affections are fixed on her
fortune and not her person.

DUENNA Signor Isaac, won't you sit?
The Duenna sits
ISAAC Pardon me, madam, I have scarce recovered my astonishment
at—your condescension, madam. (*Aside*) She has the devil's own   35
dimples, to be sure.
DUENNA Nay, you shall not stand.
Isaac sits
I do not wonder, sir, that you are surprised at my affability. I
own, signor, that I was vastly prepossessed against you; and,
being teased° by my father, I did give some encouragement to   40
Antonio. But then, sir, you were described to me as a quite differ-
ent person.
ISAAC Ay, and so you were to me, upon my soul, madam.
DUENNA But when I saw you, I was never more struck in my life.
ISAAC That was just my case too, madam; I was struck all of a heap,°   45
for my part.
DUENNA Well, sir, I see our misapprehension has been mutual. You
expected to find me haughty and averse, and I was taught to believe
you a little black snub-nosed fellow, without person, manners or
address.   50
ISAAC (*aside*) Egad, I wish she had answered her picture as well.
DUENNA But, sir, your air° is noble; something so liberal in your carriage,° with so penetrating an eye, and so bewitching a smile.
ISAAC (*aside*) I'faith, now I look at her again, I don't think she is so
ugly.   55
DUENNA So little like a Jew, and so much like a gentleman.
ISAAC [*aside*] Well, there certainly *is* something pleasing in the tone of
her voice.
DUENNA You will pardon this breach of decorum in my praising you
thus, but my joy at being so agreeably deceived has given me such   60
a flow of spirits.
ISAAC O dear lady, may I thank those sweet lips for this goodness.
(*Kisses the Duenna*) (*Aside*) Why, she has a pretty sort of velvet
down; that's the truth on't.
DUENNA O sir, you have the most insinuating° manner. But indeed   65
you should get rid of that odious beard; one might as well kiss a
hedgehog.
ISAAC Yes, ma'am. (*Aside*) The razor wouldn't be amiss for either of
us.—Could you favour me with a song?
DUENNA Willingly, sir, though I am rather hoarse. Ahem!   70
The Duenna begins to sing

ISAAC [*aside*] Very like a Virginia nightingale!—Ma'am, I perceive
you're hoarse; I beg you will not distress—
DUENNA O not in the least distressed. Now, sir. [*Sings*]

SONG

When a tender maid°
Is first essayed°   75
By some admiring swain,
How her blushes rise,
If she meets his eyes,
While he unfolds his pain.
If he takes her hand, she trembles quite;   80
Touch her lips, and she swoons outright,
           While a pit-a-pat, etc.,
Her heart avows her fright.°

But in time appear
Fewer signs of fear;   85
The youth she boldly views.
If her hand he grasp,
Or her bosom clasp,
No mantling blush ensues.
Then to church, well pleased, the lovers move,   90
While her smiles her contentment prove,
           And pit-a-pat, etc.
Her heart avows her love.

ISAAC Charming, ma'am! Enchanting! And truly your notes put me
in mind of one that's very dear to me, a lady indeed whom you   95
greatly resemble.
DUENNA How! Is there then another so dear to you?
ISAAC O, no, ma'am, you mistake me!
DUENNA No, no! You offer me your hand; then another has your heart.
ISAAC O lud! No, ma'am! 'Twas my mother I meant, as I hoped to be   100
saved.
DUENNA What, sir! Am I like your mother?
ISAAC Stay, dear ma'am! I meant that you put me in mind of what my
mother was when a girl! Yes, yes, ma'am; my mother was formerly
a great beauty, I assure you. And when she married my father about   105
thirty years ago, as you may perhaps remember, ma'am—
DUENNA I, sir! I remember thirty years ago?
ISAAC O good lack! No, ma'am! Thirty years! No, no, ma'am; it was

thirty months I said. Yes, yes, ma'am, thirty months ago on her marriage with my father, who was, as I was saying, a great beauty; but, catching cold the year afterwards in child-bed of your humble servant— 110

DUENNA Of *you*, sir, and married within these thirty months?

ISAAC [*aside*] O the devil, I've made myself out but a year old!

DUENNA Come, sir, I see you are amazed and confounded at my condescension and know not what to say. 115

ISAAC It is very true indeed, ma'am. But it is a judgement;° I look on it as a judgement on me for delaying to urge the time when you'll permit me to complete my happiness, by acquainting Don Jerome with your condescension. 120

DUENNA Sir, I must frankly own to you that I can never be yours with my father's consent.

ISAAC Good lack! How so?

DUENNA When my father in his passion swore he would not see me again till I acquiesced in his will, I also made a vow that I would never take a husband from his hand. Nothing shall make me break that oath. But if you have spirit and contrivance enough to carry me off without his knowledge, I'm yours. 125

ISAAC Hum!

DUENNA Nay, sir, if you hesitate— 130

ISAAC (*aside*) I'faith, no bad whim this. If I take her at her word, I shall secure her fortune, and avoid making any settlement° in return. Thus I shall not only cheat the lover but the father too. O, cunning rogue, Isaac! Ay, ay, let this little brain alone.° Egad, I'll take her in the mind.° 135

DUENNA Well, sir, what's your determination?

ISAAC Madam, I was dumb only from rapture. I applaud your spirit, and joyfully close with your proposal; for which thus let me, on this lily hand, express my gratitude.

Isaac kisses the Duenna's hand

DUENNA Well, sir, you must get my father's consent to walk with me in the garden. But by no means inform him of my kindness to you. 140

ISAAC No, to be sure; that would spoil all. But trust me when tricking is the word. Let me alone for a piece of cunning. This very day you shall be out of his power.

DUENNA Well, I leave the management of it all to you. I perceive plainly, sir, that you are not one that can be easily outwitted. 145

ISAAC Egad, you're right, madam; you're right, i'faith.

Enter Maid

MAID Here's a gentleman at the door, who begs permission to speak with Signor Isaac.

ISAAC O, a friend of mine, ma'am, and a trusty friend. Let him come   150
in.
  Exit Maid
He is one to be depended on, ma'am.
  Enter Carlos
(*Aside to Carlos*) So, coz.°

CARLOS I have left Donna Clara safe at your lodgings, but can nowhere find Antonio.   155

ISAAC Well, I will search him out myself anon. Carlos, you rogue, I thrive, I prosper.°

CARLOS Where is your mistress?

ISAAC There, you booby, there she stands.

CARLOS Why, she's damned ugly.   160

ISAAC (*stops his mouth*) Hush!

DUENNA What is your friend saying, signor?

ISAAC O ma'am, he is expressing his raptures at such charms as he never saw before.—Hey, Carlos?

CARLOS Ay, such as I never saw before, indeed.   165

DUENNA You are a very obliging gentleman.—Well, Signor Isaac, I believe we had better part for the present. Remember our plan.

ISAAC O, ma'am, it is written in my heart, fixed as the image of those divine beauties. Adieu, idol of my soul. Yet, once more permit me.   170
  Issac kisses the Duenna

DUENNA Sweet, courteous sir, adieu.

ISAAC Your slave eternally.—Come, Carlos, say something civil at taking leave.

CARLOS [*aside to Isaac*] I'faith, Isaac, she is the hardest woman to compliment I ever saw. However, I'll try something I had studied   175
for the occasion. [*Sings*]

SONG

Ah, sure a pair was never seen,°
So justly formed to meet by nature—
The youth excelling so in mien,
The maid in every grace of feature.   180
O how happy are such lovers,
When kindred beauties each discovers.°
For surely she

> *Was made for thee,*
> *And thou to bless this lovely creature.*   185

> *So mild your looks, your children thence*
> *Will early learn the task of duty—*
> *The boys with all their father's sense,*
> *The girls with all their mother's beauty.*
> *O, how charming to inherit*   190
> *At once such graces and such spirit.*
> *Thus while you live*
> *May fortune give*
> *Each blessing equal to your merit.*

Exeunt

2.3

A library in Don Jerome's house

Don Jerome and Ferdinand discovered

JEROME Object to Antonio?° I have said it! His poverty—can you acquit him of that?

FERDINAND Sir, I own he is not over-rich; but he is of as ancient and as reputable a family as any in the kingdom.

JEROME Yes, I know the beggars are a very ancient family in most   5
kingdoms, but never in any great repute, boy.

FERDINAND Antonio, sir, has many amiable qualities.

JEROME But he is poor. Can you clear him of that, I say? Is he not a gay, dissipated rake, who has squandered his patrimony?

FERDINAND Sir, he inherited but little; and that his generosity,° more   10
than his profuseness, has stripped him of. But he has never sullied his honour, which, with his title, has outlived his means.

JEROME Pshaw! You talk like a blockhead! Nobility without an estate is as ridiculous as gold-lace on a frieze-coat.°

FERDINAND This language, sir, would better become a Dutch or   15
English trader° than a Spaniard.

JEROME Yes; and those Dutch and English traders, as you call them, are the wiser people. Why, booby, in England they were formerly as nice as to° birth and family as we are; but they have long discovered what a wonderful purifier gold is, and now no one there   20
regards pedigree in anything but a horse.

FERDINAND True, sir; and the consequence is, that a nobleman is surer of the breed of his pony than the legitimacy of his heir.

JEROME Ferdinand, I insist on it that this subject be dropped once for all. O, here comes Isaac! I hope he has prospered in his suit.   25

FERDINAND Doubtless, that agreeable figure of his must have helped his cause surprisingly.

JEROME How now?

Ferdinand walks aside. Enter Isaac

Well, my friend, have you softened her?   30

ISAAC O yes; I have softened her.

JEROME What, does she come to?°

ISAAC Why, truly, she was kinder than I expected to find her.

JEROME And the dear pretty little angel was civil, hey!

ISAAC Yes, the pretty little angel was very civil.   35

JEROME I'm transported to hear it. Well, and you were astonished at her beauty, hey?

ISAAC I was astonished indeed! Pray, how old is Miss?

JEROME How old? Let me see—eight and twelve—she is just twenty.

ISAAC Twenty?   40

JEROME Ay, to a month.

ISAAC Then, upon my soul, she is the oldest-looking girl of her age in Christendom.

JEROME Do you think so? But I believe you will not see a prettier girl.

ISAAC Here and there one.   45

JEROME Louisa has the family face.

ISAAC (*half aside*) Yes, egad, I should have taken it for a family face, and one that has been in the family some time too.

JEROME She has her father's eyes.

ISAAC Truly, I should have guessed them to have been so. (*Aside*) And   50
if she had her mother's spectacles, I believe she would not see the worse.

JEROME Her Aunt Ursula's nose, and her grandmother's forehead to a hair.

ISAAC (*aside*) Ay, faith, and her grandfather's chin to a hair.   55

JEROME Well, if she was but as dutiful as she's handsome! And harkee, friend Isaac. She is none of your made-up° beauties; her charms are of the lasting kind.

ISAAC I'faith, so they should; for if she be but twenty now, she may double her age before her years will overtake her face.   60

JEROME Why, zounds, master Isaac, you are not sneering, are you?

ISAAC Why, now seriously, Don Jerome, do you think your daughter handsome!

JEROME By this light, she's as handsome a girl as any in Seville.

ISAAC Then, by these eyes, I think her as plain a woman as ever I beheld.   65

JEROME By St Iago, you must be blind.

ISAAC No, no; 'tis you are partial.

JEROME How! Have I neither sense nor taste? If a fair skin, fine eyes, teeth of ivory, with a lovely bloom and a delicate shape—if these, with a heavenly voice, and a world of grace, are not charms, I know   70 not what you call beautiful.

ISAAC Good lack, with what eyes a father sees! As I have life, she is the very reverse of all this. As for the dimity skin you told me of, I swear 'tis a thorough nankeen as ever I saw. For her eyes, their utmost merit is in not squinting. For her teeth, where there is one   75 of ivory, its neighbour is pure ebony, black and white alternately, just like the keys of an harpsichord. Then, as to her singing and heavenly voice, by this hand, she has a shrill cracked pipe, that sounds for all the world like a child's trumpet.

JEROME Why, you little Hebrew scoundrel, do you mean to insult me?   80 Out of my house; out, I say!

FERDINAND [joining them] Dear sir, what's the matter?

JEROME Why, this Israelite here has the impudence to say your sister's ugly.

FERDINAND He must be either blind or insolent.   85

ISAAC (aside) So, I find they are all in a story.° Egad, I believe I have gone too far.

FERDINAND Sure, sir, there must be some mistake. It can't be my sister whom he has seen.

JEROME 'Sdeath, you are as great a fool as he. What mistake can there   90 be? Did not I lock up Louisa myself, and haven't I the key in my own pocket? And didn't her maid show him into the dressing-room? And yet you talk of a mistake. No, the Portuguese meant to insult me; and, but that this roof protects him, old as I am, this sword should do me justice.   95

ISAAC (aside) I must get off° as well as I can. Her fortune is not the less handsome.

ISAAC and DON JEROME [sing]

DUET

ISAAC   *Believe me, good sir, I ne'er meant to offend.°*
           My mistress I love, and I value my friend.

	To win her, and wed her, is still my request—	100
	For better, for worse, and I swear I don't jest.	
JEROME	*Zounds, you'd best not provoke me; my rage is so high.*	
ISAAC	*Hold him fast, I beseech you; his rage is so high.*	
	Good sir, you're too hot, and this place I must fly.	
JEROME	*You're a knave and a sot, and this place you'd best fly.*	105

ISAAC Don Jerome, come now; let us lay aside all joking and be serious.

JEROME How?

ISAAC Ha, ha, ha! I'll be hanged if you haven't taken my abuse of your daughter seriously.

JEROME You meant it so, did not you?   110

ISAAC O mercy, no! A joke! Just to try how angry it would make you.

JEROME Was that all, i'faith! I didn't know you had been such a wag. Ha, ha, ha! By St Iago, you made me very angry, though. Well, and you do think Louisa handsome?

ISAAC Handsome! Venus de' Medici° was a sibyl to her.   115

JEROME Give me your hand, you little jocose rogue. Egad, I thought we had been all off.

FERDINAND [*aside*] So! I was in hopes this would have been a quarrel; but I find the Jew is too cunning.

JEROME Ay, this gust of passion has made me dry. I am but seldom   120 ruffled. Order some wine in the next room; let us drink the girl's health. Poor Louisa! Ugly, hey! Ha, ha, ha! 'Twas a very good joke indeed.

ISAAC (*aside*) And a very true one for all that.

JEROME And, Ferdinand, I insist upon your drinking success to my   125 friend.

FERDINAND Sir, I will drink success to my friend with all my heart.

JEROME Come, little Solomon. If any sparks of anger had remained, this would be the only way to quench them.

DON JEROME, ISAAC, and FERDINAND [*sing*]

TRIO

> *A bumper of good liquor°*   130
> *Will end a contest quicker*
> *Than justice, judge or vicar.*
> > *So fill a cheerful glass,*
> > *And let good humour pass.*
>
> *But if more deep the quarrel,*   135
> *Why, sooner drain the barrel*

> *Than be the hateful fellow*
> *That's crabbed when he is mellow.*°
>   *A bumper, etc.*

Exeunt

2.4

Isaac's lodgings

Enter Louisa

LOUISA Was ever truant daughter so whimsically circumstanced as I
am! I have sent my intended husband to look after° my lover; the
man of my father's choice is gone to bring me the man of my own.
But how dispiriting is this interval of expectation! [*Sings*]

SONG

> *What bard, O time discover,*°   5
>   *With wings first made thee move?*°
> *Ah, sure he was some lover,*
>   *Who ne'er had left his love.*
>
> *For what that once did prove*°
>   *The pangs which absence brings,*   10
>   *Though but one day*
>   *He were away,*
>   *Could picture thee with wings.*

Enter Carlos

So, friend, is Antonio found?

CARLOS I could not meet with him, lady; but I doubt not my friend   15
Isaac will be here with him presently.

LOUISA O shame! You have used no diligence. Is this your courtesy to
a lady who has trusted herself to your protection?

CARLOS Indeed, madam, I have not been remiss.

LOUISA Well, well; but if either of you had known how each moment   20
of delay weighs upon the heart of her who loves, and waits the
object of her love, O, ye would not then have trifled thus.

CARLOS Alas, I know it well.

LOUISA Were you ever in love then?

CARLOS I was, lady—but, while I have life, will never be again.   25

LOUISA Was your mistress so cruel?

CARLOS If she had always been so, I should have been happier.
    [*Sings*]

SONG

> *O had my love ne'er smiled on me,°*
>   *I ne'er had known such anguish;*
> *But think how false, how cruel she,*   30
>   *To bid me cease to languish—*
> *To bid me hope her hand to gain,*
>   *Breathe on a flame half-perished,*
> *And then with cold and fixed disdain*
>   *To kill the hope she cherished.*   35
>
> *Not worse his fate, who on a wreck,*
>   *That drove as winds did blow it,*
> *Silent had left the shattered deck,*
>   *To find a grave below it.*
> *Then land was cried. No more resigned,°*   40
>   *He glowed with joy to hear it.*
> *Not worse his fate, his woe, to find*
>   *The wreck must sink ere near it.*

LOUISA As I live, here is your friend coming with Antonio. I'll retire
    for a moment to surprise him.   45
        Exit Louisa. Enter Isaac and Antonio

ANTONIO Indeed, my friend Isaac, you must be mistaken. Clara
    D'Almanza in love with me, and employ you to bring me to meet
    her! It is impossible!

ISAAC That you shall see in an instant.—Carlos, where is the lady?
        Carlos points to the doors°
    In the next room is she?   50

ANTONIO Nay, if that lady is really here, she certainly wants me to
    conduct her to a dear friend of mine, who has long been her lover.

ISAAC Pshaw! I tell you 'tis no such thing. You are the man she wants,
    and nobody but you. Here's ado to persuade you to take a pretty
    girl that's dying for you.   55

ANTONIO But I have no affection for this lady.

ISAAC And you have for Louisa, hey? But take my word for it, Antonio,
    you have no chance there; so you may as well secure the good that
    offers itself to you.

ANTONIO And could you reconcile it to your conscience, to supplant   60
    your friend?

ISAAC Pish! Conscience has no more to do with gallantry° than it has
with politics. Why, you are no honest fellow, if love can't make a
rogue of you. So come; do go in and speak to her at least.

ANTONIO Well, I have no objection to that.   65
    Isaac opens the door

ISAAC There, there she is, yonder by the window. Get in, do.
    Isaac pushes Antonio in and half shuts the door
Now, Carlos, now I shall hamper him, I warrant. Stay. I'll peep how
they go on. Egad, he looks confoundedly posed. Now she's coaxing
him. See, Carlos, he begins to come to. Ay, ay, he'll soon forget his
conscience.   70

CARLOS Look! Now they are both laughing.

ISAAC Ay! So they are, both laughing. Yes, yes, they are laughing at that
dear friend we talked of. Ay, poor devil, they have outwitted him.

CARLOS Now he's kissing her hand.

ISAAC Yes, yes, faith, they're agreed. He's caught, he's entangled. My   75
dear Carlos, we have brought it about. O, this little cunning head!
I'm a Machiavel, a very Machiavel.

CARLOS I hear somebody inquiring for you. I'll see who it is.
    Exit Carlos. Enter Antonio and Louisa

ANTONIO Well, my good friend, this lady has so entirely convinced
me of the certainty of your success at Don Jerome's that I now   80
resign my pretensions there.

ISAAC You never did a wiser thing, believe me. And as for deceiving
your friend, that's nothing at all. Tricking is all fair in love, isn't it,
ma'am?

LOUISA Certainly, sir, and I am particularly glad to find you are of that   85
opinion.

ISAAC O lud, yes, ma'am; let anyone outwit me that can, I say. But
here, let me join your hands. There, you lucky rogue, I wish you
happily married from the bottom of my soul.

LOUISA And I am sure, if you wish it, no one else should prevent it.   90

ISAAC Now, Antonio, we are rivals no more; so let us be friends, will
you?

ANTONIO With all my heart, Isaac.

ISAAC It is not every man, let me tell you, that would have taken such
pains, or been so generous to a rival.   95

ANTONIO No, faith, I don't believe there's another beside yourself in
Spain.

ISAAC Well, but you resign all pretensions to the other lady?

ANTONIO That I do most sincerely.

ISAAC I doubt you have a little hankering there still.   100

ANTONIO None in the least, upon my soul.

ISAAC I mean after her fortune?

ANTONIO No, believe me. You are heartily welcome to everything she has.

ISAAC Well, i'faith, you have the best of the bargain as to beauty,   105
twenty to one. Now I'll tell you a secret. I am to carry off Louisa this very evening.

LOUISA Indeed!

ISAAC Yes, she has sworn not to take a husband from her father's hand.
So, I've persuaded him to trust her to walk with me in the garden,   110
and then we shall give him the slip.

LOUISA And is Don Jerome to know nothing of this?

ISAAC O lud, no: there lies the jest! Don't you see that, by this step, I
overreach him? I shall be entitled to the girl's fortune without
settling a ducat on her! Ha, ha, ha! I'm a cunning dog, a'n't I? A sly   115
little villain, hey?

ANTONIO Ha, ha, ha! You are indeed!

ISAAC Roguish, you'll say; but keen, hey? Devilish keen!

ANTONIO So you are indeed; keen, very keen.

ISAAC And what a laugh we shall have at Don Jerome's, when the truth   120
comes out, hey?

LOUISA Yes, I'll answer for't; we shall have a good laugh when the
truth comes out. Ha, ha, ha!
        Enter Carlos

CARLOS Here are the dancers come to practise the fandango you
intended to have honoured Donna Louisa with.   125

ISAAC O, I shan't want them; but as I must pay them, I'll see a caper°
for my money. Will you excuse me?

LOUISA Willingly.

ISAAC Here's my friend, whom you may command for any services.
Madam, your most obedient.—Antonio, I wish you all happiness.   130
[*Aside*] O the easy blockhead! What a fool I have made of him! This
was a masterpiece.
        Exit Isaac

LOUISA Carlos, will you be my guard again, and conduct me to the
convent of St Catherine?

ANTONIO Why, Louisa, why should you go thither?   135

LOUISA I have my reasons, and you must not be seen to go with me.
I shall write from thence to my father. Perhaps, when he finds what
he has driven me to, he may relent.

ANTONIO I have no hope from him. O Louisa, in these arms should
be your sanctuary.   140

LOUISA Be patient but for a little while; my father cannot force me
thence. But let me see you there before evening, and I will explain
myself.

ANTONIO I shall obey.

LOUISA [*to Carlos*] Come, friend.—Antonio, Carlos has been a lover   145
himself.

ANTONIO Then he knows the value of his trust.

CARLOS You shall not find me unfaithful.

LOUISA, ANTONIO, and CARLOS [*sing*]

TRIO

> *Soft pity never leaves the gentle breast,*°
> *Where love has been received a welcome guest.*
> *As wandering saints poor huts have sacred made,*
> *He hallows every heart he once has swayed;*°
> *And when his presence we no longer share,*
> *Still leaves compassion as a relic there.*°

150

Exeunt

3.1

A library in Don Jerome's house

Enter Don Jerome and Servant

JEROME Why, I never was so amazed in my life! Lousia gone off with
Isaac Mendoza! What, steal away with the very man whom I
wanted her to marry! Elope with her own husband, as it were! It is
impossible.

SERVANT Her maid says, sir, they had your leave to walk in the garden   5
while you was abroad. The door by the shrubbery was found open,
and they have not been heard of since.

Exit Servant

JEROME Well, it is the most unaccountable affair! 'Sdeath, there is certainly some infernal mystery in it I can't comprehend.

Enter Second Servant, with a letter

SECOND SERVANT Here is a letter, sir, from Signor Isaac.   10

Exit Second Servant

JEROME So, so, this will explain. Ay, 'Isaac Mendoza'. Let me see.
(*Reads*) 'Dearest sir, you must, doubtless, be much surprised at my
flight with your daughter.' Yes, faith, and well I may. 'I had the happiness to gain her heart at our first interview.' The devil you had!
'But she having unfortunately made a vow not to receive a husband   15
from your hands, I was obliged to comply with her whim.' So, so!
'We shall shortly throw ourselves at your feet,° and I hope you will
have a blessing ready for one who will then be—Your son-in-law,
Isaac Mendoza.' A whim, hey? Why, the devil's in the girl, I think.
This morning she would die sooner than have him, and before   20
evening she runs away with him. Well, well, my will's accomplished,
let the motive be what it will; and the Portuguese, sure, will never
deny to fulfil the rest of the article.°

Enter Servant with another letter

SERVANT Sir, here's a man below who says he brought this from my
young lady, Donna Louisa.   25

Exit Servant

JEROME How! Yes, it is my daughter's hand indeed! Lord, there was
no occasion for them both to write. Well, let's see what she says.
(*Reads*) 'My dearest father, how shall I entreat your pardon for the
rash step I have taken, how confess the motive?' Pish! Hasn't Isaac
just told me the motive! One would think they weren't together,   30

when they wrote. 'If I have a spirit too resentful of ill usage, I have also a heart as easily affected by kindness.' So, so. Here the whole matter comes out. Her resentment for Antonio's ill usage has made her sensible of Isaac's kindness. Yes, yes, it is all plain enough. Well. 'I am not married yet, though with a man I am convinced adores me.' Yes, yes, I dare say Isaac is very fond of her. 'But I shall anxiously expect your answer, in which, should I be so fortunate as to receive your consent, you will make completely happy—Your ever affectionate daughter, Louisa.' My consent! To be sure she shall have it. Egad, I was never better pleased. I have fulfilled my resolution. I knew I should. O there's nothing like obstinacy. (*Calls*) Lewis!

> *Enter Servant*

Let the man who brought the last letter wait, and get me a pen and ink below.

> *Exit Servant*

I am impatient to set poor Louisa's heart at rest. Holloa! Lewis! Sancho!

> *Enter Servants*

See that there be a noble supper provided in the saloon tonight. Serve up my best wines, and let me have music, d'ye hear?

SERVANTS Yes, sir.

JEROME And order all my doors to be thrown open. Admit all guests with masks or without masks.°

> *Exeunt Servants*

I'faith, we'll have a night of it. And I'll let 'em see how merry an old man can be. [*Sings*]

SONG

> O the days when I was young,°
>> When I laughed in fortune's spite,
> Talked of love the whole day long,
>> And with nectar crowned the night,°
> Then it was, old Father Care,
>> Little recked I of thy frown;°
> Half thy malice youth could bear,
>> And the rest a bumper drown.
>
> Truth, they say, lies in a well;°
>> Why, I vow, I ne'er could see.
> Let the water-drinkers tell;
>> There it always lay for me.°

> For when sparkling wine went round,
>   Never saw I falsehood's mask,
> But still honest truth I found
>   In the bottom of each flask.

> True, at length my vigour's flown;   70
>   I have years to bring decay.
> Few the locks that now I own,
>   And the few I have are grey.
> Yet, old Jerome, thou may'st boast,
>   While thy spirits do not tire,   75
> Still beneath thy age's frost
>   Glows a spark of youthful fire.

Exit

3.2

The piazza°

Enter Ferdinand and Lopez

FERDINAND What, could you gather no tidings of her? Nor guess where she was gone? O Clara! Clara!

LOPEZ In truth, sir, I could not. That she was run away from her father was in everybody's mouth; and that Don Guzman was in pursuit of her was also a very common report. Where she was   5
gone, or what was become of her, no one could take upon 'em to say.

FERDINAND 'Sdeath and fury, you blockhead, she can't be out of Seville.

LOPEZ So I said to myself, sir! ''Sdeath and fury, you blockhead', says   10
I, 'she can't be out of Seville'. Then some said she had hanged herself for love, and others have it° Don Antonio had carried her off.

FERDINAND 'Tis false, scoundrel! No one said that.

LOPEZ Then I misunderstood 'em, sir.   15

FERDINAND Go, fool, get home, and never let me see you again, till you bring me news of her.

        Exit Lopez

O, how my fondness for this ungrateful girl has hurt my disposition! [*Sings*]

SONG

Ah, cruel maid, how hast thou changed°   20
  The temper of my mind?
My heart by thee from mirth estranged
  Becomes, like thee, unkind.
By fortune favoured, clear in fame,°
  I once ambitious was;   25
And friends I had, that fanned the flame
  And gave my youth applause.

But now my weakness all abuse,
  Yet vain their taunts on me;
Friends, fortune, fame itself I'd lose,   30
  To gain one smile from thee.
Yet only thou shouldst not despise
  My folly or my woe;
If I am mad in others' eyes,
  'Tis thou hast made me so.   35

But days like these, with doubting cursed,
  I will not long endure.
Am I despised? I know the worst,
  And also know my cure.
If, false, her vows she dare renounce,   40
  She instant ends my pain;
For, O, that heart must break at once,
  Which cannot hate again.°

    Enter Isaac
ISAAC [*aside*] So, I have her safe and have only to find a priest to marry
  us. Antonio now may marry Clara, or not, if he pleases.   45
FERDINAND What? What was that you said of Clara?
ISAAC O Ferdinand, my brother-in-law that shall be! Who thought of
  meeting you!
FERDINAND But what of Clara?
ISAAC I'faith, you shall hear. This morning, as I was coming down, I   50
  met a pretty damsel, who told me her name was Clara D'Almanza
  and begged my protection.
FERDINAND How?
ISAAC She said she had eloped from her father, Don Guzman, but that
  love for a young gentleman in Seville was the cause.   55
FERDINAND O heavens, did she confess it?

ISAAC O yes, she confessed at once. 'But then', says she, 'my lover is not informed of my flight, nor suspects my intention'.

FERDINAND (*aside*) Dear creature! No more I did indeed! O, I am the happiest fellow.—Well, Isaac!   60

ISAAC Why, then she entreated me to find him out for her and bring him to her.

FERDINAND Good heavens, how lucky! (*Pulling him*) Well, come along! Let's lose no time!

ISAAC Zooks! Where are we to go?   65

FERDINAND Why, did anything more pass?°

ISAAC Anything more! Yes, the end on't was, that I was moved by her speeches and complied with her desires.

FERDINAND Well, and where is she?

ISAAC Where is she? Why, don't I tell you I complied with her request 70
and left her safe in the arms of her lover?

FERDINAND 'Sdeath, you trifle with me! I have never seen her.

ISAAC You! O lud, no! How the devil should you? 'Twas Antonio she wanted, and with Antonio I left her.

FERDINAND (*aside*) Hell and madness.—What, Antonio D'Ercilla?   75

ISAAC Ay, ay, the very man; and the best part of it was, he was shy of taking her at first. He talked a good deal about honour and conscience and deceiving some dear friend; but, lord, we soon overruled that.

FERDINAND You did?   80

ISAAC O yes, presently. 'Such deceit', says he. 'Pish!', says the lady, 'tricking is all fair in love'. 'But then, my friend', says he. 'Pshaw! Damn your friend!', says I. So, poor wretch, he has no chance; no, no, he may hang himself as soon as he pleases.

FERDINAND (*aside*) I must go, or I shall betray myself.   85

ISAAC But stay, Ferdinand. You ha'n't heard the best of the joke.

FERDINAND Curse on your joke.

ISAAC Goodlack! What's the matter now? I thought to have diverted you.

FERDINAND Be racked!—tortured!—damned!   90

ISAAC Why, sure you're not the poor devil of a lover, are you? [*Aside*] I'faith, as sure as can be, he is. This is a better joke than t'other. Ha, ha, ha!

FERDINAND What, do you laugh, you vile, mischievous varlet? (*Collars him*) But that you're beneath my anger, I'd tear your heart 95
out.

Ferdinand throws Isaac from him

ISAAC O mercy! Here's usage for a brother-in-law!

FERDINAND But harkee, rascal! Tell me directly where these false friends are gone, or by my soul—

Ferdinand draws his sword

ISAAC For heaven's sake, now, my dear brother-in-law, don't be in a   100
rage! I'll recollect as well as I can.

FERDINAND Be quick then!

ISAAC I will, I will! But people's memories differ. Some have a treacherous memory; now mine is a cowardly memory. It takes to its heels
at sight of a drawn sword—it does, i'faith!—and I could as soon   105
fight as recollect.

FERDINAND Zounds, tell me the truth, and I won't hurt you.

ISAAC No, no; I know you won't, my dear brother-in-law. But that ill-
looking thing there—

FERDINAND What, then, you won't tell me?   110

ISAAC Yes, yes, I will; I'll tell you all upon my soul. But why need you
listen, sword in hand?

FERDINAND Well, there now.

Ferdinand puts up his sword

ISAAC Why then, I believe they are gone to—that is, my friend Carlos
told me he had left Donna Clara—dear Ferdinand, keep your hand   115
off—at the convent of St Catherine.

FERDINAND St Catherine!

ISAAC Yes; and that Antonio was to come to her there.

FERDINAND Is this the truth?

ISAAC It is indeed; and all I know, as I hope for life!   120

FERDINAND Well, coward, take your life. 'Tis that false, dishonourable Antonio, who shall feel my vengeance.

ISAAC Ay, ay, kill him! Cut his throat and welcome!

FERDINAND But, for Clara, infamy on her! She is not worth my
resentment.   125

ISAAC No more she is, my dear brother-in-law. I'faith, I would not be
angry about her; she is not worth it indeed.

FERDINAND 'Tis false; she is worth the enmity of princes.

ISAAC True, true; so she is, and I pity you exceedingly for having lost
her.   130

FERDINAND 'Sdeath, you rascal, how durst you talk of pitying me!

ISAAC O dear brother-in-law, I beg pardon; I don't pity you in the
least, upon my soul.

FERDINAND Get hence, you fool, and provoke me no further. Nothing
but your insignificance saves you.   135

ISAAC (*aside*) I'faith, then my insignificance is the best friend I have. [*Aloud*] I'm going, dear Ferdinand. [*Aside*] What a curst, hotheaded bully it is!

    Exit Isaac

FERDINAND From this hour I disclaim all trust in man, or love for woman. But does Antonio think to triumph with impunity, when 140 he has left me no hope of joy on earth, but in revenge. [*Sings*]

SONG

    Sharp is the woe that wounds the jealous mind,°
      When treachery two fond hearts would rend;
    But O, how keener far the pang to find
      That traitor is our bosom friend.   145

    Exit

3.3

    The garden of the convent
    Enter Louisa and Clara

LOUISA And you really wish my brother may not find you out?

CLARA Why else have I concealed myself under this disguise?

LOUISA Why, perhaps, because the dress becomes you, for you certainly don't intend to be a nun for life.

CLARA If, indeed, Ferdinand had not offended me so last night.   5

LOUISA Come, come, it was his fear of losing you made him so rash.

CLARA Well, you may think me cruel, but I swear, if he were here this instant, I believe I should forgive him. [*Sings*]

SONG

    By him we love offended,°
      How soon our anger flies;   10
    One day apart, 'tis ended—
      Behold him and it dies.

    Last night your roving brother
      Enraged I bade depart;
    And sure his rude presumption   15
      Deserved to lose my heart.

    Yet, were he now before me,
      In spite of injured pride,

> *I fear my eyes would pardon,*
> > *Before my tongue could chide.*   20
>
> *With truth the bold deceiver*
> > *To me thus oft has said:*
> *'In vain would Clara slight me,*
> > *In vain would she upbraid.*
>
> *'No scorn those lips discover,*   25
> > *Where dimples laugh the while;*
> *No frowns appear resentful,*
> > *Where heaven has stamped a smile.'*

LOUISA I protest, Clara, I shall begin to think you are seriously resolved to enter on your probation.°   30

CLARA And, seriously, I very much doubt whether the character of a nun would not become me best.

LOUISA Why, to be sure, the character of a nun is a very becoming one, at a masquerade; but no pretty woman in her senses ever thought of taking the veil for above a night.   35

CLARA Yonder I see your Antonio is returned. I shall only interrupt you. Ah, Louisa, with what happy eagerness you turn to look for him!

> *Exit Clara. Enter Antonio*

ANTONIO Well, my Louisa, any news since I left you?

LOUISA None. The messenger is not returned from my father.   40

ANTONIO Well, I confess I do not perceive what we are to expect from him.

LOUISA I shall be easier, however, in having made the trial. I do not doubt your sincerity, Antonio; but there is a chilling air around poverty that often kills affection that was not nursed in it. If we   45
would make love our household god, we had best secure him a comfortable roof. [*Sings*]

SONG

> *How oft, Louisa, hast thou said°*
> > *(Nor wilt thou the fond boast disown)*
> *Thou wouldst not lose Antonio's love*   50
> > *To reign the partner of a throne.*
>
> *And by those lips that spoke so kind,*
> > *And by this hand I pressed to mine,*
> *To be the lord of wealth and power,*
> > *I swear I would not part with thine.*   55

> *Then how, my soul, can we be poor*
> *Who own what kingdoms could not buy?*
> *Of this true heart thou shalt be queen,*
> *And, serving thee, a monarch I.*

> *Thus, uncontrolled in mutual bliss,* 60
> *And rich in love's exhaustless mine,*
> *Do thou snatch treasures from my lips,*
> *And I'll take kingdoms back from thine.*

Enter Maid with a letter to Louisa. Exit Maid
My father's answer, I suppose.

ANTONIO My dearest Louisa, you may be assured that it contains 65
nothing but threats and reproaches.

LOUISA Let us see, however. (*Reads*) 'Dearest daughter, make your
lover happy. You have my full consent to marry as your whim has
chosen. But be sure come home to sup with your affectionate father.'

ANTONIO You jest, Louisa. 70

LOUISA (*gives him the letter*) Read, read.

ANTONIO 'Tis so, by heavens! Sure there must be some mistake. But
that's none of our business. Now, Louisa, you have no excuse for
delay.

LOUISA Shall we not then return and thank my father? 75

ANTONIO But first let the priest put it out of his power to recall his
word. I'll fly to procure one.

LOUISA Nay, if you part with me again, perhaps you may lose me.

ANTONIO Come then. There is a friar of a neighbouring convent is
my friend. You have already been diverted by the manners of a 80
nunnery; let us see whether there is less hypocrisy among the holy
fathers.

LOUISA I'm afraid not, Antonio; for in religion, as in friendship, they
who profess most are ever the least sincere.

Exeunt Louisa and Antonio. Enter Clara

CLARA So, yonder they go, as happy as a mutual and confessed 85
affection can make them, while I am left in solitude. Heigh-ho!
Love may perhaps excuse the rashness of an elopement from
one's friend; but, I am sure, nothing but the presence of the man
we love can support it.° Ha! What do I see? Ferdinand, as I live!
How could he gain admission? By potent gold, I suppose, as 90
Antonio did. How eager and disturbed he seems. He shall not know
me as yet.

Clara lets down her veil. Enter Ferdinand

FERDINAND Yes, those were certainly they. My information was right. (*Going*)

CLARA (*stops him*) Pray, signor, what is your business here?   95

FERDINAND No matter, no matter.—O, they stop. (*Looks out*) Yes, that is the perfidious Clara indeed.

CLARA (*aside*) So, a jealous error. I'm glad to see him so moved.

FERDINAND Her disguise can't conceal her. No, no, I know her too well.   100

CLARA [*aside*] Wonderful discernment! [*To Ferdinand*] But, signor—

FERDINAND Be quiet, good nun, don't tease me.—By heavens, she leans upon his arm, hangs fondly on it! O woman! woman!

CLARA But, signor, who is it you want?

FERDINAND Not you, not you. So, prithee don't torment me. Yet pray   105
stay. Gentle nun, was it not Donna Clara D'Almanza just parted from you?

CLARA Clara D'Almanza, signor, is not yet out of the garden.

FERDINAND Ay, ay, I knew I was right. And pray, is not that gentle-man now at the porch with her Antonio D'Ercilla?   110

CLARA It is indeed, signor.

FERDINAND So, so. Now but one question more. Can you inform me for what purpose they have gone away?

CLARA They are gone to be married, I believe.

FERDINAND Very well. Enough.—Now if I don't mar their wedding.   115
    Exit Ferdinand

CLARA (*unveils*) I thought jealousy had made lovers quick-sighted, but it has made mine blind. Louisa's story accounts to me for this error, and I am glad to find I have power enough over him to make him so unhappy. But why should not I be present at his surprise when undeceived? When he's through the porch I'll follow him, and,   120
perhaps, Louisa shall not singly be a bride. [*Sings*]

SONG

Adieu, thou dreary pile, where never dies°
The sullen echo of repentant sighs.
Ye sister mourners of each lonely cell,
Inured to hymns and sorrow, fare ye well.   125
For happier scenes I fly this darksome grove,
To saints a prison, but a tomb to love.

    Exit

3.4

A court° before the priory

Enter Isaac, crossing the stage. Enter Antonio

ANTONIO What, my friend Isaac!

ISAAC What, Antonio! Wish me joy! I have Louisa safe.

ANTONIO Have you? I wish you joy with all my soul.

ISAAC Yes, I am come here to procure a priest to marry us.

ANTONIO So, then we are both on the same errand. I am come to look   5
for Father Paul.

ISAAC Ha! I am glad on’t. But, i’faith, he must tack me° first; my love
is waiting.

ANTONIO So is mine; I left her in the porch.

ISAAC Ay, but I am in haste to get back to Don Jerome.   10

ANTONIO And so am I too.

ISAAC Well, perhaps he’ll save time and marry us both together. Or
I’ll be your father° and you shall be mine. Come along. But you’re
obliged to me for all this.

ANTONIO Yes, yes.   15

Exeunt

3.5

A room in the priory

*Friars [including Father Paul, Father Francis, and Father
Augustine] at a table drinking [and singing]°*

GLEE° and CHORUS

This bottle’s the sun of our table;°
  His beams are rosy wine;
We, planets that are not able
  Without his help to shine.
Let mirth and glee abound;   5
  You’ll soon grow bright
  With borrowed light,
And shine as he goes round.

PAUL Brother Francis, toss the bottle about,° and give me your toast.

FRANCIS Have we drank the abbess of St Ursuline?   10

AUGUSTINE Yes, yes; she was the last.

FRANCIS Then I'll give you the blue-eyed nun of St Catherine's.

PAUL With all my heart. (*Drinks*) Pray, Brother Augustine, were there any benefactions left in my absence?

FRANCIS Don Juan Corduba has left an hundred ducats to remember   15
him in our masses.

PAUL Has he! Let them be paid to our wine merchant, and we'll remember him in our cups, which will do just as well. Anything more?

AUGUSTINE Yes, Baptista, the rich miser, who died last week, has   20
bequeathed us a thousand pistoles, and the silver lamp he used in his own chamber, to burn before the image of St Anthony.

PAUL 'Twas well meant; but we'll employ his money better. Baptista's bounty shall light the living, not the dead. St Anthony is not afraid to be left in the dark, though he was—   25

> *A knocking* [*off-stage*]

See who's there.°

> *Father Francis goes to the door and opens it.* [*The other Friars conceal the tables, drink and food behind a curtain. Father Paul remains behind the curtain.*] *Enter Porter*°

PORTER Here's one without in pressing haste to speak with Father Paul.

AUGUSTINE Brother Paul!

> *Father Paul comes from behind the curtain with a glass of wine, and in his hand a piece of cake*

PAUL Here! How durst you, fellow, thus abruptly break in upon our   30
devotions?

PORTER I thought they were finished.

PAUL No, they were not. Were they, Brother Francis?

AUGUSTINE Not by a bottle each.

PAUL But neither you nor your fellows mark how the hours go. No,   35
you mind nothing but the gratifying of your appetites. Ye eat and swill, and sleep, and gormandize, and thrive, while we are wasting in mortification.°

PORTER We ask no more than nature craves.

PAUL 'Tis false. Ye have more appetites than hairs, and your flushed,   40
sleek, and pampered appearance is the disgrace of our order. Out on't! If you are hungry, can't you be content with the wholesome roots of the earth, and if you are dry, isn't there the crystal spring? (*Drinks*) Put this away (*gives a glass*), and show me where I'm wanted.   45

Porter drains the glass. Father Paul, going, turns
So, you would have drunk it, if there had been any left. Ah, glutton!
Glutton!
    Exeunt

3.6

The court before the priory
Enter Isaac and Antonio

ISAAC A plaguy while coming, this same Father Paul. He's detained
    at vespers, I suppose, poor fellow.
ANTONIO No, here he comes.
    Enter Father Paul
Good Father Paul, I crave your blessing.
ISAAC Yes, good Father Paul, we are come to beg a favour.   5
PAUL What is it, pray?
ISAAC To marry us, good Father Paul; and, in truth, thou dost look
    the very priest of Hymen.
PAUL In short, I may be called so; for I deal in repentance and
    mortification.   10
ISAAC No, no, thou seem'st an officer of Hymen, because thy pres-
    ence speaks content and good humour.
PAUL Alas, my appearance is deceitful. Bloated I am, indeed, for
    fasting is a windy recreation, and it hath swollen me like a bladder.
ANTONIO But thou hast a good fresh colour in thy face, father. Rosy,   15
    i'faith!
PAUL Yes, I have blushed for mankind, till the hue of my shame is as
    fixed as their vices.
ISAAC Good man!
PAUL And I have laboured too. But to what purpose? They continue   20
    to sin under my very nose.
ISAAC I'fecks, father, I should have guessed as much, for your
    nose seems to be put to the blush° more than any other part of your
    face.
PAUL Go, you're a wag.   25
ANTONIO But to the purpose, father. Will you officiate for us?
PAUL To join young people thus clandestinely° is not safe, and indeed
    I have in my heart many weighty reasons against it.
ANTONIO [*showing a purse*] And I have in my hand many weighty

reasons for it.—Isaac, haven't you an argument or two in our favour   30
about you?

ISAAC [*doing the same*] Yes, yes; here is a most unanswerable purse.

PAUL For shame; you make me angry. You forget that I am a Jacobin,°
and when importunate people have forced their trash—ay, into this
pocket here, or into this—why, then the sin was theirs.   35

Antonio and Isaac put money into Father Paul's pockets

Fie, now you distress me! I would return it, but that I must touch
it that way, and so wrong my oath.

ANTONIO Now then, come with us.

ISAAC Ay, now give us our title to joy and rapture.

PAUL Well, when your hour of repentance comes, don't blame me.   40

ANTONIO (*aside*) No bad caution to my friend Isaac.—Well, well,
father, do you do your part and I'll abide the consequence.

ISAAC Ay, and so will I.

Antonio and Isaac are going. Enter Louisa, running

LOUISA O, Antonio, Ferdinand is at the porch and inquiring for us.

ISAAC Who? Don Ferdinand! He's not inquiring for me, I hope.   45

ANTONIO Fear not, my love, I'll soon pacify him.

ISAAC Egad, you won't. Antonio, take my advice and run away.
This Ferdinand is the most unmerciful dog and has the cursedest
long sword, and upon my soul he comes on purpose to cut your
throat!   50

ANTONIO Never fear, never fear.

ISAAC Well, you may stay if you will; but I'll get somebody else to
marry me, for, by St Iago, he shall never meet me again, while I am
master of a pair of heels.

Isaac runs out. Donna Louisa lets down her veil. Enter
Ferdinand

FERDINAND So, sir, I have met with you at last.   55

ANTONIO Well, sir?

FERDINAND Base treacherous man! Whence can a false, deceitful soul
like yours borrow confidence to look so steadily on the man you've
injured?

ANTONIO Ferdinand, you are too warm. 'Tis true you find me on the   60
point of wedding one I love beyond my life, but no argument of
mine prevailed on her to elope. I scorn deceit as much as you. By
heaven, I knew not she had left her father's till I saw her.

FERDINAND What a mean excuse! You have wronged your friend,
then, for one whose wanton forwardness anticipated your   65

treachery. Of this indeed your Jew pander informed me; but let your conduct be consistent, and since you have dared to do a wrong, follow me, and show you have spirit to avow it.°

LOUISA Antonio, I perceive his mistake. Leave him to me.

PAUL Friend, you are rude to interrupt the union of two willing 70
hearts.

FERDINAND No, meddling priest; the hand he seeks is mine.

PAUL If so, I'll proceed no further. (*To Louisa, who shakes her head*)
Lady, did you ever promise this youth your hand?

FERDINAND Clara, I thank you for your silence. I would not have 75
heard your tongue avow such falsity. Be't your punishment to
remember I have not reproached you.

> *Enter Clara, [veiled]*

CLARA What mockery° is this?

FERDINAND Antonio, you are protected now, but we shall meet.

> *As Ferdinand is going, Clara holds him by one arm and Louisa
> by the other*

LOUISA and CLARA [*sing*]

DUET

LOUISA   *Turn thee round, I pray thee;°*   80
Calm awhile thy rage.

CLARA   *I must help to stay thee,*
And thy wrath assuage.

LOUISA   *Couldst thou not discover*
One so dear to thee?   85

CLARA   *Canst thou be a lover,*
And thou fly from me?

> *Clara and Louisa unveil*

FERDINAND How's this! My sister! Clara too! I'm confounded.

LOUISA 'Tis even so, good brother.

PAUL How! What impiety! Did the man want to marry his own sister? 90

LOUISA And aren't you ashamed of yourself not to know your own
sister?

CLARA To drive away your own mistress?

LOUISA Don't you see how jealousy blinds people?

CLARA Ay, and will you ever be jealous again?   95

FERDINAND Never, never. You, sister, I know, will forgive me. But
how, Clara, shall I presume—?

CLARA No, no; just now you told me not to tease you. 'Who do you

want, good signor?' 'Not you, not you.' O you blind wretch! But
swear never to be jealous again, and I'll forgive you.   100

FERDINAND By all—

CLARA There, that will do. You'll keep the oath just as well.

        Clara gives Ferdinand her hand

LOUISA But, brother, here is one to whom some apology is due.

FERDINAND Antonio, I am ashamed to think—

ANTONIO Not a word of excuse, Ferdinand. I have not been in love   105
myself, without learning that a lover's anger should never be
resented. But come; let us retire with this good father, and we'll
explain to you the cause of your error.

ANTONIO, CLARA, LOUISA, and FATHER PAUL (*sing*)

GLEE and CHORUS

> *Oft does Hymen smile to hear°*
> > *Wordy vows of feigned regard;*   110
> *Well he knows when they're sincere—*
> > *Never slow to give reward;*
> *For his glory is to prove*
> > *Kind to those who wed for love.*

Exeunt

3.7

A grand saloon

Enter Don Jerome, Lopez, and Servants

JEROME Be sure now; let everything be in the best order. Let all my
servants have on their merriest faces, but tell 'em to get as little
drunk as possible till after supper.—So, Lopez, where's your
master? Shan't we have him at supper?

LOPEZ Indeed, I believe not, sir. He's mad, I doubt; I'm sure he has   5
frighted me from him.

JEROME Ay, ay, he's after some wench, I suppose. A young rake! Well,
well, we'll be merry without him.

        Enter a Servant

SERVANT Sir, here is Signor Isaac.

        Enter Isaac

JEROME So, my dear son-in-law! There, take my blessing and for-   10
giveness. But where's my daughter? Where's Louisa?

ISAAC She's without, impatient for a blessing, but almost afraid to
enter.

JEROME O, fly and bring her in.
        Exit Isaac
Poor girl, I long to see her pretty face.   15

ISAAC (*without*) Come, my charmer! my trembling angel!
        Enter Isaac and the Duenna. Don Jerome runs to meet them.
        The Duenna kneels°

JEROME Come to my arms, my—(*Starts back*) Why, who the devil
have we here?

ISAAC Nay, Don Jerome, you promised her forgiveness; see how the
dear creature droops.   20

JEROME Droops indeed! Why, Gad take me, this is old Margaret. But
where's my daughter? Where's Louisa?

ISAAC Why, here, before your eyes.—Nay, don't be abashed, my sweet
wife!

JEROME Wife, with a vengeance! Why, zounds, you have not married   25
the duenna!

DUENNA (*kneeling*) O dear papa! You'll not disown me sure!

JEROME Papa! Dear papa! Why, zounds, your impudence is as great
as your ugliness.

ISAAC Rise, my charmer. Go throw your snowy arms about his neck,   30
and convince him you are—

DUENNA O sir, forgive me!
        The Duenna embraces Don Jerome

JEROME Help! Murder!
        Servants come forward

SERVANTS What's the matter, sir?

JEROME Why, here, this damned Jew has brought an old harridan to   35
strangle me.

ISAAC Lord, it is his own daughter, and he is so hard-hearted he won't
forgive her.
        Enter Antonio and Louisa. They kneel

JEROME Zounds and fury, what's here now? Who sent for you, sir, and
who the devil are you?   40

ANTONIO This lady's husband, sir.

ISAAC Ay, that he is, I'll be sworn; for I left 'em with the priest, and
was to have given her away.

JEROME You were?

ISAAC Ay. That's my honest friend Antonio; and that's the little girl I   45
told you I had hampered him with.

JEROME Why, you are either drunk or mad. This is my daughter.

ISAAC No, no; 'tis you are both drunk and mad, I think. Here's your daughter.

JEROME [*to the Duenna*] Harkee, old iniquity! Will you explain all this or not? 50

DUENNA Come, then, Don Jerome, I will; though our habits° might inform you all. Look on your daughter there, and on me.

ISAAC What's this I hear?

DUENNA The truth is, that in your passion this morning you made a small mistake, for you turned your daughter out of doors and locked up your humble servant. 55

ISAAC O lud! O lud! Here's a pretty° fellow! To turn his daughter out of doors instead of an old duenna.

JEROME And, O lud! O lud!, here's a pretty fellow to marry an old duenna instead of my daughter. But how came the rest about? 60

DUENNA I have only to add that I remained in your daughter's place, and had the good fortune to engage the affections of my sweet husband here.

ISAAC Her husband! Why, you old witch, do you think I'll be your husband now! This is a trick, a cheat, and you ought all to be ashamed of yourselves. 65

ANTONIO Harkee, Isaac! Do you dare to complain of tricking?—Don Jerome, I give you my word this cunning Portuguese has brought all this upon himself, by endeavouring to overreach you by getting your daughter's fortune without making any settlement in return. 70

JEROME Overreach me!

ANTONIO 'Tis so indeed, sir, and we can prove it to you.

JEROME Why, Gad take me, it must be so, or he could never have put up with such a face as Margaret's.—So, little Solomon, I wish you joy of your wife with all my soul. 75

LOUISA Isaac, tricking is all fair in love. Let you alone for the plot.

ANTONIO A cunning dog, aren't you? A sly little villain, hey?

LOUISA Roguish, perhaps; but keen, devilish keen.

JEROME Yes, yes, his aunt always called him little Solomon. 80

ISAAC Why, the plagues of Egypt° upon you all. But do you think I'll submit to such an imposition?

ANTONIO Isaac, one serious word. You'd better be content as you are, for believe me, you will find, that in the opinion of the world there is not a fairer subject for contempt and ridicule than a knave become the dupe of his own art. 85

ISAAC I don't care; I'll not endure this.—Don Jerome, 'tis you have

done it. You would be so cursed positive about the beauty of her
you locked up, and all the time I told you she was as old as my
mother and as ugly as the devil.   90

DUENNA Why, you little insignificant reptile.

JEROME That's right! Attack him, Margaret.

DUENNA Dares such a thing as you pretend to talk of beauty! A
walking rouleau! A body that seems to owe all its consequence to
the dropsy!° A pair of eyes like two dead beetles in a wad of brown   95
dough! A beard like an artichoke, with dry shrivelled jaws that
would disgrace the mummy of a monkey!

JEROME Well done, Margaret.

DUENNA But you shall know that I have a brother who wears a sword;
and if you don't do me justice—   100

ISAAC Fire seize your brother, and you too. I'll fly to Jerusalem to
avoid you.

DUENNA Fly where you will, I'll follow you.

JEROME Throw your snowy arms about him, Margaret.
            Exeunt Isaac and the Duenna
But, Louisa, are you really married to this modest gentleman?   105

LOUISA Sir, in obedience to your commands I gave him my hand
within this hour.

JEROME My commands!

ANTONIO Yes, sir; here is your consent under your own hand.

JEROME How! Would you rob me of my child by a trick, a false pre- 110
tence, and do you think to get her fortune by the same means? Why,
'slife, you are as great a rogue as Isaac.

ANTONIO No, Don Jerome; though I have profited by this paper in
gaining your daughter's hand, I scorn to obtain her fortune by
deceit. There, sir.   115
            Antonio gives Don Jerome a letter
Now give her your blessing for a dower, and all the little I possess
shall be settled on her in return. Had you wedded her to a prince,
he could do no more.

JEROME Why, Gad take me, but you are a very extraordinary fellow.
But have you the impudence to suppose no one can do a generous   120
action but yourself?—Here, Louisa, tell this proud fool of yours
that he's the only man I know that would renounce your fortune;
and by my soul, he's the only man in Spain that's worthy of it.
There, bless you both. I'm an obstinate old fellow when I am in the
wrong; but you shall now find me as steady in the right.   125
            Enter Ferdinand and Clara

Another wonder still! Why, sirrah! Ferdinand, you have not stole a
nun, have you?

FERDINAND She is a nun in nothing but her habit, sir. Look nearer,
and you will perceive 'tis Clara D'Almanza, Don Guzman's daughter; and, with pardon for stealing a wedding,° she is also my wife.   130

JEROME Gadsbud, and a great fortune! Ferdinand, you are a prudent
young rogue, and I forgive you.—And, i'fecks, you are a pretty little
damsel. Give your father-in-law a kiss, you smiling rogue.
            [*Clara kisses Don Jerome*]

CLARA There, old gentleman, and now mind you behave well to us.

JEROME I'fecks, those lips ha'n't been chilled by kissing beads. Egad,   135
I believe I shall grow the best-humoured fellow in Spain.—Lewis,
Sancho, Carlos,° d'ye hear, are all my doors thrown open? Our chil-
dren's weddings are the only holidays that age can boast, and then
we drain with pleasure the little stock of spirits time has left us.
            Music within
But see, here come our friends and neighbours.   140
            Enter Masqueraders
And, i'faith, we'll make a night on't, with wine and dance and
catches. Then old and young shall join us.

DON JEROME, LOUISA, FERDINAND, ANTONIO, and CLARA (*sing*)

FINALE

JEROME   *Come now for jest and smiling,°*
              Both old and young beguiling.   145
                    Let us laugh and play, so blithe and gay,
                    Till we banish care away.

LOUISA   *Thus crowned with dance and song,*
              The hours shall glide along.
                    With a heart at ease, merry, merry glees   150
                    Can never fail to please.

FERDINAND   *Each bride with blushes glowing,*
              Our wine as rosy flowing,
                    Let us laugh and play, so blithe and gay,
                    Till we banish care away.   155

ANTONIO   *Then healths to every friend*
              The night's repast shall end.
                    With a heart at ease, merry, merry glees
                    Can never fail to please.

CLARA   *Nor while we are so joyous*   160
             Shall anxious fear annoy us.
                Let us laugh and play, so blithe and gay,
                Till we banish care away.
JEROME   *For generous guests like these*
             Accept the wish to please.   165
                So we'll laugh and play, so blithe and gay,
                Your smiles drive care away.

        Exeunt

A TRIP TO SCARBOROUGH

A Comedy

THE CHARACTERS OF THE PLAY

Lord Foppington	*Mr Dodd*
Young Fashion	*Mr Reddish*
Loveless	*Mr Smith*
Colonel Townly	*Mr Brereton*
Sir Tunbelly° Clumsy	*Mr Moody*
Probe°	*Mr Parsons*
Lory	*Mr Baddeley*
La Varole°	*Mr Burton*
Shoemaker	*Mr Carpenter*
Tailor	*Mr Baker*
Hosier°	*Mr Norris*
Jeweller	*Mr Lamash*
[Postilion]°	
[Servants to Lord Foppington]	
[Servants in Loveless's lodgings]	
[Servants to Sir Tunbelly Clumsy]	
[Constable]	
[Chaplain]	

Berinthia	*Mrs Yates*
Amanda	*Mrs Robinson*
Mrs Coupler°	*Mrs Booth*
Nurse	*Mrs*
Bradshaw	
Miss Hoyden°	*Mrs Abington*
[Seamstress]°	
[Maid to Amanda]	

[SCENE: SCARBOROUGH]

Prologue

Written by David Garrick, Esq.°

Spoken by Mr King°

What various transformations we remark,
From east Whitechapel to the west Hyde Park!°
Men, women, children, houses, signs, and fashions,°
State, stage, trade, taste, the humours and the passions,°
Th'Exchange, 'Change Alley, wheresoe'er you're ranging,°   5
Court, city, country—all are changed, or changing.
The streets sometime ago were paved with stones,
Which, aided by a hackney-coach, half broke your bones.°
The purest lovers then indulged no bliss;
They run great hazard if they stole a kiss.°   10
'One chaste salute', the damsel cried, 'O fie!'
As they approached, slap went the coach awry—
Poor Sylvia got a bump, and Damon a black eye.°
But now weak nerves in hackney-coaches roam,
And the crammed glutton snores unjolted home.°   15
Of former times that polished thing, a beau,°
Is metamorphosed now, from top to toe.
Then the full flaxen wig, spread o'er the shoulders,
Concealed the shallow head from the beholders!
But now the whole's reversed: each fop appears,   20
Cropped, and trimmed up, exposing head and ears.°
The buckle then its modest limits knew;
Now, like the ocean, dreadful to the view,
Hath broke its bounds, and swallows up the shoe.
The wearer's foot, like his once fine estate,   25
Is almost lost, th'encumbrance is so great.°
Ladies may smile—are they not in the plot?
The bounds of nature have not they forgot?
Were they designed to be, when put together,
Made up, like shuttlecocks, of cork and feather?°   30
Their pale-faced grandmamas appeared with grace,
When dawning blushes rose upon the face;
No blushes now their once loved station seek—
The foe is in possession of the cheek!°

No head of old, too high in feathered state,°   35
Hindered the fair to pass the lowest gate;
A church to enter now, they must be bent,
If ev'n they should try th'experiment.°
    As change thus circulates throughout the nation,
Some plays may justly call for alteration—   40
At least to draw some slender covering o'er
That graceless wit, which was too bare before.°
Those writers well and wisely use their pens,
Who turn our wantons into magdalens;°
And howsoever wicked wits revile 'em,   45
We hope to find in you their stage asylum.°

1.1

The hall of an inn

Enter Young Fashion and Lory, Postilion following with a portmanteau

YOUNG FASHION Lory, pay the postboy°, and take the portmanteau.

LORY Faith, sir, we had better let the postboy take the portmanteau and pay himself.

YOUNG FASHION Why, sure there's something left in it.   5

LORY Not a rag, upon my honour, sir. We ate the last of your wardrobe at New Malton;° and if we had had twenty miles farther to go, our next meal must have been off the cloak-bag.

YOUNG FASHION Why, 'sdeath, it appears full.

LORY Yes, sir; I made bold° to stuff it with hay, to save appearances   10 and look like baggage.

YOUNG FASHION What the devil shall I do! [*To the Postilion*] Harkee, boy, what's the chaise?°

POSTILION Thirteen shillings, please your honour.

YOUNG FASHION Can you give me change for a guinea?   15

POSTILION O yes, sir.

LORY [*aside*] So, what will he do now?—Lord, sir, you had better let the boy be paid below.°

YOUNG FASHION Why, as you say, Lory, I believe it will be as well.

LORY Yes, yes; tell them to discharge you below, honest friend.   20

POSTILION Please your honour, there are the turnpikes° too.

YOUNG FASHION Ay, ay; the turnpikes, by all means.

POSTILION And I hope your honour will order me something for myself.

YOUNG FASHION To be sure, bid them give you a crown.   25

LORY Yes, yes; my master doesn't care what you charge them. So get along, you—

POSTILION Your honour promised to send the ostler—

LORY Pshaw, damn the ostler! Would you impose upon the gentleman's generosity?   30

    Lory pushes the Postilion out

A rascal, to be so cursed ready with his change!

YOUNG FASHION Why, faith, Lory, he had near posed me.

LORY Well, sir, we are arrived at Scarborough, not worth a guinea! I

hope you'll own yourself a happy man: you have outlived all your   35
cares.

YOUNG FASHION How so, sir?

LORY Why, you have nothing left to take care of.

YOUNG FASHION Yes, sirrah, I have myself and you to take care of
still.

LORY Sir, if you could prevail with somebody else to do that for you,   40
I fancy we might both fare the better for't. But now, sir, for my Lord
Foppington, your elder brother.

YOUNG FASHION Damn my elder brother!

LORY With all my heart; but get him to redeem your annuity however.
Look you, sir, you must wheedle him, or you must starve.   45

YOUNG FASHION Look you, sir, I will neither wheedle him nor starve.

LORY Why, what will you do then?

YOUNG FASHION Cut his throat, or get someone to do it for me.

LORY Gadso, sir, I'm glad to find I was not so well acquainted with
the strength of your conscience as with the weakness of your purse.   50

YOUNG FASHION Why, art thou so impenetrable a blockhead as to
believe he'll help me with a farthing?

LORY Not if you treat him *de haut en bas* as you used to do.

YOUNG FASHION Why, how wouldst have me treat him?

LORY Like a trout—tickle him.°   55

YOUNG FASHION I can't flatter.

LORY Can you starve?

YOUNG FASHION Yes.

LORY I can't. Goodbye t'ye, sir.

YOUNG FASHION Stay! Thou'lt distract me.° But who comes here?   60
My old friend, Colonel Townly?

    Enter Colonel Townly

My dear colonel, I am rejoiced to meet you here.

TOWNLY Dear Tom, this is an unexpected pleasure. What, are you
come to Scarborough to be present at your brother's wedding?

LORY Ah, sir, if it had been his funeral, we should have come with   65
pleasure.

TOWNLY What, honest Lory, are you with your master still?

LORY Yes, sir, I have been starving with him ever since I saw your
honour last.

YOUNG FASHION Why, Lory is an attached° rogue; there's no getting   70
rid of him.

LORY True, sir; as my master says, there's no seducing me from his
service—(*aside*) till he's able to pay me my wages.

YOUNG FASHION Go, go, sir, and take care of the baggage.

LORY Yes, sir. The baggage!   75

    [*Lory picks up the portmanteau*]

    O lord! I suppose, sir, I must charge the landlord to be very par-
ticular where he stows this.

YOUNG FASHION Get along, you rascal.

    Exit Lory, with the portmanteau

    But, colonel, are you acquainted with my proposed sister-in-law?

TOWNLY Only by character. Her father, Sir Tunbelly Clumsy, lives   80
within a quarter of a mile of this place, in a lonely old house, which
nobody comes near. She never goes abroad, nor sees company at
home. To prevent all misfortunes, she has her breeding within
doors.° The parson of the parish teaches her to play upon the
dulcimer;° the clerk° to sing, the nurse to dress, and her father to   85
dance. In short, nobody has free admission there but our old
acquaintance, Mother Coupler, who has procured your brother this
match, and is, I believe, a distant relation of Sir Tunbelly's.

YOUNG FASHION But is her fortune so considerable?

TOWNLY Three thousand a year, and a good sum of money inde-   90
pendent of her father beside.

YOUNG FASHION 'Sdeath, that my old acquaintance, Dame° Coupler,
could not have thought of me as well as my brother for such a prize.

TOWNLY Egad, I wouldn't swear that you are too late. His lordship, I
know, hasn't yet seen the lady, and, I believe, has quarrelled with   95
his patroness.

YOUNG FASHION My dear colonel, what an idea have you started!

TOWNLY Pursue it if you can, and I promise you you shall have
my assistance; for besides my natural contempt for his lordship, I
have at present the enmity of a rival towards him.   100

YOUNG FASHION What, has he been addressing your old flame, the
sprightly widow Berinthia?

TOWNLY Faith, Tom, I am at present most whimsically circumstanced. I came here near a month ago to meet the lady you
mention; but, she failing in her promise, I, partly from pique, and   105
partly from idleness, have been diverting my chagrin by offering up
chaste incense to the beauties of Amanda, our friend Loveless's
wife.

YOUNG FASHION I have never seen her, but have heard her spoken of
as a youthful wonder of beauty and prudence.   110

TOWNLY She is so indeed; and, Loveless being too careless and insensible of the treasure he possesses, my lodging in the same house has

given me a thousand opportunities of making my assiduities acceptable; so that in less than a fortnight I began to bear my disappointment from the widow with the most Christian resignation.   115

YOUNG FASHION And Berinthia has never appeared?

TOWNLY O, there's the perplexity; for, just as I began not to care
whether I ever saw her again or not, last night she arrived.

YOUNG FASHION And instantly reassumed her empire.

TOWNLY No, faith. We met; but, the lady not condescending to give   120
me any serious reasons for having fooled me for a month, I left her
in a huff.

YOUNG FASHION Well, well, I'll answer for't; she'll soon resume her
power, especially as friendship will prevent your pursuing the other
too far. But my coxcomb of a brother is an admirer of Amanda's   125
too, is he?

TOWNLY Yes; and, I believe, is most heartily despised by her. But
come with me, and you shall see her and your old friend Loveless.

YOUNG FASHION I must pay my respects to his lordship. Perhaps you
can direct me to his lodgings.   130

TOWNLY Come with me; I shall pass by it.

YOUNG FASHION I wish you could pay the visit for me, or could tell
me what I should say to him.

TOWNLY Say nothing to him. Apply yourself to his bag,° his sword,
his feather, his snuffbox; and when you are well with them, desire   135
him to lend you a thousand pounds, and I'll engage you prosper.

YOUNG FASHION 'Sdeath and furies! Why was that coxcomb thrust
into the world before me? O fortune! Fortune! Thou art a jilt, by
Gad.

    Exeunt

1.2

    A dressing-room

    Lord Foppington, in his nightgown, and La Varole

LORD FOPPINGTON Well, 'tis an unspeakable pleasure to be a man of
quality,° strike me dumb!° Even the boors of this northern spa have
learned the respect due to a title.—La Varole!

LA VAROLE Mi lor.

LORD FOPPINGTON You ha'n't yet been at Muddymoat Hall to   5
announce my arrival, have you?

LA VAROLE Not yet, mi lor.

LORD FOPPINGTON Then you need not go till Saturday.

> *Exit La Varole*

As I am in no particular haste to view my intended sposa, I shall
sacrifice a day or two to the pursuit of my friend Loveless's wife.   10
Amanda is a charming creature, strike me ugly; and if I have
any discernment in the world, she thinks no less of my Lord
Foppington.

> *Enter La Varole*

LA VAROLE Mi lor, de shoemaker, de tailor, de hosier, de seamstress,
de peru,° be all ready, if your lordship please to dress.   15

LORD FOPPINGTON 'Tis well. Admit them.

LA VAROLE Hey, *messieurs, entrez.*°

> *Enter Tailor, Seamstress, Shoemaker, Hosier, Jeweller, and
> Servants*

LORD FOPPINGTON So, gentlemen, I hope you have all taken pains to
show yourselves masters in your professions.

TAILOR I think I may presume to say, sir—   20

LA VAROLE My lor, you clown° you!

TAILOR My lord, I ask your lordship's pardon, my lord. I hope, my
lord, your lordship will please to own I have brought your lordship
as accomplished a suit of clothes as ever peer of England wore, my
lord. Will your lordship please to try 'em now?   25

LORD FOPPINGTON Ay; but let my people dispose the glasses,° so that I
may see myself before and behind; for I love to see myself all round.

> [*The Servants position the mirrors.*] *Whilst Lord Foppington
> puts on his clothes, enter Young Fashion and Lory*

YOUNG FASHION [*aside to Lory*] Hey-day! What the devil have we
here? Sure my gentleman's grown a favourite at court,° he has got
so many people at his levee.   30

LORY Sir, these people come in order to make him a favourite at court;
they are to establish him with the ladies.

YOUNG FASHION Good heaven! To what an ebb of taste are women
fallen, that it should be in the power of a laced coat to recommend
a gallant to them!   35

LORY Sir, tailors and hairdressers are now become the bawds of the
nation; 'tis they that debauch all the women.

YOUNG FASHION Thou say'st true; for there's that fop now has not,
by nature, wherewithal to move a cookmaid, and by the time these
fellows have done with him, egad he shall melt down a countess.   40
But now for my reception.

LORD FOPPINGTON [*to the Tailor*] Death and eternal tartures!° Sir, I
say the coat is too wide here by a foot.

TAILOR My lord, if it had been tighter, 'twould neither have hooked
nor buttoned.   45

LORD FOPPINGTON Rat° the hooks and buttons, sir! Can anything be
worse than this? As Gad shall jedge me, it hangs on my shoulders
like a chairman's surtout.

TAILOR 'Tis not for me to dispute your lordship's fancy.

LORY [*aside to Young Fashion*] There, sir, observe what respect does.   50

YOUNG FASHION Respect! Damn him for a coxcomb. But let's accost°
him.—[*To Lord Foppington*] Brother, I'm your humble servant.

LORD FOPPINGTON O lard, Tam, I did not expect you in England.
Brother, I'm glad to see you. But what has brought you to Scarborough, Tam? (*To the Tailor*) Look you, sir, I shall never be rec-   55
onciled to this nauseous wrapping-gown. Therefore, pray get me
another suit with all possible expedition; for this is my eternal aversion.—Well, but, Tam, you don't tell me what has driven you to
Scarborough?—Mrs Calico,° are not you of my mind?

SEAMSTRESS Directly, my lord. I hope your lordship is pleased with   60
your ruffles?

LORD FOPPINGTON In love with them, stap my vitals! Bring my bill;
you shall be paid tomorrow.

SEAMSTRESS I humbly thank your lordship.

  Exit Seamstress

LORD FOPPINGTON Hark thee, shoemaker. These shoes a'n't ugly,   65
but they don't fit me.

SHOEMAKER My lord, I think they fit you very well.

LORD FOPPINGTON They hurt me just below the instep.

SHOEMAKER (*feeling his foot*) No, my lord; they don't hurt you there.

LORD FOPPINGTON I tell thee they pinch me execrably.   70

SHOEMAKER Why then, my lord, if those shoes pinch you I'll be
damned.

LORD FOPPINGTON Why, wilt thou undertake to persuade me I
cannot feel?

SHOEMAKER Your lordship may please to feel what you think fit, but   75
that shoe does not hurt you. I think I understand my trade.

LORD FOPPINGTON Now, by all that's great and powerful, thou art
an incomprehensible coxcomb; but thou makest good shoes, and so
I'll bear with thee.

SHOEMAKER My lord, I have worked for half the people of quality in   80

this town these twenty years, and 'tis very hard I shouldn't know
when a shoe hurts, and when it don't.

LORD FOPPINGTON Well, prithee be gone about thy business.
    Exit Shoemaker
    Mr Mendlegs, a word with you. The calves of these stockings are
    thickened a little too much; they make my legs look like a porter's. 85

HOSIER My lord, methinks they look mighty well.

LORD FOPPINGTON Ay, but you are not so good a judge of those
things as I am; I have studied them all my life. Therefore pray let
the next be the thickness of a crown piece less.

HOSIER Indeed, my lord, they are the same kind I had the honour to 90
furnish your lordship with in town.

LORD FOPPINGTON Very possibly, Mr Mendlegs. But that was in the
beginning of the winter;° and you should always remember, Mr
Hosier, that if you make a nobleman's spring legs as robust as his
autumnal calves, you commit a manstrous impropriety, and make no 95
allowance for the fatigues of the winter.

JEWELLER I hope, my lord, those buckles have had the unspeakable
satisfaction of being honoured with your lordship's approbation?

LORD FOPPINGTON Why, they are of a pretty fancy; but don't you
think them rather of the smallest? 100

JEWELLER My lord, they could not well be larger to keep on your
lordship's shoe.

LORD FOPPINGTON My good sir, you forget that these matters are
not as they used to be. Formerly, indeed, the buckle was a sort of
machine, intended to keep on the shoe; but the case is now quite 105
reversed, and the shoe is of no earthly use, but to keep on the
buckle.—Now give me my watches, and the business of the
morning will be pretty well over.

YOUNG FASHION [*aside to Lory*] Well, Lory, what dost think on't? A
very friendly reception from a brother after three years' absence! 110

LORY Why, sir, 'tis your own fault. Here you have stood ever since you
came in, and have not commended any one thing that belongs to
him.
    [*Exit Jeweller*]

YOUNG FASHION Nor ever shall, while they belong to a coxcomb. [*To
Lord Foppington*] Now your people of business are gone, brother, I 115
hope I may obtain a quarter of an hour's audience of you?

LORD FOPPINGTON Faith, Tam, I must beg you'll excuse me at this
time, for I have an engagement which I would not break for the

salvation of mankind.—[*Calling offstage*] Hey! There! Is my carriage at the door?—(*Going*) You'll excuse me, brother.   120

YOUNG FASHION Shall you be back to dinner?

LORD FOPPINGTON As Gad shall jedge me, I can't tell, for it is passible I may dine with some friends at Donner's.°

YOUNG FASHION Shall I meet you there? For I must needs talk with you.   125

LORD FOPPINGTON That, I'm afraid, mayn't be quite so praper, for those I commonly eat with are a people of nice conversation;° and you know, Tam, your education has been a little at large.° But there are other ordinaries in the town, very good beef ordinaries. I suppose, Tam, you can eat beef? However, dear Tam, I'm glad to   130 see thee in England, stap my vitals!

    Exeunt Lord Foppington, [*La Varole and Servants*]

YOUNG FASHION Hell and furies! Is this to be borne?

LORY Faith, sir, I could almost have given him a knock o' the pate myself.

YOUNG FASHION 'Tis enough; I will now show you the excess of my   135
passion by being very calm. Come, Lory, lay your loggerhead to mine, and, in cold blood, let us contrive his destruction.

LORY Here comes a head, sir, would contrive it better than us both, if she would but join in the confederacy.

YOUNG FASHION By this light, Madam Coupler! She seems dissatis-   140
fied at something. Let us observe her.

    Enter Mrs Coupler

COUPLER [*aside*] So! I am likely to be well rewarded for my services, truly; my suspicions, I find, were but too just. What! Refuse to advance me a paltry sum, when I am upon the point of making him master of a galleon!° But let him look to the consequences! An   145
ungrateful, narrow-minded coxcomb!

YOUNG FASHION So he is, upon my soul, old lady. It must be my brother you speak of.

COUPLER Ha! Stripling, how came you here? What, hast spent all, hey? And art thou come to dun his lordship for assistance?   150

YOUNG FASHION No; I want somebody's assistance to cut his lordship's throat, without the risk of being hanged for him.

COUPLER Egad, sirrah, I could help thee to do him almost as good a turn without the danger of being burnt in the hand° for't.

YOUNG FASHION How, how, old mischief?   155

COUPLER Why, you must know I have done you the kindness to make up a match for your brother.

YOUNG FASHION I'm very much beholden to you, truly.

COUPLER You may be before the wedding-day yet. The lady is a great
heiress, the match is concluded, the writings° are drawn, and his   160
lordship is come hither to put the finishing hand to the business.

YOUNG FASHION I understand as much.

COUPLER Now you must know, stripling, your brother's a knave.

YOUNG FASHION Good.

COUPLER He has given me a bond of a thousand pounds for helping   165
him to this fortune, and has promised me as much more in ready
money upon the day of the marriage; which, I understand by a
friend, he never designs to pay me; and his just now refusing to pay
me a part is a proof of it. If, therefore, you will be a generous young
rogue and secure me five thousand pounds, I'll help you to the lady.   170

YOUNG FASHION And how the devil wilt thou do that?

COUPLER Without the devil's aid, I warrant thee. Thy brother's face
not one of the family° ever saw. The whole business has been
managed by me, and all the letters go through my hands. Sir Tunbelly Clumsy, my relation—for that's the old gentleman's name—   175
is apprised of his lordship's being down here, and expects him
tomorrow to receive his daughter's hand. But the peer, I find, means
to bait here a few days longer, to recover the fatigue of his journey,
I suppose. Now you shall go to Muddymoat Hall in his place. I'll
give you a letter of introduction; and if you don't marry the girl   180
before sunset, you deserve to be hanged before morning.

YOUNG FASHION Agreed, agreed. And for thy reward—

COUPLER Well, well. Though I warrant thou hast not a farthing of
money in thy pocket now. No, one may see it in thy face.

YOUNG FASHION Not a souse,° by Jupiter.   185

COUPLER Must I advance then? Well, be at my lodgings next door this
evening, and I'll see what may be done. We'll sign and seal, and
when I have given thee some farther instructions, thou shalt hoist
sail and be gone.

Exit Mrs Coupler

YOUNG FASHION So, Lory, providence, thou seest, at last takes care   190
of merit. We are in a fair way to be great people.

LORY Ay, sir, if the devil don't step between the cup and the lip,° as
he uses to do.

YOUNG FASHION Why, faith, he has played me many a damned trick
to spoil my fortune, and, egad, I'm almost afraid he's at work about   195
it again now; but if I should tell thee how, thou'dst wonder at me.

LORY Indeed, sir, I should not.

YOUNG FASHION How dost know?

LORY Because, sir, I have wondered at you so often, I can wonder at
you no more.   200

YOUNG FASHION No! What wouldst thou say if a qualm of conscience
should spoil my design?

LORY I would eat my words, and wonder more than ever!

YOUNG FASHION Why, faith, Lory, though I am a young rakehell,°
and have played many a roguish trick, this is so full-grown a cheat,   205
I find I must take pains to come up to't. I have scruples.

LORY They are strong symptoms of death. If you find they increase,
sir, pray make your will.

YOUNG FASHION No, my conscience shan't starve me neither; but
thus far I'll listen to it. Before I execute this project, I'll try my   210
brother to the bottom.° If he has yet so much humanity about him
as to assist me, though with a moderate aid, I'll drop my project at
his feet, and show him how I can do for him much more than what
I'd ask he'd do for me. This one conclusive trial of him I resolve to
make.   215

> Succeed or fail, still victory's my lot.
> If I subdue his heart, 'tis well. If not,
> I will subdue my conscience to my plot.

    Exeunt

2.1

[*Loveless and Amanda's lodgings*]

Enter Loveless and Amanda

LOVELESS How do you like these lodgings, my dear? For my part, I
am so well pleased with them, I shall hardly remove whilst we stay
here, if you are satisfied.

AMANDA I am satisfied with everything that pleases you; else I had not
come to Scarborough at all.   5

LOVELESS O, a little of the noise and folly of this place will sweeten
the pleasures of our retreat;° we shall find the charms of our retirement doubled when we return to it.

AMANDA That pleasing prospect will be my chiefest entertainment,
whilst, much against my will, I engage in those empty pleasures   10
which 'tis so much the fashion to be fond of.

LOVELESS I own most of them are, indeed, but empty; yet there are
delights, of which a private life is destitute, which may divert an
honest man, and be a harmless entertainment to a virtuous woman.
Good music is one; and truly, with some small allowance, the plays,   15
I think, may be esteemed another.

AMANDA Plays, I must confess, have some small charms, and would
have more, would they restrain that loose encouragement to vice,
which shocks, if not the virtue of some women, at least the modesty
of all.   20

LOVELESS But, till that reformation can be wholly made, 'twould
surely be a pity to exclude the productions of some of our best
writers for want of a little wholesome pruning, which might be
effected by anyone who possessed modesty enough to believe that
we should preserve all we can of our deceased authors, at least till   25
they are outdone by the living ones.°

AMANDA What do you think of that you saw last night?

LOVELESS To say truth, I did not mind it much.° My attention was
for some time taken off to admire the workmanship of nature in
the face of a young lady who sat some distance from me. She was   30
so exquisitely handsome!

AMANDA So exquisitely handsome!

LOVELESS Why do you repeat my words, my dear?

AMANDA Because you seemed to speak them with such pleasure, I
thought I might oblige you with their echo.   35

LOVELESS Then you are alarmed, Amanda?

AMANDA It is my duty to be so when you are in danger.

LOVELESS You are too quick in apprehending for me.° I viewed her
with a world of admiration, but not one glance of love.

AMANDA Take heed of trusting to such nice distinctions. But were   40
your eyes the only things that were inquisitive? Had I been in your
place, my tongue, I fancy, had been curious too. I should have asked
her where she lived, yet still without design.° Who was she, pray?

LOVELESS Indeed, I cannot tell.

AMANDA You will not tell.   45

LOVELESS By all that's sacred then, I did not ask.

AMANDA Nor do you know what company was with her?

LOVELESS I do not. But why are you so earnest?

AMANDA I thought I had cause.

LOVELESS But you thought wrong, Amanda; for turn the case, and let   50
it be your story. Should you come home and tell me you had seen
a handsome man, should I grow jealous because you had eyes?

AMANDA But should I tell you he was *exquisitely* so, and that I had
gazed on him with admiration, should you not think 'twere possible I might go one step further and inquire his name?   55

LOVELESS (*aside*) She has reason on her side. I have talked too much;
but I must turn off another way. (*To Amanda*) Will you then make
no difference, Amanda, between the language of our sex and yours?
There is a modesty restrains your tongues, which makes you speak
by halves when you commend; but roving flattery gives a loose   60
to ours, which makes us still speak double what we think. You
should not, therefore, in so strict a sense take what I said to her
advantage.

AMANDA Those flights of flattery, sir, are to our faces only; when
women are once out of hearing, you are as modest in your com-   65
mendations as we are. But I shan't put you to the trouble of farther
excuses. If you please, this business shall rest here. Only give me
leave to wish, both for your peace and mine, that you may never
meet this miracle of beauty more.

LOVELESS I am content.   70

Enter Servant

SERVANT Madam, there is a lady at the door in a chair° desires to know
whether your ladyship sees company. Her name is Berinthia.

AMANDA O, dear, 'tis a relation I have not seen these five years.—Pray
her to walk in.

Exit Servant

Here's another beauty for you; she was, when I saw her last, reck-   75
oned extremely handsome.

LOVELESS Don't be jealous now, for I shall gaze upon her too.
        Enter Berinthia
(*Aside*) Ha! By heavens, the very woman!

BERINTHIA (*saluting° Amanda*) Dear Amanda, I did not expect to
meet with you in Scarborough.   80

AMANDA Sweet cousin, I'm overjoyed to see you. (*To Loveless*) Mr
Loveless, here's a relation and a friend of mine I desire you'll be
better acquainted with.

LOVELESS (*saluting Berinthia*) If my wife never desires a harder thing,
madam, her request will be easily granted.   85
        Enter Servant

SERVANT Sir, my Lord Foppington presents his humble service° to
you, and desires to know how you do. He's at the next door,° and
if it be not inconvenient to you, he'll come and wait upon you.

LOVELESS Give my compliments to his lordship, and I shall be glad
to see him.   90
        Exit Servant
[*To Berinthia*] If you are not acquainted with his lordship, madam,
you will be entertained with his character.

AMANDA Now it moves my pity more than my mirth, to see a man
whom nature has made no fool be so very industrious to pass for an
ass.   95

LOVELESS No, there you are wrong, Amanda; you should never
bestow your pity upon those who take pains for your contempt. Pity
those whom nature abuses, never those who abuse nature.
        Enter Lord Foppington

LORD FOPPINGTON Dear Loveless, I am your most humble servant.

LOVELESS My lord, I'm yours.   100

LORD FOPPINGTON [*to Amanda*] Madam, your ladyship's very
humble slave.

LOVELESS My lord, this lady is a relation of my wife's.

LORD FOPPINGTON (*saluting Berinthia*) The beautifullest race of
people upon earth, rat me. Dear Loveless, I am overjoyed that you   105
think of continuing here. I am, stap my vitals. (*To Amanda*) For
Gad's sake, madam, how has your ladyship been able to subsist thus
long under the fatigue of a country life?

AMANDA My life has been very far from that, my lord; it has been a
very quiet one.   110

LORD FOPPINGTON Why, that's the fatigue I speak of, madam; for 'tis impossible to be quiet without thinking. Now thinking is to me the greatest fatigue in the world.

AMANDA Does not your lordship love reading then?

LORD FOPPINGTON O, passionately, madam; but I never think of   115
what I read.

BERINTHIA Why, can your lordship read without thinking?

LORD FOPPINGTON O lard, can your ladyship pray without devotion, madam?

AMANDA Well, I must own I think books the best entertainment in the   120
world.

LORD FOPPINGTON I am so much of your ladyship's mind, madam, that I have a private gallery in town, where I walk sometimes, which is furnished with nothing but books and looking-glasses. Madam, I have gilded them, and ranged them so prettily, before Gad, it is the   125
most entertaining thing in the world to walk and look at them.

AMANDA Nay, I love a neat library too; but 'tis, I think, the inside of a book should recommend it most to us.

LORD FOPPINGTON That I must confess I am not altogether so fand of, far to my mind the inside of a book is to entertain one's   130
self with the forced product of another man's brain. Now I think a man of quality and breeding may be much more diverted with the natural sprauts of his own. But to say the truth, madam, let a man love reading never so well, when once he comes to know the tawn, he finds so many better ways of passing away the four-and-twenty   135
hours, that it were ten thousand pities he should consume his time in that. Far example, madam, now, my life. My life, madam, is a perpetual stream of pleasure that glides through with such a variety of entertainments, I believe the wisest of our ancestors never had the least conception of any of 'em. I rise, madam, when in town,   140
about twelve o'clock. I don't rise sooner, because it is the worst thing in the world for the complexion. Nat that I pretend to be a beau, but a man must endeavour to look decent, lest he makes so odious a figure in the side-bax,° the ladies should be compelled to turn their eyes upon the play. So, at twelve o'clock I say I rise. Naw,   145
if I find it a good day, I resalve to take the exercise of riding, so drink my chocolate, and draw on my boots by two. On my return, I dress, and after dinner lounge perhaps to the opera.

BERINTHIA Your lordship, I suppose, is fond of music?

LORD FOPPINGTON O, passionately, on Tuesdays and Saturdays, pro-   150
vided there is good company, and one is not expected to undergo the fatigue of listening.

AMANDA Does your lordship think that the case at the opera?

LORD FOPPINGTON Most certainly, madam. There is my Lady
Tattle, my Lady Prate, my Lady Titter, my Lady Sneer, my Lady   155
Giggle, and my Lady Grin. These have boxes in the front, and,
while any favourite air is singing, are the prettiest company in the
waurld, stap my vitals! Mayn't we hope for the honour to see you
added to our society, madam?

AMANDA Alas, my lord, I am the worst company in the world at a   160
concert, I'm so apt to attend to the music.

LORD FOPPINGTON Why, madam, that is very pardonable in the
country, or at church, but a manstrous inattention in a polite assembly. But I am afraid I tire the company?

LOVELESS Not at all; pray go on.   165

LORD FOPPINGTON Why then, ladies, there only remains to add that
I generally conclude the evening at one or other of the clubs.° Nat
that I ever play deep;° indeed I have been for some time tied up°
from losing above five thousand pawnds at a sitting.

LOVELESS But isn't your lordship sometimes obliged to attend the   170
weighty affairs of the nation?°

LORD FOPPINGTON Sir, as to weighty affairs, I leave them to weighty
heads: I never intend mine shall be a burden to my body.

BERINTHIA Nay, my lord, but you are a pillar of the state.

LORD FOPPINGTON An ornamental pillar, madam; for, sooner than   175
undergo any part of the burden, rat me, but the whole building
should fall to the ground.

AMANDA But, my lord, a fine gentleman spends a great deal of
his time in his intrigues;° you have given us no account of them
yet.   180

LORD FOPPINGTON (aside) So! She would inquire into my amours;
that's jealousy. Poor soul! I see she's in love with me. (To Amanda)
Why, madam, I should have mentioned my intrigues, but I am really
afraid I begin to be troublesome with the length of my visit.

AMANDA Your lordship is too entertaining to grow troublesome   185
anywhere.

LORD FOPPINGTON (aside) That now was as much as if she had said,
'Pray make love to me'.° I'll let her see I'm quick of apprehension.
(To Amanda) O lard, madam, I had like to have forgot a secret I
must needs tell your ladyship. (To Loveless) Ned, you must not be   190
so jealous now as to listen.

LOVELESS Not I, my lord. I am too fashionable a husband to pry into
the secrets of my wife.

LORD FOPPINGTON (*to Amanda, squeezing her hand*) I am in love with
you to desperation, strike me speechless!   195

AMANDA (*giving him a box o' the ear*) Then thus I return your
passion.—An impudent fool!

LORD FOPPINGTON Gad's curse, madam, I'm a peer of the realm.

LOVELESS Hey, what the devil, do you affront my wife, sir? Nay,
then—   200

> *Loveless draws his sword and fights Lord Foppington*

AMANDA Ah! What has my folly done?—Help! Murder! Help! Part
them, for heaven's sake.

> [*Loveless wounds Lord Foppington*]

LORD FOPPINGTON (*falling back, and leaning on his sword*) Ah! Quite
through the body, stap my vitals!

> *Enter Servants*

LOVELESS (*running to him*) I hope I ha'n't killed the fool, however. Bear   205
him up.—Where's your wound?

LORD FOPPINGTON Just through the guts.

LOVELESS Call a surgeon there.

> [*Exit a Servant*]

Unbutton him quickly.

LORD FOPPINGTON Ay, pray make haste.   210

LOVELESS This mischief you may thank yourself for.

LORD FOPPINGTON I may so; love's the devil indeed, Ned.

> *Enter Probe and Servant*

SERVANT Here's Mr Probe, sir, was just going by the door.

LORD FOPPINGTON He's the welcomest man alive.

PROBE Stand by, stand by, stand by; pray, gentlemen, stand by. Lord   215
have mercy upon us! Did you never see a man run through the body
before? Pray stand by.

LORD FOPPINGTON Ah! Mr Probe, I'm a dead man.

PROBE A dead man, and I by! I should laugh to see that, egad.

LOVELESS Prithee, don't stand prating, but look upon his wound.   220

PROBE Why, what if I won't look upon his wound this hour, sir?

LOVELESS Why, then he'll bleed to death, sir.

PROBE Why, then I'll fetch him to life again, sir.

LOVELESS 'Slife, he's run through the guts, I tell thee.

PROBE I wish he was run through the heart, and I should get the more   225
credit° by his cure. Now I hope you are satisfied? Come, now let
me come at him, now let me come at him. (*Viewing Lord Foppington's wound*) Oons, what a gash is here! Why, sir, a man may drive
a coach and six horses into your body!

LORD FOPPINGTON O!   230

PROBE Why, what the devil, have you run the gentleman through with a scythe? (*Aside*) A little scratch between the skin and the ribs; that's all.

LOVELESS Let me see his wound.

PROBE Then you shall dress it, sir; for if anybody looks upon it, I won't.   235

LOVELESS Why, thou art the veriest coxcomb I ever saw.

PROBE Sir, I am not master of my trade for nothing.

LORD FOPPINGTON Surgeon!

PROBE Sir?

LORD FOPPINGTON Are there any hopes?   240

PROBE Hopes! I can't tell. What are you willing to give for a cure?

LORD FOPPINGTON Five hundred paunds with pleasure.

PROBE Why, then perhaps there may be hopes; but we must avoid a further delay.—[*To the Servants*] Here, help the gentleman into a chair, and carry him to my house presently. That's the properest   245 place—(*aside*) to bubble him out of his money.—Come, a chair; a chair quickly.

    [*Servants enter with a chair*]°

There, in with him.

    The Servants put Lord Foppington into a chair

LORD FOPPINGTON Dear Loveless, adieu. If I die, I forgive thee; and if I live, I hope thou wilt do as much by me. I am sorry you and I   250 should quarrel, but I hope here's an end on't; for if you are satisfied, I am.

LOVELESS I shall hardly think it worth my prosecuting any farther, so you may be at rest, sir.

LORD FOPPINGTON Thou art a generous fellow, strike me dumb!   255 (*Aside*) But thou hast an impertinent wife, stap my vitals!

PROBE So, carry him off, carry him off. We shall have him prate himself into a fever by and by. Carry him off.

    Exeunt Servants with Lord Foppington and Probe

AMANDA [*kneeling*] Now on my knees, my dear, let me ask your pardon for my indiscretion; my own I never shall obtain.   260

LOVELESS [*raising her*] O, there's no harm done; you served him well.

AMANDA He did indeed deserve it; but I tremble to think how dear my indiscreet resentment might have cost you.

LOVELESS O, no matter; never trouble yourself about that.

    Enter Colonel Townly

TOWNLY So, so, I'm glad to find you all alive. I met a wounded peer   265 carrying off. For heaven's sake, what was the matter?

LOVELESS O, a trifle. He would have made love to my wife before my face; so she obliged him with a box o' the ear, and I run him through the body. That was all.

TOWNLY Bagatelle° on all sides. But pray, madam, how long has this noble lord been an humble servant° of yours? 270

AMANDA This is the first I have heard on't; so I suppose 'tis his quality more than his love has brought him into this adventure. He thinks his title an authentic passport to every woman's heart, below the degree of a peeress. 275

TOWNLY He's coxcomb enough to think anything; but I would not have you brought into trouble for him. I hope there's no danger of his life?

LOVELESS None at all. He's fallen into the hands of a roguish surgeon, who, I perceive, designs to frighten a little money out of him. But I saw his wound; 'tis nothing. He may go to the ball tonight if he pleases. 280

TOWNLY I am glad you have corrected him without farther mischief, or you might have deprived me of the pleasure of executing a plot against his lordship, which I have been contriving with an old acquaintance of yours. 285

LOVELESS Explain.

TOWNLY His brother, Tom Fashion, is come down here, and we have it in contemplation to save him the trouble of his intended wedding; but we want° your assistance. Tom would have called, but he is preparing for his enterprise. So I promised to bring you to him. So, sir, if these ladies can spare you— 290

LOVELESS I'll go with you with all my heart—(aside) though I could wish, methinks, to stay and gaze a little longer on that creature. Good gods, how engaging she is! But what have I to do with beauty? I have already had my portion, and must not covet more. (To Colonel Townly) Come, sir; when you please. 295

TOWNLY Ladies, your servant.

AMANDA Mr Loveless, pray one word with you before you go.

LOVELESS (to Colonel Townly) I'll overtake you, colonel. 300
                    Exit Colonel Townly
What would my dear?

AMANDA Only a woman's foolish question. How do you like my cousin here?

LOVELESS Jealous already, Amanda?

AMANDA Not at all. I ask you for another reason. 305

LOVELESS (aside) Whate'er her reason be, I must not tell her true.

(*To Amanda*) Why, I confess she's handsome; but you must not think I slight your kinswoman, if I own to you, of all the women who may claim that character,° she is the last would triumph in my heart.   310

AMANDA I'm satisfied.

LOVELESS Now tell me why you asked.

AMANDA At night I will. Adieu.

LOVELESS (*kissing her*) I'm yours.

    Exit Loveless

AMANDA (*aside*) I'm glad to find he does not like her, for I have a great   315
mind to persuade her to come and live with me.

BERINTHIA (*aside*) So! I find my colonel continues in his airs;° there must be something more at the bottom of this than the provocation he pretends from me.

AMANDA For heaven's sake, Berinthia, tell me what way I shall take to   320
persuade you to come and live with me?

BERINTHIA Why, one in the world there is, and but one.

AMANDA And pray what is that?

BERINTHIA It is to assure me I shall be very welcome.

AMANDA If that be all, you shall e'en sleep here tonight.   325

BERINTHIA Tonight!

AMANDA Yes, tonight.

BERINTHIA Why, the people where I lodge will think me mad.

AMANDA Let 'em think what they please.

BERINTHIA Say you so, Amanda? Why then, they shall think what   330
they please; for I'm a young widow, and I care not what anybody thinks. Ah, Amanda, it's a delicious thing to be a young widow.

AMANDA You'll hardly make me think so.

BERINTHIA Pooh! Because you are in love with your husband; but that is not every woman's case.   335

AMANDA I hope 'twas yours at least.

BERINTHIA Mine, say you? Now I have a great mind to tell you a lie; but I shall do it so awkwardly, you'd find me out.

AMANDA Then e'en speak the truth.

BERINTHIA Shall I? Then, after all, I did love him, Amanda, as a nun   340
does penance.

AMANDA How did you live together?

BERINTHIA Like man and wife—asunder. He loved the country, I the town. He hawks and hounds, I coaches and equipage. He eating and drinking, I carding and playing. He the sound of a horn, I the   345
squeak of a fiddle. We were dull company at table, worse abed.

Whenever we met we gave one another the spleen,° and never agreed but once, which was about lying alone.

AMANDA But tell me one thing truly and sincerely. Notwithstanding all these jars, did not his death at last extremely trouble you?   350

BERINTHIA O yes. I was forced to wear an odious widow's band a twelvemonth for't.

AMANDA Women, I find, have different inclinations. Prithee, Berinthia, instruct me a little farther, for I'm so great a novice, I'm almost ashamed on't. Not, heaven knows, that what you call intrigues   355 have any charms for me. The practical part of all unlawful love is—

BERINTHIA O 'tis abominable; but for the speculative, that we must all confess is entertaining enough.

AMANDA Pray be so just then to me to believe 'tis with a world of innocence I would inquire whether you think those we call women   360 of reputation do really escape all other men, as they do those shadows of 'em, the beaux?

BERINTHIA O no, Amanda; there are a sort of men make dreadful work amongst 'em—men that may be called the beaux' antipathy, for they agree in nothing but walking upon two legs. These have brains, the   365 beau has none. These are in love with their mistress, the beau with himself. They take care of her reputation, he's industrious to destroy it. They are decent,° he's a fop. They are men, he's an ass.

AMANDA If this be their character, I fancy we had here e'en now a pattern° of 'em both.   370

BERINTHIA His lordship and Colonel Townly?

AMANDA The same.

BERINTHIA As for the lord, he's eminently so; and for the other, I can assure you there's not a man in town who has a better interest with the women that are worth having an interest with.   375

AMANDA He answers then the opinion I had ever of him. Heavens, what a difference there is between a man like him and that vain nauseous fop, Lord Foppington! (*Taking Berinthia's hand*) I must acquaint you with a secret, cousin. 'Tis not that fool alone has talked to me of love. Townly has been tampering too.   380

BERINTHIA (*aside*) So, so! Here the mystery comes out!—Colonel Townly! Impossible, my dear!

AMANDA 'Tis true, indeed! Though he has done it in vain; nor do I think that all the merit of mankind combined could shake the tender love I bear my husband. Yet I will own to you, Berinthia, I   385 did not start at his addresses, as when they came from one whom I contemned.

168

BERINTHIA (*aside*) O, this is better and better. Well said, innocence!—
And you really think, my dear, that nothing could abate your constancy and attachment to your husband?   390

AMANDA Nothing. I am convinced.

BERINTHIA What if you found he loved another woman better?

AMANDA Well!

BERINTHIA Well! Why, were I that thing they call a slighted wife,
somebody should run the risk of being that thing they call a   395
husband.°

AMANDA O fie, Berinthia! No revenge should ever be taken against a
husband; but to wrong his bed is a vengeance, which of all
vengeance—

BERINTHIA Is the sweetest! Ha, ha, ha! Don't I talk madly?   400

AMANDA Madly indeed!

BERINTHIA Yet I'm very innocent.

AMANDA That I dare swear you are. I know how to make allowances
for your humour.° But you resolve then never to marry again?

BERINTHIA O no! I resolve I will.   405

AMANDA How so?

BERINTHIA That I never may.

AMANDA You banter me.

BERINTHIA Indeed I don't; but I consider I'm a woman and form my
resolutions accordingly.   410

AMANDA Well, my opinion is, form what resolution you will, matrimony will be the end on't.

BERINTHIA I doubt it. But ah, heavens, I have business at home and
am half an hour too late.

AMANDA As you are to return with me,° I'll just give some orders and   415
walk with you.

BERINTHIA Well, make haste, and we'll finish this subject as we go.
     Exit Amanda
Ah, poor Amanda, you have led a country life! Well, this discovery
is lucky! Base Townly! At once false to me, and treacherous to his
friend! And my innocent, demure cousin too! I have it in my power   420
to be revenged on her, however. Her husband, if I have any skill in
countenance,° would be as happy in my smiles as Townly can hope
to be in hers. I'll make the experiment, come what will on't. The
woman who can forgive the being robbed of a favoured lover must
be either an idiot or a wanton.   425
     [*Exit*]

3.1

[Lord Foppington's lodgings]

Enter Lord Foppington and La Varole

LORD FOPPINGTON Hey, fellow! Let my *vis-à-vis* come to the door.

LA VAROLE Will your lordship venture so soon to expose yourself to the weather?

LORD FOPPINGTON Sir, I will venture as soon as I can to expose myself to the ladies. 5

LA VAROLE I wish your lordship would please to keep house a little longer; I'm afraid your honour does not well consider your wound.

LORD FOPPINGTON My wound! I would not be in eclipse another day, though I had as many wounds in my body as I have had in my heart. So mind, Varole; let these cards° be left as directed. For this evening 10 I shall wait on my father-in-law, Sir Tunbelly, and I mean to commence my devoirs to the lady, by giving an entertainment at her father's expense. And hark thee. Tell Mr Loveless I request he and his company will honour me with their presence, or I shall think we are not friends. 15

LA VAROLE I will be sure.

Exit La Varole. Enter Young Fashion

YOUNG FASHION Brother, your servant. How do you find yourself today?

LORD FOPPINGTON So well, that I have ardered my carriage to the door; so there's no great danger of death this baut,° Tam. 20

YOUNG FASHION I'm very glad of it.

LORD FOPPINGTON (*aside*) That I believe's a lie.—Prithee, Tam, tell me one thing. Did not your heart cut a caper° up to your mauth, when you heard I was run through the bady?

YOUNG FASHION Why do you think it should? 25

LORD FOPPINGTON Because I remember mine did so when I heard my uncle was shot through the head.

YOUNG FASHION It then did very ill.

LORD FOPPINGTON Prithee, why so?

YOUNG FASHION Because he used you very well. 30

LORD FOPPINGTON Well! Naw, strike me dumb, he starved me. He has let me want a thausand women for want of a thausand pound.

YOUNG FASHION Then he hindered you from making a great many ill bargains, for I think no woman worth money that will take money.

LORD FOPPINGTON If I was a younger brother, I should think so too.   35

YOUNG FASHION Then you are seldom much in love?

LORD FOPPINGTON Never, stap my vitals!

YOUNG FASHION Why then did you make all this bustle about Amanda?

LORD FOPPINGTON Because she was a woman of an insolent virtue,   40
and I thought myself piqued in honour to debauch her.

YOUNG FASHION (aside) Very well. Here's a rare fellow for you, to
have the spending of five thousand pounds a year. But now for my
business with him.—Brother, though I know to talk of business,
especially of money, is a theme not quite so entertaining to you as   45
that of the ladies, my necessities are such, I hope you'll have
patience to hear me.

LORD FOPPINGTON The greatness of your necessities, Tam, is the
worst argument in the warld for your being patiently heard. I do
believe you are going to make a very good speech; but, strike me   50
dumb, it has the worst beginning of any speech I have heard this
twelvemonth.

YOUNG FASHION I'm sorry you think so.

LORD FOPPINGTON I do believe thou art. But come, let's know the
affair quickly.   55

YOUNG FASHION Why then, my case in a word is this. The necessary
expenses of my travels have so much exceeded the wretched income
of my annuity, that I have been forced to mortgage it for five
hundred pounds, which is spent. So, unless you are so kind as to
assist me in redeeming it, I know no remedy but to take a purse.°   60

LORD FOPPINGTON Why, faith, Tam, to give you my sense of the
thing, I do think taking a purse the best remedy in the warld; for if
you succeed you are relieved that way, if you are taken—you are
relieved t'other.°

YOUNG FASHION I'm glad to see you are in so pleasant a humour;° I   65
hope I shall find the effects on't.

LORD FOPPINGTON Why, do you then really think it a reasonable
thing that I should give you five hundred pawnds?

YOUNG FASHION I do not ask it as a due, brother; I am willing to
receive it as a favour.   70

LORD FOPPINGTON Then thou art willing to receive it any how,
strike me speechless. But these are damned times to give money in.
Taxes are so great, repairs so exorbitant, tenants such rogues, and
bouquets so dear, that, the devil take me, I am reduced to that
extremity in my cash, I have been forced to retrench in that one   75

article of sweet pawder,° till I have braught it dawn to five guineas a maunth. Now judge, Tam, whether I can spare you five hundred pawnds?

YOUNG FASHION If you can't I must starve, that's all. (*Aside*) Damn him.   80

LORD FOPPINGTON All I can say is, you should have been a better husband.°

YOUNG FASHION Oons! If you can't live upon ten thousand a year, how do you think I should do't upon two hundred?

LORD FOPPINGTON Don't be in a passion, Tam, for passion is the   85
most unbecoming thing in the warld to the face. Look you, I don't love to say anything to you to make you melancholy; but upon this occasion I must take leave to put you in mind that a running horse does require more attendance than a coach-horse. Nature has made some difference 'twixt you and me.   90

YOUNG FASHION Yes. She has made you older. (*Aside*) Plague take her.

LORD FOPPINGTON That is not all, Tam.

YOUNG FASHION Why, what is there else?

LORD FOPPINGTON (*looking first upon himself and then upon his brother*) Ask the ladies.   95

YOUNG FASHION Why, thou essence-bottle, thou musk cat,° dost thou then think thou hast any advantage over me but what fortune has given thee?

LORD FOPPINGTON I do, stap my vitals.

YOUNG FASHION Now, by all that's great and powerful, thou art the   100
prince of coxcombs.

LORD FOPPINGTON Sir, I am praud of being at the head of so prevailing a party.

YOUNG FASHION Will nothing then provoke thee? Draw, coward.
      [*Young Fashion draws his sword*]

LORD FOPPINGTON Look you, Tam, you know I have always taken   105
you for a mighty dull fellow, and here is one of the foolishest plats° broke out that I have seen a lang time. Your poverty makes life so burdensome to you, you would provoke me to a quarrel, in hopes either to slip through my lungs into my estate, or to get yourself run through the guts, to put an end to your pain. But I will disap-   110
point you in both your designs; far, with the temper of a philasapher and the discretion of a statesman, I shall leave the room with my sword in the scabbard.
      Exit Lord Foppington

YOUNG FASHION So! Farewell, brother; and now, conscience, I defy
    thee.—Lory!   115
    Enter Lory
LORY Sir?
YOUNG FASHION Here's rare news, Lory. His lordship has given me
    a pill has purged off all my scruples.
LORY Then my heart's at ease again. For I have been in a lamentable
    fright, sir, ever since your conscience had the impudence to intrude   120
    into your company.
YOUNG FASHION Be at peace; it will come there no more. My brother
    has given it a wring by the nose, and I have kicked it down stairs.
    So run away to the inn, get the chaise ready quickly, and bring it to
    Dame Coupler's without a moment's delay.   125
LORY Then, sir, you are going straight about the fortune?
YOUNG FASHION I am. Away; fly, Lory!
LORY The happiest day I ever saw. I'm upon the wing already.
    Exeunt severally

3.2

A garden

Enter Loveless and Servant
LOVELESS Is my wife within?
SERVANT No, sir; she has been gone out this half-hour.
LOVELESS Well, leave me.
    Exit Servant
    How strangely does my mind run on this widow. Never was my
    heart so suddenly seized on before. That my wife should pick out   5
    her, of all womankind, to be her playfellow. But what fate does, let
    fate answer for. I sought it not. So! By heavens, here she comes!
    Enter Berinthia
BERINTHIA What makes you look so thoughtful, sir? I hope you are
    not ill.
LOVELESS I was debating, madam, whether I was so or not, and that   10
    was it which made me look so thoughtful.
BERINTHIA Is it then so hard a matter to decide? I thought all people
    were acquainted with their own bodies, though few people know
    their own minds.

LOVELESS What if the distemper I suspect be in the mind?   15
BERINTHIA Why, then I'll undertake to prescribe you a cure.
LOVELESS Alas, you undertake you know not what.
BERINTHIA So far at least, then, you allow me to be a physician.
LOVELESS Nay, I'll allow you to be so yet farther, for I have reason to
    believe, should I put myself into your hands, you would increase   20
    my distemper.
BERINTHIA How?
LOVELESS O, you might betray my complaints° to my wife.
BERINTHIA And so lose all my practice.°
LOVELESS Will you then keep my secret?   25
BERINTHIA I will.
LOVELESS I'm satisfied. Now hear my symptoms, and give me your
    advice. The first were these. When I saw you at the play, a random
    glance you threw at first alarmed me. I could not turn my eyes from
    whence the danger came. I gazed upon you till my heart began to   30
    pant. Nay, even now, on your approaching me, my illness is so
    increased, that if you do not help me I shall, whilst you look on,
    consume to ashes. (*Taking her hand*)
BERINTHIA (*breaking from him*) O, lord, let me go. 'Tis the plague, and
    we shall be infected.   35
LOVELESS Then we'll die together,° my charming angel.
BERINTHIA O Gad, the devil's in you! Lord, let me go! Here's some-
    body coming.
        Enter Servant
SERVANT Sir, my lady's come home, and desires to speak with you.
LOVELESS Tell her I'm coming.   40
        Exit Servant
    (*To Berinthia*) But before I go, one glass of nectar to drink her health.
BERINTHIA Stand off, or I shall hate you, by heavens.
LOVELESS (*kissing her*) In matters of love, a woman's oath is no more
    to be minded than a man's.
        Exit Loveless
BERINTHIA Um!   45
        Enter Colonel Townly
TOWNLY [*aside*] So! What's here? Berinthia and Loveless! And in such
    close° conversation! I cannot now wonder at her indifference in
    excusing herself to me! O rare woman. Well then, let Loveless look
    to his wife; 'twill be but the retort courteous° on both sides. (*To
    Berinthia*) Your servant, madam. I need not ask you how you do;   50
    you have got so good a colour.

BERINTHIA No better than I used to have, I suppose.

TOWNLY A little more blood in your cheeks.

BERINTHIA I have been walking!

TOWNLY Is that all? Pray, was it Mr Loveless went from here just now? 55

BERINTHIA O yes; he has been walking with me.

TOWNLY He has!

BERINTHIA Upon my word I think he is a very agreeable man! And there is certainly something particularly insinuating in his address!°

TOWNLY [aside] So! So! She hasn't even the modesty to dissemble!— 60 Pray, madam, may I, without impertinence, trouble you with a few serious questions?

BERINTHIA As many as you please; but pray let them be as little serious as possible.

TOWNLY Is it not near two years since I have presumed to address 65 you?°

BERINTHIA I don't know exactly; but it has been a tedious long time.

TOWNLY Have I not, during that period, had every reason to believe that my assiduities were far from being unacceptable?

BERINTHIA Why, to do you justice, you have been extremely trouble- 70 some; and I confess I have been more civil to you than you deserved.

TOWNLY Did I not come to this place at your express desire? And for no purpose but the honour of meeting you? And after waiting a month in disappointment, have you condescended to explain, or in the slightest way apologize for, your conduct? 75

BERINTHIA O heavens! Apologize for my conduct! Apologize to you! O you barbarian! But pray now, my good serious colonel, have you anything more to add?

TOWNLY Nothing, madam, but that after such behaviour I am less surprised at what I saw just now. It is not very wonderful that the 80 woman who can trifle with the delicate addresses° of an honourable lover should be found coquetting with the husband of her friend.

BERINTHIA Very true. No more wonderful than it was for this *honourable* lover to divert himself in the absence of this coquette with endeavouring to seduce his friend's wife! O colonel, colonel, don't 85 talk of honour or your friend, for heaven's sake.

TOWNLY [aside] 'Sdeath, how came she to suspect this!—Really, madam, I don't understand you.

BERINTHIA Nay, nay, you saw I did not pretend to misunderstand you. But here comes the lady. Perhaps you would be glad to be left with 90 her for an explanation.

TOWNLY O madam, this recrimination is a poor resource; and to

convince you how much you are mistaken, I beg leave to decline the
happiness you propose me. Madam, your servant.

Enter Amanda. Colonel Townly whispers to Amanda

BERINTHIA [*aside*] He carries it off well, however. Upon my word,   95
very well! How tenderly they part!

Exit Colonel Townly

So, cousin. I hope you have not been chiding your admirer for being
with me. I assure you we have been talking of you.

AMANDA Fie, Berinthia! My admirer? Will you never learn to talk in
earnest of anything?   100

BERINTHIA Why, this shall be in earnest, if you please; for my part I
only tell you matter of fact.

AMANDA I'm sure there's so much jest and earnest° in what you say
to me on this subject, I scarce know how to take it. I have just parted
with Mr Loveless. Perhaps it is my fancy, but I think there is an   105
alteration in his manner, which alarms me.

BERINTHIA And so you are jealous? Is that all?

AMANDA That all! Is jealousy then nothing?

BERINTHIA It should be nothing, if I were in your case.

AMANDA Why, what would you do?   110

BERINTHIA I'd cure myself.

AMANDA How?

BERINTHIA Care as little for my husband as he did for me. Look you,
Amanda. You may build castles in the air, and fume, and fret, and
grow thin, and lean, and pale, and ugly, if you please. But I tell you   115
no man worth having is true to his wife, or ever was, or ever will be
so.°

AMANDA Do you then really think he's false to me? For I did not
suspect him.

BERINTHIA Think so! I am sure of it.   120

AMANDA You are sure on't?

BERINTHIA Positively. He fell in love at the play.

AMANDA Right; the very same. But who could have told you this?

BERINTHIA Um. O, Townly! I suppose your husband has made him
his confidant.   125

AMANDA O base Loveless! And what did Townly say on't?

BERINTHIA (*aside*) So, so. Why should she ask that?—Say! Why, he
abused Loveless extremely, and said all the tender things of you in
the world.

AMANDA Did he? O, my heart! I'm very ill. I must go to my chamber.   130
Dear Berinthia, don't leave me a moment.

BERINTHIA. No; don't fear.

    Exit Amanda

So. There is certainly some affection on her side at least towards Townly. If it prove so, and her agreeable husband perseveres, heaven send me resolution! Well, how this business will end I know not; but I seem to be in as fair a way to lose my gallant colonel, as a boy is to be a rogue, when he's put clerk to an attorney.

    Exit

3.3

    A country house

    Enter Young Fashion and Lory

YOUNG FASHION So, here's our inheritance, Lory, if we can but get into possession. But methinks the seat of our family looks like Noah's ark, as if the chief part on't were designed for the fowls of the air and the beasts of the field.°

LORY Pray, sir, don't let your head run upon the orders of building° here. Get but the heiress; let the devil take the house.

YOUNG FASHION Get but the house! Let the devil take the heiress, I say. But come, we have no time to squander; knock at the door.

    Lory knocks two or three times

What the devil, have they got no ears in this house? Knock harder.

LORY Egad, sir, this will prove some enchanted castle. We shall have the giant come out by and by with his club and beat our brains out.

    Lory knocks again

YOUNG FASHION Hush, they come.

SERVANT (*from within*) Who is there?

LORY Open the door and see. Is that your country breeding?

SERVANT (*within*) Ay, but two words to that bargain.°—Tummas, is the blunderbuss primed?

YOUNG FASHION Oons, give 'em good words, Lory, or we shall be shot here a-fortune-catching.

LORY Egad, sir, I think you're in the right on't.—Ho! Mr What-d'ye-call'um, will you please to let us in? Or are we to be left to grow like willows° by your moat-side?

    Servant appears at the window with a blunderbuss

SERVANT Weel naw, what's ya're business?

YOUNG FASHION Nothing, sir, but to wait upon Sir Tunbelly, with
    your leave.   25

SERVANT To weat upon Sir Tunbelly? Why, you'll find that's just as
    Sir Tunbelly pleases.

YOUNG FASHION But will you do me the favour, sir, to know whether
    Sir Tunbelly pleases or not?

SERVANT Why, look you, d'ye see, with good words much may be   30
    done.°—Ralph, go thy waes, and ask Sir Tunbelly if he pleases to
    be waited upon. And—dost hear?—call to Nurse that she may lock
    up Miss Hoyden before the geat's open.

YOUNG FASHION D'ye hear that, Lory?
    [*The gate opens.*] *Enter Sir Tunbelly Clumsy, with Servants,*
    armed with guns, clubs, pitchforks, etc.

LORY O! (*Running behind his master*) O lord, O lord, lord, we are both   35
    dead men.

YOUNG FASHION Take heed, fool; thy fear will ruin us.

LORY My fear, sir? 'Sdeath, I fear nothing. (*Aside*) Would I were well
    up to the chin in a horse-pond.

SIR TUNBELLY Who is it here has any business with me?   40

YOUNG FASHION Sir, 'tis I, if your name be Sir Tunbelly Clumsy?

SIR TUNBELLY Sir, my name is Sir Tunbelly Clumsy, whether you
    have any business with me or not. So you see I am not ashamed of
    my name, nor my face either.

YOUNG FASHION Sir, you have no cause that I know of.   45

SIR TUNBELLY Sir, if you have no cause either, I desire to know who
    you are; for till I know your name, I shan't ask you to come into my
    house; and when I do know your name, 'tis six to four I don't ask
    you then.

YOUNG FASHION (*giving him a letter*) Sir, I hope you'll find this letter   50
    an authentic passport.

SIR TUNBELLY [*reads*] Cod's my life, from Mrs Coupler. I ask your
    lordship's pardon ten thousand times. (*To his Servant*) Here, run in
    a-doors quickly. Get a Scotch coal fire in the great parlour. Set all
    the Turkey work chairs in their places. Get the brass candlesticks   55
    out, and be sure stick the socket full of laurel.° Run. (*Turning to*
    Young Fashion) My lord, I ask your lordship's pardon. (*To Servant*)
    And—do you hear?—run away to Nurse; bid her let Miss Hoyden
    loose again.
        Exit Servant
    (*To Young Fashion*) I hope your honour will excuse the disorder of   60
    my family. We are not used to receive men of your lordship's great

quality every day. Pray, where are your coaches and servants, my
lord?

YOUNG FASHION Sir, that I might give you and your fair daughter
a proof how impatient I am to be nearer akin to you, I left my   65
equipage to follow me, and came away post with only one servant.

SIR TUNBELLY Your lordship does me too much honour. It was exposing your person to too much fatigue and danger; I protest it was.
But my daughter shall endeavour to make you what amends she can;
and, though I say it, that should not say it, Hoyden has charms.   70

YOUNG FASHION Sir, I am not a stranger to them, though I am to her.
Common fame° has done her justice.

SIR TUNBELLY My lord, I am common fame's very grateful humble
servant. My lord, my girl's young; Hoyden is young, my lord. But
this I must say for her. What she wants in art, she has by nature;   75
what she wants in experience, she has in breeding; and what's
wanting in her age is made good in her constitution.° So pray, my
lord, walk in; pray, my lord, walk in.

YOUNG FASHION Sir, I wait upon you.

> *Exeunt through the gate*

[3.4]

> [*A room in Sir Tunbelly Clumsy's house*]

> *Miss Hoyden alone*

HOYDEN Sure, nobody was ever used as I am. I know well enough
what other girls do, for all° they think to make a fool of me. It's well
I have a husband a-coming, or ecod I'd marry the baker, I would so.
Nobody can knock at the gate, but presently I must be locked up;
and here's the young greyhound can run loose about the house all   5
the day long, so she can. 'Tis very well.

NURSE (*without, opening the door*) Miss Hoyden, Miss, Miss, Miss,
Miss Hoyden!

> *Enter Nurse*

HOYDEN Well, what do you make such a noise for, ha? What do you
din a body's ears for? Can't one be at quiet for you?   10

NURSE What do I din your ears for? Here's one come will din your
ears for you.

HOYDEN What care I who's come? I care not a fig who comes, nor who
goes, as long as I must be locked up like the ale cellar.

NURSE That, Miss, is for fear you should be drank before you are ripe.   15
HOYDEN O don't you trouble your head about that. I'm as ripe as you,
     though not so mellow.
NURSE Very well. Now I have a good mind to lock you up again, and
     not let you see my lord tonight.
HOYDEN My lord! Why, is my husband come?   20
NURSE Yes, marry, is he, and a goodly person too.
HOYDEN (*hugging Nurse*) O my dear Nurse, forgive me this once, and
     I'll never misuse you again. No; if I do, you shall give me three
     thumps on the back and a great pinch by the cheek.
NURSE Ah, the poor thing, see how it melts! It's as full of good nature   25
     as an egg's full of meat.
HOYDEN But, my dear Nurse, don't lie now! Is he come, by your
     troth?°
NURSE Yes, by my truly is he.
HOYDEN O lord! I'll go and put on my laced tucker,° though I'm   30
     locked up a month for't.
          Exit Miss Hoyden running, [*followed by Nurse*]

4.1

[A room in Sir Tunbelly Clumsy's house]

Enter Miss Hoyden and Nurse

NURSE Well, Miss, how do you like your husband that is to be?

HOYDEN O lord, Nurse, I'm so overjoyed, I can scarce contain myself.

NURSE O but you must have a care of being too fond, for men nowadays hate a woman that loves 'em.

HOYDEN Love him! Why do you think I love him, Nurse? Ecod, I   5
would not care if he was hanged, so I were but once married to him.
No, that which pleases me is to think what work I'll make° when I
get to London; for when I am a wife and a lady both, ecod I'll flaunt
it with the best of 'em. Ay, and I shall have money enough to do so
too, Nurse.   10

NURSE Ah, there's no knowing that, Miss, for though these lords have
a power of wealth indeed, yet, as I have heard say, they give it all
to their sluts and their trulls, who joggle it about in their coaches,
with a murrain to 'em, whilst poor Madam sits sighing and wishing,
and has not a spare half-crown to buy her a *Practice of Piety*.°   15

HOYDEN O, but, for that, don't deceive yourself, Nurse, for this I must
say of my lord, he's as free as an open house at Christmas. For
this very morning he told me I should have six hundred a year to
buy pins.° Now, Nurse, if he gives me six hundred a year to buy
pins, what do you think he'll give me to buy fine petticoats?   20

NURSE Ah, my dearest, he deceives thee foully, and he's no better than
a rogue for his pains. These Londoners have got a gibberage° with
'em would confound a gipsy. That which they call pin-money is to
buy their wives everything in the versal° world, down to their very
shoe-knots. Nay, I have heard folks say that some ladies, if they will   25
have gallants, as they call 'em, are forced to find them out of their
pin-money too. But look, look, if his honour be not coming to you.
Now, if I were sure you would behave yourself handsomely, and not
disgrace me that have brought you up, I'd leave you alone together.

HOYDEN That's my best Nurse; do as you'd be done by.° Trust us   30
together this once, and if I don't show my breeding, may I never
be married but die an old maid.

NURSE Well, this once I'll venture you. But if you disparage me—°

HOYDEN Never fear.

Exit Nurse. Enter Young Fashion

YOUNG FASHION Your servant, madam. I'm glad to find you alone,   35
for I have something of importance to speak to you about.

HOYDEN Sir—my lord, I meant—you may speak to me about what
you please. I shall give you a civil answer.

YOUNG FASHION You give me so obliging a one, it encourages me to
tell you in a few words what I think both° for your interest and   40
mine. Your father, I suppose you know, has resolved to make me
happy in being your husband, and I hope I may depend on your
consent to perform what he desires.

HOYDEN Sir, I never disobey my father in anything but eating green
gooseberries.   45

YOUNG FASHION So good a daughter must needs be an admirable
wife. I am therefore impatient till you are mine, and hope you will
so far consider the violence of my love, that you won't have the
cruelty to defer my happiness so long as your father designs it.

HOYDEN Pray, my lord, how long is that?   50

YOUNG FASHION Madam, a thousand years—a whole week.

HOYDEN A week! Why, I shall be an old woman by that time.

YOUNG FASHION And I an old man.

HOYDEN Why, I thought it was to be tomorrow morning, as soon as
I was up. I'm sure Nurse told me so.   55

YOUNG FASHION And it shall be tomorrow morning, if you'll
consent.

HOYDEN If I'll consent! Why, I thought I was to obey you as my
husband?

YOUNG FASHION That's when we are married. Till then I'm to obey   60
you.

HOYDEN Why then, if we are to take it by turns, it's the same
thing. I'll obey you now, and when we are married you shall obey
me.

YOUNG FASHION With all my heart. But I doubt we must get Nurse   65
on our side, or we shall hardly prevail with the chaplain.

HOYDEN No more we shan't indeed, for he loves her better than he
loves his pulpit, and would always be a-preaching to her by his good
will.

YOUNG FASHION Why then, my dear, if you'll call her hither, we'll   70
try to persuade her presently.

HOYDEN O lord, I can tell you a way how to persuade her to anything.

YOUNG FASHION How's that?

HOYDEN Why, tell her she's a handsome, comely woman, and give her
half-a-crown.   75

YOUNG FASHION Nay, if that will do, she shall have half a score of them.

HOYDEN O gemini, for half that she'd marry you herself. I'll run and call her.

Exit Miss Hoyden

YOUNG FASHION So, matters go swimmingly. This is a rare girl, i'faith. I shall have a fine time on't with her at London. But no matter. She brings me an estate will afford me a separate maintenance.°

Enter Lory

So, Lory, what's the matter?

LORY Here, sir; an intercepted packet° from the enemy. Your brother's postilion brought it. I knew the livery, pretended to be a servant of Sir Tunbelly's, and so got possession of the letter.

YOUNG FASHION (*looking at it*) Oons! He tells Sir Tunbelly here that he will be with him this evening, with a large party to supper. Egad, I must marry the girl directly.

LORY O zounds, sir, directly, to be sure! Here she comes.

Exit Lory

YOUNG FASHION And the old Jezebel° with her. She has a thorough procuring countenance, however.

Enter Miss Hoyden and Nurse

How do you do, Mrs Nurse? I desired your young lady would give me leave to see you, that I might thank you for your extraordinary care and conduct in her education. Pray accept of this small acknowledgement for it at present [*giving her money*]; and depend upon my farther kindness when I shall be that happy thing, her husband.

NURSE (*aside*) Gold, by maakins!°—Your honour's goodness is too great. Alas, all I can boast of is, I gave her pure good milk, and so your honour would have said, an you had seen how the poor thing thrived, and how it would look up in my face, and crow and laugh it would!

HOYDEN (*to Nurse, taking her angrily aside*) Pray one word with you. Prithee, Nurse, don't stand ripping up old stories, to make one ashamed before one's love. Do you think such a fine, proper gentleman as he is cares for a fiddlecome tale of a child? If you have a mind to make him have a good opinion of a woman, don't tell him what one did then; tell him what one can do now. (*To Young Fashion*) I hope your honour will excuse my mismanners to whisper before you. It was only to give some orders about the family.

183

YOUNG FASHION O, everything, madam, is to give way to business; besides, good housewifery is a very commendable quality in a young lady.   115

HOYDEN Pray, sir, are young ladies good housewives at London town? Do they darn their own linen?

YOUNG FASHION O no; they study how to spend money, not to save it.

HOYDEN Ecod, I don't know but that may be better sport—ha, Nurse!   120

YOUNG FASHION Well, you shall have your choice when you come there.

HOYDEN Shall I? Then, by my troth, I'll get there as fast as I can. (*To Nurse*) His honour desires you'll be so kind as to let us be married tomorrow.   125

NURSE Tomorrow, my dear madam?

YOUNG FASHION Ay, faith, Nurse, you may well be surprised at Miss's wanting to put it off so long. Tomorrow! No, no; 'tis now, this very hour, I would have the ceremony performed.

HOYDEN Ecod, with all my heart.   130

NURSE O mercy, worse and worse.

YOUNG FASHION Yes, sweet Nurse, now, and privately. For, all things being signed and sealed, why should Sir Tunbelly make us stay a week for a wedding-dinner?

NURSE But if you should be married now, what will you do when Sir   135
Tunbelly calls for you to be wedded?

HOYDEN Why, then we will be married again.

NURSE What, twice, my child!

HOYDEN Ecod, I don't care how often I'm married, not I.

NURSE Well, I'm such a tender-hearted fool, I find I can refuse you   140
nothing. So you shall e'en follow your own inventions.°

HOYDEN Shall I? (*Aside*) O lord, I could leap over the moon.

YOUNG FASHION Dear Nurse, this goodness of yours shall be still more rewarded. But now you must employ your power with the chaplain, that he may do his friendly office too, and then we shall   145
be all happy. Do you think you can prevail with him?

NURSE Prevail with him! Or he shall never prevail with me, I can tell him that.

YOUNG FASHION I'm glad to hear it. However, to strengthen your interest with him, you may let him know I have several fat   150
livings° in my gift, and that the first that falls° shall be in your disposal.

NURSE Nay then, I'll make him marry more folks than one, I'll
  promise him.

HOYDEN Faith, do, Nurse, make him marry you too; I'm sure he'll   155
  do't for a fat living.

YOUNG FASHION Well, Nurse, while you go and settle matters with
  him, your lady and I will go and take a walk in the garden.
    Exit Nurse
  (*Giving Miss Hoyden his hand*) Come, madam. Dare you venture
  yourself alone with me?   160

HOYDEN O dear, yes, sir. I don't think you'll do anything to me I need
  be afraid on.°
    Exeunt

4.2

[Loveless and Amanda's lodgings]

Enter Amanda, her Maid following

MAID If you please, madam, only to say whether you'll have me buy
  them or not?

AMANDA Yes—no—go, teaser! I care not what you do! Prithee leave
  me.
    Exit Maid. Enter Berinthia

BERINTHIA What in the name of Jove's the matter with you?   5

AMANDA The matter, Berinthia? I'm almost mad; I'm plagued to
  death.

BERINTHIA Who is it that plagues you?

AMANDA Who do you think should plague a wife but her husband?

BERINTHIA O ho, is it come to that? We shall have you wish yourself   10
  a widow, by and by.

AMANDA Would I were anything but what I am! A base, ungrateful
  man, to use me thus!

BERINTHIA What, has he given you fresh reason to suspect his
  wandering?   15

AMANDA Every hour gives me reason.

BERINTHIA And yet, Amanda, you perhaps at this moment cause in
  another's breast the same tormenting doubts and jealousies which
  you feel so sensibly yourself.

AMANDA Heaven knows I would not!   20

BERINTHIA Why, you can't tell but there may be someone as tenderly attached to Townly, whom you boast of as your conquest, as you can be to your husband.

AMANDA I'm sure I never encouraged his pretensions.

BERINTHIA Pshaw! Pshaw! No sensible man ever perseveres to love 25 without encouragement. Why have you not treated him as you have Lord Foppington?

AMANDA Because he has not presumed so far. But let us drop the subject. Men, not women, are riddles. Mr Loveless now follows some flirt for variety, whom I'm sure he does not like so well as he 30 does me.

BERINTHIA That's more than you know, madam.

AMANDA Why, do you know the ugly thing?

BERINTHIA I think I can guess at the person. But she's no such ugly thing neither. 35

AMANDA Is she very handsome?

BERINTHIA Truly I think so.

AMANDA Whate'er she be, I'm sure he does not like her well enough to bestow anything more than a little outward gallantry upon her.

BERINTHIA (aside) Outward gallantry! I can't bear this.—Come, come, 40 don't you be too secure, Amanda; while you suffer Townly to imagine that you do not detest him for his designs on you, you have no right to complain that your husband is engaged elsewhere. But here comes the person we were speaking of.

        Enter Colonel Townly

TOWNLY Ladies, as I come uninvited, I beg, if I intrude you will use 45 the same freedom in turning me out again.

AMANDA I believe, sir, it is near the time Mr Loveless said he would be at home. He talked of accepting Lord Foppington's invitation to sup at Sir Tunbelly Clumsy's.

TOWNLY His lordship has done me the honour to invite me also. If 50 you'll let me escort you, I'll let you into a mystery as we go, in which you must play a part when we arrive.

AMANDA But we have two hours yet to spare; the carriages are not ordered till eight, and it is not a five minutes' drive. So, cousin, let us keep the colonel to play piquet with us, till Mr Loveless comes 55 home.

BERINTHIA As you please, madam. But you know I have letters to write.

TOWNLY Madam, you know you may command me, though I'm a very wretched gamester. 60

AMANDA O, you play well enough to lose your money, and that's all
the ladies require. And so, without any more ceremony, let us go
into the next room and call for cards and candles.

Exeunt

4.3

Berinthia's dressing-room

Enter Loveless

LOVELESS So. Thus far all's well. I have got into her dressing-
room; and, it being dusk, I think nobody has perceived me steal into
the house. I heard Berinthia tell my wife she had some particular
letters to write this evening before we went to Sir Tunbelly's, and
here are the implements for correspondence. How shall I muster up   5
assurance to show myself when she comes? I think she has given
me encouragement; and, to do my impudence justice, I have made
the most of it. I hear a door open and someone coming. If it should
be my wife, what the devil should I say? I believe she mistrusts me,
and by my life I don't deserve her tenderness. However, I am   10
determined to reform, though not yet. Ha! Berinthia. So, I'll step
in here till I see what sort of humour she is in.

Loveless goes into the closet. Enter Berinthia

BERINTHIA Was ever so provoking a situation! To think I should sit
and hear him compliment Amanda to my face! I have lost all
patience with them both. I would not for something° have Loveless   15
know what temper of mind they have piqued me into. Yet I can't
bear to leave them together. No; I'll put my papers away, and return
to disappoint them.

Berinthia goes to the closet

O lord! A ghost! A ghost! A ghost!

Enter Loveless

LOVELESS Peace, my angel. It's no ghost, but one worth a hundred   20
spirits.

BERINTHIA How, sir, have you had the insolence to presume to—Run
in again; here's somebody coming.

Exit Loveless. Enter Maid

MAID O lord, ma'am, what's the matter?

BERINTHIA O heavens, I'm almost frightened out of my wits! I   25
thought verily I had seen a ghost, and 'twas nothing but a black

hood pinned against the wall. You may go again. I am the fearfullest
fool!

Exit Maid. Enter Loveless

LOVELESS Is the coast clear?

BERINTHIA The coast clear! Upon my word, I wonder at your   30
assurance!

LOVELESS Why, then you wonder before I have given you a proof of
it. But where's my wife?

BERINTHIA At cards.

LOVELESS With whom?   35

BERINTHIA With Townly.

LOVELESS Then we are safe enough.

BERINTHIA You are so! Some husbands would be of another mind
were he at cards with their wives.

LOVELESS And they'd be in the right on't too; but I dare trust mine.   40

BERINTHIA Indeed! And she, I doubt not, has the same confidence in
you. Yet do you think she'd be content to come and find you here?

LOVELESS Egad, as you say, that's true. Then, for fear she should
come, hadn't we better go into the next room out of her way?

BERINTHIA What, in the dark?   45

LOVELESS Ay, or with a light; which° you please.

BERINTHIA You are certainly very impudent.

LOVELESS Nay then, let me conduct you, my angel.

BERINTHIA Hold, hold! You are mistaken in your angel, I assure you.

LOVELESS I hope not, for by this hand I swear—   50

BERINTHIA Come, come, let go my hand, or I shall hate you. I'll cry
out, as I live.

LOVELESS Impossible! You cannot be so cruel.

BERINTHIA Ha! Here's someone coming. Be gone instantly.

LOVELESS Will you promise to return if I remain here?   55

BERINTHIA Never trust myself in a room with you again while I live.

LOVELESS But I have something particular to communicate to you.

BERINTHIA Well, well. Before we go to Sir Tunbelly's, I'll walk upon the
lawn. If you are fond of a moonlight evening, you will find me there.

LOVELESS I'faith, they're coming here now. I take you at your word.   60

Exit Loveless into the closet

BERINTHIA 'Tis Amanda, as I live. I hope she has not heard his voice.
Though I mean she should have her share of jealousy in turn.

Enter Amanda

AMANDA Berinthia, why did you leave me?

BERINTHIA I thought I only spoiled your party.

AMANDA Since you have been gone, Townly has attempted to renew   65
his importunities. I must break with him, for I cannot venture to
acquaint Mr Loveless with his conduct.

BERINTHIA O no; Mr Loveless mustn't know of it by any means.

AMANDA O, not for the world. I wish, Berinthia, you would undertake
to speak to Townly on the subject.   70

BERINTHIA Upon my word, it would be a very pleasant subject for me
to talk to him on. But come, let us go back. And you may depend
on't, I'll not leave you together again, if I can help it.

Exeunt Berinthia and Amanda. Enter Loveless

LOVELESS So, so! A pretty piece of business I have overheard. Townly
makes love to my wife, and I'm not to know it for the world. I must   75
inquire into this; and, by heaven, if I find that Amanda has in the
smallest degree—Yet what have I been at here? O, 'sdeath, that's no
rule!

> That wife alone unsullied credit wins,
> Whose virtues can atone her husband's sins.   80
> Thus, while the man has other nymphs in view,
> It suits the woman to be doubly true.

Exit

5.1

A garden. Moonlight°

Enter Loveless

LOVELESS Now, does she mean to make a fool of me, or not? I shan't
wait much longer, for my wife will soon be inquiring for me to set
out on our supping party. Suspense is at all times the devil; but, of
all modes of suspense, the watching for a loitering mistress is the
worst. But let me accuse her no longer. She approaches, with one   5
smile to o'erpay the anxiety of a year.

Enter Berinthia

O Berinthia, what a world of kindness are you in my debt! Had you
stayed five minutes longer—

BERINTHIA You would have been gone, I suppose.

LOVELESS (*aside*) Egad, she's right enough.   10

BERINTHIA And I assure you 'twas ten to one that I came at all. In
short, I begin to think you are too dangerous a being to trifle with;
and as I shall probably only make a fool of you at last, I believe we
had better let matters rest as they are.

LOVELESS You cannot mean it, sure?   15

BERINTHIA No! Why, do you think you are really so irresistible, and
master of so much address, as to deprive a woman of her senses in
a few days' acquaintance?

LOVELESS O, no, madam; 'tis only by your preserving your senses that
I can hope to be admitted into your favour. Your taste, judgement,   20
and discernment are what I build my hopes on.

BERINTHIA Very modest, upon my word. And it certainly follows, that
the greatest proof I can give of my possessing those qualities would
be my admiring Mr Loveless!

LOVELESS O, that were so cold a proof.   25

BERINTHIA What shall I do more? Esteem you?

LOVELESS O no; worse and worse. Can you behold a man, whose every
faculty your attractions have engrossed, whose whole soul, as by
enchantment, you have seized on—can you see him tremble at your
feet, and talk of so poor a return as your esteem!   30

BERINTHIA What more would you have me give to a married man?

LOVELESS How doubly cruel to remind me of misfortunes!

BERINTHIA A misfortune to be married to so charming a woman as
Amanda!

LOVELESS I grant all her merit, but—'sdeath, now see what you have   35
    done by talking of her! She's here, by all that's unlucky!

BERINTHIA O Ged, we had both better get out of the way, for I should
    feel as awkward to meet her as you.

LOVELESS Ay, but if I mistake not, I see Townly coming this way also.
    I must see a little into this matter.   40

       Loveless steps aside

BERINTHIA O, if that's your intention, I am no woman if I suffer
    myself to be outdone in curiosity.

       Berinthia goes on the other side. Enter Amanda

AMANDA Mr Loveless come home and walking on the lawn! I will not
    suffer him to walk so late, though perhaps it is to show his neglect
    of me. Mr Loveless—ha! Townly again! How I am persecuted!   45

       Enter Colonel Townly

TOWNLY Madam, you seem disturbed!

AMANDA Sir, I have reason.

TOWNLY Whatever be the cause, I would to heaven it were in my
    power to bear the pain, or to remove the malady.

AMANDA Your interference can only add to my distress.   50

TOWNLY Ah, madam, if it be the sting of unrequited love you suffer
    from, seek for your remedy in revenge. Weigh well the strength and
    beauty of your charms, and rouse up that spirit a woman ought to
    bear. Disdain the false embraces of a husband. [*Kneeling*] See at
    your feet a real lover. His zeal may give him title to your pity,   55
    although his merit cannot claim your love!

LOVELESS (*aside*) So, so, very fine, i'faith!

AMANDA Why do you presume to talk to me thus? Is this your friend-
    ship to Mr Loveless? I perceive you will compel me at last to
    acquaint him with your treachery.   60

TOWNLY He could not upbraid me if you were. He deserves it from
    me, for he has not been more false to you than faithless to me.

AMANDA To you!

TOWNLY Yes, madam; the lady for whom he now deserts those charms
    which he was never worthy of was mine by right—and I imagined   65
    too, by inclination. Yes, madam, Berinthia, who now—

AMANDA Berinthia! Impossible!

TOWNLY 'Tis true, or may I never merit your attention. She is the
    deceitful sorceress who now holds your husband's heart in bondage.

AMANDA I will not believe it.   70

TOWNLY By the faith of a true lover, I speak from conviction. This
    very day I saw them together, and overheard—

AMANDA Peace, sir; I will not even listen to such slander. This is a
poor device to work on my resentment, to listen to your insidious
addresses. No, sir. Though Mr Loveless may be capable of error, I   75
am convinced I cannot be deceived so grossly in him, as to believe
what you now report; and for Berinthia, you should have fixed on
some more probable person for my rival than she who is my relation and my friend. For, while I am myself free from guilt, I will
never believe that love can beget injury, or confidence° create   80
ingratitude.

TOWNLY If I do not prove this to you—

AMANDA You never shall have an opportunity. From the artful manner
in which you first showed yourself attentive to me, I might have
been led, as far as virtue permitted, to have thought you less crim-   85
inal than unhappy. But this last unmanly artifice merits at once my
resentment and contempt.

    Exit Amanda

TOWNLY Sure there's divinity about her; and she has dispensed some
portion of honour's light to me. Yet can I bear to lose Berinthia
without revenge or compensation? Perhaps she is not so culpable   90
as I thought her. I was mistaken when I began to think lightly of
Amanda's virtue, and may be in my censure° of my Berinthia.
Surely I love her still; for I feel I should be happy to find myself in
the wrong.

    Exit Colonel Townly. Loveless and Berinthia move
    centre-stage°

BERINTHIA Your servant, Mr Loveless.   95

LOVELESS Your servant, madam.

BERINTHIA Pray, what do you think of this?

LOVELESS Truly, I don't know what to say.

BERINTHIA Don't you think we steal forth two very contemptible
creatures?   100

LOVELESS Why, tolerably so, I must confess.

BERINTHIA And do you conceive it possible for you ever to give
Amanda the least uneasiness again?

LOVELESS No, I think we never should, indeed.

BERINTHIA We! Why, monster, you don't pretend that I ever enter-   105
tained a thought.

LOVELESS Why then, sincerely and honestly, Berinthia, there is something in my wife's conduct which strikes me so forcibly, that if it
were not for shame and the fear of hurting you in her opinion, I

swear I would follow her, confess my error, and trust to her gen-   110
erosity for forgiveness.

BERINTHIA Nay, prithee don't let your respect for me prevent you; for
as my object in trifling with you was nothing more than to pique
Townly, and as I perceive he has been actuated by a similar motive,
you may depend on't I shall make no mystery of the matter to him.   115

LOVELESS By no means inform him; for though I may choose to pass
by his conduct without resentment, how will he presume to look
me in the face again!

BERINTHIA How will you presume to look him in the face again?

LOVELESS He, who has dared to attempt the honour of my wife!   120

BERINTHIA You, who have dared to attempt the honour of his mistress! Come, come; be ruled by me who affect more levity than I
have, and don't think of anger in this cause. A readiness to resent
injuries is a virtue only in those who are slow to injure.

LOVELESS Then I will be ruled by you. And when you shall think   125
proper to undeceive Townly, may your good qualities make as
sincere a convert of him as Amanda's have of me. When truth's
extorted from us, then we own the robe of virtue is a graceful habit.

> Could women but our secret counsels scan—°
> Could they but read the deep reserve of man—°   130
> To keep our love, they'd rate their virtue high;
> They'd live together, and together die!°

Exeunt

5.2

Sir Tunbelly Clumsy's house

Enter Miss Hoyden, Nurse, and Young Fashion

YOUNG FASHION This quick dispatch of the chaplain's I take so
kindly, it shall give him claim to my favour as long as I live, I assure
you.

HOYDEN And to mine too, I promise you.

NURSE I most humbly thank your honours; and may your children   5
swarm about you, like bees about a honeycomb.

HOYDEN Ecod, with all my heart. The more the merrier, I say. Ha,
Nurse?

Enter Lory, taking Young Fashion hastily aside

LORY One word with you, for heaven's sake.

YOUNG FASHION What the devil's the matter?   10

LORY Sir, your fortune's ruined, if you are not married. Yonder's your
    brother, arrived with two coaches and six horses, twenty footmen,
    and a coat worth fourscore pounds. So judge what will become of
    your lady's heart.

YOUNG FASHION Is he in the house yet?   15

LORY No, they are capitulating° with him at the gate. Sir Tunbelly
    luckily takes him for an impostor, and I have told him that we had
    heard of this plot before.

YOUNG FASHION That's right. (*To Miss Hoyden*) My dear, here's a
    troublesome business my man tells me of. But don't be frightened;   20
    we shall be too hard for the rogue. Here's an impudent fellow at the
    gate, not knowing I was come hither incognito, has taken my name
    upon him, in hopes to run away with you.

HOYDEN O the brazen-faced varlet! It's well we are married, or maybe
    we might never have been so.   25

YOUNG FASHION (*aside*) Egad, like enough.—Prithee, Nurse, run to
    Sir Tunbelly, and stop him from going to the gate before I speak
    with him.

NURSE An't please your honour, my lady and I had best lock ourselves
    up till the danger be over.   30

YOUNG FASHION Do so, if you please.

HOYDEN Not so fast. I won't be locked up any more, now I'm married.

YOUNG FASHION Yes, pray, my dear, do, till we have seized this rascal.

HOYDEN Nay, if you'll pray me, I'll do anything.

        Exeunt Miss Hoyden and Nurse

YOUNG FASHION (*to Lory*) Hark you, sirrah, things are better than   35
    you imagine. The wedding's over.

LORY The devil it is, sir!

YOUNG FASHION Not a word. All's safe. But Sir Tunbelly don't know
    it, nor must not, yet. So I am resolved to brazen the business out,
    and have the pleasure of turning the imposture upon his lordship,°   40
    which I believe may easily be done.

        *Enter Sir Tunbelly Clumsy, and Servants, armed with clubs,
        pitch-forks, etc.*

YOUNG FASHION Did you ever hear, sir, of so impudent an
    undertaking?

SIR TUNBELLY Never, by the mass. But we'll tickle° him, I'll warrant
    you.   45

YOUNG FASHION They tell me, sir, he has a great many people with
    him, disguised like servants.

SIR TUNBELLY Ay, ay, rogues enow. But we have mastered them. We
only fired a few shot over their heads, and the regiment scoured in
an instant.—Here, Tummas, bring in your prisoner.   50

YOUNG FASHION If you please, Sir Tunbelly, it will be best for me
not to confront the fellow yet, till you have heard how far his impudence will carry him.

SIR TUNBELLY Egad, your lordship is an ingenious person. Your lordship then will please to step aside.   55

LORY (aside) 'Fore heaven, I applaud my master's modesty.
          Exeunt Young Fashion and Lory. Enter Servants, [Constable,
          and Chaplain], with Lord Foppington, disarmed

SIR TUNBELLY Come, bring him along, bring him along.

LORD FOPPINGTON What the pax° do you mean, gentlemen? Is it fair
time that you are all drunk before supper?

SIR TUNBELLY Drunk, sirrah! Here's an impudent rogue for you.   60
Drunk or sober, bully, I'm a justice of the peace, and know how to
deal with strollers.

LORD FOPPINGTON Strollers!

SIR TUNBELLY Ay, strollers. Come, give an account of yourself.
What's your name? Where do you live? Do you pay scot and lot?°   65
Come, are you a freeholder or a copyholder?

LORD FOPPINGTON And why dost thou ask me so many impertinent
questions?

SIR TUNBELLY Because I'll make you answer 'em before I have done
with you, you rascal, you.   70

LORD FOPPINGTON Before Gad, all the answer I can make to 'em is
that thou art a very extraordinary fellow, stap my vitals!

SIR TUNBELLY Nay, if you are for joking with deputy lieutenants, we
know how to deal with you.—[*To the Chaplain*] Here, draw a
warrant for him° immediately.   75

LORD FOPPINGTON A warrant! What the devil is't thou wouldst be
at, old gentleman?

SIR TUNBELLY I would be at you, sirrah, if my hands were not tied
as a magistrate, and with these two double fists beat your teeth down
your throat, you dog you.   80

LORD FOPPINGTON And why wouldst thou spoil my face at that rate?

SIR TUNBELLY For your design to rob me of my daughter, villain.

LORD FOPPINGTON Rab thee of thy daughter! Now do I begin to
believe I am in bed and asleep, and that all this is but a dream.
Prithee, old father, wilt thou give me leave to ask thee one question?   85

SIR TUNBELLY I can't tell whether I will or not, till I know what it is.

LORD FOPPINGTON Why then, it is whether thou didst not write to my Lord Foppington to come down and marry thy daughter?

SIR TUNBELLY Yes, marry did I, and my Lord Foppington is come down, and shall marry my daughter before she's a day older.   90

LORD FOPPINGTON Now give me thy hand, old dad; I thought we should understand one another at last.

SIR TUNBELLY This fellow's mad. Here, bind him hand and foot.

The Servants bind Lord Foppington

LORD FOPPINGTON Nay, prithee, knight, leave fooling; thy jest begins to grow dull.   95

SIR TUNBELLY Bind him, I say; he's mad. Bread and water, a dark room, and a whip may bring him to his senses again.

LORD FOPPINGTON Prithee, Sir Tunbelly, why should you take such an aversion to the freedom of my address, as to suffer the rascals thus to skewer down my arms like a rabbit? (*Aside*) Egad, if I don't   100
waken quickly, by all that I can see, this is like to prove one of the most impertinent dreams that ever I dreamt in my life.

Enter Miss Hoyden and Nurse

HOYDEN (*going up to him*) Is this he that would have run away with me? Faugh! How he stinks of sweets!° Pray, father, let him be dragged through the horse-pond.   105

LORD FOPPINGTON (*aside*) This must be my wife, by her natural inclination to her husband.

HOYDEN Pray, father, what do you intend to do with him? Hang him?

SIR TUNBELLY That, at least, child.

NURSE Ay, and it's e'en too good for him too.   110

LORD FOPPINGTON (*aside*) Madame la gouvernante, I presume. Hitherto this appears to me one of the most extraordinary families that ever man of quality matched into.

SIR TUNBELLY What's become of my lord, daughter?

HOYDEN He's just coming, sir.   115

LORD FOPPINGTON (*aside*) My lord! What does he mean by that, now?

Enter Young Fashion and Lory

Stap my vitals, Tam! Now the dream's out.

YOUNG FASHION Is this the fellow, sir, that designed to trick me of your daughter?   120

SIR TUNBELLY This is he, my lord. How do you like him? Is not he a pretty fellow to get a fortune?

YOUNG FASHION I find by his dress he thought your daughter might be taken with a beau.

HOYDEN O gemini, is this a beau? Let me see him again. Ha! I find a   125
beau is no such ugly thing, neither.

YOUNG FASHION [*aside*] Egad, she'll be in love with him presently.
I'll e'en have him sent away to jail. (*To Lord Foppington*) Sir, though
your undertaking shows you a person of no extraordinary modesty,
I suppose you ha'n't confidence enough to expect much favour from   130
me.

LORD FOPPINGTON Strike me dumb, Tam, thou art a very impudent
fellow.

NURSE Look, if the varlet has not the frontery° to call his lordship
plain Thomas.   135

SIR TUNBELLY Come, is the warrant writ?

CHAPLAIN Yes, sir.

LORD FOPPINGTON Hold, one moment. Pray, gentlemen. My Lord
Foppington, shall I beg one word with your lordship?

NURSE O, ho, it's 'my lord' with him now; see how afflictions will   140
humble folks.

HOYDEN Pray, my lord, don't let him whisper too close, lest he bite
your ear off.

LORD FOPPINGTON I am not altogether so hungry as your ladyship
is pleased to imagine. (*To Young Fashion*) Look you, Tam, I am   145
sensible I have not been so kind to you as I ought; but I hope
you'll forgive what's past, and accept of the five thousand pounds
I offer. Thou may'st live in extreme splendour with it, stap my
vitals!

YOUNG FASHION It's a much easier matter to prevent a disease than   150
to cure it. A quarter of that sum would have secured your mistress;
(*leaving him*) twice as much won't redeem her.

SIR TUNBELLY Well, what says he?

YOUNG FASHION Only the rascal offered me a bribe to let him go.

SIR TUNBELLY Ay, he shall go, with a halter to him.—Lead on,   155
Constable.

   Enter Servant

SERVANT Sir, here is Muster Loveless, and Muster Colonel Townly,
and some ladies, to wait on you.

LORY (*aside to Young Fashion*) So, sir, what will you do now?

YOUNG FASHION Be quiet; they are in the plot. (*To Sir Tunbelly*) Only   160
a few friends, Sir Tunbelly, whom I wished to introduce to you.

LORD FOPPINGTON Thou art the most impudent fellow, Tam, that
ever nature yet brought into the world.—Sir Tunbelly, strike
me speechless, but these are my friends and my guests, and they

will soon inform thee whether I am the true Lord Foppington or   165
not.

Enter Loveless, Colonel Townly, Amanda, and Berinthia

YOUNG FASHION So, gentlemen, this is friendly; I rejoice to see you.

TOWNLY My lord, we are fortunate to be the witnesses of your lordship's happiness.

LOVELESS But your lordship will do us the honour to introduce us to   170
Sir Tunbelly Clumsy?

AMANDA And us to your lady.

LORD FOPPINGTON Ged take me, but they are all in a story.°

SIR TUNBELLY Gentlemen, you do me great honour; my Lord Foppington's friends will ever be welcome to me and mine.   175

YOUNG FASHION My love, let me introduce you to these ladies.

HOYDEN By goles, they look so fine and so stiff,° I am almost ashamed
to come nigh 'em.

AMANDA A most engaging young lady, indeed!

HOYDEN Thank ye, ma'am.   180

BERINTHIA And I doubt not will soon distinguish herself in the beau
monde.

HOYDEN Where is that?

YOUNG FASHION You'll soon learn, my dear.

LOVELESS But, Lord Foppington—   185

LORD FOPPINGTON Sir!

LOVELESS Sir! I was not addressing myself to you, sir. Pray, who is
this, gentlemen? He seems rather in a singular predicament.

SIR TUNBELLY Ha, ha, ha! So, these are your friends and your guests,
ha, my adventurer?   190

LORD FOPPINGTON I am struck dumb with their impudence, and
cannot positively say whether I shall ever speak again or not.

SIR TUNBELLY Why, sir, this modest gentleman wanted to pass
himself upon me for Lord Foppington, and carry off my daughter.

LOVELESS A likely plot to succeed, truly! Ha, ha!   195

LORD FOPPINGTON As Gad shall judge me, Loveless, I did not expect
this from thee. Come, prithee confess the joke; tell Sir Tunbelly
that I am the real Lord Foppington, who yesterday made love to
thy wife, was honoured by her with a slap on the face, and after-
ward pinked through the bady by thee.   200

SIR TUNBELLY A likely story, truly, that a peer would behave thus!

LOVELESS A curious fellow indeed, that would scandalize the
character° he wants to assume! But what will you do with him, Sir
Tunbelly?

SIR TUNBELLY Commit him certainly, unless the bride and bride- 205
groom choose to pardon him.

LORD FOPPINGTON Bride and bridegroom! For Gad's sake, Sir
Tunbelly, 'tis tarture to me to hear you call 'em so.

HOYDEN Why, you ugly thing, what would you have him call us? Dog
and cat! 210

LORD FOPPINGTON By no means, Miss; for that sounds ten times
more like man and wife than t'other.

SIR TUNBELLY A precious rogue this, to come a-wooing!
    Enter Servant

SERVANT There are some more gentlefolks below, to wait upon Lord
Foppington. 215

TOWNLY [*aside to Young Fashion*] 'Sdeath, Tom, what will you do
now?

LORD FOPPINGTON Now, Sir Tunbelly, here are witnesses, who, I
believe, are not corrupted.

SIR TUNBELLY Peace, fellow!—Would your lordship choose to have 220
your guests shown here, or shall they wait till we come to 'em?

YOUNG FASHION I believe, Sir Tunbelly, we had better not have these
visitors here yet. (*Aside*) Egad, all must out!

LOVELESS Confess, confess; we'll stand by you.

LORD FOPPINGTON Nay, Sir Tunbelly, I insist on your calling 225
evidence on both sides; and if I do not prove that fellow an
impostor—

YOUNG FASHION Brother, I will save you the trouble, by now con-
fessing that I am not what I have passed myself for.—Sir Tunbelly,
I am a gentleman, and I flatter myself a man of character; but 'tis 230
with great pride I assure you I am not Lord Foppington.

SIR TUNBELLY Oons! What's this! An impostor! A cheat! Fire and
faggots,° sir! If you are not Lord Foppington, who the devil are
you?

YOUNG FASHION Sir, the best of my condition is I am your son-in- 235
law, and the worst of it is I am brother to that noble peer.

LORD FOPPINGTON Impudent to the last!

SIR TUNBELLY My son-in-law! Not yet, I hope?

YOUNG FASHION Pardon me, sir; I am, thanks to the goodness of your
chaplain and the kind offices of this old gentlewoman. 240

LORY 'Tis true, indeed, sir; I gave your daughter away, and Mrs
Nurse, here, was clerk.°

SIR TUNBELLY Knock that rascal down!—But speak, Jezebel, how's
this?

NURSE Alas, your honour, forgive me! I have been overreached in this   245
business as well as you. Your worship knows, if the wedding dinner
had been ready, you would have given her away with your own
hands.

SIR TUNBELLY But how durst you do this without acquainting me?

NURSE Alas, if your worship had seen how the poor thing begged and   250
prayed, and clung and twined about me like ivy round an old wall,
you would say I who had nursed it and reared it must have had a
heart of stone to refuse it.

SIR TUNBELLY Oons! I shall go mad!—Unloose my lord there, you
scoundrels!   255

LORD FOPPINGTON Why, when these gentlemen are at leisure, I
should be glad to congratulate you on your son-in-law with a little
more freedom of address.

[*The Servants free Lord Foppington*]

HOYDEN Egad, though, I don't see which is to be my husband, after
all.   260

LOVELESS Come, come, Sir Tunbelly. A man of your understanding
must perceive that an affair of this kind is not to be mended by
anger and reproaches.

TOWNLY Take my word for it, Sir Tunbelly; you are only tricked into
a son-in-law you may be proud of. My friend, Tom Fashion, is as   265
honest a fellow as ever breathed.

LOVELESS That he is, depend on't, and will hunt or drink with you
most affectionately; be generous, old boy, and forgive them.

SIR TUNBELLY Never! The hussy! When I had set my heart on getting
her a title!   270

LORD FOPPINGTON Now, Sir Tunbelly, that I am untrussed, give me
leave to thank thee for the very extraordinary reception I have met
with in thy damned, execrable mansion, and at the same time to
assure thee that, of all the bumpkins and blockheads I have had the
misfortune to meet with, thou art the most obstinate and egregious,   275
strike me ugly!

SIR TUNBELLY What's this! Oons! I believe you are both rogues alike!

LORD FOPPINGTON No, Sir Tunbelly; thou wilt find to thy unspeakable mortification that I am the real Lord Foppington, who was to
have disgraced myself by an alliance with a clod, and that thou hast   280
matched thy girl to a beggarly younger brother of mine, whose title
deeds might be contained in thy tobacco-box.

SIR TUNBELLY Puppy, puppy! I might prevent their being beggars if

I chose it; for I could give 'em as good a rent-roll as your lordship.

TOWNLY Well said, Sir Tunbelly.   285

LORD FOPPINGTON Ay, old fellow, but you will not do it; for that would be acting like a Christian, and thou art a thorough barbarian, stap my vitals.

SIR TUNBELLY Udzookers!° Now six such words more, and I'll forgive them directly.   290

LOVELESS 'Slife, Sir Tunbelly, you should do it, and bless yourself.— Ladies, what say you?

AMANDA Good Sir Tunbelly, you must consent.

BERINTHIA Come, you have been young yourself, Sir Tunbelly.

SIR TUNBELLY Well, then, if I must, I must. But turn that sneering   295
lord out, however; and let me be revenged on somebody. But first, look whether I am a barbarian, or not. There, children, I join your hands, and when I'm in a better humour, I'll give you my blessing.

LOVELESS Nobly done, Sir Tunbelly; and we shall see you dance at a grandson's wedding yet.   300

HOYDEN By goles, though, I don't understand this. What, a'n't I to be a lady after all? Only plain Mrs—what's my husband's name, Nurse?

NURSE Squire Fashion.

HOYDEN Squire, is he? Well, that's better than nothing.   305

LORD FOPPINGTON [aside] Now will I put on a philosophic air, and show these people that it is not possible to put a man of my quality out of countenance.—Dear Tam, since things are thus fallen out, prithee give me leave to wish thee joy; I do it de bon cœur, strike me dumb! You have married into a family of great   310
politeness and uncommon elegance of manners; and your bride appears to be a lady beautiful in her person, modest in her deportment,° refined in her sentiments, and of a nice morality, split my windpipe!

HOYDEN By goles, husband, break his bones, if he calls me names.   315

YOUNG FASHION Your lordship may keep up your spirits with your grimace,° if you please. I shall support mine, by Sir Tunbelly's favour, with this lady and three thousand pounds a year.

LORD FOPPINGTON Well, adieu, Tam.—Ladies, I kiss your hands. Sir Tunbelly, I shall now quit thy den; but while I retain my arms,° 320
I shall remember thou art a savage, stap my vitals!

    Exit Lord Foppington

SIR TUNBELLY By the mass, 'tis well he's gone, for I should ha' been

provoked by and by to ha' dun 'un° a mischief. Well, if this is a
lord, I think Hoyden has luck o' her side, in troth!

TOWNLY She has, indeed, Sir Tunbelly.   325
      [*Music offstage*]
But I hear the fiddles; his lordship, I know, had provided 'em.

LOVELESS O, a dance, and a bottle, Sir Tunbelly, by all means.

SIR TUNBELLY I had forgot the company below. Well, what, we must
be merry then, ha?—and dance and drink, ha? Well, 'fore George,
you shan't say I do things by halves. Son-in-law there looks like a   330
hearty rogue, so we'll have a night of it; and which of these gay
ladies will be the old man's partner, ha? Ecod, I don't know how I
came to be in so good a humour.

BERINTHIA Well, Sir Tunbelly, my friend and I both will endeavour
to keep you so. You have done a generous action, and are entitled   335
to our attention;° and if you should be at a loss to divert your new
guests, we will assist you to relate to them the plot of your daughter's marriage and his lordship's deserved mortification, a subject
which, perhaps, may afford no bad evening's entertainment.

SIR TUNBELLY Ecod, with all my heart; though I am a main bungler   340
at a long story.

BERINTHIA Never fear; we will assist you, if the tale is judged worth
being repeated. But of this you may be assured, that while the
intention is evidently to please, British auditors will ever be indulgent to the errors of the performance.   345
      [*Exeunt*]

THE SCHOOL FOR SCANDAL
A Comedy

A PORTRAIT°

Addressed to a lady° with the comedy of
The School for Scandal

Tell me, ye prim adepts in scandal's school,
Who rail by precept and detract by rule,°
Lives there no character so tried, so known,
So decked with grace, and so unlike your own,
That even *you* assist her fame to raise,   5
Approve by envy, and by silence praise?°
    Attend! A model shall attract your view,
Daughters of calumny. I summon *you.*
You shall decide if this a portrait prove,
Or fond creation of the muse and love.   10
    Attend, ye virgin critics shrewd and sage,
Ye matron censors of this childish age,°
Whose peering eye and wrinkled front declare
A fixed antipathy to young and fair—
By cunning cautious, or by nature cold,   15
In maiden malice virulently bold.
    Attend, ye skilled to coin the precious tale,
Creating proof, where innuendoes fail;
Whose practised memories, cruelly exact,
Omit no circumstance, except the fact!   20
Attend, all ye who boast, or old or young,°
The living libel of a slanderous tongue!
So shall my theme as far contrasted be°
As saints by fiends, or hymns by calumny.
    Come, gentle Amoret—for 'neath that name   25
In worthier verse is sung thy beauty's fame.°
Come, for but *thee* whom seeks the muse; and while°
Celestial blushes check thy conscious smile,°
With timid grace and hesitating eye
The perfect model which I boast supply!°   30
Vain muse, couldst thou the humblest sketch create°
Of *her*, or slightest charm could imitate,
Could thy blessed strain, in kindred colours, trace°
The faintest wonder of her form or face,

Poets would study the immortal line, 35
And Reynolds own his art subdued by *thine*!°
That art, which well might added lustre give
To nature's best, and heaven's superlative,
On Granby's cheek might bid new glories rise,
Or point a purer beam from Devon's eyes!° 40
    Hard is the task to shape that beauty's praise,
Whose judgement scorns the homage flattery pays!
But, praising Amoret, we cannot err:
No tongue o'ervalues heaven, or flatters *her*!
Yet *she*—by fate's perverseness!—she alone 45
Would doubt our truth, nor deem such praise her *own*.
    Adorning fashion, unadorned by dress,
Simple from taste, and not from carelessness,
Discreet in gesture, in deportment mild,
Not stiff with prudence, nor uncouthly wild, 50
No state has Amoret, no studied mien.°
She apes no goddess, and she moves no queen!°
The softer charm that in her manner lies
Is framed to captivate, yet not surprise;°
It justly suits th'expression of her face; 55
'Tis less than dignity, and more than grace!°
    On her pure cheek the native hue is such,
That, formed by heaven to be admired so much,
The hand that made her with such partial care
Might well have fixed a fainter crimson there, 60
And bade the gentle inmate of her breast,
Enshrinèd modesty, supply the rest.
    But who the peril of her lips shall paint?
Strip them of smiles—still, still all words were faint!°
But, moving, love himself appears to teach 65
Their action, though denied to rule her speech!
And thou, who seest her speak, and dost not hear,
Mourn not her distant accents 'scape thine ear.
Viewing those lips, thou still may'st make pretence
To judge of what she says, and swear 'tis sense; 70
Clothed with such grace, with such expression fraught,
They move in meaning, and they pause in thought!
But dost thou further watch, with charmed surprise,
The mild irresolution of her eyes,
Curious to mark how frequent they repose 75

In brief eclipse and momentary close?
Ah, seest thou not! An ambushed Cupid there,
Too timorous of his charge, with jealous care
Veils and unveils those beams of heavenly light,
Too full, too fatal else for mortal sight!   80
Nor yet, such pleasing vengeance fond to meet,
In pardoning dimples hope a safe retreat.
What though her peaceful breast should ne'er allow
Subduing frowns to arm her altered brow,
By love I swear, and by his gentler wiles,   85
More fatal still the mercy of her smiles!

Thus lovely, thus adorned, possessing all
Of bright or fair that can to woman fall,
The height of vanity might well be thought
Prerogative in her, and nature's fault.°   90
Yet gentle Amoret, in mind supreme
As well as charms, rejects the vainer theme;
And, half mistrustful of her beauty's store,
She barbs with wit those darts too keen before.

Graced by those signs which truth delights to own—°   95
The timid blush and mild submitted tone—°
Whate'er she says, though sense appear throughout,
Bears the unartful hue of female doubt.
Decked with that charm, how lovely wit appears;
How graceful science, when that robe she wears!°   100
Such, too, her talents and her bent of mind
As speak a sprightly heart, by thought refined;
A taste for mirth, by contemplation schooled;
A turn for ridicule, by candour ruled;
A scorn of folly, which she tries to hide;   105
An awe of talent, which she owns with pride.

Peace, idle muse! No more thy strain prolong;
But yield a theme thy warmest praises wrong.
Just to her merit, though thou canst not raise
Thy feeble verse, behold th'acknowledged praise   110
Has spread conviction through the envious train
And cast a fatal gloom o'er scandal's reign!
And, lo, each pallid hag, with blistered tongue,
Mutters assent to all thy zeal has sung,
Owns all the colours just, the outline true,°   115
Thee my inspirer, and my model *Crewe!*

THE CHARACTERS OF THE PLAY

Sir Peter Teazle°   *Mr King*
Sir Oliver Surface°   *Mr Yates*
Joseph Surface   *Mr Palmer*
Charles Surface   *Mr Smith*
Crabtree°   *Mr Parsons*
Sir Benjamin Backbite°   *Mr Dodd*
Rowley   *Mr Aickin*
Moses°   *Mr Baddeley*
Trip°   *Mr Lamash*
Snake   *Mr Packer*
Careless°   *Mr Farren*
Sir Toby Bumper°   *Mr Gaudry*
[Two Gentlemen]
[Servant to Lady Sneerwell]
[Servant to Joseph Surface]

Lady Teazle   *Mrs Abington*
Maria   *Miss P. Hopkins*
Lady Sneerwell   *Miss Sherry*
Mrs Candour°   *Miss Pope*
[Maid to Lady Teazle]

[SCENE: LONDON]

Prologue

Written by David Garrick, Esq.°

Spoken by Mr King°

A school for scandal! Tell me, I beseech you,
Needs there a school this modish art to teach you?
No need of lessons *now* the knowing think:°
We might as well be taught to eat and drink.
Caused by a dearth of scandal, should the vapours°   5
Distress our fair ones, let 'em read the papers:
Their powerful mixtures such disorders hit,
Crave what they will, there's *quantum sufficit*.°
   'Lud', cries my Lady Wormwood, who loves tattle°
And puts much salt and pepper in her prattle.   10
Just risen at noon, all night at cards, when threshing,°
'Strong tea and scandal! Bless me, how refreshing!
Give me the papers, Lisp. How bold and free.' (*Sips*)°
'"Last night Lord L——" (*Sips*) "was caught with Lady D——."
For aching heads what charming sal volatile!' (*Sips*)   15
'"If Mrs B——will still continue flirting,
We hope she'll draw, or we'll undraw, the curtain."
Fine satire poz. In public all abuse it;°
But by ourselves—' (*Sips*) '—our praise we can't refuse it.
Now, Lisp, read *you*. There at that dash and star.' (*Sips*)°   20
'Yes, ma'am. "A certain lord had best beware,
Who lives not twenty miles from Grosvenor Square,°
For should he Lady W——find willing,
Wormwood is bitter—"' 'O, that's me. The villain!
Throw it behind the fire, and never more   25
Let that vile paper come within my door.'
Thus at our friends we laugh, who feel the dart;
To reach *our* feelings, we ourselves must smart.
Is our young bard so young to think that he
Can stop the full spring-tide of calumny?   30
Knows he the world so little, and its trade?
Alas, the devil is sooner raised than laid.
So strong, so swift, the monster there's no gagging;
Cut scandal's head off, still the tongue is wagging.

Proud of your smiles, once lavishly bestowed,   35
Again our young Don Quixote takes the road.°
To show his gratitude, he draws his pen,
And seeks this hydra, scandal, in its den,°
From his fell gripe the frighted fair to save.°
Though he should fall, th'attempt must please the brave.   40
For your applause, all perils he would through;
He'll fight—that's write—a cavalliero true,
Till every drop of blood—that's ink—is spilt for *you.*

1.1

Lady Sneerwell's house.

Lady Sneerwell at the dressing-table, Snake drinking chocolate

LADY SNEERWELL The paragraphs,° you say, Mr Snake, were all inserted?

SNAKE They were, madam; and as I copied them myself in a feigned hand, there can be no suspicion whence they came.

LADY SNEERWELL Did you circulate the report of Lady Brittle's°   5
intrigue with Captain Boastall?

SNAKE That is in as fine a train° as your ladyship could wish. In the common course of things, I think it must reach Mrs Clackit's° ears within four-and-twenty hours, and then you know the business is as good as done.   10

LADY SNEERWELL Why, truly, Mrs Clackit has a very pretty talent and a great deal of industry.

SNAKE True, madam, and has been tolerably successful in her day. To my knowledge, she has been the cause of six matches° being broken off and three sons being disinherited, of four forced elopements,   15
as many close confinements,° nine separate maintenances,° and two divorces. Nay, I have more than once traced her causing a *tête-à-tête* in the *Town and Country Magazine*,° when the parties perhaps have never seen each other's faces before in the course of their lives.   20

LADY SNEERWELL She certainly has talents, but her manner is gross.°

SNAKE 'Tis very true; she generally designs well, has a free tongue and a bold invention, but her colouring is too dark and her outline often extravagant. She wants that delicacy of hint and mellowness° of sneer which distinguish your ladyship's scandal.   25

LADY SNEERWELL Ah, you are partial, Snake.

SNAKE Not in the least. Everybody allows that Lady Sneerwell can do more with a word or a look than many can with the most laboured detail,° even when they happen to have a little truth on their side to support it.   30

LADY SNEERWELL Yes, my dear Snake, and I am no hypocrite to deny the satisfaction I reap from the success of my efforts. Wounded myself in the early part of my life by the envenomed tongue of slander, I confess I have since known no pleasure equal to the reducing others to the level of my own injured reputation.   35

SNAKE Nothing can be more natural. But, Lady Sneerwell, there is one affair in which you have lately employed me, wherein I confess I am at a loss to guess your motives.

LADY SNEERWELL I conceive you mean with respect to my neighbour Sir Peter Teazle and his family?   40

SNAKE I do. Here are two young men, to whom Sir Peter has acted as a kind of guardian since their father's death, the elder possessing the most amiable character° and universally well spoken of, the other the most dissipated and extravagant° young fellow in the kingdom, without friends or character—the former an avowed   45
admirer of your ladyship, and apparently your favourite; the latter attached to° Maria, Sir Peter's ward, and confessedly° beloved by her. Now, on the face of these circumstances, it is utterly un-accountable to me why you, the widow of a city knight° with a good jointure,° should not close with° the passion of a man of such char-   50
acter and expectations as Mr Surface—and more so why you should be so uncommonly earnest to destroy the mutual attachment° sub-sisting between his brother Charles and Maria.

LADY SNEERWELL Then, at once to unravel this mystery, I must inform you that love has no share whatever in the intercourse°   55
between Mr Surface and me.

SNAKE No!

LADY SNEERWELL His real attachment is to Maria or her fortune; but, finding in his brother a favoured rival, he has been obliged to mask his pretensions and profit by my assistance.   60

SNAKE Yet still I am more puzzled why you should interest yourself in his success.

LADY SNEERWELL Heavens, how dull you are! Cannot you surmise the weakness which I hitherto through shame have concealed even from you? Must I confess that Charles—that libertine, that extrav-   65
agant, that bankrupt in fortune and reputation—that he it is for whom I am thus anxious and malicious and to gain whom I would sacrifice everything?

SNAKE Now indeed your conduct appears consistent. But how came you and Mr Surface so confidential?°   70

LADY SNEERWELL For our mutual interest. I have found him out a long time since. I know him to be artful, selfish and malicious—in short, a sentimental knave.°

SNAKE Yet Sir Peter vows he has not his equal in England; and, above all, he praises him as a man of sentiment.°   75

LADY SNEERWELL True, and with the assistance of his sentiments and hypocrisy he has brought him entirely into his interest° with regard to Maria.

Enter Servant

SERVANT Mr Surface.

LADY SNEERWELL Show him up.   80

Exit Servant

He generally calls about this time; I don't wonder at people's giving him to me for a lover.

Enter Joseph Surface

JOSEPH SURFACE My dear Lady Sneerwell, how do you do today?— Mr Snake, your most obedient.

LADY SNEERWELL Snake has just been arraigning me on our mutual   85
attachment; but I have informed him of our real views. You know how useful he has been to us; and, believe me, the confidence is not ill-placed.

JOSEPH SURFACE Madam, it is impossible for me to suspect a man of Mr Snake's sensibility° and discernment.   90

LADY SNEERWELL Well, well, no compliments now; but tell me when you saw your mistress Maria, or—what is more material to me— your brother?

JOSEPH SURFACE I have not seen either since I left you; but I can inform you that they never meet. Some of your stories have taken   95
a good effect on Maria.

LADY SNEERWELL Ah, my dear Snake, the merit of this belongs to you.—But do your brother's distresses increase?

JOSEPH SURFACE Every hour. I am told he has had another execution° in the house yesterday. In short, his dissipation and extravagance   100
exceed anything I ever heard of.

LADY SNEERWELL Poor Charles!

JOSEPH SURFACE True, madam; notwithstanding his vices, one can't help feeling for him. Ay, poor Charles! I'm sure I wish it was in my power to be of any essential service to him, for the man who does   105
not share in the distresses of a brother, even though merited by his own misconduct, deserves—

LADY SNEERWELL O lud, you are going to be moral° and forget that you are among friends.

JOSEPH SURFACE Egad, that's true. I'll keep that sentiment till I see   110
Sir Peter. However, it is certainly a charity to rescue Maria from such a libertine, who, if he is to be reclaimed, can be so only by a person of your ladyship's superior accomplishments and understanding.

SNAKE I believe, Lady Sneerwell, here's company coming. I'll go 115
and copy the letter I mentioned to you.—Mr Surface, your most
obedient.

JOSEPH SURFACE Sir, your very devoted.
        Exit Snake
Lady Sneerwell, I am very sorry you have put any further confidence in° that fellow. 120

LADY SNEERWELL Why so?

JOSEPH SURFACE I have lately detected him in frequent conference
with old Rowley, who was formerly my father's steward, and has
never, you know, been a friend of mine.

LADY SNEERWELL And do you think he would betray us? 125

JOSEPH SURFACE Nothing more likely. Take my word for't, Lady
Sneerwell. That fellow hasn't virtue enough to be faithful even to
his own villainy. Ha! Maria!
        Enter Maria°

LADY SNEERWELL Maria, my dear, how do you do? What's the
matter? 130

MARIA O, there is that disagreeable lover° of mine, Sir Benjamin
Backbite, has just called at my guardian's with his odious uncle,
Crabtree; so I slipped out and run° hither to avoid them.

LADY SNEERWELL Is that all?

JOSEPH SURFACE If my brother Charles had been of the party, ma'am, 135
perhaps you would not have been so much alarmed.

LADY SNEERWELL Nay, now you are severe, for I dare swear the truth
of the matter is Maria heard *you* were here.—But, my dear, what
has Sir Benjamin done that you should avoid him so?

MARIA O, he has done nothing; but 'tis for what he has said. His con- 140
versation is a perpetual libel° on all his acquaintance.

JOSEPH SURFACE Ay, and the worst of it is there is no advantage in
not knowing him; for he'll abuse a stranger just as soon as his best
friend—and his uncle's as bad.

LADY SNEERWELL Nay, but we should make allowance. Sir Benjamin 145
is a wit and a poet.

MARIA For my part, I own, madam, wit loses its respect with me when
I see it in company with malice. What do you think, Mr Surface?

JOSEPH SURFACE Certainly, madam, to smile at the jest which plants
a thorn in another's breast is to become a principal in the mischief. 150

LADY SNEERWELL Pshaw! There's no possibility of being witty
without a little ill nature. The malice of a good thing is the barb°
that makes it stick. What's your opinion, Mr Surface?

JOSEPH SURFACE To be sure, madam, that conversation where the
spirit of raillery° is suppressed will ever appear tedious and insipid.   155

LADY SNEERWELL Well, I'll not debate how far scandal may be allow-
able; but in a man I am sure it is always contemptible. We have pride,
envy, rivalship, and a thousand motives to depreciate each other; but
the male slanderer must have the cowardice of a woman before he
can traduce one.   160

    Enter Servant

SERVANT Madam, Mrs Candour is below, and, if your ladyship's at
leisure, will leave her carriage.

LADY SNEERWELL Beg her to walk in.

    [*Exit Servant*]

Now, Maria, however, here is a character to your taste, for though
Mrs Candour is a little talkative, everybody allows her to be the   165
best-natured and best sort of woman.

MARIA Yes; with a very gross affectation of good nature and benevolence she does more mischief than the direct malice of old
Crabtree.

JOSEPH SURFACE I'faith, 'tis very true, Lady Sneerwell. Whenever I   170
hear the current running against the characters of my friends, I
never think them in such danger as when Candour undertakes their
defence.

LADY SNEERWELL Hush, here she is.

    Enter Mrs Candour

MRS CANDOUR My dear Lady Sneerwell, how have you been this   175
century?—Mr Surface, what news do you hear? Though, indeed,
it is no matter, for I think one hears nothing else but scandal.

JOSEPH SURFACE Just so, indeed, madam.

MRS CANDOUR Ah, Maria, child, what, is the whole affair off between
you and Charles? His extravagance, I presume. The town talks of   180
nothing else.

MARIA I am very sorry, ma'am, the town° has so little to do.

MRS CANDOUR True, true, child; but there is no stopping people's
tongues. I own I was hurt to hear it—as indeed I was to learn from
the same quarter that your guardian Sir Peter and Lady Teazle have   185
not agreed lately so well as could be wished.

MARIA 'Tis strangely impertinent for people to busy themselves so.

MRS CANDOUR Very true, child; but what's to be done? People will
talk; there's no preventing it. Why, it was but yesterday I was told
that Miss Gadabout had eloped with Sir Filigree Flirt;° but, lord,   190

there is no minding what one hears—though to be sure I had this
from very good authority.

MARIA Such reports are highly scandalous.

MRS CANDOUR So they are, child. Shameful! Shameful! But the world
is so censorious, no character escapes. Lud now, who would have   195
suspected your friend Miss Prim of an indiscretion! Yet such is
the ill nature of people that they say her uncle stopped her last
week just as she was stepping into the York diligence° with her
dancing-master.

MARIA I'll answer for't there are no grounds for the report.   200

MRS CANDOUR O, no foundation in the world, I dare swear. No more
probably than for the story circulated last month of Mrs Festino's
affair with Colonel Casino,° though to be sure that matter was never
rightly cleared up.

JOSEPH SURFACE The licence of invention some people take is mon-   205
strous indeed.

MARIA 'Tis so; but in my opinion those who report such things are
equally culpable.

MRS CANDOUR To be sure they are. Tale-bearers are as bad as the
tale-makers.° 'Tis an old observation and a very true one; but what's   210
to be done, as I said before? How will you prevent people from
talking? Today Mrs Clackit assured me Mr and Mrs Honeymoon
were at last become mere man and wife like the rest of their
acquaintances.° She likewise hinted that a certain widow in the next
street had got rid of her dropsy and recovered her shape in a most   215
surprising manner;° and at the same time Miss Tattle who was
by affirmed that Lord Buffalo had discovered his lady at a house
of no extraordinary fame,° and that Sir Harry Bouquet° and Tom
Saunter were to measure swords° on a similar provocation. But,
lord, do you think I would report these things? No, no; tale-bearers,   220
as I said before, are just as bad as tale-makers.

JOSEPH SURFACE Ah, Mrs Candour, if everybody had your forbear-
ance and good nature!

MRS CANDOUR I confess, Mr Surface, I cannot bear to hear people
attacked behind their backs; and when ugly circumstances come out   225
against one's acquaintances, I own I always love to think the best.
By the bye, I hope 'tis not true that your brother is absolutely
ruined.

JOSEPH SURFACE I am afraid his circumstances are very bad indeed,
ma'am.   230

MRS CANDOUR Ah, I heard so. But you must tell him to keep up his
spirits; everybody almost is in the same way. Lord Spindle, Sir
Thomas Splint, Captain Quinze, and Mr Nickit°—all up,° I hear,
within this week! So, if Charles is undone, he'll find half his
acquaintances ruined too; and that, you know, is a consolation.   235
JOSEPH SURFACE Doubtless, ma'am, a very great one.
　　　Enter Servant
SERVANT Mr Crabtree and Sir Benjamin Backbite.
　　　Exit Servant
LADY SNEERWELL So! Maria, you see your lover pursues you. Posi-
tively you shan't escape.°
　　　Enter Crabtree and Sir Benjamin Backbite
CRABTREE Lady Sneerwell, I kiss your hands.—Mrs Candour, I don't   240
believe you are acquainted with my nephew Sir Benjamin Backbite.
Egad, ma'am, he has a pretty° wit, and is a pretty poet too.—Isn't
he, Lady Sneerwell?
SIR BENJAMIN BACKBITE O fie, uncle.
CRABTREE Nay, egad, 'tis true. I'll back him at a rebus or a charade°   245
against the best rhymer in the kingdom. Has your ladyship heard
the epigram he wrote on Lady Frizzle's° feather catching fire? Do,
Benjamin, repeat it—or the charade you made last night extempore
at Mrs Drowsy's *conversazione*.° Come now, your first is the name
of a fish, your second a great naval commander, and—   250
SIR BENJAMIN BACKBITE Uncle, now prithee—
CRABTREE I'faith, ma'am, 'twould surprise you to hear how ready he
is at these things.
LADY SNEERWELL I wonder, Sir Benjamin, you never publish
anything.   255
SIR BENJAMIN BACKBITE To say truth, ma'am, 'tis very vulgar to
print; and as my little productions are mostly satires and lampoons
on particular people, I find they circulate more by giving copies in
confidence to the friends of the parties. However, I have some love-
elegies, which, when favoured with this lady's smiles, I mean to give   260
to the public.
CRABTREE 'Fore heaven, ma'am, they'll immortalize you; you'll be
handed down to posterity like Petrarch's Laura or Waller's
Sacharissa.°
SIR BENJAMIN BACKBITE Yes, madam; I think you will like them,   265
when you shall see them on a beautiful quarto page, where a neat
rivulet of text shall murmur through a meadow of margin.° 'Fore
Gad, they will be the most elegant things of their kind.

CRABTREE But, ladies, that's true°—have you heard the news?

MRS CANDOUR What, sir, do you mean the report of—?   270

CRABTREE No, ma'am, that's not it. Miss Nicely° is going to be married to her own footman.

MRS CANDOUR Impossible!

CRABTREE Ask Sir Benjamin.

SIR BENJAMIN BACKBITE 'Tis very true, ma'am. Everything is fixed   275
and the wedding-livery bespoke.°

CRABTREE Yes, and they *do* say there were pressing° reasons for't.

LADY SNEERWELL Why, I *have* heard something of this before.

MRS CANDOUR It can't be, and I wonder anyone should believe such
a story of so prudent a lady as Miss Nicely.   280

SIR BENJAMIN BACKBITE O, lud, ma'am, that's the very reason 'twas
believed at once. She has always been so cautious and so reserved
that everybody was sure there was some reason for it at bottom.

MRS CANDOUR Why, to be sure, a tale of scandal is as fatal to the
credit of a prudent lady of her stamp as a fever is generally to those   285
of the strongest constitutions; but there is a sort of puny sickly
reputation that is always ailing, yet will outlive the robuster characters of a hundred prudes.

SIR BENJAMIN BACKBITE True, madam. There are valetudinarians in
reputation as well as constitution, who, being conscious of° their   290
weak part, avoid the least breath of air and supply their want of
stamina by care and circumspection.

MRS CANDOUR Well, but this may be all a mistake. You know, Sir Benjamin, very trifling circumstances often give rise to the most in-
jurious tales.   295

CRABTREE That they do, I'll be sworn, ma'am. Did you ever hear how
Miss Piper came to lose her lover and her character last summer at
Tunbridge?° Sir Benjamin, you remember it?

SIR BENJAMIN BACKBITE O, to be sure, the most whimsical
circumstance.   300

LADY SNEERWELL How was it, pray?

CRABTREE Why, one evening at Mrs Ponto's assembly,° the conversation happened to turn on the difficulty of breeding Nova Scotia
sheep in this country. Says a young lady in company, 'I have known
instances of it, for Miss Letitia Piper, a first cousin of mine, had a   305
Nova Scotia sheep that produced her twins'. 'What!', cries the old
dowager Lady Dundizzy,° who, you know, is as deaf as a post, 'has
Miss Piper had twins?' This mistake, as you may imagine, threw
the whole company into a fit of laughing. However, 'twas the next

morning everywhere reported, and in a few days believed by the   310
whole town, that Miss Letitia Piper had actually been brought to
bed of a fine boy and a girl; and in less than a week there were people
who could name the father—and the farm-house where the babies
were put out to nurse.°

LADY SNEERWELL Strange indeed!   315

CRABTREE Matter of fact, I assure you.—O lud, Mr Surface, pray is
it true that your uncle Sir Oliver is coming home?

JOSEPH SURFACE Not that I know of indeed, sir.

CRABTREE He has been in the East Indies° a long time; you can
scarcely remember him, I believe. Sad comfort, whenever he   320
returns, to hear how your brother has gone on.

JOSEPH SURFACE Charles has been imprudent, sir, to be sure; but I
hope no busy° people have already prejudiced Sir Oliver against
him. He may reform.

SIR BENJAMIN BACKBITE To be sure, he may. For my part, I never   325
believed him to be so utterly void of principle as people say; and,
though he has lost all his friends, I am told nobody is better spoken
of by the Jews.°

CRABTREE That's true, egad, nephew. If the Old Jewry° were a ward,
I believe Charles would be an alderman. No man more popular   330
there. 'Fore Gad, I hear he pays as many annuities as the Irish
tontine,° and that whenever he's sick they have prayers for the
recovery of his health in the synagogue.

SIR BENJAMIN BACKBITE Yet no man lives in greater splendour. They
tell me, when he entertains his friends he can sit down to dinner   335
with a dozen of his own securities,° have a score of tradesmen waiting in the antechamber and an officer° behind every guest's chair.

JOSEPH SURFACE This may be entertainment to you, gentlemen; but
you pay very little regard to the feelings of a brother.

MARIA [aside] Their malice is intolerable.—Lady Sneerwell, I must   340
wish you a good morning. I'm not very well.
        Exit Maria

MRS CANDOUR O, dear, she changed colour very much!

LADY SNEERWELL Do, Mrs Candour, follow her; she may want
assistance.

MRS CANDOUR That I will, with all my soul, ma'am. Poor dear girl,   345
who knows what her situation may be!
        Exit Mrs Candour

LADY SNEERWELL 'Twas nothing but that she could not bear to hear
Charles reflected on, notwithstanding their difference.

SIR BENJAMIN BACKBITE The young lady's penchant is obvious.

CRABTREE But, Benjamin, you mustn't give up the pursuit for that.   350
Follow her and put her into good humour—repeat her some of your
own verses. Come, I'll assist you.

SIR BENJAMIN BACKBITE Mr Surface, I did not mean to hurt you—
but, depend upon't, your brother is utterly undone. (*Going*)

CRABTREE O lud, ay, undone as ever man was—can't raise a guinea.   355
(*Going*)

SIR BENJAMIN BACKBITE And everything sold, I'm told, that was
movable. (*Going*)

CRABTREE I have seen one that was at his house. Not a thing left but
some empty bottles that were overlooked, and the family pictures,   360
which, I believe, are framed in the wainscot. (*Going*)

SIR BENJAMIN BACKBITE And I'm very sorry to hear also some bad
stories against him. (*Going*)

CRABTREE O, he has done many mean things; that's certain! (*Going*)

SIR BENJAMIN BACKBITE But, however, as he's your brother—   365
(*Going*)

CRABTREE We'll tell you all another opportunity.

Exeunt Crabtree and Sir Benjamin Backbite

LADY SNEERWELL Ha, ha, ha! 'Tis very hard for them to leave a
subject they have not quite run down.°

JOSEPH SURFACE And I believe the abuse was no more acceptable to   370
your ladyship than to Maria.

LADY SNEERWELL I doubt her affections are farther engaged than we
imagined. But the family are to be here this evening, so you may as
well dine where you are, and we shall have an opportunity of
observing farther. In the meantime, I'll go and plot mischief, and   375
you shall study sentiments.°

Exeunt

1.2

Sir Peter Teazle's house

Enter Sir Peter Teazle

SIR PETER TEAZLE When an old bachelor takes a young wife, what is
he to expect! 'Tis now six months since Lady Teazle made me the
happiest of men, and I have been the miserablest dog ever since that
ever committed wedlock. We tiffed° a little going to church, and

came to a quarrel before the bells were done ringing. I was more   5
than once nearly choked with gall° during the honeymoon, and had
lost all comfort in life before my friends had done wishing me joy.
Yet I chose with caution a girl bred wholly in the country, who never
knew luxury beyond one silk gown, nor dissipation above the annual
gala of a race-ball. Yet now she plays her part in all the extravagant   10
fopperies of the fashion and the town with as ready a grace as if she
had never seen a bush or a grass-plat out of Grosvenor Square!° I
am sneered at by my old acquaintance, paragraphed in the newspapers. She dissipates my fortune and contradicts all my humours.
Yet the worst of it is I doubt° I love her, or I should never bear all   15
this. However, I'll never be weak enough to own it.

Enter Rowley

ROWLEY O, Sir Peter, your servant. How is it with you, sir?
SIR PETER TEAZLE Very bad, Master Rowley, very bad. I meet with
nothing but crosses and vexations.
ROWLEY What can have happened to trouble you since yesterday?   20
SIR PETER TEAZLE A good question to a married man.
ROWLEY Nay, I'm sure your lady, Sir Peter, can't be the cause of your
uneasiness.
SIR PETER TEAZLE Why, has anyone told you she was dead?
ROWLEY Come, come, Sir Peter! You love her, notwithstanding your   25
tempers do not exactly agree.
SIR PETER TEAZLE But the fault is entirely hers, Master Rowley. I am
myself the sweetest-tempered man alive and hate a teasing temper,
and so I tell her a hundred times a day.
ROWLEY Indeed!   30
SIR PETER TEAZLE Ay; and what is very extraordinary, in all our disputes she is always in the wrong! But Lady Sneerwell and the set
she meets at her house encourage the perverseness of her disposition. Then, to complete my vexations, Maria, my ward, whom I
ought to have the power of a father over, is determined to turn rebel   35
too, and absolutely refuses the man whom I have long resolved on
for her husband, meaning, I suppose, to bestow herself on his profligate brother.
ROWLEY You know, Sir Peter, I have always taken the liberty to differ
with you on the subject of these two young gentlemen. I only wish   40
you may not be deceived in your opinion of the elder. For Charles—
my life on't, he will retrieve his errors yet. Their worthy father,
once my honoured master, was at his years nearly as wild a spark;

yet, when he died, he did not leave a more benevolent heart to
lament his loss.   45

SIR PETER TEAZLE You are wrong, Master Rowley. On their father's
death you know I acted as a kind of guardian to them both, till their
uncle Sir Oliver's eastern liberality gave them an early independence. Of course, no person could have more opportunities of
judging of their hearts, and I was never mistaken in my life. Joseph   50
is indeed a model for the young men of the age. He is a man of sentiment, and acts up to the sentiments he professes; but, for the
other, take my word for't, if he had any grains of virtue by descent,
he has dissipated them with the rest of his inheritance. Ah, my old
friend Sir Oliver will be deeply mortified when he finds how part   55
of his bounty has been misapplied!

ROWLEY I am sorry to find you so violent against the young man
because this may be the most critical period of his fortune. I came
hither with news that will surprise you.

SIR PETER TEAZLE What! Let me hear.   60

ROWLEY Sir Oliver *is* arrived and at this moment in town.

SIR PETER TEAZLE How! You astonish me. I thought you did not
expect him this month!

ROWLEY I did not, but his passage has been remarkably quick.

SIR PETER TEAZLE Egad, I shall rejoice to see my old friend; 'tis   65
sixteen years since we met. We have had many a day together. But
does he still enjoin us not to inform his nephews of his arrival?

ROWLEY Most strictly. He means, before it is known, to make some
trial of their dispositions.

SIR PETER TEAZLE Ah, there needs no art to discover their merits!   70
However, he shall have his way. But pray, does he know I am
married?

ROWLEY Yes, and will soon wish you joy.

SIR PETER TEAZLE What, as we drink health to a friend in a consumption? Ah, Oliver will laugh at me. We used to rail at matri-   75
mony together, but he has been steady to his text.° Well, he must
be at my house,° though; I'll instantly give orders for his reception.
But, Master Rowley, don't drop a word that Lady Teazle and I ever
disagree.

ROWLEY By no means.   80

SIR PETER TEAZLE For I should never be able to stand Noll's° jokes.
So I'd have him think, lord forgive me, that we are a very happy
couple.

ROWLEY I understand you; but then you must be very careful not to
differ while he's in the house with you.   85

SIR PETER TEAZLE Egad, and so we must; and that's impossible! Ah,
Master Rowley, when an old bachelor marries a young wife, he
deserves—no, the crime carries the punishment along with it.
Exeunt

2.1

Enter Sir Peter Teazle and Lady Teazle

SIR PETER TEAZLE Lady Teazle, Lady Teazle, I'll not bear it!

LADY TEAZLE Sir Peter, Sir Peter, you may bear it or not, as you please; but I ought to have my own way in everything, and what's more, I will too. What, though I was educated in the country, I know very well that women of fashion in London are accountable to   5
nobody after they are married.

SIR PETER TEAZLE Very well, ma'am, very well! So a husband is to have no influence, no authority?

LADY TEAZLE Authority! No, to be sure. If you wanted authority over me, you should have adopted me and not married me. I am sure you   10
were old enough.

SIR PETER TEAZLE Old enough! Ay, there it is. Well, well, Lady Teazle, though my life may be made unhappy by your temper, I'll not be ruined by your extravagance.

LADY TEAZLE My extravagance! I'm sure I'm not more extravagant   15
than a woman of fashion ought to be.

SIR PETER TEAZLE No, no, madam; you shall throw away no more sums on such unmeaning luxury. 'Slife, to spend as much to furnish your dressing-room with flowers in winter as would suffice to turn the Pantheon° into a greenhouse and give a *fête-champêtre*° at Christmas!   20

LADY TEAZLE Lord, Sir Peter, am I to blame because flowers are dear in cold weather? You should find fault with the climate and not with me. For my part, I am sure I wish it was spring all the year round, and that roses grew under one's feet!

SIR PETER TEAZLE Oons, madam, if you had been born to this, I   25
shouldn't wonder at your talking thus. But you forget what your situation was when I married you.

LADY TEAZLE No, no, I don't; 'twas a very disagreeable one, or I should never have married you.

SIR PETER TEAZLE Yes, yes, madam; you were then in somewhat an   30
humbler style, the daughter of a plain country squire. Recollect, Lady Teazle, when I saw you first—sitting at your tambour in a pretty figured linen gown, with a bunch of keys by your side, your hair combed smooth over a roll,° and your apartment hung round with fruits in worsted of your own working.°   35

LADY TEAZLE O yes, I remember it very well, and a curious° life I led!
My daily occupation to inspect the dairy, superintend the poultry,
make extracts from the family receipt-book and comb my Aunt
Deborah's° lap-dog.

SIR PETER TEAZLE Yes, yes, ma'am; 'twas so indeed.   40

LADY TEAZLE And then you know my evening amusements—to draw
patterns for ruffles which I had not the materials to make, to play
Pope Joan° with the curate, to read a novel to my aunt, or to be
stuck down to an old spinet to strum my father to sleep after a
fox-chase.   45

SIR PETER TEAZLE I am glad you have so good a memory. Yes, madam,
these were the recreations I took you from. But now you must
have your coach—*vis-à-vis*—and three powdered° footmen before
your chair,° and in summer a pair of white cats° to draw you to
Kensington Gardens.° No recollection, I suppose, when you were   50
content to ride double behind the butler on a docked coach-horse.

LADY TEAZLE No, I swear I never did that; I deny the butler and the
coach-horse.

SIR PETER TEAZLE This, madam, was your situation; and what have
I not done for you? I have made you a woman of fashion, of fortune,   55
of rank; in short, I have made you my wife.

LADY TEAZLE Well then, and there is but one thing more you can
make me to add to the obligation; and that is—

SIR PETER TEAZLE My widow, I suppose?

LADY TEAZLE Hem, hem!   60

SIR PETER TEAZLE Thank you, madam. But don't flatter yourself, for,
though your ill conduct may disturb my peace, it shall never break
my heart, I promise you. However, I am equally obliged to you for
the hint.

LADY TEAZLE Then why will you endeavour to make yourself so dis-   65
agreeable to me, and thwart me in every little elegant expense?

SIR PETER TEAZLE 'Slife, madam, I say, had you any of these elegant
expenses when you married me?

LADY TEAZLE Lud, Sir Peter, would you have me be out of the
fashion?   70

SIR PETER TEAZLE The fashion indeed! What had you to do with the
fashion before you married me?

LADY TEAZLE For my part, I should think you would like to have your
wife thought a woman of taste.

SIR PETER TEAZLE Ay, there again—taste! Zounds, madam, you had   75
no taste when you married me.

LADY TEAZLE That's very true indeed, Sir Peter; and, after having
married you, I am sure I should never pretend to taste again! But
now, Sir Peter, if we have finished our daily jangle, I presume I may
go to my engagement at Lady Sneerwell's.   80
SIR PETER TEAZLE Ay, there's another precious circumstance;° a
charming set of acquaintance you have made there.
LADY TEAZLE Nay, Sir Peter, they are people of rank and fortune, and
remarkably tenacious of reputation.
SIR PETER TEAZLE Yes, egad, they are tenacious of reputation with a   85
vengeance, for they don't choose anybody should have a character
but themselves. Such a crew! Ah, many a wretch has rid on a hurdle
who has done less mischief than those utterers of forged tales,
coiners of scandal, and clippers of reputation.°
LADY TEAZLE What, would you restrain the freedom of speech?   90
SIR PETER TEAZLE O, they have made you just as bad as anyone of
the society.
LADY TEAZLE Why, I believe I do bear a part° with a tolerable grace.
But I vow I have no malice against the people I abuse. When I say
an ill-natured thing, 'tis out of pure good humour; and I take it for 95
granted they deal exactly in the same manner with me. But, Sir
Peter, you know you promised to come to Lady Sneerwell's too.
SIR PETER TEAZLE Well, well, I'll call in just to look after my own
character.
LADY TEAZLE Then indeed you must make haste after me, or you'll   100
be too late. So good-bye to ye.
    Exit Lady Teazle
SIR PETER TEAZLE So. I have gained much by my intended expostulations. Yet with what a charming air she contradicts everything I
say, and how pleasingly she shows her contempt of my authority.
Well, though I can't make her love me, there is a great satisfaction 105
in quarrelling with her, and I think she never appears to such advantage as when she's doing everything in her power to plague me.
    Exit

2.2

Lady Sneerwell's house
Lady Sneerwell, Mrs Candour, Crabtree, Sir Benjamin
Backbite, and Joseph Surface

LADY SNEERWELL Nay, positively,° we will hear it.

JOSEPH SURFACE Yes, yes, the epigram, by all means.

SIR BENJAMIN BACKBITE Plague on't, uncle! 'Tis mere nonsense.

CRABTREE No, no; 'fore Gad, very clever for an extempore.

SIR BENJAMIN BACKBITE But, ladies, you should be acquainted with   5
the circumstance. You must know that one day last week, as Lady
Betty Curricle° was taking the dust in Hyde Park° in a sort of
duodecimo phaeton,° she desired me to write some verses on her
ponies, upon which I took out my pocket-book and in one moment
produced the following: 10

       Sure never were seen two such beautiful ponies;
       Other horses are clowns, and these macaronies.°
       Nay, to give 'em this title, I'm sure, isn't wrong:
       Their legs are so slim, and their tails are so long.

CRABTREE There, ladies! Done in the smack of a whip, and on horse-   15
back too.

JOSEPH A very Phoebus° mounted, indeed, Sir Benjamin.

SIR BENJAMIN BACKBITE O, dear sir, trifles, trifles!

    Enter Lady Teazle and Maria

MRS CANDOUR I must have a copy.

LADY SNEERWELL [*greeting her*] Lady Teazle. I hope we shall see Sir   20
Peter.

LADY TEAZLE I believe he'll wait on your ladyship presently.

LADY SNEERWELL Maria, my love, you look grave. Come, you shall
sit down to cards with Mr Surface.

MARIA I take very little pleasure in cards. However, I'll do as your   25
ladyship pleases.

LADY TEAZLE [*aside*] I am surprised Mr Surface should sit down with
her. I thought he would have embraced this opportunity of speaking to me before Sir Peter came.

MRS CANDOUR ([*speaking to Crabtree and Sir Benjamin, while*] *coming*   30
forward) Now I'll die but you are so scandalous I'll forswear your
society.

LADY TEAZLE What's the matter, Mrs Candour?

MRS CANDOUR They'll not allow our friend Miss Vermilion° to be
handsome.   35

LADY SNEERWELL O, surely she's a pretty woman.

CRABTREE I am very glad you think so, ma'am.

MRS CANDOUR She has a charming fresh colour.

LADY TEAZLE Yes, when it is fresh put on.

MRS CANDOUR O, fie, I'll swear her colour is natural. I have seen it   40
come and go.

LADY TEAZLE I dare swear you have, ma'am. It goes of a night and
comes again in the morning.

MRS CANDOUR Ha, ha, ha! How I hate to hear you talk so. But surely,
now, her sister is, or was, very handsome.   45

CRABTREE Who? Mrs Evergreen? O lud, she's six-and-fifty if she's an
hour.

MRS CANDOUR Now, positively, you wrong her. Fifty-two or fifty-
three is the utmost, and I don't think she looks more.

SIR BENJAMIN BACKBITE Ah, there is no judging by her looks, unless   50
one could see her face.°

LADY SNEERWELL Well, well. If Mrs Evergreen does take some pains
to repair the ravages of time, you must allow she effects it with great
ingenuity; and surely that's better than the careless manner in
which the Widow Ochre° caulks° her wrinkles.   55

SIR BENJAMIN BACKBITE Nay, now, Lady Sneerwell, you are severe
upon the widow. Come, come, it is not that she paints so ill;° but
when she has finished her face, she joins it on so badly to her neck
that she looks like a mended statue, in which the connoisseur sees
at once that the head's modern, though the trunk's antique.   60

CRABTREE Ha, ha, ha! Well said, nephew!

MRS CANDOUR Ha, ha, ha! Well, you make me laugh; but I vow I hate
you for't. What do you think of Miss Simper?

SIR BENJAMIN BACKBITE Why, she has very pretty teeth.

LADY TEAZLE Yes, and on that account, when she is neither speaking   65
nor laughing (which very seldom happens), she never absolutely
shuts her mouth, but leaves it always on a jar as it were.

MRS CANDOUR How can you be so ill-natured?

LADY TEAZLE Nay, I allow even that's better than the pains Mrs Prim
takes to conceal her losses in front. She draws her mouth till it pos-   70
itively resembles the aperture of a poor's-box, and all her words
appear to slide out edgeways.

LADY SNEERWELL Very well, Lady Teazle. I see you can be a little
severe.

LADY TEAZLE In defence of a friend it is but justice. But here comes   75
Sir Peter to spoil our pleasantry!°
    Enter Sir Peter Teazle

SIR PETER TEAZLE Ladies, your most obedient. (*Aside*) Mercy on me,
here is the whole set! A character dead at every word,° I suppose.

MRS CANDOUR I am rejoiced you are come, Sir Peter. They have been
so censorious; they will allow good qualities to nobody—not even   80
good nature to our friend Mrs Pursy.°

LADY TEAZLE What, the fat dowager, who was at Mrs Codille's° last
night?

MRS CANDOUR Nay, her bulk is her misfortune; and, when she takes
such pains to get rid of it, you ought not to reflect on her.   85

LADY SNEERWELL That's very true indeed.

LADY TEAZLE Yes, I know she almost lives on acids and small whey,
laces herself by pulleys,° and often in the hottest noon of summer
you may see her on a little squat pony, with her hair platted up
behind like a drummer's,° and puffing round the Ring° on a full   90
trot.

MRS CANDOUR I thank you, Lady Teazle, for defending her.

SIR PETER Yes, a good defence, truly.

MRS CANDOUR But Sir Benjamin is as censorious as Miss Sallow.

CRABTREE Yes, and she is a curious being to pretend to be censori-   95
ous—an awkward gawky, without any one good point under heaven!

MRS CANDOUR Positively, you shall not be so very severe. Miss
Sallow is a relation of mine by marriage, and, as for her person,
great allowance is to be made, for, let me tell you, a woman labours
under many disadvantages who tries to pass for a girl at six-and-   100
thirty.

LADY SNEERWELL Though surely she is handsome still. And for the
weakness in her eyes, considering how much she reads by candle-
light, it is not to be wondered at.

MRS CANDOUR True. And then as to her manner, upon my word, I   105
think it is particularly graceful, considering she never had the least
education, for you know her mother was a Welsh milliner and her
father a sugar-baker at Bristol.

SIR BENJAMIN BACKBITE Ah, you are both of you too good-natured!

SIR PETER TEAZLE (*aside*) Yes, damned good-natured! This their own   110
relation! Mercy on me!

SIR BENJAMIN BACKBITE And Mrs Candour is of so moral a turn,
she can sit for an hour to hear Lady Stucco° talk sentiment.

LADY TEAZLE Nay, I vow Lady Stucco is very well with the dessert
after dinner, for she's just like the French fruit one cracks for   115
mottos—made up of paint and proverb.°

MRS CANDOUR Well, I never will join in ridiculing a friend; and so I
constantly tell my cousin Ogle,° and you all know what pretensions
she has to be critical° in beauty.

CRABTREE O, to be sure she has herself the oddest countenance that   120
    ever was seen. 'Tis a collection of features from all the different
    countries of the globe.

SIR BENJAMIN BACKBITE So she has indeed. An Irish front.

CRABTREE Caledonian locks.

SIR BENJAMIN BACKBITE Dutch nose.   125

CRABTREE Austrian lip.

SIR BENJAMIN BACKBITE Complexion of a Spaniard.

CRABTREE And teeth *à la Chinoise.*°

SIR BENJAMIN BACKBITE In short, her face resembles a *table d'hôte*
    at Spa,° where no two guests are of a nation.   130

CRABTREE Or a congress at the close of a general war, wherein all the
    members, even to her eyes, appear to have a different interest, and
    her nose and chin are the only parties likely to join issue.°

MRS CANDOUR Ha, ha, ha!

SIR PETER TEAZLE (*aside*) Mercy on my life! A person they dine with   135
    twice a week!

MRS CANDOUR Nay, but I vow you shall not carry the laugh off so,
    for give me leave to say that Mrs Ogle—

SIR PETER TEAZLE Madam, madam, I beg your pardon. There's no
    stopping these good gentlemen's tongues; but when I tell you, Mrs   140
    Candour, that the lady they are abusing is a particular friend of
    mine, I hope you'll not take her part.

LADY SNEERWELL Well said, Sir Peter. But you are a cruel creature—
    too phlegmatic yourself for a jest and too peevish to allow wit in
    others.   145

SIR PETER TEAZLE Ah, madam, true wit is more nearly allied to good
    nature than your ladyship is aware of.

LADY TEAZLE True, Sir Peter. I believe they are so near akin that they
    can never be united.°

SIR BENJAMIN BACKBITE Or rather, madam, suppose them man and   150
    wife, because one so seldom sees them together.

LADY TEAZLE But Sir Peter is such an enemy to scandal, I believe he
    would have it put down by Parliament.

SIR PETER TEAZLE 'Fore heaven, madam, if they were to consider the
    sporting with reputation of as much importance as poaching on   155
    manors,° and pass an Act for the Preservation of Fame, I believe
    there are many would thank them for the Bill.

LADY SNEERWELL O lud, Sir Peter, would you deprive us of our
    privileges?

SIR PETER TEAZLE Ay, madam. And then no person should be   160

permitted to kill characters or run down reputations, but qualified°
old maids and disappointed widows.

LADY SNEERWELL Go, you monster.

MRS CANDOUR But sure you would not be quite so severe on those
who only report what they hear.   165

SIR PETER TEAZLE Yes, madam, I would have law merchant° for them
too; and, in all cases of slander currency, whenever the drawer of
the lie was not to be found, the injured party should have a right to
come on any of the endorsers.°

CRABTREE Well, for my part, I believe there never was a scandalous   170
tale without some foundation.

LADY SNEERWELL Come, ladies, shall we sit down to cards in the next
room?

          Enter Servant. He whispers to Sir Peter Teazle

SIR PETER TEAZLE I'll be with them directly.

          [*Exit Servant*]

[*Aside*] I'll get away unperceived.   175

LADY SNEERWELL Sir Peter, you are not leaving us?

SIR PETER TEAZLE Your ladyship must excuse me; I'm called away by
particular business. But I leave my character behind me.

          Exit Sir Peter Teazle

SIR BENJAMIN BACKBITE Well, certainly, Lady Teazle, that lord of
yours is a strange being. I could tell you some stories of him would   180
make you laugh heartily if he wasn't your husband.

LADY TEAZLE O, pray don't mind that. Come, do let's hear 'em.

          Lady Teazle and Sir Benjamin Backbite join Mrs Candour
          and Crabtree, all talking as they are going into the next room

JOSEPH SURFACE (*rising with Maria*) Maria, I see you have no satisfaction in this society.°

MARIA How is it possible I should? If to raise malicious smiles at the 185
infirmities and misfortunes of those who have never injured us be
the province of wit or humour, heaven grant me a double portion
of dullness.

JOSEPH SURFACE Yet they appear more ill-natured than they are.
They have no malice at heart.   190

MARIA Then is their conduct still more contemptible, for in my
opinion nothing could excuse the intemperance of their tongues but
a natural and ungovernable bitterness of mind.

JOSEPH SURFACE [*kneeling°*] But can you, Maria, feel thus for others
and be unkind to me alone? Is hope to be denied the tenderest   195
passion?

MARIA Why will you distress me by renewing this subject?

JOSEPH SURFACE Ah, Maria, you would not treat me thus and oppose your guardian's, Sir Peter's, wishes, but that I see that profligate Charles is still a favoured rival.   200

MARIA Ungenerously urged. But, whatever my sentiments of that unfortunate young man are, be assured I shall not feel more bound to give him up because his distresses have lost him the regard even of a brother.

     Enter Lady Teazle

JOSEPH SURFACE Nay, but, Maria, do not leave me with a frown. By   205
all that's honest, I swear—(*aside*) Gad's life, here's Lady Teazle!

     [*Joseph Surface rises*]

[*To Maria*] You must not, no, you shall not, for though I have the greatest regard for Lady Teazle—

MARIA Lady Teazle!

JOSEPH SURFACE Yet, were Sir Peter to suspect—   210

LADY TEAZLE (*coming forward*) What's this, pray? Do you take her for me!—Child, you are wanted in the next room.

     Exit Maria

What is all this, pray?

JOSEPH SURFACE O, the most unlucky circumstance in nature. Maria has somehow suspected the tender concern which I have for your   215
happiness and threatened to acquaint Sir Peter with her suspicions, and I was just endeavouring to reason with her when you came.

LADY TEAZLE Indeed; but you seemed to adopt a very tender method of reasoning. Do you usually argue on your knees?

JOSEPH SURFACE O, she's a child, and I thought a little bombast°—   220
but, Lady Teazle, when are you to give me your judgement on my library as you promised?

LADY TEAZLE No, no; I begin to think it would be imprudent, and you know I admit you as a lover no further than fashion requires.

JOSEPH SURFACE True, a mere platonic cicisbeo°—what every   225
London wife is entitled to.

LADY TEAZLE Certainly one must not be out of the fashion. However, I have so much of my country prejudices left that, though Sir Peter's ill humour may vex me ever so, it never shall provoke me to—   230

JOSEPH SURFACE The only revenge in your power.° Well, I applaud your moderation.

LADY TEAZLE Go, you are an insinuating wretch. But we shall be missed; let us join the company.

JOSEPH SURFACE But we had best not return together.   235
LADY TEAZLE Well, don't stay, for Maria shan't come to hear any more
of your reasoning, I promise you.
    Exit Lady Teazle
JOSEPH SURFACE A curious dilemma, truly, my politics° have run me
into. I wanted at first only to ingratiate myself with Lady Teazle
that she might not be my enemy with Maria, and I have—I don't   240
know how—become her serious lover. Sincerely, I begin to wish I
had never made such a point of gaining so very good a character,
for it has led me into so many cursed rogueries° that I doubt I shall
be exposed at last.
    Exit

2.3

    Sir Peter Teazle's
    Enter Sir Oliver Surface and Rowley
SIR OLIVER SURFACE Ha, ha, ha! And so my old friend is married,
hey? A young wife out of the country! Ha, ha, ha! That he should
have stood bluff to old bachelor° so long and sink into a husband
at last!
ROWLEY But you must not rally him on the subject, Sir Oliver. 'Tis   5
a tender point, I assure you, though he has been married only
seven months.°
SIR OLIVER SURFACE Then he has been just half a year on the stool
of repentance.° Poor Peter! But you say he has entirely given up
Charles, never sees him, hey?   10
ROWLEY His prejudice against him is astonishing, and, I am sure,
greatly increased by a jealousy of him with Lady Teazle, which he
has been industriously led into by a scandalous society in the neighbourhood, who have contributed not a little to Charles's ill name.
Whereas the truth is, I believe, if the lady is partial to either of them   15
his brother is the favourite.
SIR OLIVER SURFACE Ay, I know. There are a set of malicious prating
prudent gossips, both male and female, who murder characters to
kill time and will rob a young fellow of his good name before he has
years° to know the value of it. But I am not to be prejudiced against   20
my nephew by such, I promise you. No, no! If Charles has done
nothing false or mean, I shall compound for his extravagance.°

ROWLEY Then, my life on't, you will reclaim him. Ah, sir, it gives me new life to find that your heart is not turned against him, and that the son of my good old master has one friend, however, left. 25

SIR OLIVER SURFACE What, shall I forget, Master Rowley, when I was at his years myself, egad, my brother and I were neither of us very prudent youths? And yet I believe you have not seen many better men than your old master was.

ROWLEY Sir, 'tis this reflection gives me assurance that Charles may 30 yet be a credit to his family. But here comes Sir Peter.

SIR OLIVER SURFACE Egad, so he does. Mercy on me, he's greatly altered, and seems to have a settled married look. One may read husband in his face at this distance.

Enter Sir Peter Teazle

SIR PETER TEAZLE Ha, Sir Oliver, my old friend! Welcome to 35 England a thousand times!

SIR OLIVER SURFACE Thank you, thank you, Sir Peter! And, i'faith, I am as glad to find you well, believe me.

SIR PETER TEAZLE Ah, 'tis a long time since we met—sixteen years, I doubt, and many a cross accident° in the time. 40

SIR OLIVER SURFACE Ay, I have had my share. But, what, I find you are married. Hey, my old boy! Well, well, it can't be helped, and so I wish you joy with all my heart.

SIR PETER TEAZLE Thank you, thank you, Sir Oliver. Yes, I have entered into the happy state, but we'll not talk of that now. 45

SIR OLIVER SURFACE True, true, Sir Peter; old friends should not begin on grievances at first meeting. No, no, no.

ROWLEY (*to Sir Oliver Surface*) Take care, pray, sir.

SIR OLIVER SURFACE Well, so one of my nephews, I find, is a wild rogue, hey? 50

SIR PETER TEAZLE Wild! Ah, my old friend, I grieve for your disappointment there. He's a lost young man indeed. However, his brother will make you amends. Joseph is indeed what a youth should be; everybody in the world speaks well of him.

SIR OLIVER SURFACE I am sorry to hear it; he has too good a charac- 55 ter to be an honest fellow. Everybody speaks well of him! Pshaw! Then he has bowed as low to knaves and fools as to the honest dignity of genius or virtue.

SIR PETER TEAZLE What, Sir Oliver, do you blame him for not making enemies? 60

SIR OLIVER SURFACE Yes, if he has merit enough to deserve them.

SIR PETER TEAZLE Well, well, you'll be convinced when you know

him. 'Tis edification to hear him converse; he professes the noblest
sentiments.

SIR OLIVER SURFACE Ah, plague on his sentiments! If he salutes me   65
with a scrap of morality in his mouth, I shall be sick directly. But,
however, don't mistake me, Sir Peter. I don't mean to defend
Charles's errors. But, before I form my judgement of either of
them, I intend to make a trial of their hearts; and my friend Rowley
and I have planned something for the purpose.   70

ROWLEY And Sir Peter shall own he has been for once mistaken.

SIR PETER TEAZLE O, my life on Joseph's honour!

SIR OLIVER SURFACE Well, come; give us a bottle of good wine, and
we'll drink the lads' healths and tell you our scheme.

SIR PETER TEAZLE *Allons* then.   75

SIR OLIVER SURFACE And don't, Sir Peter, be so severe against your
old friend's son. Od's my life, I am not sorry that he has run out
of the course° a little. For my part, I hate to see prudence clinging
to the green suckers of youth; 'tis like ivy round a sapling and spoils
the growth of the tree.   80

　　　Exeunt

3.1

Sir Peter Teazle's

Sir Peter Teazle, Sir Oliver Surface, and Rowley

SIR PETER TEAZLE Well then, we will see this fellow first and have our wine afterwards. But how is this, Master Rowley? I don't see the jet of your scheme.

ROWLEY Why, sir, this Mr Stanley whom I was speaking of is nearly related to them by their mother. He was once a merchant in Dublin, but has been ruined by a series of undeserved misfortunes. He has applied by letter since his confinement° both to Mr Surface and Charles. From the former he has received nothing but evasive promises of future service, while Charles has done all that his extravagance has left him power to do, and he is at this time endeavouring to raise a sum of money, part of which, in the midst of his own distresses, I know he intends for the service of poor Stanley.

SIR OLIVER SURFACE Ah, he is my brother's son!

SIR PETER TEAZLE Well, but how is Sir Oliver personally to—

ROWLEY Why, sir, I will inform Charles and his brother that Stanley has obtained permission° to apply in person to his friends; and, as they have neither of them ever seen him, let Sir Oliver assume his character, and he will have a fair opportunity of judging at least of the benevolence of their dispositions. And, believe me, sir, you will find in the youngest brother one who in the midst of folly and dissipation has still, as our immortal bard expresses it, 'a tear for pity and a hand open as day for melting charity'.°

SIR PETER TEAZLE Pshaw! What signifies his having an open hand, or purse either, when he has nothing left to give! Well, well, make the trial if you please. But where is the fellow whom you brought for Sir Oliver to examine relative to° Charles's affairs?

ROWLEY Below, waiting his commands, and no one can give him better intelligence. This, Sir Oliver, is a friendly Jew, who, to do him justice, has done everything in his power to bring your nephew to a proper sense of his extravagance.

SIR PETER Pray let us have him in.

ROWLEY [*to Servant offstage*] Desire Mr Moses to walk upstairs.

SIR PETER TEAZLE But why should you suppose he will speak the truth?

ROWLEY O, I have convinced him that he has no chance of

recovering certain sums advanced to Charles, but through the
bounty of Sir Oliver, who he knows is arrived; so that you may
depend on his fidelity to his interest. I have also another evidence°
in my power, one Snake, whom I have detected in a matter little
short of forgery,° and shall shortly produce to remove some of your   40
prejudices, Sir Peter, relative to Charles and Lady Teazle.

SIR PETER TEAZLE I have heard too much on that subject.

ROWLEY Here comes the honest Israelite.°

    Enter Moses

[*Introducing Moses*] This is Sir Oliver.

SIR OLIVER SURFACE Sir, I understand you have lately had great deal-   45
ings with my nephew Charles.

MOSES Yes, Sir Oliver; I have done all I could for him, but he was
ruined before he came to me for assistance.

SIR OLIVER SURFACE That was unlucky, truly, for you have had no
opportunity of showing your talents.   50

MOSES None at all. I hadn't the pleasure of knowing his distresses till
he was some thousands worse than nothing.

SIR OLIVER SURFACE Unfortunate indeed! But I suppose you have
done all in your power for him, honest Moses?

MOSES Yes, he knows that. This very evening I was to have brought   55
him a gentleman from the city who doesn't know him and will, I
believe, advance him some money.

SIR PETER TEAZLE What, one Charles has never had money from
before?

MOSES Yes, Mr Premium of Crutched Friars,° formerly a broker.   60

SIR PETER TEAZLE Egad, Sir Oliver, a thought strikes me. Charles,
you say, doesn't know Mr Premium.°

MOSES Not at all.

SIR PETER TEAZLE Now then, Sir Oliver, you may have a better opportunity of satisfying yourself than by an old romancing tale of a poor   65
relation. Go with my friend Moses and represent° Mr Premium, and
then I'll answer for't you will see your nephew in all his glory.

SIR OLIVER SURFACE Egad, I like this idea better than the other, and
I may visit Joseph afterwards as old Stanley.

SIR PETER TEAZLE True, so you may.   70

ROWLEY Well, this is taking Charles rather at a disadvantage, to be sure.
However, Moses, you understand Sir Peter and will be faithful.

MOSES You may depend upon me. This is near the time I was to have
gone.

SIR OLIVER SURFACE I'll accompany you as soon as you please, Moses.   75
   But hold; I have forgot one thing. How the plague shall I be able to
   pass for a Jew?

MOSES There's no need. The principal° is Christian.

SIR OLIVER SURFACE Is he? I'm sorry to hear it. But then again, a'n't
   I rather too smartly dressed to look like a moneylender?   80

SIR PETER TEAZLE Not at all. 'Twould not be out of character if you
   went in your own carriage—would it, Moses?

MOSES Not in the least.

SIR OLIVER SURFACE Well, but how must I talk? There's certainly
   some cant of usury and mode of treating° that I ought to know.   85

SIR PETER TEAZLE O, there's not much to learn. The great point, as
   I take it, is to be exorbitant enough in your demands—hey, Moses?

MOSES Yes, that's a very great point.

SIR OLIVER SURFACE I'll answer for't I'll not be wanting in that. I'll
   ask him eight or ten per cent on the loan, at least.   90

MOSES If you ask him no more than that, you'll be discovered
   immediately.

SIR OLIVER SURFACE Hey, what the plague! How much then?

MOSES That depends upon the circumstances. If he appears not very
   anxious for the supply, you should require only forty or fifty per   95
   cent; but if you find him in great distress and want° the moneys
   very bad, you may ask double.

SIR PETER TEAZLE A good honest trade you're learning, Sir Oliver.

SIR OLIVER SURFACE Truly I think so, and not unprofitable.

MOSES Then, you know, you haven't the moneys yourself, but are   100
   forced to borrow them for him of a friend.

SIR OLIVER SURFACE O, I borrow it of a friend, do I?

MOSES Yes, and your friend is an unconscionable dog, but you can't
   help it.

SIR OLIVER SURFACE My friend is an unconscionable dog, is he?   105

MOSES Yes, and he himself hasn't the moneys by him, but is forced
   to sell stock at a great loss.

SIR OLIVER SURFACE He is forced to sell stock, is he? At a great loss,
   is he? Well, that's very kind of him.

SIR PETER TEAZLE I'faith, Sir Oliver—Mr Premium, I mean—you'll   110
   soon be master of the trade. But, Moses, wouldn't you have him
   run out a little against the Annuity Bill?° That would be in character, I should think.

MOSES Very much.

ROWLEY And lament that a young man now must be at years of dis-   115
cretion before he is suffered to ruin himself.

MOSES Ay, great pity!

SIR PETER TEAZLE And abuse the public for allowing merit to an
Act whose only object is to snatch misfortune and imprudence
from the rapacious relief of usury and give the minor a chance   120
of inheriting his estate, without being undone by coming into
possession.

SIR OLIVER SURFACE So, so. Moses shall give me further instructions
as we go together.

SIR PETER TEAZLE You will not have much time, for your nephew   125
lives hard by.

SIR OLIVER SURFACE O, never fear; my tutor appears so able that,
though Charles lived in the next street, it must be my own fault if
I am not a complete rogue before I turn the corner.

    Exeunt Sir Oliver Surface and Moses

SIR PETER TEAZLE So. Now I think Sir Oliver will be convinced. You   130
are partial, Rowley, and would have prepared Charles for the other
plot.

ROWLEY No, upon my word, Sir Peter—

SIR PETER TEAZLE Well, go bring me this Snake, and I'll hear what
he has to say presently. I see Maria and want to speak with her.   135

    Exit Rowley

I should be glad to be convinced my suspicions of Lady Teazle and
Charles were unjust. I have never yet opened my mind on this
subject to my friend Joseph. I'm determined I will do it. He will
give me his opinion sincerely.

    Enter Maria

So, child, has Mr Surface returned with you?   140

MARIA No, sir; he was engaged.

SIR PETER TEAZLE Well, Maria, do you not reflect, the more you converse with that amiable young man, what return his partiality for
you deserves?

MARIA Indeed, Sir Peter, your frequent importunity on this subject   145
distresses me extremely. You compel me to declare that I know no
man who has ever paid me a particular attention whom I would not
prefer to Mr Surface.

SIR PETER TEAZLE So! Here's perverseness! No, no, Maria; 'tis
Charles only whom you would prefer. 'Tis evident his vices and   150
follies have won your heart.

MARIA This is unkind, sir. You know I have obeyed you in neither

seeing nor corresponding with him. I have heard enough to convince me that he is unworthy my regard. Yet I cannot think it culpable if, while my understanding severely condemns his vices, my   155
heart suggests some pity for his distresses.

SIR PETER TEAZLE Well, well, pity him as much as you please, but
give your heart and hand to a worthier object.

MARIA Never to his brother.

SIR PETER TEAZLE Go, perverse and obstinate! But take care,   160
madam.° You have never yet known what the authority of a
guardian is; don't compel me to inform you of it.

MARIA I can only say you shall not have just reason. 'Tis true by my
father's will I am for a short period bound to regard you as his substitute, but must cease to think you so, when you would compel me   165
to be miserable.

Exit Maria

SIR PETER TEAZLE Was ever man so crossed as I am! Everything con-
spiring to fret me! I hadn't been involved in matrimony a fortnight
before her father, a hale and hearty man, died on purpose, I believe,
for the pleasure of plaguing me with the care of his daughter. But   170
here comes my helpmate! She appears in great good humour. How
happy I should be if I could tease her into loving me, though but a
little.

Enter Lady Teazle

LADY TEAZLE Lud, Sir Peter, I hope you haven't been quarrelling with
Maria. It isn't using me well to be ill-humoured when I am not by!   175

SIR PETER TEAZLE Ah, Lady Teazle, you might have the power to
make me good-humoured at all times.

LADY TEAZLE I am sure I wish I had, for I want you to be in a charming sweet temper at this moment. Do be good-humoured now, and
let me have two hundred pounds, will you?   180

SIR PETER TEAZLE Two hundred pounds! What, a'n't I to be in a good
humour without paying for it? But speak to me thus, and i'faith
there's nothing I could refuse you. You shall have it; but seal me a
bond for the repayment.°

LADY TEAZLE O, no! [*Offering her hand to be kissed*] There, my note   185
of hand will do as well.

SIR PETER TEAZLE (*kissing her hand*) And you shall no longer
reproach me with not giving you an independent settlement;° I
mean shortly to surprise you. But shall we always live thus, hey?

LADY TEAZLE If you please. I'm sure I don't care how soon we leave   190
off quarrelling, provided you'll own you were tired first.

SIR PETER TEAZLE Well, then let our future contest be who shall be
most obliging.

LADY TEAZLE I assure you, Sir Peter, good nature becomes you. You
look now as you did before we were married, when you used to walk   195
with me under the elms and tell me stories of what a gallant you
were in your youth and chuck me under the chin—you would—
and ask me if I thought I could love an old fellow who would deny
me nothing, didn't you?

SIR PETER TEAZLE Yes, yes, and you were as kind and attentive.   200

LADY TEAZLE Ay, so I was, and would always take your part when my
acquaintance used to abuse you and turn you into ridicule.

SIR PETER TEAZLE Indeed!

LADY TEAZLE Ay, and when my cousin Sophy has called you a stiff
peevish old bachelor and laughed at me for thinking of marrying   205
one who might be my father, I have always defended you, and said
I didn't think you so ugly by any means and that I dared say you'd
make a very good sort of a husband.

SIR PETER TEAZLE And you prophesied right, and we shall certainly
now be the happiest couple.   210

LADY TEAZLE And never differ again.

SIR PETER TEAZLE No, never; though at the same time, indeed, my
dear Lady Teazle, you must watch your temper° very narrowly, for
in all our little quarrels, my dear, if you recollect, my love, you
always began first.   215

LADY TEAZLE I beg your pardon, my dear Sir Peter; indeed you
always gave the provocation.

SIR PETER TEAZLE Now, see, my angel, take care! Contradicting isn't
the way to keep friends.

LADY TEAZLE Then don't you begin it, my love!   220

SIR PETER TEAZLE There now! You—you are going on! You don't
perceive, my life, that you are just doing the very thing which you
know always makes me angry.

LADY TEAZLE Nay, you know, if you will be angry without any
reason—   225

SIR PETER TEAZLE There, now, you want to quarrel again.

LADY TEAZLE No, I am sure I don't; but if you will be so peevish—

SIR PETER TEAZLE There, now, who begins first?

LADY TEAZLE Why, you, to be sure. I said nothing but there's no
bearing your temper.   230

SIR PETER TEAZLE No, no, madam; the fault's in your own temper.

LADY TEAZLE Ay, you are just what my cousin Sophy said you would
be.

SIR PETER TEAZLE Your cousin Sophy is a forward impertinent gipsy.

LADY TEAZLE You are a great bear, I'm sure, to abuse my relations.°   235

SIR PETER TEAZLE Now may all the plagues of marriage be doubled
on me if ever I try to be friends with you any more.

LADY TEAZLE So much the better.

SIR PETER TEAZLE No, no, madam; 'tis evident you never cared a pin
for me, and I was a madman to marry you—a pert rural coquette   240
that had refused half the honest squires in the neighbourhood.

LADY TEAZLE And I am sure I was a fool to marry you—an old
dangling° bachelor who was single at fifty only because he never
could meet with anyone who would have him.

SIR PETER TEAZLE Ay, ay, madam; but you were pleased enough to   245
listen to me. You never had such an offer before.

LADY TEAZLE No! Didn't I refuse Sir Tivy Terrier,° who everybody said would have been a better match, for his estate is just as
good as yours, and he has broke his neck° since we have been
married!   250

SIR PETER TEAZLE I have done with you, madam. You are an unfeeling, ungrateful—but there's an end of everything. I believe you
capable of anything that's bad. Yes, madam, I now believe the reports relative to you and Charles, madam—yes, madam, you and
Charles—are not without grounds.   255

LADY TEAZLE Take care, Sir Peter. You had better not insinuate any
such thing! I'll not be suspected without cause, I promise you.

SIR PETER TEAZLE Very well, madam, very well; a separate maintenance, as soon as you please. Yes, madam, or a divorce. I'll make an
example of myself for the benefit of all old bachelors. Let us sep-   260
arate, madam.

LADY TEAZLE Agreed, agreed—and, now, my dear Sir Peter, we are
of a mind once more, we may be the happiest couple, and never
differ again, you know. Ha, ha! Well, you are going to be in a
passion, I see, and I shall only interrupt you. So, bye–bye!   265

Exit Lady Teazle

SIR PETER TEAZLE Plagues and tortures! Can't I make her angry
neither! O, I am the miserablest fellow. But I'll not bear her presuming to keep her temper.° No, she may break my heart, but she
shan't keep her temper.

Exit

3.2

Charles Surface's house

Enter Trip, Moses, and Sir Oliver Surface

TRIP Here, Master Moses. If you'll stay a moment, I'll try whether
Mr—what's the gentleman's name?

SIR OLIVER SURFACE Mr—(*aside*) Moses, what *is* my name?

MOSES Mr Premium.

TRIP Premium. Very well.   5

Exit Trip, taking snuff

SIR OLIVER SURFACE To judge by the servants, one wouldn't believe
the master was ruined. But, what, sure this was my brother's house?

MOSES Yes, sir. Mr Charles bought it of Mr Joseph° with the furniture, pictures, etc., just as the old gentleman left it. Sir Peter
thought it a great piece of extravagance in him!   10

SIR OLIVER SURFACE In my mind the other's economy in selling it to
him was more reprehensible by half.

Enter Trip

TRIP My master says you must wait, gentlemen. He has company and
can't speak with you yet.

SIR OLIVER SURFACE If he knew who it was wanted to see him,   15
perhaps he wouldn't have sent such a message.

TRIP Yes, yes, sir; he knows you are here. I didn't forget little
Premium. No, no, no.

SIR OLIVER SURFACE Very well. And, I pray, sir, what may be your
name?   20

TRIP Trip, sir; my name is Trip, at your service.

SIR OLIVER SURFACE Well then, Mr Trip, you have a pleasant sort of
a place° here, I guess.

TRIP Why, yes; here are three or four of us pass our time agreeably
enough. But then our wages are sometimes a little in arrear, and   25
not very great either—but fifty pounds a year, and find our own
bags and bouquets.°

SIR OLIVER SURFACE (*aside*) Bags and bouquets! Halters and
bastinadoes!

TRIP But apropos, Moses, have you been able to get me that little bill 30
discounted?°

SIR OLIVER SURFACE [*aside*] Wants to raise money too! Mercy on me!
Has his distresses,° I warrant, like a lord, and affects creditors and
duns!

MOSES 'Twas not to be done indeed, Mr Trip.   35
    Moses gives Trip the note

TRIP Good lack, you surprise me. My friend Brush° has endorsed it,°
and I thought when he put his mark on the back of a bill 'twas as
good as cash.

MOSES No, 'twouldn't do.

TRIP A small sum, but twenty pounds. Harkee, Moses, do you think   40
you couldn't get it me by way of annuity?

SIR OLIVER SURFACE [*aside*] An annuity! Ha, ha, ha! A footman raise
money by annuity! Well done, luxury, egad!

MOSES But you must insure your place.

TRIP O, with all my heart. I'll insure my place, and my life too, if you   45
please.

SIR OLIVER SURFACE [*aside*] It's more than I would your neck.

TRIP But then, Moses, it must be done before this damned register°
takes place. One wouldn't like to have one's name made public, you
know.   50

MOSES No, certainly. But is there nothing you could deposit?

TRIP Why, nothing capital of my master's wardrobe has dropped
lately.° But I could give you a mortgage on some of his winter
clothes with equity of redemption before November,° or you shall
have the reversion of the French velvet or a *post-obit* on the blue   55
and silver.° These, I should think, Moses, with a few pair of point
ruffles as a collateral security—hey, my little fellow?

MOSES Well, well.
    Bell rings [*offstage*]

TRIP Gad, I heard the bell. I believe, gentlemen, I can now introduce
you.—Don't forget the annuity, little Moses.—This way, gentle-   60
men.—Insure my place! You know—

SIR OLIVER SURFACE [*aside*] If the man be a shadow of his master,
this is the temple of dissipation indeed!
    Exeunt

3.3

[*Another room in Charles Surface's house*]

Charles Surface, Careless, Sir Toby Bumper, and Two
Gentlemen, at a table with wine, etc.°

CHARLES SURFACE 'Fore heaven, 'tis true! There's the great degen-
eracy of the age. Many of our acquaintance have taste, spirit and
politeness; but, plague on't, they won't drink.

CARELESS It is so indeed, Charles. They give in to all the substantial luxuries of the table, and abstain from nothing but wine and wit.   5

CHARLES SURFACE O, certainly society suffers by it intolerably, for now, instead of the social spirit of raillery that used to mantle over° a glass of bright burgundy, their conversation is become just like the spa water they drink, which has all the pertness° and flatulence° of champagne without its spirit or flavour.   10

FIRST GENTLEMAN But what are they to do who love play° better than wine?

CARELESS True. There's Harry diets himself for gaming and is now under a hazard-regimen.°

CHARLES SURFACE Then he'll have the worst of it. What, you   15
wouldn't train a horse for the course by keeping him from corn. For my part, egad, I am now never so successful as when I am a little merry. Let me throw on° a bottle of champagne and I never lose. At least I never feel my losses, which is exactly the same thing.

SECOND GENTLEMAN Ay, that I believe.   20

CHARLES SURFACE And then what man can pretend to be a believer in love who is an abjurer of wine? 'Tis the test by which the lover knows his own heart. Fill a dozen bumpers to a dozen beauties, and she that floats at top° is the maid that has bewitched you.

CARELESS Now then, Charles, be honest and give us your real   25
favourite.

CHARLES SURFACE Why, I have withheld her only in compassion to you. If I toast her, you must give a round of her peers,° which is impossible—on earth!

CARELESS O then we'll find some canonized vestals° or heathen god-   30
desses that will do, I warrant.

CHARLES SURFACE Here then. Bumpers, you rogues, bumpers! Maria, Maria.
    All drink

FIRST GENTLEMAN Maria who?

CHARLES SURFACE O damn the surname! 'Tis too formal to be reg-   35
istered in love's calendar. But now, Sir Toby Bumper, beware; we must have beauty superlative.

CARELESS Nay, never study, Sir Toby. We'll stand to the toast, though your mistress should want an eye; and you know you have a song will excuse you.   40

SIR TOBY Egad, so I have, and I'll give him the song instead of the lady. [*Sings*]

SONG AND CHORUS

Here's to the maiden of bashful fifteen,
  Here's to the widow of fifty,
Here's to the flaunting, extravagant quean,   45
  And here's to the housewife that's thrifty.
    Chorus *Let the toast pass,*
      Drink to the lass,
I'll warrant she'll prove an excuse for the glass!

Here's to the charmer whose dimples we prize!   50
  Now to the maid who has none, sir.
Here's to the girl with a pair of blue eyes,
  And here's to the nymph with but one, sir!
    Chorus *Let the toast pass, etc.*

Here's to the maid with a bosom of snow,   55
  Now to her that's as brown as a berry.
Here's to the wife with a face full of woe,
  And now for the damsel that's merry.
    Chorus *Let the toast pass, etc.*

  For let 'em be clumsy or let 'em be slim,   60
  Young or ancient, I care not a feather.
So fill a pint bumper quite up to the brim,
  And let us e'en toast 'em together!
    Chorus *Let the toast pass, etc.*

ALL Bravo, bravo!   65
    Enter Trip. He whispers to Charles Surface
CHARLES SURFACE Gentlemen, you must excuse me a little.—
  Careless, take the chair, will you?
CARELESS Nay, prithee, Charles, what now? This is one of your peer-
  less beauties, I suppose, has dropped in by chance.
CHARLES SURFACE No, faith, to tell you the truth, 'tis a Jew and a   70
  broker who are come by appointment.
CARELESS O damn it, let's have the Jew in.
FIRST GENTLEMAN Ay, and the broker too, by all means.
SECOND GENTLEMAN Yes, yes, the Jew and the broker.
CHARLES SURFACE Egad, with all my heart.—Trip, bid the gentle-   75
  men walk in; though there's one of them a stranger, I can tell
  you.
    [*Exit Trip*]

CARELESS Charles, let us give them some generous burgundy and perhaps they'll grow conscientious.°

CHARLES SURFACE O hang 'em, no! Wine does but draw forth a man's 80 natural qualities, and to make them drink would only be to whet their knavery.

    Enter Trip, Sir Oliver Surface, and Moses

So. Honest Moses, walk in; walk in, pray, Mr Premium.—That's the gentleman's name, isn't it, Moses?

MOSES Yes, sir. 85

CHARLES SURFACE Set chairs, Trip.—Sit down, Mr Premium.— Glasses, Trip.—Sit down, Moses.—Come, Mr Premium, I'll give you a sentiment.° Here's success to usury.—Moses, fill the gentleman a bumper.

MOSES [*draining his glass*] Success to usury. 90

CHARLES SURFACE Right, Moses. Usury is prudence and industry and deserves to succeed.

SIR OLIVER SURFACE [*drinking a little of his bumper*] Then here is all the success it deserves.

CARELESS No, no, that won't do, Mr Premium; you have demurred 95 to° the toast, and must drink it in a pint bumper.

FIRST GENTLEMAN A pint bumper at least.

MOSES O pray, sir, consider Mr Premium's a gentleman.

CARELESS And therefore loves good wine.

SECOND GENTLEMAN Give Moses a quart glass. This is mutiny, and 100 a high contempt of the chair.

CARELESS Here. Now for't. I'll see justice done to the last drop of my bottle.

SIR OLIVER SURFACE Nay, pray, gentlemen. I did not expect this usage.

CHARLES SURFACE No, hang it, Careless; you shan't. Mr Premium's 105 a stranger.

SIR OLIVER SURFACE [*aside*] Od, I wish I was well out of this company.

CARELESS Plague on 'em then! If they won't drink, we'll not sit down with 'em. Come, Harry, the dice are in the next room.—Charles, 110 you'll join us, when you have finished your business with these gentlemen.

CHARLES SURFACE I will. I will.

    Exeunt Sir Toby Bumper and Two Gentlemen

Careless!

CARELESS Well. 115

CHARLES SURFACE Perhaps I may want you.

CARELESS O you know I am always ready. Word, note, or bond; 'tis all the same to me.°

Exit Careless

MOSES Sir, this is Mr Premium, a gentleman of the strictest honour and secrecy, and always performs what he undertakes.—Mr Premium, this is— 120

CHARLES SURFACE Pshaw, have done! Sir, my friend Moses is a very honest fellow, but a little slow at expression. He'll be an hour giving us our titles. Mr Premium, the plain state of the matter is this. I am an extravagant young fellow, who wants money to borrow; you I take to be a prudent old fellow, who has got money to lend. I am blockhead enough to give fifty per cent sooner than not have it, and you, I presume, are rogue enough to take a hundred if you could get it. Now, sir, you see we are acquainted at once, and may proceed to business without farther ceremony. 125 130

SIR OLIVER SURFACE Exceeding frank, upon my word. I see, sir, you are not a man of many compliments.°

CHARLES SURFACE O no, sir; plain dealing in business I always think best.

SIR OLIVER SURFACE Sir, I like you the better for't. However, you are mistaken in one thing; I have no money to lend. But I believe I could procure some of a friend. But then he's an unconscionable dog— isn't he, Moses?—and must sell stock to accommodate you, mustn't he, Moses? 135

MOSES Yes, indeed! You know I always speak the truth, and scorn to tell a lie. 140

CHARLES SURFACE Right! People that speak truth generally do. But these are trifles, Mr Premium. What, I know money isn't to be bought without paying for't.

SIR OLIVER SURFACE Well, but what security could you give? You have no land, I suppose? 145

CHARLES SURFACE Not a molehill, nor a twig,° but what's in beau-pots out at the window.

SIR OLIVER SURFACE Nor any stock, I presume.

CHARLES SURFACE Nothing but livestock, and that's only a few point-ers and ponies. But pray, Mr Premium, are you acquainted at all with any of my connections?° 150

SIR OLIVER SURFACE Why, to say truth, I am.

CHARLES SURFACE Then you must know that I have a devilish rich uncle in the East Indies, Sir Oliver Surface, from whom I have the greatest expectations. 155

SIR OLIVER SURFACE That you have a wealthy uncle I have heard; but how your expectations will turn out is more, I believe, than you can tell.

CHARLES SURFACE O no, there can be no doubt of it. They tell me I'm a prodigious favourite, and that he talks of leaving me everything. 160

SIR OLIVER SURFACE Indeed this is the first I've heard on't.

CHARLES SURFACE Yes, yes, 'tis just so. Moses knows 'tis true—don't you, Moses? 165

MOSES O yes, I'll swear to't.

SIR OLIVER SURFACE [*aside*] Egad, they'll persuade me presently I'm at Bengal.

CHARLES SURFACE Now I propose, Mr Premium, if it's agreeable to you, to grant a *post-obit°* on Sir Oliver's life, though at the same 170 time the old fellow has been so liberal to me that I give you my word I should be very sorry to hear anything had happened to him.

SIR OLIVER SURFACE Not any more than I should, I assure you. But the bond you mention happens to be just the worst security you could offer me, for I might live to a hundred and never recover the 175 principal.°

CHARLES SURFACE O, yes, you would. The moment Sir Oliver dies, you know you'd come on me for the money.

SIR OLIVER SURFACE Then I believe I should be the most unwelcome dun you ever had in your life. 180

CHARLES SURFACE What, I suppose you are afraid now that Sir Oliver is too good a life.°

SIR OLIVER SURFACE No, indeed I am not, though I have heard he is as hale and healthy as any man of his years in Christendom.

CHARLES SURFACE There again you are misinformed. No, no, the 185 climate has hurt him considerably. Poor Uncle Oliver. Yes, he breaks apace,° I'm told, and so much altered lately that his nearest relations don't know him.

SIR OLIVER SURFACE No! Ha, ha, ha! So much altered lately that his relations don't know him! Ha, ha, ha! That's droll, egad! Ha, ha, 190 ha!

CHARLES SURFACE Ha, ha! You're glad to hear that, little Premium.

SIR OLIVER SURFACE No, no, I'm not.

CHARLES SURFACE Yes, yes, you are. Ha, ha, ha! You know that mends your chance. 195

SIR OLIVER SURFACE But I'm told Sir Oliver is coming over; nay, some say he is actually arrived.

CHARLES SURFACE Pshaw! Sure I must know better than you whether he's come or not. No, no, rely on't; he is at this moment at Calcutta—isn't he, Moses?   200

MOSES O yes, certainly.

SIR OLIVER SURFACE Very true; as you say, you must know better than I. Though I have it from pretty good authority—haven't I, Moses?

MOSES Yes, most undoubted.

SIR OLIVER SURFACE But, sir, as I understand you want a few hun-   205
dreds immediately, is there nothing you would dispose of?

CHARLES SURFACE How do you mean?

SIR OLIVER SURFACE For instance, now, I have heard that your father left behind him a great quantity of massy old plate.

CHARLES SURFACE O lud, that's gone, long ago. Moses can tell you   210
how better than I can.

SIR OLIVER SURFACE (aside) Good lack! All the family race cups and corporation bowls!°—Then it was also supposed that his library was one of the most valuable and complete—

CHARLES SURFACE Yes, yes. So it was—vastly too much so for a   215
private gentleman. For my part, I was always of a communicative° disposition, so I thought it a shame to keep so much knowledge to myself.

SIR OLIVER SURFACE [aside] Mercy on me! Learning that had run in the family like an heirloom!—Pray what are become of the   220
books?

CHARLES SURFACE You must inquire of the auctioneer, Master Premium, for I don't believe even Moses can direct you there.

MOSES I never meddle with books.

SIR OLIVER SURFACE So, so. Nothing of the family property left, I   225
suppose?

CHARLES SURFACE Not much indeed, unless you have a mind to the family pictures. I have got a room full of ancestors above; and if you have a taste for old paintings, egad, you shall have 'em a bargain.°   230

SIR OLIVER SURFACE Hey, and the devil! Sure you wouldn't sell your forefathers, would you?

CHARLES SURFACE Every man of 'em to the best bidder.

SIR OLIVER SURFACE What, your great-uncles and -aunts?

CHARLES SURFACE Ay, and my great-grandfathers and -grandmothers   235
too.

SIR OLIVER SURFACE (aside) Now I give him up!—What the plague! Have you no bowels° for your own kindred? Od's life, do you take

me for Shylock in the play, that you would raise money of me on
your own flesh and blood?°   240

CHARLES SURFACE Nay, my little broker, don't be angry. What need
you care, if you have your money's worth?

SIR OLIVER SURFACE Well, I'll be the purchaser. I think I can dispose
of the family. [*Aside*] O, I'll never forgive him this—never!

Enter Careless

CARELESS Come, Charles; what keeps you?   245

CHARLES SURFACE I can't come yet, i'faith! We are going to have a
sale above. Here's little Premium will buy all my ancestors.

CARELESS O, burn° your ancestors!

CHARLES SURFACE No, he may do that afterwards if he pleases. Stay,
Careless, we want you. Egad, you shall be auctioneer. So come along   250
with us.

CARELESS O, have with you, if that's the case. I can handle a hammer
as well as a dice-box!

SIR OLIVER SURFACE [*aside*] O the profligates!

CHARLES SURFACE Come, Moses; you shall be appraiser if we want   255
one.—Gad's life, little Premium, you don't seem to like the
business.

SIR OLIVER SURFACE O, yes, I do vastly. Ha, ha! Yes, yes, I think it
a rare joke to sell one's family by auction. Ha, ha! [*Aside*] O, the
prodigal!   260

CHARLES SURFACE To be sure, when a man wants money, where the
plague should he get assistance, if he can't make free with his own
relations!

Exeunt

4.1

Picture room at Charles Surface's

Enter Charles Surface, Sir Oliver Surface, Moses, and Careless

CHARLES SURFACE Walk in, gentlemen, pray walk in! Here they are, the family of the Surfaces up to the Conquest.°

SIR OLIVER SURFACE And, in my opinion, a goodly collection.

CHARLES SURFACE Ay, ay, these are done in the true spirit of portrait-painting—no volunteer grace,° or expression, not like the works of your modern Raphael,° who gives you the strongest resemblance, yet contrives to make your own portrait independent of you, so that you may sink the original and not hurt the picture. No, no; the merit of these is the inveterate likeness, all stiff and awkward as the originals, and like nothing in human nature beside!

SIR OLIVER SURFACE Ah, we shall never see such figures of men again.

CHARLES SURFACE No, I hope not. You see, Master Premium, what a domestic character I am. Here I sit of an evening, surrounded by my family. But come, get to your pulpit, Mr Auctioneer. Here's an old gouty chair° of my grandfather's will answer the purpose.

CARELESS Ay, ay, this will do. But, Charles, I have ne'er a hammer, and what's an auctioneer without his hammer?

CHARLES SURFACE Egad, that's true. What parchment have we here?

Charles Surface takes down a roll

'Richard, heir to Thomas . . .'° Our genealogy in full! Here, Careless, you shall have no common bit of mahogany; here's the family tree for you, you rogue. This shall be your hammer, and now you may knock down my ancestors with their own pedigree.

SIR OLIVER SURFACE [*aside*] What an unnatural rogue! An *ex post facto* parricide!°

CARELESS Yes, yes, here's a list of your generation° indeed. Faith, Charles, this is the most convenient thing you could have found for the business, for 'twill serve not only as a hammer, but a catalogue into the bargain. But come, begin. A-going, a-going, a-going!

CHARLES SURFACE Bravo, Careless! Well, here's my great uncle, Sir Richard Ravelin°—a marvellous good general in his day, I assure you. He served in all the Duke of Marlborough's wars, and got that cut over his eye at the Battle of Malplaquet.° What say you, Mr Premium? Look at him! There's a hero for you! Not cut out of° his

feathers, as your modern clipped° captains are, but enveloped in   35
wig and regimentals as a general should be. What do you bid?

MOSES Mr Premium would have you speak.

CHARLES SURFACE Why then, he shall have him for ten pounds, and
I am sure that's not dear for a staff officer.

SIR OLIVER SURFACE [*aside*] Heaven deliver me! His famous Uncle   40
Richard for ten pounds!—Very well, sir; I take him at that.

CHARLES SURFACE Careless, knock down my Uncle Richard. Here
now is a maiden sister of his, my Great-Aunt Deborah, done by
Kneller,° thought to be in his best manner, and a very formidable
likeness. There she is, you see—a shepherdess feeding her flock.   45
You shall have her for five pounds ten.° The sheep are worth the
money.

SIR OLIVER SURFACE [*aside*] Ah, poor Deborah! A woman who set
such a value on herself!—Five pound ten! She's mine.

CHARLES SURFACE Knock down my Aunt Deborah! Here now are two   50
that were a sort of cousins of theirs.—You see, Moses, these pictures were done some time ago, when beaux wore wigs, and the
ladies wore their own hair.

SIR OLIVER SURFACE Yes, truly, head-dresses appear to have been a
little lower in those days.   55

CHARLES SURFACE Well, take that couple for the same.

MOSES 'Tis good bargain.

CHARLES SURFACE Careless!—This now is a grandfather of my
mother's, a learned judge, well known on the western circuit.—
What do you rate him at, Moses?   60

MOSES Four guineas.

CHARLES SURFACE Four guineas! Gad's life, you don't bid me the
price of his wig!—Mr Premium, you have more respect for the
woolsack; do let us knock his lordship down at fifteen.

SIR OLIVER SURFACE By all means.   65

CARELESS Gone.

CHARLES SURFACE And there are two brothers of his, William and
Walter Blunt Esquires, both Members of Parliament, and noted
speakers, and—what's very extraordinary—I believe this is the first
time they were ever bought and sold.   70

SIR OLIVER SURFACE That's very extraordinary indeed! I'll take them
at your own price for the honour of Parliament.

CARELESS Well said, little Premium. I'll knock 'em down at forty.

CHARLES SURFACE Here's a jolly fellow. I don't know what relation,
but he was mayor of Manchester. Take him at eight pounds.   75

SIR OLIVER SURFACE No, no; six will do for the mayor.

CHARLES SURFACE Come, make it guineas and I'll throw you the two aldermen there into the bargain.

SIR OLIVER SURFACE They're mine.

CHARLES SURFACE Careless, knock down the mayor and aldermen. 80 But, plague on't, we shall be all day, retailing in this manner. Do let us deal wholesale. What say you, little Premium? Give me three hundred pounds for the rest of the family in the lump.

CARELESS Ay, ay; that will be the best way.

SIR OLIVER SURFACE Well, well, anything to accommodate you. They 85 are mine. But there is one portrait, which you have always passed over.

CARELESS What, that ill-looking little fellow over the settee?

SIR OLIVER SURFACE Yes, sir, I mean that, though I don't think him so ill-looking a little fellow by any means. 90

CHARLES SURFACE What, that? O that's my Uncle Oliver. 'Twas done before he went to India.

CARELESS Your Uncle Oliver! Gad! Then you'll never be friends, Charles; that now to me is as stern a looking rogue as ever I saw— an unforgiving eye, and a damned disinheriting countenance! An 95 inveterate knave, depend on't!—Don't you think so, little Premium?

SIR OLIVER SURFACE Upon my soul, sir, I do not; I think it is as honest a looking face as any in the room, dead or alive. But I suppose your Uncle Oliver goes with the rest of the lumber.

CHARLES SURFACE No, hang it, I'll not part with poor Noll. The old 100 fellow has been very good to me, and, egad, I'll keep his picture, while I've a room to put it in.

SIR OLIVER SURFACE (aside) The rogue's my nephew, after all!—But, sir, I have somehow taken a fancy to that picture.

CHARLES SURFACE I'm sorry for't, for you certainly will not have it. 105 Oons, haven't you got enough of 'em?

SIR OLIVER SURFACE (aside) I forgive him everything!—But, sir, when I take a whim in my head, I don't value money. I'll give as much for that as for all the rest.

CHARLES SURFACE Don't tease me, Master Broker; I tell you I'll not 110 part with it, and there's an end on't.

SIR OLIVER SURFACE (aside) How like his father the dog is!—Well, well, I have done. (Aside) I did not perceive it before, but I think I never saw such a resemblance.—Well, sir, here is a draft for your sum. 115

CHARLES SURFACE Why, 'tis for eight hundred pounds!

SIR OLIVER SURFACE You will not let Oliver go?

CHARLES SURFACE Zounds, no, I tell you once more.

SIR OLIVER SURFACE Then never mind the difference; we'll balance another time. But give me your hand on the bargain. You are an honest fellow, Charles. I beg pardon, sir, for being so free.—Come, Moses. 120

CHARLES SURFACE Egad, this is a whimsical old fellow.—But harkee, Premium. You'll prepare lodgings for these gentlemen?

SIR OLIVER SURFACE Yes, yes, I'll send for them in a day or two. 125

CHARLES SURFACE But hold! Do now send a genteel conveyance for them, for I assure you they were most of them used to ride in their own carriages.

SIR OLIVER SURFACE I will, I will, for all but Oliver.

CHARLES SURFACE Ay, all but the little honest nabob.° 130

SIR OLIVER SURFACE You're fixed on that?

CHARLES SURFACE Peremptorily.

SIR OLIVER SURFACE [aside] A dear extravagant rogue!—Good day.——Come, Moses. [Aside] Let me hear now who dares call him profligate! 135

> *Exeunt Sir Oliver Surface and Moses*

CARELESS Why, this is the oddest genius° of the sort I ever saw.

CHARLES SURFACE Egad, he's the prince of brokers, I think. I wonder how the devil Moses got acquainted with so honest a fellow. Ha, here's Rowley. Do, Careless, say I'll join the company in a moment. 140

CARELESS I will. But don't now let that old blockhead persuade you to squander any of that money on old musty debts, or any such nonsense, for tradesmen, Charles, are the most exorbitant fellows!

CHARLES SURFACE Very true, and paying them is only encouraging them. 145

CARELESS Nothing else.

CHARLES SURFACE Ay, ay; never fear.

> *Exit Careless*

So. This was an odd old fellow indeed! Let me see; two thirds of this is mine by right.° Five hundred and thirty pounds, 'fore heaven! I find one's ancestors are more valuable relations than I took 'em for! Ladies and gentlemen, your most obedient and very grateful humble servant. 150

> *Enter Rowley*

Ha, old Rowley! Egad, you are just come in time to take leave of your old acquaintance.

ROWLEY Yes, I heard they were going. But I wonder you can have such   155
spirits under so many distresses.

CHARLES SURFACE Why, there's the point. My distresses are so many
that I can't afford to part with my spirits; but I shall be rich and
splenetic all in good time. However, I suppose you are surprised
that I am not sorrowful at parting with so many near relations. To   160
be sure 'tis very affecting. But, rot 'em, you see they never move a
muscle; so why should I?

ROWLEY There's no making you serious a moment.

CHARLES SURFACE Yes, faith. I am so now. [*Giving him the draft*] Here,
my honest Rowley, here; get me this changed, and take a hundred   165
pounds of it immediately to old Stanley.

ROWLEY A hundred pounds. Consider only—

CHARLES SURFACE Gad's life, don't talk about it. Poor Stanley's wants
are pressing, and if you don't make haste we shall have someone
call that has a better right to the money.   170

ROWLEY Ah, there's the point! I never will cease dunning you with
the old proverb—

CHARLES SURFACE 'Be just before you're generous',° hey! Why, so I
would if I could; but justice is an old lame hobbling beldam, and I
can't get her to keep pace with generosity, for the soul of me.   175

ROWLEY Yet, Charles, believe me, one hour's reflection—

CHARLES SURFACE Ay, ay, it's all very true; but harkee, Rowley, while
I have, by heaven I'll give. So, damn your economy;° and now for
hazard.

  Exeunt

4.2

The parlour at Charles Surface's
Enter Sir Oliver Surface and Moses

MOSES Well, sir, I think, as Sir Peter said, you have seen Mr Charles
in high glory. 'Tis pity he's so extravagant.

SIR OLIVER SURFACE True; but he wouldn't sell my picture.

MOSES And loves wine and women so much.

SIR OLIVER SURFACE But he wouldn't sell my picture.   5

MOSES And game so deep.°

SIR OLIVER SURFACE But he wouldn't sell my picture. O here's
Rowley!

  Enter Rowley

ROWLEY So, Sir Oliver, I find you have made a purchase.

SIR OLIVER SURFACE Yes, yes, our young rake has parted with his   10
ancestors like old tapestry.

ROWLEY And here has he commissioned me to redeliver you part of
the purchase money—I mean, though, in your necessitous character of old Stanley.

MOSES Ah, there is the pity of all! He is so damned charitable.   15

ROWLEY And I have left a hosier and two tailors in the hall, who, I'm
sure, won't be paid, and this hundred would satisfy 'em!

SIR OLIVER SURFACE Well, well, I'll pay his debts, and his benevo-
lences too. But now I am no more a broker and you shall introduce
me to the elder brother as old Stanley.   20

ROWLEY Not yet awhile. Sir Peter, I know, means to call there about
this time.

 Enter Trip

TRIP O, gentlemen, I beg pardon for not showing you out. This
way.—Moses, a word.

 Exeunt Trip and Moses

SIR OLIVER SURFACE There's a fellow for you. Would you believe it!   25
That puppy intercepted the Jew on our coming and wanted to raise
money before he got to his master.

ROWLEY Indeed!

SIR OLIVER SURFACE Yes, they are now planning an annuity business.
Ah, Master Rowley, in my day servants were content with the   30
follies of their masters when they were worn a little threadbare,
but now they have their vices, like their birthday clothes,° with the
gloss on.

 Exeunt

4.3

A library° at Joseph Surface's

Joseph Surface and Servant

JOSEPH SURFACE No letter from Lady Teazle?

SERVANT No, sir.

JOSEPH SURFACE [*aside*] I am surprised she hasn't sent if she is prevented from coming. Sir Peter certainly does not suspect me. Yet I
wish I may not lose the heiress through the scrape I have drawn   5

myself in with the wife. However, Charles's imprudence and bad character are great points in my favour.

   Knocking [offstage]

SERVANT Sir, I believe that must be Lady Teazle.

JOSEPH SURFACE Hold! See whether it is or not before you go to the door. I have a particular message for you if it should be my brother.

SERVANT [*looking out the window*] 'Tis her ladyship, sir. She always leaves her chair at the milliner's in the next street.

JOSEPH SURFACE Stay, stay. Draw that screen before the window.

   Servant draws the screen

That will do. My opposite neighbour is a maiden lady of so curious a temper!

   Exit Servant

I have a difficult hand to play in this affair. Lady Teazle has lately suspected my views on Maria, but she must by no means be let into that secret, at least not till I have her more in my power.

   Enter Lady Teazle

LADY TEAZLE What, sentiment in soliloquy! Have you been very impatient now? O lud, don't pretend to look grave. I vow I couldn't come before.

JOSEPH SURFACE O madam, punctuality is a species of constancy, a very unfashionable quality in a lady.

LADY TEAZLE Upon my word, you ought to pity me. Do you know that Sir Peter is grown so ill-tempered to me of late, and so jealous! Of Charles too! That's the best of the story, isn't it?

JOSEPH SURFACE (*aside*) I am glad my scandalous friends keep that up.

LADY TEAZLE I am sure I wish he would let Maria marry him, and then perhaps he would be convinced. Don't you, Mr Surface?

JOSEPH SURFACE (*aside*) Indeed I do not.—O certainly I do, for then my dear Lady Teazle would also be convinced how wrong her suspicions were of my having any design on the silly girl.

   Joseph Surface and Lady Teazle sit

LADY TEAZLE Well, well, I'm inclined to believe you. But isn't it provoking to have the most ill-natured things said to one? And there's my friend Lady Sneerwell has circulated I don't know how many scandalous tales of me, and all without any foundation too. That's what vexes me.

JOSEPH SURFACE Ay, madam, to be sure, that is the provoking circumstance. Without foundation. Yes, yes, there's the mortification indeed, for when a slanderous story is believed against one,

there certainly is no comfort like the consciousness of having
deserved it.

LADY TEAZLE No, to be sure, then I'd forgive their malice; but to
attack me who am really so innocent, and who never say an ill-
natured thing of anybody—that is, of any friend! And then Sir   45
Peter too, to have him so peevish and so suspicious, when I know
the integrity of my own heart; indeed 'tis monstrous.

JOSEPH SURFACE But, my dear Lady Teazle, 'tis your own fault if you
suffer it. When a husband entertains a groundless suspicion of his   50
wife and withdraws his confidence from her, the original compact°
is broke, and she owes it to the honour of her sex to endeavour to
outwit him.

LADY TEAZLE Indeed! So that, if he suspects me without cause, it
follows that the best way of curing his jealousy is to give him reason   55
for't.

JOSEPH SURFACE Undoubtedly, for your husband should never be
deceived in you, and in that case it becomes you to be frail in compliment to his discernment.

LADY TEAZLE To be sure, what you say is very reasonable. And when   60
the consciousness of my own innocence—

JOSEPH SURFACE Ah, my dear madam, there is the great mistake. 'Tis
this very conscious innocence that is of the greatest prejudice to
you. What is it makes you negligent of forms and careless of
the world's opinion? Why, the consciousness of your innocence.   65
What makes you thoughtless in your conduct and apt to run into
a thousand little imprudences? Why, the consciousness of your
innocence. What makes you impatient of Sir Peter's temper and
outrageous at° his suspicions? Why, the consciousness of your own
innocence.   70

LADY TEAZLE 'Tis very true.

JOSEPH SURFACE Now, my dear Lady Teazle, if you would but once
make a trifling *faux pas*,° you can't conceive how cautious you would
grow, and how ready to humour and agree with your husband.

LADY TEAZLE Do you think so?   75

JOSEPH SURFACE O, I'm sure on't. And then you would find all
scandal would cease at once, for, in short, your character at present
is like a person in a plethora°—absolutely dying of too much health.

LADY TEAZLE So, so. Then I perceive your prescription is that I must
sin in my own defence, and part with my virtue to preserve my   80
reputation.

JOSEPH SURFACE Exactly so, upon my credit, ma'am.

LADY TEAZLE Well, certainly this is the oddest doctrine, and the
newest receipt for avoiding calumny.

JOSEPH SURFACE An infallible one, believe me. Prudence, like experi-   85
ence, must be paid for.

LADY TEAZLE Why, if my understanding were once convinced—

JOSEPH SURFACE O, certainly, madam, your understanding *should* be
convinced. Yes, yes; heaven forbid I should persuade you to do
anything you *thought* wrong. No, no; I have too much honour to   90
desire it.

LADY TEAZLE Don't you think we may as well leave honour out of the
argument?

JOSEPH SURFACE Ah, the ill effects of your country education, I see,
still remain with you.   95

LADY TEAZLE I doubt they do indeed, and I will fairly own to you
that if I could be persuaded to do wrong it would be by Sir Peter's
ill usage sooner than your honourable logic, after all.

JOSEPH SURFACE Then, by this hand which he is unworthy of—
          Enter Servant
'Sdeath, you blockhead! What do you want?   100

SERVANT I beg pardon, sir; but I thought you wouldn't choose Sir
Peter to come up without announcing him?

JOSEPH SURFACE Sir Peter! Oons and the devil!

LADY TEAZLE Sir Peter! O lud! I'm ruined, I'm ruined.

SERVANT Sir, 'twasn't I let him in.   105

LADY TEAZLE O I'm undone. What will become of me now, Mr
Logic? O mercy, he's on the stairs. I'll get behind here. And if ever
I am so imprudent again—
          Lady Teazle goes behind the screen

JOSEPH SURFACE Give me that book!
          Joseph Surface sits down. Servant pretends to adjust his hair.
          Enter Sir Peter Teazle

SIR PETER TEAZLE [*aside*] Ay, ever improving himself!—Mr Surface,   110
Mr Surface!

JOSEPH SURFACE O, my dear Sir Peter, I beg your pardon. (*Gaping,
and throws away the book°*) I have been dozing over a stupid book!
Well, I am much obliged to you for this call. You haven't been here,
I believe, since I fitted up this room. Books, you know, are the only   115
things I am a coxcomb in.

SIR PETER TEAZLE 'Tis very neat indeed. Well, well, that's proper.
And you make even your screen a source of knowledge—hung, I
perceive, with maps.

JOSEPH SURFACE O yes, I find great use in that screen.   120

SIR PETER TEAZLE I dare say you must, certainly, when you want to
find anything in a hurry.

JOSEPH SURFACE (*aside*) Ay, or to hide anything in a hurry either.

SIR PETER TEAZLE Well, I have a little private business.

JOSEPH SURFACE (*to Servant*) You needn't stay.   125

SERVANT No, sir.

   Exit Servant

JOSEPH SURFACE Here's a chair, Sir Peter. I beg—

   [*Sir Peter Teazle and Joseph Surface sit*]

SIR PETER TEAZLE Well, now we are alone, there *is* a subject, my dear
friend, on which I wish to unburden my mind to you—a point of
the greatest moment to my peace. In short, my good friend, Lady   130
Teazle's conduct of late has made me extremely unhappy.

JOSEPH SURFACE Indeed I'm very sorry to hear it.

SIR PETER TEAZLE Yes, 'tis but too plain she has not the least regard
for me; but, what's worse, I have pretty good authority to suspect
that she must have formed an attachment to another.   135

JOSEPH SURFACE You astonish me.

SIR PETER TEAZLE Yes, and, between ourselves, I think I have discovered the person.

JOSEPH SURFACE How! You alarm me exceedingly!

SIR PETER TEAZLE Ah, my dear friend, I knew you would sympathize   140
with me.

JOSEPH SURFACE Yes, believe me, Sir Peter, such a discovery would
hurt me just as much as it would you.

SIR PETER TEAZLE I am convinced of it. Ah, it is a happiness to have
a friend whom one can trust even with one's family secrets. But   145
have you no guess who I mean?

JOSEPH SURFACE I haven't the most distant idea. It can't be Sir Benjamin Backbite.

SIR PETER TEAZLE O, no. What say you to Charles?

JOSEPH SURFACE My brother? Impossible!   150

SIR PETER TEAZLE Ah, my dear friend, the goodness of your own
heart misleads you; you judge of others by yourself.

JOSEPH SURFACE Certainly, Sir Peter, the heart that is conscious of
its own integrity is ever slow to credit another's treachery.

SIR PETER TEAZLE True, but your brother has no sentiment; you   155
never hear him talk so.

JOSEPH SURFACE Yet I can't but think that Lady Teazle herself has
too much principle.

SIR PETER TEAZLE Ay, but what's her principle against the flattery of
a handsome, lively young fellow?   160

JOSEPH SURFACE That's very true.

SIR PETER TEAZLE And then you know the difference of our ages
makes it very improbable that she should have a great affection for
me; and, if she were to be frail and I were to make it public, why,
the town would only laugh at me, the foolish old bachelor who had   165
married a girl.

JOSEPH SURFACE That's true, to be sure; they *would* laugh.

SIR PETER TEAZLE Laugh! Ay, and make ballads and paragraphs and
the devil knows what of me.

JOSEPH SURFACE No, you must never make it public.   170

SIR PETER TEAZLE But, then again, that the nephew of my old friend
Sir Oliver should be the person to attempt such a wrong hurts me
more nearly.

JOSEPH SURFACE Ay, there's the point; when ingratitude barbs the
dart of injury, the wound has double danger in it.   175

SIR PETER TEAZLE Ay, I that was in a manner left his guardian, in
whose house he had been so often entertained, who never in my life
denied him my advice.

JOSEPH SURFACE O, 'tis not to be credited. There may be a man
capable of such baseness, to be sure; but for my part, till you can   180
give me positive proofs, I cannot but doubt it. However, if this
should be proved on him, he is no longer a brother of mine! I disclaim kindred with him, for the man who can break through the
laws of hospitality and attempt the wife of his friend deserves to be
branded as the pest of society.   185

SIR PETER TEAZLE What a difference there is between you! What
noble sentiments!

JOSEPH SURFACE Yet I cannot suspect Lady Teazle's honour.

SIR PETER TEAZLE I am sure I wish to think well of her and to remove
all ground of quarrel between us. She has lately reproached me   190
more than once with having made no settlement on her, and in our
last quarrel she almost hinted that she should not break her heart
if I was dead. Now, as we seem to differ in our ideas of expense, I
have resolved she shall be her own mistress in that respect for the
future; and if I were to die she shall find that I have not been inat- 195
tentive to her interest while living. Here, my friend, are the drafts
of two deeds which I wish to have your opinion on. By one she will
enjoy eight hundred a year independent while I live, and by the
other the bulk of my fortune after my death.

JOSEPH SURFACE This conduct, Sir Peter, is indeed truly generous!   200
(*Aside*) I wish it may not corrupt my pupil.

SIR PETER TEAZLE Yes, I am determined she shall have no cause to
complain, though I would not have her acquainted with the latter
instance of my affection yet awhile.

JOSEPH SURFACE (*aside*) Nor I, if I could help it.   205

SIR PETER TEAZLE And now, my dear friend, if you please we will talk
over the situation of your hopes with Maria.

JOSEPH SURFACE (*softly*) No, no, Sir Peter; another time, if you
please.

SIR PETER TEAZLE I am sensibly° chagrined at the little progress you   210
seem to make in her affection.

JOSEPH SURFACE (*softly*) I beg you will not mention it. What are my
disappointments when your happiness is in debate! (*Aside*) 'Sdeath,
I should be ruined every way.

SIR PETER TEAZLE And though you are so averse to my acquainting   215
Lady Teazle with your passion, I am sure she's not your enemy in
the affair.

JOSEPH SURFACE Pray, Sir Peter, now oblige me. I am really too much
affected by the subject we have been speaking on to bestow a
thought on my own concerns. The man who is entrusted with his   220
friend's distresses can never—
        Enter Servant
Well, sir?

SERVANT Your brother, sir, is speaking to a gentleman in the street and
says he knows you are within.

JOSEPH SURFACE 'Sdeath, blockhead, I'm not within; I'm out for the   225
day.

SIR PETER TEAZLE Stay, hold; a thought has struck me. You shall
be at home.°

JOSEPH SURFACE Well, well, let him up.
        Exit Servant
He'll interrupt, Sir Peter. However—   230

SIR PETER TEAZLE Now, my good friend, oblige me, I entreat you.
Before Charles comes, let me conceal myself somewhere. Then do
you tax him on the point we have been talking on, and his answers
may satisfy me at once.

JOSEPH SURFACE O fie, Sir Peter! Would you have me join in so mean   235
a trick? To trepan my brother to—

SIR PETER TEAZLE Nay, you tell me you are *sure* he is innocent. If so,
you do him the greatest service in giving him an opportunity to

clear himself; and you will set my heart at rest. Come, you shall not
refuse me. Here, behind this screen will be—   240
    Sir Peter Teazle goes to the screen
Hey, what the devil! There seems to be one listener here already.
I'll swear I saw a petticoat.

JOSEPH SURFACE Ha, ha, ha! Well, this is ridiculous enough. I'll tell
you, Sir Peter. Though I hold a man of intrigue° to be a most des-
picable character, yet you know it doesn't follow that one is to be   245
an absolute Joseph° either. Harkee. 'Tis a little French milliner, a
silly rogue that plagues me; and, having some character,° on your
coming she ran behind the screen.

SIR PETER TEAZLE Ah, you rogue! But, egad, she has overheard all I
have been saying of my wife.   250

JOSEPH SURFACE O, 'twill never go any further; you may depend on't.

SIR PETER TEAZLE No! Then, i'faith, let her hear it out. Here's a
closet will do as well.

JOSEPH SURFACE Well, go in then.

SIR PETER TEAZLE Sly rogue, sly rogue!   255
    Sir Peter Teazle goes into the closet

JOSEPH SURFACE A very narrow escape indeed! And a curious situation I'm in! To part man and wife in this manner!

LADY TEAZLE (*peeping from the screen*) Couldn't I steal off?

JOSEPH SURFACE Keep close,° my angel.

SIR PETER TEAZLE (*peeping out*) Joseph, tax him home.   260

JOSEPH SURFACE Back, my dear friend!

LADY TEAZLE (*peeping*) Couldn't you lock Sir Peter in?

JOSEPH SURFACE Be still, my life.

SIR PETER TEAZLE (*peeping*) You're sure the little milliner won't blab?

JOSEPH SURFACE In, in, my good Sir Peter! [*Aside*] 'Fore Gad, I wish   265
I had a key to the door.
    Enter Charles Surface

CHARLES SURFACE Hollo! Brother, what has been the matter? Your
fellow wouldn't let me up at first. What, have you had a Jew or a
wench with you?

JOSEPH SURFACE Neither, brother, I assure you.   270

CHARLES SURFACE But what has made Sir Peter steal off? I thought
he had been with you.

JOSEPH SURFACE He *was*, brother; but, hearing you were coming, he
did not choose to stay.

CHARLES SURFACE What, was the old gentleman afraid I wanted to   275
borrow money of him?

JOSEPH SURFACE No, sir; but I am sorry to find, Charles, that you have lately given that worthy man grounds for great uneasiness.

CHARLES SURFACE Yes, they tell me I do that to a great many worthy men. But how so, pray? 280

JOSEPH SURFACE To be plain with you, brother, he thinks you are endeavouring to gain Lady Teazle's affections from him.

CHARLES SURFACE Who, I? O lud, not I, upon my word. Ha, ha, ha! So the old fellow has found out that he has got a young wife, has he? Or, what's worse, has her ladyship discovered that she has an 285 old husband?

JOSEPH SURFACE This is no subject to jest on, brother. He who can laugh—

CHARLES SURFACE True, brother, as you were going to say. Then, seriously, I never had the least idea of what you charge me with, 290 upon my honour.

JOSEPH SURFACE (*aloud*) Well, it will give Sir Peter great satisfaction to hear this.

CHARLES SURFACE To be sure, I once thought the lady seemed to have taken a fancy to me; but, upon my soul, I never gave her the least 295 encouragement. Besides, you know my attachment to Maria.

JOSEPH SURFACE But, sure, brother, even if Lady Teazle had betrayed the fondest partiality for you—

CHARLES SURFACE Why, lookee, Joseph. I hope I shall never deliberately do a dishonourable action; but, if a pretty woman were pur- 300 posely to throw herself in my way, and that pretty woman married to a man old enough to be her father—

JOSEPH SURFACE Well!

CHARLES SURFACE Why, I believe I should be obliged to borrow a little of your morality; that's all. But, brother, do you know now 305 that you surprise me exceedingly by naming *me* with Lady Teazle, for, faith, I always understood *you* were her favourite?

JOSEPH SURFACE O, for shame, Charles; this retort is foolish.

CHARLES SURFACE Nay, I swear I have seen you exchange such significant glances. 310

JOSEPH SURFACE Nay, nay, sir, this is no jest.

CHARLES SURFACE Egad, I'm serious. Don't you remember? One day when I called here—

JOSEPH SURFACE Nay, prithee, Charles—

CHARLES SURFACE And found you together. 315

JOSEPH SURFACE Zounds, sir, I insist—

CHARLES SURFACE And another time when your servant—

JOSEPH SURFACE Brother, brother, a word with you. (*Aside*) Gad, I
    must stop him.

CHARLES SURFACE Informed me, I say, that—   320

JOSEPH SURFACE Hush! I beg your pardon, but Sir Peter has over-
    heard all we have been saying. I knew you would clear yourself, or
    I should not have consented.

CHARLES SURFACE How, Sir Peter! Where is he?

JOSEPH SURFACE Softly. There.   325

    Joseph Surface points to the closet

CHARLES SURFACE O, 'fore heaven, I'll have him out.—Sir Peter,
    come forth.

JOSEPH SURFACE No, no!

CHARLES SURFACE I say, Sir Peter, come into court.

    Charles Surface pulls in Sir Peter Teazle

    What, my old guardian, what, turn inquisitor and take evidence,   330
    incog.?°

SIR PETER TEAZLE Give me your hand, Charles; I believe I have sus-
    pected you wrongfully. But you mustn't be angry with Joseph; 'twas
    my plan.

CHARLES SURFACE Indeed!   335

SIR PETER TEAZLE But I acquit you. I promise you I don't think near
    so ill of you as I did; what I have heard has given me great
    satisfaction.

CHARLES SURFACE Egad, then 'twas lucky you didn't hear any
    more—(*half aside*) wasn't it, Joseph?   340

SIR PETER TEAZLE Ah, you would have retorted on him.

CHARLES SURFACE Ay, ay; that was a joke.

SIR PETER TEAZLE Yes, yes; I know his honour too well.

CHARLES SURFACE But you might as well have suspected him as me
    in this matter for all that—(*half aside*) mightn't he, Joseph?   345

SIR PETER TEAZLE Well, well, I believe you.

JOSEPH SURFACE (*aside*) Would they were both well out of the room.

    Enter Servant, who whispers to Joseph Surface

SIR PETER TEAZLE And in future, perhaps, we may not be such
    strangers.

JOSEPH SURFACE [*aside, to Servant*] Lady Sneerwell! Stop her by all 350
    means.

    Exit Servant

    Gentlemen, I beg pardon; I must wait on you down stairs. Here is
    a person come on particular business.

CHARLES SURFACE Well, you can see him in another room. Sir

Peter and I haven't met a long time and I have something to say to   355
him.

JOSEPH SURFACE [*aside*] They must not be left together. I'll contrive
to send Lady Sneerwell away, and return directly. (*Aside to Sir Peter*)
Sir Peter, not a word of the French milliner.

SIR PETER TEAZLE O not for the world!   360

    Exit Joseph Surface
Ah, Charles, if you associated more with your brother, one might
indeed hope for your reformation. He is a man of sentiment. Well,
there is nothing in the world so noble as a man of sentiment!

CHARLES SURFACE Pshaw! He is too moral by half, and so apprehensive of his good name,° as he calls it, that I suppose he would as   365
soon let a priest into his house as a girl.

SIR PETER TEAZLE No, no, come, come, you wrong him. No, no,
Joseph is no rake, but he is not such a saint in that respect either.
(*Aside*) I have a great mind to tell him; we should have a laugh.

CHARLES SURFACE O hang him! He's a very anchorite, a young   370
hermit.

SIR PETER TEAZLE Harkee; you must not abuse him. He may chance
to hear of it again, I promise you.

CHARLES SURFACE Why, you won't tell him?

SIR PETER TEAZLE No, but—this way—[*Aside*] Egad, I'll tell him!—   375
Harkee. Have you a mind to have a good laugh at Joseph?

CHARLES SURFACE I should like it of all things.

SIR PETER TEAZLE Then, i'faith, we will. (*Aside*) I'll be quit with°
him for discovering me. (*Whispering*) He had a girl with him when
I called.   380

CHARLES SURFACE What, Joseph! You jest.

SIR PETER TEAZLE Hush! (*Whispers*) A little French milliner. And the
best of the jest is she's in the room now.

CHARLES SURFACE The devil she is.

SIR PETER TEAZLE Hush. I tell you. (*Points*)   385

CHARLES SURFACE Behind the screen! 'Slife, let us unveil her.

SIR PETER TEAZLE No, no! He's coming. You shan't indeed.

CHARLES SURFACE O, egad, we'll have a peep at the little milliner.

SIR PETER TEAZLE Not for the world. Joseph will never forgive me.

CHARLES SURFACE I'll stand by you.   390

SIR PETER TEAZLE (*struggling with Charles*) Od's, here he is.

    Joseph Surface enters just as Charles Surface throws down the
    screen

CHARLES SURFACE Lady Teazle!—by all that's wonderful!

SIR PETER TEAZLE Lady Teazle!—by all that's horrible!

CHARLES SURFACE Sir Peter, this is one of the smartest French milliners I ever saw! Egad, you seem all to have been diverting your- 395 selves here at hide-and-seek, and I don't see who is out of the secret! Shall I beg your ladyship to inform me? Not a word! Brother, will you please to explain this matter? What, morality dumb too? Sir Peter, though I found you in the dark, perhaps you are not so now? All mute! Well, though I can make nothing of the affair, I suppose 400 you perfectly understand one another. So I'll leave you to your- selves. (*Going*) Brother, I'm sorry to find you have given that worthy man so much uneasiness! Sir Peter, there's nothing in the world so noble as a man of sentiment!

> *Exit Charles Surface. Sir Peter Teazle, Lady Teazle, and*
> *Joseph Surface stand for some time looking at each other*

JOSEPH SURFACE Sir Peter, notwithstanding I confess that appear- 405 ances are against me, if you will afford me your patience, I make no doubt but I shall explain everything to your satisfaction.

SIR PETER TEAZLE If you please.

JOSEPH SURFACE The fact is, sir, that Lady Teazle, knowing my pre- tensions to your ward Maria—I say Lady Teazle, being apprehen- 410 sive of the jealousy of your temper, and knowing my friendship to the family—she, sir, I say, called here, in order that I might explain those pretensions; but on your coming, being apprehensive, as I said, of your jealousy, she withdrew. And this, you may depend on't, is the whole truth of the matter. 415

SIR PETER TEAZLE A very clear account, upon my word, and I dare swear the lady will vouch for every article of it.

LADY TEAZLE (*coming forward*) For not one word of it, Sir Peter.

SIR PETER TEAZLE How! Don't you even think it worthwhile to agree in the lie? 420

LADY TEAZLE There is not one syllable of truth in what that gentle- man has told you.

SIR PETER TEAZLE I believe you, upon my soul, ma'am.

JOSEPH SURFACE (*aside to Lady Teazle*) 'Sdeath, madam, will you betray me? 425

LADY TEAZLE Good Mr Hypocrite, by your leave, I will speak for myself.

SIR PETER TEAZLE Ay, let her alone,° sir. You'll find she'll make out a better story than you without prompting.

LADY TEAZLE Hear me, Sir Peter. I came hither on no matter relat- 430 ing to your ward, and even ignorant of this gentleman's pretensions to her. But I came, seduced by his insidious arguments, at least to listen to his pretended° passion, if not to sacrifice your honour to his baseness.

SIR PETER TEAZLE Now I believe the truth is coming indeed.   435

JOSEPH SURFACE The woman's mad.

LADY TEAZLE No, sir; she has recovered her senses, and your own arts have furnished her with the means.—Sir Peter, I do not expect you to credit me; but the tenderness you expressed for me, when I am sure you could not think I was a witness to it, has penetrated to my   440 heart. And, had I left the place without the shame of this discovery, my future life should have spoke° the sincerity of my gratitude. As for that smooth-tongue hypocrite, who would have seduced the wife of his too credulous friend, while he affected honourable addresses to his ward, I behold him now in a light so truly despic-   445 able, that I shall never again respect myself for having listened to him.

Exit Lady Teazle

JOSEPH SURFACE Notwithstanding all this, Sir Peter, heaven knows—

SIR PETER TEAZLE That you are a villain! And so I leave you to your conscience.   450

JOSEPH SURFACE You are too rash, Sir Peter. You shall hear me! The man who shuts out conviction by refusing to—

SIR PETER TEAZLE O!

Exit Sir Peter Teazle, Joseph Surface following and speaking

5.1

The library at Joseph Surface's

Enter Joseph Surface and Servant

JOSEPH SURFACE Mr Stanley! Why should you think I would see him? You must know he comes to ask something!

SERVANT Sir, I should not have let him in, but that Mr Rowley came to the door with him.

JOSEPH SURFACE Pshaw! Blockhead, to suppose that I should now be 5
in a temper to receive visits from poor relations! Well, why don't you show the fellow up?

SERVANT I will, sir. Why, sir, it was not my fault that Sir Peter discovered my lady.

JOSEPH SURFACE Go, fool! 10

Exit Servant

Sure fortune never played a man of my policy° such a trick before. My character with Sir Peter, my hopes with Maria—destroyed in a moment! I'm in a rare humour to listen to other people's distresses. I shan't be able to bestow a benevolent sentiment on Stanley. So, here he comes, and Rowley with him. I *must* try to recover 15
myself and put a little charity into my face, however.

Exit Joseph Surface. Enter Sir Oliver Surface and Rowley

SIR OLIVER SURFACE What, does he avoid us? That was he, was it not?

ROWLEY It was, sir. But I doubt you are come a little too abruptly; his nerves are so weak, that the sight of a poor relation may be too much for him. I should have gone first, to break you to him. 20

SIR OLIVER SURFACE A plague of his nerves! Yet this is he whom Sir Peter extols as a man of the most benevolent way of thinking!

ROWLEY As to his way of thinking, I can't pretend to decide, for, to do him justice, he appears to have as much speculative° benevolence as any private gentleman in the kingdom, though he is seldom so 25
sensual as to indulge himself in the exercise of it.

SIR OLIVER SURFACE Yet has a string of charitable sentiments, I suppose, at his fingers' ends!

ROWLEY Or rather at his tongue's end, Sir Oliver; for I believe there is no sentiment he has more faith in than that 'charity begins at 30
home'.

SIR OLIVER SURFACE And his, I presume, is of that domestic sort which never stirs abroad at all.

ROWLEY I doubt you'll find it so. But he's coming. I mustn't seem to
    interrupt you; and you know, immediately as you leave him, I come   35
    in to announce your arrival in your real character.
SIR OLIVER SURFACE True; and afterwards you'll meet me at Sir
    Peter's.
ROWLEY Without losing a moment.
        Exit Rowley
SIR OLIVER SURFACE So. I don't like the complaisance° of his   40
    features.
        Enter Joseph Surface [and Servant]
JOSEPH SURFACE Sir, I beg you ten thousand pardons for keeping you
    a moment waiting. Mr Stanley, I presume?
SIR OLIVER SURFACE At your service.
JOSEPH SURFACE Sir, I beg you will do me the honour to sit down. I   45
    entreat you, sir.
SIR OLIVER SURFACE Dear sir, there's no occasion. (*Aside*) Too civil
    by half!
        [Joseph Surface and Sir Oliver Surface sit]
JOSEPH SURFACE I have not the pleasure of knowing you, Mr Stanley;
    but I am extremely happy to see you look so well. You were nearly   50
    related to my mother, I think, Mr Stanley?
SIR OLIVER SURFACE I was, sir—so nearly that my present poverty, I
    fear, may do discredit to her wealthy children. Else I should not
    have presumed to trouble you.
JOSEPH SURFACE Dear sir, there needs no apology. He that is in   55
    distress, though a stranger, has a right to claim kindred with the
    wealthy. I am sure I wish I was of that class, and had it in my power
    to offer you even a small relief.
SIR OLIVER SURFACE If your uncle Sir Oliver were here, I should have
    a friend.   60
JOSEPH SURFACE I wish he were, sir, with all my heart. You should
    not want an advocate with him, believe me, sir.
SIR OLIVER SURFACE I should not need one; my distresses would
    recommend me. But I imagined his bounty had enabled you to
    become the agent of his charity.   65
JOSEPH SURFACE My dear sir, you were strangely misinformed. Sir
    Oliver is a worthy man, a very worthy sort of man. But avarice, Mr
    Stanley, is the vice of age. I will tell you, my good sir, in confidence,
    what he has done for me has been a mere nothing, though people,
    I know, have thought otherwise; and for my part I never chose to   70
    contradict the report.

SIR OLIVER SURFACE What, has he never transmitted you bullion, rupees, pagodas?

JOSEPH SURFACE O, dear sir, nothing of the kind. No, no, a few presents now and then. China, shawls, congou tea, avadavats, and Indian crackers.° Little more, believe me.

SIR OLIVER SURFACE [aside] Here's gratitude for twelve thousand pounds! Avadavats and Indian crackers!

JOSEPH SURFACE Then, my dear sir, you have heard, I doubt not, of the extravagance of my brother. There are very few would credit what I have done for that unfortunate young man!

SIR OLIVER SURFACE (aside) Not I for one!

JOSEPH SURFACE The sums I have lent him! Indeed I have been exceedingly to blame. It was an amiable weakness! However, I don't pretend to defend it, and now I feel it doubly culpable, since it has deprived me of the power of serving *you*, Mr Stanley, as my heart directs.

SIR OLIVER SURFACE [aside] Dissembler!—Then, sir, you cannot assist me?

JOSEPH SURFACE At present, it grieves me to say, I cannot; but whenever I have ability you may depend upon hearing from me.

SIR OLIVER SURFACE I am extremely sorry.

JOSEPH SURFACE Not more than I am, believe me. To pity, without the power to relieve, is still more painful than to ask and be denied.

SIR OLIVER SURFACE Kind sir, your most obedient humble servant.

JOSEPH SURFACE You leave me deeply affected, Mr Stanley. [*To Servant*] William, be ready to open the door.

SIR OLIVER SURFACE O, dear sir, no ceremony.

JOSEPH SURFACE Your very obedient.

SIR OLIVER SURFACE Sir, your most obsequious.

JOSEPH SURFACE You may depend upon hearing from me, whenever I can be of service.

SIR OLIVER SURFACE Sweet sir, you are too good.

JOSEPH SURFACE In the meantime I wish you health and spirits.

SIR OLIVER SURFACE Your ever grateful and perpetual humble servant.

JOSEPH SURFACE Sir, yours as sincerely.

SIR OLIVER SURFACE [aside] Now I am satisfied!
        Exeunt Sir Oliver Surface [and Servant]
JOSEPH SURFACE (*alone*) This is one bad effect of a good character; it invites applications from the unfortunate, and there needs no small degree of address° to gain the reputation of benevolence

without incurring the expense. The silver ore of pure charity is an expensive article in the catalogue of a man's good qualities, whereas the sentimental French plate I use instead of it makes just as good a show and pays no tax.° 115

Enter Rowley [and Servant]

ROWLEY Mr Surface, your servant. I was apprehensive of interrupting you, though my business demands immediate attention, as this note will inform you.

JOSEPH SURFACE Always happy to see Mr Rowley. (*Reads*) How! 'Oliver Surface'! My uncle arrived! 120

ROWLEY He is indeed—we have just parted—quite well after a speedy voyage, and impatient to embrace his worthy nephew.

JOSEPH SURFACE I am astonished!—[*To Servant*] William, stop Mr Stanley, if he's not gone.

ROWLEY O, he's out of reach, I believe. 125

JOSEPH SURFACE Why didn't you let me know this when you came in together?

ROWLEY I thought you had particular business. But I must be gone to inform your brother, and appoint him here to meet his uncle. He will be with you in a quarter of an hour. 130

JOSEPH SURFACE So he says. Well, I am strangely overjoyed at his coming. (*Aside*) Never, to be sure, was anything so damned unlucky!

ROWLEY You will be delighted to see how well he looks.

JOSEPH SURFACE O, I'm rejoiced to hear it. (*Aside*) Just at this time!

ROWLEY I'll tell him how impatiently you expect him. 135

JOSEPH SURFACE Do, do; pray give my best duty and affection. Indeed I cannot express the sensations I feel at the thought of seeing him!

Exit Rowley

His coming just at this time is the cruellest piece of ill fortune!

Exit

5.2

At Sir Peter Teazle's

Enter Mrs Candour and Maid

MAID Indeed, ma'am, my lady will see nobody at present.

MRS CANDOUR Did you tell her it was her friend Mrs Candour?

MAID Yes, ma'am; but she begs you will excuse her.

MRS CANDOUR Do go again. I shall be glad to see her if it be only for
a moment, for I am sure she must be in great distress.   5
    Exit Maid
Dear heart,° how provoking! I'm not mistress of half the circum-
stances! We shall have the whole affair in the newspapers with the
names of the parties at length, before I have dropped the story at a
dozen houses.
    Enter Sir Benjamin Backbite
O, dear Sir Benjamin, you have heard, I suppose?   10
SIR BENJAMIN BACKBITE Of Lady Teazle and Mr Surface?°
MRS CANDOUR And Sir Peter's discovery?
SIR BENJAMIN BACKBITE O, the strangest piece of business to be sure.
MRS CANDOUR Well, I never was so surprised in my life! I am so sorry
for all parties; indeed I am.   15
SIR BENJAMIN BACKBITE Now I don't pity Sir Peter at all. He was
so extravagantly partial to Mr Surface.
MRS CANDOUR Mr Surface! Why, 'twas with Charles Lady Teazle was
detected.
SIR BENJAMIN BACKBITE No such thing. Mr Surface is the gallant.   20
MRS CANDOUR No, no, Charles is the man. 'Twas Mr Surface brought
Sir Peter on purpose to discover them.
SIR BENJAMIN BACKBITE I tell you I have it from one—
MRS CANDOUR And I have it from one—
SIR BENJAMIN BACKBITE Who had it from one who had it—   25
MRS CANDOUR From one immediately—but here's Lady Sneerwell.
Perhaps she knows the whole affair.
    Enter Lady Sneerwell
LADY SNEERWELL So, my dear Mrs Candour, here's a sad affair of
our friend Lady Teazle.°
MRS CANDOUR Ay! My dear friend, who could have thought it!   30
LADY SNEERWELL Well, there is no trusting appearances. Though,
indeed, she was always too lively for me.
MRS CANDOUR To be sure her manners were a little too free; but she
was very young.
LADY SNEERWELL And had indeed some good qualities.   35
MRS CANDOUR So she had indeed. But have you heard the
particulars?
LADY SNEERWELL No; but everybody says that Mr Surface—
SIR BENJAMIN BACKBITE Ay, there; I told you Mr Surface was the man.
MRS CANDOUR No, no, indeed; the assignation was with Charles.   40
LADY SNEERWELL With Charles! You alarm me, Mrs Candour.

MRS CANDOUR Yes, yes, he was the lover. Mr Surface, do him justice, was only the informer.

SIR BENJAMIN BACKBITE Well, I'll not dispute with you, Mrs Candour; but, be it which it may, I hope that Sir Peter's wound will not—   45

MRS CANDOUR Sir Peter's wound! O mercy! I didn't hear a word of their fighting.

LADY SNEERWELL Nor I a syllable!

SIR BENJAMIN BACKBITE No! What, no mention of the duel?   50

MRS CANDOUR Not a word.

SIR BENJAMIN BACKBITE O lord, yes, yes; they fought before they left the room.

LADY SNEERWELL Pray let us hear.

MRS CANDOUR Ay, do oblige us with the duel.   55

SIR BENJAMIN BACKBITE 'Sir', says Sir Peter, immediately after the discovery, 'you are a most ungrateful fellow'.

MRS CANDOUR Ay, to Charles.

SIR BENJAMIN BACKBITE No, no, to Mr Surface. 'A most ungrateful fellow; and old as I am, sir', says he, 'I insist on immediate   60 satisfaction'.

MRS CANDOUR Ay, that must have been to Charles, for 'tis very unlikely Mr Surface should go to fight in his own house.

SIR BENJAMIN BACKBITE Gad's life, ma'am, not at all. 'Giving me immediate satisfaction.' On this, madam, Lady Teazle, seeing Sir   65 Peter in such danger, ran out of the room in strong hysterics, and Charles after her, calling out for hartshorn and water! Then, madam, they began to fight with swords—

Enter Crabtree

CRABTREE With pistols, nephew. I have it from undoubted authority.

MRS CANDOUR O, Mr Crabtree, then it is all true.   70

CRABTREE Too true indeed, ma'am, and Sir Peter's dangerously wounded.

SIR BENJAMIN BACKBITE By a thrust in *seconde*,° quite through his left side.

CRABTREE By a bullet lodged in the thorax.   75

MRS CANDOUR Mercy on me! Poor Sir Peter!

CRABTREE Yes, ma'am; though Charles would have avoided the matter if he could.

MRS CANDOUR I knew Charles was the person.

SIR BENJAMIN BACKBITE O, my uncle, I see, knows nothing of the   80 matter.

CRABTREE But Sir Peter taxed him with the basest ingratitude.

SIR BENJAMIN BACKBITE That I told you, you know.

CRABTREE Do, nephew, let me speak. And insisted on an immediate—

SIR BENJAMIN BACKBITE Just as I said.   85

CRABTREE Od's life, nephew, allow others to know something too. A pair of pistols lay on the bureau; for Mr Surface, it seems, had come the night before late from Salt Hill, where he had been to see the Montem° with a friend who has a son at Eton. So, unluckily, the pistols were left charged.°   90

SIR BENJAMIN BACKBITE I heard nothing of this.

CRABTREE Sir Peter forced Charles to take one, and they fired—it seems, pretty nearly together. Charles's shot took place,° as I told you, and Sir Peter's missed. But, what is very extraordinary, the ball struck against a little bronze Pliny° that stood over the chimney   95 piece, grazed out of the window at a right angle, and wounded the postman, who was just coming to the door with a double letter from Northamptonshire.

SIR BENJAMIN BACKBITE My uncle's account is more circumstantial, I must confess; but I believe mine is the true one for all   100 that.

LADY SNEERWELL [aside] I am more interested in° this affair than they imagine and must have better information.

 Exit Lady Sneerwell

SIR BENJAMIN BACKBITE (*after a pause, looking at each other*) Ah! Lady Sneerwell's alarm is very easily accounted for.   105

CRABTREE Yes, yes, they certainly *do* say; but that's neither here nor there.

MRS CANDOUR But pray where is Sir Peter at present?°

CRABTREE O, they brought him home, and he is now in the house, though the servants are ordered to deny it.   110

MRS CANDOUR I believe so. And Lady Teazle, I suppose, attending him?

CRABTREE Yes, yes. I saw one of the faculty° enter just before me.

SIR BENJAMIN BACKBITE Hey, who comes here?

CRABTREE O, this is he; the physician, depend on't.   115

MRS CANDOUR O certainly, it must be the physician, and now we shall know.

 Enter Sir Oliver Surface

CRABTREE Well, doctor, what hopes?

MRS CANDOUR Ay, doctor, how's your patient?

SIR BENJAMIN BACKBITE Now, doctor, isn't it a wound with a small-   120 sword?

CRABTREE A bullet lodged in the thorax, for a hundred!°

SIR OLIVER SURFACE Doctor! A wound with a small-sword! And a bullet in the thorax! Oons, are you mad, good people?

SIR BENJAMIN BACKBITE Perhaps, sir, you are not a doctor.   125

SIR OLIVER SURFACE Truly I am to thank you for my degree, if I am.

CRABTREE Only a friend of Sir Peter's then, I presume. But, sir, you must have heard of this accident?

SIR OLIVER SURFACE Not a word!

CRABTREE Not of his being dangerously wounded?   130

SIR OLIVER SURFACE The devil he is!

SIR BENJAMIN BACKBITE Run through the body.

CRABTREE Shot in the breast.

SIR BENJAMIN BACKBITE By one Mr Surface.

CRABTREE Ay, the younger.   135

SIR OLIVER SURFACE Hey! What the plague! You seem to differ strangely in your accounts. However, you agree that Sir Peter is dangerously wounded?

SIR BENJAMIN BACKBITE O, yes, we agree there.

CRABTREE Yes, yes, I believe there can be no doubt of that.   140

SIR OLIVER SURFACE Then, upon my word, for a person in that situation he is the most imprudent man alive, for here he comes walking as if nothing at all were the matter.

    Enter Sir Peter Teazle

Od's heart, Sir Peter, you are come in good time, I promise you, for we had just given you over.°   145

SIR BENJAMIN BACKBITE Egad, uncle, this is the most sudden recovery!

SIR OLIVER SURFACE Why, man, what do you do out of bed with a small-sword through your body, and a bullet lodged in your thorax!

SIR PETER TEAZLE A small-sword and a bullet?   150

SIR OLIVER SURFACE Ay, these gentlemen would have killed you, without law or physic, and wanted to dub me° a doctor, to make me an accomplice.

SIR PETER TEAZLE Why, what is all this?

SIR BENJAMIN BACKBITE We rejoice, Sir Peter, that the story of the   155
duel is not true, and are sincerely sorry for your other misfortunes.

SIR PETER TEAZLE (*aside*) So, so; all over the town already.

CRABTREE Though, Sir Peter, you were certainly vastly to blame to marry at all, at your years.

SIR PETER TEAZLE Sir, what business is that of yours?   160

MRS CANDOUR Though, indeed, as Sir Peter made so good a husband, he's very much to be pitied!

SIR PETER TEAZLE Plague on your pity, ma'am; I desire none of it.

SIR BENJAMIN BACKBITE However, Sir Peter, you must not mind the   165
laughing and jests you will meet with on this occasion.

SIR PETER TEAZLE Sir, I desire to be master in my own house.

CRABTREE 'Tis no uncommon case; that's one comfort.

SIR PETER TEAZLE I insist on being left to myself. Without ceremony,
I insist on your leaving my house directly!   170

MRS CANDOUR Well, well, we are going; and, depend on't, we'll make
the best report of you we can.

SIR PETER TEAZLE Leave my house!

CRABTREE And tell how hardly you have been treated.

SIR PETER TEAZLE Leave my house!   175

SIR BENJAMIN BACKBITE And how patiently you bear it.

SIR PETER TEAZLE Fiends! Vipers! Furies! O that their own venom
would choke them.

Exeunt Mrs Candour, Sir Benjamin Backbite, Crabtree

SIR OLIVER SURFACE They are very provoking indeed, Sir Peter.

Enter Rowley

ROWLEY I heard high° words. What has ruffled you, Sir Peter?   180

SIR PETER TEAZLE Pshaw, what signifies asking? Do I ever pass a day
without my vexations?

SIR OLIVER SURFACE Well, I'm not inquisitive. I come only to tell you
that I have seen both my nephews in the manner we proposed.

SIR PETER TEAZLE A precious couple they are!   185

ROWLEY Yes, and Sir Oliver is convinced that your judgement was
right, Sir Peter.

SIR OLIVER SURFACE Yes, I find Joseph is indeed the man, after all.

ROWLEY Yes, as Sir Peter says, he's a man of sentiment.

SIR OLIVER SURFACE And acts up to the sentiments he professes.   190

ROWLEY It certainly is edification to hear him talk.

SIR OLIVER SURFACE O, he's a model for the young men of the age!
But how's this, Sir Peter? You don't join in your friend Joseph's
praise as I expected.

SIR PETER TEAZLE Sir Oliver, we live in a damned wicked world, and   195
the fewer we praise the better.

ROWLEY What, do *you* say so, Sir Peter, who were never mistaken in
your life?

SIR PETER TEAZLE Pshaw! Plague on you both! I see by your
sneering you have heard the whole affair. I shall go mad among   200
you!

ROWLEY Then, to fret you no longer, Sir Peter, we are indeed
acquainted with it all. I met Lady Teazle coming from Mr Surface's
so humbled that she deigned to request *me* to be her advocate with
you.   205

SIR PETER TEAZLE And does Sir Oliver know all too?

SIR OLIVER SURFACE Every circumstance!

SIR PETER TEAZLE What, of the closet, and the screen, hey?

SIR OLIVER SURFACE Yes, yes, and the little French milliner. O, I have
been vastly diverted with the story. Ha, ha!   210

SIR PETER TEAZLE 'Twas very pleasant!°

SIR OLIVER SURFACE I never laughed more in my life, I assure you.
Ha, ha!

SIR PETER TEAZLE O vastly diverting. Ha, ha!

ROWLEY To be sure, Joseph, with his sentiments! Ha, ha!   215

SIR PETER TEAZLE Yes, yes, his sentiments. Ha, ha! A hypocritical
villain!

SIR OLIVER SURFACE Ay, and that rogue Charles! To pull Sir Peter
out of the closet! Ha, ha!

SIR PETER TEAZLE Ha, ha! 'Twas devilish entertaining, to be sure.   220

SIR OLIVER SURFACE Ha, ha! Egad, Sir Peter, I should like to have
seen your face when the screen was thrown down. Ha, ha!

SIR PETER TEAZLE Yes, yes; my face when the screen was thrown
down. Ha, ha! O, I must never show my head again!

SIR OLIVER SURFACE But come, come. It isn't fair to laugh at you   225
neither, my old friend; though, upon my soul, I can't help it.

SIR PETER TEAZLE O, pray don't restrain your mirth on my account.
It does not hurt me at all. I laugh at the whole affair myself. Yes,
yes, I think being a standing jest for all one's acquaintances a very
happy situation. O yes, and then, of a morning, to read the para-   230
graphs about Mr S——, Lady T—— and Sir P—— will be so
entertaining!

ROWLEY Without affectation, Sir Peter, you may despise the ridicule
of fools. But I see Lady Teazle going towards the next room. I am
sure you must desire a reconciliation as earnestly as she does.   235

SIR OLIVER SURFACE Perhaps my being here prevents her coming
to you. Well, I'll leave honest Rowley to mediate between you.
But he must bring you all presently to Mr Surface's, where I am
now returning—if not to reclaim a libertine, at least to expose
hypocrisy.   240

SIR PETER TEAZLE Ah, I'll be present at your discovering yourself there with all my heart, though 'tis a vile unlucky place for discoveries.

ROWLEY We'll follow.

Exit Sir Oliver Surface

SIR PETER TEAZLE She is not coming here, you see, Rowley.   245

ROWLEY No, but she has left the door of that room open, you perceive. See, she is in tears!

SIR PETER TEAZLE Certainly a little mortification appears very becoming in a wife. Don't you think it will do her good to let her pine a little?   250

ROWLEY O, this is ungenerous in you.

SIR PETER TEAZLE Well, I know not what to think. You remember, Rowley, the letter I found of hers, evidently intended for Charles?

ROWLEY A mere forgery, Sir Peter, laid in your way on purpose. This is one of the points which I intend Snake shall give you conviction   255
on.

SIR PETER TEAZLE I wish I were once satisfied of that. She looks this way. What a remarkably elegant turn of the head she has! Rowley, I'll go to her.

ROWLEY Certainly.   260

SIR PETER TEAZLE Though, when it is known that we are reconciled, people will laugh at me ten times more!

ROWLEY Let them laugh, and retort their malice only by showing them you are happy in spite of it.

SIR PETER TEAZLE I'faith, so I will! And, if I'm not mistaken, we may   265
yet be the happiest couple in the country.

ROWLEY Nay, Sir Peter, he who once lays aside suspicion—

SIR PETER TEAZLE Hold, my dear Rowley. If you have any regard for me, never let me hear you utter anything like a sentiment. I have had enough of *them* to serve me the rest of my life.   270

Exeunt

5.3

The library at Joseph Surface's

Joseph Surface and Lady Sneerwell

LADY SNEERWELL Impossible! Will not Sir Peter immediately be reconciled to Charles, and of consequence no longer oppose his union with Maria? The thought is distraction to me!°

JOSEPH SURFACE Can passion furnish a remedy?

LADY SNEERWELL No, nor cunning either. O, I was a fool, an idiot, 5
to league with such a blunderer!

JOSEPH SURFACE Sure, Lady Sneerwell, I am the greatest sufferer;
yet you see I bear the accident with calmness.

LADY SNEERWELL Because the disappointment doesn't reach your
heart; your interest only attached you to Maria. Had you felt for her 10
what I have for that ungrateful libertine, neither your temper
nor hypocrisy could prevent your showing the sharpness of your
vexation.

JOSEPH SURFACE But why should your reproaches fall on me for this
disappointment? 15

LADY SNEERWELL Are not you the cause of it? What had you to do,
to bate in° your pursuit of Maria to pervert Lady Teazle by the
way? Had you not a sufficient field for your roguery in blinding Sir
Peter and supplanting your brother? I hate such an avarice of
crimes. 'Tis an unfair monopoly and never prospers. 20

JOSEPH SURFACE Well, I admit I have been to blame. I confess I
deviated from the direct road of wrong. But I don't think we're so
totally defeated neither.

LADY SNEERWELL No!

JOSEPH SURFACE You tell me you have made a trial of Snake since we 25
met, and that you still believe him faithful to us.

LADY SNEERWELL I do believe so.

JOSEPH SURFACE And that he has undertaken, should it be necessary,
to swear and prove that Charles is at this time contracted by vows
and honour to your ladyship, which some of his former letters to 30
you will serve to support.

LADY SNEERWELL This indeed might have assisted.

JOSEPH SURFACE Come, come; it is not too late yet.
     Knocking [offstage]
But hark! This is probably my uncle Sir Oliver. Retire to that room.
We'll consult farther when he's gone. 35

LADY SNEERWELL Well, but if he should find you out too.

JOSEPH SURFACE O, I have no fear of that. Sir Peter will hold his
tongue for his own credit's sake, and you may depend on't I shall
soon discover Sir Oliver's weak side!

LADY SNEERWELL I have no diffidence of° your abilities; only be 40
constant to one roguery at a time.

JOSEPH SURFACE I will, I will.
     Exit Lady Sneerwell

So. 'Tis confounded hard after such bad fortune to be baited° by one's confederate in evil. Well, at all events, my character is so much better than Charles's that I certainly—Hey! What! This is not Sir 45 Oliver, but old Stanley again! Plague on't, that he should return to tease me just now! We shall have Sir Oliver come and find him here and—

Enter Sir Oliver Surface [and Servant]

Gad's life, Mr Stanley, why have you come back to plague me just at this time? You must not stay now, upon my word! 50

SIR OLIVER SURFACE Sir, I hear your uncle Oliver is expected here; and though he has been so penurious to you, I'll try what he'll do for me.

JOSEPH SURFACE Sir, 'tis impossible for you to stay now. So I must beg—come any other time, and I promise you you shall be 55 assisted.

SIR OLIVER SURFACE No, Sir Oliver and I must be acquainted.

JOSEPH SURFACE Zounds, sir, then I insist on your quitting the room directly.

SIR OLIVER SURFACE Nay, sir! 60

JOSEPH SURFACE Sir, I insist on't. [*To Servant*] Here, William, show this gentleman out.—Since you compel me, sir, not one moment. (*Going to push Sir Oliver Surface out*) This is such insolence.

Enter Charles Surface

CHARLES SURFACE Hey-dey! What's the matter now? What the devil, 65 have you got hold of my little broker here! Zounds, brother, don't hurt little Premium.—What's the matter, my little fellow?

JOSEPH SURFACE So! He has been with you too, has he?

CHARLES SURFACE To be sure he has! Why, 'tis as honest a little—but sure, Joseph, you have not been borrowing money too, have 70 you?

JOSEPH SURFACE Borrowing? No! But, brother, you know here we expect Sir Oliver every—

CHARLES SURFACE O Gad, that's true! Noll mustn't find the little broker here, to be sure. 75

JOSEPH SURFACE Yet Mr Stanley insists—

CHARLES SURFACE Stanley? Why, his name's Premium.

JOSEPH SURFACE No, no, Stanley.

CHARLES SURFACE No, no, Premium.

JOSEPH SURFACE Well, no matter which, but— 80

CHARLES SURFACE Ay, ay, Stanley or Premium, 'tis the same thing, as

you say, for I suppose he goes by half a hundred names, besides
A.B.s at the coffee-houses.°

    Knock [offstage]

JOSEPH SURFACE Death! Here's Sir Oliver at the door.

    Knocking again

  Now I beg, Mr Stanley—   85

CHARLES SURFACE Ay, and I beg, Mr Premium—

SIR OLIVER SURFACE Gentlemen!

JOSEPH SURFACE Sir, by heaven, you shall go.

CHARLES SURFACE Ay, out with him certainly.

SIR OLIVER SURFACE This violence—   90

JOSEPH SURFACE 'Tis your own fault.

CHARLES SURFACE Out with him, to be sure.

    As Joseph and Charles Surface are forcing Sir Oliver Surface
    out, enter Sir Peter Teazle, Lady Teazle, Maria, and
    Rowley

SIR PETER TEAZLE My old friend Sir Oliver! Hey, what in the name
of wonder! Here are dutiful nephews! Assault their uncle at the first
visit!   95

LADY TEAZLE Indeed, Sir Oliver, 'twas well we came in to rescue you.

ROWLEY Truly it was, for I perceive, Sir Oliver, the character of old
Stanley was no protection to you.

SIR OLIVER SURFACE Nor of Premium either. The necessities of the
former couldn't extort a shilling from that benevolent gentleman,   100
and now, egad, I stood a chance of faring worse than my ancestors
and being knocked down without being bid for.

    After a pause, Joseph and Charles Surface turn to each other

JOSEPH SURFACE Charles!

CHARLES SURFACE Joseph!

JOSEPH SURFACE 'Tis now complete!   105

CHARLES SURFACE Very.

SIR OLIVER SURFACE Sir Peter, my friend—and Rowley too—look on
that elder nephew of mine. You know what he has already received
from my bounty, and you know also how gladly I would have
regarded half my fortune as held in trust for him. Judge then my   110
disappointment in discovering him to be destitute of truth, charity
and gratitude.

SIR PETER TEAZLE Sir Oliver, I should be more surprised at this
declaration if I had not myself found him selfish, treacherous and
hypocritical.   115

LADY TEAZLE And if the gentleman pleads not guilty to these, pray let him call *me* to his character.

SIR PETER TEAZLE Then I believe we need add no more. If he knows himself, he will consider it as the most perfect punishment that he is known by the world.   120

CHARLES SURFACE (*aside*) If they talk this way to honesty, what will they say to *me* by and by!

SIR OLIVER SURFACE As for that prodigal, his brother there—

CHARLES SURFACE (*aside*) Ay, now comes my turn. The damned family pictures will ruin me.   125

JOSEPH SURFACE Sir Oliver! Uncle! Will you honour me with a hearing?

CHARLES SURFACE (*aside*) Now, if Joseph would make one of his long speeches, I might recollect myself° a little.

SIR OLIVER SURFACE I suppose you would undertake to justify   130
yourself entirely.

JOSEPH SURFACE I trust I could.

SIR OLIVER SURFACE Pshaw! (*To Charles Surface*) Well, sir, and *you* could *justify* yourself too, I suppose!

CHARLES SURFACE Not that I know of, Sir Oliver.   135

SIR OLIVER SURFACE What, little Premium has been let too much into the secret, I presume.

CHARLES SURFACE True, sir. But they were family secrets and should never be mentioned again, you know.

ROWLEY Come, Sir Oliver, I know you cannot speak of Charles's   140
follies with anger.

SIR OLIVER SURFACE Od's heart, no more I can; nor with gravity either.—Sir Peter, do you know the rogue bargained with me for all his ancestors, sold me judges and generals by the foot and maiden aunts as cheap as broken china!   145

CHARLES SURFACE To be sure, Sir Oliver, I did make a little free with the family canvas; that's the truth on't. My ancestors may certainly rise in evidence against me; there's no denying it. But believe me sincere when I tell you—and upon my soul I would not say it if I was not—that if I do not appear mortified at   150
the exposure of my follies, it is because I feel at this moment the warmest satisfaction in seeing you, my *liberal* benefactor.

SIR OLIVER SURFACE Charles, I believe you. Give me your hand again. The ill-looking little fellow over the settee has made your peace, sirrah!   155

CHARLES SURFACE Then, sir, my gratitude to the original is still increased.

LADY TEAZLE (*pointing to Maria*) Yet I believe, Sir Oliver, here is one whom Charles is still more anxious to be reconciled to.

SIR OLIVER SURFACE O, I have heard of his attachment there; and, with the young lady's pardon, if I construe right that blush— 160

SIR PETER TEAZLE Well, child, speak your sentiments.

MARIA Sir, I have little to say, but that I shall rejoice to hear that he is happy. For me, whatever claim I had to his affection, I willingly resign it to one who has a better title. 165

CHARLES SURFACE How, Maria!

SIR PETER TEAZLE Hey-day, what's the mystery now? While he appeared an incorrigible rake, you would give your hand to no one else; and now that he's likely to reform, I warrant you won't have him!

MARIA His own heart—and Lady Sneerwell—know the cause. 170

CHARLES SURFACE Lady Sneerwell!

JOSEPH SURFACE Brother, it is with great concern I am obliged to speak on this point; but my regard to justice compels me, and Lady Sneerwell's injuries can no longer be concealed.

Joseph Surface goes to the door. Enter Lady Sneerwell

SIR PETER TEAZLE So! Another French milliner, egad! He has one in every room in the house, I suppose. 175

LADY SNEERWELL Ungrateful Charles! Well may you be surprised and feel for the indelicate situation which your perfidy has forced me into.

CHARLES SURFACE Pray, uncle, is this another plot of yours? For, as I have life, I don't understand it. 180

JOSEPH SURFACE I believe, sir, there is but the evidence of one person more necessary to make it extremely clear.

SIR PETER TEAZLE And that person, I imagine, is Mr Snake.— Rowley, you were perfectly right to bring him with us, and pray let him appear. 185

ROWLEY Walk in, Mr Snake.

Enter Snake

I thought his testimony might be wanted. However, it happens unluckily that he comes to confront Lady Sneerwell and not to support her.

LADY SNEERWELL (*aside*) Villain! Treacherous to me at last!—Speak, fellow, have you too conspired against me? 190

SNAKE I beg your ladyship ten thousand pardons. You paid me extremely liberally for the lie in question; but I have unfortunately been offered double to speak the truth.

SIR PETER TEAZLE Plot and counterplot, egad. I wish your ladyship joy of the success of your negotiation.

LADY SNEERWELL The torments of shame and disappointment on you all!

LADY TEAZLE Hold, Lady Sneerwell. Before you go, let me thank you for the trouble you and that gentleman have taken in writing letters to me from Charles and answering them yourself. And let me also request you to make my respects to the scandalous college of which you are president, and inform them that Lady Teazle, licentiate, begs leave to return the diploma they granted her, as she leaves off practice and kills characters no longer.

LADY SNEERWELL You too, madam? Provoking! Insolent! May your husband live these fifty years!

Exit Lady Sneerwell

SIR PETER TEAZLE Oons, what a fury!

LADY TEAZLE What a malicious creature it is!

SIR PETER TEAZLE Hey, not for her last wish?

LADY TEAZLE O, no.

SIR OLIVER SURFACE Well, sir, and what have you to say now?

JOSEPH SURFACE Sir, I am so confounded to find that Lady Sneerwell could be guilty of suborning Mr Snake in this manner to impose on us all that I know not what to say. However, lest her revengeful spirit should prompt her to injure my brother, I had certainly better follow her directly.

Exit Joseph Surface

SIR PETER TEAZLE Moral to the last drop!

SIR OLIVER SURFACE Ay, and marry her, Joseph, if you can. Oil and vinegar, egad! You'll do very well together.

ROWLEY I believe we have no more occasion for Mr Snake at present.

SNAKE Before I go, I beg pardon once for all for whatever uneasiness I have been the humble instrument of causing to the parties present.

SIR PETER TEAZLE Well, well, you have made atonement by a good deed at last.

SNAKE But I must request of the company that it shall never be known.

SIR PETER TEAZLE Hey! What the plague! Are you ashamed of having done a right thing once in your life?

SNAKE Ah, sir, consider I live by the badness of my character! I have nothing but my infamy to depend on! And if it were once known that I had been betrayed into an honest action, I should lose every friend I have in the world.

SIR OLIVER SURFACE Well, well, we'll not traduce you by saying
anything in your praise. Never fear.   235
    Exit Snake

SIR PETER TEAZLE There's a precious rogue. Yet that fellow is a writer
and a critic!
    Charles and Maria talk apart°

LADY TEAZLE See, Sir Oliver; there needs no persuasion now to
reconcile your nephew and Maria.

SIR OLIVER SURFACE Ay, ay, that's as it should be, and, egad, we'll   240
have the wedding tomorrow morning.

CHARLES SURFACE Thank you, my dear uncle.

SIR PETER TEAZLE What, you rogue, don't you ask the girl's consent
first?

CHARLES O, I have done that a long time—above a minute—ago, and   245
she has looked yes.

MARIA For shame, Charles.—I protest, Sir Peter, there has not been
a word!

SIR OLIVER SURFACE Well then, the fewer the better. May your love
for each other never know abatement.   250

SIR PETER TEAZLE And may you live as happily together as Lady
Teazle and I—intend to do.°

CHARLES SURFACE Rowley, my old friend, I am sure you congratulate me, and I suspect that I owe you much.

SIR OLIVER SURFACE You do indeed, Charles.   255

ROWLEY If my efforts to serve you had not succeeded, you would have
been in my debt for the attempt; but deserve to be happy, and you
overpay me.

SIR PETER TEAZLE Ay, honest Rowley always said you would reform.

CHARLES SURFACE Why, as to reforming, Sir Peter, I'll make no   260
promises; and that I take to be a proof that I intend to set about it.
But here shall be my monitor, my gentle guide. Ah, can I leave the
virtuous path those eyes illumine?

    Though thou, dear maid, shouldst waive thy beauty's sway,°
    Thou still must rule, because I will obey.   265
    An humbled fugitive from folly view,
    No sanctuary near, but love and *you*.
    (*To the audience*)
    You can indeed each anxious fear remove,
    For even scandal dies if you approve.
    [*Exeunt*]

Epilogue

Written by G. Colman, Esq.°

Spoken by Mrs Abington°
in the character of Lady Teazle

I, who was late so volatile and gay,
Like a trade-wind, must now blow all one way,
Bend all my cares, my studies, and my vows,
To one old rusty weathercock, my spouse.
So wills our virtuous bard—the motley Bayes°   5
Of crying epilogues and laughing plays!°
   Old bachelors, who marry smart young wives,
Learn from our play to regulate your lives!
Each bring his dear to town, all faults upon her—
London will prove the very source of honour.   10
Plunged fairly in, like a cold bath, it serves,
When principles relax, to brace the nerves.
Such is my case; and yet I might deplore
That the gay dream of dissipation's o'er;
And say, ye fair, was ever lively wife,   15
Born with a genius for the highest life,
Like me untimely blasted in her bloom,
Like me condemned to such a dismal doom?
Save money, when I just knew how to waste it!
Leave London, just as I began to taste it!   20
Must I then watch the early-crowing cock,
The melancholy ticking of a clock,
In the lone rustic hall for ever pounded,
With dogs, cats, rats, and squalling brats surrounded?
With humble curates can I now retire,   25
While good Sir Peter boozes with the squire,
And at backgammon mortify my soul
That pants for loo or flutters at a vole?
Seven's the main! Dear sound, that must expire,°
Lost at hot cockles round a Christmas fire!   30
The transient hour of fashion too soon spent,
Farewell the tranquil mind, farewell content!
Farewell the plumèd head, the cushioned tête,°

That takes the cushion from its proper seat!
The spirit-stirring drum!—card-drums, I mean—°   35
Spadille, odd trick, pam, basto, king and queen!
And you, ye knockers, that with brazen throat
The welcome visitor's approach denote,
Farewell! All quality of high renown,
Pride, pomp, and circumstance of glorious town,   40
Farewell! Your revels I partake no more,°
And Lady Teazle's occupation's o'er!°
All this I told our bard. He smiled and said 'twas clear
I ought to play deep tragedy next year.°
Meanwhile he drew wise morals from his play,   45
And in these solemn periods stalked away.°
'Blessed were the fair, like you her faults who stopped,
And closed her follies when the curtain dropped!
No more in vice or error to engage,
Or play the fool at large on life's great stage.'   50

THE CRITIC°
or
A Tragedy Rehearsed

TO MRS GREVILLE°

Madam,

In requesting your permission to address the following pages to you, which (as they aim themselves to be critical) require every protection and allowance that approving taste or friendly prejudice can give them, I yet ventured to mention no other motive than the gratification of private friendship and esteem. Had I suggested a hope that your implied approbation would give a sanction to their defects, your particular reserve, and dislike to the reputation of critical taste, as well as of poetical talent, would have made you refuse the protection of your name to such a purpose. However, I am not so ungrateful as now to attempt to combat this disposition in you. I shall not here presume to argue that the present state of poetry claims and expects every assistance that taste and example can afford it, nor endeavour to prove that a fastidious concealment of the most elegant productions of judgement and fancy is an ill return for the possession of those endowments.° Continue to deceive yourself in the idea that you are known only to be eminently admired and regarded for the valuable qualities that attach° private friendships, and the graceful talents that adorn conversation. Enough of what you have written has stolen into full public notice to answer my purpose; and you will, perhaps, be the only person conversant in elegant° literature, who shall read this address and not perceive that, by publishing your particular approbation of the following drama, I have a more interested object° than to boast the true respect and regard with which

I have the honour to be,

madam,

your very sincere

and obedient humble servant,

R. B. Sheridan

THE CHARACTERS OF THE PLAY

Dangle°	*Mr Dodd*
Sneer	*Mr Palmer*
Sir Fretful Plagiary°	*Mr Parsons*
Puff°	*Mr King*
Signor Pasticcio Ritornello°	*Mr Delpini*
French Interpreter	*Mr Baddeley*
Underprompter°	*Mr Phillimore*
[Servant to Dangle]	
[Scenemen]°	
Mrs Dangle	*Mrs Hopkins*
Italian Girls	*Miss Field, and the*
	Miss Abrams

Characters of the Tragedy

Lord Burghley	*Mr Moody*
Governor of Tilbury Fort	*Mr Wrighten*
Earl of Leicester	*Mr Farren*
Sir Walter Ralegh	*Mr Burton*
Sir Christopher Hatton	*Mr Waldron*
Master of the Horse	*Mr Kenny*
[Knight]	
Don Ferolo Whiskerandos°	*Mr Bannister, Jun.*
Beefeater°	*Mr Wright*
Justice	*Mr Packer*
Son	*Mr Lamash*
Constable	*Mr Fawcett*
Thames	*Mr Gawdry*
[Two Sentinels]	
[Two Attendants to Thames]	
Tilburina°	*Miss Pope*
First Niece	*Miss Collet*
Second Niece	*Miss Kirby*
Confidante	*Mrs Bradshaw*

[SCENE: LONDON]

Prologue

By the Honourable Richard Fitzpatrick°

The sister muses, whom these realms obey,°
Who o'er the drama hold divided sway,
Sometimes, by evil counsellors, 'tis said,
Like earth-born potentates have been misled.
In those gay days of wickedness and wit,   5
When Villiers criticised what Dryden writ,
The tragic queen, to please a tasteless crowd,
Had learned to bellow, rant, and roar so loud,
That frightened nature, her best friend before,
The blustering beldam's company forswore.°   10
Her comic sister—who had wit, 'tis true—
With all her merits, had her failings too,
And would sometimes in mirthful moments use
A style too flippant for a well-bred muse.°
Then female modesty, abashed, began   15
To seek the friendly refuge of the fan,
A while behind that slight entrenchment stood,°
Till, driven from thence, she left the stage for good.
In our more pious and far chaster times,
These sure no longer are the muse's crimes!   20
But some complain that, former faults to shun,
The reformation to extremes has run.
The frantic hero's wild delirium past,
Now insipidity succeeds bombast;
So slow Melpomene's cold numbers creep,°   25
Here dullness seems her drowsy court to keep,°
And we are scarce awake, whilst you are fast asleep.
Thalia, once so ill-behaved and rude,
Reformed, is now become an arrant prude,
Retailing nightly to the yawning pit   30
The purest morals, undefiled by wit!
Our author offers in these motley scenes°
A slight remonstrance to the drama's queens;
Nor let the goddesses be over-nice—
Free-spoken subjects give the best advice.   35

Although not quite a novice in his trade,
His cause tonight requires no common aid.
To this, a friendly, just, and powerful court,
I come ambassador to beg support.
Can he, undaunted, brave the critic's rage?   40
In civil broils with brother bards engage?
Hold forth their errors to the public eye,
Nay more, e'en newspapers themselves defy?
Say, must his single arm encounter all?
By numbers vanquished, e'en the brave may fall;°   45
And though no leader should success distrust,
Whose troops are willing, and whose cause is just,
To bid such hosts of angry foes defiance,
His chief dependence must be your alliance.

1.1

[*The Dangles' house*]

Mr and Mrs Dangle at breakfast, and reading newspapers

DANGLE (*reading*) 'Brutus° to Lord North.° Letter the second on the state of the army.'—Pshaw! 'To the first L dash D of the A dash Y.'°—'Genuine extract of a letter from St Kitts.'°—'Coxheath° intelligence.'°—'It is now confidently asserted that Sir Charles Hardy°—'—Pshaw! Nothing but about the fleet and the nation! And I hate all politics but theatrical politics.—Where's *The Morning Chronicle*?° 5

MRS DANGLE Yes, that's your gazette.°

DANGLE So, here we have it. [*Reads*] 'Theatrical intelligence extraordinary. We hear there is a new tragedy in rehearsal at Drury Lane Theatre, called *The Spanish Armada*,° said to be written by Mr Puff, a gentleman well known in the theatrical world. If we may allow ourselves to give credit to the report of the performers, who, truth to say, are in general but indifferent judges, this piece abounds with the most striking and received° beauties of modern composition.' So! I am very glad my friend Puff's tragedy is in such forwardness.°—Mrs Dangle, my dear, you will be very glad to hear that Puff's tragedy— 10 15

MRS DANGLE Lord, Mr Dangle, why will you plague me about such nonsense? Now the plays are begun° I shall have no peace. Isn't it sufficient to make yourself ridiculous by your passion for the theatre, without continually teasing me to join you? Why can't you ride your hobby-horse without desiring to place me on a pillion behind you, Mr Dangle? 20

DANGLE Nay, my dear, I was only going to read— 25

MRS DANGLE No, no; you will never read anything that's worth listening to. You hate to hear about your country. There are letters every day with Roman signatures,° demonstrating the certainty of an invasion, and proving that the nation is utterly undone. But you never will read anything to entertain one. 30

DANGLE What has a woman to do with politics, Mrs Dangle?

MRS DANGLE And what have you to do with the theatre, Mr Dangle? Why should you affect the character of a critic?° I have no patience with you! Haven't you made yourself the jest of all your acquaintance by your interference in matters where you have no business? 35

Are not you called a theatrical quidnunc,° and a mock Maecenas°
to secondhand authors?

DANGLE True; my power with the managers is pretty notorious. But
is it no credit to have applications from all quarters for my interest?° From lords to recommend fiddlers, from ladies to get boxes,   40
from authors to get answers, and from actors to get engagements.

MRS DANGLE Yes, truly; you have contrived to get a share in all the
plague and trouble of theatrical property, without the profit, or even
the credit of the abuse that attends it.

DANGLE I am sure, Mrs Dangle, you are no loser by it, however; *you*   45
have all the advantages of it. Mightn't you, last winter, have had
the reading of the new pantomime° a fortnight previous to its
performance? And doesn't Mr Fosbrook° let you take places for
a play before it is advertised, and set you down for a box for
every new piece through the season? And didn't my friend, Mr   50
Smatter,° dedicate his last farce to you at my particular request,
Mrs Dangle?

MRS DANGLE Yes; but wasn't the farce damned,° Mr Dangle? And to
be sure it is extremely pleasant to have one's house made the motley
rendezvous of all the lackeys of literature! The very high change°   55
of trading authors and jobbing critics! Yes, my drawing-room is an
absolute register-office for candidate actors and poets without character.° Then to be continually alarmed with misses and ma'ams
piping hysteric changes on Juliets and Dorindas, Pollys° and Ophe-
lias; and the very furniture trembling at the probationary starts and   60
unprovoked rants of would-be Richards° and Hamlets! And what
is worse than all, now that the manager has monopolized the Opera
House,° haven't we the signors and signoras calling here, sliding
their smooth semibreves, and gargling glib divisions in their outlandish throats—with foreign emissaries and French spies, for   65
aught I know, disguised like fiddlers and figure dancers!°

DANGLE Mercy! Mrs Dangle!

MRS DANGLE And to employ yourself so idly at such an alarming
crisis as this too, when, if you had the least spirit, you would have
been at the head of one of the Westminster associations,° or trail-   70
ing a volunteer pike in the Artillery Ground.° But you—o' my conscience, I believe if the French were landed tomorrow, your first
inquiry would be whether they had brought a theatrical troupe with
them.

DANGLE Mrs Dangle, it does not signify. I say the stage is 'the mirror   75
of nature', and the actors are 'the abstract and brief chronicles of

the time';° and pray what can a man of sense study better? Besides, you will not easily persuade me that there is no credit or importance in being at the head of a band of critics, who take upon them to decide for the whole town, whose opinion and patronage all   80 writers solicit, and whose recommendation no manager dares refuse!

MRS DANGLE Ridiculous! Both managers and authors of the least merit laugh at your pretensions. The public is their critic, without whose fair approbation they know no play can rest on the stage, and   85 with whose applause they welcome such attacks as yours, and laugh at the malice of them, where they can't at the wit.

DANGLE Very well, madam, very well.

  Enter Servant

SERVANT Mr Sneer, sir, to wait on you.

DANDGLE O, show Mr Sneer up.   90

  Exit Servant

  Plague on't! Now we must appear loving and affectionate, or Sneer will hitch us into a story.°

MRS DANGLE With all my heart. You can't be more ridiculous than you are.

DANGLE You are enough to provoke—   95

  Enter Sneer

  Ha, my dear Sneer, I am vastly glad to see you.—My dear, here's Mr Sneer.

MRS DANGLE Good morning to you, sir.

DANGLE Mrs Dangle and I have been diverting ourselves with the papers. Pray, Sneer, won't you go to Drury Lane Theatre the first   100 night of Puff's tragedy?

SNEER Yes; but I suppose one shan't be able to get in, for on the first night of a new piece they always fill the house with orders° to support it. But here, Dangle, I have brought you two pieces, one of which you must exert yourself to make the managers accept, I can   105 tell you that, for 'tis written by a person of consequence.°

DANGLE So! Now my plagues are beginning!

SNEER Ay, I am glad of it, for now you'll be happy. Why, my dear Dangle, it is a pleasure to see how you enjoy your volunteer fatigue and your solicited solicitations.°   110

DANGLE It's a great trouble; yet, egad, it's pleasant too. Why, sometimes of a morning, I have a dozen people call on me at breakfast-time, whose faces I never saw before, nor ever desire to see again.

SNEER That must be very pleasant indeed!

DANGLE And not a week but I receive fifty letters, and not a line in   115
them about any business of my own.

SNEER An amusing correspondence!

DANGLE (*reading*) 'Bursts into tears, and exit.' What, is this a tragedy!

SNEER No, that's a genteel comedy—not a translation, only 'taken
from the French'.° It is written in a style which they have lately   120
tried to run down°—the true sentimental, and nothing ridiculous
in it from the beginning to the end.

MRS DANGLE Well, if they had kept to that, I should not have been
such an enemy to the stage; there was some edification to be got
from those pieces, Mr Sneer!   125

SNEER I am quite of your opinion, Mrs Dangle. The theatre in proper
hands might certainly be made the school of morality;° but now,
I am sorry to say it, people seem to go there principally for their
entertainment!°

MRS DANGLE It would have been more to the credit of the managers   130
to have kept it in the other line.°

SNEER Undoubtedly, madam; and hereafter perhaps to have had it
recorded that, in the midst of a luxurious and dissipated age, they
preserved *two* houses° in the capital, where the conversation was
always moral at least, if not entertaining!   135

DANGLE Now, egad, I think the worst alteration is in the nicety of
the audience. No double entendre, no smart innuendo admitted; even Vanbrugh and Congreve obliged to undergo a bungling
reformation!°

SNEER Yes, and our prudery in this respect is just on a par with the   140
artificial bashfulness of a courtesan, who increases the blush upon
her cheek in an exact proportion to the diminution of her modesty.

DANGLE Sneer can't even give the public a good word! But what have
we here? This seems a very odd—

SNEER O, that's a comedy, on a very new plan; replete with wit and   145
mirth, yet of a most serious moral! You see it is called *The Reformed
Housebreaker*; where, by the mere force of humour, housebreaking
is put into so ridiculous a light, that if the piece has its proper run,
I have no doubt but that bolts and bars will be entirely useless by
the end of the season.   150

DANGLE Egad, this is new indeed!

SNEER Yes; it is written by a particular friend of mine, who has discovered that the follies and foibles of society are subjects unworthy
the notice of the comic muse, who should be taught to stoop° only
at the greater vices and blacker crimes of humanity—gibbeting   155

capital offences in five acts, and pillorying petty larcenies in two. In
short, his idea is to dramatize the penal laws,° and make the stage
a court of ease° to the Old Bailey.

DANGLE It is truly moral.

Enter Servant

SERVANT Sir Fretful Plagiary, sir.   160

DANGLE Beg him to walk up.

Exit Servant

Now, Mrs Dangle, Sir Fretful Plagiary is an author to your own
taste.

MRS DANGLE I confess he is a favourite of mine, because everybody
else abuses him.   165

SNEER Very much to the credit of your charity, madam, if not of your
judgement.

DANGLE But, egad, he allows no merit to any author but himself.
That's the truth on't—though he's my friend.

SNEER Never. He is as envious as an old maid verging on the despera-   170
tion of six-and-thirty. And then the insidious humility with which
he seduces you to give a free° opinion on any of his works can be
exceeded only by the petulant arrogance with which he is sure to
reject your observations.

DANGLE Very true, egad—though he's my friend.   175

SNEER Then his affected contempt of all newspaper strictures;
though, at the same time, he is the sorest man alive, and shrinks like
scorched parchment from the fiery ordeal of true criticism. Yet is
he so covetous of popularity, that he had rather be abused than not
mentioned at all.   180

DANGLE There's no denying it—though he is my friend.

SNEER You have read the tragedy he has just finished, haven't you?

DANGLE O yes; he sent it to me yesterday.

SNEER Well, and you think it execrable, don't you?

DANGLE Why, between ourselves, egad, I must own—though he's my   185
friend—that it is one of the most—(*aside*) he's here!—finished and
most admirable perform—

SIR FRETFUL (*without*) Mr Sneer with him, did you say?

Enter Sir Fretful Plagiary

DANGLE Ah, my dear friend! Egad, we were just speaking of your
tragedy. Admirable, Sir Fretful, admirable!   190

SNEER You never did anything in your life beyond it, Sir Fretful—
never in your life.

SIR FRETFUL You make me extremely happy; for without a

compliment,° my dear Sneer, there isn't a man in the world whose
judgement I value as I do yours. And Mr Dangle's.   195
MRS DANGLE They are only laughing at you, Sir Fretful; for it was
  but just now that—
DANGLE Mrs Dangle!—Ah, Sir Fretful, you know Mrs Dangle. My
  friend Sneer was rallying just now. He knows how she admires you,
  and—   200
SIR FRETFUL O lord, I am sure Mr Sneer has more taste and sincer-
  ity than to—(*Aside*) A damned double-faced fellow!
DANGLE Yes, yes, Sneer will jest; but a better-humoured—
SIR FRETFUL O, I know!
DANGLE He has a ready turn for ridicule; his wit costs him nothing. 205
SIR FRETFUL (*aside*) No, egad, or I should wonder how he came by it.
MRS DANGLE Because his jest is always at the expense of his friend.
DANGLE But, Sir Fretful, have you sent your play to the managers yet,
  or can I be of any service to you?
SIR FRETFUL No, no, I thank you; I believe the piece had sufficient   210
  recommendation with it.° I thank you, though. I sent it to the
  manager of Covent Garden Theatre° this morning.
SNEER I should have thought now, that it might have been cast—as
  the actors call it—better at Drury Lane.
SIR FRETFUL O lud, no! Never send a play there while I live. Harkee. 215
    Sir Fretful Plagiary whispers to Sneer
SNEER 'Writes himself'! I know he does.°
SIR FRETFUL I say nothing. I take away from no man's merit, am hurt
  at no man's good fortune. I say nothing. But this I will say: through
  all my knowledge of life, I have observed that there is not a passion
  so strongly rooted in the human heart as envy!   220
SNEER I believe you have reason° for what you say, indeed.
SIR FRETFUL Besides, I can tell you it is not always so safe to leave a
  play in the hands of those who write themselves.
SNEER What, they may steal from them, hey, my dear Plagiary?
SIR FRETFUL Steal! To be sure they may; and, egad, serve your best   225
  thoughts as gipsies do stolen children—disfigure them to make 'em
  pass for their own.°
SNEER But your present work is a sacrifice to Melpomene, and *he*, you
  know, never—°
SIR FRETFUL That's no security. A dextrous plagiarist may do any-   230
  thing. Why, sir, for aught I know, he might take out some of the
  best things in my tragedy, and put them into his own comedy.°
SNEER That might be done, I dare be sworn.

SIR FRETFUL And then, if such a person gives you the least hint or
assistance, he is devilish apt to take the merit of the whole.   235

DANGLE If it succeeds.

SIR FRETFUL Ay; but with regard to this piece, I think I can hit that
gentleman,° for I can safely swear he never read it.

SNEER I'll tell you how you may hurt him more.

SIR FRETFUL How?   240

SNEER Swear he wrote it.

SIR FRETFUL Plague on't now, Sneer, I shall take it ill. I believe you
want to take away my character as an author!

SNEER Then I am sure you ought to be very much obliged to me.°

SIR FRETFUL Hey! Sir!   245

DANGLE O, you know he never means what he says.

SIR FRETFUL Sincerely then—you do like the piece?

SNEER Wonderfully!

SIR FRETFUL But come now, there must be something that you think
might be mended,° hey?—Mr Dangle, has nothing struck you?   250

DANGLE Why, faith, it is but an ungracious thing for the most part
to—

SIR FRETFUL With most authors it is just so indeed; they are in
general strangely tenacious!° But, for my part, I am never so well
pleased as when a judicious critic points out any defect to me; for   255
what is the purpose of showing a work to a friend, if you don't mean
to profit by his opinion?

SNEER Very true. Why then, though I seriously admire the piece upon
the whole, yet there is one small objection, which, if you'll give me
leave, I'll mention.   260

SIR FRETFUL Sir, you can't oblige me more.

SNEER I think it wants incident.

SIR FRETFUL Good God! You surprise me! 'Wants incident'!

SNEER Yes; I own I think the incidents are too few.

SIR FRETFUL Good God! Believe me, Mr Sneer, there is no per-   265
son for whose judgement I have a more implicit° deference. But
I protest to you, Mr Sneer, I am only apprehensive that the
incidents are too crowded.—My dear Dangle, how does it strike
you?

DANGLE Really I can't agree with my friend Sneer. I think the plot   270
quite sufficient; and the four first acts by many degrees the best I
ever read or saw in my life. If I might venture to suggest anything,
it is that the interest rather falls off in the fifth.

SIR FRETFUL Rises, I believe you mean, sir.

300

DANGLE No; I don't, upon my word.   275

SIR FRETFUL Yes, yes, you do, upon my soul. It certainly don't fall
off, I assure you. No, no, it don't fall off.

DANGLE Now, Mrs Dangle, didn't you say it struck you in the same
light?

MRS DANGLE No, indeed, I did not. I did not see a fault in any part   280
of the play from the beginning to the end.

SIR FRETFUL Upon my soul, the women are the best judges after all!

MRS DANGLE Or if I made any objection, I am sure it was to nothing
in the piece; but that I was afraid it was, on the whole, a little too
long.   285

SIR FRETFUL Pray, madam, do you speak as to duration of time; or
do you mean that the story is tediously spun out?

MRS DANGLE O lud, no! I speak only with reference to the usual
length of acting plays.

SIR FRETFUL Then I am very happy—very happy indeed—because   290
the play is a short play, a remarkably short play. I should not venture
to differ with a lady on a point of taste; but, on these occasions, the
watch, you know, is the critic.

MRS DANGLE Then, I suppose, it must have been Mr Dangle's drawling manner of reading it to me.   295

SIR FRETFUL O, if Mr Dangle read it! That's quite another affair! But
I assure you, Mrs Dangle, the first evening you can spare me three
hours and an half,° I'll undertake to read you the whole from beginning to end, with the prologue and epilogue, and allow time for the
music between the acts.°   300

MRS DANGLE I hope to see it on the stage next.°

DANGLE Well, Sir Fretful, I wish you may be able to get rid as easily
of the newspaper criticisms as you do of ours.

SIR FRETFUL The newspapers! Sir, they are the most villainous, licentious, abominable, infernal—Not that I ever read them. No, I make   305
it a rule never to look into a newspaper.

DANGLE You are quite right, for it certainly must hurt an author of
delicate feelings to see the liberties they take.

SIR FRETFUL No! Quite the contrary. Their abuse is, in fact, the best
panegyric; I like it of all things. An author's reputation is only in   310
danger from their support.

SNEER Why, that's true. And that attack now on you the other day—

SIR FRETFUL What? Where?

DANGLE Ay, you mean in a paper of Thursday. It was completely ill-
natured to be sure.   315

SIR FRETFUL O, so much the better. Ha, ha, ha!° I wouldn't have it otherwise.

DANGLE Certainly it is only to be laughed at; for—

SIR FRETFUL You don't happen to recollect what the fellow said, do you?   320

SNEER Pray, Dangle. Sir Fretful seems a little anxious.

SIR FRETFUL O lud, no! Anxious? Not I. Not the least. I—but one may as well hear, you know.

DANGLE Sneer, do *you* recollect? (*Aside to Sneer*) Make out something.°   325

SNEER (*to Dangle*) I will. [*Aloud*] Yes, yes, I remember perfectly.

SIR FRETFUL Well, and pray now—not that it signifies°—what might the gentleman say?

SNEER Why, he roundly asserts that you have not the slightest invention or original genius whatever, though you are the greatest tra-   330
ducer of all other authors living.

SIR FRETFUL Ha, ha, ha! Very good!

SNEER That, as to comedy, you have not one idea of your own, he believes, even in your commonplace-book,° where stray jokes and pilfered witticisms are kept with as much method as the ledger of   335
the lost-and-stolen office.

SIR FRETFUL Ha, ha, ha! Very pleasant!

SNEER Nay, that you are so unlucky as not to have the skill even to *steal* with taste. But that you glean from the refuse of obscure volumes, where more judicious plagiarists have been before you; so   340
that the body of your work is a composition of dregs and sediments, like a bad tavern's worst wine.

SIR FRETFUL Ha, ha!

SNEER In your more serious efforts, he says, your bombast would be less intolerable, if the thoughts were ever suited to the expression;   345
but the homeliness of the sentiment stares through the fantastic encumbrance of its fine language, like a clown in one of the new uniforms!°

SIR FRETFUL Ha, ha!

SNEER That your occasional tropes and flowers° suit the general   350
coarseness of your style, as tambour sprigs would a ground of linsey-wolsey;° while your imitations of Shakespeare resemble the mimicry of Falstaff's page,° and are about as near the standard of the original.

SIR FRETFUL Ha!   355

SNEER In short, that even the finest passages you steal are of no service to you; for the poverty of your own language prevents their assimilating, so that they lie on the surface, like lumps of marl° on a barren moor, encumbering what it is not in their power to fertilize!

SIR FRETFUL (*after great agitation*) Now another person would be 360 vexed at this.

SNEER O, but I wouldn't have told you, only to divert you.

SIR FRETFUL I know it. I *am* diverted. Ha, ha, ha! Not the least invention! Ha, ha, ha! Very good! Very good!

SNEER Yes, no genius! Ha, ha, ha! 365

DANGLE A severe rogue! Ha, ha, ha! But you are quite right, Sir Fretful, never to read such nonsense.

SIR FRETFUL To be sure; for, if there is anything to one's praise, it is a foolish vanity to be gratified at it; and if it is abuse, why, one is always sure to hear of it from one damned good-natured friend or 370 another!

Enter Servant

SERVANT Sir, there is an Italian gentleman, with a French interpreter, and three young ladies, and a dozen musicians, who say they are sent by Lady Rondeau and Mrs Fugue.

DANGLE Gadso, they come by appointment.—Dear Mrs Dangle, do 375 let them know I'll see them directly.

MRS DANGLE You know, Mr Dangle, I shan't understand a word they say.

DANGLE But you hear there's an interpreter.

MRS DANGLE Well, I'll try to endure their complaisance till you come. 380

Exit Mrs Dangle

SERVANT And Mr Puff, sir, has sent word that the last rehearsal is to be this morning, and that he'll call on you presently.

DANGLE That's true. I shall certainly be at home.

Exit Servant

Now, Sir Fretful, if you have a mind to have justice done you in the way of answer, egad, Mr Puff's your man. 385

SIR FRETFUL Pshaw! Sir, why should I wish to have it answered, when I tell you I am pleased at it?

DANGLE True, I had forgot that. But I hope you are not fretted at what Mr Sneer—

SIR FRETFUL Zounds, no, Mr Dangle! Don't I tell you these things 390 never fret me in the least?

DANGLE Nay, I only thought—

SIR FRETFUL And let me tell you, Mr Dangle, 'tis damned affronting in you to suppose that I am hurt, when I tell you I am not.

SNEER But why so warm, Sir Fretful?   395

SIR FRETFUL Gadslife, Mr Sneer, you are as absurd as Dangle. How
    often must I repeat it to you, that nothing can vex me but your sup-
    posing it possible for me to mind the damned nonsense you have
    been repeating to me! And let me tell you, if you continue to believe
    this, you must mean to insult me, gentlemen; and then your disre-   400
    spect will affect me no more than the newspaper criticisms, and I
    shall treat it with exactly the same calm indifference and philo-
    sophic contempt. And so your servant.

        Exit Sir Fretful Plagiary

SNEER Ha, ha, ha! Poor Sir Fretful! Now will he go and vent his phi-
    losophy in anonymous abuse° of all modern critics and authors.   405
    But, Dangle, you must get your friend Puff to take me to the
    rehearsal of his tragedy.

DANGLE I'll answer for't° he'll thank you for desiring it. But come and
    help me to judge of this musical family; they are recommended by
    people of consequence, I assure you.   410

SNEER I am at your disposal the whole morning. But I thought you
    had been a decided° critic in music, as well as in literature?

DANGLE So I am; but I have a bad ear. I'faith, Sneer, though, I am
    afraid we were a little too severe on Sir Fretful—though he is my
    friend.   415

SNEER Why, 'tis certain that unnecessarily to mortify the vanity of any
    writer is a cruelty which mere dullness never can deserve; but where
    a base and personal malignity usurps the place of literary emula-
    tion,° the aggressor deserves neither quarter nor pity.

DANGLE That's true, egad!—though he's my friend!   420

        [*Exeunt*]

1.2

A drawing-room in the Dangles' house. Harpsichord, etc.

*Signor Pasticcio Ritornello, Three Daughters of Signor
Pasticcio Ritornello, French Interpreter, Mrs Dangle, and
Servants discovered*

INTERPRETER *Je dis, madame, j'ai l'honneur* to introduce *et de vous
    demander votre protection pour le Signor Pasticcio Ritornello et pour sa
    charmante famille.*°

SIGNOR PASTICCIO *Ah! Vossignoria, noi vi preghiamo di favorirci colla vostra protezione.*   5

FIRST DAUGHTER *Vossignoria, fateci queste grazie.*

SECOND DAUGHTER *Si, signora.*°

INTERPRETER Madame, me interpret. *C'est à dire*—in English—*qu'ils vous prient de leur faire l'honneur*—°

MRS DANGLE I say again, gentlemen, I don't understand a word you   10
say.

SIGNOR PASTICCIO *Questo signore spiegherà.*°

INTERPRETER *Oui*—me interpret—*nous avons les lettres de recommendation pour Monsieur Dangle de*—°

MRS DANGLE Upon my word, sir, I don't understand you.   15

SIGNOR PASTICCIO *La Contessa Rondeau è nostra padrona.*

THIRD DAUGHTER *Si, padre, e mi Lady Fugue.*°

INTERPRETER O, me interpret! *Madame, ils disent*—in English—*qu'ils ont l'honneur d'être protégés de ces dames.*° You understand?

MRS DANGLE No, sir; no understand!   20
         Enter Dangle and Sneer

INTERPRETER *Ah, voici*° *Monsieur Dangle!*

ALL ITALIANS *A! Signor Dangle!*

MRS DANGLE Mr Dangle, here are two very civil gentlemen trying to make themselves understood, and I don't know which is the interpreter.   25

DANGLE *Eh bien!*°
         Interpreter and Signor Pasticcio Ritornello speak together

INTERPRETER *Monsieur Dangle, le grand bruit de vos talents pour la critique et de votre intérêt avec messieurs les directeurs à tous les théâtres*—°

SIGNOR PASTICCIO *Vossignoria siete si famoso per la vostra conoscenza e vostra interessi presso i Direttori da*—°   30

DANGLE Egad, I think the interpreter is the hardest to be understood of the two!

SNEER Why, I thought, Dangle, you had been an admirable linguist!

DANGLE So I am, if they would not talk so damned fast.

SNEER Well, I'll explain that the less time we lose in hearing them°   35
the better, for that I suppose is what they are brought here for.
         Sneer speaks to Signor Pasticcio Ritornello. The Three
         Daughters sing trios, etc.,° *Dangle beating out of time. Servant*
         enters and whispers to Dangle

DANGLE Show him up.
         Exit Servant

Bravo! Admirable! Bravissimo! Admirablissimo!—Ah, Sneer, where
will you find such as these voices in England?

SNEER   Not easily.   40

DANGLE   But Puff is coming.—Signor, and little signoras, obligatis-
simo! Sposa Signora Danglena—Mrs Dangle, shall I beg you to
offer them some refreshments, and take their address° in the next
room?

> *Exit Mrs Dangle with Signor Pasticcio Ritornello, the Three*
> *Daughters, and French Interpreter ceremoniously. Enter*
> *Servant*

SERVANT   Mr Puff, sir.   45

> *Enter Puff*

DANGLE   My dear Puff!

PUFF   My dear Dangle, how is it with you?

DANGLE   Mr Sneer, give me leave to introduce Mr Puff to you.

PUFF   Mr Sneer is this? Sir, he is a gentleman whom I have long panted
for the honour of knowing, a gentleman whose critical talents and   50
transcendent judgement—

SNEER   Dear sir—

DANGLE   Nay, don't be modest, Sneer. My friend Puff only talks to
you in the style of his profession.

SNEER   His profession!   55

PUFF   Yes, sir; I make no secret of the trade I follow. Among friends
and brother authors, Dangle knows I love to be frank on the subject,
and to advertise myself *viva voce*.° I am, sir, a practitioner in panegyric, or—to speak more plainly—a professor of° the art of
puffing, at your service, or anybody else's.   60

SNEER   Sir, you are very obliging! I believe, Mr Puff, I have often
admired your talents in the daily prints.°

PUFF   Yes, sir, I flatter myself I do as much business in that way as any
six of the fraternity° in town. Devilish hard work all the summer,
friend Dangle! Never worked harder! But harkee, the winter   65
managers were a little sore, I believe.°

DANGLE   No, I believe they took it all in good part.

PUFF   Ay! Then that must have been affectation in them, for, egad,
there were some of the attacks which there was no laughing at!

SNEER   Ay, the humorous ones. But I should think, Mr Puff, that   70
authors would in general be able to do this sort of work for
themselves.

PUFF   Why, yes, but in a clumsy way. Besides, we look on that as an
encroachment, and so take the opposite side. I dare say now you

conceive half the very civil paragraphs and advertisements you   75
see to be written by the parties concerned or their friends? No
such thing. Nine out of ten manufactured by me in the way of
business.

SNEER Indeed!

PUFF Even the auctioneers now—the auctioneers, I say—though the   80
rogues have lately got some credit for their language, not an article
of the merit theirs!° Take them out of their pulpits, and they are
as dull as catalogues. No, sir; 'twas I first enriched their style. 'Twas
I first taught them to crowd their advertisements with panegyrical
superlatives, each epithet rising above the other, like the bidders in   85
their own auction-rooms! From *me* they learned to inlay their
phraseology with variegated chips of exotic metaphor.° By *me* too
their inventive faculties were called forth. Yes, sir, by *me* they were
instructed to clothe ideal walls with gratuitous° fruits, to insinuate
obsequious rivulets into visionary groves, to teach courteous shrubs   90
to nod their approbation of the grateful soil, or on emergencies to
raise upstart oaks where there never had been an acorn, to create a
delightful vicinage without the assistance of a neighbour, or fix the
temple of Hygeia in the fens of Lincolnshire!°

DANGLE I am sure you have done them infinite service; for now, when   95
a gentleman is ruined, he parts with his house with some credit.

SNEER Service! If they had any gratitude, they would erect a statue to
him. They would figure him as a presiding Mercury,° the god of
traffic and fiction, with a hammer in his hand instead of a
caduceus.—But pray, Mr Puff, what first put you on exercising your   100
talents in this way?

PUFF Egad, sir, sheer necessity, the proper parent of an art so nearly
allied to invention.° You must know, Mr Sneer, that from the first
time I tried my hand at an advertisement, my success was such, that
for some time after I led a most extraordinary life indeed!   105

SNEER How, pray?

PUFF Sir, I supported myself two years entirely by my misfortunes.

SNEER By your misfortunes!

PUFF Yes, sir, assisted by long sickness and other occasional disorders;
and a very comfortable living I had of it.   110

SNEER From sickness and misfortunes! You practised as a doctor and
an attorney at once?

PUFF No, egad; both maladies and miseries were my own.

SNEER Hey! What the plague!

DANGLE 'Tis true, i'faith.   115

PUFF Harkee! By advertisements. 'To the charitable and humane' and
'to those whom providence hath blessed with affluence'.

SNEER O, I understand you.

PUFF And, in truth, I deserved what I got, for I suppose never man
went through such a series of calamities in the same space of time!   120
Sir, I was five times made a bankrupt, and reduced from a state of
affluence by a train of unavoidable misfortunes! Then, sir, though
a very industrious tradesman, I was twice burnt out, and lost my
little all both times! I lived upon those fires a month. I soon after
was confined by a most excruciating disorder, and lost the use of   125
my limbs! That told very well,° for I had the case strongly attested,
and went about to collect the subscriptions myself.

DANGLE Egad, I believe that was when you first called on me.

PUFF In November last? O no! I was at that time a close° prisoner in
the Marshalsea° for a debt benevolently contracted to serve a friend!   130
I was afterwards twice tapped for a dropsy,° which declined into a
very profitable consumption! I was then reduced to—O no, then I
became a widow with six helpless children, after having had eleven
husbands pressed,° and being left every time eight months gone
with child, and without money to get me into an hospital!   135

SNEER And you bore all with patience, I make no doubt?

PUFF Why, yes, though I made some occasional attempts at felo de se.
But as I did not find those rash actions answer,° I left off killing
myself very soon. Well, sir, at last, what with bankruptcies, fires,
gouts, dropsies, imprisonments, and other valuable calamities,   140
having got together a pretty handsome sum, I determined to quit a
business which had always gone rather against my conscience, and
in a more liberal° way still to indulge my talents for fiction and
embellishment through my favourite channels of diurnal communication.° And so, sir, you have my history.   145

SNEER Most obligingly communicative indeed; and your confession,
if published, might certainly serve the cause of true charity, by res-
cuing the most useful channels of appeal to benevolence from the
cant of imposition.° But surely, Mr Puff, there is no great mystery°
in your present profession?   150

PUFF Mystery! Sir, I will take upon me to say the matter was never
scientifically treated nor reduced to rule before.

SNEER Reduced to rule?

PUFF O lud, sir, you are very ignorant, I am afraid. Yes, sir, puffing is
of various sorts.° The principal are: the puff direct, the puff   155
preliminary, the puff collateral, the puff collusive, and the puff

oblique, or puff by implication. These all assume, as circumstances
require, the various forms of letter to the editor, occasional anecdote, impartial critique, observation from correspondent, or adver-
tisement° from the party.°   160
SNEER The puff direct I can conceive.
PUFF O, yes, that's simple enough. For instance, a new comedy or
farce is to be produced at one of the theatres, though by the bye
they don't bring out half what they ought to do. The author,
suppose Mr Smatter,° or Mr Dapper, or any particular friend of   165
mine. Very well. The day before it is to be performed, I write an
account of the manner in which it was received. I have the plot from
the author, and only add, 'Characters strongly drawn . . . highly
coloured . . . hand of a master . . . fund of genuine humour . . .
mine of invention . . . neat dialogue . . . attic salt'!° Then for the 170
performance. 'Mr Dodd was astonishingly great in the character of
Sir Harry! That universal and judicious actor Mr Palmer perhaps
never appeared to more advantage than in the colonel. But it is not
in the power of language to do justice to Mr King!° Indeed, he more
than merited those repeated bursts of applause which he drew from 175
a most brilliant and judicious audience! As to the scenery, the mi-
raculous power of Mr De Loutherbourg's pencil° are universally
acknowledged! In short, we are at a loss which to admire most—
the unrivalled genius of the author, the great attention and liberality of the managers, the wonderful abilities of the painter, or the 180
incredible exertions of all the performers!'
SNEER That's pretty well indeed, sir.
PUFF O cool, quite cool, to what° I sometimes do.
SNEER And do you think there are any who are influenced by this?
PUFF O, lud, yes, sir. The number of those who go through the fatigue 185
of judging for themselves is very small indeed!
SNEER Well, sir, the puff preliminary?
PUFF O, that, sir, does well in the form of a caution. In a matter of
gallantry now, Sir Flimsy Gossamer° wishes to be well with Lady
Fanny Fête. He applies to me. I open trenches° for him with a para- 190
graph in *The Morning Post.*° 'It is recommended to the beautiful
and accomplished Lady F four stars° F dash E to be on her guard
against that dangerous character, Sir F dash G, who, however pleasing and insinuating his manners may be, is certainly not remarkable
for the *constancy of his attachments*' (in italics). Here you see Sir 195
Flimsy Gossamer is introduced to the particular notice of Lady
Fanny, who perhaps never thought of him before. She finds herself

publicly cautioned to avoid him, which naturally makes her desirous of seeing him. The observation of their acquaintance causes a pretty kind of mutual embarrassment. This produces a sort   200 of sympathy of interest, which if Sir Flimsy is unable to improve effectually, he at least gains the credit of having their names mentioned together, by a particular set, and in a particular way, which nine times out of ten is the full accomplishment of modern gallantry!   205

DANGLE Egad, Sneer, you will be quite an adept in the business.

PUFF Now, sir, the puff collateral is much used as an appendage to advertisements, and may take the form of anecdote. 'Yesterday, as the celebrated George Bon Mot° was sauntering down St James's Street,° he met the lively Lady Mary Myrtle° coming out of the   210 Park. "Good God, Lady Mary, I'm surprised to meet you in a white jacket, for I expected never to have seen you, but in a full-trimmed uniform and a light-horseman's cap!"°—"Heavens, George, where could you have learned that?"—"Why", replied the wit, "I just saw a print of you in a new publication called *The Camp Magazine*,°   215 which, by the bye, is a devilish clever thing, and is sold at No. 3, on the right hand of the way, two doors from the printing-office, the corner of Ivy Lane, Paternoster Row, price only one shilling!"'

SNEER Very ingenious indeed!

PUFF But the puff collusive is the newest of any; for it acts in the dis-   220 guise of determined hostility. It is much used by bold booksellers and enterprising poets. An indignant correspondent observes that the new poem called 'Beelzebub's Cotillion, or Prosperpine's *Fête Champêtre*'° is one of the most unjustifiable performances he ever read! The severity with which certain characters are handled is   225 quite shocking! And as there are many descriptions in it too warmly coloured for female delicacy, the shameful avidity with which this piece is bought by all people of fashion is a reproach on the taste of the times and a disgrace to the delicacy of the age! Here you see the two strongest inducements are held forth. First, that nobody   230 ought to read it, and secondly, that everybody buys it; on the strength of which the publisher boldly prints the tenth edition before he had sold ten of the first, and then establishes it by threatening himself with the pillory, or absolutely indicting himself for scan. mag.!°   235

DANGLE Ha, ha, ha! Gad, I know it is so.

PUFF As to the puff oblique, or puff by implication, it is too various and extensive to be illustrated by an instance. It attracts in titles and

presumes in patents.° It lurks in the limitation of a subscription°
and invites in the assurance of crowd and incommodation at public   240
places. It delights to draw forth concealed merit with a most disinterested assiduity, and sometimes wears a countenance of smiling
censure and tender reproach. It has a wonderful memory for parliamentary debates, and will often give the whole speech of a
favoured member with the most flattering accuracy.° But, above all,   245
it is a great dealer in reports and suppositions. It has the earliest
intelligence of intended preferments° that will reflect honour on
the patrons, and embryo promotions of modest gentlemen, who
know nothing of the matter themselves. It can hint a ribbon° for
implied services in the air of a common report,° and with the care-   250
lessness of a casual paragraph suggest officers into commands, to
which they have no pretension but their wishes. This, sir, is the last
principal class in the art of puffing, an art which, I hope you will
now agree with me, is of the highest dignity, yielding a tablature°
of benevolence and public spirit, befriending equally trade, gal-   255
lantry, criticism, and politics—the applause of genius! the register
of charity!° the triumph° of heroism! the self-defence of contractors!° the fame of orators! and the gazette of ministers!

SNEER Sir, I am completely a convert both to the importance and ingenuity of your profession; and now, sir, there is but one thing   260
which can possibly increase my respect for you, and that is your
permitting me to be present this morning at the rehearsal of your
new trage—

PUFF Hush, for heaven's sake. *My* tragedy!—Egad, Dangle, I take this
very ill. You know how apprehensive I am of being known to be the   265
author.

DANGLE I'faith, I would not have told; but it's in the papers, and your
name at length in *The Morning Chronicle*.

PUFF Ah, those damned editors never can keep a secret!—Well, Mr
Sneer, no doubt you will do me great honour. I shall be infinitely   270
happy, highly flattered—

DANGLE I believe it must be near the time. Shall we go together?

PUFF No; it will not be yet this hour, for they are always late at that
theatre. Besides, I must meet you there, for I have some little
matters here to send to the papers, and a few paragraphs to scrib-   275
ble before I go. (*Looking at memorandums*) Here is 'a conscientious
baker, on the subject of the army bread', and 'a detester of visible
brickwork, in favour of the new-invented stucco', both in the style
of Junius,° and promised for tomorrow. The Thames navigation°

too is at a stand. Misomud° or Anti-shoal must go to work again   280
directly. Here too are some political memorandums, I see. Ay. 'To
take Paul Jones° and get the Indiamen out of the Shannon,° rein-
force Byron,° compel the Dutch to—'° So! I must do that in the
evening papers, or reserve it for *The Morning Herald*, for I know
that I have undertaken tomorrow, besides, to establish the unanim-   285
ity of the fleet° in *The Public Advertiser*, and to shoot Charles Fox°
in *The Morning Post*.° So, egad, I ha'n't a moment to lose!

DANGLE Well! We'll meet in the green room.°

    Exeunt severally

2.1

The theatre

Enter Dangle, Puff, and Sneer, as before the curtain°

PUFF No, no, sir. What Shakespeare says of actors may be better
applied to the purpose of plays. *They* ought to be 'the abstract and
brief chronicles of the times'.° Therefore, when history, and particularly the history of our own country, furnishes anything like a
case in point to the time in which an author writes, if he knows his   5
own interest, he will take advantage of it. So, sir, I call my tragedy
The Spanish Armada and have laid the scene before Tilbury Fort.°

SNEER A most happy thought certainly!

DANGLE Egad, it was; I told you so.—But pray now, I don't understand how you have contrived to introduce any love into it.   10

PUFF Love! O, nothing so easy; for it is a received point among poets,
that where history gives you a good heroic outline for a play, you
may fill up with a little love at your own discretion; in doing which,
nine times out of ten, you only make up a deficiency in the private
history of the times. Now I rather think I have done this with some   15
success.

SNEER No scandal about Queen Elizabeth, I hope?

PUFF O lud, no, no! I only suppose the Governor of Tilbury Fort's
daughter to be in love with the son of the Spanish admiral.

SNEER O, is that all?   20

DANGLE Excellent, i'faith! I see it at once. But won't this appear rather
improbable?

PUFF To be sure it will; but what the plague! A play is not to show
occurrences that happen every day, but things just so strange, that
though they never *did*, they *might* happen.   25

SNEER Certainly nothing is unnatural, that is not physically
impossible.

PUFF Very true. And for that matter Don Ferolo Whiskerandos, for
that's the lover's name, might have been over here in the train of
the Spanish ambassador; or Tilburina, for that is the lady's name,   30
might have been in love with him, from having heard his character
or seen his picture, or from knowing that he was the last man in the
world she ought to be in love with, or for any other good female
reason. However, sir, the fact is, that though she is but a knight's
daughter, egad, she is in love like any princess!   35

DANGLE Poor young lady! I feel for her already, for I can conceive how great the conflict must be between her passion and her duty, her love for her country and her love for Don Ferolo Whiskerandos!°

PUFF O, amazing! Her poor susceptible heart is swayed to and fro by contending passions, like—   40

Enter Underprompter

UNDERPROMPTER Sir, the scene is set, and everything is ready to begin, if you please.

PUFF Egad, then we'll lose no time.

UNDERPROMPTER Though I believe, sir, you will find it very short, for all the performers have profited by the kind permission you   45
granted them.

PUFF Hey! What!

UNDERPROMPTER You know, sir, you gave them leave to cut out or omit whatever they found heavy or unnecessary to the plot, and I must own they have taken very liberal advantage of your   50
indulgence.

PUFF Well, well. They are in general very good judges; and I know I am luxuriant. [*Calls offstage*] Now, Mr Hopkins,° as soon as you please.

UNDERPROMPTER (*to the music*°) Gentlemen, will you play a few bars   55
of something, just to—

PUFF Ay, that's right, for, as we have the scenes and dresses,° egad, we'll go to't, as if it was the first night's performance. But you need not mind stopping between the acts.

Exit Underprompter. Orchestra play. Then the bell rings°

So!—Stand clear, gentlemen. Now you know there will be a cry of   60
'Down! Down! Hats off!° Silence!' Then up curtain, and let us see what our painters have done for us.°

The curtain rises and discovers Tilbury Fort. Two Sentinels asleep°

DANGLE Tilbury Fort! Very fine indeed!

PUFF Now, what do you think I open with?

SNEER Faith, I can't guess.   65

PUFF A clock. Hark!

Clock strikes

I open with a clock striking, to beget an awful° attention in the audience. It also marks the time, which is four o'clock in the morning, and saves a description of the rising sun and a great deal about gilding the eastern hemisphere.°   70

DANGLE But pray, are the sentinels to be asleep?

PUFF Fast as watchmen.

SNEER Isn't that odd, though, at such an alarming crisis?

PUFF To be sure it is. But smaller things must give way to a striking
    scene at the opening. That's a rule. And the case is, that two great   75
    men are coming to this very spot to begin the piece. Now it is not
    to be supposed they would open their lips, if these fellows were
    watching them. So, egad, I must either have sent them off their
    posts, or set them asleep.

SNEER O, that accounts for it! But tell us, who are these coming?   80

PUFF These are they—Sir Walter Ralegh and Sir Christopher Hatton.
    You'll know Sir Christopher by his turning out his toes—famous,
    you know, for his dancing. I like to preserve all the little traits of
    character. Now attend.

        Enter Sir Walter Ralegh° and Sir Christopher Hatton°

SIR CHRISTOPHER   *True, gallant Ralegh!*   85

DANGLE What, they had been talking before?°

PUFF O, yes; all the way as they came along. (*To the actors*) I beg
    pardon, gentlemen, but these are particular friends of mine, whose
    remarks may be of great service to us. (*To Sneer and Dangle*) Don't
    mind interrupting° them whenever anything strikes you.   90

SIR CHRISTOPHER   *True, gallant Ralegh!*
  But O, thou champion of thy country's fame,
  There is *a question which I yet must ask—*
  A question which I never asked before.
  What mean these mighty armaments,   95
  This general muster, and this throng of chiefs?°

SNEER Pray, Mr Puff, how came Sir Christopher Hatton never to ask
    that question before?

PUFF What, before the play began? How the plague could he?

DANGLE That's true, i'faith!   100

PUFF But you will hear what he thinks of the matter.

SIR CHRISTOPHER *Alas, my noble friend, when I behold*
  Yon tented plains in martial symmetry
  Arrayed; when I count o'er yon glittering lines
  Of crested warriors, where the proud steed's neigh   105
  And valour-breathing trumpet's shrill appeal
  Responsive vibrate on my listening ear;
  When virgin majesty herself I view,
  Like her protecting Pallas veiled in steel,°
  With graceful confidence exhort to arms;°   110
  When, briefly, all I hear or see bears stamp

  Of martial vigilance and stern defence,
  I cannot but surmise—forgive, my friend,
  If the conjecture's rash—I cannot but
  Surmise the state some danger apprehends!   115

SNEER A very cautious conjecture that.

PUFF Yes, that's his character—not to give an opinion, but on secure grounds. Now then.

SIR WALTER *O, most accomplished Christopher—*

PUFF He calls him by his Christian name, to show that they are on the 120
most familiar terms.°

SIR WALTER *O, most accomplished Christopher, I find*
  Thy staunch sagacity still tracks the future
  In the fresh print of the o'ertaken past.

PUFF Figurative!°   125

SIR WALTER *Thy fears are just.*

SIR CHRISTOPHER   *But where, whence, when, and what*
  The danger is, methinks I fain would learn.

SIR WALTER *You know, my friend, scarce two revolving suns,*
  And three revolving moons, have closed their course°
  Since haughty Philip, in despite of peace,°   130
  With hostile hand hath struck at England's trade.

SIR CHRISTOPHER *I know it well.*

SIR WALTER *Philip, you know, is proud, Iberia's king!*°

SIR CHRISTOPHER *He is.*

SIR WALTER   *His subjects in base bigotry*
  And Catholic oppression held, while we,   135
  You know, the Protestant persuasion hold.

SIR CHRISTOPHER *We do.*

SIR WALTER *You know, beside, his boasted armament,*
  The famed Armada, by the Pope baptized,
  With purpose to invade these realms—

SIR CHRISTOPHER   *Is sailed.*   140
  Our last advices so report.°

SIR WALTER *While the Iberian admiral's chief hope,*
  His darling son—

SIR CHRISTOPHER *—Ferolo Whiskerandos hight—*

SIR WALTER *The same—by chance a prisoner hath been ta'en,*
  And in this fort of Tilbury—

SIR CHRISTOPHER   *Is now*   145
  Confined. 'Tis true, and oft from yon tall turret's top
  I've marked the youthful Spaniard's haughty mien,

Unconquered, though in chains!

SIR WALTER   *You also know—*

DANGLE Mr Puff, as he *knows* all this, why does Sir Walter go on
telling him?   150

PUFF But the audience are not supposed to know anything of the
matter, are they?

SNEER True, but I think you manage ill; for there certainly appears no
reason why Sir Walter should be so communicative.

PUFF 'Fore Gad now, that is one of the most ungrateful observations   155
I ever heard, for the less inducement he has to tell all this, the more
I think you ought to be obliged to him; for I am sure you'd know
nothing of the matter without it.

DANGLE That's very true, upon my word.

PUFF But you will find he was *not* going on.   160

SIR CHRISTOPHER *Enough, enough! 'Tis plain, and I no more*
Am in amazement lost!

PUFF Here, now, you see, Sir Christopher did not in fact ask any one
question for his own information.

SNEER No, indeed; his has been a most disinterested curiosity!   165

DANGLE Really, I find, we are very much obliged to them both.

PUFF To be sure you are. Now then for the commander-in-chief, the
Earl of Leicester,° who, you know, was no favourite but of the
queen's. [*To the actors*] We left off—'in amazement lost!'

SIR CHRISTOPHER *Am in amazement lost.*   170
But see where noble Leicester comes, supreme
In honours and command!

SIR WALTER   *And yet methinks,*
At such a time, so perilous, so feared,
That staff might well become an abler grasp.

SIR CHRISTOPHER *And so, by heaven, think I! But soft, he's here!*   175

PUFF Ay, they envy him.

SNEER But who are these with him?

PUFF O, very valiant knights! One is the governor of the fort, the other
the master of the horse. And now I think you shall hear some better
language. I was obliged to be plain and intelligible° in the first scene, 180
because there was so much matter of fact in it; but now, i'faith, you
have trope,° figure,° and metaphor, as plenty as noun-substantives.°

    Enter Earl of Leicester, the Governor, the Master of the
    Horse, and a Knight

LEICESTER *How's this, my friends! Is't thus your new-fledged zeal*
And plumèd valour moults in roosted sloth?

Why dimly glimmers that heroic flame,   185
Whose reddening blaze, by patriot spirit fed,
Should be the beacon of a kindling realm?
Can the quick current of a patriot heart
Thus stagnate in a cold and weedy converse
Or freeze in tideless inactivity?   190
No! Rather let the fountain of your valour
Spring through each stream of enterprise,
Each petty channel of conducive daring,
Till the full torrent of your foaming wrath
O'erwhelm the flats of sunk hostility!°   195

PUFF There it is—followed up!

SIR WALTER *No more! The freshening breath of thy rebuke*
Hath filled the swelling canvas of our souls!
And thus, though fate should cut the cable of
        (All take hands)
Our topmost hopes, in friendship's closing line°   200
We'll grapple with despair, and if we fall,
We'll fall in glory's wake!

LEICESTER *There spoke old England's genius!*
Then, are we all resolved?

ALL *We are—all resolved.*   205

LEICESTER *To conquer—or be free?°*

ALL *To conquer, or be free.*

LEICESTER *All?*

ALL *All.*

DANGLE *Nem. con.,°* egad!   210

PUFF O, yes; where they *do* agree on the stage, their unanimity is
    wonderful!

LEICESTER *Then, let's embrace. And now—*
        [*Leicester kneels*]

SNEER What the plague! Is he going to pray?

PUFF Yes, hush! In great emergencies, there is nothing like a prayer!   215

LEICESTER *O mighty Mars!*

DANGLE But why should he pray to *Mars?*

PUFF Hush!

LEICESTER   *If, in thy homage bred,*
Each point of discipline I've still observed,°   220
Nor but by due promotion and the right
Of service to the rank of major-general
Have risen, assist thy votary now!

GOVERNOR [*kneeling*] *Yet do not rise. Hear me!*
MASTER OF HORSE [*kneeling*] *And me!*   225
KNIGHT [*kneeling*] *And me!*
SIR WALTER [*kneeling*] *And me!*
SIR CHRISTOPHER [*kneeling*] *And me!*
PUFF Now, pray all together.
ALL *Behold thy votaries submissive beg*   230
  That thou wilt deign to grant them all they ask,
  Assist them to accomplish all their ends,
  And sanctify whatever means they use
  To gain them!
SNEER A very orthodox quintetto!°   235
PUFF [*to the actors*] Vastly well, gentlemen. [*To Sneer and Dangle*] Is that
  well managed or not? Have you such a prayer as that on the stage?
SNEER Not exactly.
LEICESTER (*to Puff*) But, sir, you haven't settled how we are to get off
  here.   240
PUFF You could not go off kneeling, could you?°
SIR WALTER (*to Puff*) O no, sir! Impossible!
PUFF It would have a good effect, i'faith, if you could! Exeunt
  praying! Yes, and would vary the established mode of springing off
  with a glance at the pit.   245
SNEER O never mind. So as you get them off, I'll answer for it the
  audience won't care how.
PUFF Well then, repeat the last line standing, and go off the old way.
ALL [*standing*] *And sanctify whatever means we use*
  To gain them.   250
      Exeunt Sir Walter Ralegh, Sir Christopher Hatton, Earl of
      Leicester, the Governor, the Master of the Horse, and Knight
DANGLE Bravo! A fine exit.
SNEER Well, really, Mr Puff—
PUFF Stay a moment.
      The Sentinels get up
FIRST SENTINEL *All this shall to Lord Burghley's ear.*°
SECOND SENTINEL *'Tis meet it should.*   255
      Exeunt Sentinels
DANGLE Hey! Why, I thought those fellows had been asleep?
PUFF Only a pretence. There's the art of it. They were spies of Lord
  Burghley's.
SNEER But isn't it odd they were never taken notice of, not even by
  the commander-in-chief?   260

PUFF O lud, sir, if people who want to listen or overhear were not always connived at in a tragedy, there would be no carrying on any plot in the world.

DANGLE That's certain!

PUFF But take care, my dear Dangle; the morning gun is going to fire. 265
    Cannon fires

DANGLE Well, that will have a fine effect.

PUFF I think so, and helps to realize the scene.°
    Cannon fires twice
What the plague! *Three* morning guns! There never is but one! Ay, this is always the way at the theatre. Give these fellows a good thing, and they never know when to have done with it. You have no more 270 cannon to fire?

PROMPTER (*from within*) No, sir.

PUFF Now then, for soft music.

SNEER Pray what's that for?

PUFF It shows that Tilburina is coming; nothing introduces you a 275 heroine like soft music. Here she comes.

DANGLE And her confidante, I suppose?

PUFF To be sure. Here they are—inconsolable, to the minuet in *Ariadne!*°
    Soft music. Enter Tilburina and Confidante

TILBURINA *Now has the whispering breath of gentle morn°* 280
Bade nature's voice and nature's beauty rise;
While orient Phoebus with unborrowed hues
Clothes the waked loveliness which all night slept
In heavenly drapery! Darkness is fled.
Now flowers unfold their beauties to the sun, 285
And, blushing, kiss the beam he sends to wake them—
The striped carnation, and the guarded rose,°
The vulgar wallflower, and smart gillyflower,°
The polyanthus mean, the dapper daisy,
Sweet William, and sweet marjoram, and all 290
The tribe of single and of double pinks!
Now, too, the feathered warblers tune their notes
Around, and charm the listening grove. The lark!
The linnet! chaffinch! bullfinch! goldfinch! greenfinch!
—But O, to me no joy can they afford! 295
Nor rose, nor wallflower, nor smart gillyflower,
Nor polyanthus mean, nor dapper daisy,
Nor William sweet, nor marjoram—nor lark,

Linnet, nor all the finches of the grove!
PUFF Your white handkerchief, madam.   300
TILBURINA I thought, sir, I wasn't to use that till '*heart-rending woe*'.
PUFF O yes, madam. At '*the finches of the grove*', if you please.
TILBURINA   *—nor lark,*
    Linnet, nor all the finches of the grove!
        Tilburina weeps
PUFF Vastly well, madam!   305
DANGLE Vastly well indeed!
TILBURINA *For, O too sure, heart-rending woe is now*
    The lot of wretched Tilburina!
DANGLE O! 'Tis too much.
SNEER O! It is indeed.   310
CONFIDANTE *Be comforted, sweet lady; for who knows*
    But heaven has yet some milk-white day in store.
TILBURINA *Alas, my gentle Nora,*
    Thy tender youth as yet hath never mourned
    Love's fatal dart. Else wouldst thou know that, when   315
    The soul is sunk in comfortless despair,
    It cannot taste of merriment!
DANGLE That's certain!
CONFIDANTE *But see where your stern father comes;*
    It is not meet that he should find you thus.   320
PUFF Hey, what the plague! What a cut is here! Why, what is become
    of the description of her first meeting with Don Whiskerandos, his
    gallant behaviour in the sea-fight, and the simile° of the canary
    bird?
TILBURINA Indeed, sir, you'll find they will not be missed.°   325
PUFF Very well. Very well!
TILBURINA The cue, ma'am, if you please.
CONFIDANTE *It is not meet that he should find you thus.*
TILBURINA *Thou counsel'st right, but 'tis no easy task*
    For barefaced grief to wear a mask of joy.   330
        Enter Governor
GOVERNOR *How's this? In tears? O Tilburina, shame!*
    Is this a time for maudlin tenderness
    And Cupid's baby woes? Hast thou not heard
    That haughty Spain's Pope-consecrated fleet
    Advances to our shores, while England's fate,   335
    Like a clipped guinea, trembles in the scale!°
TILBURINA *Then is the crisis of my fate at hand!*

I see the fleets approach. I see—

PUFF Now, pray, gentlemen, mind. This is one of the most useful
figures we tragedy writers have,° by which a hero or heroine, in con-   340
sideration of their being often obliged to overlook things that *are*
on the stage, is allowed to hear and see a number of things that are
not.

SNEER Yes; a kind of poetical second-sight!

PUFF Yes.—Now then, madam.   345

TILBURINA   *I see their decks*
Are cleared! I see the signal made!
The line is formed! A cable's length asunder!°
I see the frigates stationed in the rear;
And now I hear the thunder of the guns!   350
I hear the victor's shouts. I also hear
The vanquished groan! And now 'tis smoke. And now
I see the loose sails shiver in the wind!
I see—I see—what soon you'll see—

GOVERNOR *Hold, daughter! Peace! This love hath turned thy brain.*   355
The Spanish fleet thou canst not see, because
It is not yet in sight!

DANGLE Egad, though, the governor seems to make no allowance for
this poetical figure you talk of.

PUFF No, a plain matter-of-fact man. That's his character.   360

TILBURINA *But will you then refuse his offer?*

GOVERNOR *I must. I will. I can. I ought. I do.*

TILBURINA *Think what a noble price—*

GOVERNOR *No more. You urge in vain.*

TILBURINA *His liberty is all he asks—*   365

SNEER All *who* asks, Mr Puff? Who is—

PUFF Egad, sir, I can't tell. Here has been such cutting and slashing,
I don't know where they have got to myself.

TILBURINA Indeed, sir, you will find it will connect very well.
                              —And your reward secure.   370

PUFF O, if they hadn't been so devilish free with their cutting here,
you would have found that Don Whiskerandos has been tamper-
ing° for his liberty and has persuaded Tilburina to make this proposal to her father. And now pray observe the conciseness with
which the argument is conducted. Egad, the pro and con goes as   375
smart as hits° in a fencing match. It is indeed a sort of small-sword
logic, which we have borrowed from the French.°

TILBURINA *A retreat in Spain!*

GOVERNOR *Outlawry here!*

TILBURINA *Your daughter's prayer!*   380

GOVERNOR *Your father's oath!*

TILBURINA *My lover!*

GOVERNOR *My country!*

TILBURINA *Tilburina!*

GOVERNOR *England!*   385

TILBURINA *A title!*

GOVERNOR *Honour!*

TILBURINA *A pension!*

GOVERNOR *Conscience!*

TILBURINA *A thousand pounds!*   390

GOVERNOR *Ha! Thou hast touched me nearly!*

PUFF There you see. She threw in '*Tilburina!*' Quick parry quart with
    '*England!*' Ha! Thrust in tierce '*A title!*' Parried by '*Honour!*' Ha!
    '*A Pension!*' over the arm! Put by '*Conscience!*'. Then flanconade°
    with '*A thousand pounds!*'. And a palpable hit,° egad!   395

TILBURINA *Canst thou*
    Reject the suppliant, *and the* daughter *too?*

GOVERNOR *No more; I would not hear thee plead in vain.*
    The father *softens, but the* governor
    Is fixed!   400

      Exit Governor

DANGLE Ay, that antithesis of persons is a most established figure.°

TILBURINA *'Tis well. Hence then, fond hopes; fond passion, hence.*
    Duty, behold I am all over thine.

WHISKERANDOS (*without*) *Where is my love? My—*

TILBURINA *Ha!*   405

      Enter Don Ferolo Whiskerandos

WHISKERANDOS   *My beauteous enemy?*

PUFF O dear ma'am, you must start a great deal more than that. Con-
    sider you had just determined in favour of duty, when in a moment°
    the sound of his voice revives your passion, overthrows your reso-
    lution, destroys your obedience. If you don't express all that in your   410
    start, you do nothing at all.

TILBURINA Well, we'll try again!

DANGLE Speaking from within has always a fine effect.

SNEER Very.

WHISKERANDOS *My conquering Tilburina! How! Is't thus*   415
    We meet? Why are thy looks averse! What means
    That falling tear, that frown of boding woe?

Ha! Now indeed I am a prisoner!
Yes, now I feel the galling weight of these
Disgraceful chains, which, cruel Tilburina,   420
Thy doting captive gloried in before.
But thou art false, and Whiskerandos is undone!

TILBURINA *O no; how little dost thou know thy Tilburina!*

WHISKERANDOS *Art thou then true? Be gone, cares, doubts and fears.*
I make you all a present to the winds;°   425
And if the winds reject you, try the waves.

PUFF The wind, you know, is the established receiver of all stolen
sighs and cast-off griefs and apprehensions.

TILBURINA *Yet must we part? Stern duty seals our doom.*
Though here I call yon conscious clouds to witness,°   430
Could I pursue the bias of my soul,°
All friends, all right of parents I'd disclaim,
And thou, my Whiskerandos, shouldst be father
And mother, brother, cousin, uncle, aunt,
And friend to me!   435

WHISKERANDOS *O matchless excellence! And must we part?*
Well, if—we must—we must; and in that case
The less is said the better.

PUFF Hey-day! Here's a cut! What, are all the mutual protestations
out?   440

TILBURINA Now, pray, sir, don't interrupt us just here; you ruin our
feelings.

PUFF *Your* feelings! But, zounds, *my* feelings, ma'am!

SNEER No, pray don't interrupt them.

WHISKERANDOS *One last embrace.*

TILBURINA   *Now, farewell forever.*   445

WHISKERANDOS *Forever!*

TILBURINA (*going*) *Ay, forever.*

PUFF 'Sdeath and fury! Gadslife! Sir! Madam! If you go out without
the parting look, you might as well dance out.° Here, here!

CONFIDANTE But pray, sir, how am *I* to get off here?   450

PUFF *You*? Pshaw! What the devil signifies how *you* get off! Edge away
at the top,° or where you will.

          Puff pushes the Confidante off
Now, ma'am, you see—°

TILBURINA We understand you, sir.
Ay, forever.   455

WHISKERANDOS AND TILBURINA (*turning back*) *Oh-h!*
    Exeunt Don Ferolo Whiskerandos and Tilburina. Scene closes°
DANGLE O charming!
PUFF Hey! 'Tis pretty well, I believe. You see I don't attempt to strike
    out° anything new; but I take it I improve on the established modes.
SNEER You do indeed. But pray, is not Queen Elizabeth to appear?   460
PUFF No, not once. But she is to be talked of forever; so that, egad,
    you'll think a hundred times that she is on the point of coming
    in.
SNEER Hang it; I think it's a pity to keep *her* in the green room all the
    night.   465
PUFF O no, that always has a fine effect; it keeps up expectation.
DANGLE But are we not to have a battle?
PUFF Yes, yes, you will have a battle at last; but, egad, it's not to be
    by land, but by sea, and that is the only quite new thing in the
    piece.°   470
DANGLE What, Drake° at the Armada, hey?
PUFF Yes, i'faith, fireships° and all. Then we shall end with the pro-
    cession. Hey! That will do, I think.
SNEER No doubt on't.
PUFF Come, we must not lose time. So now for the underplot.   475
SNEER What the plague! Have you another plot?
PUFF O lord, yes; ever while you live, have two plots to your tragedy.
    The grand point in managing them is only to let your underplot
    have as little connection with your main plot as possible. I flatter
    myself nothing can be more distinct than mine; for as in my chief   480
    plot the characters are all great people, I have laid my underplot in
    low life, and as the former is to end in deep distress, I make the
    other end as happy as a farce.—Now, Mr Hopkins, as soon as you
    please.
    Enter Underprompter
UNDERPROMPTER Sir, the carpenter says it is impossible you can go   485
    to the park scene yet.
PUFF The park scene! No, I mean the description scene here, in the
    wood.
UNDERPROMPTER Sir, the performers have cut it out.
PUFF Cut it out!   490
UNDERPROMPTER Yes, sir.
PUFF What! The whole account of Queen Elizabeth?
UNDERPROMPTER Yes, sir.

PUFF And the description of her horse and side-saddle?

UNDERPROMPTER Yes, sir.   495

PUFF So, so. This is very fine indeed! [*Calling offstage*] Mr Hopkins,
how the plague could you suffer this?

HOPKINS (*from within*) Sir, indeed the pruning knife—

PUFF The pruning knife? Zounds, the axe! Why, here has been such
lopping and topping, I shan't have the bare trunk of my play left   500
presently. Very well, sir. The performers must do as they please;
but, upon my soul, I'll print it every word.°

SNEER That I would indeed.

PUFF Very well, sir. Then we must go on. Zounds, I would not have
parted with the description of the horse! Well, sir, go on. Sir, it was 505
one of the finest and most laboured° things. Very well, sir, let them
go on. There you had him and his accoutrements from the bit to
the crupper. Very well, sir, we must go to the park scene.

UNDERPROMPTER Sir, there is the point. The carpenters say, that
unless there is some business put in here before the drop,° they   510
shan't have time to clear away the fort or sink Gravesend and the
river.°

PUFF So! This is a pretty dilemma truly!° [*To Dangle and Sneer*]
Gentlemen, you must excuse me; these fellows will never be ready,
unless I go and look after them myself.   515

SNEER O dear sir, these little things will happen.

PUFF To cut out this scene! But I'll print it; egad, I'll print it every
word!

    Exeunt

3.1

Before the curtain

Enter Puff, Sneer and Dangle

PUFF Well, we are ready. Now then for the justices.

    Curtain rises. Justices, Constables, etc., discovered°

SNEER This, I suppose, is a sort of senate scene.°

PUFF To be sure. There has not been one yet.

DANGLE It is the underplot, isn't it?

PUFF Yes. [*To the actors*] What, gentlemen, do you mean to go at once   5
to the discovery scene?°

JUSTICE If you please, sir.

PUFF O very well.—Harkee. I don't choose to say anything more; but,
i'faith, they have mangled my play in a most shocking manner!

DANGLE It's a great pity!   10

PUFF Now then, Mr Justice, if you please.

JUSTICE *Are all the volunteers without?°*

CONSTABLE   *They are.*
  Some ten in fetters, and some twenty drunk.

JUSTICE *Attends the youth, whose most opprobrious fame*
  And clear convicted crimes have stamped him soldier?   15

CONSTABLE *He waits your pleasure, eager to repay*
  The blessed reprieve that sends him to the fields
  Of glory, there to raise his branded hand
  In honour's cause.

JUSTICE   *'Tis well. 'Tis justice arms him!*
  O, may he now defend his country's laws   20
  With half the spirit he has broke them all!
  If 'tis your worship's pleasure, bid him enter.

CONSTABLE *I fly, the herald of your will.*

    Exit Constable

PUFF Quick, sir!°

SNEER But, Mr Puff, I think not only the justice, but the clown seems   25
to talk in as high a style as the first hero among them.

PUFF Heaven forbid they should not in a free country! Sir, I am not
for making slavish distinctions and giving all the fine language to
the upper sort of people.

DANGLE That's very noble in you indeed.   30

    Enter Justice's Lady

PUFF Now pray mark this scene.
LADY *Forgive this interruption, good my love;*
But as I just now passed a prisoner youth
Whom rude hands hither led, strange bodings seized°
My fluttering heart, and to myself I said,   35
'An if our Tom had lived, he'd surely been°
This stripling's height!'
JUSTICE *Ha! Sure some powerful sympathy directs*
Us both.
        Enter Son and Constable
What is thy name?   40
SON *My name's Tom Jenkins. Alias have I none,*
Though orphaned, and without a friend!
JUSTICE *Thy parents?*
SON *My father dwelt in Rochester and was,*
As I have heard, a fishmonger—no more.°   45
PUFF What, sir, do you leave out the account of your birth, parentage
and education?
SON They have settled it so, sir, here.
PUFF O! O!
LADY *How loudly nature whispers to my heart!*   50
Had he no other name?
SON   *I've seen a bill*
Of his, signed Tomkins, creditor.°
JUSTICE *This does indeed confirm each circumstance*
The gipsy told! Prepare!
SON *I do.*   55
JUSTICE *No orphan, nor without a friend art thou.*
I am thy father, here's thy mother, there°
Thy uncle—this thy first cousin, and those°
Are all your near relations!
MOTHER *O ecstasy of bliss!*   60
SON *O most unlooked-for happiness!*
JUSTICE *O wonderful event!*
        Justice, Justice's Wife, and Son faint alternately in each other's
        arms
PUFF There, you see relationship, like murder, will out.°
JUSTICE *Now let's revive; else were this joy too much!*
But come, and we'll unfold the rest within,   65
And thou my boy must needs want rest and food.
Hence may each orphan hope, as chance directs,

To find a father, where he least expects!
    Exeunt Justices, Constables, Justice's Wife, Son, etc.
PUFF What do you think of that?
DANGLE One of the finest discovery-scenes I ever saw. Why, this   70
    underplot would have made a tragedy itself.
SNEER Ay, or a comedy either.
PUFF And keeps quite clear, you see, of the other.
    Enter Scenemen,° taking away the seats
PUFF The scene remains, does it?
SCENEMAN Yes, sir.   75
PUFF You are to leave one chair, you know. But it is always awkward
    in a tragedy, to have you fellows coming in in your playhouse liv-
    eries to remove things. I wish that could be managed better. So now
    for my mysterious yeoman.
    Enter a Beefeater
BEEFEATER *Perdition catch my soul, but I do love thee.°*   80
SNEER Haven't I heard that line before?
PUFF No, I fancy not. Where, pray?
DANGLE Yes, I think there is something like it in *Othello*.
PUFF Gad! Now you put me in mind on't, I believe there is. But that's
    of no consequence! All that can be said is, that two people happened   85
    to hit on the same thought; and Shakespeare made use of it first.
    That's all.
SNEER Very true.
PUFF [*to the Beefeater*] Now, sir, your soliloquy. But speak more to the
    pit, if you please. The soliloquy always to the pit; that's a rule.   90
BEEFEATER *Though hopeless love finds comfort in despair,*
    It never can endure a rival's bliss!
    But soft, I am observed.
    Exit the Beefeater
DANGLE That's a very short soliloquy.°
PUFF Yes; but it would have been a great deal longer if he had not   95
    been observed.
SNEER A most sentimental° beefeater that, Mr Puff.
PUFF Harkee, I would not have you be too sure that he *is* a beefeater.
SNEER What! A hero in disguise?
PUFF No matter; I only give you a hint. But now for my principal   100
    character. Here he comes. Lord Burghley in person! Pray, gentle-
    men, step this way. Softly. I only hope the Lord High Treasurer is
    perfect;° if he is but perfect!
    Enter Burghley. He goes slowly to a chair and sits

SNEER Mr Puff!

PUFF Hush! [*To Burghley*] Vastly well, sir! Vastly well! A most   105
interesting gravity!

DANGLE What, isn't he to speak at all?

PUFF Egad, I thought you'd ask me that. Yes, it is a very likely thing, that
a minister in his situation, with the whole affairs of the nation on his
head, should have time to talk! But hush, or you'll put him out.   110

SNEER Put him out! How the plague can that be, if he's not going to
say anything?

PUFF There's a reason!° Why, his part is to *think*, and how the plague
do you imagine he can *think* if you keep talking?

DANGLE That's very true, upon my word!   115

Burghley comes forward, shakes his head and exits

SNEER He is very perfect indeed. Now, pray what did he mean by that?

PUFF You don't take it?°

SNEER No; I don't, upon my soul.

PUFF Why, by that shake of the head, he gave you to understand that
even though they had more justice in their cause and wisdom in   120
their measures, yet, if there was not a greater spirit shown on the
part of the people, the country would at last fall a sacrifice to the
hostile ambition of the Spanish monarchy.

SNEER The devil! Did he mean all that by shaking his head?

PUFF Every word of it, if he shook his head as I taught him.   125

DANGLE Ah, there certainly is a vast deal to be done on the stage by
dumb show and expression of face, and a judicious author knows
how much he may trust to it.

SNEER O, here are some of our old acquaintance.

Enter Sir Christopher Hatton and Sir Walter Ralegh

SIR CHRISTOPHER My *niece*, and your *niece* too!   130
By heaven, there's witchcraft in't. He could not else°
Have gained their hearts. But see where they approach,
Some horrid purpose lowering on their brows!

SIR WALTER *Let us withdraw and mark them.*

Sir Christopher Hatton and Sir Walter Ralegh withdraw

SNEER What is all this?   135

PUFF Ah, here has been more pruning! But the fact is, these two young
ladies are also in love with Don Whiskerandos. Now, gentlemen,
this scene goes entirely for what we call situation and stage effect,
by which the greatest applause may be obtained without the assistance of language, sentiment or character. Pray mark!   140

Enter the Two Nieces

FIRST NIECE *Ellena here!*
  She is his scorn as much as I; that is
  Some comfort still.
PUFF O dear madam, you are not to say that to her face! *Aside*, ma'am,
  aside. The whole scene is to be *aside.*   145
FIRST NIECE (*aside*) *She is his scorn as much as I; that is*
  Some comfort still!
SECOND NIECE (*aside*) *I know he prizes not Pollina's love,*
  But Tilburina lords it o'er his heart.
FIRST NIECE (*aside*) *But see the proud destroyer of my peace.*   150
  Revenge is all the good I've left.
SECOND NIECE (*aside*) *He comes, the false disturber of my quiet.*
  Now vengeance do thy worst.
      Enter Don Ferolo Whiskerandos
WHISKERANDOS *O hateful liberty, if thus in vain°*
  I seek my Tilburina!
BOTH NIECES   *And ever shalt!*   155
      Sir Christopher Hatton and Sir Walter Ralegh come
      forward
SIR CHRISTOPHER and SIR WALTER *Hold! We will avenge you.*
      The two Nieces draw their two daggers to strike Don Ferolo
      Whiskerandos. The Uncles, at the instant, with their two
      swords drawn, catch their two Nieces' arms and turn the points
      of their swords to Don Ferolo Whiskerandos, who immediately
      draws two daggers and holds them to the two Nieces' bosoms
WHISKERANDOS *Hold you, or see your nieces bleed!*
PUFF There's situation for you! There's an heroic group! You see the
  ladies can't stab Whiskerandos. He durst not strike them for fear of
  their uncles. The uncles durst not kill him, because of their nieces.   160
  I have them all at a deadlock, for every one of them is afraid to let
  go first.
SNEER Why, then they must stand there forever.
PUFF So they would, if I hadn't a very fine contrivance for't. Now
  mind.   165
      Enter the Beefeater with his halberd°
BEEFEATER *In the queen's name I charge you all to drop*
  Your swords and daggers!
      The two Nieces, Sir Christopher Hatton, Sir Walter Ralegh,
      and Don Ferolo Whiskerandos drop their swords and daggers
SNEER That is a contrivance indeed.
PUFF Ay, in the queen's name.

SIR CHRISTOPHER *Come, niece!*   170
SIR WALTER *Come, niece!*
        Exeunt Sir Christopher Hatton and Sir Walter Ralegh with
        the two Nieces
WHISKERANDOS *What's he, who bids us thus renounce our guard?°*
BEEFEATER *Thou must do more: renounce thy love!*
WHISKERANDOS *Thou liest, base beefeater!*
BEEFEATER   *Ha! Hell! The lie!°*
    By heaven, thou'st roused the lion in my heart!   175
    Off yeoman's habit! Base disguise off, off!
        The beefeater discovers himself,° by throwing off his upper dress
        and appearing in a very fine waistcoat
    Am I a beefeater now?
    Or beams my crest as terrible as when°
    In Biscay's Bay I took thy captive sloop?
PUFF There, egad, he comes out to be the very captain of the priva-   180
    teer who had taken Whiskerandos prisoner, and was himself an old
    lover of Tilburina's.
DANGLE Admirably managed indeed.
PUFF Now, stand out of their way.
WHISKERANDOS *I thank thee, fortune, that hast thus bestowed*   185
    A weapon to chastise this insolent.
        Don Ferolo Whiskerandos takes up one of the swords
BEEFEATER *I take thy challenge, Spaniard, and I thank*
    Thee, fortune, too!
        The Beefeater takes up the other sword
DANGLE That's excellently contrived! It seems as if the two uncles
    had left their swords on purpose for them.   190
PUFF No, egad, they could not help leaving them.
WHISKERANDOS *Vengeance and Tilburina!*
BEEFEATER   *Exactly so.*
        The Beefeater and Don Ferolo Whiskerandos fight; and, after
        the usual number of wounds given, Don Ferolo Whiskerandos
        falls
WHISKERANDOS *O cursèd parry! That last thrust in tierce*
    Was fatal. Captain, thou hast fencèd well!
    And Whiskerandos quits this bustling scene   195
    For all eter—°
BEEFEATER *—nity, he would have added, but stern death*
    Cut short his being and the noun at once!

PUFF O, my dear sir, you are too slow. Now mind me.° [*To Don Ferolo*
    Whiskerandos] Sir, shall I trouble you to die again?   200
WHISKERANDOS *And Whiskerandos quits this bustling scene*
    For all eter—
BEEFEATER *—nity, he would have added—*
PUFF No, sir, that's not it. Once more, if you please.
WHISKERANDOS I wish, sir, you would practise this without me; I   205
    can't stay dying here all night.
PUFF Very well, we'll go over it by and by.—[*To Dangle and Sneer*] I
    must humour these gentlemen!
        Exit Don Ferolo Whiskerandos
BEEFEATER *Farewell, brave Spaniard! And when next—*
PUFF Dear sir, you needn't speak that speech, as the body has walked   210
    off.°
BEEFEATER That's true, sir! Then I'll join the fleet.
PUFF If you please.
        Exit the Beefeater
    Now, who comes on?
        Enter Governor, with his hair properly° disordered
GOVERNOR *A hemisphere of evil planets reign!*   215
    And every planet sheds contagious frenzy!°
    My Spanish prisoner is slain! My daughter,
    Meeting the dead corse borne along, has gone
    Distract!
        A loud flourish of trumpets [offstage]
            But hark! I am summoned to the fort.
    Perhaps the fleets have met! Amazing crisis!   220
    O Tilburina! From thy agèd father's beard
    Thou'st plucked the few brown hairs which time had left!
        Exit Governor
SNEER Poor gentleman!
PUFF Yes, and no one to blame but his daughter!
DANGLE And the planets.   225
PUFF True. Now enter Tilburina!
SNEER Egad, the business comes on quick here.
PUFF Yes, sir. Now she comes in stark mad in white satin.°
SNEER Why in white satin?
PUFF O lord, sir, when a heroine goes mad, she always goes into white   230
    satin. Don't she, Dangle?
DANGLE Always; it's a rule.

PUFF (*looking at the book*) Yes, here it is. 'Enter Tilburina, stark mad in white satin, and her confidante, stark mad in white linen.'

    Enter Tilburina and Confidante mad, according to custom

SNEER But, what the deuce, is the confidante to be mad too?   235

PUFF To be sure she is. The confidante is always to do whatever her mistress does—weep when she weeps, smile when she smiles, go mad when she goes mad.—Now, Madam Confidante! But keep your madness in the background, if you please.

TILBURINA *The wind whistles, the moon rises. See*   240
    They have killed my squirrel in his cage!°
    Is this a grasshopper! Ha! No, it is my
    Whiskerandos. You shall not keep him.
    I know you have him in your pocket.
    An oyster may be crossed in love! Who says   245
    A whale's a bird? Ha! Did you call, my love?
    He's here! He's there! He's everywhere!
    Ah me! He's nowhere!

    Exeunt Tilburina and Confidante

PUFF There, do you ever desire to see anybody madder than that?

SNEER Never while I live!   250

PUFF You observed how she mangled the metre?

DANGLE Yes; egad, it was the first thing made me suspect she was out of her senses.

SNEER And pray what becomes of her?

PUFF She is gone to throw herself into the sea° to be sure. And that   255
brings us at once to the scene of action, and so to my catastrophe°—
my sea-fight, I mean.

SNEER What, you bring that in at last?

PUFF Yes, yes, you know my play is *called The Spanish Armada.*
Otherwise, egad, I have no occasion for the battle at all. Now then   260
for my magnificence!°—my battle!—my noise!—and my procession!°—You are all ready?

PROMPTER (*within*) Yes, sir.

PUFF Is the Thames dressed?

    Enter Thames with two Attendants

THAMES Here I am, sir.   265

PUFF Very well indeed. [*To Dangle and Sneer*] See, gentlemen, there's
a river for you! This is blending a little of the masque° with my
tragedy. A new fancy, you know, and very useful in my case; for as
there *must be* a *procession*, I suppose Thames and all his tributary
rivers to compliment Britannia with a fête in honour of the victory.   270

SNEER But pray, who are these gentlemen in green with him?

PUFF Those? Those are his banks.

SNEER His banks?

PUFF Yes, one crowned with alders and the other with a villa!° You   275
take the allusions? But hey! What the plague! [*To Thames*] You have
got both your banks on one side. [*To one of the Attendants*] Here,
sir, come round. Ever while you live, Thames, go between your
banks.°

> *Bell rings*°

There, so! Now for't! [*To Dangle and Sneer*] Stand aside, my dear
friends!—Away, Thames!   280

> *Exit Thames between his banks. Flourish of drums, trumpets,*
> *cannon, etc., etc. Scene changes to the sea. The fleets engage.*
> *The music plays 'Britons, strike home'.° Spanish fleet destroyed*
> *by fireships, etc. English fleet advances. Music plays 'Rule*
> *Britannia'.° The procession of all the English rivers and their*
> *tributaries with their emblems, etc., begins with Handel's*
> *'Water Music';° ends with a chorus to the march in 'Judas*
> *Maccabaeus'.° During this scene Puff directs and applauds*
> *everything. Then—*

PUFF Well, pretty well; but not quite perfect. So, ladies and gentlemen, if you please, we'll rehearse this piece again tomorrow.

> *Curtain drops*

APPENDIX

At the first performance the following sequence was performed in place of 2.1.513–18:

PUFF So, this is a pretty dilemma truly. Do call the head carpenter to me.

UNDERPROMPTER [*calling offstage*] Mr Butler.   515
       Enter Carpenter, dressed [*as a general*]
  Here he is, sir.

PUFF Hey, this the head carpenter?

UNDERPROMPTER Yes, sir. He was to have walked as one of the generals at the review, for the truth is, sir, your tragedy employs everybody in the company.   520

PUFF Then pray, Mr General, or Mr Carpenter, what is all this?

CARPENTER Why, sir, you only consider° what my men have to do. They have got to remove Tilbury Fort with the cannon and to sink Gravesend and the river, and I only desire three minutes to do it in.

PUFF Ah, and they have cut out the scene.   525

CARPENTER Besides, could I manage it in less, I question if the lamplighters could clear away the sun in time.

PUFF [*to the Underprompter*] Do call one of them here.

UNDERPROMPTER [*calling offstage*] Master lamplighter.

[VOICE] (*from without*) Mr Goodwin.   530
       Enter Lamplighter as a river god with a page holding up his
       train

LAMPLIGHTER Here.

PUFF Sir, your most obedient servant.—Who the devil's this?

UNDERPROMPTER The master lamplighter, sir. He does one of the river gods in the procession.

PUFF O, a river god is he?—Well, sir, you want time here, I   535
understand.

LAMPLIGHTER Three minutes at least, sir, unless you have a mind to burn the fort.

PUFF Then they have cut out the scene.

CARPENTER Lord, sir, there only wants a little business to be put in   540
here. Just as long as while we have been speaking will do it.

PUFF What, then, are you all ready now?

PROMPTER (*behind*) Yes, all clear.

PUFF O, then we'll easily manage it.

UNDERPROMPTER Clear the stage. 545

PUFF And do, general, keep a sharp look-out, and beg the river god not to spare his oil in the last scene; it must be brilliant.— Gentlemen, I beg a thousand pardons, but—

SNEER O dear, these little things will happen.

[*Exeunt*]

EXPLANATORY NOTES

The following abbreviations are used in the notes:

BD	Philip H. Highfill, Jr., *et al.*, *A Biographical Dictionary of Actors, Actresses, Musicians, Dancers, Managers and Other Stage Personnel in London, 1660–1800*, 16 vols. (Carbondale and Edwardsville, Ill., 1973–93)
Borsay	Peter Borsay, *The English Urban Renaissance: Culture and Society in the Provincial Town, 1660–1770* (Oxford, 1989)
Butterfield	H. Butterfield, *George III, Lord North and the People 1779–80* (London, 1949)
C	*The Critic*
Crane	Richard Brinsley Sheridan, *The Critic*, ed. David Crane (London, 1989)
D	*The Duenna*
Duthie	Richard Brinsley Sheridan, *The Rivals*, ed. Elizabeth Duthie (London, 1979)
Fiske 1	'A Score for *The Duenna*', *Music and Letters*, 42 (1961), 132–41
Fiske 2	*English Theatre Music in the Eighteenth Century* (London, 1973)
FS	Frances Sheridan, *Plays*, ed. Robert Hogan and Jerry C. Beasley (Newark, NJ, 1984)
F.S.	Full Score.
Hughes	Leo Hughes, *The Drama's Patrons: A Study of the Eighteenth-Century London Audience* (Austin, Tex., and London, 1971)
Koster and Coades	Frances Sheridan, *Memoirs of Miss Sidney Bidulph*, ed. Patricia Koster and Jean Coades (Oxford, 1995)
Langford	Paul Langford, *A Polite and Commercial People: England 1727–1783* (Oxford, 1992)
Letters	Richard Brinsley Sheridan, *Letters*, ed. Cecil Price, 3 vols. (Oxford, 1966)
LGC	London Guildhall Library *Critic* manuscript
Nettleton	Richard Brinsley Sheridan, *The Major Dramas*, ed. George Henry Nettleton (Boston, 1906)
Price	Richard Brinsley Sheridan, *Dramatic Works*, ed. Cecil Price, 2 vols. (Oxford, 1973)
R	*The Rivals*
Rhodes	R. Crompton Rhodes, *Harlequin Sheridan: The Man and the Legend* (Oxford, 1933)
Rhodes ed.	Richard Brinsley Sheridan, *Plays and Poems*, ed. R. Crompton Rhodes, 3 vols. (Oxford, 1928)
Rump	Eric S. Rump, 'Sheridan, Politics, the Navy and Musical

Allusions in the Final Scene of *The Critic'*, *Restoration and 18th Century Theatre Research*, 2nd ser. 6 (1991), 30–4

Russell   Gillian Russell, *The Theatres of War: Performance, Politics, and Society, 1793–1815* (Oxford, 1995)

S.D   stage direction

SS   *The School for Scandal*

Tilley   M. P. Tilley, *A Dictionary of the Proverbs in England in the Sixteenth and Seventeenth Centuries* (Ann Arbor, Mich., 1950)

TS   Thomas Sheridan, *A General Dictionary of the English Language*, 2 vols. (London, 1780)

TTS   *A Trip to Scarborough*

Act, scene, and line references for quotations from the Duke of Buckingham's *The Rehearsal*, Shakespeare's plays, and John Vanbrugh's *The Relapse* in the notes are taken from the following editions:

George Villiers, Duke of Buckingham, *The Rehearsal*, ed. D. E. L. Crane (Durham, 1976)

William Shakespeare, *The Complete Works*, ed. Stanley Wells and Gary Taylor (Oxford, 1986)

Sir John Vanbrugh, *Four Comedies*, ed. Michael Cordner (Harmondsworth, 1989)

When Sheridan was writing the plays gathered here, his father, Thomas Sheridan, was completing work on his *General Dictionary of the English Language*, 2 vols. (London, 1780). His definitions of particular words often provide an interesting slant on his son's use of the same words in his comedies. I have therefore quoted frequently from the *Dictionary* in the following notes.

The Rivals

Preface 1–2 *closet-prologue*: i.e. it performs the same service in introducing, and soliciting a good reception for, the published script as a prologue performs for the play in performance. (In this period a 'closet' was a small, private room where a gentleman or lady might, for instance, sit to read such a work as this.)

2–3 *solicits*: urges, pleads for.

5 *representation*: performance on stage.

6–7 *determined*: settled, conclusively decided.

7–8 *the cooler tribunal of the study*: the judgement of the solitary reader, which is likely to be calmer than is possible amidst the excitements and distractions of theatre performance.

8 *solicitude*: pleading, advocacy.

11–12 *as the procrastination . . . the cause*: i.e. as being like the deferral to a later date of a legal action because the plaintiff knows his case is weak.

20–2 *the withdrawing . . . hasty correction*: for information on the play's early stage history, see Introduction, pp. vii–x.

30 *a young man*: Sheridan was 23 when he wrote *The Rivals*, his first play.

34 *candour*: Sheridan sometimes uses the word in senses close to some of its modern meanings, as, for instance, at line 27 above, where it could reasonably be glossed as meaning 'frankness'. One meaning not current in the period, however, is one familiar to us—i.e. plain speaking, even if the truth communicated hurts its recipient or some third party. The predominant meanings of 'candour' and 'candid' in the 1770s are defined by Donald Davie, 'An Episode in the History of Candour', *PN Review*, 4 (1977), no. 4, 46: '*a candid* person was one who habitually gave others the benefit of the doubt, who thought the best of others until he was compelled to think worse. In this sense, "candour" was for the eighteenth century the name of a very lofty virtue indeed—equivalent indeed to the virtue of Christian *charity*.' William Empson provides a parallel definition: 'A candid person picks out the good points in a person's character and ignores the bad ones, without affectation or design. The judgements are favourable but also unbiased and sincere' (*The Structure of Complex Words* (London, 1951), 309). This phrasing spotlights the intricacy of the mental processes potentially involved and is part of an account of the process by which, in Davie's phrase, both 'candour' and 'candid' became 'suspect words, very problematical' (p. 46) during the last quarter of the eighteenth century. As Empson remarks (p. 307), 'The ingenious lady in *The School for Scandal* [i.e. Mrs Candour] had not Candour but an Affectation of it; however, this was coming to be regarded as a common danger; and the song "Save Oh save me from the candid friend" (1798) amounts to an attack on the word.'

36 *disposition*: willingness, inclination (however imperfectly executed).

41–2 *the uncommon length . . . the first night*: see Introduction, p. vii.

47 *a chasm . . . public*: i.e. a gap in the sequence of performances offered.

49 *Mr Harris's*: Thomas Harris, the manager of the Covent Garden Theatre from 1767 to 1809. In later years he was on occasion Sheridan's business partner, but more normally his chief commercial rival. A canny businessman, he worked on smaller budgets than Drury Lane, usually with fewer performers, but staged more plays. He made less profit; but his organization was not in constant turmoil like Drury Lane's, and his venture was generally more stable. For further information, see Cecil Price, 'Thomas Harris and the Covent Garden Theatre', in Kenneth Richards and Peter Thomson (eds.), *Essays on the Eighteenth-Century Stage* (London, 1972), 105–22.

55 *after the first trial*: after the play had been once tested in performance.

58–9 *no means conversant with plays in general*: an odd statement from a beginning playwright whose father was a prominent actor and had been a distinguished theatre manager in Dublin and whose mother was a playwright. In later life, however, he claimed that being 'tormented by the boys [at Harrow], as a poor player's son' had bred in him 'such an aversion to the stage . . . that, throughout his life, he had never seen a representation from beginning to end, except of his own pieces at rehearsals' (Rhodes, 11).

75 *judgement*: i.e. true unbiased assessment.

77 *virulence of malice*: predetermined malice. Organized and premeditated opposition to a first performance was not unusual in the eighteenth-century theatre. See Hughes, 55 ff.

78 *apprehensive*: conscious, sensible; fearfully anticipatory.

81 *mark*: identify, distinguish.

82 *ungenerous*: unworthy of a gentleman. Cf. lines 96–9 below.

83 *disappointment*: here, being robbed of the anticipated spectacle of Sheridan's anger.

86 *dispense with*: cope with not being the recipient of.

87 *rude*: 'harsh, inclement' (TS).

89 *fiat*: formal authorization, decree (from Latin: 'let it be done').

90 *object*: goal.

95 *spleen-swollen*: inflated by spleen; i.e. vociferously spiteful, dismissive, and angry.

96 *consequence*: importance.

98 *original*: innate.

101–2 *any national reflection . . . O'Trigger*: John Lee's coarse and inadequate playing of Sir Lucius at the first performance of *The Rivals* was a disaster, but critical disapproval also extended to the writing of the role. *The Morning Chronicle* (18 Jan. 1775), for instance, asserted that 'This representation of Sir Lucius is indeed an affront to the common sense of an audience, and is so far from giving the manners of our brave and worthy neighbours, that it scarce equals the picture of a *respectable* Hotentot; gabbling in an uncouth dialect, neither Welch, English, nor Irish.' Before the second performance, the role was effectively re-invented, and the part was also re-cast, with the Irish actor, Clinch, wooing the audience 'by a very gentlemanly brogue, and naiveté of manner' (*The London Evening Post*, 31 Jan.–2 Feb. 1775). *The Morning Chronicle* (30 Jan. 1775) now decreed that the retouching of the role 'wipes off the former stigma undeservedly thrown on the sister kingdom'.

109 *stage-novels*: i.e. sentimental comedies, the vogue for which Sheridan also mocked in the 'Prologue on the tenth night', lines 21–44. It has been

argued that 'cross fertilization between sentimental comedy and the popular novel was a recognized fact in the eighteenth century' and that indeed 'sentimental comedy may have been primarily a reading phenomenon'—hence, 'stage-*novels*'—'whose foothold in the theater was tenuous'. See Richard Bevis, *The Laughing Tradition: Stage Comedy in Garrick's Day* (London, 1980), 33, and *passim*.

115–16 *the principals in a theatre*: the managers. Cf. note to line 49 above.

121 *the precepts of judgement*: critical rules.

The Characters of the Play *Absolute*: authoritarian, imperious, dictatorial, admitting no limit to the exercise of his will.

Faulkland: he shares his name with an ill-fated central figure in the novel by Frances Sheridan, Richard Brinsley's mother, *Memoirs of Miss Sidney Bidulph* (1761). See the note to 5.1.3 S.D. below.

Acres: (1) owner of a landed estate; (2) provincial, without metropolitan polish.

O'Trigger: addicted to quarrelling and duelling (an attribute of the stage Irishman).

Fag: drudge.

Malaprop: from French *mal à propos*, i.e. inappropriate; here, verbally accident-prone.

Languish: pine away with love-sickness; 'look with softness or tenderness' (TS).

Prologue This is the version of the original prologue spoken at the first performance of the revised *Rivals* on 28 Jan. 1775 and printed in the first edition. Cecil Price discovered an incomplete manuscript text of the earlier version of it spoken at the play's very first performance on 17 Jan. 1775 and reprinted it in 'The First Prologue to *The Rivals*', *Review of English Studies*, NS 25 (1969), 192–5.

S.D. *Enter Sergeant-at-law . . . paper*: the prologue develops a legal conceit. At the behest (and payment) of the attorney (in modern terms, a solicitor), the sergeant-at-arms (barrister) works from the brief (a summary of the case) the former has given him and pleads the dramatist's case before the jury (the audience).

1 *cramp hand*: handwriting which is difficult to decipher.

5 *Dibble*: the name of the attorney, as also of a gardening tool used to make holes in which seeds are to be planted. Similarly, the attorney 'seeds' the sergeant-at-law with fees and briefs.

6 *A poet and a fee!*: the connection of poetry with poverty was proverbial.

11 *sons of Phoebus*: poets. Phoebus Apollo was the Greek god of poetry.

12 *the Fleet*: a London prison for debtors and bankrupts.

13–14 *sprig | Of bays*: laurel branch. A wreath of laurel was the traditional reward for poetic distinction. The couplet's meaning is that the barrister's pleading often benefits from some of the poet's inventive and rhetorical skills, and perhaps also that some lawyers themselves dabble in poetry.

15–16 *Full-bottomed heroes . . . | . . . curl*: The reference is to the images of lawyers in flowing wigs 'on signs' outside their premises, advertising their services. In this fantasy their flowing wigs contain a tiny sprig of laurel (sacred to poets and victors).

17–18 *in adverse days, | . . . bays*: lawyers prove much less vulnerable than poets because (1) lawyers earn more than poets; (2) lawyers can defend themselves more easily than poets; and (3) poets may need the lawyer's protective skills. Sheridan had come to London to study law, but abandoned that avenue of advancement with the success of *The Rivals*; so the couplet has a wry personal application.

20 *tie*: lawyer's tie-wig (in which the hair is gathered behind and tied with a ribbon).

23 *flourish*: speak eloquently.

26 *Used to the ground*: (1) being an experienced legal advocate; (2) being accustomed to speak prologues in this theatre.

28–31 *No tricking . . . | . . . Drury Lane*: during a legal trial a barrister's sleight of hand can evade the worst legal consequences for his client, or else he can exploit an error in the proceedings to produce a similar result. In the theatre there is no such escape from an audience's verdict. The dramatist cannot even appeal to another court to set it aside—i.e. Drury Lane (the other patent theatre) will not be interested in a play which has failed at Covent Garden.

33 *costs of suit*: i.e. enough to cover the costs of mounting the performance.

36 *transportation*: the transportation of convicted criminals to penal colonies abroad was a contemporary legal punishment.

39 *My client . . . challenge here*: defence counsel could move the dismissal of potential jurors on grounds of bias. No such right will or can be invoked in the playhouse against members of the audience.

40 *session*: (1) theatre première; (2) sitting of a court of law.

44 *all respecting*: deferring, or paying respect, to all his spectators

45 *voice*: vote

Prologue . . . on the tenth night The profits of the third, sixth, and ninth performances of a play—if it managed to survive that long—came to the dramatist, and in celebration a new prologue was often provided for the ninth performance. The false start *The Rivals* endured, followed by its successful relaunch, seems to have resulted in the original first night not being included in these calculations; so its tenth performance was the dramatist's third benefit, for which Sheridan wrote this prologue.

Mrs Bulkley: this is a departure from the established procedure of having the prologue spoken by a man and is presumably a reward to Mrs Bulkley, who played Julia, and who had been greatly praised for her 'just and elegant manner of speaking' the epilogue—itself much admired—at the first performance (*The Morning Chronicle*, 18 Jan. 1775).

1–2 *Granted our cause ... | ... no more*: with the play an established success, the original prologue's pleading for a kindly reception can now be dispensed with.

3 *pleading*: 'pleasing' (*1775* and Price). For a convincing case for reading 'pleading' here, see Peter Dixon and Vicky Bancroft, 'Sheridan's Second Prologue to *The Rivals*: A Case for Emendation', *Notes and Queries*, 234 (1989), 478–80, and Robert A. H. Smith, 'Sheridan's Second Prologue to *The Rivals*: A Further Note', *Notes and Queries*, 235 (1990), 314–15.

client: 'One who applies to an advocate for counsel and defence' (TS).

7 *on this form*: Mrs Bulkley points to her right, where a life-size relief or cut-out figure of the comic muse, with her 'light mask' (l. 11 below), adorned the Covent Garden proscenium arch.

quaint and fly: ingenious and sharp-witted.

12 *Or hides the conscious blush*: Allardyce Nicoll, *The Garrick Stage: Theatres and Audience in the Eighteenth Century* (Manchester, 1980), 28, reproduces a 1763 drawing of the Covent Garden stage, in which comedy holds her mask with a crooked arm in a way which could suggest either that she was about to don it herself or was offering it to the spectators to conceal the blushes her wit and satire provoke.

11–12 *While her light mask ... | ... provokes*: 'While her light masks or covers Satire's strokes, | All hides the conscious blush, her wit provokes' (Price and *1775*). For the reasons for emending Price's version, see the articles cited in the first note to l. 3 above. ('... or ... or' means '... either ... or'; and 'conscious' means 'guiltily self-aware'.)

17 *Bid her be grave*: if one were to tell her to be grave.

23 *Her emblems view*: this, and the following lines, suggest that some representation of the 'sentimental muse' may have been provided on stage. Unlike comedy and tragedy (see notes to ll. 7 and 41), her figure did not permanently adorn the Covent Garden proscenium arch.

24 *'The Pilgrim's Progress' and a sprig of rue*: John Bunyan's enormously popular Christian allegory (1678–84) and the plant which is traditionally

an emblem of sorrow and repentance are offered by Sheridan as fit symbols of the lachrymosely moralistic comedy he mocks.

28 *her sister's*: tragedy's (the sister dramatic genre to comedy). In Sheridan's account, sentimental comedy erodes the traditional generic distinctions which separate comedy and tragedy. The logical conclusion is that in due course its conclusions will turn as bloody as tragedy's (ll. 32–4). For an authoritative account of how Sheridan's mockery of sentimental comedy fits within a larger critical trend in the 1770s, see Robert D. Hume, 'Goldsmith and Sheridan and the Supposed Revolution of "Laughing" against "Sentimental" Comedy', in *The Rakish Stage: Studies in English Drama, 1660–1800* (Carbondale and Edwardsville, Ill., 1983), 312–58.

31–4 *Harry Woodward . . . | . . . Green*: all the performers named played roles in *The Rivals*.

41 *their favourite*: the figure of tragedy decorated the opposite arch at Covent Garden to that which displayed comedy.

1.1. S.D. *Bath*: in 1775 Bath was the 'queen of the spas' and 'the most fashionable of all provincial towns'. It 'had burst its traditional physical limits, filling the surrounding orchards, fields, and hills with some of the most urbane classical architecture to be found in Europe'. It was also 'a consumer's paradise, with an expanding volume and variety of fine craftsmen and retailers' (Borsay, 31–2 and 35).

S.D. *Coachman crosses the stage*: 'The stage direction at the very start of *The Rivals*, "Coachman crosses the stage", has been taken as a merry, private reference to a prank of his courting days, when he disguised himself as a coachman in order to be with his forbidden love, Elizabeth' (Katharine Worth, *Sheridan and Goldsmith* (London, 1992), 120). Certainly Sheridan's own experience of a long courtship, filled with jealousy, self-doubts, and family quarrels—and the public notoriety it caused, via a sensational elopement to France and Sheridan's two duels with another of Elizabeth Linley's suitors—are part of the comedy's hinterland.

2 *Od's*: an abbreviated form of 'God's' (used in softened oaths).

old: long-established, of long acquaintance. Fag is usually played by a young actor.

4 *Excuse my glove*: Fag is pulling rank on the Coachman, as he does later (l. 34 below) in assuming that his fellow-servant will not share Fag's ability to read. Cf. also his comments at 2.1.20–1.

10 *Ay!*: 'used either for "yes" or, as here, for emphasis, "certainly"' (Duthie).

10–13 *Master thought . . . warning*: the imminent recurrence of Sir Anthony's gout—'A periodical disease attended with great pain' (TS)—made him decide urgently on a trip to the famous spa town with its medicinal waters.

30 *trusted you*: confided secrets to you.

33 *L-O-V-E*: 'LOVE' (*1775*); i.e. Fag condescendingly spells it out to his fellow servant. Dolby's acting edition (1814) indicates what is required phonetically: 'EL O VE EE'.

35 *Jupiter*: the chief of the ancient Roman gods, who donned numerous disguises to make love to mortal women. Sheridan had revised *Ixion*, a burlesque play by his friend Nathaniel Halhed, in which Jupiter wooed Major Amphitryon's wife. See Price, ii. 793–6.

41 *half-pay*: in the eighteenth-century 'some two-thirds of the commissions held in the British Army were had by purchase . . . If an officer wished to retire from active service, but keep some part of his pay and retain his investment without selling, he went on to the "half-pay list". Here he kept himself "on reserve" as it were, ready to return on active service if called and hence given half pay as a retaining fee' (J. A. Houlding, *Fit for Service: The Training of the British Army, 1715–1795* (Oxford, 1981), 100–1).

46 *the stocks*: government stock, sold to fund the national debt.

48 *out of gold*: off gold plate.

51 *has a set of thousands*: 'A team of six horses worth thousands of pounds' (Nettleton).

52 *draw kindly with*: work well in harness with (a coachman's term); i.e. get on well with. Thomas's language elsewhere in the scene bears the signs of his trade, as, for example, at ll. 32 and 58.

63 *the Pump Room*: the room in which the spa's waters were dispensed to those who sought relief from them, and also a place of general social assembly. For one account of a visit there at 'eight in the morning', see Tobias Smollett, *The Expedition of Humphry Clinker*, ed. Angus Ross (Harmondsworth, 1967), 68–9.

64 *the Parades*: the splendid North and South Parades, which ran parallel to each other near the River Avon, were constructed in the 1740s and soon became 'the principal place of public resort in the city' (Borsay, 166).

66–7 *Their regular hours . . . after eleven!*: regulations, dating from the long and formative reign of Beau Nash (1705–61) as Master of Ceremonies at Bath, constrained all public assemblies to end by 11 p.m., though private visiting could be prolonged beyond that.

67 *gentleman*: personal servant, valet.

70 *Du Peigne*: 'of the comb' (French), reflecting the servant's nationality.

72 *polish*: acquire social refinement.

73–4 *a wig, Thomas?*: 'Up to the 1770s it was unfashionable for men not to wear a wig; then suddenly even a tonnish servant such as Fag in Sheridan's *The Rivals* would not have been seen dead wearing one' (Roy Porter, *English Society in the Eighteenth Century* (Harmondsworth, 1982), 166).

78 *Od rabbit it!*: God drat (= damn) it!

78–9 *When the fashion . . . the box!*: i.e. when the legal profession had adopted the fashion, I knew it would inevitably be taken up by coachmen (who sat on 'the box' at the front of the coach). (The play on 'got foot' and 'mount' blithely treats the coachmen as if they were the lawyers' social superiors.)

84–5 *they . . . ben't . . . tho'ff*: those . . . aren't . . . though (dialect).

85–6 *Jack Gauge the exciseman*: he would use the 'gauge' to measure the capacity of beer, wine, and spirits casks in order to calculate the duty to be levied on them.

86 *his carrots*: his own red colour of hair.

87 *college*: i.e. of doctors or surgeons.

89 *hold—mark!*: wait—look!

94 *Gyde's Porch*: 'Gyde kept the old (or lower) assembly rooms on the Lower Walks' (Price), which also had a handsome garden and a secluded walk along the river. They had been redecorated to keep up with current fashion in the early 1770s.

1.2.1 *transferred*: this is the reading of *1775*, which has been glossed as 'crossed, walked over', though *OED* offers no authority for such an intransitive usage. It could also be *1775*'s mistranscription of 'traversed', a thought encouraged by the substitution of that verb at this point in *1776* (from corrections usually assumed to be Sheridan's). But, as Price (i. 64) pointed out, Sheridan, 'sensitive to the connection between vocabulary and social standing', was unlikely to allow a maidservant who did not know the meaning of 'sal volatile' to use so literary a word as 'traversed', though that, of course, might be part of her feigned 'simplicity'. He therefore surmised that it could be 'the compositor's misreading of Sheridan's scribbled insertion of the much commoner word "traips'd"'.

2 *circulating library*: 'Circulating libraries were ideally suited to a public pursuing reading as a recreation. . . . Such establishments were especially popular in the resorts, where there was plenty of spare time to be filled. . . . At Bath the libraries became places of resort in their own right' (Borsay, 134).

4 *The Reward of Constancy*: no book with quite this title has been identified; but since all the other books mentioned in the scene are real it seems unlikely that this one is invented. Nettleton proposed that the reference was to 'the sub-title of *The Happy Pair; or, Virtue and Constancy rewarded. A Novel. By Mr Shebbeare*—noticed in the *Supplement to The Universal Magazine* (January–June, 1771)'.

6 *The Fatal Connection*: '(1773), by Mrs. Fogerty', identified by Nettleton, who quotes the verdict of *The London Magazine* (Sept. 1773)—'Romantic nonsense, as usual'—and the claim of *The Monthly Review* (Aug. 1773)

348

that 'Surely Mrs. Fogerty was begotten, born, nursed, and educated in a circulating library, and sucked in the spirit of romance with her mother's milk.'

8 *The Mistakes of the Heart*: by Pierre Henri Treyssac de Vergy (1769). Nettleton quotes *The Town and Country Magazine* (Apr. 1769): 'This writer imitates Rousseau and Richardson. His performance is not without merit, and we might commend it to the ladies if there were not some scenes too luxuriant for the eye of delicacy.'

9 *Mr Bull*: 'Lewis Bull, who also sold books and knick-knacks. His shop was opposite Gyde's rooms on the Lower Walks' (Duthie).

9–10 *Miss Sukey Saunter*: her name—'Sukey' is a diminutive form of Susan—was used to sign a letter in *The Morning Post* (3 Feb. 1775), rebuking Sheridan for his 'unjust, and very impertinent' attack in *The Rivals* on circulating libraries and for inconsistency in 'his sentiments' (Nettleton).

11 *The Delicate Distress*: by Elizabeth Griffith (1769), described in *The Monthly Review* (Sept. 1769) as 'an interesting tale, embellished with an agreeable variety of characters' (Nettleton).

12 *The Memoirs of Lady Woodford*: anonymous (1771). *The Monthly Review* (June 1771) reported that 'Tenderness and simplicity are the principal characteristics of this innocent novel' (Nettleton).

13–14 *Mr Frederick's*: William Frederick had a shop at 18 The Grove. By 1770 he had 'amassed 9,000 books and 1,000 modern novels and romances' (Phyllis Hembry, *The English Spa 1560–1815: A Social History* (London, 1990), 149).

15 *dog's-eared it*: turned down the corners of its pages; made it worn or grubby.

22 *The Gordian Knot*: by Richard Griffith, husband of Elizabeth (1769), and published as the second half of a four-volume set with *The Delicate Distress*. To *The Monthly Review* (Sept. 1769) it seemed 'a more complicated and more elaborate, but less sprightly and less pleasing history' than his wife's work (Nettleton).

Peregrine Pickle: *The Adventures of Peregrine Pickle* (1751) by Tobias Smollett. Some readers and reviewers criticized the overt vulgarity of many of its episodes—for example, one in which Peregrine bores holes in his aunt's chamber-pot—and in 1758 Smollett published a revised and expurgated version of the novel. There is nothing to indicate which version Lydia is reading.

23 *The Tears of Sensibility*: four novels translated from the French of Baculard D'Arnoud by John Murdoch (1773). Nettleton gathers varied contemporary opinions, including the comment, from *The Monthly Review* (Apr. 1773), that 'The Author aims, for the most part, to keep his

Readers on the rack. He deals only in those virtues and vices which aston-ish and exercise our sensibility in the extreme. He therefore defeats his own purpose. A tale made up wholly of wonders, never excites admira-tion; and a novel, which in every page is to harrow up the soul, leaves it in great quietness.'

23 *Humphry Clinker*: by Tobias Smollett, his final novel, published in 1771, the year of his death. Part of its action is set in Bath.

23–4 *The Memoirs . . . by Herself*: a central and detachable segment of Smol-lett's *Peregrine Pickle*, comprising scandalous recollections of the life and love affairs of Lady Vane, published with her consent and assistance, and perhaps partly drafted by her. The novelist Samuel Richardson judged them 'the very bad Story of a wicked woman'.

25 *The Sentimental Journey*: by Laurence Sterne (1768); enormously popular, but also controversial. Sterne died soon after its publication, and *The London Magazine*'s posthumous review of the book judged 'that Sterne, when he appeared before his Maker, needed the help of a record-ing angel whose tears would blot out his sins' (Arthur H. Cash, *Laurence Sterne: The Later Years* (London and New York, 1986), 332–3).

26 *glass*: mirror.

27 *The Whole Duty of Man*: an enormously popular religious conduct book, attributed to Richard Allestree, and originally published in 1659. It went through many editions in the eighteenth century. In an early treatise, Sheridan recommended its use in the education of girls (*Letters*, i. 56). J. R. Moore suggested, in *Notes and Queries*, 202 (1957), that Sheridan is recollecting an incident in Daniel Defoe's *The Family Instructor*, in which a 'mother had burned her elder daughter's sentimental and licentious books, and had replaced them with a prayer-book, *The Practice of Piety*, and *The Whole Duty of Man*'.

40 *You were denied to me at first*: i.e. the servants initially told her that Lydia was not receiving visits.

44 *wait on*: visit, pay his respects to.

dressed: i.e. changed out of his travelling clothes.

48 *connection*: relationship; dealings.

49 *intercourse*: relationship; association.

52 *Lady Macshuffle's rout*: a 'rout' was a large evening party or reception; and the hostess, as her name suggests, was an Irish lady who was a slow and rather dragging dancer.

56 *a Delia or a Celia*: conventional names for a mistress in pastoral and love poetry. Sheridan used Delia as a romantic name for Elizabeth Linley during their courtship.

61 *teased*: often in this period a verb of stronger meanings than now; so, here, 'harassed, tormented'.

63 *interest*: influence; friendship.

72 *paying his addresses to*: wooing.

84 *till of age:* i.e. before her twenty-first birthday.

93 *resolution*: decision (to come to Bath).

95–6 *your own mistress . . . Sir Anthony*: Unlike Lydia, she is 'of age' (cf. note to l. 84 above), and therefore able to determine her own marriage choice without financial consequences. Until marriage, however, she remains under the protection of her guardian, Sir Anthony.

100 *contracted*: formally engaged.

101 *consequent embarrassments*: subsequent difficulties. This is presumably her euphemistic way of referring to the problems caused by Faulkland's temperament. 'Embarrassments' was most frequently used of financial difficulties; but that seems inappropriate to the comfortable circumstances of both Julia and Faulkland.

103 *generous*: 'noble of mind, magnanimous, open of heart' (TS); i.e. showing the characteristics which prove Faulkland to be 'Not of mean birth, of good extraction', another of TS's glosses for this adjective.

107 *unhackneyed*: inexperienced; i.e. the passion is still fresh and new to him.

111 *return*: reciprocation; response.

114 *temper*: temperament, mental disposition.

100–17 *Nay, you are wrong . . . his attachment*: Sheridan, seeing Julia's account of Faulkland's character had been cut in an acting text *c.*1787, is reputed to have entered this marginal comment in the manuscript: 'The only speech in the play that cannot be omitted. The pruning-knife, Damme, the Axe! the Hatchet' (Rhodes, 144). Cf. Puff's exclamation in matching circumstances (*C* 2.1.498).

135 *paying my respects to Mrs Malaprop*: making a courtesy call on Mrs Malaprop (on Julia's arrival in Bath).

136 *her select words . . . mispronounced*: cf. the description of Mrs Tryfort in Frances Sheridan's *A Journey to Bath*, 1.5: ''tis the vainest poor creature, and the fondest of hard words, which without *mis*calling, she always takes care to misapply' (FS 168). Sheridan's conception of Mrs Malaprop is generally indebted to the character in his mother's play.

139 *coz*: friend (an abbreviation of 'cousin'; but often used in the period, as here, between close acquaintances not related by blood).

144 *Roderick Random*: *The Adventures of Roderick Random*, Smollett's first novel, published in 1748. An enormously popular work, it had reached its eighth London edition by 1770.

145 *The Innocent Adultery*: a translation (probably Samuel Croxall's 1722 one) of Paul Scarron's *L'Adultère Innocente*, 'a thoroughly indecent romance' (Nettleton). For a rake's use of this book in an adulterous escapade, see

William Congreve's *The Old Bachelor* (1693), 4.4, a play Sheridan revived early in his management of Drury Lane.

146 *Lord Aimworth*: '*The History of Lord Aimworth, and the Honourable Charles Hartford, Esq., in a Series of Letters*. By the author of *Dorinda Catsby*, and *Ermina, or the Fair Recluse*, 3 vols. (1773)' (Price).

Ovid: there were numerous eighteenth-century translations of Ovid's poetry, especially the *Metamorphoses*; but perhaps Lydia is most likely to be reading his love poems, especially the *Amores (Loves)* and the *Ars Amatoria (The Art of Love)*.

147 *The Man of Feeling*: by Henry Mackenzie (1771); an immediate success, and often reprinted. For Robert Burns, this novel of sentiment was 'a book I prize next to the Bible'. Sir Walter Scott described the title character as 'a hero constantly obedient to every emotion of his moral sense'.

148 *Mrs Chapone*: her *Letters on the Improvement of the Mind. Addressed to a young Lady* were published in two volumes in 1773. Their subjects (Nettleton) included 'the regulation of the heart and affections', 'the government of the temper', 'oeconomy', 'politeness and accomplishments', 'geography and chronology', and 'the manner, and course of reading history'. Most aptly to the present context, as *The Gentleman's Magazine* (May 1773) noted, they were 'addressed from an aunt to her niece'. It also observed that their 'language is the language of the heart; and the instructions are conveyed in so kind and engaging a manner, that they cannot fail of being extensively useful'. According to *The Monthly Review* (July 1773), 'these letters have a tendency to do much more essential service than the general run of novels and romances'. For a recent discussion of the *Letters*, see Sylvia Harcstark Myers, *The Bluestocking Circle: Women, Friendship, and the Life of the Mind in Eighteenth-Century England* (Oxford, 1990), 229–39.

Fordyce's Sermons: *Sermons to Young Women*, 2 vols. (1765) by James Fordyce, a Presbyterian cleric. They were in their seventh edition by 1771. Much preoccupied with fallen women, they 'are probably as erotically charged as the "lewd" sentimental novels which he believed made the woman who read them a prostitute in her heart' (Koster and Coades, pp. xxvii–xxviii). For the argument that this passage is recollected in another Lydia's response to the same book in Jane Austen's *Pride and Prejudice*, see the articles by E. E. Phare and Frank W. Bradbrook, respectively, in *Notes and Queries*, 209 (1964), 182–3 and 421–3.

150 *torn away*: i.e. the pages have been used to make curl papers, employed instead of hair-rollers.

152–3 *Lord Chesterfield's Letters*: *Letters to his Son* (1774), by Philip Stanhope, 4th Earl of Chesterfield. Their publication provoked a storm of controversy, including Samuel Johnson's famous judgement that 'they teach the morals of a whore, and the manners of a dancing-master'. Mrs Chapone—see note to l. 148 above—had also published criticism of them. The book might therefore seem an odd choice for Lydia to display for her aunt to see; but the answer may lie in Sheridan's criticism elsewhere of Chesterfield's 'insistence on absolute parental authority' (Jack D. Durant, *Richard Brinsley Sheridan* (Boston, 1975), 21–2).

154 *deliberate*: TS offers two relevant meanings: (1) 'circumspect, wary', in which case Mrs Malaprop speaks ironically, and (2) 'slow'.

161 *illiterate*: for, obliterate. But it also sounds like Mrs Malaprop's inspired application of the adjective as a verb—i.e. if Lydia were unable to read and hence uninfluenced by romantic fantasies, Ensign Beverley would mean nothing to her. Sheridan's mother had been forbidden by her father to learn the alphabet or how to write; her brothers defied his orders and surreptitiously taught her. Cf. Sir Anthony's opinions on the subject, ll. 193–6 below.

169 *pretend*: profess, claim; plan.

172 *extirpate*: for, extricate or exculpate; 'extirpate' means 'kill, exterminate'.

173 *controvertible*: for, incontrovertible. But she speaks wiser than she knows, since 'controvertible' means 'debatable'.

175 *friends*': 'relatives'.

177 *my aversion*: an object of repugnance to me.

182 *are sensible*: know, are conscious of.

184 *unknown what tears I shed!*: she means, officially at least, (1) I shed my tears in secret and/or (2) the tears I shed were innumerable, but contrives also to say (3) I didn't shed any tears.

187–8 *belie . . . belie*: misrepresent . . . give the lie to.

192 *intricate*: sometimes glossed as a mistake for 'ingrate' (=ungrateful); but 'intricate' meaning 'perplexingly complex, therefore deceitful' fits her feelings very well.

197–8 *absolute misanthropy*: the adjective plays—deliberately or inadvertently—on Sir Anthony's surname. See Introduction, pp. x–xi. 'Misanthropy' (the condition) should be 'misanthrope' (the individual); but then that too may be a mistake for 'misogynist'.

201 *half-bound volumes, with marble covers*: 'with the spine and corners bound in leather, and the rest covered in marbled paper; i.e. novels' (Duthie).

205–6 *an evergreen tree of diabolical knowledge*: a compacted allusion to two famous biblical passages: Genesis 2: 17 and Psalms 37: 35.

209 *laconically*: for, ironically. 'Laconically' means 'tersely, concisely'.

212 *Observe me*: listen to me, pay careful attention to what I say.

213 *progeny*: perhaps, for prodigy; though 'progeny' meaning 'offspring' makes a kind of sense here—i.e. no daughter of Mrs Malaprop's should

make pretensions to learning. The same solecism is committed by Mrs Tryfort in Frances Sheridan's *A Journey to Bath* (FS 175).

215 *simony*: simony is the buying and selling of church offices. Perhaps she intends 'cyclometry' (measurement of circles) or 'ciphering' (working with numbers, arithmetic).

216 *fluxions*: 'in mathematicks, the arithmetick or analysis of infinitely small variable quantities' (TS); though another meaning ('constant change-ability') is probably in her thoughts.

paradoxes: TS defines 'paradox' as 'A tenet contrary to received opinion', which renders it unnecessary to assume, as numerous editors have done, that its use here is a mistake and that Mrs Malaprop intended 'parallaxes', a parallax being 'the distance between the true and apparent place of any star viewed from the earth' (TS).

inflammatory: arousing, stimulating, tending to heat the blood and arouse the senses.

220 *ingenuity and artifice*: both words have positive and negative senses. Mrs Malaprop intends the former, but the latter are apt to Lydia's handling of her. Thus, 'ingenuity' could mean 'wit, invention', or 'fraud, cunning', and 'artifice' 'skill, art', or 'trick, ability to deceive'.

221 *supercilious*: for, superficial.

222 *geometry*: for, geography.

223 *contagious*: for, contiguous. But 'contagious' may reflect very well Mrs Malaprop's sense of the dangers which may flow in from abroad (as, for instance, in translations of French romances).

224 *orthodoxy*: for, orthography; though perfect obedience to decorum is indeed what she desires of Lydia.

226 *reprehend*: for, apprehend. But also present is the idea that this ideal Lydia would 'reprehend' much of what the present Lydia proudly pronounces.

228 *superstitious*: presumably for, superfluous. But the word also meant '(too) fastidious, punctilious' and in context here could be read as 'conserva-tive, backward-looking'.

235–6 *no positive ... Mr Acres*: i.e. no irretrievable commitment to marry Lydia to Mr Acres.

249 *conciliating*: restoring to amicability and peace by soothing treatment. Mrs Malaprop is either being ironic or needed a word like 'pacifying' or 'subduing'.

251 *invocations*: i.e. lover's supplications, as to a goddess.

252 *illegible*: for, ineligible. But 'illegible' meaning 'indecipherable, incom-prehensible' is lurking in Mrs Malaprop's mind somewhere.

260 *intuition*: for, tuition. But also at work here is her resentment that Lydia intuits so much about her aunt's feelings.

263 *artifical*: some editors have judged this a slip for 'artful'; but 'artificial' could itself mean 'cunning, skilful', hence 'deceitful'.

272 *presently*: immediately.

275 *malevolence*: for, benevolence.

276 *locality*: for, loquacity.

284 *twelve*: i.e. shillings.

286 *a quarter's pay*: three months' pay (for Lucy, not the ensign). The latter would earn £60–65 per year.

291 *gold pocket-pieces*: 'coins no longer current, or similar small objects, carried as lucky charms' (Duthie).

2.1.21 *'recruit'*: in three meanings: (1) enlist 'men' for the army; (2) obtain new 'money' by marriage with an heiress; (3) restore health ('constitution') by relaxation and pleasure at Bath.

25–6 *to give the thing an air*: to lend the lie plausibility and style.

26–7 *disbanded chairmen*: dismissed or unemployed carriers of sedan-chairs. The latter were a favoured mode of transport at Bath.

27 *minority waiters*: 'minority' has sometimes here been glossed as 'out of employment'; but a more plausible possibility is 'very young or junior'— i.e. at the bottom of the servants' hierarchy, and so vulnerable to being tempted into an apparently more exciting life.

27–8 *billiard-markers*: billiard-scorers.

31–3 *whenever I . . . the bill*: Fag compares his invention and amplification of the 'recruiting' lie to the forging of a bill of credit (or cheque), where the forger also fakes extra supporting signatures testifying to, and guaranteeing, the bill's reliability.

47 *character*: public reputation (the word's most frequent meaning in these plays)

52 *mistress*: i.e. Julia, Faulkland's fiancée.

64 *character*: identity.

70 *the reversion . . . my side*: my anticipated inheritance, on my father's death, of a good fortune.

83–4 *my sum . . . this cast:* my entire happiness on this one throw of the dice.

96–7 *aspiration*: breath; therefore, movement.

131 *Od's whips and wheels*: the first of Acres's 'referential' oaths (l. 286 below), whereby the objects he invokes in swearing accord with the subject which currently preoccupies him.

132 *the Mall*: tree-bordered walk alongside St James's Park in London.

137 *solicit your connections*: desire to know you better.

146 *the German Spa*: the name of a continental town with mineral springs (now in Belgium), which lent its name as a generic term for other such resorts.

164 *crickets*: Acres has the insect's proverbial merriment in mind. Cf. Tilley, C825.

185 *squallante . . . quiverante*: Acres manufactures mock-Italian musical terms from squalling, rumbling, and quivering (none of them as complimentary as he presumably intends).

185–6 *this time month*: a month ago.

187 *Piano's*: in musical terminology, 'piano' means 'soft, quiet'.

190 *Is not . . . love?*: he is recalling the opening line of Shakespeare's *Twelfth Night*: 'If music be the food of love, play on'.

194–5 *purling stream*: a hackneyed phrase from pastoral and love poetry.

196 *'When absent . . . delight'*: the sixth song from *Twelve Songs set to Music by William Jackson of Exeter: Opera Quarta* (London, n.d.), 14–19. Its first stanza reads: 'When absent from my soul's delight, | What terrors fill my troubled breast; | Once more returned to thy loved sight, | Hope too returns, my fears have rest'.

198 *'Go, gentle gales!'*: the fifth song in Jackson's *Twelve Songs*. The words, with some variations, derive from the third of Alexander Pope's *Pastorals* (1709), ll. 17–22. The relevant section is the song of Hylas for his absent love. Jackson's first two stanzas read: 'Go, gentle gales; go, gentle gales, | And bear my sighs away; | To Delia's ear, to Delia's ear, | The tender notes convey. | As some sad turtle his long-lost love deplores | And with deep murmurs fills the sounding shores, | Thus far from Delia to the wood I mourn, | Alike unheard, unpitied, and forlorn.'

200 *My heart's . . . free*: the third air in the first scene of Isaac Bickerstaff's enormously popular *Love in a Village* (1762), it is sung by Rosetta, who has run away from her 'parents to avoid an odious marriage' and is now being pursued by an elderly seducer she disdains. Its complete text is as follows: 'My heart's my own, my will is free, | And so shall be my voice; | No mortal man shall wed with me, | Till first he's made my choice. | Let parents rule, cry nature's laws, | And children still obey; | And is there then no saving clause | Against tyrannic sway?' Price cites in this connection a passage from *The Gazetteer*, 21 Sept. 1771: the 'ill-effects, which romance and novel-reading, has upon the minds of the fair sex has been often and justly exposed; but there is another part of their study, which, is in my opinion, of a similar nature . . . I mean the fashionable songs and airs which young ladies are taught from their childhood to sing, and get by heart'. Price reports that the author 'mentions "My heart's my own" as among the fifteen that seem to him to be "extravagant" and "inflammatory"'.

202 *pipe and balladmonger*: i.e. her musical taste is coarse and lowly—on a level with street-ballads—and she is behaving as if she were a professional entertainer. *OED*'s first recorded use of 'balladmonger' is

Hotspur's contemptuous use of it—'these same metre ballad-mongers'—in *1 Henry IV*, 3.1.126, a passage probably in Sheridan's mind here.

214 *race-ball*: regular series of horse-races were key features of the social calendar at major provincial cities and were accompanied by lavish entertainments, including balls.

221 *expose yourself so*: lay yourself open to ridicule in this way.

227 *insure her for that*: vouch for her ability at that.

228 *minuet . . . country dancing*: a minuet is a slow, stately dance for two, whereas in country dancing couples stood in long lines opposite each other and then mingled and exchanged partners. It is this swapping and promiscuous mingling which alarm Faulkland. It is also relevant that Mrs Bulkley, who played Julia, had by 1775 achieved most applause for her brilliance as a dancer.

swimmings: 'swimming' could mean 'a smooth gliding movement' or 'dizziness, giddiness', either or both of which would be apt here.

234 *cotillion*: an eighteenth-century French social dance with elaborate steps and figures.

235 *monkey-led*: i.e. led in the dance by dandies and fops (mere apes of fashion).

235-6 *To run the gauntlet*: i.e. to dance with one's partner between two rows of other dancers. The phrase derives from the military and naval punishment in which the victim runs between two lines of his fellows who strike out at him with sticks or knotted cords. In Faulkland's perfervid imagination, the other dancers—those 'amorous palming puppies' (l. 236)—reach out to a willing Julia with a different kind of design on her body. ('Palming' means (1) touching or stroking with the palm and (2) deceitful, capable of trickery.)

237 *managed*: of a horse: put through the exercises of the *manège*, i.e. 'the strict practice of the riding school' (Price); hence, here, performing obligingly at the behest, and to the command, of the 'amorous palming puppies'.

238 *delicate*: fastidious.

245-6 *The atmosphere . . . chain!*: Price offers a helpful quotation from *A New and Complete Dictionary of Arts and Sciences* (2nd edn., 1763), 1050: 'These exhalations, or subtle effluvia, constitute electricity . . . They seem to adhere to the extremities of the bodies which they surround, and from which they recede, in the form of sparks'. TS's definition of 'electricity' is also relevant: 'A property in bodies, whereby, when rubbed, they draw substances, and emit fire'. (There is also a pun on 'spark': (1) electrical phenomenon; (2) fine gentleman.)

262 *forestalled me*: i.e. tied me down from pursuing other women. In eighteenth-century usage 'to forestall someone' was 'to seize or gain possession of (some thing or person) before another'.

264 *frogs and tambours*: a 'frog' was an ornamental coat-fastening, and a 'tambour' was either an embroidery-frame or embroidery done using such a frame.

264–5 *ancient madam*: Bob's mother.

266–7 *cashier . . . incapable*: i.e. discard the country clothes he is still wearing. He is thus behaving in line with the social agenda established at Bath by Beau Nash, by which he used 'negative propaganda . . . to stigmatize rural dress and habits' (Borsay, 261).

270 *kindly*: naturally.

273 *triggers and flints*: the reference is to firearms, since Bob intends to challenge Beverly to a duel. The flint produced the spark which ignited the gunpowder and fired the bullet.

277 *genteel*: gentlemanlike, fashionable (not ironic or deprecatory).

278 *militia*: auxiliary military force raised from the civilian population in each county.

283–4 *according to the sentiment*: i.e. according to the subject which was being treated or the emotion being conveyed.

285 *the 'oath . . . sense'*: Cf. Alexander Pope, *An Essay in Criticism* (1711), ll. 364–5: ''Tis not enough no Harshness gives Offence, | The *Sound* must seem an *Eccho* to the *Sense*'.

302 *bumpers*: glasses filled to the brim; therefore, here, toasts (all of which Captain Absolute must drain off).

327 *a small pittance*: reckoning that the captain's army income would be about £190 a year, Duthie concludes that 'his total income, with the £50 a year that his father gives him . . . is about the lowest level that a gentleman could manage to live on, allowing for the expenses of dress, a servant, and social life'.

331 *make some figure*: present an impressive appearance.

336 *sensible of my attention*: grateful for my consideration; responsive to my care for you.

366 *inclinations*: liking, affections.

369 *business*: (1) other engagements; (2) serious matters; (3) commercial transactions.

371–2 *not worth redeeming*: Sir Anthony pretends to treat literally his son's use of 'pledged'—i.e. he has given the 'angel' his vows as a warrant or security for his continued fidelity and love. But, according to Sir Anthony, even if the 'angel' now forecloses—i.e. refuses to return those vows because of the captain's failure to perform what he promised—no great loss will be incurred, since only words were involved in the transaction. And, in any case, the 'angel' made vows too, and the captain will still have those.

390–1 *the Crescent*: 'Royal Crescent in Bath, an architectural innovation, built 1767–74 by the younger John Wood' (Duthie). In it 'thirty houses were combined into a sweeping linear edifice with a major axis of 538 feet and 114 giant ionic columns separating 105 bays. Though it was all pure façade, since nothing substantial lay to the rear, here was a public front that no English country mansion could match' (Borsay, 236–7).

391 *the bull's in Cox's museum*: opened in 1772 in Spring Gardens, London, by the jeweller James Cox, and 'the most elegant of eighteenth-century London exhibitions in respect to both contents and clientele' and 'the talk of London for three full years', it displayed automatons which 'were also splendid works of art', including 'Gorgeously caparisoned bulls'. See Richard D. Altick, *The Shows of London* (Cambridge, Mass., and London, 1978), 69–72.

400 *laughing in your sleeve*: secretly mocking me.

415 *fly out*: erupt in anger.

427 *five-and-threepence*: i.e. a quarter of a guinea.

435 *intriguer*: lover, seducer, Don Juan.

441 *turnspit*: a dog employed to turn a roasting-spit. Cf. 'puppy triumvirate' (l. 442), where 'puppy' means (1) small dog and (2) conceited, empty-headed young man.

442 *area*: sunken enclosure giving access to the house's basement.

448 *vents his spleen*: unleashes, disburdens, his anger.

2.2.3 *notice in form*: i.e. formal confirmation of the fact (by her receiving her first bribe from him).

6 *'dear Dalia'*: she mimics his Irish accent. Apart from 'embassadress' (l. 10 below), there is no other attempt to render Sir Lucius's pronunciations in the early texts' spelling.

13 S.D. *simply*: foolishly, like a simpleton.

28 *incentive*: provocative (a perfectly good contemporary usage; not a malapropism).

29 *induction*: Mrs Malaprop presumably wants the word to mean something on the lines of 'capacity to induce, seductive power'; but this is substantially beyond its normal range of meanings.

30 *commotion*: perhaps for, emotion; but 'commotion' meaning 'mental or emotional disturbance' also fits the context.

superfluous: for, superficial.

32 *punctuation*: for, punctilio or punctiliousness.

33 *infallible*: absolutely to be relied upon; or a slip for 'ineffable'.

33–4 *worthy . . . my affections*: i.e. passing every test needed to earn my affections.

44 *pressed*: forcibly compelled or enlisted, as by the press-gang.

45 *habeas corpus*: 'writ requiring the investigation of the legitimacy of a person's detention, by which his or her release may be secured' (*OED*).

50 *nice*: choosy, fastidious, scrupulous.

58 *seed such a gemman!*: saw such a gentleman. This is part of the 'simplicity' Lucy assumes in such encounters.

73 *call him out*: challenge him to a duel.

3.1.11 *at twelve years old*: military commissions could be purchased and bestowed on minors. 'Infants might be gazetted cornets or ensigns, and in this way get a head start in the seniority which sped on an officer's first promotion' (Houlding, *Fit for Service*, 102).

15–16 *Never . . . never*: an echo of the words of Shakespeare's King Lear over the dead Cordelia: 'Thou'lt come no more. | Never, never, never, never, never' (*The Tragedy of King Lear*, 5.3.283–4).

25 *condescension to me*: gracious behaviour to me (as your inferior).

32 *absolute*: (1) total and (2) apt to a son of the Absolutes.

43 *country*: neighbourhood.

58 *insinuations*: amorous suggestiveness or promise.

85–6 *a singularity*: i.e. (1) her having only one eye; (2) being odd in that respect.

89 *block*: (1) blockhead; (2) piece of wood, like the ones on which dress uniforms ('regimentals') were brushed.

107 *the Grove*: Orange Grove, near Bath Abbey, and 'not far from the North Parade, a fashionable resort named after the Prince of Orange' (Nettleton).

109–10 *set . . . down*: Sir Anthony sarcastically uses military vocabulary, in which 'set down' meant 'encamp before a town for a siege'.

112 *Promethean torch*: in Greek mythology, Prometheus stole fire from the gods to bestow it on mankind.

3.2.44 *roving*: infidelity, fickleness.

51 *a point*: a compass point; therefore, here, the minutest of distances.

54 *title*: claim (based on his having saved her life).

59 *person*: physical appearance, properties of body.

62–3 *Where . . . of a man*: where nature's gift of physical beauty to a man prompts admiration from others.

64 *this vain article*: the beauty which (1) causes vanity in its possessor and (2) provokes worthless, unsignifying praise from others.

67 *an Ethiop*: to European eyes (attuned to 'fairness' as their norm of beauty) the epitome of ugliness.

69 *contract*: formal engagement to marry.

73 *restraint*: 'Abridgement of liberty' (TS); i.e. his being bound by the agreement to marry Julia.

92 *countenance*: approval, support, authorization.

3.3.2 *accommodation*: perhaps for, recommendation. But 'accommodation' could mean 'something that ministers to one's comfort'—i.e. an alliance with the Absolutes will please Mrs Malaprop greatly.

ingenuity: frankness, openness. What she misses, however, is another sense in which 'ingenuity' (=capacity for trickery) applies to him.

12 *ineffectual*: for, intellectual. But somewhere at work in her mind is the regrettable fact that most contemporary men did indeed wish their wives to be 'ineffectual', i.e. no threat to their own power.

20 *specious*: (1) pleasing to the eye; (2) deceptively attractive.

23 *pineapple*: for, pinnacle; though architects used pineapple shapes to decorate the tops of pillars, towers, etc.—a fact which may be lurking behind Mrs Malaprop's choice of words.

25 *strolling*: vagrant, itinerant.

27 *silly*: (1) sad, deserving of pity; (2) insignificant.

30 *exploded*: possibly for, exposed; but one current meaning of 'explode' (= cry down, reject scornfully) fits the sentence.

31 *conjunctions*: for, injunctions.

32-3 *preposition*: for, proposition.

34 *particle*: part of a series of misappropriations of grammatical terms; cf. 'conjunctions' and 'preposition' earlier, and the pun on 'decline' (l. 33), i.e. (1) refuse and (2) inflect (a noun, adjective, or pronoun through its different cases).

36 *hydrostatics*: for, hysterics. 'Hydrostatics' was 'The science of weighing fluids' and 'bodies in fluids' (TS).

37 *persisted*: for, desisted; but 'persisted' is, of course, what Lydia has indeed done.

38 *interceded*: for, intercepted; but, since 'interceded' could mean 'acted as a go-between', her slip teasingly anticipates the letter's boast about making her perform this function (ll. 76-7) and her acting unknowingly in this way later in the scene.

55 *design*: 'scheme formed to the detriment of another' (TS).

68 *reprehend*: for, comprehend or apprehend.

69 *oracular*: for, vernacular. But an eighteenth-century meaning of the adjective—'ambiguous or mysterious'—has its aptness to Mrs Malaprop's characteristic style of language.

69 *derangement of epitaphs*: for, arrangement of epithets.

77 *assurance*: presumption, impudence; self-confidence.

85–6 *in the nick*: at the critical moment.

86 *laid by the heels*: thwarted, outwitted, disgraced.

    fairly: aptly, suitably; handsomely; justly.

91 *try her temper*: explore her 'disposition of mind' (TS); test how well her composure holds under strain.

99 *below*: waiting downstairs.

136 *Briefly*: in short, to speak concisely.

145 *condescending*: graciously accommodating.

146 *licensed*: i.e. as her husband.

148 *portion*: dowry.

183 *contain*: restrain myself.

191 *allegory*: for, alligator; though the Egyptian variety is actually the crocodile.

3.4. S.D. *as just dressed*: Acres's country clothes have now been abandoned, and he wears dandified fashionable dress.

1 *I become it so*: i.e. that these fashionable clothes suit me.

3 *monkeyrony*: David means to be complimentary, but accidentally inserts 'monkey' in place of the first two syllables of 'macaroni'. 'Macaroni' was a current name for an extravagant dandy, addicted to Continental, especially Italian, fashions, and flaunting his contempt for conservative, insular values. On the macaroni cult, see Langford, 576–8.

4 *print-shops*: shops which sold prints and engravings, the subjects of which included representations of famous people. David loyally hopes that his master will now be admitted to that select band.

6 *all in all*: of supreme importance.

7 *the old lady*: Bob's mother.

8 *Mrs Pickle*: the cook.

10 *Dolly Tester*: a chambermaid ('tester' meant 'the cover of a bed' (TS)). But it also meant 'a sixpence', the tip Bob bestowed on his 'favourite' for other services associated with a bed.

11 *hold a gallon*: wager a gallon (of ale).

12 *Phillis*: Bob's favourite hunting-dog (cf. 4.1.61).

14 *polishing*: acquiring social refinement. But David in his reply applies the word more literally.

16 *De la Grace*: 'of social poise' (French). He is a dancing-master.

17 *balancing, and chasing, and boring*: they are all dance movements. 'Balancing' derives from French 'balance', meaning 'a swaying step from

one foot to the other; 'chasing' from French 'chasse', 'a sliding step in which one foot displaces the other; and 'boring' from 'bourrée', a lively dance in three-quarter time.

23 *Sink, slide, coupee*: more dance movements: respectively, (1) bend the knees; (2) step smoothly to one side; (3) resting on one foot, pass the other forward or backward, making a bow to your partner.

26 *a good stick*: a lively and reliable dancer. Cf. 'play a good stick', meaning 'play one's part well'.

27 *never valued*: wasn't worried about, took in my stride.

your cross-over . . . left: movements in country dancing.

31 *pas*: in French (1) dance-step; (2) no; not. (The dancing-master has clearly had frequent occasion to correct Acres's errors.)

33 *antigallican*: anti-French; with an allusion to the Laudable Association of Anti-Gallicans, founded by a group of London tradesmen during the 1745 invasion crisis. Its aim was to discourage the importation and consumption of French produce and manufactures and encourage British ones. It regarded the adoption of French fashions and styles as a form of cultural treason and a profligate pollution of national identity.

40 *Cupid's jack-o'-lantern*: ignis fatuus, will-o'-the-wisp; 'burning marsh gas by which travellers, who mistake it for a light, are led astray' (Duthie).

41 *quagmire*: (1) wet boggy land which gives way underfoot; (2) awkward, perplexing situation.

59 *wear no swords here*: the wearing of swords was forbidden at Bath under regulations to prevent duelling introduced by Beau Nash.

61 *to be sure*: certainly.

71 *I fire apace*: my anger grows rapidly.

73–4 *of my side*: on my side.

76 *Alexander the Great*: Clinch, who appeared as Sir Lucius from the second performance, had frequently played Alexander in Nathaniel Lee's *The Rival Queens* (1677) on the London stage, a part in which his violence was much remarked. According to *The Westminster Magazine*, Oct. 1774, 'if he is not less violent, he will inevitably tear himself, and his parts to rags'.

80 *a grenadier's march*: Sir Lucius's yoking of Achilles and Alexander the Great reminds Acres of the first line of 'The British Grenadiers': 'Some talk of Alexander, and some of Achilles'.

84 *Blunderbuss Hall*: Sir Lucius's ancestral mansion.

86 *the New Room*: 'The Upper Assembly rooms at Bath, built by John Wood (d. 1782), and opened in 1771' (Price). 'Sheridan himself wrote some humorous verses on the occasion, which appeared in *The Bath Chronicle*, Oct. 1771' (Nettleton).

91 *balls and barrels*: bullets and gun-barrels.

93 *milk of human kindness*: cf. Lady Macbeth's fear that her husband's 'nature' 'is too full o'th' milk of human kindness | To catch the nearest way' (*Macbeth*, 1.4.15–17).

94 *I could do such deeds*: Acres is recollecting, imprecisely, Lear's threat that 'I will do such things— | What they are, yet I know not; but they shall be | The terrors of the earth' (*The Tragedy of King Lear*, 2.2.454–6).

104 *damme*: i.e. damn me!

116 *pretensions*: (competing) claims.

118 *Kingsmead Fields*: when he lived in Bath, Sheridan lodged in Kingsmead Street, which looked on to open fields.

120 *crest . . . seal*: Acres presses his ring with the family crest into the wax with which he seals the challenge.

126 *let the worst come of it*: even if the worst happens.

130–1 *to carry your message*: i.e. thus performing one of the functions of a second in a duel.

133 *at the expense of my country*: i.e. sneering at my Irishness.

134 *fall in with*: happen to meet.

138–9 *Well, for the present*: i.e. farewell.

4.1.7 *cormorants*: seabirds, proverbially regarded as insatiable; therefore, used for human beings with insatiably predatory dispositions.

8–9 *quarter-staff, or short-staff*: fighting with a long heavy pole tipped with iron, or a smaller version of the same.

10 *sharps and snaps*: swords and pistols.

19 *courtier-like*: the unreliability of courtiers was a proverbial joke.

22 *Pleasant enough*: quite amusing, quite a joke.

23 *Boh!*: 'An exclamation intended to startle' (*OED*).

25 *whips over to*: transfers itself to; i.e. is now counted to the credit of my enemy, since he has conquered me.

25–30 *honour . . . without it*: behind these exchanges lie Falstaff's soliloquies on honour (*1 Henry IV*, 5.1.127–40, and 5.3.30–8).

34 *Under favour*: if I may venture to say so; with your permission.

36 *ounce of lead*: bullet.

44–5 *double-barrelled . . . pistols!*: in his excitement David mismatches his adjectives and nouns.

63 *Crop*: Acres's horse.

72 *croaking raven*: cf. Lady Macbeth's 'The raven himself is hoarse | That croaks the fatal entrance of Duncan | Under my battlements' (*Macbeth*, 1.5.36–9) in the same scene from which Acres quoted earlier. Cf. 3.4.93

above, and note. Sheridan's father had written on the correct enunciation of these lines in his *Lectures on the Art of Reading* (2nd edn.; London, 1781), 65.

74–5 *St George*: as befitted a renowned dragon-slayer, St George was celebrated as a military saint.

82 *wrought me to it*: worked me up to it; persuaded me to do it.

87 *mortal defiance*: challenge to the death.

95–6 *not quite so proper*: (1) because he would be acting in a duel against a brother officer; (2) because he would be acting against himself.

99 *Whenever he*: (1) when he; (2) if he ever.

4.2. 6 *caparisons*: for, comparisons. TS defines 'caparison' as 'A sort of cover for a horse'.

10 *alacrity*: 'Cheerfulness, sprightliness, gayety' (TS).

10–11 *adulation*: it has sometimes been assumed that this is a mistake for 'admiration'; but 'adulation' may be exactly what Mrs Malaprop is pleased to think she has received from Captain Absolute.

12 *physiognomy*: for, phraseology. It may, however, indeed be the Captain's face which has most impressed her.

13 *what Hamlet says*: Mrs Malaprop is quoting, with characteristically inventive inaccuracy, Hamlet's description of his dead father to his mother: 'See what a grace was seated on this brow— | Hyperion's curls, the front of Jove himself, | An eye like Mars, to threaten or command, | A station like the herald Mercury | New lighted on a heaven-kissing hill; | A combination and a form indeed | Where every god did seem to set his seal | To give the world assurance of a man' (3.4.54–61).

16 *similitude*: editors usually assume Mrs Malaprop intended 'similarity'. But TS glosses 'similitude' itself as meaning 'Likeness, resemblance'.

34 *Pay your respects!*: i.e. greet Sir Anthony respectfully.

37 *my alliance*: i.e. marrying into my family, becoming kin to me.

40 S.D. *seems to expostulate*: the character does expostulate; it is the actor of the part who seems to. For the same eighteenth-century usage, cf. the S.D. at l. 80 below.

45 *affluence*: for, influence.

64 *directly*: immediately; without an intermediary; face to face.

68 *sirrah*: 'A compellation of reproach and insult' (TS).

98 *Bedlam*: the foreshortened name of a London asylum for lunatics, the Hospital of St Mary of Bethlehem.

103 *for your mother*: in defence of your mother's chastity.

111 *singular*: unique; distinctive.

113 *disinterested*: 'unbiased (here, by mercenary considerations)' (Duthie).

114 *more elevated character*: i.e. both in reassuming his own true rank and as her husband.

116 *Upon my soul . . . fellow!*: cf. Lord Foppington's line, when confronted by another act of impersonation: 'Strike me dumb, Tam, thou art a very impudent fellow' (*The Relapse*, 4.6.79–80).

135 *compilation*: sometimes read as a mistake for 'appellation'; but 'compilation' in the sense of 'compiling, putting together' fits perfectly well here.

141 *clever*: 'Dextrous, skilful; just, fit, proper, commodious; well-shaped, handsome' (TS).

143 *gallant*: 'inclined to courtship' (TS).

144–6 *not anticipate . . . the future*: 'a self-contradictory proposition, or bull' (Duthie).

151–2 *'Youth's . . . made for joy'*: the potency of Sir Anthony's itch to be 'gallant' is shown by this recollection of the song sung by the promiscuous highwayman Macheath and his whores in John Gay's *The Beggar's Opera* (1728), 2.4. The words of the full song are as follows: 'Youth's the season made for joys, | Love is then our duty; | She alone who that employs | Well deserves her beauty. | Let's be gay, | While we may; | Beauty's a flower, despised in decay. | Let us drink and sport today, | Ours is not tomorrow. | Love with youth flies swift away; | Age is naught but sorrow. | Dance and sing; | Time's on the wing; | Life never knows the return of spring'.

155 S.D. *handing*: leading or taking by the hand.

163 *romance*: living in a fictional world; indulgence of fantasy.

165 *such settlements as—*: i.e. the legal arrangements concerning control of her fortune after their marriage will be arranged exactly as she wills and entirely to her advantage.

167 *forms*: normal formalities.

168 *licence*: i.e. marriage licence.

178 *imposition*: 'cheat', 'imposture' (TS).

183 *fondly*: foolishly; with affection.

202 S.D. *puts . . . up again*: restores it to the place from which he had taken it

220 *analysed*: presumably for, paralysed.

226 *Cerberus*: in Greek mythology, the three-headed watchdog which guards the entrance of Hades.

4.3.3 *Carmine*: 'A powder of a bright red or crimson colour' (TS).

7–8 *the old serpent . . . red cloth*: vipers were believed to be attracted by red cloth; so women, themselves serpent-like since their seduction by the serpent in the Garden of Eden, are similarly bewitched by soldiers' red uniforms.

9 *probability of succeeding*: look of success.

41–2 *name your time and place*: i.e. for their duel. This was the right of the person who had received the challenge.

44 *the Spring Gardens*: 'A summer meeting-place for public breakfasts, teas, concerts, and fireworks. It lay on the Bathwick side of the Pulteney Bridge (Price)'.

44–5 *shall scarcely be*: are unlikely to be.

48 *gets wind*: becomes known about.

61 *a resource*: 'Some new or unexpected means that offer' (TS).

62 *knocked o' the head*: killed.

69 *finely obliqued*: elegantly, conveniently, and deftly turned askew or away.

79 *go with me*: i.e. to act as my second in the duel.

81 *accommodated*: brought to a peaceful agreement or conclusion.

110–11 *'not unsought be won'*: Faulkland is quoting, from John Milton's *Paradise Lost*, viii. 500–7, Adam's rapt account of his first encounter with the newly created Eve: 'She heard me thus, and though divinely brought, | Yet innocence and virgin modesty, | Her virtue and the conscience of her worth, | That would be wooed, and not unsought be won, | Not obvious, not obtrusive, but retired, | The more desirable, or to say all, | Nature her self, though pure of sinful thought, | Wrought in her so, that seeing me, she turned.'

125–7 *If her love . . . doubts forever*: Faulkland's metaphor plays on the difference between true and counterfeit coins. As the king's name is not dishonoured when stamped on legitimate coins, so, if Julia's love is confirmed as not counterfeit, she will be fully worthy of bearing Faulkland's (sur)name through marriage. And, once they are married, he will discard his doubts forever.

5.1.3 S.D. *Enter Faulkland*: It is in this scene that the actions of Sheridan's character come closest to those of his namesake in Frances Sheridan's *Memoirs of Miss Sidney Bidulph* (1761). In that novel's final stages, Faulkland, under pursuit for murder, prepares to flee the country for Holland. His plight prompts Miss Bidulph to promise to marry him; but her hesitation about performing this promise immediately draws from Faulkland the accusation that 'the woman whom my soul worships, and to whom I sacrificed all my hopes of happiness, repays me with ingratitude' (Koster and Coades, 435). For such intensities and their tragic sequel, *The Rivals* substitutes its Faulkland's comic self-delusions and self-punishing stratagems.

S.D. *muffled up*: i.e. as if it was necessary to conceal his identity from potential pursuers.

5 *a long farewell*: Faulkland owes the phrase to Shakespeare's *Henry VIII*, 3.2.352.

7 *forfeited*: since (as he pretends) he has killed someone in a duel.

20 *fulfilled*: i.e. by their marriage.

38 *forfeited by this unhappy act*: i.e. as part of the legal penalty for your crime.

44 *rude*: ungentle, unkind.

54 *proved you to the quick*: tested you to the limit; probed your innermost thoughts.

54–5 *this useless device*: this redundant deceit (since it has only proved again what has been so often demonstrated previously).

67 *imposition*: deception; infliction of an unjust burden.

73–4 *providence*: divine direction.

83 *With this conviction*: being convinced of this.

87 *licensed power*: i.e. as her husband.

91–2 *As my faith . . . another*: for other examples of the proposition that 'a woman of real delicacy shou'd never admit a second impression on her heart', see C. J. Rawson, 'Some Remarks on Eighteenth-Century "Delicacy," with a Note on Hugh Kelly's *False Delicacy*', *Journal of English and Germanic Philology*, 56 (1962), 7–8.

101 *awful*: commanding respect and wonder.

104 *heaven-gifted*: bestowed as a gift by heaven; endowed with heavenly gifts.

107 *a principal*: one of the combatants in the duel.

107–8 *reverse . . . here*: i.e. by becoming himself the victim of another's sword.

109 *like the moon's*: which makes men 'lunatic', i.e. 'Mad, having the imagination influenced by the moon' (TS), from Latin 'luna' (moon).

110 *subtler*: more acutely perceptive, more capable of making fine distinctions, more gifted in 'sensibility' (l. 111).

128–9 *confidence*: confiding in me.

135–6 *Smithfield bargain*: a sharp bargain in which the buyer may be deceived; and, hence, a marriage in which money is the main consideration.

136–7 *sentimental*: i.e. arousing and fulfilling all the most exquisite of emotions.

138 *Conscious*: privy to, sharing in, human thoughts.

Scotch parson; in England, it was illegal for people under 21 to marry without the consent of their parents or guardians; but no such law applied in Scotland.

143–4 *a bishop's licence . . . cried three times*: Hardwicke's Marriage Act of 1753 provided that couples intending to marry could either seek a bishop's licence, which permitted them to marry in the church of the parish where one of them lived, or have their banns read ('cried') on three successive Sundays in the church in which they wished to be married.

164–5 *parricide*: for, homicide.

165 *simulation*: 'That part of hypocrisy which pretends that to be which is not' (TS). Presumably Mrs Malaprop chooses to believe that the captain's impersonation of Beverley is in some way responsible for his involvement in the duel.

166 *antistrophe*: for, catastrophe. TS defines 'antistrophe' as 'In an ode sung in parts, the second stanza of every three'.

168 *enveloped*: for, developed (meaning 'revealed, unfolded'); though 'enveloped' (meaning 'covered up') fairly reflects the obfuscatory qualities the circumlocutory Fag then proceeds to display.

173 *interested in*: concerned in; implicated in.

177–8 *flourishing*: rhetorically elaborating.

182 *perpendiculars*: for, particulars.

190 *on terms*: on good terms; but also, because (or provided) he pays me my wages.

200–2 *firearms . . . crackers besides!*: David gets carried away and lists everything beginning with 'fire' that he can think of. 'Firelocks' are muskets, and 'fire-engines' implements for creating a fire. A 'fire-office' is a fire-insurance office, and 'fire-screens' are screens for sheltering ladies' complexions from the heat of a fire in a hearth, while 'Crackers' are fireworks.

203 *favour*: look, appearance.

211 *participate*: for, precipitate, but 'participate' may signal Mrs Malaprop's unwillingness to get too close to such violence.

212–13 *desperately given*: in the mood to kill.

213 *Philistine*: 'like the Biblical Philistines, very belligerent (and also alien, being Irish)' (Duthie).

218 *putrefactions*: for, petrifactions; i.e. fossils and stalactites in the Derbyshire Peak District, already amply featured in guidebooks. In Jan. 1779, Drury Lane mounted a spectacular pantomime with De Loutherbourg designs, *The Wonders of Derbyshire; or, Harlequin in the Peak*, in which Sheridan may have had a hand. It was based on views of the county, including two tavern scenes. The one for Poole's Cavern was especially praised as 'taken with great exactness' (*The London Magazine*, Jan. 1779).

220 *felicity*: perhaps (as editors suggest) for, velocity. But 'felicity' (meaning 'happiness, bliss' and 'good fortune') also fits the context.

222 *do you look*: not a question, but an instruction.

229 *exhort*: for, escort. But 'exhorting' her (meaning 'urging her forwards'), given her nervousness about the duel, may be what will be required of her guide.

230 *envoy*: for, convoy (meaning 'escort'). But 'envoy' (meaning 'messenger or agent sent on behalf of another') may also signal her desire that he goes before them to encounter danger first.

230 *precede*: for, proceed.

5.2. S.D. *The South Parade*: the splendid backdrop for this scene won special praise at the first performance.

1–2 *A sword . . . mad dog*: see the note to 3.4.59 above.

4 S.D. *takes a circle*: walks round in a circle.

29 *make matters up*: effect a reconciliation.

48 *divert*: entertain, amuse.

69 *please you*: may it please you, let it be acceptable to you.

79–80 *the mayor . . . beadles*: another of David's lists. He invokes all the civic officers he can recollect, from the highest to the lowest, who may have an interest in public order.

81 *Give me your shoulder!*: Sir Anthony needs help because of his gout.

5.3.1 *forty yards*: i.e. between the duellists as they aim.

19 *the gentleman's friend and I*: i.e. the two seconds.

29 *pickled*: 'preserved in brine (formaldehyde had not then been discovered)' (Duthie).

30 *lie here in the Abbey*: be buried in Bath Abbey.

39 *files*: lines of soldiers (ranged one behind another).

S.D. *an attitude*: a set or pre-rehearsed posture.

42 *quite out*: totally wrong.

57 *lief*: willingly.

81 *that*: if only.

90 S.D. *(To Faulkland)*: Sir Lucius assumes that Faulkland, whom he does not know, must be Beverley.

122 *backs and abettors*: supporters and adherents. Sheridan may have in mind the recurrent use of 'back' in Congreve's *The Old Bachelor*, where Sir Joseph Wittoll uses it to describe Captain Bluffe, who in effect operates as his protection against threats from others.

142–5 *counsellor . . . amicable suit*: Sir Lucius introduces a legal metaphor by dubbing his sword 'counsellor' ('one that is consulted in a suit of law' (TS)), and Captain Absolute extends it by talking of 'an amicable suit', which means 'one settled out of court', and, therefore, without a contest (or, here, a duel).

146–7 *Knock 'em . . . in particular*: David's excitable use of 'knock down' fluctuates between (1) knock down their swords and (2) fell the duellists themselves.

147–8 *bind . . . behaviour*: David characteristically combines the idea of restraining or tethering his master with the common legal phrase, 'bind someone over to his good behaviour', i.e. require a promise of good behaviour from them.

149 *Put up*: sheathe your sword.

152 *I serve his majesty*: i.e. an officer cannot but respond to a challenge. The *Articles of War*, however, expressly forbade any participation in duels by officers, a prohibition often ignored in practice.

165 *let's have . . . before ladies*: (1) because talk of 'honour' triggers fighting; and (2) because 'honour' also means 'chastity', and such matters are not to be spoken of before ladies. But the syntactical form she happens upon also suggests that men should not act honourably before ladies.

166 *intimidate*: terrify (the normal eighteenth-century meaning).

169 *delusions*: for, allusions; but also carrying the sense that 'the past' was full of 'delusions', Mrs Malaprop's no less than Lydia's.

182 *support a real injury*: i.e. fight a duel when he had deliberately intended to offend or had really offended.

191 *obligation*: an act which obliges the other party to respond with similar generosity.

193 *dissolve my mystery*: 'dissolve' here means (1) cause to disintegrate and (2) undo, bring to an end; and 'mystery' 'an enigma, any thing artfully made difficult' (TS).

199 *the soft impeachment*: for 'soft' TS offers 'delicate, elegantly tender', and for 'impeachment' 'publick accusation, charge preferred'—i.e. Mrs Malaprop pleads happily guilty to having conducted an amorous correspondence under the name of Delia.

200 *be easy*: i.e. he won't be troubling her with his attentions.

201 *Van Dyke*: the seventeenth-century painter; for, vandal.

217 S.D. *All retire but Julia and Faulkland*: i.e. the others leave the central playing-area free for Julia and Faulkland.

246-7 *Our partners . . . each other*: i.e. Julia and Lydia have moved away from Faulkland and Captain Absolute and are talking together.

Epilogue The epilogue, and Mrs Bulkley's delivery of it, were greatly admired. *The Morning Chronicle*, 18 Jan. 1775, for instance, declared it to be 'one of the most excellent and poetical Epilogues we ever remember to have heard'.

Mrs Bulkley: cf. note to heading of 'Prologue on the tenth night'.

1 *our poet*: the dramatist.

5 *whether damned or not*: whether or not successful with spectators and critics.

11 *John Trot*: TS defines 'to trot' as 'to walk fast, in a ludicrous or contemptuous sense'; so the choice of name identifies its owner's lack of dignity and social grace.

15 *vanquished victor*: a recollection of John Dryden's *Alexander's Feast* (1697), ll. 99–115: 'The Prince, unable to conceal his pain, | Gazed on the fair | Who caused his care, | And sighed and looked, and sighed and looked, | Sighed and looked, and sighed and looked again: | At length, with love and wine at once oppressed, | The vanquished victor sunk upon her breast.'

17–20 *The jolly toper . . . | . . . sparkling brim*: the hardened and addicted drinker urges his more sluggish companions to down their drink faster. But soon they have drunk so much that he can only push them on to yet more consumption by challenging each of them in turn to propose a toast to their mistress (their 'Chloe'). Since, in such challenges, each drinker must drink off a full glass or cup (a 'bumper') in response to each toast, the 'jolly toper' is happy for the present; but, as in the epilogue's previous examples, he could not have achieved what he desired without the existence of women.

22 *counsel with a lady's eyes*: converse in private with a lady's charms; indicate which way the wind is blowing via the looks on his mistress's face (with the further implication that she in fact controls the flow of success or failure to his various dependants, cf. ll. 23–5 below). In l. 25 a 'pension' means a salary or stipend, and a 'place' is an 'office' or 'publick employment' (TS).

34 *pressed*: hugged, embraced.

37 *the ditty which his Susan loved*: cf. John Gay's ballad, 'Sweet William's Farewell to Black-eyed Susan', ll. 31–42: 'If to far India's coast we sail, | Thy eyes are seen in diamonds bright, | Thy breath is Africk's spicy gale, | Thy skin is ivory, so white. | Thus every beauteous object that I view | Wakes in my soul some charm of lovely Sue. | Though battle call me from thy arms, | Let not my pretty Susan mourn; | Though cannons roar, yet safe from harms, | William shall to his dear return. | Love turns aside the balls that round me fly, | Lest precious tears should drop from Susan's eye.'

39 *The boatswain*: not the 'tar', but the sailor of superior rank who gives him his commands. The tar's song ('cadence') softened the boatswain's characteristic 'tone'. In Gay's poem, the boatswain appears only to give 'the dreadful word' (l. 43) that the ship must depart, leaving Susan behind.

40 *fairly*: justly.

42 *list*: hear, pay attention to.

The Duenna

The Characters of the Play [*Friars*]: see note to 3.5, opening S.D., below.

Duenna: 'An old woman kept to guard a younger' (TS).

1.1. The performance was preceded by an overture by Thomas Linley junior. The full score is 'available as it was published in parts by S., A. and P. Thompson. Sets are very rare, and the only one I can trace is in the University Music School at Cambridge, and this lacks the second oboe. . . . The middle movement is for wind alone' (Fiske 1). The vocal casting of the opera's principal roles was as follows: Don Jerome baritone, Ferdinand tenor, Louisa soprano, the Duenna mezzo, Clara coloratura soprano, Antonio tenor, Isaac Mendoza baritone, and Carlos tenor.

5 *strangely*: extremely; surprisingly, unaccountably.

12 S.D. *without*: off-stage.

17 S.D. *masks and music*: i.e. friends in masks and musicians.

18 *Symphony*: 'Concert of instruments, harmony of mingled sounds' (TS).

19 *Tell me, my lute*: set by Thomas Linley jun. A full score, requiring 'flutes and strings', is in British Museum MS Egerton 2493 (Fiske 1).

32 *The breath of morn*: the first words read 'The crimson morn' in the version of the songs 'For the VOICE, HARPSICHORD, or VIOLIN' published on 23 Dec. 1775, where this and the following '*What vagabonds* . .' are printed as 'two pieces, but continuous'. Both are 'Probably composed for the words, perhaps by Linley sen.' (Fiske 1).

35 *I own no light*: i.e. I will not admit/acknowledge that any light irradiates the world.

36 *thy numbers*: your song.

38–9 *Phoebus . . . in light*: Apollo, son of Leto and Jupiter; god of the sun, as also of music and poetry. As the sun-god, he coursed daily across the sky; hence, 'moves in light'.

1.2.25 *Could I her faults remember*: 'By Linley jun.; F.S. [i.e. full score] in Egerton 2493 (horns and strings)' (Fiske 1).

39 *Bajazet in the cage*: Bayezid I (1347–1403), the first Ottoman sovereign to be titled 'sultan', was defeated and captured by Timur. He died in captivity some months later. The story was best known to eighteenth-century theatregoers and readers via Nicholas Rowe's often performed *Tamerlane* (1701), which climaxes with Tamerlane (Timur) imposing on Bajazet 'The doom thy rage designed for me . . . : | Closed in a cage, like some destructive beast, | I'll have thee borne about, in public view, | A great example of that righteous vengeance, | That waits on cruelty, and pride, like thine'. The cage does not appear on stage, but the 'print' referred to here clearly illustrated the tyrant's fate graphically.

43 *that her brat . . . her fortune*: that the stepmother's child might gain the fortune which is rightly Clara's.

49 *rated*: reproved, rebuked, scolded.

50 *confident*: presumptuous, impudent.

61 *assurance*: presumption, impudence.

67 *my life for it*: i.e. I would pledge my life on it.

73 *I ne'er could any lustre see*: 'I could never lustre see' (Thompson), which led Fiske 1 to speculate that 'the tune was probably an old one, and the words had to be adapted to fit it'. Fiske 2, however, is inclined to favour Linley sen. as the composer.

78 *untouched by art*: unassisted by make-up.

84 *again*: in response, in reciprocation.

89–90 *you have . . . your sister*: i.e. my love for your sister guarantees I will not be your rival for Clara.

105 *Friendship . . . of reason*: 'By Linley jun.; F.S. in Egerton 2493 (bassoons and strings)' (Fiske 1).

120 *Though cause . . . appears*: the music is by William Jackson of Exeter. 'F.S. in his "Third Set of Songs" (Op. 7) to the words "Fair Delia my Breast so alarms" (British Museum, H.1266.a). Scored for two violins and bass; harpsichord essential' (Fiske 1).

1.3.15 *a party in the whole*: completely our accomplice, committed to the whole plot.

18 *wish you joy*: congratulate you on your marriage (a set phrase).

20 *Thou canst . . . fortune's store*: 'Composed in the popular Scotch style' (Fiske 1); perhaps by Thomas Linley sen. (Fiske 2).

34 *as undelivered*: as if it had not yet been delivered and opened.

36 *catgut*: the dried and twisted intestines of sheep, horse, or ass, used for the stringing of musical instruments.

39 *incantations*: 'enchantment[s]' (TS); but also playing on 'to chant' meaning 'to sing'.

40–1 *as they say . . . the ears*: 'The most perfect process is as follows: as much as possible of the brain is extracted through the nostrils with an iron hook, and what the hook cannot reach is rinsed out with drugs' (Herodotus on mummification in ancient Egypt, in *The Histories*, trans. Aubrey de Sélincourt and revised by A. R. Burn (Harmondsworth, 1972), 160).

47 *sentiments*: opinions.

61 *he is . . . his own art*: i.e. his own tricks undo or make a fool of him.

70 *engrafting on a crab*: 'engrafting' plays on (1) producing (fruit) by grafting and (2) procreating; and 'crab' plays on (1) wild apple, noted for its sour, astringent flavour and (2) sour, cross-grained person.

108 *had as lief*: would have been equally glad if.

122 *with a vengeance*: of the extremest kind.

creature: puppet, agent, dependant.

126 *a decoy-duck*: a person who entices others into mischief.

134 *become*: befit, grace, look well on.

137 *cry aloof*: cry 'Be off', warn to be off.

sons of gallantry: i.e. potential seducers.

138 *spring guns*: guns discharged by bodily contact or with a wire, etc., attached to the trigger (used as traps for poachers or trespassers).

140 *wanton sibyl*: lascivious prophetess or fortune-teller; or foreteller (and, hence, provoker) of rebellious and lascivious future events.

woman of Endor: 'The witch consulted by Saul before the battle of Gilboa: see 1 Samuel 28.7' (Price).

156 *If a daughter . . . your life*: 'Scotch Air, "Hooly and Fairly", 1st pub. 1757; Beard sang it at Ranelagh Gardens. Later arr. Haydn for Thomson' (Fiske 2).

174 *speed you well*: good fortune be with you; may your plots prosper.

177 *equip myself*: dress myself in the appropriate style.

1.4. S.D. *The court*: the courtyard.

1–2 *The world . . . original sin*: a recollection of John Milton's *Paradise Lost*, xii. 646–7: 'The world was all before them, where to choose | Their place of rest, and providence their guide' (describing the enforced departure of the fallen Adam and Eve from Paradise).

5 *turned away*: dismissed.

1.5.2 *mother-in-law*: stepmother.

7 S.D. *retire*: i.e. they move upstage or to one side of it; they don't exit.

11 *prudery*: 'Overmuch nicety in conduct' (TS).

22 *in masquerade*: i.e. as if dressed for going to a masked ball; in disguise.

26 *only that I have just*: if I hadn't myself just.

33 *When sable . . . restoring*: 'Scotch or more probably English Air, 'De'il tak' the wars' (Fiske 2), printed in Thomas D'Urfey, *Wit and Mirth: or Pills to Purge Melancholy* (London, 1719–20), i. 294–5.

81 *habit*: adornment; i.e. in decorating it with a beard.

104 *positively*: irretrievably, indisputably.

122 *St Iago*: St James, the patron saint of Catholic Spain.

132 *Had I . . . falsehood framed*: 'Irish tune, "Gramachree Molly"; Moore later wrote for it "The Harp that once through Tara's Halls". Intro. an oboe solo' (Fiske 2). 'W. T. Parke, in his "Musical Memoirs" (II, p. 14) says he was always applauded for his cadenzas on the oboe in this song, i.e. in the orchestral opening' (Fiske 1).

138 *aged*: pronounced as one syllable.

152 *on all hands*: from every source.

157 *this scrape*: this embarrassment, the blame for this.

160 *My mistress . . . to her*: 'Three items in' the 1775 printing of the *Duenna* songs, but really one. 'By Linley jun.; F.S. in Egerton 2493. The sections scored for strings; oboe, bassoons and strings; horns and strings' (Fiske 1). For Sheridan's instructions to his father-in-law on how this passage should be set, see Introduction, p. xvii.

165 *In . . . confide*: place trust in, have faith in; offer confidences to.

2.1.28 *Give Isaac . . . can boast*: 'Not traced. Perhaps by Linley senior' (Fiske 1).

40 *a throne*: i.e. a hump.

63 *Dominion was given*: only in W. Fraser Rae's 1902 transcription of the Frampton Court MS (now lost) of *The Rivals*; no information available about its musical setting.

67 *Its worship disown*: i.e. refuse to be a worshipper at beauty's shrine.

76–7 *a Virginia nightingale*: the cardinal, *Cardinalis cardinalis*, which has a strong, clear song.

85 *Lauretta, come*: no entrance for the maid is provided in the early texts, and it is sufficient for us to imagine her waiting offstage.

86 *to make love with*: to pay court to your mistress with.

88 *When the maid whom we love*: 'Unidentified' (Fiske 2).

2.2.1 S.D. *goes to the door*: the Rae transcription of the Frampton Court MS has '*Maid crosses the Stage and goes to the Door in the back Scene*'. From the mid-eighteenth century the 'use of practicable doors in the scene . . . increased. Tate Wilkinson writes of a flat with two folding doors in the middle which was in use at Covent Garden in 1747' (Sybil Rosenfeld, *A Short History of Scene Design in Great Britain* (Oxford, 1973), 80–1).

4–5 *the Inquisition*; 'the court established in some countries subject to the pope for the detection of heresy' (TS). 'It lasted in Spain from the Middle Ages to 1835' (Price).

7 *for the soul of me*: i.e. even to save my soul.

17 *mollifies apace*: relaxes her severity swiftly.

18 *attitude*: posture.

21 *so*: in such a welcoming and congenial manner.

22 *condescension*: gracious, accommodating behaviour.

40 *teased*: harried, persecuted. Cf. note to *R* 1.2.61.

45 *struck all of a heap*: astonished; but also, prostrated with dismay.

52 *air*: demeanour.

52–3 *liberal in your carriage*: genteelly relaxed and easy in your behaviour.

65 *insinuating*: TS defines 'to insinuate' as 'to gain on the affections by gentle degrees'.

74 *When a tender maid*: ' "On a Bank of Flowers" by Galliard, sung in Settle's *The Lady's Triumph* (1718). Thomson thought it was Scotch and got Kozeluch to arr. it' (Fiske 2).

75 *essayed*: approached; courted; put to the test.

82–3 *a pit-a-pat . . . | . . . heart avows*: by its palpitations her heart confesses.

117 *a judgement*: a divine judgement or punishment.

132 *settlement*: husband's financial arrangements for his wife, made at the time of marriage, especially for her jointure, i.e. 'Estate settled on a wife to be enjoyed after her husband's decease' (TS).

134 *let . . . alone*: i.e. this little brain can be relied on to contrive great plots without help from others.

135 *in the mind*: while she is of this mind, in this mood.

153 *coz*: see note to *R* 1.2.139.

156–7 *I thrive, I prosper*: cf. the boast of Shakespeare's Edmund: 'I grow, I prosper. | Now gods, stand up for bastards' (*The Tragedy of King Lear*, 1.2.21–2).

177 *Ah, sure . . . never seen*: 'By Michael Arne, written in the Scotch style for Allan Ramsay's "The Highland Laddie", and published in "The Flow'ret" (*c*.1753) when "Master Arne" was only about thirteen. The original is for voice and bass only' (Fiske 1).

182 *kindred beauties each discovers*: each displays beauties so closely allied to, or matching, those of the other.

2.3.1 *Object to Antonio?*: i.e. what can I urge against Antonio? (He is repeating the question Ferdinand has just asked him.)

10 *generosity*: living in, and up to, the style of a gentleman, as his birth demands.

14 *frieze-coat*: frieze is a coarse woollen cloth with a nap; so not the kind of material from which rich men's clothes would be made.

16 *trader*: 'One engaged in merchandise or commerce' (TS); not, in Ferdinand's terms, a gentleman.

19 *nice as to*: fastidious about.

32 *come to*: behave good humouredly and welcomingly, prove accommodating.

57 *made-up*: fabricated.

86 *all in a story*: agreed (in cahoots) in telling the same lies.

96 *get off*: escape from this predicament.

99 *Believe me . . . to offend*: 'F.S. in Egerton 2493. Freely arranged by Linley junior from a much longer canon by John Travers, "When Bibo thought

fit from the world to retreat" (words by Matthew Prior), to be found in his "Eighteen Canzonets for Two and Three Voices" (British Museum, 805.e.). For strings alone' (Fiske 1).

115 *Venus de' Medici*: a nude Venus, and a celebrated work of ancient Greek sculpture; lead copies of it were a fashionable ornament in eighteenth-century English gardens. (For 'sibyl', see note to 1.3.140 above.)

130 *A bumper of good liquor*: 'Not traced.' The 1775 printing of the *Duenna* songs 'gives opening and closing bars on four staves for strings, and the rest can easily be scored on the same pattern' (Fiske 1).

138 *crabbed when he is mellow*: 'morose' even when 'melted down with drink' (TS).

2.4.2 *look after*: seek out.

5 *What bard, O time discover*: 'By Tommaso Giordani, who was then living in London. F.S. in "Favourite Songs" from his "La Marchesa Giardiniera", first performed at the Haymarket Theatre, 14 March 1775; 8 performances by end of season. Scored for flutes, horns and strings' (Fiske 1).

5–6 *What bard . . . | . . . thee move?*: O time, reveal what poet it was who first imagined you as moving with wings?

9 *prove*: experience.

29 *O had . . . on me*: 'Scotch song, "The bush aboon Traquair". The tune had been used by Allan Ramsay in "The Gentle Shepherd", and when Linley senior rescored this ballad opera for Drury Lane in 1781 he left out "The bush aboon Traquair", presumably because by then it was associated with' Sheridan's play. It is likely that 'it was not sung after Leoni's day' (Fiske 1).

40 *land was cried*: i.e. the sighting of land was proclaimed.

49 S.D. *to the doors*: either the proscenium doors or practicable doors in the scenic flats. For the latter, see note to 2.2.1 S.D. above.

62 *gallantry*: 'courtship, refined address to women' (TS).

126 *a caper*: a high dancing-step; so, here, some dancing.

149 *Soft pity . . . gentle breast*: a catch by William Hayes, 'from his "Epitaph on Sophocles" (British Museum, H.1994.a.(135))', the original words of which begin: 'Wind, gentle Evergreens, to form a shade | Around the tomb where Sophocles is laid' (Fiske 1). In a letter to his father-in-law, Sheridan explained that 'They are to sing "Wind, gentle evergreen" just as you sing it (only with other words), and I wanted only such support from the instruments, or such joining in, as you should think would help to set off and assist the effort. I inclose the words I had made for "Wind, gentle evergreen," which will be sung, as a catch, by Mrs. Mattocks, Dubellamy, and Leoni. I don't mind the words not fitting the notes so well as the original ones' (*Letters*, i. 90).

152 *swayed*: ruled, governed.

154 *as a relic there*: at the first performance, as *The Gazetteer*, 21 Nov. 1775, reported, there was at this point 'A new Spanish Dance by Signor and Signora Zucelli, Mr. Dagueville, Signora Vidini, etc.' *The Morning Chronicle*, 22 Nov. 1775, judged that it 'was unpleasing' and 'too long stretched' and that 'it had better be omitted'.

3.1.17 *throw ourselves at your feet*: kneel before him to beg a paternal blessing.

23 *fulfil . . . the article*: make the financial arrangement (as regards property settled on his wife at marriage) expected of a wealthy husband. Cf. note to 2.2.132, above.

50–1 *Admit . . . without masks*: i.e. he is throwing his house open to all comers.

54 *O the days . . . young*: 'By Linley senior; Sheridan wrote the words to fit his song "Prithee, pretty man", which does not seem to survive' (Fiske 1). 'F.S. in LGC' ('a MS in the younger Linley's hand of Act III only in London's Guildhall Library (Gresham 376)') (Fiske 2). Sheridan wrote to his father-in-law that 'I think it will do vastly well for the words: Don Jerome sings them when he is in particular spirits; therefore the tune is not too light, though it might seem so by the last stanza—but he does not mean to be grave there, and I like particularly the returning to "O the days when I was young!" We have mislaid the notes, but Tom [i.e. Linley jun.] remembers it. If you don't like it for words, will you give us one? but it must go back to "O the days," and be *funny*' (*Letters*, i. 89–90).

57 *nectar*: the drink of the gods; therefore, here, delicious wine.

59 *recked I of*: did I care for.

62 *Truth . . . in a well*: cf. the proverbial 'Truth lies at the bottom of a well' (Tilley T582).

65 *There . . . for me*: i.e. he never disturbed it, he didn't drink water.

3.2. S.D. *The piazza*: 'The New Piazza' (*1794*); but presumably the same setting as that for 1.5.

12 *have it*: say that.

20 *Ah, cruel maid . . . changed*: 'By Jackson of Exeter. F.S. (two violins and bass) in his first set of songs (Op. 1, 1755) to Parnell's words "My days have been so wondrous free" (British Museum, W.1266.a)' (Fiske 1).

24 *clear in fame*: unblemished in reputation.

43 *again*: in reciprocation (for maltreatment by another).

66 *pass*: happen.

142 *Sharp . . . jealous mind*: 'By Linley junior. F.S. in Egerton 2493 (horns and strings).' It is likely 'that it was soon cut, no doubt because it was so difficult' (Fiske 1).

3.3.9 *By him we love offended*: 'By Rauzzini, the famous castrato who settled in Bath about the time Linley left. F.S. in 'Favourite Songs' from his "Piramo e Tisbe" (British Museum, G.555.a.), first performed at the Haymarket Theatre, 16 March 1775; 7 performances by the end of the season . . . Scored for flutes, oboes, bassoon, horns and strings' (Fiske 1).

30 *probation*: noviciate, period of testing before a nun's full admission to a convent.

48 *How oft . . . said*: 'Scotch Song, "The Birks of Endermay" (or Invermay)'; full score, arranged by Linley jun. in LGC (Fiske 2).

89 *support it*: render it endurable.

122 *Adieu . . . never dies*: ascribed by a nineteenth-century source to Sacchini, but not confirmed. 'F.S. in LGC' (Fiske 2). 'Very difficult, both for singer and oboist' (Fiske 2). Sheridan instructed his father-in-law that 'Miss Brown sings' her song 'in a joyful mood: we want her to show in it as much execution as she is capable of, which is pretty well; and, for variety, we want Mr. Simpson's hautboy to cut a figure, with replying passages, etc., in the way of Fisher's '*M'ami, il bel idol mio*,' to abet which I have lugged in "Echo", who is always allowed to play her part' (*Letters*, i. 92). Sheridan's next letter reveals that Linley sen. had taken him more literally than he had intended: 'You misunderstood me as to the hautboy song; I had not the least intention to fix on "Bel idol mio." However, I think it is particularly well adapted, and, I doubt not, will have a great effect' (i. 92–3).

3.4. S.D. *court*: courtyard.

7 *tack me*: marry me (slang).

13 *be your father*: i.e. give away the bride.

3.5. S.D. *Friars . . . and singing]: 1794* and Price simply read '*Friars*' here. The three friars named in this edition's S.D. are assigned dialogue subsequently; but it seems likely that other friars were also onstage in this scene (Price, i. 228). The friars wore blue robes at the first performance. We owe this detail to a writer in the *St James's Chronicle*, 12–14 Dec. 1775, who complained about the inaccuracy of this costuming and also strenuously objected to the satiric and (in his view) unjust portrayal of the friars. The earliest Italian versions of *The Duenna* excise these characters completely. However much these scenes catered to anti-papist prejudice, Sheridan himself was a lifelong advocate of Catholic Emancipation.

S.D. *GLEE*: a part-song, especially an unaccompanied one, for three or more voices.

1 *This bottle's . . . our table*: by Linley jun.; 'ascribed to him by Ritson and Shield in *Select Collection of English Songs* iii (1783); F.S. *not* in LGC' (Fiske 2).

9 *toss the bottle about*: pass the bottle round the table.

26 *See who's there: 1794* and Price provide no direction about what further action needs to occur here; but the *1794* stage direction at l. 29 below makes it clear that something must. A reconstructed text of the play for performance outside London, printed in *The European Magazine* (May 1783), provides the following sequence here: '*Knocking at the door; the table, &c. drawn behind a curtain. Brother Francis unlocks the door.*' This has been used as the model for the editorial stage direction here.

S.D. *Porter*: described as '*meagre and pale*' in another reconstructed text of *The Duenna* (Dublin, 1787), 35.

38 *mortification*: fasting; mortifying the flesh and its appetites.

3.6.22–3 *your nose . . . blush*: the characteristic insignia of the drunkard.

27 *clandestinely*: clandestine marriages, which the 1753 Marriage Act had sought to eliminate, were ones which were legally binding, but conducted in a manner which broke canon law. They were performed by someone at least purporting to be a clergyman, but in secret, not public, without prior reading of banns or valid licence—see note to *R* 5.1.143–4—and so on. For further discussion, see Lawrence Stone, *Road to Divorce: England 1530–1987* (Oxford, 1990), 96–120.

33 *Jacobin*: friar of the order of St Dominic.

68 *spirit to avow it*: i.e. in a duel.

78 *mockery*: 'imitation, counterfeit appearance, vain show' (TS).

80 *Turn thee . . . pray thee*: 'By Linley junior. F.S. in Egerton 2493 (flutes, horns and strings)' (Fiske 1).

109 *Oft does . . . to hear*: '"Geminiani's Minuet", first (?) pub. 1725 as "Gently touch the warbling Lyre"'; full score, arranged by Linley jun., in LGC (Fiske 2).

3.7.16 S.D. *The Duenna kneels*: i.e. to ask 'her father's' blessing.

52 *habits*: costume, dress.

58 *pretty*: crafty; fine.

81 *the plagues of Egypt*: see Exodus 7–12.

94–5 *A body . . . the dropsy*: 'dropsy' is a medical condition characterized by an excess of watery fluid, which leads to emphatic swelling of the body. Hence, Margaret's insult is that the only mark of distinction (i.e. 'consequence') he possesses is (diseased) bulk.

130 *with pardon for stealing a wedding*: asking forgiveness for marrying secretly.

137 *Carlos*: one of Don Jerome's servants, and not Isaac's friend.

144 *Come now . . . and smiling*: 'the melody is from Thomas Morley's "Now is the Month of Maying"; FS *not* in LGC' (Fiske 2).

A Trip to Scarborough

The Characters of the Play *Tunbelly*: 'tun' means (1) 'A large cask; two pipes, the measure of four hogsheads' and (2) ' a drunkard, in burlesque' (TS).

Probe: 'A slender wire by which surgeons search the depth of wounds' (TS).

La Varole: Sheridan's softened version of Vanbrugh's La Vérole, i.e. syphilis.

Hosier: maker of, and dealer in, hose, i.e. stockings.

[Postilion]: 'one who guides a post-chaise' (TS).

Coupler: matchmaker.

Hoyden: noisy, rude, boisterous girl.

[Seamstress]: woman whose trade is seaming or sewing.

Prologue This prologue from *1781* was, in fact, the second which Garrick wrote for the play. A draft of the first survives in manuscript and is reprinted in Price ii. 561–3.

David Garrick, Esq.: the greatest and most versatile of eighteenth-century British actors, Garrick was also a brilliant theatre manager, talented playwright, and highly accomplished writer of prologues and epilogues, who dominated the British stage for some thirty years. His reign at Drury Lane ended in 1776, when his key managerial responsibilities were assumed by Sheridan. Garrick himself had adapted numerous pre-1700 plays—including Shakespeare's *The Taming of the Shrew* and Wycherley's *The Country Wife*—for performance on the contemporary stage. After his death Sheridan composed his *Verses to the Memory of Garrick Spoken as a Monody* for performance at Drury Lane on 11 Mar. 1719.

Mr King: Thomas King, a superb comic actor, a mainstay of the Drury Lane company, and Garrick's closest and most trusted professional friend. James Boaden, *Memoirs of the Life of John Philip Kemble, Esq.* (London, 1825), i. 60, praised him as 'the very best speaker of prologues and epilogues that was ever heard. His manner added to the keenness of the rhymed couplet, and he presented the successive pictures of the ludicrous with so much truth, and without stooping in the least to mimicry, that his forty lines on such occasions composed a little drama perfect in itself, which had a charm independent of its relation to the play it accompanied.'

  2 *east Whitechapel to the west Hyde Park*: i.e. from poverty-stricken neighbourhoods in the east to the most fashionable ones in the west of the capital city.

3 *signs*: shop signs. TS defines 'a sign' as 'a picture hung at a door, to give notice what is sold within'.

4 *State*: 'the principal persons in the government' (TS).

5 *Th'Exchange*: the Royal Exchange in Cornhill, the hub of the London mercantile world, where merchants trading to different regions each had their separate walks.

'Change Alley: beside the Royal Exchange in Cornhill. Bartering in stocks took place there in the open air.

8 *hackney-coach*: a two-horse, four-wheeled coach kept for hire.

10 *run*: ran.

13 *Sylvia . . . Damon*: type names for lovers.

7–15 *The streets . . . | . . . unjolted home*: on the transformation of at least some London streets in this period, see M. Dorothy George, *London Life in the Eighteenth Century* (Harmondsworth, 1965), 107–8.

16 *a beau*: 'A man of dress' (TS).

18–21 *Then the full . . . and ears*: see note to *R* 1.1.73–4.

26 *encumbrance*: (1) load (of buckle upon shoe) and (2) burden of debt (upon the 'nice fine estate'), accumulated by his profligate life-style.

30 *cork*: used for the heels of ladies' shoes.

34 *The foe*: the devil.

35 *head of old*: tiered wig in former times.

38 *If ev'n they . . . th'experiment*: if, that is, they were ever to attempt to attend church service. (TS defines 'even', used adverbially, as 'A word of strong assertion, verily; supposing that; notwithstanding.)

42 *That graceless wit . . . bare before*: a recollection of a line by Alexander Pope, 'How Van wants grace, who never wanted wit!' (*The First Epistle of the Second Book of Horace Imitated*, l. 289).

44 *wantons into magdalens*: whores into repentant sinners.

46 *asylum*: 'A sanctuary, a refuge' (TS).

1.1.1 *postboy*: 'boy that rides post' (TS); i.e. the postilion.

7 *New Malton*: 'Or Malton, a market town twenty-miles from Scarborough' (Price).

10 *made bold*: took the liberty.

13 *chaise*: i.e. carriage-fare. TS defines 'a chaise' as 'A carriage of pleasure drawn by one horse'.

18 *below*: i.e. by the inn-staff (who will add it to Fashion's bill).

21 *turnpikes*: fees charged at toll-gates on the journey (a fairly recent innovation on the road to Scarborough).

55 *Like . . . him*: a way of catching trout.

60 *distract me*: drive me mad.

70 *attached*: devoted; but also punning on 'attached' meaning 'arrested, seized by the law' (and on 'rogue' meaning 'vagrant').

83–4 *breeding within doors*: education in her father's house.

85 *dulcimer*: 'A musical instrument played by striking the brass wire with little sticks' (TS).

clerk: clergyman's assistant, 'layman who reads the responses to the congregation in church, to direct the rest' (TS).

92 *Dame*: Madam.

134 *bag*: money-bag; or small pouch (used to hold the back-hair of a wig).

1.2.2 *quality*: superior rank.

strike me dumb!: i.e. may I be struck dumb (if this isn't true)! The 'strike me . . .' formula is a recurrent verbal trait of Vanbrugh's Lord Foppington, which Sheridan takes over, sometimes bowdlerizes, and also sometimes varies with his own inventions.

15 *peru*: La Varole's mangling of 'peruke(-maker)', i.e. wig-maker.

17 *messieurs, entrez*: sirs, enter.

21 *clown*: peasant, oaf.

26 *people dispose the glasses*: servants arrange the mirrors.

29 *a favourite at court*: and therefore with influence over appointments, etc., which would lead others to attend his 'levee' (defined by TS as 'the concourse of those who crowd around a man of power in a morning').

42 *tartures*: Sheridan's Foppington, like Vanbrugh's, on occasion affectedly substitutes 'a' for 'o' in this fashion (plus some other similar vowel switches). Neither dramatist is totally consistent in his spellings, and an actor would be likely to standardize Foppington's pronunciation somewhat more than the texts of either *The Relapse* or *A Trip to Scarborough* do.

46 *Rat*: affected pronunciation of 'rot' (='drat, confound').

51 *accost*: 'address', 'salute' (TS).

59 *Calico*: 'An Indian stuff [i.e. material] made of cotton' (TS); therefore, here a name for a dealer in fashionable cloth.

93 *the winter*: i.e. the social season.

123 *Donner's*: 'The Assembly Rooms at Scarborough' (Price); a fashionable place of meeting. This is a rare touch of local colour. Scarborough does not play the role in this comedy that Bath did in *The Rivals*. Sheridan had lived in Bath; but, as far as we know, he never visited Scarborough.

127 *nice conversation*: select range of acquaintance.

128 *at large*: 'without restraint' (TS); socially indiscriminate.

145 *galleon*: 'Galloon' (*1781* and Price), which TS defines as 'A kind of close lace, made of gold or silver, or of silk alone'. To the present editor, 'galleon' (i.e. 'treasure-ship') seems more plausible here; hence the emendation.

154 *burnt in the hand*: branded (as a judicial punishment).

160 *writings*: legal documents governing the financial settlement accompanying the marriage.

173 *family*: household.

185 *Not a souse*: no money at all, not a single coin.

192 *the cup and the lip*: cf. the proverbial 'Many things happen between the cup and the lip' (Tilley T191).

204 *rakehell*: 'A wild, worthless, dissolute, debauched fellow' (TS).

210–11 *try . . . to the bottom*: test my brother to the limits, probe my brother's nature thoroughly.

2.1.7 *our retreat*: our country retirement. 1.1 of *The Relapse* shows us Amanda and Loveless in that 'retreat', which protects Loveless, with his promiscuous past, from renewed subjugation to metropolitan temptations.

15–26 *truly, with . . . living ones*: in *The Relapse* the parallel conversation (2.1.18–28) concerns the possible impurity of the contemporary drama. Sheridan keeps much of Vanbrugh's dialogue, but re-routes the debate so that its primary focus is on how the 1770s stage should deal with its late seventeenth-century inheritance. See Introduction, pp. xxvi–xxvii.

28 *mind it much*: pay much attention to it.

38 *apprehending for me*: becoming concerned for me.

43 *design*: 'scheme formed to the detriment of another' (TS).

71 *chair*: sedan-chair.

79 S.D. *saluting*: greeting with a kiss.

86 *his humble service*: his compliments.

87 *at the next door*: visiting at the next house or lodgings.

144 *side-box*: at the theatre, and a natural choice of location for those who delighted in self-display, since some of the side-boxes lay behind the front of the forestage and were therefore in full view of most of the other spectators.

167 *clubs*: gambling-clubs (as his following comments make clear).

168 *deep*: for very large stakes.

    tied up: constrained, limited.

170–1 *attend . . . nation*: i.e. be present in the House of Lords.

179 *intrigues*: love-affairs.

188 *make love to me*: woo me.

225–6 *more credit*: greater reputation.

247 S.D. [*Servants . . . a chair*]: i.e. they bring a sedan-chair onto the stage.

270 *Bagatelle*: 'A trifle. Not English' (TS).

271 *servant*: suitor, admirer.

290 *want*: need.

309 *that character*: i.e. the reputation of handsomeness.

317 *airs*: affectation of indifference; moodiness.

347 *spleen*: 'a fit of anger; melancholy, hypochondriachal vapours' (TS).

368 *They are decent*: i.e. their behaviour fits within normal social decorums.

370 *a pattern*: 'a specimen', 'an example' (TS).

395–6 *that thing they call a husband*: a cuckold.

404 *humour*: 'jocularity'; but also 'general turn or temper of mind' (TS).

415 *return with me*: come back here to lodge with me tonight.

421–2 *in countenance*: in reading faces.

3.1.10 *cards*: calling-cards, visiting-cards.

20 *this baut*: this bout, this time.

23 *caper*: jubilant high step in dancing.

60 *take a purse*: i.e. commit a robbery.

64 *relieved t'other*: i.e. by being executed.

65 *pleasant a humour*: so humorous, so witty, a mood.

76 *sweet pawder*: perfumed powder used as a cosmetic.

82 *husband*: manager of your resources.

96 *musk cat*: the animal from which the perfume is derived.

106 *plats*: Foppington's pronunciation of 'plots'.

3.2. 23 *complaints*: (1) symptoms; (2) marital discontents.

24 *lose all my practice*: since confidentiality is indispensable to both the doctor and the adulteress.

36 *die together*: at this point in *The Relapse*, 3.2.112–13, Loveless is playing on the common seventeenth-century pun on 'die' (meaning 'reach sexual climax'), which Berinthia then weaves further variations on in her subsequent soliloquy (ll. 130–5). Sheridan cuts the latter. His retaining Loveless's line presumably means that the original equivocation on 'die' would not have been immediately apparent to a 1770s audience.

47 *close*: (1) intimate; (2) secret.

49 *retort courteous*: Townley owes the phrase to Shakespeare's Touchstone (*As You Like It*, 5.4.90).

59 *insinuating in his address*: seductive in his manner of wooing.

65–6 *address you*: pay court to you, woo you.

81 *delicate addresses*: decorous courtship.

103 *jest and earnest*: i.e. such a mingling of tones.

116–17 *no man . . . will be so*: on the manuscript submitted to the censor, 'the Deputy Licenser of Plays, Edward Capell, placed brackets round' this, adding the comment that 'This ought to be suppressed' (L. W. Conolly, *The Censorship of English Drama 1737–1824* (San Marino, 1976), 151–2). The fact that it was included in the published text does not mean that his instruction was disobeyed in the playhouse. The line is Vanbrugh's, not Sheridan's.

3.3.3–4 *Noah's ark . . . field*: see Genesis 7.

5–6 *orders of building*: the classical orders of architecture (Doric, Ionic, Corinthian); i.e. what the house looks like.

16 *two words to that bargain*: cf. the proverbial 'Two words to a bargain' (Tilley W827).

22 *like willows*: i.e. the conventional posture of the forlorn and discontented lover.

30–1 *with good words . . . done*: playing on a variety of proverbs about 'good words', including 'Good words are worth much and cost little' and 'Good words cool more than cold water'; see Tilley W803–12.

56 *stick . . . laurel*: as at festival times (such as Christmas).

72 *Common fame*: public reputation.

77 *constitution*: 'temper of body, with respect to health; temper of mind' (TS).

3.4.2 *for all*: notwithstanding that, however much.

27–8 *by your troth*: on your oath.

30 *tucker*: 'A small piece of linen that shades the breasts of women' (TS).

4.1.7 *what work I'll make*: what I'll get up to.

15 *Practice of Piety*: an enormously popular devotional work by Lewis Bayly, first published early in the seventeenth century, and often reprinted.

19 *buy pins*: 'pin-money' was the term for the allowance a husband allotted to his wife for her personal expenditure.

22 *gibberage*: Nurse's variation on 'gibberish'.

24 *versal*: whole.

30 *do . . . by*: cf. the proverbial 'Do as you would be done to' (Tilley D395).

33 *if you disparage me—*: if your behaviour lets me down, lessens my reputation.

40 *both*: i.e. to be both.

82–3 *separate maintenance*: normally, the financial support a husband gave his wife when they formally separated. Fashion calmly anticipates a complete inversion of gender roles.

85 *packet*: letter.

92 *Jezebel*: perhaps used here as a general term of distaste. It usually means either (1) wicked or shameless woman or (2) woman who wears heavy make-up.

100 *by maakins!*: i.e. by makings (a meaningless exclamatory oath).

141 *inventions*: plans, designs.

150–1 *fat livings*: well-paid church employments, to which Foppington, as a substantial property-owner, would have the right of making appointments.

151 *falls*: falls vacant.

162 *on*: of.

4.3.15 *for something*: for a reason I won't specify.

46 *which*: whichever.

5.1 S.D. *Moonlight*: by the mid-eighteenth century stage lighting could be varied to distinguish, when necessary, between night and full daylight. But De Loutherbourg's work at Drury Lane—see Sheridan's Playhouses, above p. xlix, and note to *C* 1.2.77—vastly increased the sophistication of the lighting effects available there.

80 *confidence*: i.e. confiding or trusting (in a friend).

92 *censure*: 'judgment, opinion' (TS).

94 S.D. *Loveless and Berinthia move centre-stage*: this edition; '*Enter* LOVELESS and BERINTHIA' (*1781* and Price). But l. 40 above indicates that Loveless, and therefore presumably Berinthia also, remain concealed onstage to observe the Amanda/Townly encounter.

129 *secret counsels*: innermost thoughts.

130 *reserve*: 'something concealed in the mind' (TS).

132 *They'd*: they and their virtue would.

5.2.16 *capitulating*: a slip, worthy of Mrs Malaprop, which Sheridan inherited from Vanbrugh. Lory means 'negotiating' but manages to predict imminent defeat for their conspiracy.

40 *turning . . . lordship*: making Foppington out to be the impostor.

44 *tickle*: (ironic) chastise, thrash.

58 *pax*: i.e. pox (=syphilis).

65 *scot and lot*: 'parish payments' (TS), levied proportionately to an individual's ability to pay. Sir Tunbelly is scornfully asking Foppington if he is of sufficient estate to pay this tax.

75 *warrant for him*: i.e. for his arrest and imprisonment.

104 *sweets*: perfumes.

134 *frontery*: Nurse's personal version of 'effrontery'.

173 *all in a story*: see note to D 2.3.86.

177 *stiff*: 'formal' (TS).

202–3 *scandalize the character*: bring discredit upon the rank and identity.

232–3 *Fire and faggots*: 'faggots' specifically meant 'kindling used in burning heretics'. Sir Tunbelly would like to incinerate someone.

242 *clerk*: see note to 1.1.85 above.

289 *Udzookers*: Sir Tunbelly's variation on 'gadzooks', an exclamation of uncertain origin.

312–3 *deportment*: 'Conduct . . . demeanour, behaviour' (TS).

317 *grimace*: affected composure.

320 *arms*: coat of arms.

323 *dun 'un*: done him.

336 *attention*: politeness, courtesy.

The School for Scandal

A Portrait This poem was written to accompany a handsome manuscript copy of *The School for Scandal* presented to Mrs Crewe by Sheridan soon after the play's première. It circulated in manuscript soon thereafter, but did not appear in print until 1814.

   a lady: 'Frances Anne Crewe (1748–1818), wife of John, later first Lord Crewe (1742–1829)' (Price). She was for a time Sheridan's mistress.

 2 *rail . . . by rule*: abuse others and destroy their reputations according to the set rules of scandalmongering.

 6 *Approve by envy*: authenticate 'her fame' by the palpable envy it provoked in you.

12 *censors*: critics, censurers.

21 *or . . . or*: either . . . or.

23 *my theme*: Frances Anne Crewe.

25–6 *Amoret . . . | . . . fame*: Elizabeth Sheridan 'gave the name of Amoret to Mrs Crewe in her poem "Laura to Silvio", praising her 'gentle step and hesitating grace' (Rhodes ed., iii. 199–200); so that may be the 'worthier verse' (l. 26) Sheridan refers to. Price, however, pointed out that 'Charles Fox . . . also wrote verses to "Amoret", which are mentioned by Horace Walpole in a letter of 27 May 1775, to William Mason.'

27 *but*: except for.

28 *conscious*: alert, conveying intelligence.

30 *boast*: 'exalt' (TS).

31 *couldst thou*: if you could.

33 *blessed strain, in kindred colours*: highest, most impassioned language, in a rhetorical style matched to her virtues.

36 *Reynolds*: 'Sir Joshua Reynolds (1723–92) painted three portraits of Mrs Crewe' (Price).

39–40 *Granby's cheek . . . | . . . Devon's eyes*: Reynolds painted portraits of Mary Isabella, wife of Charles Manners, Marquis of Granby, and Georgina, wife of William Cavendish, fifth Duke of Devonshire. 'The beauty of' the latter's 'eyes was constantly mentioned' (Price).

51 *state*: pomposity of bearing.

52 *moves no queen*: does not move as if she were a queen.

54 *surprise*: take possession by force (as in a military attack).

56 *dignity*: 'grandeur of mien' (TS).

64 *were*: would be.

90 *Prerogative in her*: her special and appropriate privilege, natural right.

95 *which truth delights to own*: i.e. which are the characteristic properties and tokens of female virtue.

96 *submitted tone*: decorously submissive, or unassertive, manner of speaking.

100 *science*: skill or knowledge (acquired by study).

115 *Owns*: confesses, admits.

The Characters of the Play *Teazle*: i.e. he and his wife tease—irritate and grate upon—each other. A 'teasel' is a plant with prickly leaves, and the head of the fuller's teasel is used for teasing cloth.

Surface: all three characters bearing this surname are not what they seem. Both Sir Oliver and Joseph indulge in different forms of impersonation; and Charles's rakish exterior masks his true nature.

Crabtree: he displays the properties of the fruit the tree bears. As it is bitter and sour, so he purveys unpleasant stories about his acquaintances.

Backbite: 'To censure or reproach the absent' (TS).

Moses: a generic name for a Jewish moneylender.

Trip: 'to run lightly' (TS), so, nimble, fleet; but also 'To fall by losing the hold of the feet; to fail, to err, to be deficient' (TS).

Careless: 'negligent, heedless, unmindful; cheerful, undisturbed; unmoved by, unconcerned at' (TS).

Bumper: see note to *R* 2.1.302.

Candour: see note to *R* Preface, l. 34.

Prologue

David Garrick, Esq: see note to *TTS*, Prologue.

Mr King: see note to *TTS*, Prologue.

3 *knowing*: 'Skilful, well instructed' (TS).

5 *the vapours*: modish illnesses 'caused by . . . diseased nerves, melancholy, spleen' (TS).

8 *quantum sufficit*: Latin for ' "As much as suffices," *i.e.* "plenty" ' (Nettleton).

9 *Wormwood*: (1) an aromatic plant with a proverbially bitter taste; (2) source of bitter mortification or vexation.

11 *threshing*: tossing restlessly or uneasily (in bed).

13 *Lisp*: a type-name for a maid. (She affects, and inadvertently parodies, fashionable speech.)

18 *poz*: fashionable slang abbreviation of 'positively'.

20 *dash and star*: 'A frequent method of reference to the principals in fashionable intrigues' in newspaper reports (Nettleton). Cf. note to 1.1.18 below.

22 *Grosvenor Square*: one of London's most exclusively fashionable and aristocratic neighbourhoods.

36 *Don Quixote*: i.e. just as the honourably intentioned but deluded hero of Miguel de Cervantes' great comic novel (1605–15) sallied forth to undertake deeds of knight errantry, so Sheridan, flattered by previous successes, sets off in his new play to right one of the wrongs of his time.

38 *hydra*: a monster (in Greek mythology) with many heads, which grew again as fast as they were cut off. Cf. ll. 33–4 above.

39 *fell gripe*: fierce claws.

1.1.1 *paragraphs*: (in eighteenth-century newspaper or periodical usage) short articles with no headline; printed items of news. Contemporaries identified Snake as 'the editor of a morning paper' (Rhodes, 71–2).

5 *Brittle's*: frail, weak, liable to surrender to sexual temptation.

7 *as fine a train*: as completely on course; as well advanced.

8 *Clackit's*: TS defines 'to clack' as 'to let the tongue run'.

14 *matches*: intended marriages.

16 *close confinements*: secret births.

separate maintenances: see note to *TTS*, 4.1.82–3.

18 *Town and Country Magazine*: this was published monthly. Notorious among its regular features was the 'tête-à-tête' in each issue, in which a sexual scandal in high society was exposed with engravings of the main

participants under easily decodable pseudonyms. The magazine's editor thanked Sheridan for having 'immortalized' it 'upon the stage' but defended the accuracy of his stories (Rhodes ed., ii. 15). 'In January 1777, four months before the performance of *The School for Scandal*, the tête-à-tête represented "Malgrida" and "Thalia"; "Malgrida," scholar, orator and politician, was Lord Shelburne, afterwards Marquis of Lansdowne, and his mistress, "Thalia, wife of Mr. A——n, musician." was Mrs. Abington, the original Lady Teazle' (Rhodes, 72).

21 *gross*: 'inelegant' (TS).

24 *mellowness*: relaxation, ease; geniality; 'Ripeness, softness by maturity' (TS).

21-9 *her manner . . . laboured detail*: both speakers make use of quasi-technical terms from art criticism ('design', 'invention', 'colouring', 'outline', etc.).

43 *character*: reputation.

44 *extravagant*: 'roving beyond just limits or prescribed methods; irregular, wild; wasteful, prodigal, vainly expensive' (TS).

47 *attached to*: in love with, enamoured on.

confessedly: i.e. Maria herself acknowledges it to be so.

49 *a city knight*: presumably a merchant who had received a knighthood, and therefore, in fashionable circles, not on an even footing with those whose rank was derived from birth. Bateson surmises that 'Sneerwell, a woman of breeding and brains, had perhaps been compelled' to such a marriage 'because of her tarnished reputation' (cf. ll. 32-5 above); but this is to stray far beyond what the text warrants.

50 *jointure*: see note to D 2.2.132.

close with: come to an agreement with; embrace.

52 *attachment*: intimacy, devotion; 'Adherence, regard' (TS).

55 *intercourse*: dealings. (The word had not acquired its later sexual meaning.)

70 *so confidential*: so totally in each other's confidence.

73 *sentimental knave*: i.e. he lavishly dispenses moralistic aphorisms but only uses them as a mask behind which he can pursue his own treacherous agenda.

75 *man of sentiment*: a nicely balanced phrase, since it can mean both (1) a man who professes moral views and (2) a man of deeply humane and compassionate feeling. Sir Peter's error is to deduce from the fact that Joseph is clearly (1) that therefore he must also be (2).

77 *into his interest*: onto his side, into serving his designs.

90 *sensibility*: refinement of feeling; 'quickness of perception' (TS).

99 *execution*: an 'execution' was the seizure of the goods of a debtor in default of payment. 'Distress' (cf. l. 98 above) could carry the same

meaning. Charles is in the midst of an extended sequence of such actions by his creditors.

108 *be moral*: indulge in moralizing.

119–20 *put any further confidence in*: confide yet more secrets to.

128 S.D. *Enter Maria*: 'She is able to enter unannounced because of her intimacy with Sneerwell' (Bateson).

131 *lover*: suitor.

133 *run*: ran.

141 *libel*: '*OED* cites this passage as example of "popular use"; "slander" would be the *correct* term' (Bateson).

152 *barb*: she is playing on two senses of the word: (1) backward-projecting point of an arrow, which makes its extraction difficult; (2) wounding remark.

155 *raillery*: 'satirical merriment' (TS).

182 *the town*: the fashionable upper-class society of London.

190 *Sir Filigree Flirt*: filigree is 'delicate ornamental work (with beads, precious stones, etc.)'; hence, anything delicate, intricate, highly wrought. As a verb, 'to flirt' meant (1) to behave amorously; but also (2) to sneer, scoff, gibe.

198 *York diligence*: the more expensive, but swifter, stage-coach to York. They were presumably on their way to Scotland; see note to *R* 5.1.138.

202–3 *Festino's . . . Casino*: 'festino' means 'feast, entertainment'; while 'casino' similarly means 'a public music or dancing saloon'. 'Casino' was also a two-handed card-game.

209–10 *Tale-bearers . . . tale-makers*: Mrs Candour's aphorism borrows the syntactical shape of the proverbial 'A taleteller is worse than a thief' (Tilley T55).

212–14 *Mr and Mrs Honeymoon . . . acquaintances*: i.e. their marriage is now wracked with disputes and quarrels.

214–16 *a certain widow . . . manner*: i.e. an unfortunate pregnancy had been passed off as 'dropsy', which causes the body to swell through an excess of watery fluid.

217–18 *Buffalo . . . fame*: Lord Buffalo is, like his namesake, a horned beast— i.e. endowed with cuckold's horns—because of his wife's adultery. ('No extraordinary fame' means 'of ill repute'.)

218 *Sir Harry Bouquet*: Sheridan re-used the name for a character in *The Camp* (1778). For 'bouquet', see note to 3.2.27 below.

219 *to measure swords*: to fight a duel.

232–3 *Spindle . . . Nickit*: Charles's friends are all addicted gamblers in desperate financial straits. 'Spindle' presumably derives his name from the rod or pin on which a gaming-wheel revolves; while 'Splint' may testify to either his dire financial situation (i.e. just held together) or to the horse-disease of that name (i.e. his favourite gambling was on horse-racing and he backed losers). 'Quinze' is the name of a card-game resembling pontoon, and 'Nickit' plays on 'nick', a particular throw of the dice in the game called hazard, and 'to nick' meaning 'to cheat'.

233 *all up*: totally bankrupt.

238-9 *Positively you shan't escape*: Maria has started to leave, but her hostess won't permit her to.

242 *pretty*: 'Neat, elegant' (TS).

245 *a rebus or a charade*: both are word puzzles, in which punning or other riddling clues are provided to identify each syllable. 'Sir Benjamin added the grace of rhyme to his enigmas' (Bateson).

247 *Frizzle's*: 'to frizzle' was 'to form (hair) into small crisp curls'.

249 *conversazione*: an at-home, a social gathering for discussion of the arts and literature, with occasionally an accompanying musical entertainment, recently introduced from Italy.

263-4 *Petrarch's Laura or Waller's Sacharissa*: his love for the unidentified but presumably real Laura was the inspiration for the love-poetry of Francesco Petrarca (1304-74), while Edmund Waller (1606-87) wrote poems to Dorothy Sidney, eldest daughter of the Earl of Leicester, under the name of Sacharissa. Neither poet's passion was consummated, a poor omen for Sir Benjamin.

267 *margin*: (1) outer border of page; (2) river-bank.

269 *that's true*: i.e. I've just thought of something you must be told.

271 *Nicely*: fastidious, delicately discriminating.

276 *wedding-livery bespoke*: the wedding-clothes have been ordered.

277 *pressing*: (1) urgent; (2) physically burdensome.

290 *conscious of*: guiltily aware of.

298 *Tunbridge*: the 'only real pretender to Bath's crown' among the spa towns; but, although 'able to attract a nationwide and prestigious clientele, it never expanded at the rate of the Somerset spa' (Borsay, 32).

302 *Ponto's assembly*: 'ponto' in quadrille is the ace of trumps when trumps are either diamonds or hearts.

307 *Dundizzy*: a devastating combination of 'dun', which TS glosses as 'dark, gloomy', therefore, here, 'murky of intelligence', and 'dizzy', for which TS offers 'thoughtless'.

314 *put out to nurse*: i.e. to be breast-fed by a poor woman hired for the purpose (and also to be concealed, so that the mother would not be shamed).

319 *East Indies*: this term covered the whole of SE Asia to the east of and including India.

323 *busy*: mischief-making, meddlesome, officious (as in 'busybody').

328 *the Jews*: i.e. the community of Jewish moneylenders in London.

329 *the Old Jewry*: a short street, near the Bank of England, where many Jews lived.

331–2 *Irish tontine*: a form of lottery, the subscribers to which were paid annuities as long as they lived, with the survivors' amounts increasing as other contributors died. Originally it was introduced by the Irish authorities in an attempt to reduce the national debt; an English version followed in 1765.

336 *securities*: friends who have acted as sureties for the many loans Charles has taken out.

337 *officer*: bailiff.

369 *not quite run down*: (1) not quite exhausted; (2) not totally discredited.

376 *sentiments*: see note to 1.1.75 above.

1.2.4 *tiffed*: rowed, had a tiff.

6 *gall*: bitterness of spirit, rancour (supposed to reside in the gall bladder).

12 *Grosvenor Square*: see note to Prologue, l. 22, above.

15 *doubt*: fear.

76 *steady to his text*: loyal to his professed principles.

77 *be at my house*: be my guest, lodge with me.

81 *Noll's*: Oliver's.

2.1.19–20 *the Pantheon*: in Oxford Street; opened in 1772, it was used for large fashionable gatherings. Price quotes from *The Public Advertiser*, 29 Jan. 1772: 'The much-talked-of Receptacle of fashionable Pleasure the Pantheon . . . The whole Building is composed of a Suite of 14 Rooms . . . each affording a striking Instance of the Splendour and Profusion of modern Times'. 'Critics were appalled by its extravagance and pointlessness. Most people, it was observed, simply went to the Pantheon to see and be seen' (Langford, 578).

20 *fête champêtre*: a large-scale and lavish open-air entertainment or festival. For comment on it as an instance of 'an apparently limitless desire for new sensations' in the 1770s, see Langford, 575–6.

34 *roll*: round cushion or pad.

35 *in worsted of your own working*: i.e. on woollen wall-hangings or tapestries you yourself had made.

36 *curious*: (1) exquisite, fine; (2) queer, strange.

38–9 *Aunt Deborah's*: not a fashionable name, and with something of a Puritan tinge.

43 *Pope Joan*: card-game using a compartmented tray, played by three or more persons.

48 *powdered*: i.e. with powdered wigs.

49 *chair*: sedan-chair.

white cats: this has to mean 'horses' or 'ponies'; but, while 'cattle' is used in the period as a collective noun which could include 'horses', no parallel for the use of 'cats' (as a fashionable abbreviation of 'cattle'?) in this sense has been found. Price wonders whether Sheridan may be responding to the final line in this passage from George Colman's prologue to Garrick's *Bon Ton* (1775): 'Nature it [i.e. *bon ton*] thwarts, and contradicts all reason; | 'Tis stiff French stays, and fruit when out of season; | A rose, when half a guinea is the price; | A set of bays, scarce bigger than six mice.'

50 *Kensington Gardens*: pleasure gardens attached to Kensington Palace, open to the public, though pedestrians only were permitted.

81 *precious circumstance*: splendid state of affairs.

88–9 *those utterers ... reputation*: Sir Peter blends scandalmongers and the criminals who disperse ('utter') counterfeit money, fake ('coin') such currency, and debase authentic coins by trimming ('clipping') their outer rim. Defacing the king's coinage was a capital offence, hence the reference to being transported 'on a hurdle' to execution in l. 87 above.

93 *bear a part*: contribute; sustain my share of the group activity.

2.2.1 *positively*: absolutely, without contradiction.

7 *Curricle*: light, open, two-wheeled carriage, usually drawn by two horses abreast.

Hyde Park: see note to l. 90 below.

8 *duodecimo phaeton*: small four-wheeled open carriage.

12 *macaronies*: for 'macaronis', see note to *R* 3.4.3. Sheridan adapted these four lines from a short poem of his own. Their original wording was: 'Sure never were seen two such sweet little Ponies | Other horses are clowns, these macaronis. | And to give them this title I'm sure isn't wrong, | Their legs are so slim and their tails are as long.'

17 *Phoebus*: see note to *D* 1.1.38–9.

34 *Vermilion*: a brilliant red or scarlet; indicating either the natural colour of the lady's complexion or that she has been using the rouge-pot too freely.

50–1 *there is ... her face*: i.e. her face is so plastered with obscuring and remedial cosmetics that her own skin cannot be glimpsed.

55 *Ochre*: TS defines 'ochre' as 'A kind of earth slightly coherent, and easily dissolved in water'—i.e. the lady's face is in a state of imminent dissolution. In addition, its colour is scarcely healthy, since the pigments grouped under this name range from yellow to deep orange red or brown.

caulks: stops up, fills in.

57 *paints so ill*: applies cosmetics so ineptly.

76 *pleasantry*: 'Gaiety, merriment; lively talk' (TS).

78 *A character dead at every word*: Sir Peter is recollecting Alexander Pope's *The Rape of the Lock* (1714), iii. 16: 'At ev'ry word a reputation dies'.

81 *Pursy*: 'shortbreathed and fat' (TS).

82 *Codille's*: in the card-game ombre, the losing of the game by the person who undertakes to win it is called 'codille'.

88 *laces herself by pulleys*: i.e. is so fat she can only fasten her corset with the help of pulleys.

90 *like a drummer's*: Bateson aptly cites the opening couplet of the fragment from which Sheridan derived ll. 11–14 above: 'Then, behind, all my hair is done up in a plat, | And so, like a cornet's, tuck'd under my hat'.

the Ring: 'The fashionable drive in Hyde Park, shut in by railings and fine trees' (Price). 'One set of coaches circled the drive in one direction, and another set in the opposite direction, thus affording the fashionable a chance to exchange greetings' (Nettleton).

113 *Stucco*: 'A kind of fine plaster for walls' (TS); i.e. the lady is concealing her deficiencies with heavy make-up.

115–16 *French fruit . . . proverb*: Price quotes a letter from Horace Walpole to Lady Ossory: 'Paragraphs of news . . . are like mottoes too wrapped in sugar, which everybody breaks, finds nothing worth reading, and yet goes on cracking.'

118 *Ogle*: TS defines 'to ogle' as 'To view with side glances as in fondness'.

119 *critical*: 'Exact, nicely judicious, accurate'; 'captious inclined to find fault' (TS).

123–8 *An Irish front . . . à la Chinoise*: it is unclear what an Irish forehead would be; perhaps, in line with the stereotype of the stage Irishman, 'brazen' or 'boastful'. 'Caledonian locks' means 'long hair, like a Scots Highlander's'. A 'Dutch nose' is flat or snub-nosed. An 'Austrian lip' displays the 'Protrusion of lower lip characteristic of the Habsburg (Imperial) family' (Bateson). A Spanish complexion is dark of hue (from infusion of Moorish blood). And Chinese teeth were allegedly stained black.

129–30 *table d'hôte at Spa*: a common table for guests at a hotel. For 'Spa', see note to *R* 2.1.146.

133 *join issue*: join forces, take the same side.

149 *united*: i.e. married.

155–6 *poaching on manors*: 'By an act of 1670 a man had to be lord of a manor, or have a substantial income from landed property, even to kill a hare on his own land'; and throughout the eighteenth century 'a mass of other statutes re-enacted and stiffened the penalties for unqualified hunting' (Douglas Hay, 'Poaching and the Game Laws on Cannock Chase', in

Douglas Hay *et al.*, *Albion's Fatal Tree: Crime and Society in Eighteenth-Century England* (Harmondsworth, 1975), 189.

161 *qualified*: i.e. possessed of the qualities necessary.

166 *law merchant*: 'the body of rules regulating trade and commerce between different countries' (*OED*).

167–9 *in all cases . . . endorsers*: a series of puns on financial and scandalmongering senses. Thus, 'currency' means (1) circulation (of slander) and (2) money as medium of exchange, 'drawer' (1) deviser (of the lie) and (2) person who derives funds from cashing in a bill of exchange, and 'endorsers' (1) those who give authority to scandal by repeating it and (2) those who sign a bill of exchange on the back to guarantee that it will be paid. Finally, 'to come on' means (1) attack and (2) demand recompense for.

184 *society*: company; but also, the 'school'.

194 S.D. [*kneeling*]: Lady Teazle's later remark (l. 219) establishes that Joseph kneels at some point during this duologue, and this seems, on balance, the most likely moment, though other options could, of course, work in performance. The moment of his rising—here placed at l. 206—is also not specified by Sheridan.

220 *bombast*: 'Fustian, big words' (TS); grandiloquent behaviour.

225 *platonic cicisbeo*: i.e. the recognized gallant and escort, but not lover, of a married woman.

231 *The only revenge in your power*: i.e. cuckolding Sir Peter.

238 *politics*: tactics, stratagems.

243 *rogueries*: 'Knavish tricks; waggery, arch tricks' (TS).

2.3.3 *bluff to old bachelor*: loyal to bachelordom.

7 *seven months*: cf. "Tis now six months' (1.2.2).

8–9 *the stool of repentance*: used to exhibit the penitent in the penance ritual the church still imposed on its delinquent members.

19–20 *has years*: is old enough, is sufficiently experienced.

22 *compound for his extravagance*: (1) not be offended by his extravagance; (2) settle his debts.

40 *cross accident*: adverse happening or occurrence.

77–8 *run out of the course*: left the straight and narrow path of absolute virtue.

3.1.7 *confinement*: imprisonment (for debt).

16 *obtained permission*: i.e. from his gaolers.

21–2 *'a tear . . . charity'*: the quotation derives from the dying Henry IV's description of his apparently dissolute son, Prince Hal, in Shakespeare's *2 Henry IV*, 4.3.31–2.

26 *relative to*: in relation to, with regard to.

38 *evidence*: witness.

40 *forgery*: a capital offence in the eighteenth century.

43 *the honest Israelite*: the character of Moses almost led to the play's being banned. He was rumoured to be based on Benjamin Hopkins, alleged to make usurious loans to minors, and currently fighting for re-election, with government support, as Chamberlain of the City of London. Accordingly, the licence to perform the play was withheld, and Sheridan's personal intervention with the Lord Chamberlain was needed before it was granted. For further details of the incident, see Price, i. 300–3.

60 *Crutched Friars*: 'A continuation of Jewry Street, running from Aldgate to Mark Lane' (Price).

62 *Premium*: 'Something given to invite a loan or bargain; a reward proposed' (TS).

66 *represent*: impersonate, pretend to be.

78 *principal*: the person for whom Moses is the go-between.

85 *treating*: negotiating.

96 *want*: i.e. that he needs.

112 *Annuity Bill*: discussed in Parliament in April and passed on 12 May, this protected minors from paying more than 10 shillings per £100 per annum to moneylenders and was aimed at Hopkins and his kind.

161 *madam*: as the tone of their exchanges grows chiller, Sir Peter switches from addressing her as 'Maria' to the more formal 'madam' (i.e. sarcastically treating her as if she were an adult, and thus rebuking her for the independent-minded way in which she is behaving).

183–4 *seal me . . . repayment*: i.e. by kissing him. She wittily deflects him by offering her hand to be kissed in her next speech, where she plays on the normal meaning of 'note of hand' (i.e. promissory note signed by her hand).

188 *independent settlement*: a settlement which will secure her an independent income of her own.

213 *temper*: disposition, temperament.

232–5 *Ay, you . . . my relations*: there is a theatrical tradition that at one rehearsal of this scene Sheridan interrupted Mrs Abington when she reached 'How dare you abuse my relations?' and gave her this advice; 'No, no, that won't do at all! It mustn't be *pettish*. That's shallow—shallow. You must go up stage with, "You are just what my cousin Sophy said you would be," and then turn and sweep down on him like a volcano. "You are a great bear to abuse my relations! How *dare* you abuse my relations!"' (Ellen Terry, *The Story of My Life* (Woodbridge, Suffolk, 1982), 31).

243 *dangling*: TS defines a dangler as 'A man that hangs about women' and 'to dangle' as 'to be an humble follower'.

247 *Sir Tivy Terrier*: Tivy is an abbreviation of 'tantivy', i.e. a rapid gallop, headlong rush, and he owes his surname to the terrier's capacities as a hunting-dog.

249 *broke his neck*: in a fall from his horse while hunting.

268 *temper*: equanimity, poise.

3.2.8 *Mr Joseph*: as the elder brother Joseph inherited his father's house.

23 *a place*: employment.

27 *bags and bouquets*: both are terms for wigs in which the back hair was gathered in an ornamental silk bag or purse.

30–1 *bill discounted*: Trip has asked Moses to act as go-between in getting a promissory note of his cashed in ahead of the date on which it falls due. This was called 'discounting', because the money obtained would be less than the face value of the bill. As Sir Oliver's following aside implies, Trip is playing well out of his social league and aping the financial practices of his social superiors.

33 *distresses*: see note to 1.1.99 above.

36 *Brush*: Charles's valet, whose responsibilities include brushing his master's clothes.

endorsed it: see note to *R* 2.2.167–9.

48 *damned register*: established under the provisions of the Annuity Bill. See note to l. 112 above.

52–3 *nothing capital . . . dropped lately*: one of the perks of being an upper servant was that some of their employers' discarded clothing came to them. 'Capital' here means 'sufficient to provide the basis of this kind of financial transaction'.

53–4 *a mortgage . . . November*: i.e. he would hand over some of his master's winter clothes, on condition he could redeem them, at an appropriate price, before his master, on the onset of winter, noticed their absence.

54–6 *you shall have . . . silver*: i.e. these clothes are sure soon to be Trip's, so he would guarantee to hand them over immediately to Moses. ('Reversion' means an anticipated inheritance (usually, after another's death), and '*post-obit*' was a bond to repay borrowed money on the death of a specified person from whom the borrower anticipates an inheritance.)

3.3. S.D. *Charles Surface . . . etc.*: Price, following manuscript sources, prints only 'CHARLES—CARELESS—*etc. etc.*' here.

7 *mantle over*: form over (like froth on the top of a drink).

9 *pertness*: 'spriteliness without force' (TS).

flatulence: 'windiness; pomposity, pretentiousness' (TS).

11 *play*: gambling.

14 *a hazard-regimen*: a course of diet to make him fit to play the card-game called 'hazard', in which the chances are complicated by arbitrary rules.

18 *throw on*: throw the dice, having drunk.

24 *floats at top*: stays in your memory through the alcoholic haze.

28 *you must . . . her peers*: i.e. each of the others must in turn propose a toast to another woman who is her equal.

30 *canonized vestals*: virgin saints.

79 *grow conscientious*: develop a conscience.

88 *sentiment*: striking or aphoristic thought; here, a toast.

95–6 *demurred to*: raised an objection to; refrained from drinking off your whole glass in response to.

117–18 *you know . . . to me*: he lives up to his name in being carelessly willing to act as security in any deal Charles may strike.

132 *of many compliments*: i.e. who indulges in many preliminary flourishes.

147 *twig*: plentiful timber on an estate was a potentially lucrative source of income.

151–2 *are you . . . my connections?*: do you know who any of my relatives are?

170 *post-obit*: see note to 3.2.54–6 above.

176 *principal*: sum originally loaned.

182 *too good a life*: likely to be too long-lived.

187 *breaks apace*: weakens, declines, swiftly.

212–13 *race cups and corporation bowls*: cups won in horse races and bowls bestowed on holders of civic offices or those a town or city wishes to honour.

216 *communicative*: 'Inclined to make advantages common, liberal of knowledge, not selfish' (TS).

229–30 *a bargain*: as a bargain.

238 *bowels*: compassion, sympathetic feelings.

239–40 *Shylock . . . blood*: cf. Shylock's bargain with Antonio in Shakespeare's *The Merchant of Venice*, 1.3.143–50.

248 *burn*: damn, to hell with. But, in his next speech, Charles responds as if Careless had used the verb literally.

4.1.2 *up to the Conquest*: back to the Norman Conquest of 1066.

5 *no volunteer grace*: no gratuitous graces or inventive embellishments (to render the portrait unrealistic).

6 *modern Raphael*: Sir Joshua Reynolds, a close friend of the Sheridans; see note to *A Portrait*, l. 36.

16 *gouty chair*: one designed to suit the needs of a sufferer from gout, appropriate for its adopted use here because of its extended leg rest.

20 '*Richard, heir to Thomas . . .*': an in-joke, since the dramatist was himself son, though not heir, to Thomas Sheridan.

24–5 *ex post facto parricide*: i.e. if Charles's father were not already dead, his son's behaviour would kill him.

26 *generation*: family, line of descent.

31 *Ravelin*: 'A ravelin was a fortification with two faces at an angle to the main structure' (Price).

33 *the Battle of Malplaquet*: an allied victory in the War of the Spanish Succession, under the command of Marlborough and Prince Eugene, on 11 Sept. 1709. The casualties on both sides were formidable and assisted in turning English opinion against the continuation of the war.

34 *cut out of*: deprived of.

35 *clipped*: pared down, diminished.

44 *Kneller*: the great portrait painter Sir Godfrey Kneller (1646–1723). He 'painted many ladies in landscapes and pastoral settings, but not as shepherdesses' (Bateson).

46 *ten*: i.e. 10 shillings.

130 *nabob*: 'A civil or military official of the East India Company, who made a fortune during his stay in India' (Price). Their reputation was growing steadily worse during the 1770s; so the attachment of 'honest' to the noun here is emphatic.

136 *genius*: character, bent.

148–9 *two thirds . . . right*: a third of the £800 goes to Moses as his commission.

173 '*Be just . . . generous*': The Oxford Dictionary of English Proverbs, rev. F. P. Wilson (3rd edn.; Oxford, 1970), 416, lists it as a proverb, but cites this passage as its first example!

178 *economy*: frugality; good economic management.

4.2.6 *so deep*: (1) so addictedly; (2) for such large sums.

32 *birthday clothes*: the king's official birthday in January was the peak of the social season, and especially lavish clothes bought for the attendant celebrations presumably were not designed to be re-worn and descended to the servants as the perquisites of their office. Cf. note to 3.2.52–3 above.

4.3. S.D. *A library*: the setting of this scene in a library infuriated Percy Bysshe Shelley. As Thomas Love Peacock, '*Memoirs of Shelley*' and Other Essays and Reviews (London, 1970), 45, recorded, 'When, after the scenes which exhibited Charles Surface in his jollity, the scene returned, in the fourth act, to Joseph's library, Shelley said to me "I see the purpose of this comedy. It is to associate virtue with bottles and glasses, and villainy with books." I had great difficulty to make him stay to the end.'

51 *the original compact*: the agreement on which the marriage was founded.

69 *outrageous at*: infuriated about; excessive in your response to.

73 *faux pas*: act which risks compromising your reputation; indiscreet action.

78 *a plethora*: a medical condition characterized by excess of blood.

112–13 S.D. (*Gaping, and throws away the book*): 'Gaping' means 'yawning'. His throwing away the book is at odds with Joseph's professed devotion to books; and 'One eighteenth-century actor playing Joseph turned his page down carefully before laying the book aside; an action in line with the neatness Joseph boasts of, but losing Sheridan's point about the holes that show from time to time in his carefully prepared Surface' (Katharine Worth, *Sheridan and Goldsmith* (London, 1992), 40).

210 *sensibly*: palpably, appreciably.

228 *be at home*: i.e. admit his visit.

244 *man of intrigue*: i.e. a man who indulges in surreptitious love-affairs.

246 *absolute Joseph*: i.e. on the model of the biblical Joseph, who rejected the advances of his master's wife who 'caught him by his garment, saying, Lie with me' (Genesis 39: 12)

247 *character*: public reputation (to lose).

259 *close*: hidden.

331 *incog.*: i.e. incognito; here, unobserved, from concealment.

364–5 *apprehensive of his good name*: worried about maintaining his reputation.

378 *quit with*: revenged on.

428 *let her alone*: rely on her.

433 *pretended*: (1) which he professed; (2) which he feigned.

442 *should have spoke*: would have spoken, would have made evident.

5.1.11 *policy*: tactical sagacity, prudent and expedient conduct.

24 *speculative*: theoretical.

40 *complaisance*: 'Civility, desire of pleasing' (TS).

75–6 *congou tea, avadavats, and Indian crackers*: Black China tea, Indian song-birds, and fireworks imported from India.

111 *address*: social deftness.

112–15 *The silver ore . . . tax*: the reference is to the highly controversial plate tax of 1756, which imposed an annual levy on the quantity of silver plate owned by a household. Joseph rejects practical charity as imposing too heavy a tax on the man who performs it and confines himself to benevolent sayings, which resemble cheap imported plate in attracting no further financial consequences. Also in play here is the idea of sentimental comedy—*comédie larmoyante*—as being itself of French derivation.

5.2.6 *Dear heart*: an exclamation of dismay.

11 *Mr Surface*: i.e. Joseph (his title as the elder brother and the principal heir).

29 *our friend Lady Teazle*: for an argument in favour of reading 'our friend Teazle' here, see Geraldine Murray, 'A Sheridan Emendation', *Notes and Queries*, 234 (1989), 482–3.

73 *in seconde*: 'A "thrust in *seconde*" is one delivered under one's opponent's blade, and with the knuckles upwards, the wrist turned downwards' (Price).

89 *the Montem*: 'the procession, on Whit Tuesday, by Eton boys to Salt-hill. On the way they collected money for the senior collegers' (Price).

90 *charged*: loaded. They were carried—or, at least, so Crabtree's story goes—by Joseph, ready for firing, as protection against highwaymen on his alleged journey.

93 *took place*: found its aim.

95 *Pliny*: 'the classical letter-writer . . . widely regarded as a model of epistolary elegance'; so an appropriate object for the bullet to bounce off in the direction of the postman bearing the double letter (J. R. Moore, 'Sheridan's "Little Pliny"', *Notes and Queries*, 59 (1944), 164).

102 *interested in*: concerned in; personally implicated in the consequences of.

113 *one of the faculty*: a doctor.

122 *for a hundred*: for a wager of £100.

145 *given you over*: written you off as mortally wounded.

152 *dub me*: nominate me, invest me with the title of.

180 *high*: angry.

211 *pleasant*: entertaining, a good joke.

5.3.3 *is distraction to me*: drives me mad.

16–17 *What had you . . . bate in*: what reason had you to slacken in.

40 *diffidence of*: lack of confidence in.

43 *baited*: tormented, harassed; mocked.

83 *A.B.s at the coffee-houses*: business advertisements in the newspapers were often signed A.B. and a coffee-house given as the place at which the advertiser could be contacted.

129 *recollect myself*: summon back my concentration and invention, regroup my thoughts.

237 S.D. *apart*: i.e. they have separated from the others to speak intimately together.

251–2 *as Lady Teazle and I—intend to do*: the pause in the middle of the line is crucial to its comic effect. It lures the audience into thinking that Sir Peter is about to make an ill-advised boast about past marital harmony, an expectation he can then triumphantly defeat by the line's last three words. For interesting commentary on the line in performance, see John Dolman, Jr., 'A Laugh Analysis of *The School for Scandal*', *Quarterly Journal of Speech*, 16 (1930), 438.

264 *waive thy beauty's sway*: relinquish or refuse to exercise the command over me your beauty gives you.

Epilogue *Colman*: George Colman the Elder (1732–94), a highly talented comic dramatist and manager of the Covent Garden Theatre, 1767–74, and of the Haymarket Theatre, 1777–89. His plays include a first-rate marriage comedy, *The Jealous Wife* (1761), and *Polly Honeycombe* (1760), to which some think Sheridan was indebted for some aspects of his portrait of Lydia Languish.

Mrs Abington: one of the most praised performers of her generation. James Boaden, *The Life of Mrs Jordan* (London, 1831), i. 16–17, testified that she 'unquestionably possessed very peculiar and hitherto unapproached talent. She, I think, took more entire *possession* of the stage, than any actress I have seen; there was, however, no assumption in her dignity; she was a lawful and graceful sovereign, who exerted her full power, and enjoyed her established prerogatives.' He also wrote that 'common-place was not the station of Abington. She was always beyond the surface; untwisted all the chains which bind ideas together; and seized upon the exact cadence and emphasis by which the point of dialogue is enforced.' She became an arbiter of fashion; her decision to wear a *'remarkably low'* wig as Lady Teazle 'exhibited such evident marks of propriety that all the high heads in the house looked more like caricatures upon dress than real fashion' (*BD*, i. 18).

5 *motley Bayes*: though presumably invoked affectionately here, 'Bayes' is the name under which Buckingham satirized John Dryden in *The Rehearsal* (1671). Dryden was Sheridan's favourite poet, so perhaps that turns the recollection into a compliment. ('Motley' was the parti-coloured dress of the professional jester or comedian.)

6 *crying epilogues*: a jibe at Sheridan's epilogue to George Ayscough's tragedy, *Semiramis* (1776), for which see Price, ii. 823–4.

29 *Seven's the main*: 'The main was the number (five to nine) called by the caster in hazard, before the dice were thrown. "If seven is thrown for a Main, and four the Chance, it is two to one against the Person who throws" (*Hoyle's Games Improv'd*, rev. Thomas Jones (1778), 210)' (Price).

33 *cushioned tête*: lady's hair or wig, worn high over a pad and elaborately ornamented. Cf. *TTS*, Prologue, ll. 35–8.

35 *card-drums*: 'Card parties at private houses' (Price).

41 *Your revels . . . no more*: cf. 'Our revels now are ended' (*The Tempest*, 4.1.148).

39–42 *Farewell . . . | . . . occupation's o'er*: a parodic variation on Othello's lament on being convinced of Desdemona's infidelity (3.4.352–62).

44 *I ought . . . next year*: Abington only played comic roles.

46 *periods*: sentences.

The Critic

'Johnson had laid down in his *Dictionary* (1755) that "C, according to English orthography, never ends a word". Was Sheridan attacking a rule that was now falling into obsolescence and, by his insistence on the modern spelling [of 'critic'], dubbing Johnson's pronouncement antiquarian nonsense?' (James Morwood, *The Life and Works of Richard Brinsley Sheridan* (Edinburgh, 1985), 105).

Dedication *Mrs Greville*: Frances Greville (*c*.1724–89), mother of Sheridan's mistress, Frances Anne Crewe, to whom he had dedicated *The School for Scandal*. Roger Lonsdale (ed.), *Eighteenth Century Women Poets: An Anthology* (Oxford, 1989), 190–4, provides a biographical sketch of Frances Greville and reprints two of her poems, including 'A Prayer for Indifference', according to Lonsdale (p. 190) 'the most celebrated poem by a woman in the period'.

14–16 *a fastidious concealment . . . endowments*: apart from 'A Prayer for Indifference' Mrs Greville published almost none of her poems.

18 *attach*: draw and secure.

21 *elegant*: 'appropriate to people of refinement and cultivated taste' (*OED*); 'Pleasing with minuter beauties; nice, not coarse, not gross' (TS).

23 *interested object*: self-interested aim.

The Characters of the Play *Dangle*: TS defines 'to dangle' as 'to hang upon any one, to be an humble follower'. The model for the part was said to be Thomas Vaughan, author of a farce, *The Hotel*, produced at Drury Lane in Nov. 1776 under Sheridan's management, and a theatrical devotee and haunter of the green room.

Sir Fretful Plagiary: for Richard Cumberland as the target of Sheridan's satire in this role, see Introduction, p. x.

Puff: TS defines 'to puff' as 'to swell or blow up with praise; to swell or elate with pride'.

Pasticcio Ritornello: a pastiche is a musical composition made up of pieces derived from or imitating various sources; a ritornello is an instrumental refrain, interlude, or prelude, especially in a vocal work. (There were constant influxes of Continental musicians into London in the late eighteenth century; and Sheridan as manager of the King's Theatre in the Haymarket will have been a principal target of their solicitations.)

Underprompter: for the work of the prompter and his assistants, see note to 2.1.53 below.

Scenemen: scene shifters, stage-crew.

Ferolo Whiskerandos: in Spanish 'férula' means both 'birch rod' and 'rule, domination'. The surname offers a clue to the required make-up. In this role Bannister mimicked William Smith's performance of Richard III.

Beefeater: 'A yeoman of the guard' (TS), i.e. one of the armed force which protected the Tower of London.

Tilburina: 'the damsel of Tilbury, as it were' (Crane). Miss Pope's playing of the role reportedly mocked Mrs Crawford's characteristic playing of tragic heroines.

Prologue The obvious candidate to speak the prologue was Thomas King (see note to TTS, Prologue).

Richard Fitzpatrick: Richard Fitzpatrick (1748–1813) was the second son of the 1st Earl of Upper Ossory. He was an intimate friend of the politician Charles James Fox, as also of George Selwyn, both of whom are alluded to later in the play (see notes to 1.2.209 and 286). Fitzpatrick and Fox 'lived in the same lodgings in Piccadilly, and had kindred tastes for society, gambling, literature, and the theatre . . . Fitzpatrick had entered the army in 1765, and, though opposed to the war in America, served there in 1777'. He later 'attained the rank of Lieutenant-General and the post of Secretary of War' (Nettleton). A letter survives in which Sheridan invites Fitzpatrick to 'come and abuse' *The Critic* in performance, misquoting in the process his own Sir Fretful: 'Nothing is so pleasant as a judicious Critic who—' (*Letters*, i. 128–9; cf. 1.1.254–5 below).

1 *The sister muses . . . | . . . obey*: the muse of comedy, Thalia, and the muse of tragedy, Melpomene, rule the playhouse world.

5–10 *In those gay . . . forswore*: the Duke of Buckingham's mockery of John Dryden's capacities as a playwright in the character of Bayes—and, more broadly, of heroic and tragic playwriting in his time—in *The Rehearsal* (1671) provides the crucial precedent on which *The Critic* is founded. *The Rehearsal* was still a repertory piece in the 1770s, and Bayes had been a favourite role of Garrick's. The success of *The Critic*, however, finally displaced it from the stage.

14 *flippant*: sportive, playful; treating serious matters lightly and disrespectfully.

17 *slight entrenchment*: insubstantial defence.

25 *numbers*: lines of verse.

26 *dullness . . . keep*: cf. Alexander Pope's *The Dunciad* (1742-3), where the goddess of dullness bestows on her adherents 'the soft gifts of Sleep' (iii. 419); and also the domain of nonsense in John Dryden's *MacFlecknoe* (1682), 'Where their vast courts the mother-strumpets keep' (l. 72).

32 *motley scenes*: see note to *SS*, Epilogue, l. 5.

45 *By numbers*: by the sheer scale of the opposing forces.

1.1.1 *Brutus*: a pseudonym used by the Whig pamphleteer, probably Sir Philip Francis (1740-1818), who mainly wrote under the name of Junius when attacking the government and person of Lord North in letters to *The Public Advertiser* between 1769 and 1771. The name had also been used to sign a letter to the same paper on 6 Sept. 1779, 'satirizing the military discipline of the Westminster and Middlesex volunteers' (Price). For the latter, see notes to l. 70 below.

Lord North: Frederick North, second Earl of Guilford (1732-92), chief minister of George III at the date of the play, and a much vilified figure, blamed in particular for the fallible conduct of the American war and the ill-preparedness and confusion of the country's response to the threat of a Spanish and French invasion in the summer of 1779. Sheridan wrote for *The Englishman*, a periodical published between 13 March and 2 June 1779 to attack North's administration.

2-3 *the first . . . A dash Y*: John Montagu, 4th Earl of Sandwich (1718-92), first Lord of the Admiralty, 'the target of ceaseless invective aimed at his notorious corruption' (Nettleton).

3 *a letter from St Kitts*: the sugar trade from the West Indies was of crucial financial significance to Britain. But the American war hit the trade hard, and sugar imports declined sharply. American privateers attacked shipping whenever they could, and French forces also damaged the English fleet there in the summer of 1779, making territorial gains, including Grenada, the richest sugar-island after Jamaica. The English fleet pulled back to St Kitts for repairs. The news in Dangle's letter is therefore unlikely to be good. There was 'bitter resentment' at home 'at what was considered Byron's "abandoning" of the [Grenada] garrison, which put up a brave defence against overwhelming odds' (Patrick Crowhurst, *The Defence of British Trade 1689-1815* (Folkestone, 1977), 199).

Coxheath: France's recognition in 1778 of the independence of Britain's American colonies and declaration of war against Britain led to the establishment of military camps along the routes of a possible invasion in southern England. One of these was at Coxheath, near Maidstone. There large-scale military manoeuvres were practised in preparation for war. These manoeuvres became a major spectator sport, attracting people from a wide social range, including nobility and gentry travelling from London and the resort towns of the south coast. The camp grew into a miniature city, with its own butchers, bakers, tailors, fishmongers, etc., supplying the needs of those who had flocked there. For a time this was the fashionable place to be. The London theatres responded by transferring the Coxheath Camp to their stages. The Patagonian puppet theatre in Exeter Change offered a new three-act comic opera, *A Tour of Coxheath; or, The Humours of a Modern Camp*, in Jan. 1779, featuring 'a Grand Perspective View of the Encampment, and an Exact Representation of their Majesties passing the Line' (*The Morning Post*, 22 Jan. 1779); and there was a Sadler's Wells entertainment of Aug. 1778, *A Trip to Coxheath*, which concluded with a distant view of the camp. Sheridan scripted and De Loutherbourgh designed *The Camp* (premièred at Drury Lane on 15 Oct. 1778), which climaxed with an elaborate scenic display of Coxheath. It was a triumph, with fifty-six performances that season. For more information on the Coxheath phenomenon, see Russell, 33–51.

4 *intelligence*: information, news.

4–5 *Sir Charles Hardy*: recently appointed commander of the Channel fleet at the age of 64, and ineffectual and unaggressive in his discharge of his office in the face of the threatened French and Spanish invasion force. One of his subordinate officers lamented that 'So much indifference at so dangerous a crisis is astonishing and alarming' (Butterfield, 58).

6–7 *The Morning Chronicle*: 'William Woodfall (1746–1803) was its dramatic critic and subjected the plays that he saw to careful and dispassionate examination. The newspaper was said, in its issue of 5 Nov. 1777, to have "the honour of taking the lead as a theatrical reviewer"' (Price).

8 *gazette*: 'A paper of news, a paper of publick intelligence' (TS).

11 *The Spanish Armada*: Puff's choice of subject is richly topical. In June 1779 the threat of invasion by a partly Spanish fleet provoked the Earl of Shelburne to enter 'into a minute account of the internal state of this country, when it was threatened by the Spanish Armada' in the House of Lords in June 1779, and George III wrote that 'It was the vigour of mind shown by Queen Elizabeth and her subjects, added to the assistance of Divine Providence, that saved this island when attacked by the Spaniards' (Butterfield, 42 and 51). With an eye on the threat of 'Invasion from our inveterate Enemies', *Lloyd's Evening Post*, 29 Sept.–1 Oct., provided an 'Account of the Trophies taken from the Spaniards, in 1588, at their Grand Invasion'. The theatre followed suit with *The Prophecy; or, Queen Elizabeth at Tilbury*, a pantomime pastiche presented at Sadler's Wells in the summer of 1779. The scenery includes a view of Tilbury Fort and the surrounding country, and the climax displayed the English fleet triumphant on the seas, with the French and Spanish fleets dismasted and defeated. The manager of Sadler's Wells and likely contriver of *The Prophecy* was Thomas King, the original Puff in *The Critic*, and for whom the role was clearly designed.

15 *received*: accepted and ratified by critical precept and approval; already used in, and plagiarized from, other plays.

16–17 *in such forwardness*: in such an advanced state of preparation.

20 *Now the plays are begun*: the season at Drury Lane ran from mid-September to the end of May.

28 *with Roman signatures*: letters to the editors in newspapers were often signed—cf. note to l. 1 above—with Roman pseudonyms. The crisis of Sept. and Oct. 1779 prompted a particularly energetic flow of them.

33 *the character of a critic*: cf. Bayes in *The Rehearsal*, 1.1.307–17: 'there are, now-a-days, a sort of persons, they call Critiques, that, I gad, have no more wit in them than so many Hobby-horses; but they'll laugh you, Sir, and find fault, and censure things, that, I gad, I'm sure, they are not able to do themselves. A sort of envious persons, that emulate the glories of persons of parts, and think to build their fame, by calumniating of persons, that, I gad, to my knowledge, of all persons in the world are, in nature, the persons that do as much despise all that as—a—In fine, I'll say no more of 'em.'

36 *quidnunc*: gossip, newsmonger (from Latin 'quid nunc?', meaning 'what now?').

Maecenas: patron (from the name of the Roman patron of the poets Virgil and Horace).

39–40 *for my interest*: i.e. to use my influence and connections to the letter-writers' advantage.

47 *pantomime*: eighteenth-century pantomimes typically began with relatively serious material, often retelling stories derived from classical mythology, while the second half metamorphosed the deities into *commedia dell'arte* figures, and Harlequin and Columbine then danced and mimed their way through a hectic sequence of spectacular settings and actions, frequently spoofing the serious plot along the way. For another format, equally spectacular and farcical, see the account of *Harlequin a Sorcerer* (1752) in Cecil Price, *Theatre in the Age of Garrick* (Oxford, 1973), 71–3. For Sheridan's own contribution to the genre, see John McVeagh, '*Robinson Crusoe*'s Stage Debut: The Sheridan Pantomime of 1781', *Journal of Popular Culture*, 24 (1990), 137–52.

48 *Mr Fosbrook*: Thomas Fosbrook, a trusted employee of both Garrick's and Sheridan's at Drury Lane. In 1779 he was box bookkeeper and numberer (i.e. he counted the spectators to ensure that ticket receipts tallied with the numbers present).

51 *Smatter*: (1) foolish talk, chatter; (2) dabbler, trifler.

53 *damned*: a flop in performance, hissed off the stage.

55 *high change*: i.e. exchange, 'the place where the merchants [here, theatre practitioners of various kinds] meet to negotiate their affairs' (TS).

'Jobbing' (l. 56), therefore, plays on (1) buying and selling stocks and (2) doing any bits of work that are offered.

57–8 *without character*: without reputation; unrecommended, not possessed of references; without any distinctive quality to recommend them.

59 *Dorindas, Pollys*: Dorinda is a character in George Farquhar's *The Beaux' Stratagem* (1707), and Polly Peachum is a leading figure in John Gay's *The Beggar's Opera* (1728). The two plays were among the century's most often performed works.

61 *Richards*: Richard IIIs. David Garrick made his London debut, and Thomas Sheridan, the playwright's father, his professional debut, in this Shakespearian role.

62–3 *the manager . . . Opera House*: Sheridan and Thomas Harris bought the King's Theatre in the Haymarket on 4 Feb. 1778 and opened it with opera that autumn. The venture did not pay; Harris withdrew at the end of the first season, and Sheridan himself sold out to William Taylor on 7 Nov. 1781. The project is chronicled in Curtis Price, Judith Milhous, and Robert D. Hume, *Italian Opera in Late Eighteenth-Century London*, i. *The King's Theatre, Haymarket 1778–1791* (Oxford, 1995).

66 *figure dancers*: a 'figure dance' is one consisting of several distinct figures or divisions.

70 *Westminster associations*: volunteer militia, raised to meet the crisis with France and Spain.

71 *Artillery Ground*: an area used for military exercises near Moorfields in London.

75–7 *the stage . . . of the time'*: Dangle is quoting Hamlet on 'the purpose of playing'—'to hold as 'twere the mirror up to nature' (3.2.20–2)—and on 'the players' as 'the abstracts and brief chronicles of the time' (2.2.525–7). These allusions were a late addition, since they do not appear in the copy of the play submitted for licensing to the Lord Chamberlain the day before the first performance. But the text already contained many other echoes of *Hamlet*, which was the mainpiece which *The Critic* accompanied at its première.

92 *hitch us into a story*: weave gossip around us, make us the subject of his gossip.

103 *orders*: free tickets (especially for first performances) given to people who could be relied upon to applaud the show, a practice in which Sheridan freely indulged as Drury Lane manager, including for the early performances of *The School for Scandal*.

106 *consequence*: important rank.

110 *solicited solicitations*: i.e. importuning (the theatre managers, etc.) because you yourself have been importuned by others to do so.

119–20 *'taken from the French'*: 'The operative word is "taken". A translation acknowledges its origin; this does not' (Crane).

120–1 *lately . . . run down*: see note to *R*, Prologue, l. 28.

127 *school of morality*: cf. Winworth's assertion at the end of Hugh Kelly's *False Delicacy* (1768) that 'the stage should be a school of morality'.

128–9 *people . . . their entertainment*: an early fragment by Sheridan survives in which a playwriting Scotchman defends his principles to a doubtful theatre manager (Price, ii. 804): 'no Sir it ever was my opinion that the stage should be a place of Rational entertainment, instead of which I am very sorry to say most people go there for their diversion, accordingly I have formed my commedy so that It is no laughing gig[g]ling piece of work, He must be a very light man that shall discompose his muscles from the beginning to the end.'

131 *line*: style of comedy.

134 *two houses*: playing on 'houses' meaning (1) theatres and (2) private homes. The insinuation is that only at Drury Lane and Covent Garden in contemporary London are there 'houses' (in either sense) where moral decorums are sustained.

137–9 *No double . . . reformation!*: Sheridan is mocking himself. Cf. his bowdlerization of Vanbrugh's *The Relapse* as *A Trip to Scarborough* and his chastening of the texts of the three Congreve plays he revived at Drury Lane.

154 *stoop . . . at*: swoop down on.

157 *dramatize the penal laws*: i.e. cover all the categories of indictable offences in a series of comedies; produce a series of plays which will reform all varieties of criminal conduct.

158 *a court of ease*: Sheridan's variation on 'chapel of ease' (meaning one provided for parishioners who live far from the parish church). Hence, the stage will punish and reform criminals the principal London criminal court (the 'Old Bailey') does not manage to reach.

172 *free*: 'unrestrained', 'frank' (TS).

193–4 *without a compliment*: without any flattery, speaking truthfully.

210–11 *the piece . . . with it*: i.e. its quality recommends itself.

211–12 *the manager of Covent Garden Theatre*: cf. note to *R*, Preface, 49.

216 *'Writes . . . he does*: i.e. the Drury Lane manager, Sheridan himself.

221 *you have reason*: since it is, of course, Sir Fretful's dominant fixation.

226–7 *as gipsies . . . their own*: Sheridan gilds the joke here by having Sir Fretful plagiarize even as he denounces plagiarism. Thomas Moore, *Memoirs of . . . Richard Brinsley Sheridan* (3rd edn.; London, 1828), 276, identified the relevant lines in Charles Churchill's *The Apology* (1761):'Like gipsies, lest the stolen brat be known, | Defacing first, then claiming for their own'.

228–9 *he, you know, never—*: i.e. Sheridan never writes tragedy.

232 *tragedy . . . comedy*: Ian Donaldson explores 'the century's most common theatrical joke: that it was difficult nowadays to know whether a play was meant to be tragic or comic' ('Drama from 1710 to 1780', in Roger Lonsdale (ed.), *Dryden to Johnson* (London, 1971), 191–3). Cf. also 'Our poets make us laugh at Tragoedy, | And with their Comedies they make us cry' (*The Rehearsal*, Prologue, 13–14). Also relevant is the oft-told tale of Richard Cumberland, Sir Fretful's original, striving to suppress his children's laughter at *The School for Scandal*—'What are you laughing at, my dear little folks? you should not laugh, my angels; there is nothing to laugh at'—which reputedly earned the rejoinder from Sheridan that 'It was very ungrateful in Cumberland to have been displeased with his poor children for laughing at *my comedy*; for I went the other night to see *his tragedy*, and laughed at it from beginning to end' (*Sheridania* (London, 1826), 67).

237–8 *hit that gentleman*: get the better of, or outmanœuvre, Sheridan.

243–4 *character . . . to me*: Sir Fretful means 'high reputation as an author'; but Sneer responds as if he had meant 'other people's knowledge that I am an author'.

250 *mended*: improved, enhanced.

254 *tenacious*: i.e. stubborn in defending every word they have written.

266 *implicit*: absolute, unquestioning.

297–8 *three hours and an half*: grossly, of course, beyond the acceptable length for a play; but, in part, a self-reflexive joke from a dramatist who had apologized for the 'uncommon length of' *The Rivals* 'as represented the first night' (*R*, Preface, 41–2).

299–300 *the music between the acts*: entr'acte music was usual, even in tragedy.

301 *next*: i.e. as the next new play to be performed.

316 *Ha, ha, ha!*: in *The Rehearsal*, Bayes resorts to laughing as he narrates the actors' refusal to act a previous play of his (2.2.30–6).

324–5 *Make out something*: invent something.

327 *signifies*: is significant, matters.

334 *your commonplace-book*: cf. Bayes's displaying of 'my book of *Drama Common places*; the Mother of many other Plays' (*The Rehearsal*, 1.1.84–6).

347–8 *like a clown in one of the new uniforms*: like a peasant in one of the gaudy and fantastical uniforms affected by the aristocratic camp-followers at Coxheath Camp. See note to l. 3 above.

350 *tropes and flowers*: rhetorical and figurative embellishments.

351–2 *tambour . . . linsey-wolsey*: 'Elaborate embroidery on a very ordinary fabric of wool and linen' (Price).

353 *the mimicry of Falstaff's page*: the page-boy is given by Prince Hal to Falstaff, who suspects a mischievous intent: 'If the Prince put thee into my service for any other reason than to set me off, why then, I have no judgement' (*2 Henry IV*, 1.2.12–14). When Hal next sees the page, Falstaff's transformation of him is arresting: ''A had him from me Christian, and look if the fat villain have not transformed him ape' (2.2.63–5).

358 *marl*: 'A kind of clay much used for manure' (TS).

405 *in anonymous abuse*: i.e. in a newspaper article or periodical essay.

408 *answer for't*: assure you, guarantee, take it on my responsibility.

412 *decided*: unhesitating; definite, self-assured.

418–19 *literary emulation*: the (natural) desire to outgo others' literary achievements.

1.2.1–3 *Je dis . . . famille*: I say, madam, I have the honour to introduce, and request your protection for, Signor Pasticcio Ritornello and his charming family.

4–7 *Ah! . . . signora*: 'Ah! Your ladyship, we beg you to grace us with your patronage.' 'Your ladyship, do us these favours.' 'Yes, madam.' (Sheridan's Italian is approximate, but he presumably intended his Italian characters to speak accurately. His phrasings have therefore been adjusted here, where necessary, to produce more idiomatic Italian.)

8–9 *C'est à dire . . . l'honneur—*: that is to say, in English, that they beg you to do them the honour—

12 *Queste . . . spiegherà*: this gentleman will explain.

13–14 *nous avons . . . Dangle de—*: we have letters of introduction for Mr Dangle from—

16–17 *La Contessa . . . Fugue*: 'Countess Rondeau is our patron.' 'Yes, father, and my Lady Fugue.'

18–19 *ils disent . . . dames*: they say, in English, that they have the honour of being favoured by these ladies.

21 *voici*: here is.

26 *Eh bien!*: ah well!

27–8 *le grand bruit . . . théâtres—*: the great reputation of your critical talents and of your influence with the managers of all the theatres—

29–30 *Vossignoria . . . da—*: your lordship is so famed for your critical judgement and your influence over the managers at—

35 *the less . . . hearing them*: the sooner we hear them.

36 S.D. *The . . . sing trios, etc.*: 'In the early performances the trio here was in French, sung by Carlo Delpini, Ann Field (?–1789) and one of the Miss

Abrams, no doubt Harriet (1760?–1825), with a duet following it in Italian sung by Miss Field and Miss Abrams' (Crane). The trio and duet were so popular that they were published separately in 1779, thus becoming the first part of the play to be printed. The music was by Tommaso or Giuseppi Giordani. The 1779 translation of the trio's words runs as follows: 'I left my Country and my Friends to play on my Guitar | Which goes tang tang tang | Which goes tang tamarre. | I here am known and call'd by all, | By the name of my tinkling Guitarr. | Little Nancy said to me one Day, | Come and play on your Guitarr.' The English version of the Italian duet is: 'Flat'rer why dost thou deceive me? | Why betray my constant love? | Why with sighs and well feign'd Sorrow | Hast thou sworn thy faith to prove? | False betrayer, thou base deceiver, | Ev'ry grief I owe to thee.'

43 *take their address*: receive, or cope with, their civilities; find out where they live.

58 *viva voce*: aloud, openly, undisguisedly.

59 *a professor of*: i.e. someone whose profession is.

62 *prints*: newspapers.

64 *fraternity*: of fellow writers and/or puffers.

64–6 *all the summer . . . believe*: summer theatre at the Haymarket was regularized with a grant of letters patent to Samuel Foote in 1766. Puff's work as publicist for these summer performances has presumably included unflattering comparisons with the winter season offerings at Drury Lane and Covent Garden.

81–2 *not an article of the merit theirs*: 'The ridicule of the language of auctioneers was pointed at Robert Langford, who had made an effort to gain some financial control at Drury Lane' (Price, ii. 471). See, also, *Letters*, i. 104–7.

86–7 *inlay . . . metaphor*: 'like a kind of linguistic marquetry' (Crane).

89 *gratuitous*: 'free and abundant, not laboured for' (Crane); but also 'asserted without proof' (TS).

93–4 *the temple . . . Lincolnshire*: Hygeia was the Roman goddess of health; while Lincolnshire, with its low-lying fenland, was notoriously dank and unhealthy. Price suggested that there might also be 'a glancing allusion to James Graham's, the quack doctor's, establishments in the Adelphi, the "Temple of Health and Hymen" and later, in Pall Mall, "the Electrical Temple of Health"'.

98 *Mercury*: messenger of the classical deities, and patron of lying, hence of 'traffic' (i.e. 'Commerce, merchandising' (TS)) and 'fiction' (i.e. 'a falsehood, a lie' (TS)).

102–3 *sheer necessity . . . invention*: cf. 'necessity is the mother of invention' (Tilley N61).

126 *told very well*: (1) was an effective story to tell; (2) brought in the money very well.

129 *close*: 'shut fast' (TS).

130 *the Marshalsea*: 'debtors' prison on the south bank of the Thames' (Price).

131 *was . . . dropsy*: had the excess fluid in the body, which is characteristic of the condition known as dropsy, drained off.

134 *pressed*: (1) press-ganged; (2) pressed in bed (hence, the numerous children).

138 *answer*: yield the expected profit.

143 *liberal*: (1) gentlemanly; (2) profitable; (3) unfettered.

144–5 *channels of diurnal communication*: daily newspapers.

146–9 *and your confession . . . imposition*: exception was taken to this passage at the first performance. According to *The Morning Chronicle* (2 Nov. 1779), 'The whole piece was received with the greatest applause, excepting only that part of Puff's advertisement of himself, in which he ridicules in the lump, those addresses to the humane and benevolent which occasionally appear in the daily prints,—to this a great part of the audience opposed a long and virtuous hiss; their displeasure however was converted into expressions of approbation, when Mr. King seized a lucky moment to "promise to tell Mr. Sneer, that he did not mean to deaden his feelings, or lessen his humanity; that he intended merely to awaken his prudence, and instruct him in future to make a proper enquiry into the truth of the cases stated in such advertisements before he parted with his money for the relief of the parties from whom the advertisements came".' There is an early tradition that Sheridan, foreseeing the possibility of such a reaction, had prepared King's apparent improvisation for him. He, however, 'obviously preferred his original thoughts when he came to print the work' (Price, i. 27); and, to judge from newspaper notices (Price, ii. 480–1), he persisted with it in performance also. Price, ii. 513, reprints an example of the kind of newspaper petition 'To the Affluent and Humane' in which Puff claims to excel.

149 *mystery*: trade skill; special art.

154–5 *puffing . . . of various sorts*: what follows is 'A kind of parody of Touchstone's dissertation on the lye in quarrelling' (*General Evening Post*, 30 Oct.–2 Nov. 1779). See *As You Like It*, 5.4.49–101.

159–60 *advertisement*: information; 'notice of any thing published in a paper of intelligence' (TS).

160 *party*: (1) person involved or concerned; (2) political grouping or faction.

165 *Smatter*: 'to smatter' was 'To have a slight, superficial knowledge; to talk superficially or ignorantly' (TS).

170 *attic salt*: elegant wit.

171–4 *Mr Dodd . . . Mr King*: the three actors singled out for praise are on stage at this moment—Dodd as Dangle, Palmer as Sneer, and King as Puff. The 'Sir Harry' and 'colonel' invoked here are nominally in a play of Puff's invention; but Dodd had played Sir Harry Bouquet in Sheridan's *The Camp* (1778). The most famous 'Sir Harry' in the eighteenth-century repertoire was Sir Harry Wildair in Farquhar's sustainedly popular *The Constant Couple* (1699), though Dodd seems never to have played the role. Palmer had, however, appeared as Colonel Standard in the same play. Mark S. Auburn, *Sheridan's Comedies: Their Contexts and Achievements* (Lincoln, Nebr., and London, 1977), 185–6, suggests that the puff here may be for Elizabeth Griffith's *The Times* (Drury Lane, 2 Dec. 1779), probably just beginning rehearsal when *The Critic* was staged. Its cast included Colonel Mountfort (played by Palmer) and Sir Harry Granger, for which King might then have been pencilled in, though the role was finally taken by another actor.

177 *Mr De Loutherbourg's pencil*: Philippe Jacques De Loutherbourg was engaged by Garrick as scene designer at Drury Lane in 1771. For some account of his radical innovations in the job, see Sheridan's Playhouses, p. xlix above. *The Morning Chronicle*, 17 Feb. 1776, praised De Loutherbourg as 'The first artist who showed our theatre directors that by a just disposition of light and shade, and critical preservation of perspective the eye of the spectator might be so effectually deceived in a playhouse as to take the produce of art for real nature'. 'A newspaper advertisement of the first production of *The Critic* has these significant lines: "The Scenery designed by Mr. De Loutherbourg and executed under his Direction"' (Nettleton). For further discussion of his career, see Christopher Baugh, 'Philippe James de Loutherbourg and the Early Pictorial Theatre: Some Aspects of its Cultural Context', *Themes in Drama*, 9 (1987), 99–128.

183 *to what*: in comparison to what.

189 *Sir Flimsy Gossamer*: both his Christian and surname mean 'trivial, light, insubstantial, insignificant'.

190 *open trenches*: i.e. begin the siege.

191 *The Morning Post*: an extraordinarily successful newspaper, 'circulated mainly in London's fashionable West End, and specializing in '"anecdotes" and "personalities," that is, gossip and abuse' (Lucyle Werkmeister, *The London Daily Press 1772–1792* (Lincoln, Nebr., 1963), 5.

192 *stars*: 'The abbreviations of the text for "Lady Fanny Fête" and "Sir Flimsy Gossamer" follow the method in vogue in the Têtes-à-Têtes in *The Town and Country Magazine*' (Nettleton). See *SS*, Prologue, 20, and 1.1.18, and notes.

209 *George Bon Mot*: 'clearly George Selwyn, a noted wit; Boswell, in his London journal for 5 January 1763, calls him "one of the brightest geniuses in England, of whom more good sayings are recorded than anybody"' (Crane).

209–10 *St James's Street*: built in the 1690s, and in the 1770s still at the heart of fashionable London.

210 *Myrtle*: 'A fragrant tree' (TS); also, the tree of Venus, goddess of love.

211–13 *a white jacket . . . cap*: i.e. he expected that, like other fashionable ladies, she would be at Coxheath Camp, adorned in her own variation on military uniform. See note to 1.1.3 above, and also Russell, 38–41, on the actual and alleged behaviour of women at Coxheath.

215 *The Camp Magazine*: Coxheath Camp generated its own publicity, guides, and newspapers.

223–4 *Fête Champêtre*: see note to *SS* 2.1.20.

235 *scan. mag.*: *scandalum magnatum* (defamation of magnates), i.e. prosecution for uttering or disseminating a malicious report against the crown, peers, judges, or other principal officers of the realm.

239 *patents*: a patent was a governmental grant conferring some exclusive right or privilege.

It lurks . . . a subscription: i.e. by strictly limiting the number of potential subscribers (to, say, the publication of a book), it encourages people to desire to be one of the select few permitted to become a subscriber.

243–5 *It has . . . accuracy*: i.e. the speeches are largely or wholly the product of the reporters' invention.

247 *preferments*: promotions, appointments.

248 *embryo promotions*: 'promotions as yet hardly in the realm of the possible' (Crane).

249 *ribbon*: decoration, public honour.

250 *in the air of a common report*: as if it was already commonly discussed or known.

254 *yielding a tablature*: providing a vivid portrait.

256–7 *register of charity*: the means by which acts of charity are recorded.

257 *triumph*: victory parade or celebration.

279 *contractors*: parties to a contract or bargain.

Junius: see note to 1.1.1 above.

The Thames navigation: 'Trinity House was attacked in the newspapers for not dredging the Thames adequately: see the *Public Advertiser*, 26 Oct. 1779' (Price).

280 *Misomud*: i.e. hater of mud (like 'Anti-shoal', one of Puff's pseudonyms).

282 *Paul Jones*: John Paul Jones (1747–92), Scottish-American naval adventurer and privateer. For two years before the première of *The Critic*, he had menaced British shipping as he cruised about the British Isles.

Indiamen out of the Shannon: Jones's activities threatened the English coast; so presumably some merchant ships of the East India Company had been forced by him to take shelter in the Shannon.

283 *Byron*: John Byron (1723–86), vice-admiral, and commander of the West Indies fleet in 1778–9. See note to 1.1.3, above.

compel the Dutch to—: 'To "surrender Paul Jones"' (Nettleton), who cites *The Public Advertiser*, 16 Oct. 1779: 'Orders have been sent to our Ambassador at the Hague, directing him to apply to the States for the immediate Surrender of Paul Jones'.

285–6 *establish . . . fleet*: i.e. support the government's line by denying the internal divisions and dissension which had riven the Channel fleet during the naval crisis of the preceding summer.

286 *Charles Fox*: Charles James Fox (1749–1806), leading Whig politician, and (from 1780) Sheridan's friend and political ally. He fiercely attacked governmental policy in these years.

287 *The Morning Post*: 'The Morning Post was as well known for scurrilous personal attacks as was *The Public Advertiser* for communications on matters of public interest, or *The Morning Chronicle* for theatrical intelligence. In politics *The Morning Post* supported the ministry, and hence would be glad "to shoot Charles Fox"' (Nettleton).

288 *green room*: waiting-room for performers not currently on stage.

2.1. S.D. *before the curtain*: a curtain, traditionally green, hung within the proscenium. It was drawn up after the prologue and then usually not lowered until the play's end, though occasionally it descended between the acts to prepare an especially spectacular scene-change.

2–3 *'the abstract . . . the times'*: see note to 1.1.75–7, above.

7 *Tilbury Fort*: 'Built in the reign of Henry VIII to defend the mouth of the Thames' (Price). 'Here Queen Elizabeth assembled her troops at the time of the Armada (1588)' (Nettleton).

36–8 *how great . . . Whiskerandos!*: cf. the dilemma of Volscius in *The Rehearsal*, 3.5.94–7: 'Shall I to Honour or to Love give way? | Go on, cries Honour; tender Love saies, nay: | Honour, aloud, commands, pluck both Boots on.'

53 *Mr Hopkins*: William Hopkins, prompter and copyist at Drury Lane from 1760 to 1780. He never actually appears on stage in *The Critic*, but speaks from the wings at 2.1.497, and 3.1.544 (Appendix). 'He' had had an onstage role, but impersonated by an actor, in Garrick's *A Peep Behind the Curtain; or, The New Rehearsal* (1767). The prompter prepared prompt

copies, saw to the copying of parts, generally assisted the theatre manager, and covered many of the responsibilities of the modern stage manager.

55 S.D. *to the music*: to the musicians in the playhouse orchestra.

57 *scenes and dresses*: scenery and costumes.

59 S.D. *the bell rings*: the normal signal that the performance is about to begin, the bell was rung by the prompter.

60–1 *a cry of . . . Hats off!*: from spectators whose view of the stage is obstructed by other spectators.

62 *for us: 1781* marks a new scene here; but since the action is continuous, and Puff, Dangle, and Sneer remain on stage, Act 2 is here printed as a single unit.

S.D. *Two Sentinels asleep*: a somnolent echo of the opening of *Hamlet*.

67 *awful*: awe-struck; terror-stricken.

69–70 *a description . . . hemisphere*: Price offers in comparison this passage from Richard Cumberland, *The Battle of Hastings* (1778), 3.1: 'Invention never yok'd | A fairer courser to Apollo's car, | When with the zephyrs and the rosy hours | Through heav'n's bright portal he ascends the east, | And on his beamy forehead brings the morn.'

84 S.D. *Sir Walter Ralegh*: c.1552–1618, knighted in 1584, later captain of the Queen's Guard, and 'in many ways the typical Elizabethan adventurer' (Crane).

S.D. *Sir Christopher Hatton*: 1540–91; appointed Lord Chancellor in Apr. 1587. 'In February of that year he had spoken at length in the House of Commons on the peril of a Spanish invasion. Hence his "cautious conjecture" of danger is highly ridiculous. He was called "the dancing chancellor" because the attention of Queen Elizabeth was attracted to him by his graceful dancing in a mask at court' (Nettleton).

86 *before*: i.e. before their entry. Cf. *The Rehearsal*, 2.1.23–9: '*Physician* Sir, to conclude. *Smith* What, before he begins? *Bayes* No, Sir; you must know, they had been talking of this a pretty while without. *Smith* Where? in the Tyring-room? *Bayes* Why ay, Sir. He's so dull! Come, speak again.'

89–90 *Don't mind interrupting*: feel no hesitation about interrupting.

95–6 *What mean . . . throng of chiefs?*: cf. *Hamlet*, 1.1.69–78.

109 *Pallas*: Pallas Athene, goddess of war.

110 *When virgin majesty . . . | . . . to arms*: under the threat of the Spanish Armada, Queen Elizabeth I, mounted on a war-horse and armed ('veiled in steel'), reviewed her troops at Tilbury Fort in Aug. 1588. Her speech to them was reprinted in *The Public Advertiser*, 17 Sept. 1779, as an apparently similar threat loomed. *The Prophecy*—see note to 1.1.11 above—versified Elizabeth's oration in bombast which included the boast that 'To herself then let England be true, | In spite of each threat and bravado,

| Protected by Heaven and you, | I'll laugh at the Spanish Armada' (Price, ii. 466).

120–1 *He calls . . . familiar terms*: cf. the entry of the two kings of Brentford hand in hand, in *The Rehearsal*, 2.2.7–9, with one calling the other 'sweetheart', and Bayes's explanation that the mode of address 'is familiar, because they are both persons of the same quality'.

125 *Figurative*: in *The Rehearsal*, 4.2.16, Bayes similarly proclaims 'Antithesis!' to direct attention to the rhetorical splendours of his writing.

128–9 *two revolving suns,* | *. . . moons*: cf. *Hamlet*, 3.2.148–55.

129 *course*: race, circuit.

130 *haughty Philip*: Philip II of Spain (1527–98), the architect of the attack on England in 1588.

133 *proud, Iberia's*: the comma first appears in *1781* and perhaps 'signals the added twist of rhetorical peculiarity the actor was moved to give the line on the stage' (Crane), though it may equally always have been part of Sheridan's plan.

141 *advices*: intelligence reports.

167–8 *the Earl of Leicester*: Robert Dudley, Earl of Leicester (*c.*1532–88), captain-general of the army (composed of 16,500 men) at Tilbury when the Spanish invasion appeared imminent.

180 *obliged to be plain and intelligible*: in *The Rehearsal*, Bayes shows similar impatience with the obligation to write plainly: 'If I writ, Sir, to please the Country, I should have follow'd the old plain way; but I write for some persons of Quality, and peculiar friends of mine, that understand what Flame and Power in writing is: and they do me the right, Sir, to approve of what I do' (1.1.286–90). He revisits the topic to similar effect later (5.1.102–6).

182 *trope*: 'A change of a word from its original signification' (TS).

figure: 'in rhetorick, any mode of speaking in which words are detorted from their literal and primitive sense' (TS).

noun-substantives: i.e. common nouns.

195 *flats*: smooth low ground exposed to inundations' (TS).

200 *closing line*: i.e. as in a line of warships closing on the enemy.

206 *free*: i.e. by embracing death.

210 *Nem. con.*: *nemine contradicente*; i.e. with no one contradicting.

220 *discipline*: military craft or skill.

235 *orthodox quintetto*: in fact, in *1781* there are six kneelers; but it had been a genuine quintet in an earlier version when the Master of the Horse had not joined the others in kneeling. The prayer itself is scarcely 'orthodox', with these Protestant warlords praying, not to the Christian God, but to

Mars, and blithely concluding with a request that the end should be taken to justify the means.

241 *You could . . . could you?*: Price compares Henry Jones, *The Earl of Essex* (1753), 2.1, where Southampton enters, kneels, then asks: 'Permit me, madam, to approach you thus'. In *The Rehearsal*, 3.5.103, S.D., Volscius '*Goes out hopping with one Boot on, and the other off*'.

254 *Lord Burghley's ear*: 'William Cecil, Lord Burghley (1520–98), Elizabeth's Secretary of State and Lord Treasurer, whose intelligence network was famous' (Crane).

267 *helps realize the scene*: increases the realism of the setting.

278–9 *the minuet in 'Ariadne'*: a famous piece from the overture to Handel's opera *Arianna in Creta* (1734). It was used constantly in the theatres, 'and not only in the intervals; it was also much used as quiet background music . . . the pianissimo ending of this minuet is memorable' (Fiske 2, 260).

280 *Now . . . gentle morn*: Miltonic echoes have been detected in this parodic speech. Compare, for instance, *Lycidas*, ll. 139–51, and *Paradise Lost*, iv. 641–56. There may also be a debt to *The Winter's Tale*, 4.4.116–27. But Sheridan is principally recollecting Ophelia's mad-scene (*Hamlet*, 4.5.21–72 and 155–98).

287 *guarded*: (1) protected by thorns; (2) ornamented.

288 *vulgar*: 'mean, low' (TS); ordinary, commonplace.

323 *simile*: cf. Bayes's delight in similes: 'That's a general Rule, you must ever make a *simile*, when you are surpris'd; 'tis the new way of writing' (*The Rehearsal*, 2.3.15–17). 'Simon Simile' in *The Morning Chronicle*, 4 Dec. 1775, had criticized the songs in *The Duenna* for their lack of simile: 'a song without a simile is like a play without a plot; the animating principle is wanting, and no graces of thought or language can make it entertaining' (Price, i. 210). In *Ixion*, the burlesque fragment by Halhed and Sheridan, the playwright is called Simile.

325 *they will not be missed*: i.e. their omission will not cause any problems.

336 *Like a clipped . . . scale!*: this animate guinea, whose edge has been clipped, trembles because it will not weigh its due weight. The bathetic comparison between this and a climactic moment in English history exemplies Puff's literary incompetence, but is also a satirical thrust at the British government's ill-preparedness in the crisis of the summer of 1779.

339–40 *This is . . . writers have*: Price compares Ralegh speaking to Burghley in Henry Jones, *The Earl of Essex*, 1.1: 'My heart exults; I see, | I see, my lord, our utmost wish accomplish'd! | I see great Cecil shine without a rival, | And England bless him as her guardian saint.'

348 *line*: line of battle.

372–3 *tampering*: plotting; offering bribes.

375–6 *as smart as hits*: cf. Bayes in *The Rehearsal*, 3.1.10–16: 'it might properly enough be call'd a prize of Wit; for you shall see 'em come in upon one another snipsnap, hit for hit, as fast as can be. First one speaks, then presently t'others upon him, slap, with a Repartee; then he at him again, dash with a new conceipt: and so eternally, eternally, I gad, till they go quite off the Stage.'

377 *borrowed from the French*: Crane points out a more immediate source in Cumberland's *The Battle of Hastings*, 5.1: '*Edgar* My honour and my oath— | *King* Thy life— | *Edgar* My love.'

392–4 *parry quart . . . flanconade*: 'quart' and 'tierce' are fencing terms for standard positions for the sword-arm in parrying; while a 'flanconade' is a thrust in the side.

395 *a palpable hit*: cf. Osric's judgement on Hamlet's first successful thrust at Laertes: 'A hit, a very palpable hit' (5.2.232).

401 *figure*: rhetorical effect, stylistic trick.

408 *in a moment*: in *The Rehearsal*, 3.5.43–7, Parthenope's entry immediately provokes from Volscius this reponse: 'Bless me! how frail are all my best resolves! | How, in a moment, is my purpose chang'd! | Too soon I thought my selfe secure from Love. | Fair Madam, give me leave to ask her name | Who does so gently rob me of my fame?'

425 *I make . . . the winds*: Price again compares a passage from Henry Jones's *The Earl of Essex*, 2: 'I scorn the blaze of courts, the pomp of kings; | I give them to the winds.'

430 *conscious*: privy to, and sharing in, human thoughts (a contemporary poetic usage).

431 *bias*: 'propension, inclination' (TS).

448–9 *If you . . . dance out*: in *The Rehearsal*, Bayes has comparable difficulties with actors' handling of exits and entrances (3.4.5–8, and 5.1.344–52).

452 *at the top*: i.e. upstage.

455 *you see—*: Puff presumably demonstrates that 'parting look' for the actors.

456 S.D. *Scene closes*: see Sheridan's Playhouses, p. xlviii, above.

458–9 *strike out*: carve out, invent.

469–70 *the only quite new thing in the piece*: a sea-battle may have been a novel effect; but from the mid-1770s onwards there had been a vogue for plays showing ships at sea, including at Covent Garden Thompson's *The Syrens* (1776) and Dibdin's *The Seraglio* (1776). At Drury Lane in 1773, in *Alfred*, complete models of ships took part in a naval review. In 1794, Sheridan and De Loutherbourg collaborated on *The Glorious First of June*, which climaxed with a magnificent staging of one of Lord Howe's naval victories, accompanied by a choral rendition of 'Rule Britannia'.

471 *Drake*: just as Puff insouciantly contrives to keep Elizabeth I offstage, so, despite his apparent promise here, he finds no role for Sir Francis Drake, one of the key players in the eventual sea-battle against the Spanish Armada. Cf. the criticism in *Scot's Magazine*, Feb. 1778: 'Why Mr. Cumberland has chosen to call this play *The Battle of Hastings*, we do not see. To be sure we hear something of such a battle in the last act, but almost the whole of the tragedy consists of love-scenes between a disguised prince, and a couple of fond maidens. The Rival Beauties would have been a more proper name for it. The French are blamed for filling their tragedies with love; Mr. Cumberland appears inclined to keep them in countenance' (quoted in Stanley Thomas Williams, *Richard Cumberland: His Life and Dramatic Works* (New Haven, 1917), 141–2).

472 *fireships*: 'Against the Armada the English used old ships filled with inflammable material, which were then floated downwind towards the Spanish ships' (Crane).

502 *I'll print it every word*: *The Critic* itself was fairly long for an afterpiece and was often trimmed in performance. Puff's repeated refrain, therefore, also mirrors the relationship between the printed and performed states of the play of which he is a part. A substantial difference between performance and reading texts of a play is in any case frequent in this period.

506 *laboured*: carefully worked, produced with great effort. But the word also already carried its modern meaning, 'lacking spontaneity, heavy'.

510 *before the drop*: some extra material is needed, to be performed before the lowered curtain or a drop scene lowered on two rollers, in order to allow time for the scene-change behind it. It is reported that, in identical circumstances, Sheridan himself improvised the words for a song to bridge a scene-change in the annual pantomime of 1779 (Rhodes, 85).

511–12 *sink Gravesend and the river*: scenic elements like this were raised and lowered through a series of longitudinal apertures or flaps across the stage. See Colin Visser, 'Scenery and Technical Design', in Robert D. Hume (ed.). *The London Theatre World, 1660–1800* (Carbondale and Edwardsville, Ill., 1980), 100. (Gravesend is on the south bank of the Thames, not far from Tilbury Fort.)

509 *So! This . . . truly!*: at the first performance, instead of the dialogue printed from this point onwards in *1781*, the act concluded with the alternative material printed in the Appendix below, pp. 336–7.

3.1.1 S.D. *Justices, Constables, etc., discovered*: thus, *1781*. It is unclear how many justices and constables Sheridan requires. He provides dialogue for only one justice and one constable; but later in the scene a line-up of 'all your near relations' (l. 59) is demanded. Are these the mute justices and constables, or perhaps courtroom spectators?

2 *senate scene*: as, for example, in Thomas Otway's enormously popular tragedy, *Venice Preserved* (1682), 4.2.

6 *discovery scene*: i.e. a scene pivoted on some great revelation.

12 *volunteers*: 'Forcible enlistment was common during wartime as a cheap alternative to even starting a prosecution, as a punishment sometimes substituted at the time of trial, and as a common condition of a pardon from a sentence of transportation, confinement to the hulks, or death' (Douglas Hay, 'War, Dearth and Theft in the Eighteenth Century: The Record of the English Courts', *Past and Present*, 95 (May 1982), 141–2).

24 *Quick, sir!*: despite his promise to 'fly', the constable is clearly milking his exit.

34 *rude*: rough, harsh.

36 *if our Tom had lived*: that Sheridan was here targeting J. Home's successful tragedy, *Douglas* (1756), was immediately registered (Price, ii. 482). Its Act 2 discovery scene gives us a mother imagining that if her son had survived 'He might have been like this young gallant stranger | And paired with him in features and in shape'. The stranger, who is, of course, her son, soon has the lines: 'My name is Norval: on the Grampian Hills | My father feeds his flocks'. Cf. ll. 41–5 below.

45 *fishmonger*: cf. *Hamlet*, 2.2.175. Also, in *The Rehearsal*, 3.4.17, Prettyman announces that 'Altho a Fisherman, he is my Father'.

51–2 *bill . . . | . . . creditor*: Crane observes that the 'name Tomkins clearly provided the "Tom" and the "kins" of the lost boy's present name'. He also, however, assumes that 'bill' here means 'bill of exchange' and is consequently puzzled it should be signed 'Tomkins, *creditor*'. But 'bill', then as now, could also mean 'list of services or items for which payment is requested'. The alleged problem therefore vanishes.

57 *I am thy father*: Price compares Cumberland's *The West Indian* (1771): '*Stockwell*—I am your father. | *Belcour* My father! Do I live? | *Stockwell* I am your father. | *Belcour* It is too much . . .'.

57–8 *there | Thy uncle*: see note to l. 1, S.D., above.

63 *relationship . . . out*: cf. the proverbial 'Murder will out' (Tilley M1315).

73 S.D. *Scenemen*: scene shifting was mainly carried out in full view of the audience by theatre employees, who wore liveries (like, for example, footmen in aristocratic households). Hence, Puff's complaint about the awkwardness of their appearing on the same set as his fictional Elizabethans.

80 *Perdition . . . thee*: from *Othello*, 3.3.91–2. *Othello* was the mainpiece which preceded the second performance of *The Critic* on 1 Nov. 1779; so the audience will indeed have heard the familiar line recently on that occasion.

425

94 *a very short soliloquy*: in *The Rehearsal*, 2.4.77–8, Shirly enters to soliloquize briefly—'Hey ho, hey ho: what a change is here! Hey day, hey day! I know not what to do, nor what to say'—before exiting from the stage and the play. Earlier, Prettyman manages four lines of soliloquy before announcing, 'I am so surpris'd with sleep, I cannot speak the rest' (2.2.8–9).

97 *sentimental*: sententious.

103 *perfect*: the spectators are likely to understand this in the still familiar theatrical sense—i.e. 'totally in control of his lines'. It is only after experiencing the actor's mute impersonation of Burghley that they will understand Puff must instead have meant something on the lines of 'perfectly rehearsed in his part'. See also Introduction, pp. xlii–xliii. In *The Rehearsal*, 5.1.190–2, Johnson advises Bayes: 'if I were in your place I would make 'em go out again without ever speaking one word'.

113 *There's a reason!*: possibly simply 'It is all quite logical'; but Crane suggests the meaning is 'What a foolish opinion' (which would require the following stress: '*There's* a reason').

117 *take it?*: comprehend it?

131 *witchcraft*: cf. *Othello*, 1.3.62–4.

154 *hateful liberty, if*: liberty is hateful, if.

165 S.D. *halberd*: 'A battle-ax fixed on a long pole' (TS).

172 *renounce our guard?*: drop our fighting posture?

174 *The lie!*: i.e. he has accused me of lying!

176 S.D. *discovers himself*: reveals his true identity.

178 *crest*: 'pride, spirit, fire'; 'the ornament of the helmet in heraldry' (TS), i.e. the visible evidence of my true rank.

196 *For all eter—*: a Shakespearian parallel is the death of Hotspur midphrase in *1 Henry IV*, 5.4.85, with the abortive thought being completed by Prince Hal. An eighteenth-century precedent (cited by Price) is in Henry Brooke, *Gustavus Vasa, the Deliverer of his Country* (1739), 3.2: 'Tell him—for once, that I have fought like him, | And wou'd like him have— | Conquer'd—he shou'd have said—but there, O there, | Death sto—pt him short'.

199 *Now mind me*: pay careful attention to what I say.

210–11 *the body has walked off*: Crane points out that the 'dead also walk off in *The Rehearsal*' (5.1.346–52) and that 'at one point they even dance' (2.5.7–10).

214 S.D. *properly*: 'Fitly, suitably' (TS); as is decorous or according to convention.

216 *sheds contagious frenzy!*: spreads madness on earth like an epidemic.

228 *stark mad . . . in white satin*: this was indeed the reigning convention, as, for instance, in the dressing of the mad Ophelia (Marvin Rosenberg, *The*

Masks of Hamlet (Newark, NJ, 1992), 774)—a spectacle offered earlier in the evening on which *The Critic* was premièred.

241 *squirrel*: Price compares Richard Steele's *The Funeral* (1701), 5.3: '*Enter Widow in deep Mourning, with a dead Squirrel on her Arm'*.

255 *She . . . into the sea*: *The Rehearsal* produces two reports of women drowned in the sea (4.1.92, and 5.1.375). Ophelia's death is also in Sheridan's mind here.

256 *catastrophe*: 'The change of revolution, which produces the conclusion or final event of a dramatick piece' (TS).

260–1 *Now then for my magnificence!*: cf. Bayes's delighted boast that 'I'l shew you the greatest Scene that ever *England* saw: I mean not for words, for those I do not value; but for state, shew, and magnificence' (*The Rehearsal*, 5.1.1–4).

261–2 *procession*: on the vogue for spectacular processions in the mid- to late-eighteenth-century theatre, see Hughes, 112–18.

267 *the masque*: the eighteenth century saw a demand for musical masques or interludes as theatrical afterpieces. These included Dalton's radical reworking of Milton's *Comus* for Drury Lane. See Allardyce Nicoll, *A History of English Drama 1660–1900*, ii. *Early Eighteenth Century Drama* (3rd edn.; Cambridge, 1961), 258–60.

274 *one . . . villa*: the north bank of the Thames was a fashionable area for out-of-town housing for the wealthy. On the Surrey side there were alder coppices, grown to supply the gunpowder mills at Chilworth.

277–8 *go between your banks*: cf. Bayes's explanation that 'by the very nature of this Dance, the Earth must be sometimes between the Sun and the Moon, and the Moon between the Earth and Sun' (*The Rehearsal*, 5.1.291–4).

279 S.D. *Bell rings*: the prompter used his bell to cue and co-ordinate his stage team and the actors at such moments as this. Cf. note to 2.1.59 S.D. above.

280 S.D. *'Britons, strike home'*: Henry Purcell's 'show-stopping trumpet-song . . . so much admired in the eighteenth century, a huffing song to end all huffing songs' in the third act of John Fletcher's *Bonduca*, an '80-year-old play about Queen Boadicea and the invading Romans reworked for the 1690s' (Roger Savage, 'The Theatre Music', in Michael Burden (ed.), *The Purcell Companion* (London, 1995), 358–9), and possibly originally mounted in this revision 'as part of the general thanksgiving for William III's recent victory over the French at Namur' (Rump, 31). The Fletcher play, in a more radical revision, had been successfully staged by George Colman the Elder at the Haymarket in the summer of 1778. Garrick's prologue for it, according to *The London Evening Chronicle* (30 July–1 Aug. 1778), 'presents Bonduca as a heroic warrior whose deeds should inspire a modern audience'; and 'the performance of "Britons, strike home" had a glorious effect, and was encored by all the house' (Rump, 31).

280 S.D. '*Rule Britannia*': originally composed by Thomas Arne for *The Masque of Alfred* (libretto by James Thomson and David Mallet), another celebration of a national hero's defiance of invading foreigners—in this case, Danes. In the original text the navy and naval power are celebrated; but far greater emphasis is given to this in Mallet's 1751 revision, a change continued in the text for Garrick's revival in 1773. In both 1751 and 1773 'Alfred . . . claims that it is "naval strength, that must our peace assure" ', and there is a prophecy of the navy's future role as underpinning England's status as the 'great arbitress of nations'. The 1773 revival accordingly concluded with 'a De Loutherbourg scene which represented the grand naval review of 1773' (Rump, 33).

S.D. '*Water Music*': a suite of twenty-one movements, first performed on the Thames, 22 Aug. 1715, when George I and the royal family sailed from Limehouse to Whitehall.

S.D. *the march in '*Judas Maccabaeus*'*: Handel's oratorio, composed in the summer of 1746, narrates the victory of the eponymous Israelite hero over the Syrians, but also celebrates the Duke of Cumberland's recent defeat of the Young Pretender's army at Culloden. The march 'is an anticipatory celebration of Judas's triumphant return from battle'. It remained enormously popular, having 'been performed three times already in the earlier part of 1779' (Rump, 31–2). Members of the Linley family had sung in it.

Appendix

522 *you only consider*: please think, you only need to work out.

GLOSSARY

abroad away from home, out of the house
a-coming on the way
address courtship
adieu goodbye
advance lend (money)
affecting moving
allemande vigorous German dance
allons (French) let us go, come on
amour love-affair
an if
anchorite hermit, recluse
anon instantly; in a short time
an't if it
a'n't aren't
antipodes opposite side of the earth
antique ancient, antiquated
apace swiftly, promptly
apropos incidentally, by the way; to the point, on that subject
appraiser valuer
article particular, respect, detail; clause, item
artificial skilful; cunning; contrived; affected, insincere; duplicitous
assembly social gathering
assiduities constant attentions, persistent endeavours to please
assign specify, explain
assignation lovers' meeting
attorney lawyer
aught anything
averse adverse, hostile, contrary
avow acknowledge; confess, admit; maintain
Bacchus classical god of wine
backgammon board-game with draughtsmen and dice
baggage saucy woman
bait (vb.) interrupt a journey for food, rest, or pleasure
ball bullet
band headband
banter make fun of
bastinado truncheon; cudgelling; caning on the soles of the feet

basto ace of clubs
bate slacken
bauble showy trinket
baulk frustrate, disappoint
beau man of fashion and (often affected) elegance
beau monde fashionable world
beau-pot ornamental flower vase
Beelzebub the devil
beholden indebted, obliged
beldam ancient woman; hag, virago
benevolence charitable gift
benignity kindly feeling; generous deed
beside in addition, besides
blackamoor black African
black art magic, necromancy
blade dashing, pleasure-seeking man
blast gust of wind
blonde piece of silk lace
blunderbuss short gun with a large bore, firing many balls or slugs at once; noisy blusterer
boatswain ship's petty officer or warrant officer
bob wig with the bottom locks turned up into bobs or short curls
boding premonition, presentiment
bolster long firm cushion
bond promissory note
booby idiot
bravo hired ruffian, desperado
breeding education
broadsword cutting-sword with a broad blade
broker financial middleman
brook endure
bubble cheat
bumper glass or cup filled to the brim
bureau writing-desk
burn it drat it
by present
by goles an oath, a softened form of 'By God'
by the bye incidentally
by the mass an exclamation, marking

emphasis or expressing surprise or
outrage

by this light an exclamation of surprise
and emphasis

call out challenge (to a duel)

cant dialect, lingo

canting singing; whining

caper high dancing-step or -jump

cardinal woman's cloak, made of
scarlet cloth, with a hood

carding playing cards

cast throw of the dice

catch round to be sung by three or
more voices

cavalliero cavalier, knight errant

chagrin melancholy; mortification; ill-
humour, vexation

chairman man employed to carry a
sedan chair

chanting singing

character reputation, public image

charge order, command

charioteer coachman

cheer (vb.) comfort, console; enliven,
inspirit

chief commander

chirrup sing or talk merrily

chuck give a playful touch (under the
chin)

circuit journey of a judge in a
particular district to hold courts

circumstance particular, detail

cit citizen of London; tradesman

cloak-bag bag to convey a coak and/or
other clothes

clod dolt; peasant

close with accept, embrace

closet small private room

clown peasant; oaf

cocked ready to fire

cod softened form of 'God' for oaths

coin devise, fabricate

come to behave good-humouredly,
prove accommodating

commonplace-book notebook for
recording memorable passages or
quotations

complaisance civility, desire of
pleasing

compunction remorse of conscience

conducive tending to promote or
encourage

confounded confused, perplexed

conjure beseech, implore; summon;
make appear, as if by incantation or
magic

constitution quality of health, vitality;
disposition, temperament

consumption wasting disease

contemn disdain

contrivance inventive capacity, cunning

copyholder someone who holds
property by tenure from the lord of
the manor

corse corpse

cotillion brisk dance for four or eight
people

countenance face; appearance

coxcomb fool; fop

coz cousin; friend

crew company, gang

crisis turning-point; decisive moment

cropper strap looped under the horse's
tail

cross (n.) thwarting, contradiction

crown five-shilling piece

cursed (adv.) wretchedly, perversely,
damnably

curst (adj.) perversely bad-tempered,
malignant

curst (adv.) damnedly, confoundedly

dame wife, lady

dame prior abbess

dark-lantern lantern equipped with
means of concealing its light

dastardly cowardly

debauch seduce

de bon cœur (French) willingly, gladly

de haut en bas (French)
condescendingly

demur hesitation; objection

design plot

designing scheming, crafty

desperate extremely dangerous

despite contempt, scorn

deuce devil

devoir duty; act of civility; (pl.)
courteous attentions

dimity fine cotton or blend of cotton
and linen

din stun with noise; repeat continually so as to weary

dirty dishonourable, base

discharge pay off, settle with

disinterestedness freedom from self-interested motivation

dismission dismissal from employment

dispatch promptness, speed in performance

disposition temper of mind

disputant debater

dissembling deceitful

distemper sickness, infection

distract (adj.) mad, insane

distract (vb.) drive mad

divers several

divert entertain, amuse; enjoy; turn aside, dispel

divine conjecture, guess

division singer's execution of a rapid melodic passage

docked with shortened tail

dolt fool, idiot

double-faced hypocritical

doubt fear

dowager widow holding title, rank, or property, derived from her late husband

dower dowry

draft bill of exchange, cheque

drawling sluggish, crawling, dragging

ducat gold or silver coin, formerly current in most European countries

dumb show mime

dun (n.) debt-collector; importunate creditor

dun (vb.) pester, plague, beseech (for money)

durst dared

ecod a variant of 'egad' (see below)

e'en even

e'er ever

e'er a any

egad a softened oath: 'By God!', or 'A God!'

else otherwise

empire absolute dominion

enforce press home; emphasize; intensify, strengthen

engage promise, guarantee

engross monopolize

enjoin instruct, bind

enow enough, in sufficient number

ensign infantry officer of the lowest commissioned rank

envenomed poisoned; tainted

equipage clothing, costume; articles for personal ornament or use; retinue of servants

ere before

essence-bottle scent-bottle

exceptionable objectionable; liable to arouse a hostile response

expedition speed

exploded discredited, rejected with scorn

expostulation reproof

fain gladly, willingly

fancy taste; invention (in artistic design)

fandango lively Spanish dance for two, usually accompanied by guitars and castanets

farrago confused mixture, hotchpotch

farrier blacksmith and horse doctor

fast securely

faugh an exclamation expressing disgust

felo de se suicide

fête festival, celebration

fiddlecome nonsensical

fieldpiece small cannon

figured patterned

flimsy paltry; frivolous

fluting singing; playing flute or pipe

fly flee; hurry

fond foolish; affectionate

foot (vb.) dance

fopperies follies, dandyish nonsense

foppery foolish rite or practice

'fore George exclamation expressing asseveration

forsooth in truth, indeed; truly

forswear renounce, abjure

freak whim, capricious prank

front face; forehead

furies exclamation of anger, indignation or frustration (from the name of the classical goddesses of vengeance and punishment)

gad a softened form of 'God', used exclamatorily

gadsbud a softened form of 'God's body', used exclamatorily

gadso a softened oath, expressing asseveration, annoyance, or surprise

gala festivity, rejoicing

gallant lover, admirer, seducer

gallantry amorous courtship, wooing, seduction

game gambling

gamester card-player, gambler

gawky (n.) awkward or stupid person; lout

gemini a mild oath or exclamation

generous gentlemanly; gallant; magnanimous; free from meanness or prejudice

get beget, sire

gibbet (vb.) hang; expose to mockery

gi't give it

gipsy fickle or changeable woman; hussy

glee part-song, especially an unaccompanied one, for three or more voices

glibly smoothly, fluently

good lack an exclamation expressing regret, dissatisfaction, or surprise

goodly handsome

gouvernante (French) governess

grass-plat piece of ground covered with turf

guinea coin worth 21 shillings or £1.05

gust sudden outburst or fit

habit dress

halter noose

hamper burden, shackle

hand handwriting

ha'n't haven't

harkee listen carefully (i.e. what follows seems to the speaker especially important)

harridan haggard, ill-tempered old woman

hartshorn aqueous solution of ammonia; smelling salts

hazard dice-game with arbitrary rules

hearty robust, healthy

hedge in insert, insinuate

heigh-ho a sigh, expressing boredom, weariness, or disappointment

helpmate spouse

hey-day exclamation of surprise or joy

Hibernian Irishman

hight (archaic) called

hollo a cry commanding attention

horrid exciting horror; hideous, shocking

hot cockles rustic game in which one player is blindfolded and has to guess which of the others struck him or her

humour temperament; habitual frame of mind; particular inclination; facetiousness

hunting-frock hunting coat or tunic

Hymen the ancient Greek god of marriage

idle ineffectual; worthless

i'fecks in faith, truly

illiberality meanness of spirit

imprecation cursing; expression of hostility

in a-doors into the house

incommodation inconvenience

incomprehensible boundless; unfathomable

indite write; compose

instant (adv.) immediately

intercourse dealings

interest influence; share

interjectural interjectional, parenthetical

in the lump in the mass; wholesale

jackanapes ape, monkey; impudent fellow

Jacobin friar of the order of St Dominic, Dominican

jangle altercation, bickering

jangling grumbling, disputing

jar quarrel, disagreement

jet point, gist

jilt trickster, cheat; faithless woman

jocose jocular, fond of joking

Jove/Jupiter chief of the Roman gods

keen acute, alertly intelligent

knock down dispose (of an article) to an auction bidder by a knock with a hammer

languish pine with grief or unfulfilled, hopeless love

laurel wreath of victory; emblem of honour

level (n.) target; action of aiming; line of fire

level (vb.) position a weapon for firing; aim

liberal showing the characteristics of a gentleman; generous

licentiate holder of a certificate of competence from a college to practise a particular profession or skill

lief (adj.) glad, willing

lief (adv.) willingly

livery distinctive clothing of a particular employer's servants

loggerhead stupid head

loo fashionable card-game

looby lout, awkward rustic

lookee attend, take notice

lounge (n.) place for lounging and idling away the time

lounge (vb.) idle

lud lord (a softened oath)

lustre radiance, splendour

luxuriant exuberantly inventive or productive

Machiavel brilliant, unscrupulous plotter

main great, complete, remarkable

make a shift contrive, manage

malady illness, sickness

mansion-house house of the squire or lord of the manor

mantling suffusing, flushing

marry exclamation of asseveration, surprise, or indignation

Mars Roman god of war

masquerade masked ball, masked gathering

masquerader adept of disguise

massy solid and weighty; bulky

match marriage; alliance

material serious, significant

maudlin weeping; mawkishly sentimental

meet fit, appropriate

memorandum note to help the memory

mercy exclamation expressing surprise, fear, or worry

mien bearing, appearance

milliner someone who sells ribbons and dresses for women

mitigate mollify, lessen in severity

modish fashionable

monitress female guide

mort great deal

murrain curse, plague, pestilence

muses Greek goddesses, the inspirers of learning and the arts, especially poetry and music

nankeen pale yellowish cotton cloth

newsman journalist

nice choosy, fastidious, scrupulous, delicate

nicety fastidiousness; scrupulosity; over-refinement; prudery

nick critical or apt moment

occasion need, necessity; opportunity

odd trick in whist, the thirteenth trick, won by one side after each side has won six

od's an abbreviated form of 'God's' (used in softened oaths)

od's life a euphemistic form of 'God's life'

odso a mild oath, a softened form of 'Godso'

off-hand extempore, straightaway

on a jar ajar, slightly open

on't on it

oons an oath, an abbreviated form of 'God's wounds'

opprobrious infamous, shameful

ordinary eating-place, restaurant

orient (of the sun) rising; radiant, resplendent

ostler stableman or groom at an inn

o't of it

outlandish foreign; bizarre

out on't an exclamation expressing rebuke, abhorrence, or lamentation

overreach outwit, get the better of

overset capsize

own admit, confess

paduasoy rich corded silk, or a dress made of it

paint apply cosmetics

palliate extenuate, excuse

pam knave of cards in loo

pan part of a firearm which holds the gunpowder

panegyric eulogy, high praise

particular special

pate head, skull

peevish querulous, irritable; perverse, obstinate

penchant liking, inclination

perplex bewilder, torment

phlegmatic apathetic, sluggish

physician doctor

piece play; gun

pink prick, stab

pipe voice

piquet card-game for two players

pish an exclamation expressing contempt, impatience, or disgust

pistole gold coin; specifically, Spanish two-escudo piece

plagiary plagiarism

plaguy (adj.) extremely great; troublesome

plaguy (adv.) exceedingly

plate utensils for table and domestic use

play gambling

playing gambling

pleasant delightful, amusing, laughable

pleasantry good-humoured ridicule; pleasure, entertainment

pointer large gun dog

polish (vb.) become refined

poltroon spiritless coward

pooh exclamation expressing impatience, contempt, or disgust

poor's-box box for the collection of money to relieve the poor

portmanteau bag or case for carrying clothing, etc.

pose perplex; nonplus

positively absolutely, without contradiction

post with maximum speed

postilion person who rides the (leading) nearside horse drawing a coach

pother commotion, uproar

pounded impounded, confined

power large amount, great deal

prate chatter; speak boastfully

pray please inform me

prepossession favourable predisposition

presently without delay, immediately

press hasten; strive

pretty excellent, admirable; neat, elegant

prime load

prithee I ask you; please

probation testing

process way of proceeding

proper handsome, fine; decorous, respectable

Proserpine queen of the classical underworld

protest declare, affirm

pshaw an exclamation expressing contempt, impatience, or disgust

punctilio fine point of honour or decorum

puny weak, feeble; raw, novice

purling flowing swirlingly and murmuringly

puzzle baffle, confound

quean hussy; prostitute

quietus release from life; death wound

quinsy inflammation of the throat

raillery satirical merriment; good-humoured ridicule

rake Don Juan, seducer

rakehell debauchee

rally banter, joke, mock, jest at

ranting singing loudly; revelling, rioting

rascal scoundrel, rogue, knave

ready quick, prompt, agile

receipt prescription; recipe

receipt-book recipe-book

regard admire, respect, esteem

relative to in relation to, with regard to

rent-roll (record of) income derived from rent on property

reprehension censure, reprimand

resource expedient, device

return reciprocation, recompense

rivulet small stream or river

rocket firework

rogue rascal, imp

roguish playfully mischievous; waggish

romancing fantastical

rosy glowing; hopeful, propitious

rouleau cylindrical packet of gold coins

roundly plainly, without reserve; vigorously

ruffle ornamental frill for garment's neck or wrist

running horse race- or hunting-horse

run out rail, inveigh

sable black

saloon reception room

sal volatile smelling salts

'scape elude, escape from

scoff object of ridicule

scour depart in haste, flee

scrape awkward predicament or escapade

scruple be squeamish about; refrain from

scurvy worthless, contemptible, paltry

'sdeath an exclamation of impatience, a softened form of 'God's death!'

severally in different directions

sham as masquerade as, pass oneself off as

shift contrivance

shoe-knot ornamental ribbon to decorate a shoe

side-front profile

signor sir

singular unique; idiosyncratic

slattern careless of time, idling; untidy, sluttish

sloop small warship

small-sword light sword used in fencing and duelling

snub-nosed with a short, turned-up nose

something (adv.) somewhat

sot fool, blockhead

spadille ace of spades in the card-games ombre and quadrille

spark fast liver

sparkler bright, sparkling eye

spinet small harpsichord, with the strings set obliquely to the keyboard

spleen anger; malice; melancholy

splenetic peevish, testy

sposa bride

squire country gentleman; 'gentleman next in rank to a knight' (TS)

stamp type, character

start (n.) impulse; sudden involuntary bodily movement

start (vb.) move suddenly and involuntarily as a result of surprise, fright, etc.

station rank

stay halt, detain

stock block of wood; senseless idiot

strain flow of impassioned language

stroller vagrant, itinerant

stuff money, cash

stupefy deaden, render torpid

sue for request, beseech, petition for

sugar-baker sugar-refiner

sundry separate, several

sup take supper

surtout overcoat

swain lover, wooer

tabor small drum

tar sailor

tax with censure for, accuse of

tease torment, worry

temper temperament; mood

tête-à-tête private or intimate encounter or conversation

thou'dst you would

thread-paper thin paper strip containing skeins of sewing thread

'tis it is

'tisn't it is not

title-deed document recording ownership of property

to be sure certainly

to boot as well, in addition

toilet dressing-table

tol-de-rol a merry, meaningless refrain

ton fashionableness

topping pruning

touchstone instrument for testing; test

toy trifle

traducer slanderer

train series, sequence; retinue

transported enraptured

trepan ensnare, trap

trifle with (v.) play with; make light of, render trivial; dally, fool around

trim rebuke, scold

435

trull whore

Turkey-work English wool imitation of Oriental carpets, used as chair coverings

'twas it was

unallayed pure, complete

unconscionable unreasonably excessive; egregious, blatant; having no conscience, unscrupulous

under favour if I may venture to say so, with your permission

unfold discover, reveal

unget unbeget

unmeaning unintelligent; meaningless; unthinking

unsocial antisocial

untoward perverse; unlucky

untrussed unbound, untethered

upbraiding reproachful

vagabond vagrant, itinerant; criminal

valetudinarian person in poor health, especially one constantly or unduly anxious about his or her own health

varlet rogue, scoundrel, mean-spirited fellow

vent unburden; discharge

Venus classical goddess of love

veracity truthfulness, honesty

veriest truest; completest; most extreme

verily truly

vicinage neighbourhood

virago domineering woman; fierce, abusive woman

vis-à-vis light horse-drawn carriage for two people sitting face to face

vole winning of all the tricks in certain card-games

votary devoted follower; worshipper

wag droll, mischievous person

wainscot wood wall panelling

want lack, need

wa'n't wasn't, weren't

warrant guarantee, promise, assure

wedlock marriage

wheedle coax, persuade by flattery; deceive

whey watery part of milk which remains after the formation of curds

whimsical capricious; uncertain, liable to change; odd, quaint; amusing

whip (adv.) instantly, suddenly

whip (n.) coachman

whit jot

wink at pretend not to observe

wish joy to congratulate

with a vengeance with a great curse; in an extreme degree

without off-stage

wonted habitual, usual

woolsack seat made of a bag of wool for the use of judges attending the House of Lords

wrapping-gown nightgown

wrath (adj.) intensely angry

writ written, etched, scored

zooks an exclamation expressing vexation or surprise (an abbreviated form of 'gadzooks')

zounds an exclamation expressing surprise, indignation, or asseveration (an abbreviated form of 'God's wounds')

The Oxford World's Classics Website

www.worldsclassics.co.uk

- Information about new titles
- Explore the full range of Oxford World's Classics
- Links to other literary sites and the main OUP webpage
- Imaginative competitions, with bookish prizes
- Peruse the Oxford World's Classics Magazine
- Articles by editors
- Extracts from Introductions
- A forum for discussion and feedback on the series
- Special information for teachers and lecturers

www.worldsclassics.co.uk

American Literature

British and Irish Literature

Children's Literature

Classics and Ancient Literature

Colonial Literature

Eastern Literature

European Literature

History

Medieval Literature

Oxford English Drama

Poetry

Philosophy

Politics

Religion

The Oxford Shakespeare

A complete list of Oxford Paperbacks, including Oxford World's Classics, Oxford Shakespeare, Oxford Drama, and Oxford Paperback Reference, is available in the UK from the Academic Division Publicity Department, Oxford University Press, Great Clarendon Street, Oxford OX2 6DP.

In the USA, complete lists are available from the Paperbacks Marketing Manager, Oxford University Press, 198 Madison Avenue, New York, NY 10016.

Oxford Paperbacks are available from all good bookshops. In case of difficulty, customers in the UK can order direct from Oxford University Press Bookshop, Freepost, 116 High Street, Oxford OX1 4BR, enclosing full payment. Please add 10 per cent of published price for postage and packing.